READINGS
IN
ECONOMIC
DEVELOPMENT

edited by

Theodore Morgan   George W. Betz   N. K. Choudhry
University of Wisconsin   *University of Wisconsin*   *University of Buffalo*

Wadsworth Publishing Company, Inc.
Belmont, California

L. C. Cat. No.: 63-8482

Printed in the United States of America

PREFACE

Not so long ago, useful articles and other readings in the field of economic development were scarce. But in the past half-dozen years increasing work in the field has resulted in a rapidly mushrooming volume of such material. Concurrently, the effect of the rise of public and professional interest in the facts, problems, and possibilities of economic advance in underdeveloped countries can be seen in the changes in course offerings and curriculum organization in our colleges and universities.

We who teach in the field at Wisconsin have wanted, in one convenient volume for the use of our students, a well-balanced collection of articles and excerpts from longer publications; this anthology is the result. The aim of this book is to present in one place the most useful collection possible of articles and excerpts on economic development; which will, all together, illuminate and give insight over the complete range of fact, theory, and policy.

We have thought that the following materials have a special claim on space: distinguished contributions, with which all students in the field ought to be acquainted; significant contributions to controversies, which are numerous in this unsettled subject; and worthy articles originally published in foreign journals, and hence not generally available in the United States.

We have checked our judgment and improved our choices by drawing on the advice of G. B. Baldwin, P .T. Bauer, Reynold E. Carlson, Rendigs Fels, Michael Hoffman, Bert Hoselitz, Simon Kuznets, Wilfred Malenbaum, Max Millikan, Ragnar Nurkse, Kenneth Parsons, Hans Singer, and William O. Thweatt. We are indebted to each of them for his assistance.

CONTENTS

DEFINITIONS AND PROBLEMS OF UNDERDEVELOPMENT

Cases: The Economy and Society

The Measurement of Income and Income Change

Population

THEORY OF DEVELOPMENT

Social Factors in Growth

Innovation and Investment

Growth Models

International Trade and Economic Growth

Occupational Distribution in the Course of Growth

Land and the Peasants

DEVELOPMENT POLICY

Programming

Population Policy

Financial Policy

Planning and Plans

DEFINITIONS
AND
PROBLEMS
OF
UNDERDEVELOPMENT

CASES: THE ECONOMY AND SOCIETY

1. Latin America versus the United States

Sanford A. Mosk*

It is the aim of this paper to set forth an explanation of the striking contrast in economic experience between the United States and Latin America. There are, to be sure, substantial differences among the Latin-American countries themselves. Every country in Latin America has its own peculiar features and conditions, and in the pages which follow some of the important differences will be brought out. For the most part, however, I shall deal with the Latin-American countries as a group, justifying this treatment on the ground that there has been a solid core of historical experience common to all of them.

To explain the sharp contrast between the United States and Latin America with respect to material development and standards of living, we must look mainly to institutional conditions which were established early and which have shown a strong tendency to persist.

I

The typical landholding system of Latin America dates from the early days of European settlement. In the Spanish colonies the men who participated in the original conquest of territory for the crown, like those who served under Cortés in Mexico and Pizarro in Peru, were rewarded with sizable grants of land and with the right to force Indians to work for them, and thus they became the nucleus of a landed aristocracy. The conquistadors, as they were called, went far beyond what was intended by the crown, both in taking land and in forcing natives to work, and in doing so they established a pattern of behavior for their descendants and for other Spaniards who made their way to the New World.

The ownership of a landed estate in colonial Latin America was not only a source of wealth but it was a mark of social distinction as well. The man who made a fortune in mining bought land and with it prestige. From the ranks of the landed families came many of the leading civilian officials, the high army officers, and prominent church authorities. Essentially, therefore, it was the landed aristocracy that comprised the top layer of the social structure in colonial Latin America. If they were few in numbers, they were all-powerful in wealth and in political affairs. They defied royal decrees and edicts at will, sometimes not even bothering to go through the form of obedience. For practical purposes, they were a law unto themselves.

*From the *American Economic Review,* Papers and Proceedings, May 1951, pp. 367-383. The author was late Professor of Economics at the University of California.

It was pointed out above that those who participated in the Spanish conquest were given the right to draft Indian labor and that other Spaniards acquired similar privileges. Some Indians, because of isolation or other special conditions, escaped the burden of forced services, but the majority were reduced to a status of unfreedom resembling that of serfdom in medieval Europe. The Indian was attached to the landowner or the mine owner by a personal bond. The formal procedure by which he was recruited, the amount of labor time he was required to give, the kind of services he was called upon to perform, and so on, differed from place to place and from time to time. An almost bewildering variety of names was used to designate his status. Such differences did not, however, obscure the fundamental similarity in the position of all conquered Indian groups. They made up a lower class, sharply and permanently differentiated from their European masters.

In addition to serfdom, slavery was also found in the Ibero-American colonies, but it was the Negro rather than the Indian who was the slave. Enslavement of Indians, although it occurred in the Spanish colonies, was disapproved by the crown, and the legislation forbidding this practice seems to have been reasonably well enforced. As regards the social and economic system of Latin America, the difference between slavery and forced Indian labor was not important. Both institutions made possible a social structure consisting of a small landed class and a large lower class, with hardly anyone between and with rigid barriers to upward movement in the social scale.

Those in the upper class were usually persons of European ancestry, but men of mixed blood, or even pure Indian or pure Negro blood, were also found among the colonial aristocracy. The line between the upper and lower classes was economic rather than racial. Nevertheless, a racial fiction was maintained. Indian chiefs and their descendants and other persons with Indian or Negro blood who managed to acquire wealth could become honorary white men by getting a certificate of blood purification from the crown or some other appropriate agency. The pretense that such persons were white, in spite of the color of their skin, is a significant fact about the social system of colonial Latin America because it shows how firm was the line between the upper and lower class. It was thought of as a line between whites and nonwhites, not merely a line between the wealthy and the poor.

Before the end of the colonial period in the Spanish possessions, peonage was introduced, partly as a supplement for serfdom and partly as a replacement for it. Peonage provided a means of getting around the growing body of Spanish legislation designed to restrict the use of Indian serfs. The servile bond between the estate owner and the Indian who worked in his fields was replaced by a wage relation. The Indian, in theory, became a hired laborer working for cash wages. But, in one way or another, he also became a debtor to his employer, and, once caught up in a chain of debt, he could rarely escape. His labor obligation to a particular landowner became permanent, and he was tied to the landowner no less than the Indian serf who preceded him.

There were some places in colonial Latin America where the *latifundio* was not developed and where the land was occupied by small, independent farmers of Spanish stock. Costa Rica and parts of Colombia are the prize examples. But they were exceptions. The predominant rural institution was the large holding. And with the *latifundio* was found Indian serfdom or Indian peonage or Negro slavery or, as in Chile, a semiservile form of mestizo tenancy. Wealth, property, and income in colonial Latin America were highly concentrated in the small group at the top of the social system, made up of landed gentry and others closely associated with them in political, social, and military affairs. All these qualities combined to make up a social organization best described as semifeudal in nature.

When the Latin-American colonies gained their independence in the nineteenth century, the semifeudal system of landholdings and social classes was not at all disturbed. The wars of independence in Latin America were not a social revolution. They began as a revolt of creole leaders against Spanish authority, and they did not change essentially in nature during the several years of struggle before independence was won. They were not fought by the Indian, and they were certainly not fought for him. New individuals rose to power during and after the conflict, some nominal legal changes were made with respect to the status and treatment of Indians, but nothing was altered in the fundamental institutions of Latin America by the movement for independence.

Moreover, around the middle of the nineteenth century new trends in world economic development began to run their course, causing an extension and refinement of the basic conditions found in Latin America in the colonial period. The application of new technology to transportation—railroads, steamships, refrigeration, and so on—created a network of cheap, regular, and effective transport services. This network of world transport was an integral part of the international economy prevailing from about the middle of the nineteenth century to the outbreak of the first World War in 1914. Comparatively free conditions for international trade, ease of migration, and a large flow of capital from Western Europe to underdeveloped parts of the world were the interrelated components of the international economy which favored new lines of economic development everywhere.

Under earlier conditions, many parts of the world, especially continental interiors, had had only slender commercial contacts with Western Europe. Now, with suitable transport, trade, and other conditions, such regions became linked to the vital economy of Western Europe, to which they shipped an ever growing volume of raw materials and foodstuffs. The effect on the use of their soil, mineral, and timber resources was profound. Resources which had lain untouched were now brought into exploitation. New lines of production were undertaken and old ones expanded.

In Latin America, as in other areas of colonial economy, a strong impulse was given to the commercialization of economic life. It is true that subsistence production remained dominant over production for markets, in the sense that the total amount of labor time spent on raising subsistence crops was much greater than that devoted to commercial output. Nevertheless, the gain in commercial production was large after the middle of the nineteenth century. If the first influences were felt in export production, they soon spread to production for domestic markets. The transportation, handling, and, in some cases, the production of export products were carried out increasingly by persons divorced from subsistence farming. Employment increased in other service industries, such as utilities and communications, governments expanded their functions and personnel, and the growth of cities was stimulated. Thus the expansion of foreign markets was followed by an expansion of domestic markets, especially for foodstuffs.

The greater commercialization of economic life in Latin America after the middle of the nineteenth century brought about a substantial extension of the system of large landholdings. Far from giving away, the colonial system of landholdings was greatly strengthened. In some cases, new large holdings were fashioned out of public domain. Lands which had remained public property because they had not been worth exploiting now appeared attractive to private owners. Titles were acquired in a variety of ways. Some were outright gifts from a government inclined to be generous with persons of power and prestige, some were purchased for cash, others were given as compensation for military services, while still others were considered as payment for undertaking the survey of public lands. In some cases, too, large grants were made to individuals or companies for colonization purposes. Such grants presumably should have led to settlement by small farmers, but more often than not they led to additional land engrossment. Both Argentina and Mexico offer striking illustrations of the abuse of colonization land grants.

In some parts of Latin America, estates were enlarged or newly created after the middle of the nineteenth century by depriving Indian villages of lands which they had possessed since before the conquest and which they had managed to hold throughout the colonial period. The most striking development of this kind took place in Mexico during the thirty-five year rule of dictator Porfirio Díaz, when the Mexican government gave positive encouragement and assistance to the *hacendados* (estate owners) in stripping Indian villages of their customary lands.

In Bolivia, as in Mexico, many Indian communities lost their traditional landholdings in the latter part of the nineteenth century, and by roughly the same kinds of tactics and practices. Students of the Bolivian development have shown how the destruction of Indian community tenures followed the improvement in means of transportation, giving access to markets and thereby making such lands valuable to others. By 1921, when George McBride published his well-known study on agrarian conditions in Bolivia, the only Indian community lands left in the country were found in isolated and undesirable places. The desirable lands all had been taken away from the Indians during the preceding half-century.

Similar destruction of Indian tenures took place during the same period in Peru and Ecudor. In each country, geographic and institutional peculiarities affected the outcome, giving it a character of its own, but the broad result was the same in all cases. For example, in some of the Andean valleys the large holdings were tiny compared with the great *haciendas* of Mexico, but they were nevertheless large in relation to local topographic conditions, and they were created by means similar to those employed in Mexico.

Just as the system of large landholdings was extended after the middle of the nineteenth century, so did the system of peonage become more widespread. Both developments were fostered by the same fundamental influence; that is, the expanding market economy. They were opposite sides of the same coin. In some cases the encroachment on traditional Indian lands was motivated by a desire to get more Indian labor rather than by a desire to have more land for cultivation. Deprived of the lands which had provided them with subsistence, the Indians had no alternative but to become peons for the owner of a nearby *latifundio*.

Furthermore, the bonds which kept the peon subservient to the landowner were tightened after the mid-nineteenth century, since his labor was now more essential than ever for the operation of the estate. If the average *latifundio* in Latin America did not become rationalized in technology, it did become more rational in the use of its labor force as the landowners came to appreciate the satisfactions of enlarged cash incomes. If the relation between landowner and peon continued to be a semifeudal one, the feudal quality of mutual privileges and obligations became clouded and distorted by the nominal wage-contractual relation between the two. The peon became firmly fixed in his status in the social system. The machinery for keeping the peon in debt was made more effective in some places by setting up stores at which he was required to make all his purchases. Control over the peon was extended by laws relating to employment and vagrancy and in other ways. The enforcement of these laws was sometimes carried out by extralegal and unconstitutional methods, but until recently Latin-American governments paid little attention to legal niceties when dealing with peonage.

The developments in peonage just summarized took place, of course, in the areas of Indian concentration. In other places where an expansion of commercial agriculture also occurred but where there were no substantial numbers of Indians to draw on, the need for a larger labor supply was met by immigration, with the immigrants coming in as farm laborers or tenants. The experience of Argentina in this connection is especially illuminating.

Argentina had an extremely local and undeveloped economy until about 1880. Thereafter, a rapid transition set in, and within a generation a remarkable transformation had taken place. By the time of the first World War, Argentina was a major supplier of meat and grain for world markets. Following the Hispanic-American tradition, as we have already observed, the system of large landholdings was continued and extended under the new commercial influences. But the expansion of grain production called for a much larger labor supply than had been required by the typical cattle ranch of the earlier period, and since Argentina was a sparsely populated country, the additional hands required to till the soil were provided by immigration. Italians and Spaniards made up the bulk of the immigrants, coming in mostly as agricultural wage earners. Some of the Italians were merely seasonal workers who dovetailed employment in the harvesting of flax, wheat, and corn in the Southern Hemisphere with the cultivation of lands in their native Italy during the remainder of the year. These immigrants who came and went with the seasons in Argentina, just like their fellow Italians who migrated seasonally to France, were known as "the swallows."

The immigrants who settled down in Argentina rarely became landowners. Many started as farm laborers and remained permanently in that class. Others who started as farm laborers—perhaps the majority who did so—after a time became tenants. Still others were tenants from the beginning. Some of the tenants were cash renters; others were sharecroppers. But whatever the rental contract might have been, the tenant, with minor exceptions, remained a tenant and his sons also became tenants rather than owners. The large estates were not broken up to make way for independent farmers. Tenancy was an end, not a means to a higher status.

It is not my intention to suggest that the tenancy which developed in Argentina—and which continues to this day—has had the same social and economic consequences as peonage in other parts of Latin America. Studies of agrarian history and conditions in Argentina, such as Carl Taylor's book, *Rural Life in Argentina,* show that many tenants have done reasonably well from the financial viewpoint, and that some have even become wealthy. Nevertheless, the obstacles to ownership have had serious results. The Argentine tenant, like tenants in many other countries, has had little security of tenure. The usual consequences of uncertain tenure have appeared. Tenants have been loath to make improvements on farms they may not be able to operate for more than one year, and they have shown little interest in better farming methods, such as crop diversification and conservation practices.

Even more important, perhaps, have been the intangible results of permanent tenancy. The aspiration to become a landowner is a deep-seated desire among the tenants of Argentina, as any number of studies show. This ambition has been frustrated for the vast majority of the rural population. Talents and abilities which could have been brought out have remained latent and unused. Surely, a dynamic quality has been lost to the Argentine economy as a consequence of the tenancy system.

In addition, in the long run, tenancy has made its contribution to political unrest and instability in Argentina, as in many other parts of the world. It is not the only factor, but it must bear some of the responsibility. The upheavals that have taken place and the uncertainty they have left in their wake obviously have been unfavorable to the economic development of Argentina.

Finally, it is reasonable to ask whether the Argentine system of landholdings did not prevent her from taking full advantage of the big wave of European emigration in the two generations prior to World War I. Given the size and quality of her agricultural resources, Argentina could have been expected to recruit more than the 3,700,000 immigrants who reached her shores during that period. It is true that Argentina was second only to the United States as an immigration country, but she was a pretty poor second, because in the same period about six times as many immigrants entered the United States. Moreover, those who went to Argentina were less permanent. Argentine migration statistics show that approximately 45 per cent of the immigrants returned to their native lands, while re-emigration from the United States is estimated at only 30 per cent. We know that many of the immigrants who went to Argentina expected to set up farms of their own, and that they were encouraged in this belief by numerous so-called "colonization" projects. Disappointment was often followed by re-emigration. If Argentina had been able to provide greater opportunity for independent farmers, her immigrant population would have been more permanent as well as more numerous.

If time permitted, a similar analysis could be made of the immigration experience of Brazil—the second immigration country in Latin America. It would differ from the Argentine case in certain important details. Tenancy, for example, has been less common in Brazil over the whole period since the middle of the nineteenth century, and the growth of tenancy in the last thirty years has involved a movement up the social ladder from farm laborer to tenant. Thus the typical Brazilian tenant does not seem to sense the land hunger which is felt so keenly by the farm tenant in Argentina. In spite of such differences, however, the same broad conclusion holds for Brazil as for Argentina. Neither country attracted as many immigrants as its agricultural resources would warrant; neither country benefited from European emigration nearly as much as it might have.

If Argentina and Brazil were only moderately attractive to the European of small means seeking an opportunity to better himself, the countries where peonage prevailed were even less so. Such countries were repellent to potential immigrants, who saw little prospect for advancement in a community of landlords and serfs. Thus other Latin-American nations profited even less than Argentina and Brazil from the accumulated knowledge, skills, and labor power which Europeans took with them when they emigrated overseas.

Just as the countries of Latin America failed to make the most of international migration after 1850, so did they fail to make the most of the opportunities which technical improvements and an expanding world economy afforded for attaining higher average standards of living. The fundamental barriers to material progress in Latin America were institutional. Latin America remained a semifeudal society, with all the trappings thereof. The landed aristocracy, all-powerful in political and military affairs, exerted also the decisive influence in economic affairs.

The remainder of this favored class indulged, as one would expect, in conspicuous consumption. They invested readily in land, since it was socially the most respectable thing to do; and since they typically spent a good deal of time abroad, they were prone to keep funds outside the country and to hold foreign securities. No one knows how much capital has been exported from Latin America, but for "capital poor" countries it probably has been a substantial sum. Real property apart, the landed families of Latin America have had little interest in domestic investment. Small wonder, therefore, that it was mostly foreign capital, not domestic, which developed transportation, commerce, and mineral production in Latin America in the late nineteenth century and early part of the twentieth.

What has gone before is an analysis of basic institutions established in colonial Latin America and of the way in which these institutions were refined by the course of economic development after the middle of the nineteenth century. In many parts of Latin America they remain intact to this day. In some countries, developments of the last twenty-five years or so suggest that far-reaching changes are beginning to take place. These developments, representing a trend toward economic diversification in general and industrialization in particular, were accelerated during World War II. The heritage of the past, however, is not easily written off. The most serious economic problems which plague these countries nowadays are precisely those which come out of the long, semifeudal past.

To illustrate these problems—which is all that can be done in this paper without going afield from the main theme—I may call attention to the limited size of the internal market now found in Latin-American countries. A broad middle-class market is lacking. The depressed rural population offers new customers for the output of new factories. There are, of course, many steps which can be taken to raise rural buying power, but they are not likely to mean much unless accompanied by a land reform program. Even after a substantial amount of land reform has been accomplished, the restraining effects of the past make themselves felt in the lack of education, subservience to traditional methods of farming, the tendency to raise subsistence crops, poor health and sanitary conditions which impede efficient work, and so on. The experience of Mexico—the one country in Latin America which has carried out a land reform program—is illuminating in this connection, even granting that the Mexican case has been influenced by special conditions which need not prevail elsewhere.

Other illustrations of the influence of past conditions can be found in the difficulties of adjusting to the work habits required in modern industry and in acquiring a sense of responsibility about spending cash income. Here I need only point out the well-nigh universal complaint from factory owners in Latin America that they are unable to get suitable foremen and also that their absentee and turnover rates are extremely high. Similar obstacles to economic development appear today in the mobilization of capital resources. The preference for investing in land, as we have observed, and the habit of keeping funds abroad are both results of the long experience of a feudal nature in Latin America.

II

If we turn now to the United States, the early history of the British mainland colonies shows that attempts were made in some places to establish a system of landholdings and social classes resembling the surviving feudal forms in England at that time. These attempts failed, except in the South. This exception will be dealt with rather fully later, since it is illuminating with respect to the theme of this paper.

Granting that the impulse to establish relic feudal forms was found in the English colonies as well as in the Spanish and Portuguese, it must be recognized that it was weaker in the English case than in the others. The English economy at the end of the sixteenth century was much more diversified than the Spanish. Feudal remnants persisted, but they were not dominant as in Spain. Trade and industry were not only more developed but were more respectable socially. Merchants who had acquired wealth were becoming landowners and were getting incorporated into the landed aristocracy, thus weakening the feudal outlook of the old landed families. The scale of social values transplanted to the English colonies, therefore, was less rigid than the Spanish. The ownership of land was less important, and it soon became possible for a merchant in the English colonies to enjoy top social distinction without being a landowner at all. The difference in degree between the English and Spanish attitudes toward ⸗land ownership was not by itself decisive in bringing about a different course of economic and social evolution in the two sets of colonies, but it did assume importance in combination with other conditions.

Among these other conditions was the character of the Indian civilizations found in the area of Spanish conquest. In some places—notably Mexico, Guatemala, and the Andean country—the Spaniards came upon dense concentrations of aborigines, living in villages and towns, cultivating crops such as corn, beans, squash, and potatoes, and trained to perform a variety of craft and construction tasks. Once conquered, they could easily be parceled out and forced to work for their European masters—all the more easily because they were accustomed to working under compulsion for their own chieftains in the days before the conquest. In other parts of the Spanish dominions there were no great concentrations of Indians, but mostly the natives were sufficiently sedentary so that they could be captured and put to work. Later, if necessary, they were supplemented or replaced by Negro slaves. Throughout the Hispanic New World, in spite of some exceptions, it is clear that aboriginal conditions lent themselves to creating a laboring population of servile character, thus facilitating the introduction of feudal institutions.

In British North America, there were no densely-settled Indians like those of central Mexico or Peru. The will to take advantage of Indian labor was possibly not as universal among the early English colonists as among the Spanish and Portuguese, but certainly it was not lacking. Attempts were made, by Puritan groups as well as others, to captivate natives and enslave them. These efforts, however, were rarely successful. By stubborn fighting and by taking to flight, the Indians resisted being put to work by the white settlers. They were exterminated or they were driven back, but they could not be converted into a permanent servile population.

Geographic conditions also influenced the institutions which Europeans established in their colonial possessions of the New World. The tropical climate found in much of Hispanic America favored the production of sugar for export to Europe. Raising and processing of sugar cane could be done on a large scale using relatively large amounts of labor, and thus the use of Indian serfs or Negro slaves was encouraged. Other tropical and semitropical export crops of colonial Latin America, such as cacao, indigo, and cotton, had similar labor requirements and were also cultivated by unfree workers. In addition, the great discoveries of precious metals in the Spanish colonies caused thousands of Indians to render forced labor in the mines.

In British North America, except in the South, climatic conditions made it impossible to raise export crops calling for large amounts of labor. Similarly, during the early period there were no big strikes of gold and silver which might have led to widespread use of slaves in mining.

The three factors I have mentioned—namely, the weaker English impulse to introduce feudal institutions, different Indian civilizations, and different geographic conditions—adequately account for the difference between the social system established in the British mainland colonies and that of colonial Hispanic America.[1] The difference became apparent early. Subsequently, cumulative developments in each area tended to magnify the difference. Thus migration to the British colonies took on a selective character. Those who were most dissatisfied with aristocratic privilege at home and who were enterprising enough to pull up stakes and risk a new life across the Atlantic responded readily to the urge to migrate, especially to the northern and middle colonies. Yeoman farmers, artisans, and urban petty *bourgeoisie,* all of whom were prominent in the immigrant stream, gave additional strength to the social, economic, and political institutions already taking root in this part of the American continent.

The system of small landholdings which took hold during the colonial period was continued and extended after independence through the disposal of public domain by the federal government. It is well known that the public land policy was fraught with errors of judgment, shattered ideals, corruption, inadequate protection of the public interest in mineral and timber resources, and so on. Speculative interests were often benefited at the expense of settlers. In some places the method of disposing of public lands resulted in tenancy rather than ownership of small farms. These and other criticisms have justly been made of the public land policy by many writers. Nevertheless, the recognition of pre-emption rights and also the Homestead Act, in spite of numerous drawbacks, gave continued scope for the establishment of small holdings during the nineteenth century. The pattern of landholdings in this country was created before the national period of our history began, but the public land policy deserves credit as a means of extending this basic landholding system.

The wide distribution of land ownership in the United States epitomizes the dominant middle-class character of American social organization. If, as many have pointed out, there were cultural drawbacks to this kind of society, there were also well-known advantages of a material nature, expressing themselves in the economic development of the nation and in comparatively high average standards of living. The broad middle-class market in this country was a potent force in the development of mass production methods in manufacturing. As industry advanced after the Civil War, it found right at hand a mass market. Other factors, to be sure, played a part in creating this mass market. Highly productive resources certainly were important. Nevertheless, if the social organization here had been like that of Latin America, with a similar distribution of ownership of land and other resources, it is inconceivable that this country could have had a mass market. Under such conditions the rate of industrial development would have been greatly retarded.

We should also call to mind some of the advantages which this country enjoyed because there were no important social obstacles to the pursuit of opportunity and the acquisition of wealth. Birth and social position did not determine the outcome of a man's career regardless of other qualities. Those born to wealth doubtless had advantages over others, but the others were not faced with social barriers which made it impossible for

[1]Clarence Haring has an illuminating discussion of this question in his synthetic account of Spanish colonization in the New World, entitled *The Spanish Empire in America* (New York, 1947).

them to move upward in the income scale. Thus it was the United States, above all, that Europeans regarded as the land of opportunity, and it is not surprising that migration across the North Atlantic overshadowed by far all other movements of population in the period of great overseas migrations prior to World War I.

Just as the social system of the United States attracted immigrants, adding their manpower and skills to the productive capacity of the country, so must it have served to bring out the energies and latent talents of those who were already here. In Latin America, the depressed peon, with no prospect of betterment, was hardly to be blamed for schooling himself in ways of getting back at his master by slowing down in his work and shrugging off responsibility. The habits of mind and the kinds of behavior ingrained in a people by four centuries of serfdom and peonage are bound to cling tenaciously, and there is no question but that they constitute a stubborn handicap to the efforts now being made in Latin America to industrialize and to improve production in other ways as well.

The emphasis given in this paper to social organization and the related system of landholdings finds additional support in the economic history of our own South. Climate and soil early made it possible for tidewater Maryland and Virginia to become a center of tobacco production, and favorable natural conditions led to the raising of rice and indigo farther south along the coastal strip of the Carolinas and Georgia. All three crops found a ready market in Europe, and all three could be raised profitably with the use of comparatively large amounts of labor. Thus the plantation and Negro slavery became characteristic institutions of the South during colonial times. In the nineteenth century, the same system of production, with its attendant social structure, became attached to cotton raising, spreading widely through the tier of southern states.

The ante-bellum plantation system of the South resembled the *latifundia* of Latin America. The two were not precisely identical. Nevertheless, they matched each other at critical points, and the similarity between the South and Latin America was far greater than between South and North in this country. To be sure, there were many small independent farms in the South. Most of these, however, were subsistence farms located in the poorer areas. Where good soils and good location combined to make an area attractive for agricultural development, such as along the Mississippi and its tributaries, the small farmer could not share the opportunities enjoyed by the typical Northern farmer. By and large, the small farmers of the South were a depressed class.

The planter aristocracy, differentiated sharply from the small white farmers as well as from the Negro slaves, betrayed characteristics similar to those of the landed families of Latin America. They were famous for gracious hospitality and other kinds of conspicuous consumption. Social considerations made them interested in investing in land and in slaves, rarely in anything else. There were individual exceptions, of course, but the planters as a whole regarded commerce and industry as beneath the dignity of a gentleman and as a threat to a way of life that had aesthetic and enduring social values of its own.

If there was a tendency to monoculture and one-sided economic development in the South inherent in the advantages of specializing in cotton production, surely this tendency was greatly exaggerated by the social and landholding system. The South, I venture to say, could have produced just about as much cotton as it did even if it had had a more diversified economy. There is every reason to believe that the South would have attracted European immigrants if it had not been populated mainly by Negro slaves and subsistence farmers. Under different social conditions, there would have been more capital rather than less available for economic activities other than cotton raising. As it was, it is not surprising that when the Civil War broke out the South was far behind the North in the building of a railroad network and even farther behind in manufacturing development.

The tenacity of Southern institutions is shown by the course of development after the Civil War. The abolition of slavery did not do away with the plantation system, but led rather to a variation in form. The slave was replaced by the tenant, especially the sharecropper, and peonage became a characteristic feature of the Southern agrarian structure. In this respect, as in others, there was a close parallel to the experience of Latin America, where the course of evolution ran from Indian serfdom to peonage. Furthermore, tenancy in the South was a permanent status rather than a step toward ownership. This feature, too, offered a parallel with Latin America and a contrast with the remainder of the United States.

As industry began to develop in the South after the Civil War, earlier institutions made their influence felt in the establishment of mill villages and in paternalism. True, these developments were favored by circumstances arising out of the war itself, as Broadus Mitchell has pointed out in his volume on *The Industrial Revolution in the South;* but they were also an outgrowth of the depressed condition and lack of education of the subsistence farmers who made up the bulk of the wage-earning class in the new textile mills. Here, again, an interesting parallel can be drawn with Latin America, where numerous cases of paternalism have been found in the new industrial developments of recent years. There was, to be sure, some paternalism in the early development of cotton mills in New England, but it was of short duration, and it did not spread to other industries and other areas of industrial development in the North. In the South, although paternalism may be dying out nowadays, it has shown a strong tendency to persist. We may expect a similar tendency, probably a stronger one, wherever paternalism has appeared in the new industrial structure of Latin America.

In what has gone before, I have stressed the parallel development of socioeconomic institutions in Latin America and in the South of the United States. This emphasis was not intended to suggest that the two regions have had an identical historical experience. There have been many elements of difference, such as the profound influence which the Catholic Church has had upon Latin-American culture and attitudes. But in spite of such differences, the similarities have been striking. Both areas show the effects of a semifeudal social and landholding system in restraining economic development in modern times, and both show how stubborn such institutions are in loosening their grip.[2]

[2]Ed. note: Further material considers, and rejects, the thesis that natural resource and other physical conditions could explain the divergence of development of the two areas.

2. Factors in the Economic Development of Ceylon

*P. T. Ellsworth**

I

The central problem now emerging in Ceylon, toward whose solution any development program must be directed, may be put in Malthusian terms as a race between population and productivity. Until recently this was not so. Although population has grown steadily over the past half century and more, so have the means of providing for its sustenance. International specialization has been mainly responsible. Steadily rising exports of tea, rubber, and coconut products have made possible growing imports of rice and other foodstuffs in the face of lagging domestic production of these necessities, until in recent years some 60 per cent of the island's food requirements have been obtained in this manner.

Now, chiefly as a result of the advance of science along two fronts, the situation has undergone drastic change. During and since the war, the use of DDT has so reduced the incidence of malaria as to bring down the death rate by nearly half. Accordingly, the annual rate of increase of population has risen sharply; instead of the prewar figure of about 1.7 per cent, since the war it has amounted to 2.8 per cent. Changes in the age composition of the population may be expected to moderate this figure somewhat; so that for the foreseeable future an annual increase of population of about 2.4 per cent must be reckoned with.

On the side of exports, the development of synthetic rubber now threatens to bring to a halt further expansion of this source of overseas income, while tea production is approaching the limit set by available land, and aging palm groves combine with growing home consumption to threaten declining exports.

The International Bank Mission to Ceylon sees the solution to the divergent trends of food requirements and export prospects principally in augmented production of domestic agriculture. This is to be achieved partly by colonization of the underutilized portions of the island and partly by increased productivity on the food-producing lands already under cultivation. The program is, however, far more than purely agricultural. It fully recognizes that economic development is a process of "balanced growth," and includes substantial provisions for improvement of transportation, the expansion of electric power, and more adequate facilities for health and education, as well as specific measures to stimulate industrial growth.

Whether the recommended program is adequate to halt a possible decline in the standard of living, or better yet, to raise standards somewhat, is debatable. Tailored to the resources likely to be available to the country, it calls for annual investment of some Rs. 550 million per annum, or about 11 to 12 per cent of gross national product. Assuming a moder-

*From the *American Economic Review,* Papers and Proceedings, May 1953, pp. 115-124. The author is Professor of Economics, University of Wisconsin.

ately optimistic capital-output ratio of four to one, annual increments to income should rise gradually from Rs. 125 to 150 million a year. Since merely to provide for the growth of population will require an annual increase of about Rs. 100 million, this means, in the words of the report itself, that "the margin for waste and inefficiency will be very narrow." For per capita productivity to be raised, not only will there have to be "constant attention to the careful selection of better tools, equipment and methods," but these new methods will have to be widely adopted and the better tools and equipment used with a high degree of effectiveness.

This raises questions which are neither financial, technical, nor even primarily economic, but which are rather predominantly cultural. Assuming that the Mission's report embodies sound judgment as to the availability of finance, the limitations and possibilities dictated by geography, and reasonable prospects of technical aid, the success or failure of its program will largely depend upon whether the modern methods and techniques necessary to raise productivity can be assimilated by the people of Ceylon. For it is their daily productive efforts which must be made more efficient and hence more fruitful, and it is their willingness and ability to adopt better procedures and to use new instruments upon which this outcome will depend. Willingness and ability of a whole people to change its way is essentially a cultural problem, as Hoselitz has vividly shown. In the case of Ceylon, the crucial questions to be answered are: To what extent is there conflict between Ceylonese values, customs, and institutions and the values and attitudes required by essentially Western techniques? Can indigenous institutions be used by introduce new methods or to adapt these methods to Ceylonese requirements? Does there exist or can there be created in time a corps of leaders in the economic life of the community with the ability and the enthusiasm necessary to elicit cooperation from the rank and file?

Let us approach an answer to these questions by first surveying the changes required and the obstacles interposed in the fields of agriculture and industry. Then we can consider the human and institutional resources available for effecting change and the provisions suggested for improving them.

II

In agriculture, progress is hoped for in two main directions. First, continuance and expansion of colonization schemes will place cultivators with inadequate land on newly irrigated plots or on land suitable for dry-farming. But since the area suitable for irrigation comprises only about 600,000 acres, while the extension of dry-farming is limited to areas with reasonably dependable rainfall, this string to the bow is not a complete answer. It is estimated that the combined crop potential of all unused lands will be roughly not more than half of those now producing for domestic consumption. Also, because of limitations of finance, available technical staff, and the need for experimentation and training of colonists for dry-farming, exploitation of this potential cannot be achieved for a good many years.

This means that to increase food production in the near future, considerable reliance must be placed on a second phase of agricultural expansion: improved productivity on lands now being cultivated. The Mission sets as a minimum target for rice from existing paddy land an increase of 10 per cent in yields in the next six years.

Social and cultural obstacles to the success of such an agricultural program are formidable. The Ceylonese peasant is notoriously conservative and guided by tradition; he dislikes change and is not easily moved by economic considerations to alter his customary ways, being far from an "economic man" in the Western sense. Pride in doing a job well for its own sake or a spirit of workmanship is scarcely one of his traits; he is satisfied if he performs according to established routines. In this he is reinforced by the influence of Buddhism—the predominant religion of Ceylon—with its emphasis upon adherence to certain established rules of conduct and its deprecation of worldly desire.

The result of these characteristics may be seen in the failure of proven methods on demonstration farms to be widely copied. Reinforcing the peasant's conservatism and his weak response to economic motivation is a cultural factor which impedes the spread of knowledge about improved methods. He fears the "evil eye" will strike him with disaster if he appears to boast. Hence, unlike the Western farmer who has profited from new techniques, he keeps his good fortune to himself and fails to become an enthusiastic and ever multiplying emissary of progress.

Similarly in the field of health: years of strenuous effort by government health officers to encourage the building of latrines, backed by the provision of free materials, has induced villagers to construct only a negligible number. In spite of the prevalence of intestinal parasites and unremitting propaganda associating their inroads with his insanitary habits, the villager continues to follow the ways of his ancestors.

These cultural impediments not only obstruct the improvement of yields on land already farmed, but they are likely to be carried over into the newly colonized areas, since these are being peopled by cultivators from the settled regions who have little or no land, so far as possible in groups from single or neighboring villages. Arrangements are being made in the colonized areas, however, for closer supervision of farming operations.

To induce a conservative and comparatively uneconomic-minded peasantry to alter its procedures and to adopt improved methods, better implements, and superior strains of seed is not impossible, as experience in India and elsewhere demonstrates. But to overcome this conservatism and inertia, particularly to do so at a speed consonant with the goals of a development program, requires the presence of a sufficiently numerous, devoted, and energetic "spearhead" group of trained leaders. Moreover, if they are to achieve results consistent with their efforts, they must understand the peasant's outlook, approach him sympathetically, and develop unusual skills of persuasion.

A principal constituent of such a spearhead group in Ceylon is the agricultural extension staff of the Department of Agriculture. It consists of about 150 field officers, assisted by some 330 field demonstrators and food production overseers. Although more numerous, in proportion to the rural population, than county agents in the United States (1 per 11,800 as against 1 per 18,200), they confront a far more difficult task and are too few in number. In the words of the Mission's report:

So far as . . . the dissemination of information is concerned, a shortage of practical agricultural extension staff to demonstrate on the peasant's own plot the efficacy of such improved seed, implements and practices is one of the great handicaps in implementing this very wise policy. . . . The task is large, and officials are well aware of the difficulty in building a staff fully adequate to handle the development program at the desired speed. In the aggregate, professional, technical and applied knowledge still is far below the standard required for a successful assault upon the forces of ignorance and inefficiency that hold back progress. . . .

If the extension staff is too small, it is equally true that its approach is inappropriate. Instead of adopting the method so successfully used in India's Uttar Pradesh, of discovering the peasant's "felt need," of helping him to realize it, and then, having gained his confidence, of persuading him of the benefits of changes in techniques and even in the crops to be raised, the Department's workers operated on a comparatively autocratic principle. As government officials in a society dominated by status, in which government service confers exceptional prestige, they feel superior to the simple cultivator, and establish a working relationship of the all-knowing government official telling the lazy and ignorant peasant what to do. "Drives" to get people to do this or that are common, regardless of their interests. Contests are sponsored, but since competitive zeal is not a characteristic of the Ceylonese peasant, they evoke little enthusiasm.[1]

Cultural obstacles to change are perhaps pointed up most conspicuously in certain features of the family system, especially in relation to a rather obvious means of moderating the race between population and production; namely, the exercise of control over the rate of population increase. On this, the Mission makes an "earnest plea that Ceylon follow the example of her neighbor, India, in a bold effort to convert her people to the principle and practice of family planning," persuading the individual "to act by propaganda and by making available advice and facilities." It recognizes that this is a policy "calling for great courage and tact," but believes it is one "which can do more to raise the living standards and well-being of the Ceylonese of the future than any other action or influence within the power of the government." In view of the Mission's estimate that population growth in the next decade may be of the order of 2 to 2.5 millions, while potentially available irrigated and dry land "can hardly support more than 1.5 million," this conclusion certainly appears to be well founded.

In Ceylon's family system, however, male dominance is outstanding. The father is unquestioned head of the household; he replaces his wife's father in authority, and to her husband she owes entire allegiance. And to this head of the household, children are an unquestioned asset. All the burdens fall on the mother; the father views his children as an extension of his ego, the source of status in the community, and as possible contributors to enhance status of his kin through well-arranged marriages. Sons, in particular,

[1]See Murray Straus, "Cultural Factors in the Functioning of Agricultural Extension," in *Rural Sociology*.

add to his stature, and more, are a source of help in his work, of security in his old age. So although most women simply feel helpless in the face of destiny, view large numbers of children with decidedly moderate enthusiasm, and might be won over to control of family size, men welcome numerous progeny. It is the dominant male whose opposition would have to be overcome. Surely this factor poses a serious stumbling block to propaganda, advice, and facilities. As one writer puts the matter, the problem "is not essentially educational, but one of obtaining acceptance of birth limitation in a society tied to large family values"—and tied by the loyalties and interests of the strongest element in the family.[2]

I turn now to the industrial sector. Growth of industry will be comparatively limited in Ceylon, since suitable local raw materials and fuels are few, the potential market is limited, and capital resources are relatively scarce. Yet, in the view of the Mission, well-chosen industrial expansion will be desirable in years to come, especially as the empty lands fill up and new employment opportunities for the growing population have to be found.

III

In the industrial field as well as the agricultural, at least the immediate limits to growth are more social and cultural than economic. Perhaps most needed for success is an increase in the technical skills that are so important in modern industry as well as in a progressive agriculture. In the words of the report:

In most fields, the rate of development is actually limited less by finances than by lack of local technology at all levels. To carry out the various projects there are not enough research scientists, designing and operating engineers, agricultural or manufacturing specialists, or construction engineers. Equally scarce are technical supervisors, draftsmen, control chemists, field foremen, tractor operators and even skilled workmen. To remedy this must be one of the first tasks.

This shortage of well-distributed technical skills is only partly due to very limited facilities for vocational training. Much of it can be explained by the very history of the island's past development, which has been one of continued agricultural specialization. But there has been only a slow and inadequate response to growing opportunities for the use of industrial and technological skills. For an explanation of this, we must look to the special bias of the educational system, the influence of caste, and the special prestige of government service.

Ceylon's educational system has been, to paraphrase the words of its own Special Committee on Education, excessively uniform, excessively academic, and almost entirely without relation to the practical aspects of life. Arts and crafts have been neglected, opportunities to give instruction a practical bent overlooked, and the curriculum has been dominated by the highly academic requirements of a university entrance examination. Neglect of practical subjects may be partly, but only partly, attributed to the origins of Ceylon's educational system in mission schools patterned on a nineteenth century British model. Doubtless more important is the

<hr>

[2]Bryce Ryan, "Institutional Factors in Sinhalese Fertility," *Milbank Memorial Fund Quarterly,* October, 1952.

exceptionally strong prejudice against manual labor, in which caste distinctions against certain manual occupations play an important role.

Not only in its influence upon the school curriculum but also in its character as a determinant of social values has caste impeded the growth of a more adequate supply of skilled workers and of supervisory employees. Although not as rigid or as closely knit as India's caste system, that of Ceylon exercises a strong influence in certain matters, such as marriage and choice of occupation. The dominant caste in Ceylon is that of cultivators; such skilled workers as carpenters, blacksmiths, and goldsmiths come much lower down the scale, not to mention the still lower fishermen, potters, laundrymen, and the like.

Co-ordinate with the bias of the educational system and the influence of caste in restricting the formation of a class of skilled and technical workers is the unusual prestige accorded government employment in Ceylon. One meets it on every side. Wage laborers prefer a government job, hoping it will give them the security not obtainable in private employment. A study of high school pupils in four provinces showed that 75 to 100 per cent of the boys preferred the government to any other employer. But perhaps the best guide is the all but universal system of dowry, which in putting a price on the groom accurately reflects the community's estimate of the security and prestige of his employment. Here even government clerks command a premium over comparable nongovernment workers, while for a husband in the higher reaches of administrative service, the prospective father-in-law will endow his daughter most handsomely.

All these influences may be seen at work in the ambitions of secondary school pupils, which correspond but poorly with the opportunities likely to be open to them. According to a study by Professor T. L. Green, of the University of Ceylon, 52 per cent of a fairly large sample of high school children aspired to employment in service occupations, whereas only 15 per cent of the population are employed in this group.[3] If several low-rated types of work are excluded, the concentration is even greater—about 50 per cent of aspirations directed toward occupations which employ less than 6 per cent of the total, among which those of doctor, lawyer, engineer, teacher, and government clerk and inspector rated especially high. On the other hand, only 25 per cent of the pupils cared to enter the basic productive lines which account for 64 per cent of Ceylon's active workers. Only in the distributive trades, such as transportation and commerce, did employment preferences and employment opportunities correspond closely (23 and 21 per cent respectively).

Now, of course, secondary school pupils are not representative of the entire population, and the disparity between ambitions and opportunities shown by these figures could doubtless be duplicated to some degree in other countries, even the United States. I merely use them to illustrate the low repute in which skills and supervisory labor are held. As Professor Green says:

Ceylon is in urgent need of high-level productive workers, the highly skilled workers and the well-educated foreman types who are of such im-

[3]The data presented here are from an unpublished paper, "Curriculum and Social Needs in Ceylon"; the sample referred to consisted of 1,365 pupils drawn from all provinces.

portance in technological cultures. . . . Of this class of worker, many of whom are the products of high-level education in the West, there is no sign in Ceylon, nor will there be while manual work is despised and ill rewarded and while academic education is looked on as a method of escape from caste and poverty because, by leading to high professional level work, it confers status and financial reward.

But a lack of workers with suitable technical and managerial skills is by no means the only socially rooted obstacle to industrial development. As in most other underdeveloped countries, there is among Ceylonese business-men relatively little of that spirit of enterprise and venturesomeness which leads their peers in Western countries in a restless search for opportunities to produce new goods or to introduce new and improved methods. Willing-ness to risk capital in new and untried production is slight. Instead, invest-ment in tea or rubber estates, in paddy land, in importing or speculating in merchandise is much preferred.

Ceylon's predominantly agricultural past, with its lack of industrial opportunities, no doubt goes a long way toward explaining these tendencies. So do the comparatively high yields, especially in recent years, from estate production and from speculative activities. More deep-seated is a senti-mental attachment to the land, derived from centuries-long dependence on its bounty and from the high rank of the cultivator caste.

Operating to repress a spirit of enterprise are some of the basic traits of Ceylonese culture. Where one's rank in society is determined by status, whether decreed by caste or by other sources of social values, individualism in all its manifestations takes a back seat. Buddhism, too, tends to de-em-phasize personal striving. Whereas individual effort is highly prized and highly rewarded in the West, in Ceylon and other Eastern societies it ranks relatively low in the scale of social values.

Also working to discourage industrial enterprise is the high value placed on government employment. The prestige associated with participation in the activities of colonial rulers accounts for this in part, but the security motive is also powerful, perhaps reflecting some underlying tendency toward insecurity among the Sinhalese people. In any event, self-employ-ment ranks exceedingly low as an alternative to the youth of Ceylon.[4]

IV

Social and cultural obstacles to rapid change in Ceylon are formidable. If the value system were rigid and incapable of alteration or adaptation or the prospect of recruiting sufficient leaders to spearhead change exceedingly dim, the outlook might be hopeless. There are, however, many signs that traditional customs are undergoing erosion: there is a substantial group of youthful and energetic sponsors of change both in and out of government and recruitment of additional personnel and development of appropriate methods of inducing necessary change are going on concurrently in several different sectors.

On the side of institutional change, the isolation of the village and there-

---

[4]According to T. L. Green, op. cit., an average of less than 10 per cent of a representative sample of secondary school boys chose self-employment, as against upwards of 75 per cent in favor of government employment.

with the hold of its traditional values is gradually diminishing. Thus a survey of four widely scattered villages[5] indicates strong approval of factory employment, if near at hand, even for daughters; approval of merit as against caste status as the basis for civil service employment; and approval of success achieved through self-effort as opposed to inherited class position. Through isolated chinks in the old pattern, there is a strong tendency for these to spread. This is enhanced in Ceylon by the comparatively high literacy of the population and by its relatively good system of communications and transport.

Ceylon fortunately possesses two recently developed agencies of change which promise to play a role of increasing importance. These are its co-operative societies and its rural development societies. There are three principal types of co-operatives: retail stores, credit societies, and production and marketing societies. From the point of view of helping the cultivator acquire better seed and implements and encouraging him to make effective use of them, the last two are the most important; these today reach one out of each four or five villagers. Because they use local personnel which knows what the peasant wants and what his problems are, these agencies have developed a grass-roots approach which takes suggestions as well as gives them. This is their great strength, for it is through local people who have the peasant's confidence that he can be most effectively induced to change his habitual routine. But it is also their weakness, for there is a shortage of local people who are sufficiently literate, honest, forceful, and responsible to assume local leadership. This means inefficiency and comparative failure in some local societies and inability to extend them as rapidly as would be desirable. There is no solution short of a gradual spread of literacy and a gradual increase in technical competence among the local populace.

But the co-operative societies are not alone in the field. More than five thousand rural development societies, under the guidance and direction of a hundred-odd officers of the government's Department of Rural Development, enlist the efforts of local people in making their communities better and more productive places in which to live. They do so by planning, organizing, and executing projects such as the construction of roads, wells, latrines, recreation facilities, and the like. The government, in addition to lending the assistance of its central staff, now furnishes some of the materials needed and is training several thousand village workers for these communal tasks at various training centers. Plans now under way look toward increasing the number of these societies to cover most of Ceylon's 20,000-odd villages.

Another parallel attack on the problem of agricultural improvement is being sponsored by the United Nations. This is the Fundamental Education Project, administered by Dr. Spencer Hatch and a staff of six technicians. Its purpose is to train Ceylonese nationals both in the technique of improving agriculture and conditions of village life and in the equally important technique of skillfully imparting this knowledge to the villager, so that he may receive the education fundamental to the betterment of his way of living. These trainees will become the natural leaders of co-opera-

[5]Bryce Ryan, "Ceylonese Value System," *Rural Sociology,* March, 1952.

for personal rights and private property, flouting of oral or written contractual obligations and exploitation of one Nigerian by another." They also make the point that "the need for self-help is not understood by the African business-man who looked to the government, and the government alone, for financial assistance in the expansion of his business instead of joining with others in a partnership or other form of common enterprise."

The relation of these presumed deficiencies to pre-existing social patterns, however, is nowhere explored. The explanation given fails to note the existence of this question, much less provide suggestions for the resolution of what, to the Mission, was a basic conflict. Rather the explanation proceeds, with serene disregard for psycho-cultural factors, to dismiss the problem of the need for self-help, for instance, by stating that "the heavy reliance on government is ... to some extent explicable as the response of a people still under tutelage and exposed to the complexities of European culture." No one would deny the relevance of these points. But one may well ask why pre-existing attitudes toward the rulers the present government has displaced were ignored as contributing factors. The relationships between the individual and his kin and local groups (which among the Ibo, for example, have resulted precisely in setting up various "forms of common enterprise" no less involving private partnership relations whose absence the Mission deplores) may have gone unrecognized, because they take forms dictated by the traditional modes of social structuring.

The problem of the motivation of labor in terms of adapting old patterns to the demands of a new kind of discipline has been much discussed. The relation of motivation to the expression of wants through increasing opportunities for access to a wide variety of commodities is obvious, as is its relation to the tradition of saving for a rainy day. The point is clearly expressed in the Agricultural Productivity Committee's supplement to the report of the Uganda Development Council (1954):

Although factual data on the subject are imprecise, there are indications that in many parts of the Protectorate African cash income exceeds expenditures. ... The incentive therefore for the majority of farmers to increase their cash incomes is limited; leisure and time for social intercourse ... are more valuable to them than money after their limited cash wants have been met. The family system in the rural areas still provides security against old age so that there is little need to save even on that. According to the information given to us, the average peasant works from three to four hours a day and, until the general pattern of his wants can be changed, this is not likely to be much increased.

THE MEASUREMENT OF INCOME AND INCOME CHANGE

4. On Measuring Economic Growth

*G. Warren Nutter**

Economic growth may be thought of as improvement in economic welfare or as expansion in productive capabilities. Thanks to a rich literature on the matter, we have been generously informed about the pitfalls in measuring gains in welfare.[1] It is appealing to believe that some of them are avoided when growth is measured in terms of productive capabilities: here there is seemingly no problem of changing or otherwise incomparable tastes, since the thing being measured is the capacity to satisfy wants, not the degree of satisfaction itself. Moreover, this would seem to be a "neutral" measure with the same meaning for every economy at any time: in each case what is supposedly being measured is the growing ability of an economy to fulfil whatever demands might be placed upon it.[2]

The question then arises whether this is what production indexes are supposed to measure. They measure something, and there seems to be general agreement that it is not economic welfare in the normal sense. There is also an intense interest in economic growth, and production indexes are continually referred to as measures of it.

The discussion that follows centers on these issues. In large part, it is simply a restatement of well-known, often trite, propositions; it has seemed useful to repeat them, nonetheless, in order to preserve continuity of thought and to reveal my full line of reasoning. The drift of the argument is that there is no simple way to measure growth in productive capabilities and that existing measures are by no means "neutral."

I. The Meaning of Growth in Productive Capacity

A. The nature of productive capacity. It is quite natural to think of an economy as having, at any moment, definite limits to its productive capa-

---

*From the *Journal of Political Economy,* February 1957, pp. 51–63. © 1957 by The University of Chicago. Reprinted by permission of The University of Chicago Press. The author is Professor of Economics, University of Virginia.

[1] See, e.g., J. R. Hicks' "The Valuation of the Social Income," *Economica,* New Ser., VII (May, 1940), 105–24; Simon Kuznets, "On the Valuation of Social Income—Reflections on Professor Hicks' Article," *Economica,* New Ser., XV (February and May, 1948), 1–16 and 116–31; and I. M. D. Little, "The Valuation of Social Income," *Economica,* New Ser., XVI (February, 1949), 11–26.

[2] To be sure, it has been pointed out in the recent literature on index numbers, including the articles cited in n. 1, that there are a number of theoretical difficulties encountered in intertemporal comparisons of productive capabilities. But the "neutrality" of the concept has typically been stressed (see e.g., Little, *op. cit.,* pp. 19–21; Abram Bergson, *Soviet National Income and Product in 1937* [New York: Columbia University Press, 1953], pp. 44–45 and 53–54; and Gregory Grossman, "National Income," in Abram Bergson [ed.], *Soviet Economic Growth* [Evanston, Ill.: Row, Peterson & Co., 1953], p. 4).

bilities. We conceive, that is, of a production frontier consisting of all the possible baskets of goods that could be produced if the economy exerted its best efforts: all baskets short of, or bordering on, the frontier are within the economy's productive capacity; all baskets beyond the frontier are outside its capacity. This notion is simple enough and has great analytical significance. As with all economic concepts, the trouble comes when it is put into operation in a world that does not stand still. Time, as we look backward, reveals changes of all sorts, and this makes it difficult to separate the constant from the inconstant in the notion of capacity. Time, as we look forward, means opportunities for change, and this leads to confusion in defining the production frontier.

If the concept of productive capacity is to be useful, some variables on which it depends must obviously be impounded elsewhere. The traditional and most fruitful approach is to define productive capacity in terms of the given technology, resources, and institutional structure. This definition raises apparent problems when it is applied to an actual historical setting (as it must be when growth is being measured), because the "givens" are in fact changing continuously, at least in "developed" economies. Hence, in the strictest sense, productive capacity could have meaning only at an instant of time, and the production frontier would degenerate to the basket of goods actually being produced at that instant. Carried to this extreme, the concept makes no more sense than at the other extreme, where everything is left free to vary over limitless time. The way out, as in all useful theory, is to compromise and to define productive capacity as applying to an adjustment period long enough to allow for "broad" shifts in the structure of outputs but still short enough to rule out "significant" growth of technology and resources. It need not be added that setting the length of this period is an empirical problem and, as such, depends on the economy in question.

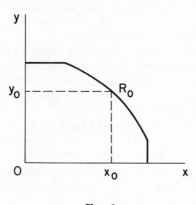

Fig. 1

It is clear that the adjustment period to be used depends also on the matter being analyzed. In some cases, the period must be kept "short," in others "long"; and we may speak loosely about "short-run" and "long-run" productive capacity. This notion differs, however, from the short and long runs of price theory, which are linked to the passage of analytical, not historical, time.[3] But there is no point in theoretical hairsplitting here, because

[3]There is no reason why productive capacity cannot be conceived of in a purely static sense, without reference to any historical context; and one could, by appropriately defining *ceteris paribus* conditions, devise as many static "runs" as he wished, including one allowing for an indefinitely long adjustment period. But it is hard to see the relevance of such abstract static concepts to economic problems of measuring economic growth, which deal with theorizing

the general argument to follow does not stand or fall on any precise conception of the notion of productive capacity. There is much room for differences of approach on this matter without affecting the relevant conclusions.

With these introductory remarks in mind, we may go on to consider the characteristics of productive capacity. So that the discussion may be carried beyond broad generalities, let us suppose we are dealing with an economy that is undergoing continuous change in technology and resources. For simplicity we may imagine that only two products, X and Y, are produced, both being "final" products. Productive capacity may then be pictured as the production frontier curve shown in Figure 1. The basket of goods "now" being produced lies, let us suppose, on the frontier—in particular, at Point R_0, representing outputs x_0 and y_0. The curve then tells us that, given an adjustment period of (say) a year, the basket R_0 could be transformed into any alternative basket on or below the curve.[1] Only the area above the curve is excluded from the productive possibility of the given technology and resources.

The shape of a production frontier is determined by the opportunity (or transformation) cost of X in terms of Y. Figure 1 follows the usual assumption that (marginal) opportunity costs rise with output, and hence the curve is concave downward. This seems to be a reasonable generalization in view of the limited adjustment period, but it perhaps oversimplifies the conditions in a many-product economy. Since nothing of any great moment in the present discussion hinges on the precise shape of the production frontier in all directions, I shall not probe the matter further at this point.

Since the production frontier is defined for a span of truly historical time, the relations shown on it are not reversible. That is to say, if the economy were to convert R_0 into some other basket, taking a year to do so, it could then reconvert to something larger than—to the northeast of—R_0 if it chose to. In the economy we are talking about, the production frontier is continuously edging upward; in analysis this movement is artificially halted for a span of time and expressed instead as an upward shift at the end of the period.

It will be noted that the production frontier contains a maximum x and a maximum y, which means that the opportunity cost of each product becomes infinite at some output. This output is, of course, what we commonly refer to as "capacity" for the product in question, as determined by existing plant and facilities and by such moving of resources as can be accomplished within the allowable adjustment period.

A production frontier may have either a forward-looking or a backward-looking meaning. Looking backward, one conceives of a specific frontier

---

applied to historical time. In particular, the notion of different stages of equilibrium does not have the same force or meaning in this area of analysis as in, say, price theory.

[1] There is presumably a different curve associated with each basket of goods that might alternatively be produced now, since the form of capital goods will presumably vary, if ever so slightly, with the output mix. This is a refinement that may well be ignored, however; it is not clearly relevant to the matters being discussed.

in the past marking off all the baskets an economy could have produced, had it chosen to; looking forward, one conceives of a frontier in the future marking off the baskets it could produce, were it to choose to. For each date in the past, there is a unique frontier; but this is not the case for each date in the future: the nature of any future frontier depends on many actions to be taken in the meantime. This is a question not merely of growth in resources and technology but also of foresight and premeditation, especially where radical shifts in an economy's structure are required. An example is conversion to a war economy or later reconversion. Other relevant things equal, the earlier the preparation for conversion or reconversion is undertaken, the farther away (within limits) will be the production frontier in the vicinity of the basket of goods aimed at. To speculate further on this matter would quickly take us into the complex issues of central planning as opposed to a market system, which would serve no purpose in this paper. It is enough to say that the production frontier for next year depends on what output mix the economy now decides, in one way or another, it would like to have then, and on the actions taken to further this decision.

Productive capacity is, of course, not always fully employed: the basket of goods being produced sometimes lies inside the production frontier. For both practical and analytical reasons, it is useful to distinguish voluntary and involuntary unemployment and to exclude the former from productive capacity as such. Thus a rise in unemployment, taken in its conventional sense, may be viewed as leaving a specific production frontier unchanged and as having its only effect on the movement of the frontier over time. A rise in leisure, on the other hand, may be viewed as constricting a production frontier, that is, as reducing productive capacity.

Productive capacity plus leisure make up what can be termed "economic capacity." Economic capacity could be pictured formally in Figure 1 by adding a third axis to measure hours of leisure. The curve presently shown represents productive capacity for a given level of leisure: an increase in leisure would move the curve to the southwest; a decrease would move it to the northeast. In this view, leisure is treated as outside the productive sphere of the economy but at the same time as part of productive potential in the broadest sense. It is certainly clear that choice of leisure generally involves sacrifice of goods that could otherwise be produced.

A final question arises whether productive capacity should take account of trade with other economies. The production frontier may be viewed as the baskets of goods available before trade, on the one hand, or after trade, on the other. The view preferred depends on the problems being studied. There is much to be said—as far as the range of problems being discussed in this paper is concerned—for concentrating on strictly internal productive capabilities. Desirable as this may be, it is not really possible either conceptually or empirically; the effects of trade cannot be fully isolated, mainly because traded items include "intermediate" as well as "final" products. We must therefore be content with a hybrid concept at best: productive capacity at existing or contemplated levels of trade.

B. *Growth in productive capacity.* In the broadest sense, growth in productive capacity consists in an upward shift in the production frontier. There are countless kinds of shifts possible—presumably there is a unique shift for every set of economic decisions. But this view, besides being useless, is wrong; for many decisions counteract one another, and the effects wash out. It should be possible, if theorizing is at all possible in this area, to select the few most important factors determining growth and to analyze their combined effects. This is indeed what economists have done over the generations, though it must be added that the empirical base of theorizing—and hence the theorizing—has been, and still is, notably weak.

In line with the traditional content of theory, we may say at the most general level that productive capacity grows in some fashion when the stock of resources (human and non-human) expands, and when technology improves. This statement merely starts us on the way by setting up two boxes into which casual factors are to be filed, leaving the most important questions unanswered. We may proceed further, while still bypassing many issues, by noting that the growth in productive capacity brought about by these two factors involves, with minor exceptions, growth in "capacity" outputs of all products. That is to say, one characteristic of growth is that, for all practical purposes, the entire production frontier shifts upward; the new frontier does not intersect the preceding one anywhere. This may not be strictly true for the shortest run frontiers, since they depend heavily for their shape on the specific forms of resources; but it would surely be applicable even here with the passage of several periods.

For concreteness, let us set the adjustment period underlying the production frontier at a year, and suppose accordingly that the frontier shifts at the end of each year. Growth of productive capacity from one year to the next year may then be pictured as in Figure 2, where the production frontier is represented as q_0^* for year zero and as q_1^* for year one. The only matter of importance for the present is that q_1^* lies entirely above q_0^*.

Growth in productive capacity depends in the first instance, of course, on investment in so-called "tangible" capital. This in turn is determined by the structure of the basket of goods actually being produced. If we think of X as capital goods and Y as consumer goods, then the larger x is in year zero, the greater will be the shift in the production frontier at the end of year zero—other relevant things being the same. Thus the shift will be of one magnitude if basket R_0 is produced; larger if a basket to the southeast is produced; and smaller if a basket to the northwest is produced. The exact nature of the shift—the shape of q_1^* relative to that of q_0^*—will depend on the forms of capital goods produced as well as on the aggregate level of capital goods production. As noted previously, however, this is a short-run matter: in a forward-looking sense, the effects of specific forms of investment can be erased over a moderate period of growth.

The nature of growth in productive capacity similarly depends on what is happening to the ratio of human to nonhuman resources, proper account being taken of leisure. Resources never all grow at the same rate, if only because some are "fixed" by nature or variable only at nature's caprice. In a broader sense, there is no inherent link between capital and population. Hence, if changes in technology are ignored, there is no reason to expect an "equal" shift in the production frontier in all directions. That is, growth in productive capacity should not be expected to be homogeneous in the mathematical sense. This is shown in Figure 2 by the fact that, loosely speaking, q_1^* lies further from q_0^* to the right of R_0 than it does to the left.

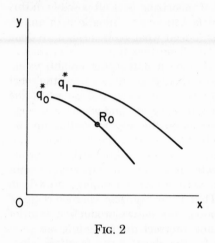

FIG. 2

The second great force underlying growth is technological progress. Technology is knowledge—in particular, knowledge of how to produce things. It should be taken as encompassing productive techniques in the narrow sense while leaving out broader matters of basic institutional structure, which are best treated separately. Of course, it is not easy to separate technological development from growth in resources, for a large measure of new technology becomes concretely embodied in new forms of resources and products. I shall ignore this difficulty without belittling it.

The precise effect of technological progress on movement of the production frontier is again neither obvious nor simple. It is plausible to suppose that technological advance is uneven, proceeding much more rapidly in some directions than in others. Observation of the world about us, both casual and careful, confirms this expectation.[5] We may therefore expect the production frontier to shift unevenly in response to technological improvements, just as it does in response to growth in resources.

Very little is known about the circumstances favoring technological progress, and this must perhaps always remain a highly speculative matter. By nature, technological advance is the result of exploration: explicit results can be planned for only within very narrow bounds, for the results cannot be known until they are discovered. An important distinction can be drawn between research and development, roughly corresponding to exploration and purposive adaptation; but even in the developmental stage the scope of planning is severely limited, the findings remaining to the end only hazily foreseen. The most important factors in technological progress would seem to be sound research procedures, specialization of tasks, communication of findings, and entrepreneurship in seeking discoveries and in putting them to work.

As noted already, technological progress means the continual introduction of new products. Growth therefore takes the form not only of expanded capacity to produce existing goods but also of ability to produce new ones. Examined closely, this distinction (like most) fades at the margins, since

[5]The most convincing evidence comes from the wide dispersion of rates of growth in resource productivity for individual industries (see John Kendrick, *Productivity Trends: Capital and Labor* ["Occasional Papers," No. 53 (New York: National Bureau of Economic Research, 1956)], p. 17).

few products remain unchanged for long. Nevertheless, the distinction has real content and, indeed, must have if the notion of growth itself is meaningful; otherwise there would be nothing but change, a movement from one set of unique conditions to another. The answer is, of course, that most products change so gradually that we may consider them, for most practical problems, as constant over interesting periods. In any case, the movement of the production frontier involves taking on new dimensions—adding new products—as well as expanding in the existing ones.

Several generalizations emerge from this brief and superficial discussion. First, in the normal course of events we may expect growth to involve an outward shift in the entire production frontier. Second, the magnitude and form of the shift depend on the growth of resources and on technological progress, both of which are uneven in direction. Third, productive capacity itself grows unevenly in different directions. More precisely, the opportunity costs at each basket of goods change, at least in some directions, as the production frontier expands. This conclusion is derived from evidence all about us showing changes in relative costs as the economy grows, and also from evidence showing differential growth in productivity in specific industries.[6] It may therefore be taken as established that the effects of even growth in resources and of uneven technological progress have not wholly offset each other in the economies we know something about.

II. Conventional Measures of Growth

A. *The nature of a production index.* A production index is essentially a device for transforming diverse rates of growth for individual products into a single rate applying to every product. Put another way, it measures growth in terms of a standard basket of goods by translating whatever basket is actually produced into an equivalent multiple of the standard basket. A production index therefore rests on certain implicit assumptions about the shape of the production frontier and the nature of its growth over time. While the implication about shape differs with the index-number formula used, in every case growth is implied to be equal in all directions. The problems of measurement arise from the fact that the implications about the shape and growth of the production frontier are at best only rough approximations to reality.

Let us consider, first, the production index based on linear aggregates of output, the most common type used. Here growth is measured by comparing sums of weighted outputs, the weights being fixed. Expressed in symbols,

$$Q = \frac{q_1}{q_0} = \frac{mx_1 + ny_1}{mx_0 + ny_0},$$

(1)

where Q stands for the production index relating year one to year zero; q for aggregate output; m and n for weights attached to outputs of X and

[6] Changes in relative costs by themselves would not be sufficient evidence, since they might be traceable to the altered structure of the basket of goods being produced. Differential growth in productivity (defined as output per unit of inputs-in-general) cannot be so readily attributed to shifts in the product mix.

Y, respectively; and the subscripts 0 and 1 for years zero and one, respectively.

The aggregate outputs q_0 and q_1 can be considered as representing production frontiers with constant opportunity costs m/n. These frontiers are pictured in Figure 3. The basket of goods produced in year zero is shown as R_0; the basket produced in year one as R_1. The basket R_0 is taken to be equivalent to any other basket on the line q_0, which is defined in equation (1). If basket R_0 had been transformed in year zero to any other basket, it is supposed that it would have been necessary to accept m/n fewer units of y for each addition unit of x—that is, m/n is taken to be the opportunity cost of X in terms of Y. Similarly, the basket R_1 is taken to be equivalent to any other basket on q_1, with the same opportunity costs applying. I shall refer to the lines q_0 and q_1 as "index frontiers," to distinguish them from actual production frontiers.

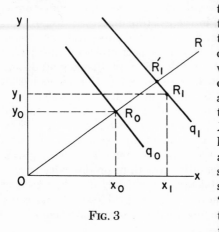

FIG. 3

The construction of the production index amounts to transforming R_1 into some multiple of R_0, so that both x and y are measured as increasing by the same percentage. This means that the index is an estimate of what would have happened if the ratio of x and y had remained constant. In Figure 3 the measuring process amounts to constraining the path of expansion to the ray OR, which is done by transforming R_1 into R'_1.[7] It is clearly implied that R'_1 could have been produced in year one in place of R_1; hence we see again that the index frontier q_1 presumably represents a production frontier.[8]

It is convenient for graphic presentation to show the production index as the distance to the index frontier for year one divided by the distance to

[7]Conceptually, it makes no difference whether growth is thought of as being measured in terms of R_0 or in terms of R_1, and the argument could equally well be developed on the basis of a ray passing through R_1 with an implied transformation of R_0 into some other basket on q_0. For the sake of simplicity, this point will not be pursued.

[8]Saying that R'_1 could have been produced instead of R'_1 is not entirely the same as saying that R_1, once produced, could be quickly transformed into R_1. The production index would be founded on a sterile concept, however, unless the latter were also implied to be true. Nobody is much interested in what could have been, unless, in the relevant sense, it could also still be.

[9]It may be readily seen that the distance (r) to an index frontier is proportional to the aggregate output (q) designating that frontier, and that the factor of proportionality is a function solely of the output ratio (yx) along which the distance is measured. For

$$r = \sqrt{x^2 + y^2} = x\sqrt{1 + \left(\frac{y}{x}\right)^2},$$

the index frontier for year zero, the distances being measured along a ray holding the output ratio constant.[9] In Figure 3 the index number Q would then be OR'_1/OR_0. It can now be seen that the construction of a production index amounts to generating a set of index frontiers implying equal growth in all directions. For suppose that OR is rotated in either direction, carrying R_0 and R_1 with it, while they remain on their respective index frontiers; then the magnitude OR'_1/OR_0 remains the same, since it is equal to q_1/q_0. Put more simply and loosely, no matter where the baskets of goods actually produced might lie on two index frontiers, the production index would come out the same.

B. *Problems of measurement.* Let us consider next some of the problems raised by the nature of production indexes. The first class of problems arises from the implication of constant opportunity costs, which, as we have seen, is contrary to the nature of things. This leads to an inherent ambiguity in any index number, flowing from the fact that the measure of growth will differ for different baskets of goods on the same production frontiers. That is to say, the index number depends on the baskets actually produced, not on the levels of productive capacity they represent.

Figure 4 is the same as Figure 3, with the addition of production frontiers q_0^* and q_1^*. It has been supposed that the production index is weighted with the opportunity costs prevailing in year zero when basket R_0 was produced; hence at R_0 the index frontier for year zero is tangent to the production frontier for the same year. The same opportunity costs will not necessarily prevail at basket R_1 (though they could), and, for convenience of argument, it has been supposed that they do not. The essential point to be made here is that the production index will vary with the position of R_1 on the production frontier q_1^*, as can be seen from the fact that OR'_1 will vary. This means that there is no unique index number associated with any given shift in the production

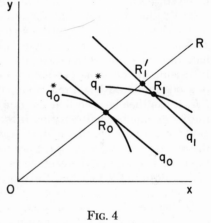

FIG. 4

$$q = mx + ny = x\left[m + n\left(\frac{y}{x}\right)\right];$$

$$\therefore q = \frac{m + n(y/x)}{\sqrt{1 + (y/x)^2}} \cdot r.$$

If, therefore, the distances r_1 to q_1 and r_0 to q_0 are measured along a ray holding y/x constant, then

$$\frac{r_1}{r_0} = \frac{q_1}{q_0}$$

frontier; or, put the other way round, the index number calculated from observed baskets of goods gives only one of many possible measures of the actual growth in productive capacity.

It is important to stress that this is not a weighting problem, though weights may, of course, influence the index number. Suppose, for instance, that R_1 were at the point on the production frontier q_1^* where opportunity costs are the same as R_0; then the index number would be the same no matter which year was used in choosing weights, since the weights would be the same. Similarly, suppose R_1 were at the intersection of OR with q_1^*; then there would also be only one index number no matter what weights were used, since both outputs would show the same percentage increase. For all other points the index number may be different when year-one weights are used instead of year-zero weights.[10] But this is something quite aside from the main point being made, which is that, for any given weighting system, the index number varies with the position of R_1 (or R_0) on its production frontier.

The assumption of even growth of productive capacity, implicit in production indexes, raises a second class of problems in that the index number depends on the structure of production. To see the major problem involved, let us suppose that the opportunity cost of X is declining historically, in the sense that for any given output of Y the slope of the production frontier is diminishing as the frontier moves outward over time. This situation is shown in Figure 4. Let us suppose in addition—to eliminate the "index-number problem"—that the outputs of X and Y are both increasing at the same percentage rate: in terms of Figure 4, all baskets of goods produced lie on the same path of expansion, that is, on a ray like OR. It can then be seen that the rate of growth in production indicated by the index number will vary with the path of expansion followed: as the path OR is rotated to the right, the rate increases; as it is rotated to the left, the rate decreases. Hence the more heavily the output of X is emphasized, the higher will be the percentage rates of growth in the outputs of *both* X and Y, despite the fact that the growth in productive capacity is the same in every case. It must be stressed that the differences here are "real," reflecting uneven growth in productive capacity; they are not the results of "index-number bias." No measure can eliminate the inherent ambiguity surrounding the movement of the production frontier, since the movement cannot be summarized in a single unique measure.

A third class of problems arises from the fact that the dimensions of productive capacity change while it grows. Suppose a new product is introduced in year one into our simple two-product economy. Since this product did not exist in year zero, no account will be taken of it in the production index, which is based on a fixed list of products. The index will

[10]The discussion here has reflected the conventional approach to weighting, which limits the choice to that between base-year and given-year weights. As will perhaps become increasingly clear from the discussion to come, one may quite justly raise the question whether either of these weighting systems has any inherent superiority over a compromise system—that is, whether the problem of choice should be put so starkly as it is in the conventional approach. In any event, the main point of this paragraph remains no matter what alternative weighting systems one has in mind.

therefore understate growth on this count. This has nothing to do with the fact that the output of new products tends to grow faster than the output of old ones, a familiar generalization; rather it has to do with our inability, in a changing economy, to construct any index number that accounts for all uses of resources at all times. The more radically the uses of resources are changing (that is, the more rapidly the dimensions of productive capacity are increasing), the more inadequate the measure of growth in productive capacity.[11]

In discussing these three major classes of problems, I have restricted myself to production indexes constructed on the arithmetic formula. It may be useful to digress very briefly in order to show that the primary conclusions are not affected by using the geometric formula, once so popular. As in the case of the arithmetic formula, even growth of productive capacity is assumed. In other respects matters are worsened, since the shape of the index frontier is the reverse of the shape of the production frontier. Using the same symbols as those in equation (1), we may express the geometric index as follows:

$$(2) \qquad Q = \frac{q_1}{q_0} = \frac{(x_1^m y_1^n)^{(1/m+n)}}{(x_0^m y_0^n)^{(1/m+n)}}.$$

It is seen from this that each index frontier q is represented as a rectangular hyperbola; when shown graphically, as in Figure 5, the index frontier is convex downward, whereas the production frontier it is supposed to represent is concave. Only under very improbable conditions will such an index frontier be a first-order approximation of a production frontier, and the relation between index numbers computed on geometric and arithmetic bases cannot be summarized in any manner that has economic meaning. It is indeed difficult to justify use of a geometric production index, for it solves none of the problems posed by the arithmetic index and introduces some additional ones of its own.

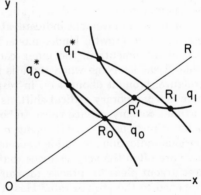

Fig. 5

Let me conclude this discussion of conventional measures of growth by noting that I have concentrated on problems in the abstract, without dwelling on the well-known difficulties in moving from idealized variables to their empirical counterparts. Outputs are available in general only for rather long accounting periods—usually a year—and hence represent the average rate over the entire period; weights can only approximate relevant marginal costs, both because they must be rather arbitrarily chosen as to

[11]This consideration argues strongly for the use of deflated value of output or chained-link indexes instead of the standard formulas based on fixed weights and a fixed list of products.

time and place and because available data may not be closely related to marginal costs; production is sometimes not taking place at the limits of productive capacity; and so on. These problems are of a different order from those discussed in the abstract, but they influence measures of growth all the same. They are neglected here, not because they are unimportant, but because they have been so well attended to elsewhere.

III. Some Tentative Generalizations

We are bound to ask ourselves what can reasonably be done with measures of economic growth if they are cloaked in such obscurity. The extreme view would argue that growth cannot be measured, that index numbers should be thrown away as useless. This is obviously nonsense, for we all know production indexes are useful. A wiser counsel is to use them with caution and only where needed. This warning has, indeed, long been raised, but it has usually grown out of concern for "bias" in weighting systems. The traditional problems of weighting are important, but one may wonder, in the light of other problems, whether they have not been too strongly stressed to the exclusion of more disturbing fundamental questions. We must at least always ask ourselves what it is we are trying to measure, and then inquire how well it can in fact be measured. In overlooking these questions, we have developed some bad habits, in particular when it comes to comparing growth in different economies.

In measuring growth for an individual country that is following a reasonably stable path of expansion, a production index has a rather clear meaning. Its movement up or down indicates, at worst, the direction of growth; the changes in movement indicate, at best, whether there is acceleration or retardation in growth. Under moderately favorable conditions the magnitude of movements in the index can also be taken more or less at face value. Troubles come when there is a long-range alteration in productive structure, brought about, say, in response to major innovations; or when there is a temporary radical shift, as in conversion from a peacetime to a wartime economy, or vice versa. In both cases there are substantial changes in the directions of growth being measured, and these may show up as spurious indications of sudden acceleration or retardation. Unfortunately, these are often the very changes that stir up most interest and create the most urgent pleas for precise measures. The question is raised: What has happened to the growth rate? Has it jumped from 3 per cent a year to 5 per cent, or only to 4½ per cent? Any simple and precise answer to these questions is bound to tell only part of the story, and that part is likely to be misleading.[12]

It is wise under all conditions to lay stress on the structure of growth, and this is in fact what we do. Whenever possible, separate indexes are usually prepared for different sectors of the economy: manufacturing, min-

[12]A classic example of faulty behavior under conditions of a radical shift in production structure is provided by the Federal Reserve Board index of industrial production covering World War II and the immediate postwar years (see Geoffrey Moore, *Production of Industrial Materials in World Wars I and II* ["Occasional Papers," No. 18, (New York: National Bureau of Economic Research, 1944)]).

ing, agriculture, services, and so on. The more narrowly these sectors are defined (excluding possibly the extreme of individual products), the more meaningful the individual indexes; for each then refers to a more or less evenly growing and relatively flat segment of the production frontier. The pattern of such growth rates is an important way of summarizing growth in productive capacity as a whole. To be sure, it is by no means free from ambiguity, but at the minimum it tends to reveal the sources of ambiguity.

So much for measuring growth in a single country. Again, as has been long recognized, the most serious dangers lie in comparisons between countries or between widely separated periods for the same country. It has become common to express differences in growth rates in very precise terms: country A's growth rate is said to be 1½ percentage points higher than country B's, and so on. Quite apart from the question of the relative adequacy of data on which the basic measures rest, such comparisons have little meaning unless careful attention is given to the productive structures in the countries involved.

One economy may, for example, be undergoing a radical metamorphosis, while the other is simply growing in size. This is not merely a matter of taking account of a country's "stage of economic development," about which little is really known. The main point is the one already made: a radical change in productive structure means a shift in the dimensions in which growth is measured and a probable "distortion" in the production index.

Along similar lines, one economy may be placing heavier emphasis than the other on products whose costs are falling. It is true that, to the extent that these products are capital equipment, there may "really" be a greater growth in productive capacity in the one economy than there would otherwise be. In any event, other things being equal, it is possible, as we have seen, for *all* outputs to grow more rapidly in an economy if production is shifted more heavily in favor of products whose opportunity costs are declining over time.

Finally, one economy may be more austere than another, limiting its efforts to a smaller range of activities. Again, to the extent that production indexes do not reflect the expenditure of resources on improving the quality of existing products and on introducing new ones, the austere economy will, other things being equal, show a faster growth rate. A related problem arises from the fact that the austere economy is probably operating close to its full economic capacity: at most, leisure does not increase so rapidly in the austere economy as elsewhere. For many problems it is necessary that this be recognized, perhaps by including leisure in the production index.

These considerations have special significance for one of the burning issues nowadays: whether Communist economies are outstripping capitalist economies. On all scores, conventional measures of growth seem to favor the Communist economies. Consider, for instance, a comparison between the Soviet Union and the United States. At least during the interwar period, the Soviet economy was undergoing a radical transformation, moving from handicraft to mechanized production, from agriculture to industry, and so on. Whenever choice has been possible, it has steadily emphasized products for which the largest reductions in costs could be expected. And it has been the very model of austerity: products are as simple as possible; quality improves slowly, if at all; efforts are concentrated on the existing line of products, with few new ones being introduced except in special areas; and leisure has shown little tendency to increase.

By contrast, over the same period the American economy has moved along a more or less steady path of development, with radical changes only in wartime, business cycles aside. The structure of production has been dictated essentially by consumers, who insist on consuming some things in larger quantity even though their costs are not declining. The trend of costs is not the sole—or the dominating—determinant of growth in production; consumer tastes have a way of entering the picture. Left on his own, the consumer does not freely choose the austere road, either; he insists, to the dismay of planners, on ever increasing variety and frills and—even more perversely—on more and more leisure.

The moral of the story is that there is no "neutral" measure of growth in productive capacity. This, too, is a will-o'-the-wisp. In comparing economies, one must somehow standardize the dimensions in which growth is being measured. The way this should be done will depend on the problems at hand. In any case, the job cannot be defaulted to the harried statistician, after he is given a mechanism for cranking out the answer in a single number. The job requires patience, judgment, and willingness to work with more than one indicator of growth.

5. The Role of National Income Estimates in the Statistical Policy of an Underdeveloped Area[1]

Dudley Seers*

Techniques of national income analysis have become a useful, in fact, an essential, part of the applied economics of the United States, Western Europe and other "developed" industrial economies. It is accordingly tempting for those working in underdeveloped areas, but who have studied and practised economic statistics in developed areas, to try to apply these techniques, even though the economic problems and statistical resources are very different. They are likely, therefore, to attach a good deal of importance to estimating the national income, whether they are working

*From the *Review of Economic Studies,* Vol. XX, 1952–53, pp. 159–168. The author is Professor of Economics, Center for Quantitative Study of Economic Structure and Growth, Yale University.

[1]The argument of this paper owes a great deal to many discussions, both abroad and in Oxford, with Miss Peter Ady, who collaborated with me in preparing preliminary social accounts for Burma, and with Mr. C. R. Ross, who collaborated with me on the same task for the Gold Coast. I have talked about the main theme at some length with Mr. Searle, the Chief Statistician of the Colonial Office. Professor Frankel and Mr. Worswick, of Oxford, have also read an earlier draft of the paper and discussed the conclusions with me, as have Professor Langley, of the College of Arts and Sciences (Baghdad), and Mr. Billington, of the Government Statistician's Office of the Gold Coast. It was also read and discussed at a meeting of the discussion group in Oxford, convened by Professor and Mrs. Hicks. I must add the customary disclaimer that, whilst I have benefited greatly from these discussions, nobody else is responsible for the paper's conclusions.

as private or official statisticians[2]: manuals on national income practice usually encourage them to do so, by giving little or no consideration to the special problems of underdeveloped areas.

Estimates of the national income of an underdeveloped area are often prefaced by a general discussion of the uses of national income estimates. I propose to discuss the merits usually claimed for such estimates, merits based on experience in developed countries: only after asking ourselves to what extent these uses apply to the problems of an underdeveloped area, can we decide how important a place national income estimates should have in its statistical policy.

I. The Uses of National Income Estimates in a Developed Economy

Comparisons between the total product and some economic category are useful as indications of magnitude in discussing developed economies. Are they also useful for underdeveloped countries? The meaning of such comparisons depends on which of the aggregates is being used; "geographical" income, the income arising in the territory, or "national" income, the income of those normally resident. For developed countries such a distinction is not important in practice, because aggregates differ only slightly from one another in actual size (and often not much harm is done if the difference is ignored). In the case of underdeveloped countries, however, the profits and interest on foreign capital are usually substantial, so that "geographical" income is very different from "national" income; and the two aggregates may move differently, according to the relative growth or decline of this property income payable abroad. The size of the national income, and thus the meaning of such comparisons, depends also on how far the definition of "income" has been pushed into the field where activity for cash payment shades into activity which is not marketed. This field is a broad and changeable one for underdeveloped territories, because of the considerable activity of all kinds—especially food production and building —not sold for cash. Moreover, the statistical material is so thin for parts of all underdeveloped economies that estimates of the national income, on any definition, are subject to large and varying errors. For all these reasons, a statement that a certain quantity "represents x per cent of the national income" may tell us much less than it appears to.

Secondly, *per caput* income estimates are used for international comparisons. May this not be rather dangerous if any of the countries are underdeveloped? Apart from the difficulties in interpreting the "national income" for the reasons mentioned above (not to speak of difficulties arising from the uncertainty of population estimates[3], such comparisons are not at all straightforward. They involve in effect some system of price-weighting for the various commodities. But immediately the question arises: what system of price-weights? By contrast to prices of manufactures, the prices of primary products move so violently from year to year (often from

[2]Perhaps I should add that I approached economic statistics of underdeveloped countries in this spirit, and only gradually, and reluctantly, became doubtful about it.

[3]And, indeed, of differences of coverage for "national income" and "population": often the latter includes the activities of people so far from the "market economy" that no measure of their activities is available.

minute to minute) that the answer will depend almost entirely on what weighting system is used.[1] Finally, there are difficulties of interpretation. In "real" comparisons, we probably have at the back of our minds the desire to compare efficiency or welfare, yet neither similarity of the conditions of production nor constancy of wants can be assumed if climatic and social conditions are very different. Moreover, as Professor Kuznets has argued, many of the tertiary services in the more developed countries, such as transport, are really "cost" rather than "income" items[5]; and the borderline between marketed activity, and, therefore, between items included in and excluded from the national product and unpaid family work, varies greatly from country to country, particularly in food processing. In the hands of authorities, such international comparisons may yield correlations which throw light on the circumstances of economic progress, and they tell us something about relative efficiencies and standards of living, but they are very widely abused. Do they not on the whole mislead more than they instruct, causing a net reduction in human knowledge?[6]

Thirdly, national income is a useful indicator of changes in a single country over time. Here again, the first step, separating price and quantity changes so as to construct a series in "fixed prices," is a severe practical problem. Secondly, because of changes in the terms of trade (often the chief short-run influence on national expenditure) we get quite different series for "real income" and "real expenditure." Moreover, quantities of output may well be correlated with prices, so that the shape of the "real income" series will largely depend on which period prices are used as weights. Is there, then, much meaning in any one answer to the question; what would be the national incomes in years $A, B, C, \ldots N$, if we measure them all in the prices of year A? The fundamental difficulty is the same as for international comparison: in a few years an underdeveloped country may have changed so much that for the purposes of the underlying assumptions in economic analysis it can no longer be considered the same country.[7]

We usually want to push the argument a stage further, and throw some light on productivity by relating an output series to a series of the volume of labor used. There are several problems here. Discontinuities on the output of primary products, due to crop diseases or mineral finds, will affect the national product, because the range of products in underdeveloped economies is by definition narrow. Turning to the denominator of a pro-

[1] A practical point is that it is often very difficult to get appropriate "annual average" prices of primary products, either for the weights of a quantity index or for the relatives of a price index, because the available information is usually an unweighted average of a selection of prices (e.g. "closing" prices for each day), whereas we would really want prices weighted by quantity sold. "Average values" of exports are to some extent free from this objection, and they may indeed be the best prices to use, but they are unfortunately often only rather indirectly related to the actual f.o.b. market values of the commodity concerned, and they may not be carefully calculated.

[5] e.g. *National Income: A Summary of Findings*, p. 116.

[6] The case against drawing conclusions about "welfare" from international national income comparisons has been put forcibly, and perhaps conclusively, by Professor Frankel in a paper read to the Royaumont Conference of the International Association for Research in Income and Wealth (1951), published in *Oxford Economic Papers*, Vol. 4, No. 1, February, 1952.

[7] Similar difficulties about "overhead" tertiary services will also arise.

ductivity ratio, in developed countries the structure of the labour force with respect to skill is fairly constant; its membership does not change greatly in the short run, and it is usually engaged on activities which eventuate quite rapidly in measurable output. In underdeveloped countries, on the other hand, not only does the skill structure change rapidly, but the people in various jobs are often quite different from one year to the next, because of labour migration or simply high rates of turnover. Moreover, they are engaged on activities yielding output with various delays (without even a constant average time-lag)." In view of these snags, can the productivity of labour be usefully measured from the national income?

In historical analysis of national income in developed countries perhaps the most useful applications have been on the "expenditure" side, relating the aggregate to components such as consumption (the "consumption function") or investment ("multiplier analysis"). Similar functions may be difficult to obtain for an underdeveloped country. The links between investment and national expenditure will be very much weaker: the profitability of investment will be determined by external markets, rather than by the internal level of activity, and the secondary "multiplier" effects of investment will largely operate overseas, because so much investment consists of imported capital goods (including building materials). Nor can we expect a stable relation between consumption and total national expenditure: changes in national expenditure due to changes in export prices certainly cause changes in consumption, but the relation between them depends on how much of the price change is absorbed by company or marketing board profits, on how rapidly the price change percolates through into local expenditure, and on what changes are induced in income distribution and in the public's spending habits."

In fact, if we pause for a moment to consider the possibilities of "model building" more closely, can we hope for firm structural relations to hold? The institutions of most underdeveloped countries are changing at a violent pace. If "cash" farming is spreading, if there are rapid extensions of retail markets and changes in their organisation, if the public's attitudes to economic stimulants are still evolving, then can one expect *average* coefficients linking different economic categories, coefficients which have been calculated from several years' experience, to mean a great deal?

We run some danger of overlooking this central weakness because of the words we use: we need the help of metaphors when we think about an economy, and in carrying over a metaphor from the economies of developed economies we may tacitly be carrying over a description. The very words "mechanism" or "model" convey the mental picture of a great piece of machinery. It is not at all certain whether this is the most useful mental picture even for a developed economy; it suggests a misleading stability

"This is true of labour in the primary industries themselves, for a large proportion of the labour force is usually engaged in activities such as shaft-sinking or ground-clearing. Many agricultural labourers have, in fact, moved to other jobs (or out of the labour force altogether) before their activities result in an increase in measurable output. But it is truer still of the economy as a whole, because total activity responds with noticeable jerks to the opening of ports or transport facilities.

"The first year that peasant incomes rise, for example, there are purchases of consumer durables (such as bicycles or gramophones), which may saturate the demand for durables.

of structure. But it is surely the wrong picture and implies the wrong statistical policy, for an economy changing rapidly—with, so to speak, rubber connecting rods which are being pulled into new shapes by the very operation of the "machine." The changing relations between the parts are precisely what interest us in a developing economy—yet these relations are assumed fixed in a national income "model."[10]

Such "models" are in any case hardly needed to explain economic developments. The explanation of the trade cycles of primary producers is usually obvious enough: fluctuations in the markets of the main customers, generally the United States and Western Europe, supplemented by internal inventory fluctuations. The economic history of a primary producer, whether trends or cycles are being studied, can generally be explained in terms of the history of the main commodities: do we need a single summary indicator of activity, as we do for a diverse economy?

Lastly, the most important application of national income analysis has been to show the policy alternatives for developed countries (*vide* the national product sections in the annual "Economic Surveys" of the United Kingdom[11]). Briefly, the Economic Surveys have started with a forecast of the coming year's product in "real" terms, and after an adjustment has been made for the terms of trade, the "real expenditure" is allocated between various end-uses.[12] In underdeveloped areas, we run up against the same difficulties as for historical analysis: the "real" product cannot be expected to change relatively slowly, by some simple function of employment, and the change in product will in any case probably be swamped by almost unpredictable changes in the terms of trade. Coming on to the use of resources, their allocation between end-uses would be limited by immobility at least as great as for industrial countries—peasants cannot be considered readily available for urban construction.[13] So national income models are not likely to be very useful for economic planning.

This discussion suggests that estimates of the national product of underdeveloped areas may not always have the uses which have been found for them in developed areas. Of course they are not useless, and, if experience in developed countries is any guide, we may find other uses in time, at present unsuspected. But, when we turn to considerations of policy for underdeveloped areas, we have to treat one fact as datum: statistical resources are very scarce. The central problem for statistical policy is how to distribute a limited amount of professional skill so that it is of maximum help to those framing economic policy. The optimum distribution can hardly allow many resources to be devoted to purposes which are not of great and obvious value. The onus seems to be on those who believe otherwise to show why national income estimation should receive the high pri-

[10]Perhaps we should think in biological, even embryological, rather than mechanical, metaphors to help us picture such economies.
[11]Especially the earlier ones, in which more of the programme was revealed.
[12]This technique is described by E. F. Jackson in Studies in Income and Wealth, Series I. The technique implicit in the President's Economic Reports to Congress is similar.
[13]Another reason for the more limited significance of income aggregates in underdeveloped economies is that the resources are so highly specific to particular industries. There is always some temptation to ignore this and, when we have completed aggregative processes, to treat the result as homogeneous.

ority it often does. The case for giving it this priority is not self-evident, and certainly does not follow from a general description of the uses of the national income based on experience elsewhere.

II. Social Accounting in Underdeveloped Areas

To leave the matter there would, however, be rather unhelpful. For as soon as we broaden the question to ask what is the role of "social accounting" in the statistical policy of an underdeveloped area, it can be answered more constructively.

What interests us in an underdeveloped area is not so much the total value of production as the relations between various parts of the economy. In order to throw light on problems of economic policy the questions arising are: what are the sources of the demand for imports and for domestic food? What happens to the proceeds of export sales? What are the existing and potential sources of saving and taxation?

To answer these questions we need a consolidated income-and-expenditure account for the output of each of the main export products: then, grouped around these, and interlocking with them, accounts for foreign trade, for the public authorities and for the transport system. If the main items in these accounts can be estimated we have gone a long way towards setting up a framework within which various economic magnitudes can be compared—for example, the respective effects on the total purchasing power of (say) a £1 million rise in Government expenditure on social services, as against a 10 per cent rise in the wages of mineworkers, or a 1s. per lb. rise in the price of an export crop.

But we shall have done more than that: we shall have completed a large part of a set of accounts describing the country's economic transactions. If these accounts can be completed, we fill in many of the items in the accounts of the remaining sectors of the economy, because what is income to one sector of the economy is expenditure to another; and we shall then be within sights of completing a set of tables constituting a financial matrix like those devised by Professor Leontief for the United States.

It may seem strange that it should be possible to attempt in an underdeveloped economy the sort of technique which is only just being introduced in the most highly developed economies. The explanation lies, firstly, in the high production of economic transactions which are international (and, therefore, recorded in the trade statistics), and, secondly, in the possibility that the accounts of one or two large mineral companies or agricultural marketing boards cover another substantial fraction of all economic transactions. A set of accounts for sectors of the economy is, in fact, feasible, either (a) if the economy is highly developed, which generally implies a comprehensive documentation by censuses of production, tax statistics, budget studies, etc.; or (b) if the economy is hardly developed at all. A comprehensive matrix of transactions would probably not be even a possibility for economies which have developed sufficiently to supply many of their own needs from local industries, but have not a comprehensive system of economic statistics.

This approach implies that as a first priority, instead of trying to fill the gaps in the "national income," statistical resources should be devoted to strengthening and extending foreign trade statistics—particularly to improving valuation and classification.[14] Since an underdeveloped country *ipso facto* relies on the proceeds of exports for much of her income, and on imports for most consumer goods (other than food) and for nearly all capital goods, the trade returns supply much of the information which has to be taken elsewhere from tax statistics(on sources of income), from censuses of production and distribution, or the statistics collected by trade associations and retailers (on supplies to the home market). Trade statistics also readily yield "average value" and volume indices, and these enable at least a start to be made on the study of price and quantity movements for the export industries, for capital investment and for personal consumption (other than food). The second priority is the consolidation of company and/or marketing board accounts; and the third is the classification of the public accounts into "current" and "capital" accounts, and (within the current account) into conventional economic categories— transfer payments, indirect taxes and subsidies, current purchases of local goods, purchases of imports, etc.

These tasks all yield fairly high dividends per unit of professional skill; they are all intrinsically worth doing, for they enable a more empirical approach to be adopted to the particular problems of trade policy and financial policy; and they make it easier for some of the choices of general economic policy, covering several fields, to be expressed quantitatively.[15]

The next statistical steps would depend on what are the main economic problems of the area. For a large number of underdeveloped economies, the most pressing danger, which may actually drive officials to ask the statistician's help, is inflation (or deflation). With the statistics so far described, a fairly comprehensive memorandum could be written on the problem of economic stability (and its implications for budgetary policy). There is one major gap still to be filled, the value of building work, which will probably have to be pieced together from clues on the value of local and imported building materials, the size of the labour force, and the structure of building costs.

With this information, a "savings-and-investment" account can be constructed for the economy in the recent past, because all items but one are now available, the exception being "personal saving," which, as in all such frameworks (even for developed economies), is the final residual. With the help of an account like this for past years, the significance of recent changes can be assessed; and, putting in predictions and assumptions for a future period, the significance of possible developments outside the Government's control can be seen, and the implications of various policies for capital investment, taxation, importing capacity, etc., can be drawn.

Here, perhaps, we may usefully follow new techniques of applied economies in developed countries, techniques devised to deal with the same problem of general inflation or deflation. In such techniques, forecasts and

[14]E.g., the classification of imports into capital goods and consumer goods. Unfortunately the new Standard International Trade Classification is not quite compatible with this division, but this topic would take another paper.
[15]Quite apart from other reasons, one strong case for a statistical policy that yields high short-run returns is the need to show results to colonial administrators or local politicians, who may be hostile to the innovation of an official statistical department and resentful of demands for information.

assumptions for a future period are brought together in a savings-and-investment account to show how large personal savings would have to be for the economic programme to be financed. Any excess of this need for savings over the expected supply of personal savings is considered an "inflationary gap," and indicates that there is a danger of a general excess of demand. In one way, this technique is especially applicable to the problems of many underdeveloped countries, for there may not be much doubt about the level of personal savings which can be expected. A notable characteristic of many underdeveloped areas is that savings habits are weak and savings institutions few, and we might not be far wrong to assume as a working hypothesis that voluntary savings will be zero. Consequently any set of policies which, *taken together,* imply a large demand on the public for savings, would create a presumptive danger of inflation: it would in effect mean a supply of consumer goods inadequate to absorb personal income. The programme need not necessarily be abandoned, or even modified (e.g. by increasing the budget surplus). The authorities may believe that the rate of personal saving can be increased by patriotic appeals, and they may in any case assume that some inflationary pressure on the economy is necessary to stimulate private investment and to increase the supply of labour. The point of this procedure is that it would provide a rough guide to the amount of inflationary demand implied by an economic programme,[16] so that those responsible for policy can gain some idea of the size of the main forces generating and absorbing purchasing power, and envisage some of the consequences of any economic programme. And apart from the short-run problems, the central longer-run problem of finding adequate sources of domestic savings can also be illustrated from a table of this type.

In practice the most difficult item to forecast may be the "export surplus" or "import surplus," because of the instability of export prices. But this may not be such a drawback as it looks, because variations in export prices are often to a large extent absorbed by export duties, mineral taxes, company profits and marketing board surpluses—particularly in the short run. They may, therefore, be largely offset by variations on the other side of an investment-and-savings account.

The reader may have noticed that I have said nothing about the valuation of local food supplies, and that forecasts of local food sales have not come into this procedure. This may seem a very big gap, but the reason is that one usually cannot rely on food farmers for savings: increases in their sales are matched by increases in their purchases. An expansion of cash sales may lead to some immediate "saving," because of the increase in the cash balances of the farming community (especially if the expansion is due to farmers entering the cash market for the first time); it may increase the sources of saving and taxes; and any extra loop in the flows of money may reduce the instability of the market economy. But such effects seem likely to be relatively small, and they seem neither to involve abandoning the basic assumption—a very low marginal propensity to save—nor in

---

[16]Conversely, if the projected account implies negative personal saving, it would almost certainly be interpreted as "deflationary," particularly if there is a general absence of liquid assets in the area.

themselves to indicate a high priority for the estimation of such sales. Those guiding economic policy are concerned with the motive forces in the short-run balance of the economy, and the food market is rather where these forces meet than where they originate.

There may, of course, be other reasons for attempting to value local food sales. It may be necessary to fill in the picture of the economy's structure, especially if there are special problems of food supply which are of great importance, and if quantitative information will help in their solution. Moreover, the entry into the market of a new cash food farmer does change the nature of the inflationary problem, even if it does not alter the relation between the total supply of consumer goods and the total demand for consumer goods: an expansion of food sales helps satisfy the demand for food, while in the farmers' hands the purchasing power is likely to augment the demand for imported textiles. Such particular market problems seem likely, however, to be of secondary importance to the general balance of the consumers' market, in the sense that if the general problems are solved, many particular problems will be solved, or at least eased. Many of the "local" problems are, however, very much more difficult to solve, and, in as far as they can be handled, their solutions (such as correcting inadequate market facilities or poor communications) are often too obvious to need statistical illustration.[17] Nor is such information at all easy to collect; valuation of food sales is often laborious, and may be almost impossible, if weights and measures are not standard, or if price quotations fluctuate violently from customer to customer.[18] By contrast it is easier to cast the general market problems in quantitative terms, and they may *have* to be put quantitatively—for example, it may be necessary to decide on the right level of taxation, too great an increase being as disastrous as too small an increase.

The criterion of maximising the practical usefulness of the allocation of scarce statistical resources, as opposed to the criterion of minimising the inaccuracy of national income estimates, generally suggests a low priority for field work on food sales, at least until diminishing returns are reached on trade statistics, the public accounts and company accounts. One may want, however, to pencil in a round figure for the sales of local foods (and other domestic products) in order to complete the structure of accounts. This would make it possible to consolidate the accounts into groups such as "Public Authorities," "Enterprises," etc., like the "social accounts" published in the United States and the United Kingdom.[19] A further step of consolidation would yield the table of "national income and expenditure."[20]

[17] A more important refinement may be to work out the balance of demand for the whole market in different regions, if geographical rigidities prevent the flow of consumer goods to regions of shortage. Fortunately, the very rigidities often involve information on the flow of goods (through the "bottleneck" port or across the ferry or along the single-line railway) amounting virtually to statistics of "overseas" trade, and making possible a separate set of social accounts.

[18] One strictly needs, moreover, the volume sold at each price.

[19] Except that in underdeveloped countries "Enterprises" almost certainly ought to be split into "exporting" and "other," if the main framework of economic transactions is to be revealed.

[20] This approach is illustrated in detail in a report by C. R. Ross and the author, *The Financial and Physical Problems of Development in the Gold Coast.*

This is surely in any case the way to estimate the national income, even if the national income is one's primary interest. Working out such accounts for each industry shows up at once the main gaps, and also prevents double counting: for example, if one has to trace the sales of (say) rail transport, one can hardly fall into the trap of including in the national income both the "added value" of the railways and the output of other industries at a price including rail freight.[21] The critical point of principle is not what accounting system to use, but what importance to attach to estimating local food output. On the principles suggested here, the national income should be considered the by-product of research and not the occasion for fieldwork otherwise hard to justify.

As a by-product it is not necessary to be spurned: one practical reason is that it is often more convenient to show economic forecasts in terms of the "national income," because the "national income" may be more familiar than a set of income flows to the administrator. But that is a matter of presentation and raises quite different issues: my concern is with how research is done, not how it should be presented.

Another obvious gap is that so far nothing has been said about "subsistence output," the well-known morass which those estimating national incomes of underdeveloped areas either skirt, rush across, or die in. Surely the country's food supply is not irrelevant to its economic problems? I have argued only that it is not very relevant to the short-term problems of inflationary and deflationary tendencies. There is a second set of problems such as: what will be the source of food in the future? What will be the population and how much food will it need? Should the emphasis be on agricultural or industrial investment? These are also problems on which statistical research can throw some light.

On the face of it, forecasting the national income might appear to offer the best approach. But an increase of (say) 10 per cent *per caput* in the national income may still leave as large a proportion of the population starving, even if the distribution is the same. We are not interested in *how much* national income, so much as in *what sort* of income. The problem of food may be the central one for at least several decades, particularly since clothing, housing and fuel may have a limited significance, in at least the tropical areas. Other sorts of consumption may, therefore, be of very minor importance until the food problem has been solved.[23] It would probably even be unwise to count on being able to purchase food imports with exports: dependence on imported foods (as Englishmen well know) means economic and strategic insecurity. The safest basis for a future programme is to aim at feeding the population from local supplies, and this implies forecasting food output, not national output. For this type of problem, we are concerned, of course, with total food supplies, subsistence and cash.

Forecasts of food supplies need not be cast in financial terms. They can

[21]Other items that are easily "double counted" are sacking, animal feeding-stuffs, and timber for building.

[22]The third main group of problems which would concern the economic statistician are those concerned with overseas reserves, currently backing servicing of foreign loans, etc. I shall not discuss this group here.

[23]To put the same point another way, the price-weights given to food in real comparisons may well understate the importance of food, because of highly unequal distribution of cash income.

in any case hardly be made by applying a productivity trend to the past or present total values of food output: the method will probably be to forecast the staple food crops, and then sum the forecasts to yield a total of food output which can be compared with the past or present totals. This is in effect an index-number problem, and, instead of price-weights, one might apply calorie-weights (or protein-weights) so as to make one's comparison show the nutritive change in "calorie-*per-caput*" terms, which may well be the most useful single way of illustrating the problem. On the other hand, there may not be the necessary conversion factors showing the calories per quantum of the main foods; it may not be practicable to put the forecasts in categories with roughly constant nutritional conversion factors; and any single nutritional measure is of limited use (vitamin contents, etc., are also relevant), particularly since the public's eagerness, even its willingness, to eat various foods is ignored in such calculations.

The forecasts may, therefore, be best stated in monetary terms. The question then becomes: what set of price-weights will yield the most useful comparison? The most obvious weights would be the average prices operating over a fairly long period in a large organised market—say, the market of the chief town. These prices will reflect, at least to some extent, consumer preferences better than small markets will, and probably nutritive values as well (including characteristics other than calorific values). They will also be as easy to collect as food prices ever are in underdeveloped areas. But, if there are special or temporary factors operating on the main market (such as the dominant influence of a racial group with abnormal food habits), one might consider that another set of prices, perhaps a quite arbitrary set, would yield a comparison of total food production with greater meaning. Such a comparison starts with a current or recent year as a base, and all food products, whether sold for cash or not, could be valued at these prices, even if prices are quite different in many districts.[24] There is no reason why, if the crop information is available, this comparison should not reach back into the past as well, or be carried forward year-by-year into the future. A system of weights probably ought, however, to be kept until it became hopelessly inappropriate, thus avoiding the frequent recalculations, and the frequent mental adjustments, which are needed when weights are often changed. This seems the answer to the bothersome problem of how to value subsistence output in an economy without a single food market if, as has been argued above, we do not need estimates of subsistence output to illustrate short-run problems of economic stability, and if intertemporal and international comparisons of national income do not in themselves justify a high priority being given to estimates of the national product.[25]

The current interest in estimating the national product for underdeveloped areas stems partly from the belief that such estimates are needed in a period of development. It has been argued above that they are not neces-

[24]Though if one wants a consistent accounting structure for short-run problems, one may also attempt to value cash sales at the prices actually charged.

[25]The national income expert might argue, that this treatment of food imputes a non-existent transport charge, if price-weights based on a central market price are used to value the whole of output. But this argument would misconceive the purpose of such a calculation, which is to enable a comparison of food consumption, not of production.

sarily required for either short-run or long-run programmes. But can they be used in some way as a measure of the progress of development? Apart from the difficulties of interpreting movements in the national product discussed above, such movements are only indirectly linked to development—they may be due to other causes than the development programme and (more important) the effect of development is far more extensive than can be indicated by short-run changes in the national income. Thus, building a factory permits an increase in national income when the factory is ready for production, but it also provides experience for the building industry during construction, and leads to new industrial and technical jobs, raising the technical level of the local population, and at a further remove it reduces the dependence on imported supplies and (possibly) the sensitivity to cyclical fluctuations. But it may make the shortage of housing and other social amenities more acute, particularly if the factory attracts to a town more workers than it can employ, and urbanisation helps to destroy the existing social structure, with all that this implies. In brief, many of the main effects of development are on variables which are conventionally excluded from the national product, but, nevertheless, are of great, perhaps overwhelming, importance.

It is, in fact, probably safer not to claim that development problems can be decided statistically, let alone on "national product" criteria. The consequences of various decisions for the labour market, for foreign exchange earnings and expenditure, for the level of incomes, possibly even for prices, can be assessed. But in the end, after all the facts have been collected, someone has to sit back and look at the complete picture, including many economic but immeasurable considerations, and many non-economic considerations, before deciding on the scale and type of development.

To say that statistics cannot imply the answer themselves to such complex and controversial problems is not to say that they are useless for such problems, still less that they are useless for all problems. I have tried to indicate how the problems of inflation and of food supply might be cast in quantitative terms. If there is no such factual guidance, administrative decisions will be taken in blindness and ignorance, solely on intuition. But the most useful policy, granted the shortage of qualified people, is to concentrate on improving specific rather than aggregative data: much help cannot be given to the administration, or much goodwill gained for a statistical department, unless statistical policy is designed for the problems of the territory and the statistical resources available.

6. Tables

World Income Distribution*

Countries with GNP per head	% of World Population	% of Real GNP
of: $150 or less	26.6	6.3
151–300	33.7	10.4
301–600	8.7	6.4
601–1,200	15.1	21.9
Above 1,200	15.9	55.0

*From P. N. Rosenstein-Roden, "International Aid for Underdeveloped Countries," *Review of Economics and Statistics*, May 1961, p. 118. Campbridge, Mass.: Harvard University Press, copyright, 1961, by The President and Fellows of Harvard College. Reprinted by permission of the publishers.

World Gross National Product and Population, 1961*

	Population (millions)	% of World Total	GNP Real Terms $ U.S. billion	% of World Total	Real GNP per head U.S. $'s
Developed countries					
West Europe	261	8.7	385	22.0	1,472
Oceania	16	.5	24	1.4	1,513
United States	185	6.2	515	29.4	2,790
Canada	18	.6	38	2.1	2,048
Japan	95	3.2	58	3.3	613
South Africa	15	.5	9	.5	598
	590	19.7	1,029	58.7	
Communist bloc					
USSR	215	7.2	212	12.1	986
Eastern Europe	100	3.3	82	4.7	825
China	694	23.2	116	6.6	167
North Korea	9	.3	2	.1	211
North Vietnam	17	.6	3	.2	199
	1,035	34.6	415	23.7	
Under-developed countries					
Africa	206	6.9	34	1.9	164
America	210	7.0	89	5.1	425
Asia	780	26.1	120	6.8	154
Europe[1]	67	2.2	34	1.9	501
Middle East	106	3.5	29	1.7	257
	1,369	45.7	306	17.5	
World total	2,993	100.0	1,750	100.0	

*From P. N. Rosenstein-Roden, "International Aid for Underdeveloped Countries," *Review of Economics and Statistics*, May 1961, p. 118. Campbridge, Mass.: Harvard University Press, copyright, 1961, by the President and Fellows of Harvard College. Reprinted by permission of the publishers.
[1]Greece, Spain, Portugal, Yugoslavia.

Growth in Population, National Product, and Product Per Capita, 19 Countries, Approximately First Half of 20th Century*

| | PERCENT CHANGE PER DECADE IN | | |
	POPULATION	NATIONAL PRODUCT	NATIONAL PRODUCT PER PERSON
1. Sweden (gross domestic product)	6.6	37.8	29.2
2. Union of South Africa (GNP)	20.9	49.7	23.8
3. Norway	8.2	33.5	23.4
4. Japan	13.3	37.9	21.7
5. Russia and USSR	12.3	33.1	18.6
6. Canada	20.9	41.4	17.0
7. Denmark (net domestic product)	11.9	30.6	16.7
8. United States	15.0	33.8	16.4
9. Ireland and Eire	−1.6	14.6	16.3
10. Switzerland	7.7	24.4	15.3
11. Italy	7.0	22.2	14.2
12. New Zealand	18.7	32.7	11.8
13. United Kingdom, excluding Southern Ireland	5.6	17.2	11.0
14. France, including Alsace-Lorraine	0.6	11.1	10.4
15. Australia	17.2	28.4	9.5
16. Netherlands	14.3	24.6	9.0
17. Hungary	6.2	15.5	8.7
18. Germany	9.8	19.9	8.3
19. Spain	8.8	14.9	5.6

*Source: S. Kuznets: *Quantitative Aspects of the Economic Growth of Nations*, I. "Levels and Variability of Rates of Growth," in *Economic Development and Cultural Change*, October 1956, Table 1, p. 10.

Where available, "national income" was used as the measure of production. This is total net output at factor costs, or the total of all goods at cost to ultimate consumers plus net capital formation, including changes in claims against foreign countries. . . . For two countries domestic, rather than national, product is used: that is, there is exclusion of adjustment for net flow of income across boundaries.

The period covered includes wars, revolutions, and other dislocations. Changes in quality are not usually recorded in price data. The shift from household to (private or public) market production introduces a possible upward bias.

I. Factor and Locational Needs, Various Manufacturing Industries

Table 1. Frequency Distribution of Rankings of Industries in Five Countries,[1] 1936–37, in Order of Increasing Amounts of Capital Per Employed Person[2]†

INDUSTRIAL CATEGORY	RANK										
	1	2	3	4	5	6	7	8	9	10	11
1. Clothing and bedding	****c										
2. Furniture, woodwork, pottery, glass, and miscellaneous		c*	*	*							
3. Leather, fur, and rubber		***			*c						
4. Textiles			c	*	*	*	*				
5. Light metals and electrical products			*	*	*			c			
6. Semi-manufactured metals and engineering					*	*c	*				
7. Building materials			*	c				**			
8. Paper, stationery, and printing						*	**	*	c		
9. Metal extraction									***		c
10. Food, drink, and tobacco							c			***	*
11. Chemicals										c*	***

†Source: Adapted from K. Mandelbaum, *The Industrialization of Backward Areas* (Oxford, 1945). This and the following tables are from K. A. Bohr, "Investment Criteria for Manufacturing Industries in Underdeveloped Countries," *Review of Economics and Statistics*, May 1954. Cambridge, Mass.: Harvard University Press, copyright, 1954, by the President and Fellows of Harvard College. Reprinted by permission of the publishers.

[1]Australia, Canada, Hungary, Palestine and Rumania. Palestinian statistics are not comparable in all classifications.

[2]Capital is valued in various ways in the separate countries, e.g., total capital assets, fixed capital assets only, or fixed capital plus inventories.

c=Canada.

*=Other countries.

Table 2. Selected Industries in Order of Percentage of Skilled and Supervisory Workers to Total Gainfully Employed: U.S., 1930*

PROFESSIONAL PERSONS, FOREMEN, AND SKILLED WORKERS AS PER CENT OF TOTAL GAINFULLY EMPLOYED	INDUSTRY	
Less than 10%	Turpentine farms and distilleries	Pottery
	Gloves	Tanning
	Shirts, collars, and cuffs	Silk
	Cigars and tobacco	Lace and embroidery
	Hats	Woolen and worsted
	Shoes	Cotton
	Leather goods	Slaughter and
	Knitting mills	packinghouses
	Fish-curing and packing	Buttons
	Fertilizers	Brick, tile, and terra cotta
10 to 20%	Hemp, jute, and linen	Paint and varnish
	Paper boxes	Glass
	Paper and pulp	Soap
	Carpets	Rayon
	Fruit and vegetable canning	Sawing and planing
	Ropes and cordage	Quarrying
	Textile dyeing, finishing, and	Lime, cement, and
	printing	artificial stone
	Rubber	
20 to 30%	Sugar and sugar-refining	Blast furnaces and steel
	Charcoal and coke	rolling mills
30 to 40%	Electrical machinery and	Jewelry
	supplies	Tinware and enamelware
	Flour and grain	Automobiles
	Agricultural implements	Furniture
Over 40%	Printing, publishing, and	Marble and stone
	engraving	Suits, coats and overalls

*Source: National Resources Planning Board, *Industrial Location and National Resources* (Washington, 1942).

II. Backward and Forward Linkage

*Average Degree of Interdependence of Economic Sectors
in Italy, Japan, and the United States**

	INTERDEPENDENCE THROUGH PURCHASES FROM OTHER SECTORS[1] (BACKWARD LINKAGE)	INTERDEPENDENCE THROUGH SALES TO OTHER SECTORS[2] (FORWARD LINKAGE)
1. *"Intermediate manufacture"* (backward and forward linkage both high)		
Iron and steel	66	78
Nonferrous metals	61	81
Paper and products	57	78
Petroleum products	65	68
Coal products	63	67
Chemicals	60	69
Textiles	67	57
Rubber products	51	48
Printing and publishing	49	46
2. *"Final manufacture"* (backward linkage high, forward linkage low)		
Grain mill products	89	42
Leather and products	66	37
Lumber and wood products	61	38
Apparel	69	12
Transport equipment	60	20
Machinery	51	28
Nonmetallic mineral products	47	30
Processed foods	61	15
Shipbuilding	58	14
Miscellaneous industries	43	20
3. *"Intermediate primary production"* (forward linkage high, backward linkage low)		
Metal mining	21	93
Petroleum and natural gas	15	97
Coal mining	23	87
Agriculture and forestry	31	72
Electric power	27	59
Nonmetallic minerals	17	52
4. *"Final primary production"* (backward and forward linkage both low)		
Fishing	24	36
Transport	31	26
Services	19	34
Trade	16	17

*Source: Chenery and Watanabe, "International Comparisons of the Structure of Production," p. 11. Reproduced by permission of the authors. [Ed. note: This table has been adapted from the author's article published in *Econometrica*, October 1958, p. 493.]
[1]Ratio of interindustry purchases to total production (%).
[2]Ratio of interindustry sales to total demand (%).

POPULATION

7. Demographic Dimensions of World Politics

Philip M. Hauser*

Politics in general, as well as world politics, is a branch of engineering—social engineering—not of science. Yet the consideration of the demographic aspects of world politics is not an inappropriate subject for a scientific journal. It is the purpose of this article to point to ways in which the findings of the science of demography illuminate various aspects of the world political scene.

There are various ways in which this subject can be developed, but I have arbitrarily chosen to discuss population factors in relation to politics, broadly conceived, on the global and on the international levels, respectively. By "global" problems I mean those that concern the earth as a whole; by "international" problems I mean those that arise among the various political subdivisions of the globe.

Global Considerations

There is no world government charged with the task of achieving world order and performing other civil governmental functions for the earth as a whole. This, however, does not mean that there are no political problems of a global, as distinguished from an international, character. Some such global problems are in fact dealt with by the United Nations and its specialized agencies, which are, of course, organizations of individual sovereign nations rather than organs of world government. Examples of global problems—problems which transcend and cannot be contained within national boundaries—include health, weather, fallout, and the newly emergent problems of outer space. It is easy to demonstrate that the contemporary rate of world population growth also constitutes a global problem—one which would be of great concern to a world government if we had one, and one which is of increasing concern to various organs of the United Nations and the specialized agencies.

Although the first complete census of mankind has yet to be taken, it is possible to reconstruct, with reasonable accuracy, the history of world population growth. This history may be encapsulated in the following estimates of the population of the earth: at the end of the Neolithic period in

*The author is Professor and Chairman of the Department of Sociology, University of Chicago. This article is adapted from his vice-presidential address to Section K of the American Association for the Advancement of Science, delivered December 27, 1959, during the Chicago meeting. Reprinted from *Science* by permission.

Europe (8000 to 7000 B.C.), 10 million; at the beginning of the Christian era, 200 to 300 million; at the beginning of the modern era (1650), 500 million; in 1950, 2.5 billion.

These four numbers constitute a measurement of one of the most dramatic aspects of man's existence on the globe, and they explain the purple language of the demographer in describing the changes in rates of population growth during the modern era as a "demographic revolution" or "population explosion."

The basis for the demographer's emotionally surcharged language may be summarized as follows.

1. The present population of the world could be produced from an initial population of two dozen individuals increasing at the rate of 0.02 percent per year over a period of 100,000 years, and man has been on the earth for at least 200,000 to 1 million years.

2. The rate of population growth has increased enormously over the three centuries of the modern era (1650–1950), during which time it averaged about 0.5 percent per year. Over this period the rate of growth increased from about 0.3 percent per year between 1650 and 1750 to 0.9 percent per year between 1900 and 1950. World population growth averaged 1 percent per year between 1930 and 1940. Now, a 1-percent return per year, even compounded, would by our standards represent a meager return on investment. But it constitutes a fantastically rapid rate of population increase. One hundred persons multiplying at 1 percent per year, not over the period of 200,000 to 1 million years of man's occupancy of this globe but merely for the 5000 years of human history, would have produced a contemporary population of 2.7 billion persons per square foot of land surface of the earth! Such an exercise in arithmetic, although admittedly dramatic and propagandistic, is also a conclusive way of demonstrating that a 1 percent per year increase in world population could not have taken place for very long in the past; nor can it continue for very long into the future.

The demographer's concern is not based only on considerations of the past. It is even more justified by postwar developments in population growth.

Table 1. Population, Income, and Energy Consumed Per Capita, by Continent, about 1950. Source of Data, United Nations, Except Where Otherwise Indicated

AREA	TOTAL POPULATION No. (THOUSANDS)	(%)	AGGREGATE INCOME DOLLARS (MILLIONS)	(%)	PER CAPITA INCOME ($)	ENERGY CONSUMED PER CAPITA (KW-HR.)
World	2497	100.0	556	100.0	223	1676
Africa	199	8.0	15	2.7	75	686
North America	219	8.8	241	43.3	1100	10,074
South America	112	4.5	19	3.4	170	741
Asia	1380	55.3	69	12.4	50	286
Europe (exclusive of U.S.S.R.)	393	15.7	149	26.8	380	3117
U.S.S.R.	181	7.2	56	10.1	310	1873
Oceania	13	0.5	7	1.3	560	3543

Since the end of World War II the rate of population increase has continued to accelerate and has reached a level of about 1.7 percent per year. There is justification, indeed, for pointing to a new population explosion in the wake of World War II of a greater magnitude than that previously observed. At the rate of world population increase for the period 1800–1850, for example, the present population would double in 135 years; at the 1900–1950 rate, in 67 years; and at the postwar rate, in only 42 years.

Projection of the post-World War II rate of increase gives a population of one person per square foot of the land surface of the earth in less than 800 years. It gives a population of 50 billions (the highest estimate of the population-carrying capacity of the globe ever calculated by a responsible scholar) in less than 200 years! This estimate, by geochemist Harrison Brown, is based on the assumptions that developments in the capturing of solar or nuclear energy will produce energy at a cost so low that it would be feasible to obtain all the "things" we need from rock, sea, and air, and that mankind would be content to subsist largely on food products from "algae farms and yeast factories!"

Moreover, the United Nations estimates of future world population indicate even further acceleration in the rate of world population growth during the remainder of this century. Between 1950 and 1975 the average annual percentage of increase, according to the United Nations "medium" assumptions, may be 2.1 percent, and between 1975 and 2000, almost 2.6 percent. Such rates of increase would double the population about every 33 and 27 years, respectively.

It is considerations of this type that would make it necessary for a world government to exercise forethought and planning, which constitute rational decision making, in facing the future. This, of course, is the purpose of the projections. The figures do not show what the future population of the world will be—for the world could not support such populations. They do demonstrate that man, as a culture-building animal, has created an environment in which the rhythm of his own reproduction has been modified in such a manner as to point to crisis possibilities.

Crisis Possibilities

The crisis possibilities are of several forms, each posing major world political problems. The first, we may note, is the ultimate crisis, which would result from the fact that the globe is finite and that living space would be exhausted. Unless one is prepared to argue that future technological developments will enable man to colonize other globes, it is clear that present rates of population increase must come to a halt by reason of lack of space. No facts or hopes as to man's ability to increase his food production and to increase other types of goods and services can indefinitely increase man's *lebensraum* (or could do so even if we accept the absurd assumption that man, at terrific cost, could burrow into the earth, live in man-made layers above it, or live on the seas).

In the short run, let us say to 1975 or to 2000, world population will be confined to much more manageable numbers .The United Nations projects, on the basis of its medium assumptions, a world population of about 3.8 billion by 1975 and 6.3 billion by 2000.

In the short run there is no problem of exhausting the space on the globe, nor is there reason to fear serious decreases in world per capita food supply, as is evidenced by projections of The Food and Agricultural Organization and others concerning foodstuffs. But there is great reason to be pessimistic about the possibility of greatly increasing the average world level of living during the remainder of this century.

In 1950, world per capita income was estimated at $223. In North America, per capita income was $1100. Had each person on the globe enjoyed the North American level of living in 1950, as measured by per capita income, the aggregate world product in 1950 would have supported only 500 million persons, as contrasted with the actual world population of 2.5 billion. For average world income to have matched income in North America, aggregate income would have had to be increased about fivefold. To bring world per capita income by 1975 to the level enjoyed in North America in 1950 would require about a 7.5-fold increase of the 1950 level in 25 years. To do the same by 2000 would require a 12-fold increase in the 1950 world income within 50 years.

Even if the more modest income level of Europe ($380 per capita in 1950) were set as the target, great increases in productivity would be necessary, because of prospective rates of population increase, to raise average world income to the required level by 1975 or 2000. To achieve this goal by 1975, world income would have to be increased 2.5-fold over the 1950 level, and to achieve it by 2000, the required increase would be greater than fourfold. A decline in the rate of world population growth to that of the period of 1800 to 1850—namely, to 0.5 per cent—would decrease by three-fourths and four-fifths, respectively, the projected world-income requirements for attaining this goal by 1975 or 2000.

These considerations not only show the enormous difficulty of materially increasing the world level of living on the basis of present rates of population increase but indicate, also, the weakness of the argument that a solution to the population problem is to be found in more equitable distribution of the world's food supply or of goods and services in general. The equitable distribution of world income in 1950 would, to be sure, have raised the per capita income of Latin America by 31 per cent; of Africa, almost threefold, and of Asia, four- to fivefold, but it would still have produced a per capita income per annum of $223, only one-fifth that in North America and only three-fifths that in Europe (exclusive of the U.S.S.R.). The miserably low level of living of most of the world's population is attributable not so much to maldistribution as to low aggregate product, the result of the low productivity of most of the world's peoples.

These political problems of a global character may perhaps be better understood through consideration of their international aspects, special attention being given to the plight of the two-thirds of the world's population resident in the underdeveloped areas of the world, in Asia, Africa, and Latin America.

International Considerations

The short-run implications of present rates of world population growth are manifest in specific forms and in varying degrees of intensity among the various regional and national subdivisions of the globe. The distribution of the world's population and of the world's utilized resources, manifest in differentials in levels of living, is the result, of course, of millennia of human history. The demographic dimensions of international politics may best be comprehended against the background of differences among peoples in levels of living and the significance of these differences at this juncture in world history (Table 1).

To note the extremes, North America in 1950, with about 16 percent of the earth's land surface, contained less than 9 percent of the world's population but about 43 percent of the world's income. Asia, in contrast, with about the same proportion of the world's land surface (18 percent), had 55 percent of the world's population but only 12 percent of the world's income. Per capita income in Asia was at a level of about $50 per year as contrasted with a level of $1100 in North America. Despite the fact that such comparisons are subject to considerable error, there is no doubt that a tremendous difference in per capita income existed, of a magnitude perhaps as great as 20 to 1.

The major factor underlying this difference is indicated by the contrast in the difference in nonhuman energy consumed in North America and Asia, respectively—over 10,000 kilowatt-hours per capita per year for the former in contrast to less than 300 for the lattter. The availability of nonhuman energy for the production of goods and services is perhaps the best single measurement available of differences in capital investment, knowhow, and technology which account for the great differences in productivity and, consequently, in the size of the aggregate product available for distribution.

The other relatively underdeveloped continents of the world also had relatively low shares of world income as compared with their proportion of world population. Africa, with a per capital income of about $75 per year, and South America, with $170, were also well below not only the level for North America ($1100) but also the levels for Europe (exclusive of the U.S.S.R.) ($380), the U.S.S.R. ($310), and Oceania ($560). There is a high correlation among these areas between per capita income and amount of nonhuman energy consumed (Table 1).

These differences in levels of living, as it turns out, are in general inversely related to present and prospective rates of population increase. The populations of the relatively underdeveloped continents of the world are increasing at a more rapid rate than those of the economically advanced continents (Table 2). Between 1950 and 1975, to use the medium projections of the United Nations, while the population of Northern America is increasing at an average annual rate of 1.7 percent and that of Europe, at 1.2 percent, that of Asia will be growing at an average annual rate of 2.4 percent, that of Africa at 2.1 percent, and that of Latin America at 3.4 percent. Between 1975 and 2000, while the rate of increase for Northern America will average 1.2 percent per year and that for Europe, 1.0 percent, the rate for Asia will be 3.0 percent, that for Africa 2.8 percent, and that for Latin America 3.8 percent, a rate at which the population would double about every 18 years.

As I have indicated above, rapid increase in world population imposes a

Table 2. Estimated Population and Population Increases, by Continent, 1900 to 2000

AREA	POPULATION (MILLION)					AN ANNUAL INCREASE (%)[1]			
	1900	1925	1950	1975	2000	1900– 1925	1925– 1950	1950– 1975	1975– 2000
World	1550	1907	2497	3828	6267	0.9	1.2	2.1	2.6
Africa	120	147	199	303	517	0.9	1.4	2.1	2.8
Northern America	81	126	168	240	312	2.2	1.3	1.7	1.2
Latin America	63	99	163	303	592	2.3	2.6	3.4	3.8
Asia	857	1020	1380	2210	3870	0.8	1.4	2.4	3.0
Europe (including U.S.S.R.)	423	505	574	751	947	0.8	0.6	1.2	1.0
Oceania	6	10	13	21	29	2.3	1.4	2.4	1.6

[1]Arithmetic mean of percentage of increase for 25-year periods.

severe burden on efforts to raise levels of living. It is easy to demonstrate that the burden would become an impossible one for the economically underdeveloped areas should their rates of population increase follow the trends indicated in the United Nations projections.

For example, Asia, merely to maintain her present low level of living, must increase her aggregate product by 60 percent between 1950 and 1975, and by an additional 75 percent between 1975 and 2000. To raise her per capita income to the European level for 1950 while continuing to experience her rapid population growth, Asia would have to increase her 1950 aggregate income 12-fold by 1975 and 21-fold by 2000. Africa, to do the same, must increase her aggregate income eight-fold by 1975 and 13-fold by 2000, and Latin America would have to increase her aggregate income fourfold by 1975 and eightfold by 2000.

To achieve a per capita income equal to that of Northern America in 1950 while experiencing the projected population growth. Asia would have to increase her aggregate income 35-fold by 1975 and 62-fold by 2000. Africa, to achieve a similar goal, would require 22-fold and 38-fold increases, respectively, in aggregate income, and Latin America, 12-fold and 23-fold increases.

These considerations provide additional justification for the use by the demographer of the phrase *population explosion;* and they certainly indicate the hopeless task which confronts the underdeveloped areas in their efforts to achieve higher levels of living while experiencing rapid population growth. The control of rates of population growth would unquestionably decrease the magnitude of the task of achieving higher levels of living in the underdeveloped areas, especially in those with populations that are large relative to resources.

Increasingly large proportions of the population in the underdeveloped areas of the world are becoming concentrated in urban places. The continued acceleration in the rate of world urbanization during the first half of this century was mainly attributable to urbanization in the underdeveloped areas, which proceeded at a pace considerably above that in the developed areas. I have had occasion to make projections of the urban population of the world and of Asia to 1975; these are presented in Table

3 as illustrative of what is in prospect in the underdeveloped areas of the globe. For the rate of urbanization in Latin America and Africa is, also, accelerating.

Table 3. Summary of Projections of Urban Population for the World and for Asia, 1975

CITIES (CATEGORY)	POPULATION (MILLIONS) PROJECTION FOR 1975		1950	ESTIMATE OF INCREASE IN POPULATION, 1950–1975 (MILLIONS)		ESTIMATE OF INCREASE IN POPULATION, 1950–1975 (%)		PROPORTION OF TOTAL POPULATION IN CITIES PROJECTION	
	Upper	Lower		Upper	Lower	Upper	Lower	1975[1]	1950
The World									
100,000 and over	745	488	314	431	174	138	55	19	13
20,000 and over	1155	779	502	653	277	130	55	30	21
Asia									
100,000 and over	340	176	106	234	70	222	66	15	8
20,000 and over	544	283	170	374	113	220	66	25	13

[1]Figures are based on the "upper" projection, which assumes urbanization of an increasing proportion of the population.

The projections for Asia indicate that in the 25 years between 1950 and 1975, in cities either of 100,000 and over or of 20,000 and over, urban population will increase by at least two-thirds and may perhaps triple. The lower projection is based on the assumption that the proportion of urban population in Asia will be the same in 1975 as it was in 1950. Under this assumption the projected increase would result from total population growth alone. But if it is assumed that the rate of urbanization in Asia will increase as it did between 1900 and 1950 while the total population continues to grow at the rate projected by the United Nations, then tripling of Asia's urban population is indicated.

Thus, while the nations of Asia are attempting to improve their miserable urban living conditions, their urban populations will continue to increase explosively—perhaps to triple within a period of less than one generation.

In the economically more advanced nations of the world, urbanization is both an antecedent and a consequent of technological advance and of a high level of living—a symbol of man's mastery over nature. In the underdeveloped nations, however, urbanization represents instead the transfer of rural poverty from an over-populated and unsettled countryside to a mass urban setting. In the economically underdeveloped areas of the world, urbanization is outpacing economic development and the city is more a symbol of mass misery and political instability than of man's conquest of nature.

The prospect for individual nations, while variable, is in general the same—one of explosive growth. Between 1955 and 1975, according to the United Nations medium projections, the population of China will increase by 294 million persons and that of India, by 177 million. That of Pakistan will increase by 45 million persons, and that of Indonesia, by 40 million, in these 20 years. Japan, although she has now greatly slowed down her rate of population growth, will, despite her already great population pressure, increase by an additional 27 million. To confine our attention to the Far East for the moment, smaller countries with the most explosive increases include South Korea, Taiwan, and Ceylon. Each of these nations is faced with a task of tremendous proportions merely to maintain her present level of living, let alone to greatly increase it while continuing to grow at the projected rates.

Political Instability

What will happen if the underdeveloped areas in Asia are frustrated in their efforts to attain a higher standard of living?

Warren S. Thompson devotes his latest book to providing an answer to this question. The larger of these nations are not apt to remain hungry and frustrated without noting the relatively sparsely settled areas in their vicinities—the nations in the South-East Asian peninsula: Burma, Thailand, and the newly formed free countries of Indochina, Laos, Cambodia, and Vietnam. (Vietminh, that is North Vietnam, is already engulfed by Communist China.) Even parts of thinly settled Africa may be subject to the aggressive action of the larger and hungrier nations as feelings of population pressure mount. Moreover, Communist China, the largest nation in the world by far, faced with the greatest absolute population increases to add to her already heavy burdens in striving for economic development, may not confine her attentions only to the smaller nations within her reach. Her present actions relative to her boundaries with India and possible tensions over her boundaries with the U.S.S.R. contain explosive possibilities.

It is Thompson's conclusion that the larger nations in the Far East, including Japan, India, and Pakistan as well as China, may resort to force to achieve access to additional resources under sufficient population pressure. The smaller countries may not be able to resort to force but are almost certain to require outside aid to prevent chaos. Furthermore, while neither Indonesia nor the Philippines is in a position to be aggressive or is easily accessible to aggressors, both, under mounting population pressures, are likely to continue to experience growing internal political instability.

Population pressure as a factor in political instability is not confined to the Far East. Populations of the Middle East and North Africa—the Muslim area (exclusive of Pakistan)—may increase from 119 million in 1955 to 192 million by 1975, an increase of 73 million or 61 percent in 20 years. As Irene Taeuber has noted, this is an area "where internal instabilities and conflicts of religious and ethnic groups create recurrent crises for the region and world." Taeuber observes that the immediate political instabilities in this area are attributable more to "diversities among the peoples and the nations than to population pressure or population growth." But she points to the importance, in the decades that lie ahead, of economic advances to lessen tension in this region and to the barrier that rapid population growth may contribute to that development.

Latin America, although in large part still a sparsely settled area of the world, is already experiencing problems associated with rapid population growth which give promise of worsening. For Latin America, as has been reported above, is faced with a population increase of 86 percent between

1950 and 1975 and of 95 percent, almost a doubling, between 1975 and 2000. Especially difficult in Latin America are the problems posed by accelerating rates of urbanization. Recent measurements of rate of urban growth in Latin America indicated that of 15 countries for which data were available, urban population in one, Venezuela, was increasing at 7 percent per year, a rate which produces a doubling about every 10 years; seven had growth rates which would double their population in less than 18 years; and only two (Chile and Bolivia) had rates of urban growth of less than 1 percent per year. Growth rates (total and urban) of the magnitude which Latin America is experiencing are likely to add appreciably to the difficulty of raising living levels and are likely to worsen already existent political instabilities that threaten internal order and may affect world peace.

Finally, a fourth region of political instability to which the population factor is a contributing element, and one where it will be increasingly manifest, is sub-Saharan Africa. Middle Africa is sparsely settled, but increasing knowledge about the area indicates high birth rates, decreasing death rates, and explosive growth. The United Nations projections indicate a population increase from 154 million in 1955 to about 202 million in 1975, or an increase of 31 percent. The familiar syndrome of underdeveloped areas—malnutrition, disease, and urban and rural squalor on the one hand and aspirations for independence and economic development on the other—are now emergent in this most primitive continent of the globe. And here, as in the other underdeveloped areas, rapid population growth is likely to intensify political unrest.

In southern Africa another type of population problem is also a major element in a political problem that has grave implications for world order as well as for the stability of the Union of South Africa. This is the problem arising from the conflict between the indigenous people and European settlers manifest in apartheid. Rapid and differential rates of growth of native and European populations are likely to intensify rather than to allay conflict in southern Africa. . . .

The Alternatives

The "why" of the population increase, in an immediate sense, is readily identifiable. It is to be found in the great increase in "natural increase"—in the gap between fertility and mortality. Quite apart from the precise timing of changes in the relations between mortality and fertility, it is clear that explosive growth can be dampened only by decreasing natural increase. This is true for the world as a whole in the ultimate sense, with differences in timing for different parts of the world. For suggested solutions to the problems of present and prospective rates of population growth in the various subdivisions of the world through migration, foreign trade, redistribution of wealth, and similar means hold forth little promise, if any, even in the short run.

There are only three ways to decrease natural increase: (i) by increasing the death rate; (ii) by decreasing the birth rate; and (iii) by some combination of the two.

Although it is true that decreased death rates were largely responsible for the population explosion in the past and are foreseen to be a large factor in the future, the adoption of a policy to increase mortality, or to diminish efforts to increase longevity, is unthinkable. Unless one is prepared to debate this, two of the three ways of decreasing natural increase are ruled out. For two of them involve an increase in death rates.

If longevity gains are to be retained, then, the only way to reduce explosive population growth is to decrease the birth rate. That is, the "death control" mankind has achieved can be retained only if it is accompanied by birth control. This proposition, even though it flows directly from the demographic facts of life, in view of prevalent value systems provokes heated debate of the type manifest in the press. Birth control has recently, indeed, made the front pages of the world press.

What is important about the value controversy under way is that it definitely affects global and international policy and action on matters of population and, therefore, on the crucial political problems involved. The most significant thing about all the available methods of birth control —a fact mainly obscured in the present public controversy—is that they are by no means adequate to the task of slowing down explosive world population increase, especially that in the underdeveloped areas. The great mass of mankind in the economically less advanced nations which are faced with accelerating rates of growth fail to limit their birth rates not because of the factors at issue in the controversy we are witnessing but because they do not have the desire, the know-how, or the means to do so. The desire to control fertility, arising from recognition of the problem, is, however, increasing. Japan is already well down the road to controlling its birth rate, although by methods which are not enthusiastically endorsed either by the Japanese themselves or by other peoples. China, India, Pakistan, and Egypt have population limitation programs under way or under serious consideration, and other underdeveloped areas are showing increasing interest in this problem. The changes in value systems which will create mass motivation to adopt methods of family limitation are not easily brought about, but they are at least under way.

Birth control methods in use in the economically more advanced nations are not, in the main, well adapted for use in the underdeveloped areas. But the results of increased research and experimentation with oral contraceptivs are encouraging, and there may soon be a breakthrough on obtaining adequate means for the task of limiting population growth in the underdeveloped areas.

Conclusion

The demographer and the increasing number of his allies, in directing attention to the implications of world population growth, are in fact pointing to major global and international political problems—problems that cannot be ignored. Needless to say, the solution to the problems is not to be found in appeals to the traditions of the past, sacred or secular. The solution is to be found in the policies and actions which man himself, as a rational animal, must work out and implement. The mind of man, which has conceived remarkable methods for increasing life expectancy, is probably ingenious enough to devise methods by which the population explosion can be controlled within the framework of man's diverse value systems.

8. The Amazing Decline of Mortality in Underdeveloped Areas

Kingsley Davis[*]

Only a short time ago the fundamental cause of declining death rates was considered to be economic development. The history of the West pointed to a direct influence of economic change on health; namely, the better diets arising from the gains in agriculture, transportation, and commerce during the eighteenth and nineteenth centuries. In addition, there were indirect influences brought by the general rise in real income per capita, to which the revolution in methods of manufacture contributed substantially. This rise in real income made possible the growth of public sanitation, medical science, and more healthful living conditions. "It is no disparagement of medical science and practice," says Thompson, "to recognize that the great decline in the death rate that has taken place during the last two centuries in the West is due, basically, to improvement in production and economic conditions."[1]

This view, so long as it is an interpretation of Western history, seems essentially correct. It is perhaps correct in any long view. But when it is applied to contemporary underdeveloped areas, it is wrong; for the truth is that these areas do not need to become economically developed to reduce their death rates drastically. The failure to realize this fact has led to erroneous prediction. In 1931, for example, Bowen predicted that "the rate of proliferation of these [backward] peoples will fall off sharply." (*Op. cit.*, page 213; also, page 221.) Nearly all forecasts of the future population of underdeveloped areas—forecasts made in the thirties and forties—have proved to be too low, mainly because the trend of mortality was not foreseen. In an interesting account of the fight against tropical diseases in various parts of the British Empire, an account published in 1949, Stephen Taylor and Phyllis Gadsden reiterate that a rise in the general standard of living is necessary if public health work is to accomplish much (*Shadows in the Sun*, Geo. G. Harrap, 1949).

The view that declining death rates in underdeveloped areas depend on general economic progress in those areas arises in part from a careless application of principles taken from Western history. It also perhaps derives from the grip which Malthus' "means of subsistence" has had on thought about population. In the last analysis, Malthus tended to reduce all positive checks on population growth to lack of means of subsistence. He paid little attention to disease as a cause of mortality and certainly very little

*From the *American Economic Review*, Papers and Proceedings, May 1956, pp. 305–318. The author is Professor of Sociology at the University of California.
[1]Warren S. Thompson, *Population Problems* (McGraw-Hill, 4th ed., 1953), p. 77. This author provides, pp. 77–82, a convincing argument for this point of view. A similar position, less fully presented, was taken by Ezra Bowen, *An Hypothesis of Population Growth* (Columbia University Press, 1931), especially p. 201; and by Burnham N. Dell and George F. Luthringer, *Population, Resources and Trade* (Little, Brown, 1938), p. 62.

attention to disease as a factor independent of lack of subsistence.[2] If all causes of death were a function of the means of subsistence, then obviously a reduction in mortality would depend directly on economic development; but such is not the case. The failure to give adequate attention to causes of death has led, at least in population theory, to a rather sterile overemphasis on the matter of food supply.

Still another reason for economic determinism with respect to mortality trends has been the underestimation of the role of cultural diffusion across international borders. Often the effect of foreign influence on the population of a particular country has been thought of in terms of international trade. Although the importance of such trade is undeniable, it nevertheless remains true that scientific communication and medical co-operation among nations have played a large role in the reduction of mortality especially in recent times. Such communication and co-operation do not depend upon a rise in the level of living or in international trade of the country benefiting from them. It depends, rather, on the economic means of the more advanced countries which offer this kind of help.

Finally, there has been a tendency to overestimate the costs and difficulties of public health programs in underdeveloped areas. Since medical services are costly in advanced countries, especially on the therapeutic side, it has been assumed that they will necessarily be too dear for underdeveloped economies. But recent history has shown that with ingenuity and newer developments in medical technology, the practice of preventive and curative medicine on a mass basis can be carried out at relatively low per capita cost.

In any case, expert opinion failed to foresee the recent trend in the death rate in underdeveloped areas. This trend has been revolutionary, and it has occurred without commensurate economic development.

The Rapid Decline of Mortality

The rapidity with which the death rate has declined in most of the underdeveloped areas, including many areas with a high ratio of population to resources, has been unprecedented. It has never been matched at any time in the now advanced countries. The exact trend is difficult to measure in the absence of good statistics, but the evidence is sufficiently abundant and accurate to establish beyond a doubt the general decline.

The best known case is that of Ceylon. There the crude death rate fell by 34 per cent in one year (from 1946 to 1947)! This was no fluke, because the death rate continued to fall. In 1945 the rate was 22.0 per 1,000 population, which was about normal for the country: during the previous fourteen years it had averaged 22.2. After 1946 the mortality fell precipitously until in 1954 it was down to 10.4 per 1,000, a reduction of 53 per cent in nine years. The United States has no recorded death rate as high as 22.0 during the period of registration since 1900; the highest recorded rate is

[2] E. F. Penrose, *Population Theories and Their Application* (Stanford: Food Research Institute, 1934), pp. 17–19, 36–43, has analyzed the defectiveness of Malthusian reasoning in this regard. More recently Marston Bates, *The Prevalence of People* (Scribner's, 1955), pp. 68 ff., has pointed out that few species of animals or insects live up to the means of subsistence. Mostly, he says, they are killed off by other animals or insects.

for 1900, when it was 17.2 per 1,000. Massachusetts had a recorded rate of 21.7 in 1875, but the subsequent decline was exceedingly slow compared to what has happened recently in Ceylon.

The case of Ceylon is interesting, not only because of the rapid drop in mortality, but because the island probably has the best statistics in South Asia. We know the causes involved, as we shall see presently. But the essential point is that this case is not at all an isolated one, for there are other instances of spectacular declines in mortality. During the 1940–50 decade the death rate dropped in Puerto Rico by 46 per cent; in Formosa, by 43 per cent; in Jamaica, by 23 per cent. In order to avoid the effect of spectacular cases, I have taken eighteen underdeveloped areas, chosen not because they had unusual declines in mortality but because they were representative of different areas and had fairly constant boundaries and a relatively continuous series of registered death statistics.[3] When the decline in the death rate from one year to a year five years later was averaged for these eighteen countries, the following results were found:

Years Compared	Percentage Decline in Crude Death Rate
1935 with 1940	8.3
1940 " 1945	5.6
1945 " 1950	24.2
1950 " latest date[1]	14.0

Since 1935, despite depression and war, the drop in mortality has apparently been averaging about 13 per cent for each half decade. Undoubtedly, these areas had long had declining death rates prior to 1935, but the pace of change seems to have accelerated after that date, and the acceleration since 1945, when World War II ended, has been little short of remarkable, as the average decline of 24 per cent between 1945 and 1950 shows.

It seems highly unlikely that these sharp declines in mortality in the eighteen countries chosen are a result of bad statistics. The statistics are certainly bad on the whole, and one has real hesitation about including data from such places as the Philippines, Egypt, and Thailand. But in many of the areas chosen the data are relatively good, and though there may have been some disorganization in vital statistics associated with the depression and the war, one would think that on the whole, especially since 1945, the registration has generally improved and that the statistics would be more likely to minimize the decline than to exaggerate it.

The unprecedented character of these drops in the death rate can be seen by looking at the past history of the now advanced countries. In the United States, for example, the greatest drop in the crude death rate since 1900,

[3]The countries included were as follows: Barbados, Costa Rica, Ceylon, Cyprus, Egypt, El Salvador, Fiji Islands, Jamaica, Malaya, Mauritius, Mexico, Panama, Philippines, Puerto Rico, Surinam, Taiwan, Thailand, Trinidad-Tobago.

[1]In nine cases the latest date was 1954; in six it was 1953; in two it was 1952; and in one it was 1951. In cases where 1954 data were lacking, the percentage decline was raised by assuming that the same rate of change would hold for five years. This was done in order to make the final period comparable with the previous three.

taking arbitrary half-decade intervals, occurred between 1910 and 1915, the decline being 10.2 per cent. Sweden had large drops in the more distant past; for instance, the rate for 1805 was 25.3 per cent below that for 1800. But in Sweden in the eighteenth and nineteenth centuries, a sharp fall in the death rate tended to be followed immediately by a sharp rise, so that the secular trend was very slight. This is shown by the fact that from 1750 to 1950 the average loss during any four successive half decades never exceeded 6.9 per cent; and in Switzerland, from 1871 on, it did not exceed 8.6 per cent. These results should be compared to the figures just given for the eighteen underdeveloped countries where the average loss per half decade during the twenty years covered is 13 per cent. It is the persistence of the downward trend, as well as its magnitude, that impresses us in the currently underdeveloped areas.

So far we have considered single-year death rates five years apart. Let us now compare five-year averages. The average percentage declines in successive five-year death rates are given in Table 1 for our eighteen underdeveloped countries. The first thing to notice is that over a period of thirty years there was always a decline from any half decade to the next. Data on the Northwest European countries going back to 1740–44 show that there was no thirty-year period in which a decline always occurred between half decades. A second thing to note is that, over the entire thirty years, the total decline was 47 per cent. In Northwest European countries the maximum average percentage decline over any thirty-year period since 1740–44 was that between 1890–94 and 1920–24, when the decline was 34 per cent.[5] A third point is that, for our underdeveloped countries, the de-

Table 1. Average Percentage Decline of Crude Death as
Between Specified Periods, in Eighteen
Underdeveloped Countries

	NUMBER OF COUNTRIES[1]	AVERAGE PERCENTAGE DECLINE FROM PREVIOUS PERIOD[2]
Half decade changes		
1920–24	—	—
1925–29	15	6.0
1930–34	16	4.6
1935–39	18	6.3
1940–44	16	8.5
1945–49	16	15.2
1950–54	18	20.1
Average		10.1
Thirty-year change		
1920–24	—	—
1950–54	15	46.9

[1]Eighteen countries were used, but in some cases data were missing for one or the other of the periods compared. The list of eighteen countries is given in footnote 3 in the text.
[2]The percentage change in average crude death rate was computed for each country. Then the percentages were added and divided by the number of countries involved in each comparison.

[5]The countries in our list were Denmark, Norway, and Sweden up to 1830–39. In 1840–49, England and Wales were added; in 1850–59, Netherlands was added; and in 1870–79, Switzerland was added.

clines were not sharp in the twenties. The downward course gained momentum in the late thirties and then became a landslide in the forties and fifties. An average drop in the death rate of 20 per cent from 1945–49 to 1950–54 is staggering in view of the preceding long decline. For our Northwest European countries, the biggest decline as between any two successive half decades was 23 per cent, from 1740–44 to 1745–49, but this was followed by fifteen years of rising mortality. We can only conclude that the Northwest European countries never experienced such large persistent declines in mortality as the underdeveloped countries have shown recently. (Mention should be made of the fact that Japan, which is also a latecomer to the scene of declining mortality, showed between 1920–24 and 1950–54 a drop of 59 per cent in her crude death rate.)

Of course, we have been dealing with crude death rates. They are the only index of mortality readily available for a number of backward countries and are more abundantly available up to date. The crude rates, however, should not be misconstrued. In the first place, since deaths are underregistered in most preindustrial areas, the actual rates are not necessarily to be taken at face value. They have been used here merely to represent trends, and they are as likely to minimize the trends as to exaggerate them. In the second place, the crude rate, as is well known, reflects the age structure as well as actual mortality. In the case of our underdeveloped countries, the period dealt with is so short and fertility has remained so constant that the age structure has not had much chance to become changed. Consequently, the comparison of the crude rates of one period with those of another, in the case of the underdeveloped countries, is not vitiated by changes in the age structure. In the case of the industrial countries, crude rates may safely be compared as between one time and another, provided the two periods are not widely separated; but one should not compare, for example, the crude rate of Sweden in 1870 with the rate in 1940, because the age structure of the Swedish population was profoundly modified by the latter date. Similarly, one cannot compare the crude rates of industrial and preindustrial countries today. The industrial nations have much older populations, whereas the nonindustrial countries, especially those which have recently lowered their mortality sharply and have maintained a high fertility, have extremely young populations. It follows that the same age-specific death rates will yield a much higher crude death rate in the industrial population than in the other, and the difference tends to become greater as the force of mortality is reduced. Thus the fact that some underdeveloped areas now have crude rates as low or lower than the advanced Western peoples does not mean that their mortality is actually similar. (See the discussion of death rates in relation to age structure in United Nations, *Demographic Yearbook*, 1951, pages 9–12.) For instance, we have compared, in Table 2, the crude death rates in certain industrial countries with those in four underdeveloped countries where deaths are well registered. It can be seen that though the crude death rates of the underdeveloped areas are as low as those of the urban-industrial countries, those areas nevertheless have a shorter average length of life.

George J. Stolnitz recently analyzed the mortality trends in advanced and backward countries by means of life tables. ("A Century of Inter-

Table 2. Comparisons Based on Crude Death Rate
and on Average Length of Life

	CRUDE DEATH RATE		AVERAGE YEARS LIVED AFTER BIRTH (MALES)	
	DATE	RATE	DATES	NUMBER
Underdeveloped countries				
Trinidad and Tobago	1954	9.8	1950–52	56.3
Ceylon	1954	10.4	1952	57.6
Costa Rica	1954	10.6	1949–51	55.7[1]
Jamaica	1953	10.4	1945–47	51.2
Urban-industrial Countries				
United States	1954	9.2	1951	65.9
United Kingdom	1954	11.4	1952	67.1
France	1954	12.0	1950–51	63.6
Sweden	1954	9.6	1946–50	69.0

[1]Males and females

national Mortality Trends: I," *Population Studies,* July, 1955, pages 24–55.) Since very few nonindustrial countries have a series of reliable life tables covering different periods, his evidence was necessarily scanty. Nevertheless, his conclusions definitely substantiate those reached here. He points out that in Eastern and Southern Europe the long-term gains in average length of life, leaving aside periods of war, have been "much more rapid" than in Northwestern Europe at a comparable stage of development. Furthermore, he finds that since 1940 survival rates have increased in the countries of Latin America, Asia, and Afria at such a rate as to narrow substantially the gap between them and the countries of Northwest European culture. He says, in fact: "There are mounting signs that the middle of this century has marked a revolutionary turning point in the life chances of the world's impoverished nations." (*Op. cit.,* page 47.)

The Causes of the Amazing Decline

The decline of mortality in the underdeveloped areas has not been equally great in all areas. It has been less in India and Egypt than in Ceylon; it has probably been less in China and Indonesia than in Malaya and Mexico. But significant declines have occurred nearly everywhere, and in many regions their speed has been startling. . . .

In general, then, it seems clear that the great reduction of mortality in underdeveloped areas since 1940 has been brought about mainly by the discovery of new methods of disease treatment applicable at reasonable cost, by the diffusion of these new methods from the advanced countries to the unadvanced through international organizations and scientific communication, by international financial help furnished through international organizations and governments and private foundations, and by the use of experts and medical personnel furnished primarily by the industrial countries. The reduction could be rapid, because it did not depend on general economic development or social modernization in the underdeveloped areas. It did not depend on training local medical personnel or local research or local prosperity. It was an example of a rapid cultural diffusion of death-control techniques which did not depend on the diffusion of other cultural elements or basic changes in the institutions and customs of the people affected. Though in the literature on public health there is still great lip service paid to the necessity of general economic improvement and community welfare in the control of disease, the truth is that many scourges can be stamped out with none of this, just as diseases in cattle can be eliminated.

The Demographic Consequences of Declining Mortality

The consequences of rapidly declining mortality in underdeveloped regions can be understood only in conjunction with what is happening to fertility. In this regard, two points seem clear: First, the drop in the death rate has tended to go much farther without a significant decline in the birth rate than was the case in the West. Second, the traditional birth rates in most underdeveloped areas appear to be, and to have been, higher than they ever were in Northwestern Europe.

The first point appears clear from available data. Stolnitz has shown for eleven Western countries the dates when the sharpest increases in life expectancy were made (*op. cit.*, page 32). In eight out of the eleven, the sharpest rise in life expectancy at birth for males was after 1915; and in none did the sharpest rise occur wholly before 1900. (The results are essentially the same for life expectancy at age 0 for females.) An analysis of crude death rates reveals much the same thing. In the case of Sweden, for example, the average percentage decline in the mean death rate as between successive decades was as follows: 1740–99, 3.7; 1800–1849, 3.1; 1850–99, 4.3; 1900–1949, 7.7. In other words the most rapid decline in mortality in Western countries occurred in the twentieth century. It is known that the birth rate had started its downward course long before this. In Sweden, for example, the crude birth rate definitely turned down around 1860, and more defined analysis suggests that there was some reduction beginning as early at 1801. (See N. B. Ryder, "The Influence of Declining Mortality on Swedish Reproduction," in Milbank Memorial Fund, *Current Research in Human Fertility*, 1955, especially pages 71–72.) By the time the most rapid descent of the death rate occurred, the birth rate was already greatly reduced. In Norway the crude birth rate had dropped to the low twenties, and in Sweden and Switzerland it had fallen to less than twenty.

But the preindustrial birth rate in Northwestern Europe seems never to have been so high in the first place as that of Asia, North Africa, and much of Latin America today. Birth rates of 40 to 60 per 1,000 population are still found in many of the latter areas, whereas in Denmark the highest birth rate recorded in the eighteenth century was 33.6 in 1780; the highest in Sweden in that century was 38.7 in 1751, and the highest in Norway was 37.8 in 1756. (For the eighteenth-century rates, see H. Gille, "The Demographic History of the Northern European Countries in the Eighteenth Century," *Population Studies*, June, 1949, page 63.) In other words, "almost all the underdeveloped areas *now* have fertility rates well above the corresponding Western European rates before decline set in about 1880–1890." (Norman S. Buchanan and Howard S. Ellis, *Approaches to Economic Development,* Twentieth Century Fund, 1955, page 107.)

Since the death rate in underdeveloped areas is falling precipitously while the birth rate, already extremely high to begin with, is either not falling at all or is doing so very slowly, the rate of natural increase is much faster in these regions than it ever was in the past in the now urban-industrial areas. The extremity of the natural increase can best be grasped by comparing it with what happened in the now industrial countries, as in Table 3. Clearly, the excess of births over deaths in most of our underdeveloped countries has been in recent years four to ten times what it was in Northwestern Europe prior to 1800. It has even been two to three times what it was in Northwestern Europe during the heyday of population growth in the latter region, 1850–99. We cannot fail to conclude, then, that neither preindustrial Europe nor industrial Europe ever had the rate of natural increase that the preindustrial countries of the world today are showing.

Table 3. *Natural Increase for Different Periods,*
*Developed and Underdeveloped Countries**

	AVERAGE NATURAL INCREASE PER 1,000 PER YEAR					
	1735–99	1800–49	1850–99	1900–49	1940–49	1950–54[3]
Industrial countries						
England and						
Wales	—	10.2[1]	12.7	6.5		
Denmark	2.8	8.5	12.2	10.9		
Norway	6.6	9.3	14.0	9.0		
Sweden	5.6	8.1	11.5	6.9		
Switerland	—	—	7.9[2]	7.0		
Average	5.0	9.0	11.7	8.1		
Underdeveloped countries						
Barbados					14.7	18.6
Ceylon					19.9	27.8
Costa Rica					27.6	37.3
Cyprus					19.6	20.2
Egypt					16.1	26.0
El Salvador					25.0	33.2
Fiji					27.5	29.6
Jamaica					17.4	22.1
Malaya					22.6	29.6
Mauritius					12.3	33.0
Mexico					24.6	28.7
Panama					24.9	26.2
Puerto Rico					26.0	27.6
Surinam					20.6	27.0
Taiwan					25.0	35.0
Thailand					14.9	18.9
Trinidad and						
Tobago					22.7	26.6
Average					21.3	27.5

*Sources: For 1940 to 1954, UN *Demographic Yearbook,* 1953 and 1954. For earlier years statistical yearbooks of various countries and H. Gille, "Demographic History of the Northern European Countries in the Eighteenth Century," *Population Studies,* June, 1949.
[1]For 1841–50 only.
[2]For 1871–99 only.
[3]For 1954 or the latest year available. See footnote 8 in text.

In many of the densely settled underdeveloped countries, indeed, the rate of natural increase is approaching or has achieved something like 30 per 1,000 per year. Thus in 1954 or the latest year available, seventeen underdeveloped countries had an average natural increase of 27.5 per 1,000.[6] These countries were chosen, it must be remembered, not because they showed high growth rates, but because, among the underdeveloped nations, they tended to have better than average birth and death statistics and represented different regions. Their statistics are far from perfect; in many cases the rates of natural increase are probably in error by substantial margins. But there is no reason to think that on the whole the births are any better registered than the deaths. The contrary may be true, which would mean that the rates given would be underestimates of natural increase. Furthermore, the evidence is overwhelming: all of these countries report extremely high rates of natural increase.

To appreciate the significance of these rates of natural increase, one should remember that a growth of 30 per 1,000 per year will double the population in twenty-three years and quadruple it in forty-six years. The United States, often thought to have established a record in population growth,[7] never had, even in its heyday and with the help of immigration, a faster increase than many of our underdeveloped areas are showing by the sheer excess of births over deaths. Here are the figures for the United States during its greatest population boom:

	AVERAGE POPULATION GROWTH PER 1,000 PER YEAR DURING PRIOR DECADE
1800	30.1
1810	31.0
1820	28.6
1830	28.9
1840	28.2
1850	30.6
1860	30.4

These figures include net immigration and so are higher than the natural increase alone would be. Lack of data on births and deaths prevents our knowing the rates of natural increase in the United States during our period of most rapid growth. Nevertheless, they are apparently equaled by the natural increase of many underdeveloped areas today. This circumstance would not seem strange if the underdeveloped areas were sparsely populated and had rich resources and expanding frontiers; but this is obviously not the case in places like Ceylon, Egypt, Jamaica, El Salvador, Taiwan, and a host of other backward areas. In such places the recent rapid population growth is a totally different matter from

[6]The list is the same as that previously used, except that the Philippines was omitted because of gross defectiveness in birth registration. Of the seventeen countries included, data were available for 1954 in nine cases; for 1953 in five cases; for 1952 in two cases; and for 1952 in one case.
[7]"It is likely that population growth was never more rapid in any nation than among the youthful population of this New World, from the days of colonial settlement to the time of the Civil War. . . ." (National Resources Committee, *The Problems of a Changing Population,* 1938), p. 6.

what it was in the United States from 1790 to 1860. It is not a response to seemingly unlimited economic opportunity but rather an unfortunate by-product of the importation of scientific death control. There appears to be nothing in the economic future of most underdeveloped countries to suggest that they can achieve substantially higher levels of living with populations that are tending to double every twenty-five to thirty years.

Future Possibilities

No doubt the reduction of mortality in underdeveloped areas can be carried still further, though possibly at slower rates. The life expectancy of these areas is still considerably lower than that of industrial nations. Unless, therefore, their birth rates begin to fall, the rates of natural increase may climb still higher. There is some evidence that fertility is beginning to drop (e.g., in Puerto Rico, Jamaica, Cyprus), but the signs are small as yet and are matched by slight apparent increases elsewhere (e.g., Trinidad, Fiji, Ceylon). Actually, the improvement of health, with no other changes, tends to increase reproduction.

If, as we have seen and contrary to earlier expectations, drastic reductions in mortality can be made without marked economic development in the countries concerned and without much change in the traditional birth rates, does this mean that the death rate is permanently disassociated from economic progress? Can populations continue to grow rapidly without a corresponding economic growth?

The answer is clearly no. The demographic trends of recent decades in underdeveloped areas are of necessity temporary. They result from the brief effect, the shot in the arm, which the conquest of disease by imported techniques can give. But people can die of other things than disease. They can die of starvation or from war, and they can die from a loss of the very disease controls which once saved them. As one analyst of mortality in Ceylon puts it: "What would happen, for example, if a future war prevented the importation of supplies of D.D.T.?"[8] Unless the demographic ledger is balanced by a change in birth rates, it may turn out that the gains in mortality in recent years will prove transitory. Economic development alone cannot be counted on to save a situation over which it has so little control and by which it is itself greatly influenced.

[8] H. Cullumbine, *An Analysis of the Vital Statistics of Ceylon* (a volume of the Ceylon Journal of Medical Science, December, 1950), p. 245.

THEORY
OF
DEVELOPMENT

SOCIAL FACTORS IN GROWTH

9. Social Implications of Economic Growth

Bert F. Hoselitz*

... Economic growth is essentially a process which forms part of the history of a society and more insights may be gained about the nature of the process of economic growth from historical studies than from either generalizations drawn from hypothetical situations resulting in a framework of arbitrary assumptions characteristic of stationary analysis in economics, or from the tacit or explicit assumption that currently underdeveloped countries are in any but the most fundamental socio-cultural aspects the images of earlier historical stages of currently developed countries. But if the study of economic growth can be furthered significantly by concentration on historical patterns of development, we must guard against falling into the other extreme of regarding each process of economic growth as so unique that its study may not yield the recognition of factors which lend themselves to general application.

Four Propositions

One attempt to derive a generally applicable set of propositions from historical study has been undertaken by Professor Simon Kuznets. Among the statements which he believes are generally applicable from his survey of historical development patterns, notably in those countries which now have the highest per capita real incomes, Professor Kuznets stresses especially the following four:

1. The main advances in real income were achieved in the last 150 to 200 years. This would lead to the social and economic history of the world of more than 200 years ago or—if we stipulate a more or less long gestation period—of say 300 years ago, and is of little significance for our problem.

2. The main advances were made in association with the introduction of industrialism, that is, a "wide application of knowledge, based on empirical science, to the problem of economic and social technology."

3. The introduction of a system of industrialism, characterized by these traits requires a "cultural milieu in which existing values do not impede an open-minded view on nature, a dispassionate consideration of empirical findings, and a strong desire to enhance the material welfare of man."

These two propositions are most widely accepted and universally agreed upon as conditions and/or results of economic advancement. In fact, the attempts of most underdeveloped countries today are directed towards the

*From *The Economic Weekly*, February 14, 1959, and February 21, 1959. The author is Professor of Economics, Research Center in Economic Development and Cultural Change, University of Chicago.

acquisition of a sizeable sector of industry and one of the chief obstacles which they encounter is the impediment imposed upon this endeavor by the tenacity of traditional so-called "irrational" cultural valuations on the part of many persons in economically little advanced societies. The joint efforts of the technical aid programmes of the United Nations, the World Bank, the Food and Agriculture Organization, and other agencies are directed, therefore, towards the provision of improved technologies, while the complementary efforts of Unesco are directed at a simultaneous eradication of illiteracy and the provision of more adequate educational and research services, so as to lay the groundwork for cultural change.

4. The last general finding of Professor Kuznets is the proposition that the adoption of a system of industrialism apparently requires a system of private enterprise as the main form of economic organization and democracy (in the western sense) as the prevalent form of political organization. Taken together, these propositions amount to stating that the only society which has so far proven to be capable of developing the productive forces of the economy sufficiently to show a sizeable gain in real income has been modern western free enterprise capitalism.

Not Representative Enough

A further task which remains, is to determine whether the four factors which were singled out by Kuznets are related to one another in some peculiar fashion, or whether they are, in turn, all dependent in some clearly identifiable way on some other variable not specifically stressed by him. We are here confronted with the problem of developing a theory of capitalist development, a task which has been undertaken by many men of genius, but which has not been crowned with conclusions which find general and undisputed acceptance. All the great theories of capitalist development by men like Malthus and Ricardo, Marx and his disciples, Sombart, Weber, and others, have found more or less convincing critics; and a synthetic theory which would incorporate all that is good in the various "one-sided" theories has not been proposed and may be impossible to develop.

The very procedure chosen by Professor Kuznets, that is, his study of the past growth processes of only those countries which, on a cross-sectional basis show the highest per capita incomes, is, in part responsible for this outcome. Although it is plausible to expect that most can be learned about the history of the growth process if the most advanced countries are selected for study, an analysis of the predominant social relations in these advanced countries would have shown that they exhibit similar political and socio-economic foundations, and a generalization of our insights in the development process would have required comparison with countries which, on the one hand, have shown clear signs of economic growth, although, on the other, they may not yet have reached a level high enough to be ranked among the approximately 15 countries with the highest per capita incomes.

Japan and Soviet Union

The two countries which have, doubtless, shown signs of rapid growth, although in terms of per capita income they have not caught up yet with western Europe and North America, are Japan and the Soviet Union. The fact that Japan experienced a period of rapid economic growth following the restoration of the Meiji is generally admitted and clearly appears from the figures which Professor Clark has published and to which reference was made a little earlier. Although on the basis of a measure in the customary per capita income terms, Japan is still below the countries of western Europe, Anglo-Saxon North America and Australasia, it has attained a level of productivity which is substantially higher than that of any comparable oriental society.

As concerns the Soviet Union there is considerable dispute of the precise magnitude of economic advancement since the inauguration of the first Five Year Plan. In part, this is due to the scarcity and incompleteness of Russian statistical data, in part to the arbitrary value assigned to the monetary unit, and in part, doubtless, to some bias with which most students approach Soviet data. However, from a neutral and fairly unbiased, as well as rather well-informed source, the Economic Commission for Europe of the United Nations, we may conclude that the Soviet Union has made rapid and impressive economic progress in the last thirty years. Comparing the output of several strategic raw materials and fuel in the Soviet Union and the seven most highly industrialized countries of western Europe (which, in 1951, had together a population approximately equal to that of the USSR) the Economic Commission for Europe concludes that, in 1951, "the output of coal, electricity and steel in the Soviet Union is about one-half of that in western Europe and is increasing at a much faster rate than can be expected for western Europe," and that "there are indications that, if present rates of expansion are maintained, by the end of this decade the production and consumption of major industrial raw materials in the Soviet Union will be equal or superior to that in the seven most industrialized countries of western Europe." On the basis of this evidence and the undoubted industrial inferiority of Russia at the time of the revolution and even thereafter, the fact of rapid economic progress in the Soviet Union cannot be doubted.

But if we confine our historical analysis and the attempt to derive generalizations from it not merely to the few western countries which had (on the basis of the United States Department of State computations) per capita real incomes of more than $200 in 1939, but include also the historical analysis of Japanese and Russian development we may be forced to alter some of the generalizations offered by Professor Kuznets. Economic development, as viewed here, is interpreted as a process exhibiting a noticeable improvement of output achieved ordinarily in a short period of time, whereas in the view of Kuznets the additional condition is set that a minimum level of per capita real income be reached or exceeded. A less rigorous definition of economic advancement results in admitting the possibility that certain factors may be operative which may prevent an economy from reaching a certain level of development, although they do not prevent development altogether. For example, on the basis of the data supplied by Colin Clark, the highest figure of Japanese output per man-year ever reached was 649 International Units. This figure, which was obtained in 1943 is roughly six and a half times that of annual output per member of the labour force at the beginning of the Japanese process of growth, in 1887. But it remains below the annual product per man-year which in the United States and Great Britain was reached before the middle of the nineteenth century. Moreover, past economic progress in the United States and Great Britain, as well as chances for future progress in these countries are much better than in Japan, so that it may justly be doubted whether Japan ever will catch up with the United States and Great Britain.

Coal-Oil-Steel Complex

This last statement rests on an implicit assumption, that is, that future chances of growth are best in those societies which have already made the most rapid and far-reaching progress in the past. Let us recall that the first general proposition cited from Professor Kuznets related to the relative recency of the growth process in the most advanced countries. This clearly establishes its close association with the process of industrialization, but beyond that, with the use of a technology appropriate to the specific resource endowment of the industrially most advanced countries. This can be stated in other words by saying that, on the basis of resources, relatively most abundant in the advanced countries, a technology was developed which tended to be peculiarly suited for the industrial and with it the general economic advancement of these countries. At the same time, and given this technology, the less advanced countries are in a less favourable condition as concerns their chances to reach the level of development of the more favoured societies and, indeed, may never catch up with them. Moreover, just as industrialization, by making use of a technology more fully in tune with the resource complex of the developed countries, gave them an impetus which permitted them to out-distance in the last 150 or 200 years the poorer countries, so the continued impact of basically the same technology permits them to further outdistance the poorer countries as time goes on. Although the specific distribution of non-renewable natural resources among presently advanced and underdeveloped countries does not prevent the poorer countries from experiencing economic growth through industrialization and the introduction of western technology, it may put limitations on the eventual level of advancement which these countries can reach, as well as on the speed with which they may reach significantly more elevated levels of output, provided this technology, especially, the coal-oil-steel complex, remains the basis of industrial growth. If coal and oil could be replaced by other sources of power, say fissionable materials, and if iron and its derivatives could be replaced by some other basic structural material, which is more generally available in the poorer countries, say aluminium, a technological revolution may take place which might alter the relative chances of ultimate economic progress through industrialization of the poorer countries.

So long as we assume that, in its basic framework, an industrial technology based on coal, oil, and iron as chief raw materials remains dominant, we must conclude that economic growth, though possible as such in all societies, may not enable all of them to reach the same level of advancement (in terms of per capita real output). In the light of this reasoning we can also explain why the Soviet Union appears to have a better prospect of catching up with and perhaps out-distancing some of the western European countries than Japan, India, or the countries of South East Asia. A similar analysis could also be applied to the spectacular rise of the United States and the somewhat less spectacular rise of Germany. Since it is impossible to predict, within any tolerable limits of accuracy, what would be the eventual prospects of advancement of the various countries if the technological framework of industrialization changed radically, the alternative growth patterns which may be specific are all founded upon accepting the predominant western technology as given.

Assuming technology to be given, there are two further variables which have a fundamental impact on the specific pattern of economic growth. The first is often loosely stated as relating to the man-land ratio, or the population density per resource unit at the beginning of the growth process, and the other relates to the degree of autonomy and spontaneity with which the growth process is inaugurated. Stated in somewhat different terms, the first set of variables determines whether the growth process is primarily intrinsic, i.e., whether it consists primarily in an intensification of economic activity within a given geographical space, or whether it is primarily expansionist, i.e., whether it consists primarily in an extension of the economic "frontier" and a gradual spatial expansion of the area in which more advanced technology and economic organization are applied. The process of capitalist development in the western world, as a whole, exhibits both the intrinsic and the expansionist growth patterns, and I consider it to be the chief merit of W. W. Rostow's recent book, "The Process of Economic Growth," to have shown not only the existence of these two patterns of economic development, but also to have related them to fluctuations in other variables of great economic significance, such as prices, etc. But if the growth process of western capitalism as a whole may be said to exhibit both intrinsic and expansionist features, different countries in the western world show wide variations. In some of them, for example, Germany, or Switzerland, intrinsic patterns are considerably more important than in other countries such as, for example, the United States or Australia, where an extension of the frontier, is a clear characteristic of the development process.

It would, of course, be a mistake to assume that every country or region whose economic history has been surveyed exhibits either an intrinsic or expansionist growth pattern in pure form. The case of Britain is an example where a slim balance between intrinsic and expansionist development prevailed. Although in the older industrial centres—London, Bristol, Sheffield, Birmingham, for example—intrinsic patterns of development preponderated, several expansionist episodes are clearly discernible: the draining of the fens must be regarded as a process of internal colonization; and the growth of coal and iron production in South Wales, the north-east of England and Scotland, as well as the development of textile and other industries in the new industrial centre of Lancashire and elsewhere, which set in motion such a vast movement of internal migration must also be considered as an extension of the internal geographical frontier. Finally, in the nineteenth century, the growth of foreign investment and the impact of the returns from this investment had profound influences upon further British economic growth.

Switzerland and Germany, the Scandinavian countries and Belgium, but also France and even Japan display predominantly intrinsic patterns of growth. Some countries, like Belgium and Denmark and Switzerland had only very limited possibilities of "internal colonization." But even some of the larger countries, such as France, for example, were so evenly settled before the advent of the industrial revolution that relatively few "new" areas within the country's boundaries were opened up in the course of economic progress. Foreign investment and colonial expansion played a role, but were, on the whole, much more limited in scope than in Britain. To be sure, the acquisition of Korea and Taiwan, and later the domination of Manchuria by Japan, were important events influencing strongly the capacity of economic growth of the centre. But the main growth process was concentrated on the homeland. With the exception of Hokkaido whose new fields land-hungry peasants gobbled up during the past century, Japan's farm land has been fully exploited for centuries; and the growth of industry was superimposed upon the earlier domestic commerce and handicrafts of such cities as Tokyo (Edo), Osaka, Kyoto, and others which even before the downfall of the shogunate had populations of around a million persons.

The Westward Movement

In contrast to these countries, the growth pattern of the United States, Canada, and Australia, is profoundly different. It is not necessary to recount here in any detail the history of the settlement of North America or Australia, but the greatness of the population shifts and associated expansion of settlement may be gauged, if we recall that in 1860 at the eve of the vast industrial upsurge in the United States, Chicago had barely more than 100,000 inhabitants, Minneapolis, Cleveland, and Detroit were little more than villages, and Los Angeles, Denver and Seattle, only dots on a map. The importance of this development pattern for our purposes is not so much to point to the addition of vast areas to the economically effective area of a country, nor to derive inspiration from the heroism and romance of the westward movement. It is important rather because it depended on the appearance of a singular mass phenomenon: the willingness and, indeed, the eagerness of entire communities of persons to relinquish the security of familiar surroundings and to settle in the wilderness or almost-wilderness.

To explain the westward movement by population pressure or even by purely economic motives such as looking for an escape from low wages or low agricultural yields must be rejected. To be sure, the westward movement had economic effects for those who took part in it as well as for those who remained behind. For settlement in the west seemed to offer a chance to many who had knowledge of at least the rudiments of agriculture. And although the majority of the migrants were farmers or farmers' sons, the urban workers benefited nevertheless from their movement westwards, because without it they would have swelled the ranks of the urban proletariat in the East. Thus, in contributing to the easing of pressure on wages in the older settled centres and in sustaining the idea that those who moved took a chance, but also might possibly win a new world, the extension of the frontier exerted a strong influence on the old American doctrine of equality of opportunity and strengthened it.

Force of Egalitarian Ideology

But the interaction between the principle of equal opportunity—one of the ideological fundamentals on which American society was built—and the motives which pushed people towards the unknown west was more complex. It was so generally admitted that everyone could improve his economic position, in the long run, provided he was industrious, honest and frugal, that the doctrine of equal opportunity may be seen to have been at the very core of the expansionist pattern of American economic growth. During more than a century, Americans who could have spent their lives rather comfortably in the familiar surroundings of the friends and acquaintances of long standing, left their towns and villages and went into the new and inhospitable western regions where they often lived in isolation and always had to face a hard struggle with nature, Indians, or pillaging raiders. One may submit that the decision to move west involved almost always hardships and privations, at least for some time, and that whatever "dividends" were gained in the process, accrued only rarely to the first settlers, and usually only to their children or grandchildren. Here becomes applicable a German proverb which was usually applied to emigrants: Der erste hat den Tod, der zweite hat die Not, der dritte hat das Brot. (The first has death, the second has misery, the third has bread.)

From a purely economic viewpoint many of the migrants thus acted very irrationally when they went west. Obviously some went, because they felt that their domestic economic situation was hopeless. Others tried to escape a family or other interpersonal relations with which they could not cope. Some ran away from a place where they had been involved in a crime or other dishonest act; and again others were religious fanatics or plain adventurers who looked for a free and dangerous life. In the case of many or perhaps all migrants strong personal motives played a role. But the factor which permitted all these widely divergent motives to become translated into externally analogous actions was the force of an egalitarian ideology which had its roots in the social thought evolved prior to and during the American Revolution. In its most general form it was a joining of some parts of the old Puritan doctrine to the newer one of Thomas Jefferson and his circle. In its more specific form it induced the peopling of the west, the search for opportunity and success in that vast empty area to the west towards which Americans felt drawn themselves as if by manifest destiny.

And in the long run this expectation of success was confirmed. The gradual settling of the American west contributed not only to the maintenance and even improvement of relatively elevated real incomes of those who remained behind, but also, in the long run, to the prosperity of those who had travelled west themselves. Many did not live to experience this prosperity, but their children and grandchildren benefited from the endurance of the first settlers and became living proof that this endurance, this abstinence had paid off. By the end of the nineteenth century, much of the early movement had disappeared, but so had the worst risks and hardships.

In exchange the grains and meats of the west, its minerals and fruits, had begun to conquer the markets of the world.

In Russia

I cannot enter into an equally extended discussion of the parallel process in Canada and Australia, but an investigation of the peopling of British North America and the continent of Australia would show the prevalence of similar factors as those operative in the United States. Even the penetration of Siberia in its early stages, during the eighteenth and nineteenth century seems to have been supported by an egalitarian and libertarian ideology, which was in full contrast to the official tsarism, and present-day bolshevism. But the chief expansion into Russian Asia occurred in the last twenty years under bolshevik rule. There it was carried not any more by an ideology of freedom and opportunity, but by the compelling power of the state.

But the very fact that the Soviet Union did experience economic growth on the expansionist pattern, and Japan on the intrinsic pattern is proof that the former is not indispensably bound up with an ideology such as that prevalent in nineteenth century America, or that the latter has as a necessary prerequisite the evolution of a spirit of capitalism. Wherever "autonomous" growth has occurred, there ideologies have had a deep influence and force. But we can also have "induced" development, that is, rather than relying on the unplanned, and as it were, accidental, combination of factors producing a system of social values conducive to development, we may rely on the conscious organization and ordering of the forces and capacities of a society with the aim of economic progress.

Japan as Model

We obtain, therefore, four fundamental patterns of economic development, depending upon whether economic growth is autonomous or induced, and whether it is intrinsic or expansionist. Great Britain and the countries of western Europe represent the autonomous-intrinsic type of development; the United States, Canada, and Australasia the autonomous-expansionist type; Japan the induced-intrinsic type; and the Soviet Union the induced-expansionist type. We cannot predict with too much accuracy which of these types the various currently underdeveloped countries will follow. But in view of the relatively dense settlement of many underdeveloped countries, and in view of the increasing role which conscious planned economic development plays in them, we may expect to see a prevalence of the induced-intrinsic type of development. This means that the experience of Japan, rather than any other country will serve as a model for the policies to be followed in presently underdeveloped countries.

I believe I have shown in the preceding sections that economic development, especially if it involves industrialisation, implies a rapid, and in a sense, revolutionary process which, if it is to take root in a society, must penetrate widely and deeply and hence affects the social, structural and cultural facets of a society. In other words, economic development consists not merely in a change of production techniques, but also, in the last resort, in a reorientation of social norms and values. Any analysis of economic development if it is to be fruitful and complete must include a set of propositions relating changes in production techniques to changes in values.

Oversimplification

Most past attempts at bringing about economic development can be viewed as proceeding from either one of these extremes. Current proposals, especially those made by some publicists who are well-intentioned but often ill-informed, and even those made by some spokesmen for government agencies or international organizations, appear to be based on notions very close to a theory of economic determinism. If the underdeveloped countries were only supplied with capital in appropriate form valued at several billion dollars annually—so the argument runs—their economy and presumably their society would be changed drastically. Even a conservative interpretation of this view comes to the result that economic changes, notably the introduction of new techniques and new capital instruments are a necessary prerequisite, and indeed the most likely path by which social behaviour patterns and cultural norms can be changed. However, it is doubtful whether the transformation of a society can be explained in such simple fashion and there is no doubt that the obstinacy with which people hold to traditional values, even in the face of a rapidly changing technology and economic organization, may impose obstacles of formidable proportions.

It may be asked whether a more fruitful procedure may not be the attempt to alter values first and to expect that this will create a climate favourable for new economic forms and processes. But it appears, from theoretical reflection and historical experience, that this method has little chance of success. We have the testimony of our most distinguished anthropologists who argue that a diffusion of values or value systems is impossible. The historical experiences, notwithstanding the success of some individual missionaries, confirm this. In those instances in which religious conversions of whole societies were attempted, as in the case of the Spanish and Portuguese colonies, the long-run effects on social structure and the economy have been small; we also note failure of attempts to remodel only secular values, while leaving the religion undisturbed, as was the case in upper Burma, where the British tried to replace traditional quasi-tribal social relations by a social system based on the free market and the rule of law. The result was negative; Burma experienced social disorganization on a large scale, culminating in gang warfare and a formidable increase of violent crimes; the expected positive results were not forthcoming. Although there was great improvement in output, there was little improvement in the level of living of the average Burman and the allocation of developmentally most significant functions continued to be influenced strongly by status considerations rather than considerations of equity and efficiency.

Non-Economic "Factors"

If we try to interpret the aspirations of the presently economically less advanced countries, we find there also a strange ambiguity which appears to be the result of partial unawareness of the close interconnectedness of economic advancement and cultural change. For the spokesmen of the poorer countries most emphatically favour economic progress resulting in an elevation of general levels of living, and blame their poverty on previous colonial status or quasi-colonial imperialistic exploitation. At the same time their rejection of colonialism, and imperialism manifests itself in a heightened sense of nationalism, the symbolic expression of which consists in the repudiation of foreign philosophies and external behaviour patterns and the reaffirmation of traditionally honoured ways of acting and thinking.

For example, the nationalism in Gandhi's independence movement was associated with the return to highly inefficient methods of traditional Indian activity, and in present-day Burma, independence is not only accompanied by a resumption of traditional names and dress, but by a strengthening of Buddhism, a religion which reflects an ideology totally opposed to efficient, progressive economic activity. The realization of economic advancement thus meets with numerous obstacles and impediments. Many of these obstacles are in the realm of economic relations; there is scarcity of capital, there is a demand for new skills and new techniques, there is a need for better roads and improved systems of communication, for public utilities and new sources of power. But some of the impediments to economic progress are beyond the area of economic relations. If the observation is made that among the prerequisites of economic development is the growth of a middle class, or the evaluation of a spirit of venturesomeness, or the elimination of corruption among officialdom, we are confronted with changes in the social organization and culture of a people rather than its economy. I propose to discuss in the remainder of this paper some of these non-economic "factors" which are yet too little explored, but which appear to exercise a strong negative and positive influence on the attainment of economic betterment.

Introducing Innovation

If we ask how technological or economic innovations are introduced in a society we immediately encounter two problems. One is the question of which innovations will be adopted with different degrees of ease, and which will be rejected and the other is the question of what person or group of persons performs the tasks of adopting and further spreading the new techniques in a society. Within the context of this paper the first question is of subordinated importance, since we are not dealing with specific innovations but the general problem of development and all underdeveloped countries are eager to accept more modern forms of economic activity, although for diverse reasons some of them may reject one or the other type. For example, though India may reject or hesitate to adopt modern methods of meat packing, it is eager to introduce other industries.

But the second question, who carries the main burden in the process of innovation, is of great interest to us; evidence for this is the fact that in discussing economic development emphasis has so often been placed on the presence or absence of certain social groups exhibiting particular attitudes (e.g., venturesomeness) or performing special roles (e.g., bureaucracy, "middle class"). In somewhat different terms, we may say that economic development requires the formation of a social group which constitutes the spearhead of different kinds of innovations.

Social Mobility

It is plain from these considerations that one of the pre-requisites of economic and technical advancement is a high degree of social mobility. If, for whatever reasons, social advancement of people in less privileged ranks in society is made difficult, or if the cleavages in status, power, and wealth between different social groups are great, an impediment to economic development of considerable magnitude is thereby in existence. Very primitive societies apart, the main status-determining factors are wealth, political power, and education. The ideal form of the liberal state is based on the assumption that each of these factors will be in the hands of a different social group or class and that in addition to the separation of powers in the political field, there will be a "balance" of social power and status. It will be remembered that an important aspect of the Marxian criticism of "bourgeois capitalism" was based on the assertion that this separation did not exist, or existed only in appearance and that, in Engels' words, "the modern state no matter what its form is essentially a capitalist machine, the state of the capitalists."

Now whether or not this statement was true of the nations of nineteenth century Europe, the social situation on which it is based is true of many underdeveloped countries today. In many of the countries of Asia, the Near East and Latin America, wealth, political power, and education are concentrated in a small group of people, and not infrequently the very individuals who control political power are also the richest and best educated men in the society. But this very monopoly of status-conferring factors is an impediment to economic development. The gap between the privileged and the masses, between the rulers and the ruled, is immense and there is nothing to fill it. But even to the extent to which this gap is being filled by an incipient middle class consisting chiefly of educators, government officials, and members of the intelligentsia, this group must, in order to assure its maintenance, either align itself with the ruling group or suffer being pushed into positions of harsh antagonism to that group. Hence intellectuals often attain positions of leadership among the discontented, the unprivileged, the poor; hence the appeal the communist ideology exerts on intellectuals in underdeveloped countries; hence also the enhanced social cleavage which becomes little, if at all, mitigated by the rise of the middle class. The cleavage of the world into two antagonistic camps becomes reflected in the political and ideological issues in a developing country and the possibility of evolutionary development towards higher levels of living disappears more and more as a practical third alternative between either the maintenance of social status quo or the revolution which threatens to throw the country into the arms of communism.

Inadequate Knowledge

Another obstacle to economic development which is located in conditions in underdeveloped countries is the nature of their aspirations and the form in which the realization of these aspirations is pictured. In more concrete terms this may be stated by saying that economic development plans are often unrealistic and divorced from the more immediate needs and productive capacities of these countries. I have drawn attention earlier to the ambiguity of simultaneously aiming at economic progress and the preservation of national and cultural traditions. But there is also an ambiguity in the thinking of many leaders of underdeveloped countries between the objectives of developmental efforts and practicable attainments. The point is sometimes stated in a rather drastic form by emphasizing the fact that many development plans fostered by underdeveloped governments give a high priority to the establishment of steel mills and other forms of heavy industry even though such plants may have little justification on the basis of considerations of efficiency and rational allocation of resources. We may look at this matter from two points of view. We may either regard the wish for a steel mill as a childish, irrational desire which only merits ridicule. But we may also regard it as a symbolic expression of the wish for industrialization, and the implicit acknowledgement of the fact that little is known about the priorities and time sequence of such a process. I would regard it as evidence of the latter alternative, and here the obstacle to fruitful development is founded on defective knowledge and consequent inability to make rational workable plans.

In spite of numerous surveys of natural resources, soil types, and other environmental factors, knowledge of the natural endowment as well as the human resources of most underdeveloped countries is very imperfect. The United Nations and its specialized agencies have often been confronted by this fact. A mission of experts sent to Haiti produced a voluminous report on developmental possibilities in that country. Yet the chief impression one gains from reading the report of that mission is the frequent repetition of the statement that fruitful recommendations cannot be made because of the absence of reliable information. Similarly, the International Bank of Reconstruction and Development and the Food and Agriculture Organization have been hamstrung in actually carrying through developmental projects for which funds would have been available, simply because workable projects which could withstand the careful scrutiny of experts were not forthcoming.

Lag in Concomitant Adjustments

Ignorance is always an obstacle to rational action. But in the case of economic development it is doubly fatal, because in this case action cannot be postponed for political or moral reasons. The consequence is that on the one hand programmes are undertaken in fields where obvious needs for improvement exist (such as public health, for example) which, however, cannot maintain themselves because the necessary concomitant adjustments in the economy lag behind, and on the other hand that short-run programmes are initiated which tend to lead to such allocation of resources (and hence to certain new rigidities and vested interest) as to make the attainment of the long-run objective more difficult. Evidence for both contingencies is frequent.

As concerns public health programmes, the attempts at control of tropical diseases are very instructive. For example, yaws and malaria are dreaded diseases in Haiti. A campaign to control yaws in the Marbial valley failed to have lasting results, although innoculation with antibiotics led to temporary relief, because the economic status of the mass of the population was not elevated enough to permit them to meet the most elementary standards of cleanliness. A swamp drainage project designed to eliminate carriers of malaria fell into disrepair after a few years, the drainage canals got choked up and large expenditures turned out to have been in vain. Owing to indifference, corruption, and mismanagement the project was not kept going properly after its foreign initiators had left.

Short-Run and Long-Run Aims

Examples of the conflict between short-run and long-run aims are also numerous. For many "one-crop" countries it presents a real dilemma. The long-run objective of economic development programmes for these countries is greater diversification of production, to make them less dependent on one or two or three staple exports, the prices of which are determined on the world market, subjecting, in this way, the international accounts of the one-crop country to great uncertainties and often violent fluctuations. At the same time the major export industry deserves full support in the short-run because it is the chief asset producing foreign exchange which, in the absence of generous loans or foreign aid, provides the wherewithal for economic development. The experience with coffee planters in some Latin-American countries and rubber planters in some countries of South East Asia shows the restraining influence on long-run plans of economic diversification exercised by vested interests in an important export industry.

Mexican Dilemma

Another instance of conflict between short-run and long-run objectives of economic development plans is reported by Wilbert E. Moore. Moore believes that the *Ejido,* although it

alleviated the immediate economic ills of the Mexican rural population . . . it did . . . make possible a re-establishment of the partially isolated village, agricultural underemployment, and all the conservative traditions of a land-hungry peasantry. . . . All indirect evidence indicates that in terms of long-run developments the *Ejido* was a strongly conservative move in the strict sense; that is, the possible increase in market orientation, improved education, and productive technique seems to have been offset by re-establishing the traditional village.

Professor Moore here again points to the fact that the implementation of short-run objectives creates vested interests which impede the full realization of the long-run developmental goals. But the nature of the vested interests in this case is very different from that of the vested interests fostered by the extension of an export crop in a "one-crop" country. In the latter case these vested interests are based chiefly on the expectation of economic gain, in the former case they consist in the rejuvenation of a traditional way of life which, in many of its aspects, is opposed to economic progress.

I believe that the dilemma found by Professor Moore in Mexico poses a general problem, notably for areas in which an extension of agricultural settlement is still possible. The fact that some underdeveloped countries, in spite of great rural population density in certain localities, have still considerable areas of uncultivated arable land, is often regarded as fortunate. In a country like India or Egypt, where further horizontal expansion of agriculture is virtually impossible, economic development is pushed necessarily into the channels of industrialization accompanied by intensification of agriculture, i.e., the application of policies resulting in higher yields per acre. This process is accompanied in all likelihood by a rapid increase of the population, and, since industrialization is associated with urbanization, by an increase in the required quantity of real output per family or productively employed individual. It is probable that under these conditions increase in agricultural productivity will not be commensurate with increase in demand for products grown on the land (foods, fibres, hides, and skins, chemical raw materials, such as oils and lumber), and the scarcity of economically usable land becomes a serious bottleneck to development. On the other hand, countries in which substantial areas of unused land are still available can syphon off part of the developing population surplus by settling it on new lands, and can simultaneously expand the output of agricultural raw materials with the increasing demand for such materials by developing industry.

Looked at purely from the viewpoint of the strategy of resource allocation planning in the short run, this group of countries (among which belong most countries of South East Asia, the Middle East, and Latin America) is therefore in a position in which rational planning may mitigate the economic sacrifices involved in industrialization. But the existence of an agricultural frontier and the knowledge that such a frontier exists exerts an influence on policies actually made. As Professor Moore has shown in his book, referred to earlier, recruitment of large masses of peasants and primitives for industry is a hard task. Resettlement may not be much easier, but it may be more acceptable to some native peoples than induction into the industrial labour force. To the extent, therefore, to which local population pressure is mitigated by resettlement—as for example by moving people in the Philippines from Luzon to Davao, or in Indonesia from Java to the outer islands—the traditional agricultural way of life with its preindustrial and non-rational aspects (in Max Weber's sense) is given a new lease on life and industrial progress made more difficult.

Conflict of Values

In essence the conflict between the two ways of life is a conflict of values. Just as Hinayana Buddhism in Burma, with its other-worldly orientation, calls forth a philosophy of life which is not conducive to economic advancement, so the strengthening of traditional methods of small scale agriculture reinforces the system of values which have flowered into great cultural achievements in the past, but which it has been impossible to adapt to rational, efficient economic activity. This conflict in values has sometimes been expressed as the antagonism between city and countryside, the mutual estrangement between the urban and the rural inhabitant. To a contemporary American, and perhaps also to a contemporary European, this distinction may appear spurious. But it is a difference which is obvious to a student of the social structure of oriental societies since it implies a wide difference in ways of life. In Western Europe the transition from one way of life to the other—and the values implied in each of them—took place during three or four hundred years, and was aided by enclosure acts, "Bauern legen," pauperization, the adaptation of the Calvinist ideology to the objectives of the commercial and industrial middle class, and other measures which turned the rolling green hills of Warwickshire and the Tyneside into the "Black Country" and the fields and wastes of Lancashire into the cotton centre of the world. I am not expressing nostalgic regrets over the passing of the European middle ages, but I am trying to indicate that parallel with the external change in the landscape the minds and aspirations of men, the things they valued and were taught to value, changed; and with this in mind it is perhaps not quite wrong to say that the England or France of the thirteenth century resembled more the present Middle East or South East Asia, than the England or France of our day.

As has been pointed out earlier, value systems offer special resistances to change, but without wishing to be dogmatic, I believe, it may be stated that their change is facilitated if the material economic environment in which they can flourish is destroyed or weakened. This seems to be the experience from the history of Western European economic development, and it seems to be confirmed by the findings of students of colonial policy and administration, and research results on the impact of industrialization in underdeveloped countries. Economic development plans which combine industrialization with an extension of traditional or near-traditional forms of agriculture are thus creating a dilemma which in the long run may present serious repercussions on the speed and facility with which ultimate objectives can be reached. This does not mean that, wherever this is possible, extension of agricultural production should not be undertaken in combination with industrialization. But rural resettlement should be regarded as a form of industrialization rather than an extension of traditional methods of farming. In view of existing pressures and the absence in almost all underdeveloped countries of an efficient administrative apparatus the difficulties which such a programme confronts are obvious.

Acquisition of New Skills

Reference to the experience of the transition from mediæval to modern economic organization in Western Europe brings to mind another important factor which may prove to be a serious obstacle to technological advancement. This obstacle is found in the changes required in methods of work and levels of skill which necessarily accompany technical change and alterations in the scope and form of economic activity. Little needs to be said here about these two points since much of the relevant evidence has been collected by Professor Moore in his book. From these remarks it appears that these obstacles, although real, are less significant than those opposing economic development because of vested interests of an elite, or the vigour of a non-industrial system of values. To a certain extent resistances against new modes of technical and economic processes and changing kinds and levels of skill are specific aspects of the two last-named factors. But since from the socio-psychological point of view economic development may be interpreted above all as a change in the division of social labour, some special attention to skills and modes of work appears to be in order.

Confining ourselves, at first, to a discussion of skills, the first question which might be raised to whether economic development requires a transition from less complex to more complex skills or vice versa. This question is impossible to answer because there exists no generally agreed upon classification of skills in terms of their complexity, and even if it existed the answer would be ambiguous. Certainly the manual skill of a handloom weaver is superior to that of a man who runs a powerloom, but the skill of the mechanic who tends the powerloom and keeps it in repair is probably superior to that of the handloom weaver. In general, it may be said, that mechanization by "putting the skill into the machine" has two opposite effects. It simplifies many manual operations and makes possible the rapid training of large numbers of unskilled or semi-skilled workers. It thus creates a large demand for people whose skill level is indifferent and who can acquire the necessary manipulatory accomplishments by a process of on-the-job training. At the same time it requires the development of a group of men, foremen, engineers, technical maintenance men, petty administrators and others capable of rendering services which often require not only a high level of dexterity but a considerable variety of aptitudes. The dexterity and ingenuity of the African native mechanic who, in some relatively isolated place in the Sudan, repairs and keeps going with some wire and pieces of sheet metal a model T Ford, which in the United States would be considered fit only for the junk heap, cannot be denied. But men like him belong to the same class as the Chinese ivory worker who produced the most delicately carved decorations on a cigarette-case, and the anonymous mediæval stone-cutter who chiselled the capitals of the Gothic cathedrals of France.

A Social Problem

It is granted that human capacity for the exercise of highly skilled tasks, that human ingenuity, human intelligence is fairly evenly distributed over the globe. The problem of developing a group of skilled technicians is not a psychological question of the capacity of persons in underdeveloped countries to learn, but a social problem; the creation of attitudes and material and psychological compensations which will make the choice of such careers attractive. In others words, the question we must ask is not: "How can the people of technically less advanced countries learn the modern techniques?" but: "Will they learn them, and how can they be induced to want to learn them?"

It will readily be acknowledged that if the question is put in this form the answer which is suggested involves a whole series of complex socialpsychological processes, which may be regarded as special cases of the general problem of the development and institutionalization of culturally deviant behaviour. It would go beyond the proper boundaries of this paper to enter into a detailed discussion of the processes which determine the genesis and direction of deviant motivations, but I believe that the identification of the problem area in which the acquisition of new skills and work methods falls indicates the magnitude of the problem and suggests the variety of obstacles which must be overcome to provide for the institutionalization of a new pattern of division of social labour. . . .

10. Religious Belief and Economic Behavior in a Central Javanese Town: Some Preliminary Considerations

Clifford Geertz

I

Modjokuto, a small town in East-Central Java studied by the writer in 1953-1954,[1] lies at the extreme eastern edge of a great irrigated rice plain through which a rambling, circular swinging river flows northward towards the Java sea. A half-day's drive from Surabaja, the Republic of Indonesia's second city and best port, Modjokuto marks the point at which the flat, fertile countryside begins to tilt upward toward the cluster of active volcanoes which tower over it to the east and whose periodic eruptions provide much of its fertility.

A commercial, educational, and administrative center for eighteen surrounding villages, the town has a population of almost 20,000, of whom about 18,000 are Javanese, 1,800 Chinese, and the remainder a handful of Arabs, Indians, or other minorities. Its spatial form is determined by the juncture of three poorly paved, secondary roads: from Surabaja, the provincial capital; from the regional capital fifteen miles to the west; and from a large inland city on the other side of the eastern mountains.

The town is surrounded on three sides by thousands of small mud-walled rice fields, most of them not more than twenty-five yards square. Flooded in the rainy season by means of an age-old irrigation system of gullies, springs, and water traps, improved by Dutch-introduced cement dams and steel sluice-gates, these fields are cultivated almost entirely in rice for six months of every year. In the dry season, which is pronounced in East Java, the land does not lie fallow but is planted in maize, soybean, peanuts, onions, peppers, or yams—usually two or three of these in turn. Almost all land holdings are small—under three acres—and although there is, particularly near the town, considerable sharecrop tenancy, the

*From *Economic Development and Cultural Change*, January 1956, pp. 134–157. © by The University of Chicago. Reprinted by permission of The University of Chicago Press. The author is Professor of Anthropology, University of Chicago.

[1]The town name is a pseudonym. The field work period ran from May 1953 until September 1954, with a two-month gap in July and August of 1953, and was undertaken as part of a cooperative project of six anthropologists and a sociologist under the sponsorship of the Center for International Studies of the Massachusetts Institute of Technology. A full description of the town, prepared by the entire project, is in the process of preparation. I wish to thank Robert Jay and Neal Smelzer for comments on an earlier draft of this paper.

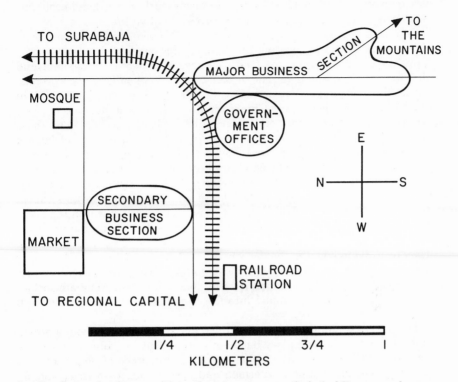

TO SURABAJA

TO THE MOUNTAINS

MOSQUE

MAJOR BUSINESS SECTION

GOVERN-
MENT
OFFICES

E

N—————S

W

SECONDARY
BUSINESS
SECTION

MARKET

RAILROAD
STATION

TO REGIONAL CAPITAL

1/4 · · · 1/2 · · · 3/4 · · · 1

KILOMETERS

landlords involved are neither absentee nor are their holdings any larger, with one or two not so very dramatic exceptions, than those of the peasants themselves.

On the fourth side of Modjokuto, the southwest, lies either forest or dry, broken, largely unirrigable land, on which, in the early part of this century, an extensive plantation system, in coffee, rubber, and sugar, was built up. Dutch-owned, Dutch-managed, and Javanese-worked, this network of plantations and sugar mills had a heavy impact on Modjokuto's economy before the war. As the town was only founded toward the latter half of the nineteenth century, the interaction between the small-scale, intensive, wet-rice farming system practiced by the independent Javanese peasant and the large-scale, extensive, cash-crop estate agriculture of the Dutch has shaped the region's economic history almost since the beginning.

The Dutch are gone from Modjokuto now, their estate and factory system shaken by the depression and shattered by the war and revolution. What remains is a peasantry very used to both money and to foreign goods, tremendous underemployment, both rural and urban, and an over-complex economic system in which the Chinese minority controls the main streams of trade. The Chinese form the heart of Modjokuto's economic circulatory system, pressing goods, many of them imported, down through its arteries, pulling back goods, the greater part of them agricultural, through its veins and passing them on to the large urban centers for further distribution; Javanese commercial activity becomes relevant only between the ends of the two channels—where they braid out into a complex network of tiny, doubled-over, and marvelously interwound economic capillaries reaching into the small crevices of native life.

Both business districts are lined with small, open-front, wooden stores, almost all of them Chinese run. Inside the stores one finds hardware, home furnishings, various types of food, jewelry, false teeth, automobile and bicycle parts, building materials, textiles, drugs from sulfa to such promising herbs as crocodile tongue and cat's beard. Even more important in terms of economic power, the Chinese control the trade in dry-season crops grown in Javanese fields, and their mills process the rice from those fields (although for the past few years a great part of the actual buying has been done under government contract, and, nominally, under government control). They own almost all the trucking, almost all the string-and-bailing-wire, jitneys which carry a great proportion (with the busses and the train) of inter-local travel, and almost all the bicycle rickshaws which, Javanese peddled, provide the bulk of passenger transport within the town. The larger small-scale factories in town and outside it—rice, lumber, soda pop, bread, charcoal—are, with a few notable exceptions, in their hands. They own the movie, the theater where the Javanese plays are given, and they manage the carnival when it comes to town. They are prevented from total domination of the economy by only one restriction: they are forbidden, by a Dutch law continued into the Republican period, to hold farm land.

The Javanese stores, almost all of them marginal, number about a dozen, most of them in the secondary business section. But the core of native-run commercial life is the market, where each day hundreds of professional or semi-professional Javanese salesmen and speculators, both male and female, bargain vigorously in a desperate attempt to earn a living or part of a living out of small-scale person-to-person trade. Textiles, daily food supplies, and dry season crops probably form the bulk of the business, but buttons, dried fish, mats, baskets, perfumes, religious books, cooked food and hot coffee, chairs and tables, nails, ready-made clothing, meat, patent medicines, leather goods, parasols, pots and pans—in fact, almost everything portable—are each day passed from hand to hand to someone's (usually small) profit.

In the market you can have your hair cut, your bicycle fixed, and your pants mended while you wait. For an Indonesian quarter you can rent a spot under a tree or a wooden shed and sell cigarettes for a penny more than you just paid for them in a Chinese store across the street. You can buy a basket of corn in the morning and sell it at noon, never leaving the market—getting your profit out of the slight rise in price which every day takes place as the market day wears on (if you are a friend or a paying acquaintance of the man who runs the scales, you may make something out of the greater weight the corn has when you sell it than when you bought it). Or, for two rupiah a day (and a few hundred capital) you can become one of the aristocrats of the market with a three-meter stall of your own, selling imported and domestic textiles for as much more than they are worth as you can wheedle an unwary peasant into paying. For the Modjokuto Javanese, buyer or seller, the market is the very model of commercial life, the source of nearly all his ideas of the possible and proper in economic behavior.

Aside from petty commerce, three other non-agricultural activities play an important part in the Javanese sector of the economy: simple manual labor, independent craft and repair work, and white-collar office work. The manual laborers, if they find work at all, may be employed by the Chinese in their rice factories, lumber yards, or other enterprises, by the government fixing roads, building irrigation dams, or sweeping streets, or by one of the scattered here today, gone tomorrow Javanese cottage industries. A great many are employed by the narrow gauge railroad which runs four short passenger trains a day from the regional capital through Modjokuto to the main Surabaja line fifteen miles northward. Many too are servants for their richer townsmen, though the departure of the Dutch has markedly reduced job opportunities in this field. The independent artisans—carpenters, chauffeurs, bricklayers, blacksmiths, watchmakers, barbers, tailors—are spread unevenly throughout the town, for they mostly work in their own homes, accepting jobs as they come fitfully to them, and drifting uneasily into unskilled occupations if forced to by economic pressure.

The white-collar clerks, teachers, and government officials form the intellectual and social elite of Modjokuto, inheritors of a political tradition in which the ability to read and write was confined to a hereditary court class, born to rule and venerated for doing so. Many of the old caste marks of the literati are nearly gone now—the variously colored parasols symbolizing rank, the deep bow of the inferior to touch the knee of the standing superior, the proclamation of pedigree through the use of court title, the tongue-tied shame of the peasant in the presence of the government official—but the general attitude of respect and subservience on the part of the uneducated toward the educated remains.

The number of the educated has been rather rapidly increasing of late with the post-revolutionary expansion of the school system. In Modjokuto there are a half-dozen six-grade government elementary schools, a government technical school at the junior high level, three private junior high schools, a government school for elementary teachers, and scattered other private schools including Chinese and Catholic elementary schools. Further, each of the surrounding villages has a school of its own, and there are still a number of old-style religious schools in the area, recently semi-modernized. The result of this sudden florescence of educational activity is that teachers, on the one hand, and advanced students, on the other, form two of the most clearly defined and dynamic social groups within the society, perhaps the two groups least closely bound to the Indonesian past, and whose relationships with the rest of the society are the most ambiguous.

There are two major government offices in Modjokuto, for it is both a district and a subdistrict capital. The subdistrict, the lowest level to which the wholly appointive national bureaucracy reaches, administers eighteen villages all lying within ten miles of the town. The district administers four contiguous subdistricts, including that of Modjokuto itself, and is in turn subordinate to the regional government. In addition, the regional headquarters of the central government police force is in Modjokuto, as are the government pawnshop and the government hospital for the area. Offices concerned with the repair of roadways, the building and maintenance of irrigation systems, the improvement of agriculture and the administration of the market further swell the total of white-collar workers employed or underemployed by the government, as do the Post Office and the office of the local representative of the Ministry of Religion.

These five major occupational types—farmer, petty trader, independent artisan, manual laborer, and white-collar clerk, teacher or administrator— represent the Javanese population of Modjokuto, grouped according to their economic activity. The crystallized typology of work patterns reflects the underlying organization of the economic system of the town of which it is an outcome. Similarly, the same population grouped according to their world outlook—according to their religious beliefs, ethical preferences, and political ideologies—yield three main cultural types which reflect the moral organization of Javanese culture as it is manifested in Modjokuto, the general ideas of order in terms of which the Javanese farmer, laborer, artisan, trader, or clerk shapes his behavior in all areas of life. These types, being so essentially Javanese, need Javanese terms to name them, terms the Javanese themselves apply: *abangan, santri, prijaji.* . . .

III

The traditional Javanese agricultural system was one in which the chief technical problem to be faced was that of labor organization. With a relatively small population (at least up until the time of the Dutch forced culture system in the mid-nineteenth century, a period from which nearly all rapid economic change in rural Java can be dated) a remarkably fertile volcanic soil and an adequate water supply, neither access to land nor questions of the differential employment of capital were serious issues. The central issue was how to organize the comparatively large rural labor force needed to work wet rice in irrigated terraces.

To meet this problem, there came to be built up a set of land and work distribution mechanisms by means of which intensive labor could be brought to bear on particular fields at the necessary points in time, as well as mechanisms of communal distribution of the harvests from these fields, which would be able to maintain individual subsistence in periods of low labor demand. Complex land-ownership rotation systems, communal work requirements, elaborate reciprocal labor lending customs among both kith and kin, sharply defined rights to work on lands of one's relatives, and specifically outlined payments in kind for specific contributions of labor made possible an agricultural system demanding periodic applications of intensive labor from a relatively small and immobile population.

The *abangan* village came to be comprised of a group of approximately equal status subsistence farmers, each with more or less identical political, social, economic, and religious rights and duties, all locked together in an intricate system of mutual aid and assistance in order to make efficient wet rice agriculture possible. The remarkable characteristic of traditional village agriculture in Java—aside from the double growing season—was (and is) the narrow margin between overpopulation and underpopulation. With the given techniques (of which a good example is the method of harvesting rice stalk by stalk with a knife the size of a razor), the number of people required to open a new wet rice field and work it adequately nearly equaled the number who could subsist from its output at a level the peasant would accept as decent, and both numbers were rather large.

In such a situation the tendency will be to provide for small increments in population by increasing the intensity of the cultivation rather than by extending cultivation to new lands, thus slowly narrowing the gap between over- and underpopulation still further. In any case, the possibilities of absorbing a larger population through bringing more land into wet rice cultivation was limited in Java from the beginning because tropical land untreated with volcanic ash is rather infertile, and much of the southern part of the island is porous limestone. In addition, the peculiar form in which the Dutch cast their economic impact upon Javanese rural society further stimulated both population growth and the tendency to absorb that growth through increasingly intensive farming. By attempting to force Javanese peasants into producing export crops on their own lands in their own manner, rather than introducing a self-contained plantation system complete with imported labor (as the British did, for example, in Malaya), the Dutch both sharply stimulated Javanese population growth and provided the agricultural means, through introduction of new plants and growing methods from their own intensive farming background, for greater intensification of traditional Javanese farming.

But, intensification, too, has its limits, and so the Javanese village has come into this century with a rapidly increasing population, now clearly too great for its agricultural foundation, a set of values which commit those who hold them to a communalistic rather than an individualistic approach to economic problems, and methods of farming no longer able to increase output significantly. Unable either emotionally or technologically to reorganize agriculture on an extensive plantation basis, and unable too to increase output through further intensification, the *abangan* has been forced to solve his population problem by lowering his standards concerning what he will accept as a decent level of living for one of a set of equally privileged peasants. Rather than the rapid concentration of wealth and the formation of an impoverished, alienated rural proletariat as one finds in so many other "underdeveloped" areas, we have had in East and Central Java a process of near equal fractionization of land holdings and of the wealth which they represent. Thus the farmer has been able, by and large, to maintain his religious, political, social, and economic equality with his fellows, and the level of living of all concerned has sunk.

This general pattern of response to a worsening economic situation through a division of the economic pie into smaller and smaller pieces might well be called "shared poverty." The *abangan*, committed to world outlook which emphasizes a close interdependence among separate families in the same village, tends to share food equally when he has it and share its absence equally when he doesn't have it, not out of a general commitment to humanitarianism or to cooperation as such, but out of a traditionalized mode of solving problems. Java's twentieth century impoverishment lacks some of the tense drama and spectacular injustice of countries with great wealth differences and large-scale landholdings, but the impoverishment is just as real, and so, ultimately, is the injustice; it is merely that Javanese do all things quietly, subtly, politely, and communally—even starve.

The effect of this "shared poverty" pattern is clearly evident in Modjo-kuto. In the village at the edge of town in which I lived, somewhat more than half of the peasants were nominally landless, yet even with the relatively heavy urbanization, the long contact with foreign influences, both Dutch and Chinese, not more than 10% of the land was held by individuals non-resident in the village itself, and there was only one landholding which could be called at all large, and it ran only to about 30 acres. Almost all the rest of the holdings were between one and three acres, and yet a large proportion of these small holdings were sharecropped on a half-half basis.

Actually, the relationships between nominal ownership of the land and working of the land were enormously more complicated; both sides of the equation were usually further fractionated. The owner might rent the land to one man. This man would then find a tenant to work it for him on a half-half basis (actually, the system of tenant payment was rather complicated and varied according to location and type of land, responsibility for various capital equipment—most particularly seed—length of time tenant and landlord had been associated, and the like; but the half-half arrangement was both the norm and the mode). The tenant in turn would then subcontract out blocks of the work on either a cash payment or a further share arrangement. A man and his womenfolk might be found to plant, weed, and harvest for 1/5 the crop; a man and his oxen might be hired to plow for 150 rupiah, and the harvest was always accomplished by a mass of people, each receiving 1/10 of what they harvested as a share. Thus the fractionization of output of these small pieces of land grows to rather fabulous proportions, with a whole series of people making a poor living rather than one or two making a good one.

Further, there is a strong moral obligation on a man, particularly if he has a job in town or if he has more than two acres or so, not to work his own land but to hire a tenant. The one large landholding is split into small holdings and tenanted out, even though the owner admitted that a foreman-worker system would have been far more efficient. The reason given was that if a labor system were used the tenants in their revenge would destroy the harvests or steal them, as they had on a number of other occasions when land was worked on a foreman system. The tenant too was obligated to farm out certain blocks of the work, particularly to relatives, and even if he paid wages in cash, the amount of the wages was tied directly to the amount of rice it would buy so that there was, in many cases explicit and conscious, an attempt to maintain a "fair shares" relationship in terms of the output of the land in kind between the various claimants to that output. In short, the land tenancy system is, in part, an attempt to replicate rural village patterns in a more urban situation and is supported by the same ethic which had supported those patterns in the simpler past.

Even in the wholly urban, non-agricultural context of the market, the same replication occurs. To understand the Javanese market, one must see it not merely as a specific geographic location at which daily trading takes place, but as a patterned type of economic activity, with its own peculiar formal characteristics, a pattern of economic activity only partly localized in the market proper. Javanese sell things to other Javanese on street corners, in homes, at sidewalk stands, in stores, over a cup of restaurant coffee, on village roads, in fact, everywhere. The market is merely the concentrated center and the visible model of a trading institution much wider than itself, and so when one sees "market," one refers to the whole range of Javanese small trading activities.

The goods flow into this "market" from various sources, but very few of them have not at one point or another passed through Chinese hands, and the local products—almost entirely agricultural—come to them in the end as well. Not in all cases, however, are the Chinese involved locally. Much of the cloth is bought in Surabaja by the Javanese directly, from Chinese stores there; a few larger-scale native traders sell crops directly to urban wholesalers; and Chinese from the cities and larger towns come often to Modjokuto (or send agents) to trade with the Javanese market people.

Once the goods enter the wholly Javanese market complex they do not go directly to the ultimate consumer, but circulate among the professional traders, each transaction nibbling away at the profit margin; the economic return for passing the goods from the large Chinese distributors to the ultimate consumers, small enough in the first place, gets divided among several people. Further, most of the capital these petty traders employ is in the form of credit extended by the Chinese wholesaler, the latter being unwilling to lend cash now that the Dutch are no longer present to enforce contracts. The Javanese trader keeps a running debt balance with the Chinese trader, a balance carefully managed on both sides not to grow so large as to encourage flight on the part of the Javanese and not shrink so small as to leave the Javanese without any control over the Chinese. In sum, the complexity of economic structure for a fairly simple economic function is surprisingly great.

In a sense the same subcontracting pattern which fractionates the returns from land operates here to fractionate the return from retail distribution. The main Javanese traders are those who have debt balances with the Chinese, the larger the balance the Chinese allows the larger is the scope of the trader's activities. But it is only in the exceptional case that the goods derived from this relation to the Chinese go directly into consumer hands. Almost always they go into the hands of other Javanese traders who hold a smaller debt balance with the larger trader. And so it goes all the way down the line. The goods pass from hand to hand, their course regulated by debt manipulations, leaving only a very small profit behind at any point along that course. Again, the moral obligation upon the Javanese trader to cut others in on a good deal shows that this response is not wholly rational, wholly economic, but is supported by a motivational pattern rather deeply ingrained in many Javanese individuals. It is, in fact, the commercial interpretation of an ethic originally created as a response to purely agricultural demands.

Finally, the "industrial" sector of the Modjokuto economy is a very thin reed indeed, but even here one can see the power of the *abangan* ethic. One of my informants set up a cigarette factory in a shed behind his house. He began with two workers—girls—rolling the cigarettes by hand, in corn sheathes provided by the workers themselves. The factory grew to employ a work force of twenty girls, the number being determined not by economic considerations but by the entrepreneur's and the girls' notions of the "correct" number which should be employed, given the amount of work involved. The result was an extremely uneconomically operated factory. Unable to accumulate enough capital to provide sufficient tobacco to keep twenty girls working even six hours a day at full capacity, the entrepreneur merely apportioned out regulated quantities of the available tobacco to each girl each day, and the girls worked at a very slow speed, producing only 1000 cigarettes in a working day where they might easily have produced 1500-2000.

Instead of trimming his work force to fit the dimensions of his industry, my informant, the entrepreneur, decided—quite consciously—that twenty workers was a "fair" number to employ. If he employed less than this number, the girls would always be demanding he hire a relative or friend of theirs; as soon as the number of workers was "high enough" in the girls' eyes, he could refuse such demands without fear of criticism. He thus increased his overhead and cut his profits (and his workers wages, as they were paid piece rate). The outcome was typical: twenty workers and an entrepreneur made a semi-adequate living, and no one made a good one, with the added consideration in this case that this economically inefficient operation reduced even further the opportunities for the entrepreneur to amass enough capital to increase output and hire more workers. As a matter of fact, the business failed after awhile, and the Javanese entrepreneur fled his Chinese creditors.

So it is that the *abangan* ethic affects the whole range of economic activity in Modjokuto. In agriculture, in trade, and in manufacturing, it emphasizes and legitimizes a pattern of economic behavior derived from past experience in a different setting; it organizes new experiences in old forms and meets new challenges with old responses. But it is not the only ethic extant in Modjokuto, for not all village Javanese projected rudely into the twentieth century have clung unreservedly to old beliefs, nor, as Java has been civilized since shortly after the time of Christ, has the background of all Javanese been wholly rural. The *santri* world view reflects an attempt to readjust and reinterpret the village ethic in terms of considerations derived both from foreign religious influence and from a longer experience in trade, and the *prijaji* world view has grown up in an urban environment focused on the great Hinduized court centers of East and Central Java.

V

Islam, it has been said, lies on Java like a veil, concealing little and shaping nothing; where Hinduism brought a civilization, Islam brought but a religion. The degree to which this aphorism has become progressively untrue over the past fifty years is a measure of the degree to which one can speak of a *santri*, as opposed to an *abangan*, world outlook in Javanese society. The self-conscious, religiously sophisticated, exclusivist Moslem is a child of this century, although Indonesia has been nominally Islamic since the sixteenth.

Until the latter part of the nineteenth century, the religious system of Java struck a balance between Islamic, Hinduistic, and animistic elements, in which the man who had memorized a little Arabic, or did his prayers somewhat more regularly, or went blindly and incomprehendingly on the pilgrimage to Mecca, was but a slightly differentiated specialist, useful to chant at a *slametan* or a death, or to organize the local version of the annual religious tax, or perhaps to provide a particularly exotic and efficacious remedy picked up in some crowded Meccan dormitory. Slightly more well-to-do perhaps, somewhat more serious religiously, maybe, a little more powerfully magically, quite probably, his interest in Islam was but a personal interpretation of the general village beliefs. As his less interested neighbors, his religious concern was both mystical and cabalistic and magical and materialistic; of the Moslem law, theology, and ethics he knew little and cared less. He was but another *abangan*, going more regularly to *slametans* than to mosques.

In time, this all changed, but the process by which the present day *santri* group has come to be rather sharply set off from the non-*santri* groups has not been a wholly rural one, but rather has found a basis in both the rural and urban sectors of the society. The recent history of Islam in Java has been one of the appearance of a still embryonic rural yeomanry on the one hand, and of a small class of free urban traders on the other, and their increasing inter-relationship legitimized in terms of a common religious bond. Since about 1910 both these groups, the rural and the urban, have been progressively influenced by reformist ideologies streaming out of the great Islamic centers of learning in the Middle East, and so there has arrived upon the Javanese social scene a still small, precarious, and fragile middle class of slightly wealthy peasants, small shopkeepers, and weak independent entrepreneurs, largely comprised of rather pious, self-conscious, aggressive, and often quite religiously sophisticated Muslim modernists.

The rural part of this development owes its existence to the fact that the problems connected with Western stimulated economic change were not always met in the villages by a simple reassertion of traditional values. In many cases they were met, instead, by increasing emphasis on the more Islamic elements of the traditional religious system at the expense of the other elements in the system, together with an attempt to justify a new social and economic ethic in terms of this altered religious emphasis. Two particular Moslem institutions—the system of rural religious education and the pilgrimage to Mecca—played an especially important role in this process. A shift to increased concern with things Islamic as opposed to things more generally Javanese led to a greater interest in the teaching of a more purely Islamic tradition and the provision of content for such teaching naturally depended upon increased contact with the center of the Moslem world. In turn, the necessity for accumulating wealth to go on the pilgrimage led to economic and social consequences which further strengthened the preference for things Islamic in the group to which they accrued.

Speaking concretely, the financial demands of the ever more attractive pilgrimage induced into the *santri* family a distinct emphasis on a value the Javanese call *gemi. Gemi*, which means obsessive thrift, was if anything disvalued by the *abangan*, who usually despised the *santri* as a solemn miser hoarding his money merely to gain useless prestige from having completed a fool's errand, but for the *santri* it was a central concern. For him it was a source of pride to work hard, dress simply, eat sparingly, and to avoid large ceremonial and festival expenditures. A man who by such means saved enough money to go to Mecca for a year or so at the age of fifty or sixty was immensely respected by the rural Moslem community.

Upon his return, the *hadji* (as Meccan pilgrims are called) became the center for a kind of local cult, for not only was he more holy for his trip, but he was more learned in correct Islamic practice as defined in the capital of Islamic civilization. A local Moslem school (*pondok*) was likely to form about him as a teacher, in which each morning and evening youths aged six to twenty-five chanted books in an Arabic they did not understand, books brought back to them by the returned *hadji* who as often did not understand Arabic either. These *pondok* varied in size from small one-room bamboo shacks where boys came only in the evenings to chant for an hour or so to large stone buildings built on land deeded officially to God, in which the students lived continuously, chanting up to five and six hours a day. In time there would grow up a kind of religious complex of mosque, school, teacher, and students, the latter—many of them come from goodly distances—living ascetically, doing their own housework and earning their way by working in the surrounding fields, either those of the *Hadji* himself or of other well-to-do supporters of the school.

Now, there have been religious schools of this general sort scattered throughout the Javanese countryside for centuries. In nearly every village there was an old man who considered himself learned in some mystical or magical art, nominally Islamic, who had set himself up as a teacher to his neighbors, and it was out of this general tradition, originally Buddhist, that the *santri* community elaborated the explicitly Moslem *pondok*. In an effort to distinguish it sharply from other types of religious schools, which they came to hold as *kaffir* (a concept of religious exclusiveness rather foreign to traditional Javanese "theology," which, if not always tolerant in practice, was usually relativistic in theory), they created a sub-culture around the *pondok* which took on a definitely Near Eastern cast. Arabic music, dances, and religious dramatic performances were introduced and Hindu-Javanese art forms rejected; imitation of Arabian clothing and some types of Arabian food became popular; and the young *santris* developed the kind of cult of body development, strength displaying, and masochistic endurance testing which is so often associated with semi-secret fraternities around the world. The *abangans* called them Arabs—whom they didn't like either—and said that like their Near Eastern cousins they were interested more in getting rich than religious.

However that may be, this valuation of individual effort, thrift, and simplicity—combined with a tendency to avoid land fractionization and easy accessibility to a labor pool of non-landowning students—did yield the *hadji* and his supporters a larger personal fortune than was possible for the general run of peasant. The rich *hadji*, surrounded by a group of satellite landholders and young laborer students, could build up a system of agricultural production (often with home industry attached) which took the form of a kind of small-scale plantation. For the most part these small plantations, if that is what they should be called, did not grow so very large, nor did the *Hadji* and his followers become so very rich, at least in the Modjokuto area. But the system had enough of an impact to create a fairly sharp economic distinction between *abangan* and *santri* which supported and strengthened the cultural distinction. Almost all the more wealthy peasants around Modjokuto today are *santris* or sons of *santris*, and "rich man" and "*hadji*" are nearly synonymous terms. . . .

Turning to the urban side of the picture, the *santri* community within the town of Modjokuto was originally made up not of local peasants forced off the land, but almost entirely of migrant traders from larger urban centers, men whose families had been in small trade for at least two or three generations. They came to Modjokuto in the first place as young men, travelling out as agents of their father, of their uncle, or their cousin, who had an established business back in Demak or Gresik or Kudus. Actually, they were not true agents, but small independent traders, for the *santri* method of introducing young relatives into the business, even sons, was neither to take them in as junior partners, nor to provide them with an initial lump of capital sufficiently large to start a going business, nor to employ them as commission or salary salesmen; rather they presented them with a half dozen pieces of cloth (pairs of shoes, cartons of cigarettes), marked them down on the books for a debt corresponding to an only slightly preferential version of the local retail price of the merchandise, and then sent them out to sell the goods for as much as the market would bear. In time, the capital got returned and the boy began to buy his own cloth, shoes, or cigarettes out of his miniscule profits. It is the hard knocks school of business education, a sink-or-swim method, and whatever its shortcomings it inured the apprentice to living perpetually on the economic margin; it equipped him with the psychology necessary to survive in a petty capitalist society.

But with six pieces of cloth bought at retail a young man could not survive among the old hands in Kudus. The apprentice traders were driven out to the more marginal towns and small cities toward the South and East where distance from commercial centers and ports, low intensity of competition, and local ignorance combined to permit a higher profit margin. Travelling light, they learned the ropes from older traders and from their co-religionists, the Arabs. "They used to say we were just like Arabs," one old *santri* trader said gleefully. "We dressed in rags, ate one meal a day of rice and corn with no trimmings, and walked for miles peddling our stuff every place we had a chance. We weren't liked much, but we all got rich." Fiercely independent, they moved back and forth between their home base and Modjokuto less and less frequently, and in time tended to settle permanently in Modjokuto, perhaps marry a local girl (usually from a rural *santri* family), and go off only now and then on buying trips to the larger centers. Often partly specialized according to origin (Kudus men sold cigarettes, Gresick men sold fish, and Bawean men sold cloth), the urban *santris* formed a rather tight in-group, set off (residentially as well as socially) from both the peasants and the government clerks and progressively disliked by both.

Stimulated by the market the Dutch factories and plantations provided, this little group flourished up until the depression. In the twenties there were nearly a dozen native stores in town, some of them rivaling the Chinese in the size and diversity of their inventories—almost all *santri-*run. The *santris* controlled the cigarette, cheap cloth, and small hardware businesses, and, except for luxury textiles, they dominated the fairly extensive trading that went on among the various local markets in the area. They built restaurants, started repair shops, tailored clothes, and cobbled shoes, and some even owned a truck or two. Some of the larger stores were able to supply, in part, more "rational" pricing mechanisms than those provided by bargaining over each individual item, to employ salesmen to go out into the countryside and sell the peasants in their homes, and to keep written books. Economic development and religious reform went hand in hand: by 1930 Islamic modernism with its attendant economic and political ideologies was well rooted in the *santri* community. Each of the various phases of the national movement (as well as of the counter-movement) found its counterpart in Modjokuto, where there occurred a remarkable efflorescence of associational life—among all groups, as a matter of fact—which has continued on into the present day.

The depression and the consequent departure of Dutch capital stunted this development half-grown; a number of the stores and restaurants failed, the Chinese muscled in on the cigarette trade, and a flood of landless *abangans,* released from jobs as Dutch servants and seasonal agricultural workers, pushed into the town to engage in commercial activities previously in largely *santri* hands. The pattern of economic life changed somewhat from one of sharp competition between aggressive and independent entrepreneurs running businesses with a certain degree of elaborated economic organization toward one of mutually interdependent impermanent traders set directly in the general all-over market complex without any mediating structure at all.

But the *santri* element, built for survival, has remained rather strong, considering the circumstances. There are today perhaps seven Javanese establishments worthy of the name "store" left in Modjokuto—six are *santri* owned. Much of the cheap textile business is still in Islamic hands, but on a rather smaller scale. And, not only are there a number of *santri* free craftsmen—shoemakers, tailors, barbers, bike repairmen—but a certain amount of small sweatshop industry continues to flourish under strictly Moslem management. In fact, in Modjokuto town today one can find a continuum of types of Javanese retail trading activity ranging from the "market complex" type to what might be called the "store complex" type, and this continuum correlates remarkably well with variations in religious belief from an *abangan* to a *santri* pole. As one moves toward the store complex, *santri* domination of economic activity grows steadily greater, although, as in any society, many of the cases are mixed ones and embarrassing exceptions occur.

The market is, of course, patronized by everyone, but most particularly it is oriented to rural and to lower class town trade; the informality, the bargaining, the generally cheaper quality of goods sold, all are directed, ultimately toward bit selling to a generally poor clientele. On the other hand, the best Javanese stores (they sell shoes and textiles mostly), situated among the Chinese in the main business section, are generally directed toward the upper-class town populace or toward the few rural rich. Their formality, their tendency toward fixed prices, their fancy glassed-in display cases, and their more expensive line of goods are adjustments to a clientele beginning to feel slightly superior to the jostling commonness of the market. In the secondary business section, particularly along the outside of the market in shops rented from the government, there are a few "transitional" stores which try to combine selling to both publics, the rural and the upper-class urban, but which are still in large part inside the market complex. . . .

VII

Prijaji in the narrow sense signifies someone who can trace his ancestry to kings and who consequently is permitted to write his name with a title before it, but it has come to be applied more generally to government officials, clerks, and, to an extent, to teachers—in short, to the whole of the literati. This little group, originally comprised of relatives and retainers of the Hindu-Javanese sultans, was the chief native agency of colonial government, the chosen instrument of indirect foreign rule, and so has been deeply affected both by the mystical aesthetics of pre-Islamic court culture and by the functional prerequisites of the hierarchical, paternal, bureaucratic, and remarkably efficient political administration introduced by the Dutch. The progeny of this ideological miscegenation turned out to be a carefully ranked caste of obsessively polite literate administrators and educators combining an inward-looking pantheistic imagination with a status-worried bureaucratic conscience. . . .

VIII

In considering the *prijaji* economic position within the Javanese society generally, one immediately comes to wonder why they are so unlanded an aristocracy, relatively speaking. Their economic base lies, even today, almost wholly in the government bureaucracy. A few have accumulated a little land, a small number may have fairly extensive holdings, and the king has always had his estate, but by and large, Java's traditional ruling class has not been able to build up a truly feudal relationship to the peasant masses. In Modjokuto, although some *prijaji* have managed to buy a dozen acres or so as an economic cushion, there is almost no tendency for the urban clerk to develop serious property interests in the rural hamlet. Now, as in the past, the relations between the village and the town are almost wholly administrative and commercial.

The reasons for this situation are to be found wholly in history, a history still insufficiently clarified. The degree of political development reached by native Javanese "states"—if any such there were—prior to the coming of the Hindus; the form the contact with the Hindus took—whether the immigrants were mainly traders or priests, whether they settled mainly on the coasts or moved quickly inland, whether they were many or few; and the degree to which the early courts were integrated into the society generally, are still all moot questions. But it seems clear that at no point have the ties between the courts and the people been well defined and stable ones. Whatever bonds have existed between the villagers and the nobles

have been brittle and opportunistic rather than permanent and traditionalized. As the courts rose and fell the villagers shifted allegiance from one
kingdom to the next, giving temporary allegiance to the one at the moment
most able to provide maximum protection in return for taxes paid or
services rendered.

With some exceptions, then, true feudalism was never able to get off the
ground in Java. The *prijaji* have been almost entirely an urban class and
a permanent rural gentry living on the land has never appeared. Instead
the tie between town and country has been a loose one in which temporary
occupants of the lower ranks of the urban bureaucracy negotiated with
relatively self-contained rural village units for support in exchange for
protection, and it was this system the Dutch rationalized by eliminating
the competition between bureaucracies. Even today the distinction between
local and national regional government is very strong in peasant minds,
and the crucially difficult link in government is that between the lowest
rank of the centrally appointed and wholly urban bureaucracy and the
elected leaders of the various village governments. Now, as in the past, the
central government and the *prijaji* outlook which justifies it sits uneasily
in the general social context of Javanese peasant society, with much less
actual control over the behavior of the villager than it would seem at first
glance to have. Without the intricate ties between the urban and rural
gentry one finds, for example in China, or without the deeply rooted,
clearly defined, land-rights-linked social code of reciprocal obligations of
feudal Europe, the *prijaji* has always found outward submission, exaggerated respect, and placating excuses easier to obtain from the *abangan*
than actual obedience.

At any rate, and for whatever reasons, the *prijaji* are not today a class of
large landholders, and their economic base lies almost entirely in the
governmental bureaucracy. To this general statement one not so very important exception must be made. The court culture, with its emphasis on
art and on dress gave rise to a native textile craft now known the world
over as *batik*. Produced by drawing designs slowly and carefully in wax
onto a piece of muslin and then dying the cloth—and repeating this process
several times with different designs and different color dyes—*batik* was originally worn almost entirely by *prijaji*. *Batik* making became, as a result, a
rather important home industry in the great court centers. Often these
industries were run by wives of lower echelon court attendants and officials
whose underpaid husbands were occupied with their obligations to king
and country, and so a somewhat peculiar pattern of female-dominated
luxury textile industry grew up.

With the development of simpler and faster methods of production and
the expansion of the market for *batik* beyond the court, the *santris* more
and more pushed their way into the industry, until today many of the
largest concerns are *santri*-run; but the low level *prijaji*, somewhat accidentally in on the ground floor, managed to hold on to a certain part of
the business. Before the war in Modjokuto, *batik* was sold almost entirely
by a few *prijaji* women who bought the material from Central Javanese
cities; now *batik* is sold mainly by *santris* and *abangans* in the market,
though for the finest work one has to go to the homes of somewhat more

upper-class women who still supplement their husband's meager salaries with a little genteel *batik* trading.

Thus, *prijaji* activity in both the rural, agricultural, and urban small trade sectors of the Javanese economy has been rather marginal at best. But with the coming of the twentieth century this group benefited almost exclusively, from greater educational opportunities, from the expanded demand for clerks and technical help induced by the Dutch plantation-factory enterprises, and from the ever expanding role of the government in the country's economic life. The *prijaji* became the doctors, lawyers, and engineers, as well as the accountants, personal secretaries, and sugar chemists, and when the revolution finally came they became also the civil servant inheritors of a governmental structure which had come to play a leading part in the organization of economic activities in the society in general and in the cities in particular. If the *santris* were the vanguard of petty capitalism in Java, the *prijajis* became, more or less accidentally and passively, the group most readily identifiable with the form of large-scale corporation centered administered capitalism which has marked the Western industrial countries in this century.

Not, of course, that the economic structure typical of Western Europe and the United States has appeared to any great degree in Java, or most particularly in Modjokuto, or that the *prijaji* represent a class of managers in the Western sense. But industrialization of any significant scope occurring today in the Javanese sector of the Indonesian economy is almost inevitably under the aegis of the central government, for the government is the only social institution capable of mobilizing the capital and, perhaps, of providing the directive personnel, and, as a result, larger enterprises are almost always directly or indirectly capitalized by the government and organized along lines similar to those of the civil bureaucracy, from whose ranks their managers are most often recruited.

In Modjokuto, there are two Javanese owned factories whose scale of operation is noticeably greater than that of petty cottage industry—one is a large rice and sugar mill and one a beer crate manufacturing concern. Both are somewhat mechanized, the first with diesel and electrically driven milling machines for both sugar and rice, the latter with electrically run power-saws imported from West Germany, and both employ more than fifty workers. The first industry is owned and run by a man who is at once head of the regional chapter of the Nationalist political party (a largely *prijaji* organization), a representative on the executive board of the regional governing council, and a man with a marked *prijaji* outlook on life; his chief technical assistant is a former *prijaji* employee of a Dutch sugar factory. The second industry is run by an ex-official of the very forestry department upon whose decisions the fate and prosperity of his enterprise depends, as it is his ability to obtain wood—almost all of it government owned—at economic prices which enable him to survive.

In addition, both industries were government subsidized in part. Clearly a familiarity with the methods of the government bureaucracy as well as an ability to manipulate it both in its own terms and by means of personal contacts is a rather more important skill for a would-be Javanese entrepreneur than those one learns in small-scale, self-capitalized trade and cottage production.

The entrance of non-*prijaji* groups onto the political stage and the growth of a universal educational system since the revolution may serve to moderate this process somewhat, but with a near monopoly of what little advanced technical training the Dutch provided the Javanese, with the highest developed skills of bureaucratic manipulation, and with a majority of the posts in the civil service in their hands, the *prijaji* are almost bound to play a major role in economic development in a country where the private sector of the economy is not likely to prove able to finance large-scale enterprises. If so, the pattern of industrial organization in Java, if ever it appears at all, may take a form consonant with the over-all rank conscious *prijaji* ethic as previously defined and the group of inward-looking mystic bureaucrats seemingly so unsuited to either agricultural or petty capitalist forms of economic organization may find the more complex phases of economic development more congenial. Or perhaps they will merely suffocate them.

IX

The *abangan, santri,* and *prijaji* world outlooks are the major cultural orientations present in contemporaary Modjokuto. Not only economic practices and occupational types, but political parties, social organizations, women's groups, residential areas, and familial relations tend to be organized and grouped according to these general rubrics. But it must be understood that these orientations are not hermetically sealed ideological systems, perfectly logical, perfectly articulated, and perfectly realized from which the social, economic, and political structures of Modjokuto are mere deductions. No more than the Westerner's, is the Javanese individual's social behavior but the outcome of his ethical preferences and metaphysical assumptions; as the Westerner's, his actions are always and everywhere the complex result of ideological, religious, economic, political, familial, and wholly individualistic considerations. . . .

11. Change and the Contented

Maurice Zinkin[*]

The great requirement for development is change; and Asia is beginning to realise it. Change is not easy. Asia has in the past been contented. Westerners and the Westernised have called this contentment pathetic. That does not make it less real, or the reasons for it less valid. Divine discontent in Asia is new, it still works very unevenly in the different layers of society, it brings with it the grave risk that the educated may become discontented enough to revolt before the peasants have become discontented enough to develop. But at least now it is there, working its way deeper and deeper into Asian society, creating the demand for a new life, for plans and

*From Maurice Zinkin, *Development for Free Asia* (London: Chatto & Windus, Ltd., 1956), Chapter 1. The author was a member of the Indian Civil Service, 1937–47, and has since been in business in India.

reforms, steel mills and fertiliser. Thailand alone is still sunk deep enough in peasant happiness not to have to bother with economics.

Asia's contentment has in the past been responsible for much of its failure to develop. Those who are already satisfied for their own present and their children's future, have no reason to sacrifice today's enjoyment for tomorrow's advantage, and without that no economic advance is possible.

The Westerner tends to miss the point. He is accustomed to see only poverty and dirt in the East. He goes into a village and imagines that its people could go Communist tomorrow; yet the only foundation for his so imagining is that that is what he would do in their place. He does not realise that he is looking at a community, most of whose people still today have the deepest of all satisfactions; they have a place in a community; in the East unlike the West a man knows where he stands with his neighbours. He may not like them or they him; they still have to accept him and he them.

The Eastern peasant, where he has enough land, was, and is, right to be contented. He lives in a community which is largely self-governed. Village affairs are still very considerably left to the village council, or the village elders. He is master of his own time and his own labour. He can, if he is fair-minded and capable, attain to a position of authority and consideration amongst his neighbours, a position which may appear of no great importance to the district officials in the great world outside but usually is all that he or his family wants. In most areas he has above him neither squire nor parson; in many areas he does not have below him any large section of society so visibly poor—on his standards—that it burdens his conscience. His position is of course far from perfect. His officials are often corrupt, his moneylender usually extortionate, his landlord's agent (if he is a tenant) normally quite unconscionable; and, wherever there is war, in the present as in the past, he is looted by every side. But, nevertheless, he is the backbone of society; and he knows it.

That is why he is so highly resistant to change. Any class which is the backbone of society is bound to insist on a high degree of conformity if it is not to disintegrate into its constituent vertebrae. Any class which consists largely of small and equal owners will tend to look with some suspicion upon those who by their ability rise out of the common ranks, and with great approbation on those who reach age and respectability by following, with shrewdness but without doubts, in the traditional paths of their ancestors.

Until perhaps the middle of the nineteenth century everywhere, and today still in such places as Thailand, this old life gives complete satisfaction to its adherents. The Hindu division of a man's life into student, householder, service to society, and the attempt to obtain salvation, was one which covered every aspect of a man's nature. That it no longer gives universal satisfaction is due primarily to two factors, both of them quite recent. First, most of Asia has filled up. There is no longer room for the indefinite multiplication of peasant holdings. If the new generation is to be provided for, some method other than traditional peasant agriculture is required. Second, the industrial and scientific revolution which has occurred in the West in the last couple of hundred years has revealed to the whole world that the poverty, which has throughout man's history been accepted with reasonable cheerfulness as the inevitable lot of the many, need be accepted no longer. Such countries as the United States and Sweden and England provide examples of places where nearly everybody gets enough to eat, enough to wear, and a decent house to live in, where everybody can read and write and nobody need die for lack of the attention of a doctor. These are doubtless material benefits, less important perhaps than the spiritual discipline of Zen Buddhism or the mystical successes of so many Hindu saints. By no means everybody in the West is impressed by them, and there are many in the East who respond with a violent negative to what they consider to be Western materialism. But that is not the view of the majority. Most people in Asia are like most people in Europe and America. They like to have enough to eat; they prefer sulpha drugs to dying of dysentery; they even enjoy the cinema and the comics. As Western material standards are made more and more vivid to them by the steadily improving means of communication which are making the modern world one, they more and more demand that these benefits shall be made available to them too. They are not impatient; they are prepared to wait, prepared to accept that it will be many years before they reach the present standards or economic level of the more successful countries. But they do demand that something should be done; that they should be able to see some progress, some improvement, not just in their lifetimes but actually within the next few years.

Economic development has therefore become in almost all the countries of Asia the dominating question of the day. The leaders are determined to change; and now at last it looks as if the people may be willing to follow. Elections can be fought on five-year plans; villages are willing to help to pay for schools and maternity clinics; the peasant will accept the advice of Extension Service officers on seed and rotations and the breeding of cattle, in a way he previously did only in Japan; the need for savings has crept into political speeches; the popular press talks of productivity, and underemployment, and the need for technicians. Economics have arrived. The people would like to develop. They are not yet quite sure how; they are sometimes appalled by the difficulty of the road; they are occasionally tempted by Communism, which promises to push them along the road by force, and thus guarantees them that they will not be allowed to get discouraged by obstacles; they are always determined to place upon their politicians and bureaucrats a burden of leadership, of pulling and showing and directing them along the right way which the more fortunate politicians and bureaucrats of the West do not have to bear. However, the stirrings are there. Whether they get these by persuasion the Indian way, or by liquidation the Chinese way, or by firm direction the Japanese way, Asians now want to develop badly enough to be prepared to pay the price.

INNOVATION AND INVESTMENT

12. Theoretical Note on Time-Preference, Productivity of Capital, Stagnation and Economic Growth

*Wassily Leontief**

Among the many factors which determine the growth or stagnation—as the case may be—of a national economy, its rate of saving out of current income and the subsequent increase in income resulting from the investment of these savings play an important role. A relatively simple method of graphic presentation and analysis makes it possible to articulate, without explicit resource to algebra or calculus, the various effects which different configurations of these two determinants can have on the state of the economy and its development over time. Like any other purely theoretical inquiry, this analysis only helps us to draw certain, possibly not immediately obvious, conclusions from alternative sets of hypothetical assumptions.

Figure 1 depicts the preferences of a given national economy between present and future levels of consumption in terms of a conventional set of social indifference curves. It deviates only in one respect from the graph used by Irving Fisher in his classic exposition of his theory of interest. The variables, Y and C, whose magnitudes are measured along the horizontal axis, represent respectively the level of real income and the amount of goods consumed in the present period. The variables Y' and C' measured vertically describe future income or consumption; "future," however, not in the sense of a single "second" period—as shown on Fisher's diagram—but in the sense of a steady, even flow which, beginning with the year following the present one, can be maintained in equal annual amounts in perpetuity.

Accordingly, every point between the coordinate axes in Figure 1 denotes a specific combination of a given present year's income (or consumption) level with a fixed level of annual income (or consumption) flow to be enjoyed in perpetuity from the next year on. Each indifference line represents a set of equally desirable combinations of present consumption levels and future consumption streams, the positions on higher indifference lines being naturally preferable to those on the lower.

The movement, from right to left, along any one of the negatively sloped straight lines, such as $P_1P'_1$ or $P_2P'_2$ accordingly describes an exchange of a batch of present goods for a constant stream of future goods or, in other words, the exchange of a capital sum for a perpetual series of equal annual interest payments. The (absolute) magnitude of the slope of each one of

*From the *American Economic Review,* Papers and Proceedings. March 1958, pp. 105–111. The author is Professor of Economics, Harvard University.

these exchange lines can consequently be interpreted as representing an annual real rate of interest. Given a free choice between alternative positions on a given exchange line, the income receivers would accordingly reach the highest attainable—under the given circumstances—level of welfare at tangency points, such as P'_1, P'_2 or P'_3.

Any point, such as P_1, P_2 or P_3, situated on the 45° line drawn from the origin, describes a stationary position in which the present (Y) and the future (Y') levels of income and consumption are identical. Actually faced with a choice between the maintenance of such a stationary state and a movement to some other position located along the exchange line which goes through it, income receivers will perpetuate the stationary state only if, as at P'_3, it happens also to be the point of tangency between the exchange line and the indifference curve which passes through that point. In other cases, they can improve their welfare by consuming less than their entire present income in order to secure a higher level of future income and consumption streams. Or, on the contrary, they might improve their situation by borrowing against the future, so as to allow the present consumption to exceed the rate of current revenue.

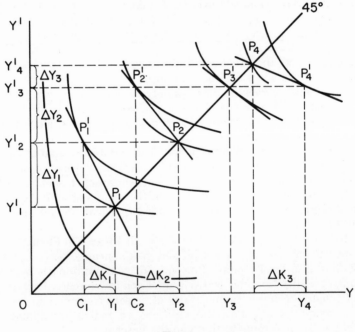

Fig. 1

Thus, starting, for example, from the initial position P_1 and facing the exchange line which passes through that point, the representative independent income recipient or the central planning authority—whichever it may be—will move from P_1 to P'_1. It will allocate to immediate direct consumption that part of present income OY_1 which is measured by the distance from O to C_1; the rest of it, C_1Y_1, or ΔK_1, will be saved and exchanged against future income. The rate of the potential income stream to be received in the next, and all later, years will be raised by ΔY_1 from OY'_1 to OY'_2. Point P_2, again located on the 45° line thus represents the prospective position of the country in the second year.

Before pursuing further the sequence of given income, saving and increased income, let us turn to Figure 2 which describes the relationship between the total stock of capital invested and the net output (income) which it can produce on the basis of the existing technology in cooperation with the given supply of all other factors. Along the horizontal axis, we

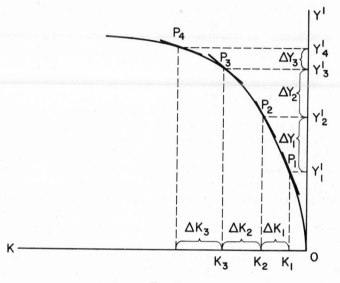

FIG. 2

measure from right to left (in order to facilitate the subsequent comparison with Figure 1) the total stock of capital, and along the vertical axis the annual rate of net output, i.e., net income. The bending of the curve describes the well-known technical relationship between the stock of productive capital and the flow of output produced with its help. The slope of that curve at any point represents the marginal productivity of the particular amount of capital which corresponds to it.

Point P_1 in Figure 1 refers to the same state of the economic system as point P_1 in Figure 2. In this position, the total stock of capital amounts to K_1 and it produces a net income flow of Y_1 units per annum. The potential increase in output, which could be brought about by an increase in the existing stock of capital, can be read off Figure 2: Specifically, the ratio between the amount of invested savings and the resulting rise in future income flow is represented—at least for changes which are not very large—by the slope of the capital-output curve at point P_1. It is that slope which, when transferred to Figure 1, describes the real rate of interest, the ratio at which the present consumption can be foregone in favor of additional future income, or, in other words, the slope of the line along which the country moves (see Figure 1) from P_1 to P'_1. The saving, ΔK_1, when added on Figure 2 to the original amount of capital, K_1, increases the total stock to K_2 and the corresponding annual rate of income flow—from Y'_1 to Y'_2. Measured on Figure 1 along the horizontal axes this is the increase from Y_1 to Y_2.

The income and consumption, represented by the position of point P_2 in Figures 1 and 2 could be maintained, as far as the country's productive power is concerned, from now on into the future without any further change. The combination of the marginal productivity of capital and time-preference, as shown at point P_2 in Figures 1 and 2, is, however, such that instead of consuming all of that increased income our developing economy will move on to point P'_2, i.e., save and invest again, increase its stock of capital from K_2 to K_3 and its income from Y_2 to Y_3. By the third year, it thus will find itself at P'_3. The slope of the indifference curve passing through that point in Figure 1 has been drawn so as to be equal to the slope of the capital-output curve at the corresponding point (P_3) in Figure 2. Hence the marginal productivity of capital is equated to marginal time-preference if the representative consumer, i.e., the country as a whole, chooses to consume neither more nor less than its entire current income. It is, in other words, an equilibrium position, a stationary state which can and will be maintained *ad infinitum* as long as no new factors enter the picture. Such a new factor might be a shift of the structural conditions, i.e., a change in the form of the production function in Figure 2 or a variation in the shape of the indifference curves in Figure 1. Or it might consist in the creation of new "initial conditions": sudden destruction—as the result of war—of some part of the existing stock of capital or, on the contrary, acquisition of additional capital from foreign sources, a developmental grant received from abroad.

On our graphs, the creation of such new initial conditions would be described, for example, as a shift from P'_3 to point P_2 or, say, to point P_4. In either case, if left to its own devices, the economy would return at once or by successive steps to its original position at P'_3. The difference between the movement from P_2 to P'_3 and from P_4 to P'_3 is that, in the latter case, having been pushed beyond the point of stable equilibrium, the system will come back to it through a process of capital consumption, i.e., by sacrificing some of the future income stream in order to be able to maintain during the transitory period a "present" level of consumption above its "current" income; while in the former case it would approach the stable equilibrium position, P'_3, from below, i.e., through a process of capital accumulation.

The economy of course does not necessarily find an equilibrium position. It might have none, or more than one, but in the latter case unstable as well as stable equilibria will necessarily be present. We call a state of unstable equilibrium one in which, in the absence of any change in its internal structure and without even the slightest variation in the initial conditions, the system would maintain itself *ad infinitum,* but from which it would tend to depart on the slightest provocation. It is analogous to the position of the proverbial egg, precariously balanced on its narrow end.

To work out in full the implications of the previous analysis, let us now turn to Figure 3. Along the horizontal axis, we measure the national income, Y. Of the two interlaced curves, MP represents the marginal productivity of capital, i.e., the slope of the capital-output line (Figure 2) as it gradually bends toward the horizontal with the increase in Y. TP measures the marginal time-preference, i.e., the slope of the indifference curves as they cross the 45° line in Figure 1 at various levels of income Y. The third curve below, identified by the letter D, represents the vertical distance (difference) between the first two (i.e., the excess of TP over MP); the points, a, b, and c, at which the D-curve crosses the zero axis mark those income levels at which the marginal productivity of capital is equal to the marginal time-preference when the country consumes exactly its entire income. They mark, in other words, the possible equilibrium positions of the system. The D-curve passes below the zero line at those income levels at which the marginal time-preference (or more precisely the slope of the indifference lines at points where they cross the 45° stationary income locus) is smaller than the corresponding marginal productivity of capital. As can be seen from Figure 1, in all such cases there will be some positive amount of saving. And as a result of it, the income will necessarily grow. Over all those intervals in which the D curve rises above the zero line, current consumption, on the contrary, will exceed net current output, the stock of capital will be diminished and income will consequently fall. The direction of the ensuing upward, or downward, change in income is indicated in Figure 3 by arrows.

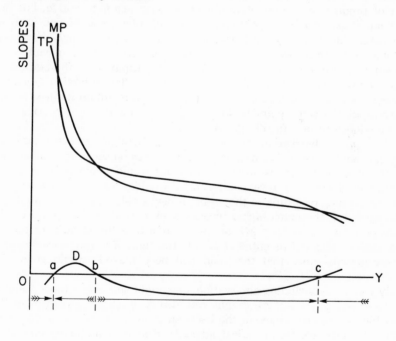

Fig. 3

To simplify the explanation of the interplay of the two sets of basic structural relationships represented, respectively, in Figures 1 and 2, the functioning of the economy has been viewed as if it had proceeded step by step. Such period analysis introduces, however, complications of its own which would be absent if the processes of production, consumption and investment were described in continuous terms. With due apology to the mathematically interested reader (who, however, should be able to work out all intermediate details himself), we will now interpret the curves in Figure 3 as if they reflected, as they well might, the properties of a continuous process. [The reader will note that the specific shapes of these curves do not actually correspond to those of the particular set of consumer-preference relationships and the production function depicted in the other graphs. While the combination of the structural relationships shown in Figures 1 and 2 yield only one equilibrium position (P'_3), Figure 3 shows the existence of three such positions, a, b, and c.]

Starting with a very small stock of capital and income inferior to that corresponding to the lowest equilibrium point, a, the system would proceed to expand toward a. If in its initial position the economy were located some place between a and b, it would also tend to move toward the former point. In this case, the process is a regressive one characterized by gradual diminution of the stock of productive capital, reduction in the rate of output (income) and incidentally—as the MP curve shows—an increase in the real rate of interest. Once a is reached in either way, the system would "stagnate" at that low but stable equilibrium position. When pushed to the left by the action of some outside force, such for example as an accidental loss of productive capital, it would move back again toward a, but not beyond. If, as beneficiary of a foreign loan or gift, it should find itself in the possession of some additional capital and correspondingly increased income, our country would at once proceed to "live above its means," i.e., consume its capital and gradually reduce its output until the stationary state at a would again be reached. Even a constant flow of foreign aid could, in such case, do no more than help the system to maintain its income and consumption at some point between a and b, without, however, releasing any tendency toward further growth.

These latter observations apply, however, only to gifts or loans not large enough to push the rate of output beyond b. Once on the other side of that unstable equilibrium position, the economy would begin to save, accumulate and increase its revenue; in short it would proceed to develop under its own power. According to the graph, a new stable equilibrium would be approached at the much higher income level, c. Had the structural conditions been such as to keep MP above TP, and thus the D-curve below the zero line, throughout its entire stretch to the right of b, the process of economic growth—once that threshold had been passed—would go on indefinitely.

By way of a concluding observation, one might suggest, without detailed explanation, how the three graphs can also be used to trace through the possible effects of changes in the basic structural conditions of the economy. For instance technological advance, described as an upward shift of the capital-output curve in Figure 2, might—and most likely actually would—affect the shape of the MP and the D-curve in Figure 3. The equilibrium positions a, b, and c would shift. Depending on the magnitude and the nature of the change, some of these positions of stationary state might even disappear or new ones might be created.

To the extent to which a rise in the productivity of capital enables the economy to increase its income without any addition to its stock of capital, technological advance will shift the system at once to the right along the horizontal axis in Figure 3 from whatever position it had previously occupied. In fact, however, new technology as a rule requires a new type of equipment and different kinds of skills. That means that its introduction will depend itself on the current rate of saving and accumulation.

A further pursuit of these speculative arguments must clearly yield diminishing returns. The effort involved in construction and interpretation of more complicated graphs might better be spent on observation and explanation of the real world.

13. Two Concepts of External Economies[1]

Tibor Scitovsky*

The concept of external economies is one of the most elusive in economic literature. Our understanding of it has been greatly enhanced by the active controversy of the twenties over the nature of the "empty economic boxes"; but full clarity has never been achieved. Definitions of external economies are few and unsatisfactory. It is agreed that they mean services (and disservices) rendered free (without compensation) by one producer to another; but there is no agreement on the nature and form of these services or on the reasons for their being free. It is also agreed that external economies are a cause for divergence between private profit and social benefit and thus for the failure of perfect competition to lead to an optimum situation; but for this there are many reasons, and it is nowhere made clear how many and which of these reasons are subsumed under the heading of "external economies." Nor do examples help to clarify the concept. The literature contains many examples of external economies; but they are as varied and dissimilar as are discussions of the subject. Some give the impression that external economies are exceptional and unimportant; others suggest that they are important and ubiquitous. Indeed, one might be tempted to explain this strange dichotomy by ideological differences between authors; but such an explanation would be both unwarranted and unnecessary. For, with the increasing rigor of economic thinking and separation of the different branches of economic theory, it is becoming increasingly clear that the concept of external economies does duty in two entirely different contexts. One of these is equilibrium theory, the other is the theory of industrialization in underdeveloped countries. It is customary to discuss these two subjects at different levels of abstraction and on the basis of very different sets of assumptions: no wonder that "external economies" stand for very different things in the two contexts. Indeed,

*From the *Journal of Political Economy*, April 1954, pp. 143–151. © 1954 by The University of Chicago. Reprinted by permission of The University of Chicago Press. The author is Professor of Economics, University of California.

[1]I am indebted to Professor Bernard Haley and Mr. Ralph Turvey for many helpful suggestions. The responsibility for errors, however, is entirely mine. [T.S.]

I shall argue that there are two entirely different definitions of external economies, one much wider than the other; and that external economies as defined in the theory of industrialization include, but go far beyond, the external economies of equilibrium theory. The latter have been discussed and rigorously defined in Professor Meade's "External Economies and Diseconomies in a Competitive Situation";[2] but, since they form part of external economies as defined in the theory of industrialization, we shall deal with them briefly here.

I

Equilibrium theory, in both its general and it partial form, is a static theory, concerned with the characteristics of the economic system when it is in equilibrium. Most of its conclusions are based on the assumptions of (1) perfect competition on both sides of every market and (2) perfect divisibility of all resources and products. These assumptions underlie the main conclusion of general equilibrium theory, viz., that the market economy leads to a situation of economic optimum (in Pareto's sense), provided that every economic influence of one person's (or firm's) behavior on another person's well-being (or firm's profit) is transmitted through its impact on market prices. Expressed differently, equilibrium in a perfectly competitive economy is a situation of Paretian optimum, except when there is interdependence among the members of the economy that is direct, in the sense that it does not operate through the market mechanism. In general equilibrium theory, then, direct interdependence is the villain of the piece and the cause for conflict between private profit and social benefit.

One can distinguish four types of direct (i.e., nonmarket) interdependence (and one of these—the last one in the following enumeration—is known as "external economies") : (1) The individual person's satisfaction may depend not only on the quantities of products he consumes and services he renders but also on the satisfaction of other persons. In particular, the high income or consumption of others may give a person pain or pleasure; and so may his knowledge that some others are less well off than he is. This is known as the "interdependence of consumers' satisfaction." (2) A person's satisfaction may be influenced by the activities of producers not only through their demand for his services and supply of the products he buys but also in ways that do not operate through the market mechanism. These may be called the producer's "direct" (i.e., nonmarket) influence on personal satisfaction and are best known by the example of the factory that inconveniences the neighborhood with the fumes or noise that emanate from it. (3) The producer's output may be influenced by the action of persons more directly and in other ways than through their offer of services used and demand for products produced by the firm. This is a counterpart of the previous case, and its main instance is inventions that facilitate production and become available to producers without charge. (4) The output of the individual producer may depend not only on his input of productive resources but also on the activities of other firms. This is a counterpart of case 1 and may be called "direct interdependence among

[2] *Economic Journal,* LXII (1952), 54–67.

producers" but is better known under the name of "external economies and diseconomies."[3]

Of these four cases of direct interdependence, the first, interdependence among consumers, is undoubtedly important. It is (together with the case mentioned in n. 3) among the main reasons for the current controversy in welfare economies and the reluctance of economists to make any welfare statements concerning the consumer. Nowadays, welfare statements are usually confined to the field of production, where the main conclusion of general equilibrium theory seems to stand on firmer ground, primarily because the remaining three cases of direct interdependence (all of which involve the producer) seem exceptional and unimportant. The second case seems exceptional, because most instances of it can be and usually are eliminated by zoning ordinances and industrial regulation concerned with public health and safety. The third case is unimportant, because patent laws have eliminated the main instance of this form of direct interdependence and transformed it into a case of interdependence through the market mechanism.[4] The fourth case seems unimportant, simply because examples of it seem to be few and exceptional.

The last statement appears at first to be contradicted by the many examples of external economies and diseconomies quoted in the literature; but most of these are *not* examples of direct interdependence among producers, which is the only meaning that can be attributed to the term "external economies" within the context of equilibrium theory. It will be useful in this connection to have a rigorous definition of direct interdependence among producers. Meade gave such a definition when he defined external economies; and I can do no better than to reproduce it. According to him, external economies exist whenever the output (x_1) of a firm depends not only on the factors of production $(l_1, c_1, \ldots)$ utilized by this firm but also on the output (x_2) and factor utilization $(l_2, c_2, \ldots)$ of another firm or group of firms.[5] In symbols,

$$x_1 = F \ (l_1, c_1, \ldots ; \qquad x_2, l_2, \ldots) \ ,$$

where the existence of external economies is indicated by the presence of the variables to the right of the semicolon. Since $F(*)$ is a production function, external economies as here defined are a peculiarity of the production function. For this reason it is convenient to call them "technological external economies."[6] While this will distinguish them from another category of external economies to be introduced presently, we must bear in mind that technological external economies are the only external economies that can arise, because of direct interdependence among producers and within the framework of general equilibrium theory.

[3] A fifth and important case, which, however, does not quite fit into the above classification, is that where society provides social services through communal action and makes them available free of charge to all persons and firms.

[4] i.e., Patent laws have created a market and a market price for the inventor's services, which in the absence of such laws would often be free goods. The case where the results of government-sponsored research into industrial and agricultural methods are made gratuitously available to industrialists and farmers belongs in the category mentioned in n. 3 above.

[5] *Op. cit.*

[6] The term is used in Jacob Viner's "Cost Curves and Supply Curves," *Zeitschrift für Nationalökonomie*, III (1931), 23–46.

The examples of external economies given by Meade are somewhat bucolic in nature, having to do with bees, orchards, and woods. This, however, is no accident: it is not easy to find examples from industry. Going through the many examples of external economies quoted in the literature, I found only two that fit the above definition: the case in which a firm benefits from the labor market created by the establishment of other firms and that in which several firms use a resource which is free but limited in supply.[1] For a more detailed discussion the reader is referred to Meade's article, which will, I think, convince him of the scarcity of technological external economies.

II

The other field in which the concept of external economies occurs frequently is the theory of industrialization of underdeveloped countries, where the concept is used in connection with the special problem of allocating savings among alternative investment opportunities. This last is one of the many practical problems to which economists are wont to apply the conclusions of general equilibrium theory. Most of them realize, of course, that general equilibrium theory is limited in its assumptions and applicability; but the only limitation taken seriously by most economists is that imposed by the assumption of perfect competition; and this—as is well known—is not always a necessary condition for the conclusions of equilibrium theory to hold good. In particular, many economists regard a uniform degree of monopoly as all that is necessary for market forces to bring about an optimum allocation of investment funds; and this weaker condition is held to be more nearly fulfilled in our society. Whether for this reason or for some other, the private profitability of investment is usually considered a good index of its social desirability, at least as a general rule.

To this rule, however, the exceptions are too great and obvious to be ignored, especially in underdeveloped countries; and it is customary to impute most of them to external economies. While the nature of these external economies is often discussed, I have been unable to find a definition of the concept in the literature dealing with underdeveloped countries. It is possible, however, to infer a definition from the many examples, discussions, and obiter dicta. It seems that external economies are invoked whenever the profits of one producer are affected by the actions of other producers. To facilitate comparison with Meade's definition, we can express this in symbols by the function

$$P_1 = G\ (x_1, l_1, c_1, \dots\ ;\ x_2, l_2, c_2, \dots),$$

which shows that the *profits* of the firm depend not only on its own output and factor inputs but also on the output and factor inputs of other firms; and we shall say that in the context of underdeveloped countries external economies are said to exist whenever the variables to the right of the semicolon are present.

[1] Instances of this are the oil well whose output depends on the number and operation of other wells on the same oil field; the fisherman whose catch depends on the operations of other fishermen in the same waters; and the firm that uses a public road (or other publicly owned utility) and is partly crowded out of it by other firms using the same road.

This definition of external economies obviously includes direct or non-market interdependence among producers, as discussed above and defined by Meade. It is much broader, however, than his definition, because, in addition to direct interdependence among producers, it also includes interdependence among producers through the market mechanism. This latter type of interdependence may be called "pecuniary external economies" to distinguish it from the technological external economies of direct interdependence.[8]

Interdependence through the market mechanism is all-pervading, and this explains the contrast between the exceptional and often awkward examples of external economies cited in discussions of equilibrium theory and the impression one gains from the literature on underdeveloped countries that the entrepreneur creates external economies and diseconomies with his every move.

What is puzzling, however, is that interdependence through the market mechanism should be held to account for the failure of the market economy to lead to the socially desirable optimum, when equilibrium theory comes to the opposite conclusion and *relies* on market interdependence to bring about an optimum situation. Pecuniary external economies clearly have no place in equilibrium theory. The question is whether the concept is meaningful elsewhere. To answer this question we must first investigate the nature of the pecuniary external economies, to which interdependence through the market mechanism give rise.

Investment in an industry leads to an expansion of its capacity and may thus lower the prices of its products and raise the prices of the factors used by it. The lowering of product prices benefits the users of these products; the raising of factor prices benefits the suppliers of the factors. When these benefits accrue to firms, in the form of profits, they are pecuniary external economies—Marshall called, or would have called, them (together with the benefits accruing to persons) consumers' and producers' surplus, respectively. According to the theory of industrialization, these benefits, being genuine benefits, should be explicitly taken into account when investment decisions are made; and it is usually suggested that this should be done by taking as the maximand not profits alone but the sum of the profits yielded and the pecuniary external economies created by the investment.

This prescription seems to be in direct conflict with the results of equilibrium theory. For, according to the latter and subject to its usual assumptions and limitations, market interdependence in the competitive system insures that the maximization of profit by each firm and of satisfaction by each person brings about an optimum situation, which, as is well known, is sometimes described as a situation in which consumers' and producers' surpluses are maximized. In other words, equilibrium theory tells us that in equilibrium the sum of consumers' and producers' surpluses will be maximized, although they do not enter explicitly, as part of the maximand, the economic decisions of any producer.[9] Assuming that these conflicting

[8]Cf. Viner, *op. cit.*
[9]Cf. J. R. Hicks, "The Rehabilitation of Consumers' Surplus," *Review of Economic Studies,* VIII (1941), 108–16. We need not enter here the debate on the usefulness of this terminology. Nor is it necessary to stress that this way of

views are both right, the conflict can be resolved only if we should find that the limitations of general equilibrium theory render it inapplicable to the problems of investment. This, indeed, must often be so; but in the following we shall single out three special cases, which seem especially important and in which the above conflict is resolved.

a. One reason why the conclusions of general equilibrium theory may be inapplicable to the practical problem of investment is that the former's assumption of perfect divisibility is not always fulfilled. Perfect competition leads to a position of economic optimum, because under perfect competition the marginal conditions of economic optimum are contained (in the absence of direct interdependence) in the marginal conditions of profit maximization by producers and satisfaction maximization by householders. Indivisibilities, however, may prevent the producer from fulfilling these marginal conditions. For example, he may find himself unable to equate marginal costs to price and, instead, face the choice of producing either less or more than the output that would equate these two quantities. In such a case one of the available alternatives will still yield him a higher profit than all others; but this need no longer be the one that is also the best from society's point of view. Hence the need, in such cases, to take society's point of view explicitly into consideration.

This fact was recognized as early as 1844 by Dupuit.[10] He was looking for a criterion of the social desirability of investment in such public utilities as canals, roads, bridges, and railways—the typical examples of indivisibilities in economics—and he found this criterion not in the actual profitability of such investments but in what their profitability would be in the hypothetical case in which the operator of the utility practiced price discrimination and thus appropriated to himself the consumers' surplus that would normally (i.e., in the absence of price discrimination) accrue to the users of the public utility. In other words, Dupuit's test of social desirability is whether the sum of profit and consumers' surplus is positive.[11] Dupuit's test and his use of the consumers' surplus concept underlying it were vindicated by Professor Hicks,[12] but neither Hicks nor Dupuit makes clear the role of indivisibilities in rendering the above test necessary. For this last point, as well as for an excellent statement of the entire argument, the reader should consult chapter xvi of Professor Lerner's *Economics of Control.*[13]

b. The second reason for the inapplicability of general equilibrium

---

stating the result of perfect competition is characteristic of partial equilibrium analysis.

[10] Cf. Jules Dupuit, "De la mesure de l'utilité des travaux publics," *Annales des ponts et chaussées,* 2d ser., Vol. VIII (1844); reprinted in *International Economic Papers,* No. 2 (1952), pp. 83–110.

[11] This is so whether the consumers' surplus accrues to persons or represents external economies accruing to firms.

[12] Cf. J. R. Hicks, "L'Économie de bien-être et la théorie des surplus du consommateur," and "Quelques applications de la théorie des surplus du consommateur," both in *Économie appliquée,* No. 4 (1948), pp. 432–57.

[13] A. P. Lerner, *Economics of Control* (New York: Macmillan Co., 1944). Lerner's solution is slightly different and, I believe, more correct than Dupuit's, in that he takes account also of producers' surplus. It might be added in passing that the type of indivisibility considered by Dupuit establishes a relation among the users of the public utility that is similar in all essentials to direct interdependence among consumers.

theory to the problems of investment is that the former is a static or equilibrium theory, whereas the allocation of investment funds is not a static problem at all. According to equilibrium theory, the producer's profit-maximizing behavior brings about a socially desirable situation *when the system is in equilibrium*; or, to give this result a more dynamic, if not entirely correct, interpretation, profit-maximizing behavior brings closer the socially desirable optimum if it also brings closer equilibrium. Investment, however, need not bring the system closer to equilibrium; and, when it does not, the results of equilibrium theory may not apply.

Profits are a sign of disequilibrium; and the magnitude of profits, under free competition, may be regarded as a rough index of the degree of disequilibrium.[14] Profits in a freely competitive industry lead to investment in that industry; and the investment, in turn, tends to eliminate the profits that have called it forth. Thus far, then, investment tends to bring equilibrium nearer. The same investment, however, may raise or give rise to profits in other industries; and to this extent it leads away from equilibrium. For example, investment in industry A will cheapen its product; and if this is used as a factor in industry B, the latter's profits will rise. This, then, is a case where the price reduction creates, not a consumers' surplus proper, accruing to persons, but pecuniary external economies, benefiting firms. Is this difference sufficient to render the conclusions of general equilibrium theory inapplicable?

To answer this question, we must pursue the argument a little further. The profits of industry B, created by the lower price of factor A, call for investment and expansion in industry B, one result of which will be an increase in industry B's demand for industry A's product. This in its turn will give rise to profits and call for further investment and expansion in industry A; and equilibrium is reached only when successive doses of investment and expansion in the two industries have led to the simultaneous elimination of profits in both. It is only at this stage, where equilibrium has been established, that the conclusions of equilibrium theory become applicable and we can say (on the usual assumptions and in the absence of direct interdependence) that the amount of investment profitable in industry A is also the socially desirable amount. This amount is clearly greater than that which is profitable at the first stage, before industry B has made adjustment. We can conclude, therefore, that when an investment gives rise to pecuniary external economies, its private profitability understates its social desirability.

Unfortunately, however, the test of social desirability applicable in the previous case is not applicable here, although it would probably give a better result than a simple calculation of profitability. This can easily be seen by comparing the situation under consideration with that which would obtain if industries A and B were integrated (although in such a way as to preserve the free competition assumed so far). In this case the pecuniary external economies created by investment in industry A would become "internal" and part of the profits of the investors themselves. Investment in A would be more profitable and pushed further than in the absence of integration; but, *without investment and expansion also in*

[14]However, the absence of profits is not a sufficient condition of equilibrium.

industry B, it would not be pushed far enough. For what inhibits investment in A is the limitation on the demand for industry A's product imposed by the limited capacity of industry B, the consumer of this product;
just as investment in industry B is inhibited by the limited capacity of
industry A, the supplier of one of industry B's factors of production. These
limitations can be fully removed only by a simultaneous expansion of both
industries. We conclude, therefore, that only if expansion in the two industries were integrated and planned together would the profitability of investment in each one of them be a reliable index of its social desirability.

It hardly needs adding that the relation between industries A and B
discussed above illustrates only one of the many possible instances of
pecuniary external economies that belong in this category. Expansion in
industry A may also give rise to profits (i) in an industry that produces
a factor used in industry A, (ii) in an industry whose product is complementary in use to the product of industry A, (iii) in an industry whose
product is a substitute for a factor used in industry A, or (iv) in an industry whose product is consumed by persons whose incomes are raised by
the expansion of industry A—and this list does not include the cases in
which the expansion causes external *dis*economies. It is apparent from this
list that vertical integration alone would not be enough and that complete
integration of all industries would be necessary to eliminate all divergence between private profit and public benefit. This was fully realized
by Dr. Rosenstein-Rodan, who, in dealing with the "Problems of Industrialisation of Eastern and South-Eastern Europe,"[15] considered most
instances of pecuniary external economies listed above and advocated that
"the whole of the industry to be created is to be treated and planned like
one huge firm or trust."[16] To put this conclusion differently, profits in a
market economy are a bad guide to economic optimum as far as investment
and industrial expansion are concerned; and they are worse, the more
decentralized and differentiated the economy.

This entire argument can be restated in somewhat different terms. In an
economy in which economic decisions are decentralized, a system of communication is needed to enable each person who makes economic decisions
to learn about the economic decisions of others and coordinate his decisions with theirs. In the market economy, prices are the signaling device
that informs each person of other people's economic decisions; and the
merit of perfect competition is that it would cause prices to transmit information reliably and people to respond to this information properly. Market
prices, however, reflect the economic situation as it is and not as it will be.
For this reason, they are more useful for co-ordinating current production
decisions, which are immediately effective and guided by short-run considerations, than they are for co-ordinating investment decisions, which
have a delayed effect and—looking ahead to a long future period—should
be governed not by what the present economic situation is but by what
the future economic situation is expected to be. The proper co-ordination
of investment decisions, therefore, would require a signaling device to
transmit information about present plans and future conditions as they
are determined by present plans; and the pricing system fails to provide

[15]*Economic Journal,* LIII (1943), 202–11.
[16]*Ibid.,* p. 204.

this.[11] Hence the belief that there is need either for centralized investment planning or for some additional communication system to supplement the pricing system as a signaling device.

It must be added that the argument of this section applies with special force to underdeveloped countries. The plant capacity most economical to build and operate is not very different in different countries; but, as a percentage of an industry's total capacity, it is very much greater in underdeveloped than in full industrialized economies. In underdeveloped countries, therefore, investment is likely to have a greater impact on prices, give rise to greater pecuniary external economies, and thus cause a greater divergence between private profit and social benefit.

c. I propose to consider yet another reason for divergence between the profitability of an investment and its desirability from the community's point of view; but this is very different from those discussed in the last two sections and has to do with the difference between the national and international points of view. In appraising the social desirability of an economic action from the international point of view, all repercussions of that action must be fully taken into account, whereas, from the national point of view, the welfare of domestic nationals alone is relevant and the losses suffered and benefits gained by foreigners are ignored. The two points of view need not necessarily lead to different appraisals; but they usually do when the economic action considered is the allocation of investment funds among purely domestic, import-competing, and export industries. From the international point of view, all external economies and diseconomies must be taken into consideration; from the national point of view, one must count only the external economies and diseconomies that accrue to domestic nationals and leave out of account the pecuniary external economies accruing to foreign buyers from the expansion of export industries and the diseconomies inflicted on foreign competitors by the expansion of import-competing industries. Accordingly, investment in export industries is always less, and that in import-competing industries is always more desirable from the national, than from the international, point of view.

In discussions on investment policy this difference between the national and international points of view usually appears in the guise of a difference between the criteria of social benefit and private profit. For social benefit, when considered explicitly, is usually identified with national benefit in our society, whereas private profit, although an imperfect index of social desirability, accounts or fails to account for external economies and diseconomies without national bias and therefore probably comes closer to registering the social welfare of the world as a whole than that of a single nation. Hence investment tends to be more profitable in export industries and less profitable in import-competing industries than would be desirable from a narrow nationalistic point of view.

It is worth noting that this argument is in some respects the reverse of the argument of Section II*b* above. There it was the failure of profit cal-

<hr />

[11] Professor Kenneth Arrow pointed out to me, however, that, in a formal sense, futures markets and futures prices could provide exactly such a signaling device.

culations to take into account pecuniary external economies that caused the divergence between private profit and social benefit; here the divergence is caused by the entry into the profit criterion of pecuniary external economies and diseconomies that accrue to foreigners and should therefore be excluded from social accounting concerned with national, rather than world, welfare. The argument is well known as the "terms-of-trade argument" and has been used to explain the failure of foreign investments in colonial areas to benefit fully the borrowing countries.[18] The divergence between national welfare and private profit depends on the foreigners' import-demand and export-supply elasticities; and it can be offset by an appropriate set of import and export duties. This has been shown by Mr. J. de V. Graaff, in his "Optimum Tariff Structures."[19] De Graaff presents his optimum tariff structure as one that will bring about that flow of goods and services which optimizes[20] the nation's welfare; but the same tariff structure will also bring about the allocation of investment funds that is optimal from the national point of view.

[18]Cf. H. W. Singer, "The Distribution of Gains between Investing and Borrowing Countries," *American Economic Review (Proceedings)*, XL (1950), 473–85.
[19]*Review of Economic Studies*, XVII (1949–50), 47–59.
[20]In Pareto's sense.

14. Why Do We Disagree on Investment Policies for Development?

*Harvey Leibenstein**

I. Introduction

The question of investment policy for the economic development of underdeveloped areas is still, at least in my opinion, a very much unsettled matter. That this should be the case is hardly surprising since the "correct policy," if such exists, depends on the solution of a number of intellectual problems that have as yet not been solved. It is *not* my purpose, in this paper, to set forth and argue for the "correct" investment allocation policy. On the contrary I hope to show that given the present imperfect state of our knowledge with respect to the factors that are significant in economic development it is impossible to come to a definitive conclusion on this matter. Different scholars may be warranted in holding different positions with respect to investment policies. If this be so then it follows that the "orthodox position," i.e., the position that emphasizes the *usual* interpretation of the marginal productivity criterion, has not been demonstrated to be the correct one, nor, by the same token, has any alternative position been proven to be correct beyond any shadow of doubt. Perhaps this is platitudinous and obvious. I hope so. But some of the recent, and not so recent literature on the subject, as well as both casual

*From the *Indian Economic Journal,* April 1958, pp. 369–386. The author is Professor of Economics, University of California, Berkeley.

and serious conversations with a number of economists, has suggested to me that this is not quite the case. Many appear to hold very strong views on the matter—often very much stronger than our present knowledge would seem to warrant. It is this feeling that prompts the present attempt to analyze why different investigators may logically and reasonably reach different conclusions on this question.

II. Alternative Decision Environments

Apart from errors in logic there are two main reasons why people come to, or appear to come to, different conclusions with respect to the same problem; different interpretations of significant concepts, or because they start from different premises. We shall leave until later the matter of semantics. The matter of premises or assumptions is far from simple in this connection. What is involved, often implicitly, is not a difference in a single assumption, or a single set of assumptions of the *same* kind, but different premises and views of the problem that come under a variety of headings. Indeed, the word assumptions or premises may be misleading in this connection, and therefore I shall use the notion of a "decision environment" to indicate what I have in mind. The following schematic outline indicates what I mean by a decision environment, and the discussion that follows suggests its relevance to the investment decision problem.

Schematic Outline of the Problem

A. *The Situation or Situation Class*
B. *The Decision Environment*

Normative
Aspects

1. Social objective or objectives
   (a) General statement of the objective(s)
   (b) Side conditions or constraints on the objective or its components
   (c) Means of evaluating components of the objective(s)
2. Values, restraints, and views, regarding the use of instruments to achieve the objective(s)
3. Time commitment and conditions connected with the time elements

Economic
Aspects

1. Target variables through which one judges the objective and its furtherance
2. View of the economic system
   (a) Equation system
   (b) Characteristics of the behavior equations
   (c) Assessment of the value of the parameters
3. Costs, benefits, and effects of direct (and permissible) instruments

C. *Policy*

The outline suggests the main elements that may be involved in an investment policy. The specific economic situation that the country finds itself in is, of course, a crucial factor. That is to say, it would be foolish to make a specific investment allocation without taking into account the specific facts at the time the decision is made. On a higher level of abstraction we would consider a class of situations that a country might find itself in, and attempt to establish investment criteria for that class. But the point of this paper is that a knowledge of the situation is not enough to determine an investment decision, nor is a knowledge of the characteristics of the situation class sufficient to determine investment criteria. Other matters are vitally involved, and it is these other matters that I refer to as the decision environment. In a short paper one cannot be exhaustive. The points listed in the outline above are intended only to be suggestive. However, they are probably sufficient to show why reasonable and logical men who agree on the situation class might very well disagree on investment policies. But we should not jump to any conclusions at this stage. There is more to the problem than simply the fact that different individuals may differ with respect to the decision environment.

The decision environment can be divided into two parts: A normative aspect, and an economic one. The division is far from perfect, and we may argue about its exact boundary, but it will do for our purposes. One aspect of the decision environment depends on norms, aims, values, and so on. It depends on the social goals and value of the society. To that extent it is normative rather than objective or scientific. On the other hand, the economic aspect depends on our view of how the economy operates. If economies were a completed science, and all the necessary facts were available, then we might all agree on the economic aspect, although we might still differ on the normative aspect.

1. Consider the problem of choosing the development objective. There are a large number of possible objectives. But the problem is also complicated by the fact that the statement of such objectives will have a number of dimensions. For example we may consider maximizing the aggregate output stream, or the aggregate *per capita* income stream or the aggregate *per capita* consumption stream, or the average length of life, etc. But statements such as these are usually incomplete. One problem is the treatment of time. In other words, if we consider the maximization of the aggregate output stream, the question arises over what period of time it is to be maximized. Usually, we conceive of some discounting procedure and attempt to maximize the present value of the output stream. In any event something has to be said in the statement of the objective as to how the time dimension is to be handled.

Another complicating feature lies in the fact that the variable to be maximized is rarely to be considered by itself in the absence of all other considerations. In other words, what we usually ask to do is to maximize some variable subject to a number of stated constraints. Thus we might attempt to maximize the present value of the output stream subject to the constraint that the income distribution is not worsened in the process.

The objective may have more than one component (or variable) that is to be optimized. In that event some way of assessing the relative importance of different components has to be determined. Clearly, economists, as well as citizens, might differ on the appropriate objectives for development.

2. Development is not an ultimate objective that supersedes all other considerations. Not all possible means to achieve given ends are legitimate.

We shall see that the constraints that we impose on the means that we can employ may affect our investment policy.

What is involved here is in part the age old question between agenda and non-agenda. That is to say, with respect to what variables are we to assume that the government or the state can interfere and control and what variables are we to assume are determined by the freely chosen actions and activities of the individuals involved. We shall also see that these sets of questions are in part related to our view of the development processes.

This point may perhaps best be indicated by a few examples. We may assume, for example, that the size of the population is determined entirely from within the system. Or we may assume that the population size can somehow be controlled by governmental action and that therefore it is a variable whose value is determined exogenously. Another possibility is that the level of consumption of population is determined within the system. Of we may assume that it is determined in part socially through a system of taxes and subsidies. Similarly we may perhaps argue that the rate of saving is determined by individual action or that it is determined by government interference. In general we can see that with respect to many variables we can make either an assumption of control or an assumption of lack of control. It will turn out that in some instances, *but not all,* we get different results depending on which set of assumptions we make.

3. The time element enters the problem in a variety of ways. At the extremes we might consider a single, once and for all investment decision apart from any other decision, as against an investment policy to cover an infinite series of investment decisions. We shall see that there are cases where it does make a distinct difference whether the decision or criterion to be applied is with respect to an isolated case, or part of a series of decisions.

4. If the social objective is stated in broad terms then there arises the problem of interpreting the objective in terms of one or more economic variables. For example, if our objective is to maximize the "standard of living" of the populace, how is this to be interpreted in economic terms? For example, how is leisure to be valued in such circumstances? We shall not go into detail in this matter, but clearly there are great possibilities for differences of opinion in this regard.

5. Really significant differences may arise with respect to our view of the development process. What will be the train of consequences that will result from a given investment allocation? The theory of economic growth is not at present in such a state that all would readily agree on this matter. The number of possible dynamical systems that we could invent is certainly very large. Given different views of economic development processes we may (but need not always) arrive at different investment criteria. We will see that whether or not different development theories lead to different criteria will depend, in part, on the other components of the decision environment.

6. The employment of direct instruments, for example, the attempt by the state to determine directly the rate of savings, or the birth rate, is usually not costless, although such costs are often ignored in discussions. Economists may legitimately differ on the costs and consequences of direct instruments, even in those cases where the normative aspects of the deci-

sion environment permits their use. The importance of this aspect will become clearer as we proceed.

There are an infinite number of decision environments that are possible. Obviously, it would be too tedious and time consuming to consider one by one all the possible decision environments that can be obtained by varying slightly its components. As a result we shall limit ourselves to examining only a few possibilities, picked in part because they help to illustrate some interesting points.

We will find that there does not exist a one-to-one correspondence between the alternative combinations of objectives, theories, socially determined parameters, etc., and the allocation criteria that can be deduced from them. Rather, we shall see that there are many-to-one correspondences. Namely, there are sets of combinations which lead to different criteria. That is to say we can outline a set of objectives, theories, and social constraints, and so on, for which a given allocation criteria may be correct for each of the combinations within the set. But there is more than one such set, and as a consequence there is more than one "reasonable" allocation criterion. However, the fact that there are often a number of decision environments consistent with a given criterion may sometimes have given the impression that the criterion is universally (or almost universally) applicable.

III. The Investment Allocation Problem

Before we proceed any further it is well to indicate the exact nature of the problem we have in mind. We begin with a given decision environment. Next, we assume that there is a given investment fund available, and that some central agency is in a position to influence or determine the allocation strategy. We differentiate between the allocation strategy and the mechanism of allocation. These are really two separate matters, although they are in some cases related to each other. For present purposes we are concerned only with allocation strategies and not with the question of the optimal mechanism under which to carry out the appropriate strategy. Thus we are not concerned with whether the government actually makes the allocations, or whether these are made through the mechanism of private enterprisers operating on their own, or operating under a system of subsidies and taxes, etc.

The given investment fund available at the outset can be allocated among a number of industries or uses. The two main aspects of the allocation problem solved simultaneously, in practice, are (1) the allocation between industries and (2) the allocation among techniques. Any concrete allocation must involve choosing the technique while one chooses simultaneously the industry. But to simplify the discussion we shall assume, except where we specifically indicate otherwise, that the allocation is to be made among industries. That is, we assume that for each industry the technique of production is given, unless otherwise stated.[1]

<hr/>

[1]We can get around this problem by defining "industry" in such a way so that the production of a commodity with a different technique implies a different industry. The reader may substitute this interpretation for the one in the text if he wishes.

Now we have to distinguish between an "allocation plan" and an "allocation." By an allocation plan we have in mind any specific allocation of the investment fund among the industries. Thus if A is an allocation plan, we may write $a_1, \ldots a_k$ as the details of this allocation plan. In other words, a_i denotes the amount of the investment fund that is to be used for the addition of capital in the ith industry. We view a_i as a specific allocation and A as an allocation Plan. There are, of course, innumerable allocation plans that are possible and our problem is to pick that allocation plan which most meets the objective contained in the decision environment. The general allocation problem is to find a criterion or principle (i.e., a strategy) by which to order or rank alternative allocation plans. Usually the allocation plans are in themselves of so complex a nature, or their consequences taken as a whole are so complex, that it is not possible to rank alternative plans directly. An alternative (and usual) procedure is to find a means of evaluating the consequences, for example, the income stream, of a specific allocation. By comparing the consequences of alternative allocations, and by shifting units of investment from one allocation to another until the consequences are equated at the margin an optimum is obtained. In this manner the ranking of allocation plans is achieved indirectly.

More specifically, the usual scheme is to assume that there is a specific consequence that follows from a specific allocation. Let us write c_i for the consequence that follows from the allocation a_i. Once we know the set of consequences c_i, for all i, and once we are able to tell what happens when we shift a small amount of investment from industry i to industry j, or *vice versa*, we are then able to apply the well known equi-marginal principle in order to obtain a maximum.[2] But it is important to observe that this really does not tell us very much about the solution of the problem in any concrete situation. What it does do is merely suggest some of the questions that have to be answered in order to approach a solution. For example, (1) What are the consequences to be considered for any specific allocation? (2) How are these consequences generated by the economic system as a whole? That is to say, how do we visualize the process that generates the stream of consequences resulting from a specific allocation? (3) Are the consequences unique and unalterable by social action or can they be changed, to some extent, by interference of a social agency? (4) For any given allocation what is the variety and range of consequences and how are these consequences related to each other? etc.

The time element enters the problem in several significant ways. We have already alluded to the fact that the time factor may enter implicitly or explicitly in the determination of the development objective. One consequence of this is that we have to devise means by which to judge alter-

[2] At no point should we argue against the applicability of the equimarginal principle, or some variant thereof. The appropriateness of the calculus to maximum problems is not in question. Even in those cases where it appears that the marginal productivity criterion is not applicable, we should not argue against the "marginal" aspect of the criterion. The argument rather is always to be understood to be with respect to the content of the criterion and not the application of the marginal concept as such. The marginal concept may be said to be contentless. Economists' arguments should not be about the mathematics of maximization.

nate output streams; for example, through a discounting technique, that enables us to evaluate alternate streams in terms of their present values.

But the time element enters the picture in a more fundamental sense. There is a time aspect to our view of the allocation problem. Namely, are we to be concerned with a single allocation plan or a sequence of them? That is, the determination of the allocation plan for one year may be very different, if we determine it as a once-and-for-all matter, apart from future plan, or if we determine it in connection with a series of future plans. In other words, the strategy for a single year need not be the same as the strategy for that year when we are simultaneously considering the strategy for *n* years.

Now, the time elements probably determine the extent to which the indirect effects of an allocation plan should be taken into account. It is likely that the greater the time period that is considered the more significant are the indirect aspects of the problem, and the less applicable are the *ceteris paribus* assumptions. But the longer the series of allocation decisions to be made, the greater the possibility of taking into account and influencing some of the indirect effects.

We now state in a few words the crux of our analysis. We distinguish between the *direct* and *indirect* consequences that we attribute to specific allocations. By a direct consequence we have in mind the increase in the output stream in a given industry that results from the allocation of investment to that industry. The indirect consequences are all of the other effects that may be attributed to this allocation, either by itself or in connection with the rest of a specified allocation plan, or series of plans. The heart of the matter is whether the indirect consequences are significant for development purposes. The differences between the few models that we shall elaborate, and the allocation criteria appropriate to them, and between a host of other possible models, will rest almost entirely on the extent to which the indirect consequences of given allocation are taken into account.

To elaborate this idea, we might specify briefly some of the indirect consequences that come to mind. The allocation plan may affect (1) the future investment as well as the future output stream. (2) It may affect the propensities to consume and the propensities to save. (3) The allocation plan and the accumulation of capital that results thereby, may change the environment in which work takes place and in this way may possibly affect, (a) intensity of effort, (b) the energy of the work force, (c) the degree to which the labour force is willing to adhere to work discipline, (d) the degree to which they develop feather bedding and innovation-retarding practices, (e) the nature of work morale, (f) the degree of economic and social mobility, and a host of other similar factors. (4) The allocation, by affecting the structure of capital, will affect the productivity of the labour force from the point of view of establishing a new relationship between the capital structure and the skill structure of the work force. (5) Finally, the allocation plan, and its consequent capital accumulation, may affect the social and cultural environment under which the economy operates, and in turn affect various aspects of the quality of the population. We shall elaborate on some of these matters as we proceed.

IV. Some Alternative Models Considered

If there were no space and time limitations, then we might consider, one by one, a large number of decision environments. But in view of such limitations a rather brief characterization and comparison of only a few decision environments will have to suffice. We shall consider two for which the social marginal productivity criterion is correct, and then sketch one environment for which the social marginal productivity criterion does not apply. Finally we shall discuss some of the critical elements that would determine the applicability of social marginal productivity or other criteria.

Model I—A neo-classical type model. For our first decision environment we shall assume: (1) that the objective of development is to maximize the present value of the *aggregate* output stream; and (2) that there exists some acceptable discounting procedure, and discount rate.

The theory we have in mind for this particular decision environment is that which comes closest to the static, conventional, micro-economic (textbook variety) model of the economic process. We assume the existence of factors of production, human and non-human, which form the stock of potential inputs. These inputs are combined in the production process in order to yield the stream of outputs. Investment, in this model, is defined as the net addition to the stock of nonhuman inputs. It is further assumed that during the time period involved the quality, size, and nature of the work force remains constant.

The consequence of investment, in this case, is simply, and only, to add to the stock of capital goods. The allocation problem here is reduced to a comparison of those income streams that result as a consequence of alternate allocation plans, and to the choice of a strategy that leads to that allocation plan whose output stream has a present value that is equal to or greater than that of all alternative allocation plans. The conventional marginal productivity principle is clearly effective here. The allocation of funds to a given industry results in an increase in the present value of that output stream. At the margin one can determine the present value of the output stream that results from the marginal input of investment in that industry. By comparing the marginal productivities thus defined, that is, the addition to the present value of the output stream that results from the application of a marginal increment to the capital stock, and allocating the capital fund so that the marginal productivities are equal for all industries, we maximize the addition to the output stream.

In this case only the *direct* consequences of any specific allocation are taken into account. Note the assumption that the total consequences of an allocation plan are no larger than the sum of direct consequences of each of the specific allocations. That is to say, there are no social economies or social diseconomies that enter the picture. The marginal productivity of an allocation and the *social* marginal productivity of that allocation are one and the same thing in this particular case. However, this is not always the situation, and we must allow for those instances.

It is not altogether clear from the literature how the word "social" in "social marginal productivity" is to be interpreted. There are at least two meanings that we could attach to the adjective "social." (1) We can assume that the marginal product of an allocation has a different social valuation than its individual private valuation. This may be because of effects of the production activity which are not taken into account in determining private costs and prices. The usual examples are such things as smoke nuisances, noise, etc. There exist in production processes costs which, because of their nature, are not borne privately. Likewise there may be social benefits of the same nature.

The other meaning that may be attached to the adjective "social," in this context, is that the output of the allocation plan is not the same as the sum of the outputs of each of the individual allocations, when they are considered apart from the other allocations that make up the allocation plan. This involves the well-known complementarities of production between industries.

Assuming that we add into our evaluation of the marginal product the differences between the social valuation and the private valuation we then obtain the application of the well-known social marginal productivity criterion. It is to be observed that in the first case it is quite simple to add the difference between the social and the private values of the marginal product since these are applied to the specific allocation themselves, apart from the other allocations that occur within the investment plan, while, in the second case, it is much more difficult because we cannot know the social valuation for a given allocation without knowing the rest of the investment plan. That is to say, for every alternative investment plan, here exists an alternative social valuation of the particular allocation under consideration.

The important consideration for our purposes is that it is assumed that the social valuation of a specific allocation depends only on differences between social and private costs, social and private benefits, and on the complementaries of production. Notice that the social valuations of the results of investment do not depend, in this model, on the effects of the allocation plan on the size, nature, quality, or desires of the work force, and populace as such. It is this last aspect that will differentiate, in great part, this decision environment from the one that we shall consider below under model 3.

Model 2—Neo-classical model—per capita output maximized. The decision environment we now consider is exactly the same as the one above with the sole exception that the objective of development is to maximize the present value of the *per capita* output stream rather than the present value of the aggregate output stream. It turns out that the result of this case is exactly the same as in the decision environment considered above. This is due to the fact that changes in population and the work force are independent of the allocation plan. Similarly, it follows that any objective involving the population, or some property, characteristic, or a quality of the population, will lead to the same allocation criterion as above as long as such characteristics and properties are assumed to be independent of the allocation plan.

Model 3—The strong interdependence model. Under this heading we outline a decision environment very different from the ones considered previously.

The objective is the same as in model 2—namely, the maximization of the present value of the *per capita* output stream. However, the vision of the economic process is very different in this case.

The crucial difference here is that we assume that the allocation plan in the first period will affect a number of variables that were assumed to be independent in the previous models. To be specific we assume that the allocation plan in period one affects in a significant way the following aspects in subsequent periods:

1. The propensity to consume in subsequent periods.
2. The inducement to invest in subsequent periods.
3. The size of the population and labour force in subsequent periods.
4. The quality of the work force in subsequent periods. To be specific, the energy level of the work force, its morale, its responsiveness to discipline, etc. Last but not least, the educational and skill level of the work force.

Once we insert into our decision environment the interdependence of the investment plan in one period and the nature of the inputs in subsequent periods then we have a completely different situation from that in the models considered above. To see this consider for a moment the possibility that arises from the fact that population growth is no longer exogenously determined. For example, allocation plan A may maximize the present value of the aggregate output stream but induce a large rate of population growth, while allocation plan B may lead to a smaller increase in the aggregate output stream but induce a more than proportionately smaller increase in population growth. Allocation plan B will then be preferred to A if our objective is to maximize *per capita* output. The marginal productivity criterion, as this is usually defined, no longer suffice under such circumstances.

At this juncture a semantic note is in order. The concept of productivity is rarely, if ever, considered to be identical with the totality of consequences that follows from a given allocation plan. Rather, by the productivity of a given set of inputs we usually mean the flow of outputs that results directly from the combination of the inputs. It does not take into account other consequences that are not directly related to the flow of outputs. That is to say, it is rarely, if ever, suggested that the concept of productivity should also include the behaviour of the factors of production in their capacities as consumers, investors, procreators, and so on. Clearly this is in accordance with the ordinary and common sense usage of the word "product" and "productivity." Thus it follows that when the aggregate product stream, in the sense just indicated, is not the sole consideration then an allocation criterion that involves only the product stream, (or productivity), such as the marginal productivity criterion, cannot be universally applicable.

The correct allocation criterion under decision environment 3 is much more difficult to determine and state than under the others. Here we have to look for that allocation plan that leads to a time pattern of capital growth *per capita,* and of growth in the quality of the population, again *per capita,* so that the present value of the output stream *per capita* is maximized. There are two streams that are of primary importance. First, we have to consider the regular re-investment stream. That is to say, we have to take into account the extent to which the allocation plan affects the investment rates and amounts, on a *per capita* basis, in the future. Second, we have to consider what might be called the human re-investment stream. That is to say, we have to take into account the extent to which the consumption patterns, as well as the investment patterns, that are consequences of the allocation plan, affect the quality of the population, and in turn, the productive capacity of the population—all of these in *per capita* terms. For present purposes we need not attempt to spell out the exact criterion applicable to this decision environment. It should be clear from the foregoing that many more considerations are involved here than are usually taken into account in the application of the marginal productivity criterion. Certainly the marginal productivity criterion, as defined here, will not always give the correct result under these circumstances.

However, the semantic aspect of the debate must not be lost sight of. That is to say, part of the argument may have to do with differences in the way we use words. For example, a great deal depends on how we interpret the word "social" in the social marginal productivity criterion. If by social rather than private marginal productivity valuations we are to understand the inclusion of all the factors that we have considered in the last decision environment then, of course, the social marginal productivity criterion will always give the right result. But in this case are we not stretching the meaning and interpretation of the word "social"? It seems to me that the only thing that "social" suggests is the fact that there may be some valuations which for society as a whole are different from the valuations as determined by private decision making entities. All that the adjective "social" really tells us is to be on guard and not accept the private valuations of productivity. It does not tell us, nor does it spell out, what are the factors to be taken into account in the determination of social valuations rather than the private valuations. Clearly, on this latter aspect, there may be legitimate differences of opinion. Problems arise because such differences are often not made explicit.

V. Review of Critical Elements

Semantic illusions may lead us to believe that we differ on allocation criteria when in fact we are merely using words differently. But apart from such semantic tangles the differences may be real ones when they are based on different decision environments. However, we have seen that different decision environments are in themselves not always sufficient to lead to different investment criteria. In other words, there is not a one-to-one correspondence between decision environments and appropriate allocation criteria. Rather, there are many decision environments for which the same allocation criterion may be applicable. (It is this feature that may be responsible, in part, for the belief in the near universality of some criteria.) For example, decision model 1 and 2 considered above implied the same allocation criterion and policy although the objectives in these decision environments were different. The reason for this was that the difference in the objectives was connected with a variable (population) that was assumed to be exogenous to the system and hence could not be affected by the investment plan.

Whether or not different decision environments lead to different allocation criteria and policies will depend, in great part, on the interaction between four broad factors: (1) the significance of the indirect consequences of the allocation plan (or plans), (2) the possibilities and costs of using direct social instruments (e.g., government action) to determine the values of variables or parameters, (3) the differences in the view of the economic development process (i.e., in different development theories), and (4) differences in objectives.

(a) *Indirect consequences of allocations and direct social instruments.* Items (1) and (2) above are very closely connected because the operation of the second may nullify the significance of the first. That is, if the indirect consequence of an allocation plan is important, but if the values of the variables or parameters so affected can be altered by the use of direct social instruments which are costless, then the indirect consequences can always be counteracted. For example, compare models 2 and 3 in the previous section. The objectives in both models are the same, but in model 3 some of the indirect consequences of the allocation plan are assumed to be important, and to affect variables (population size, investment rate, etc.) that are assumed to be exogenous to the system in model 2. The two models do imply different investment criteria and policies. But if we had assumed (as part of the decision environment) with respect to model 3 that the government could by direct action determine the size of the population, the quality of the labour force, the rate of investment, and so on, and if the costs of doing so were trivial, then the same investment criteria and policies would have been applicable in both cases. But, of course, some may believe that the use of direct social instruments for some of these purposes may not be possible, or that they should not be used for ideological reasons, or if possible and permissible they may be costlier than taking into account the indirect consequences of the allocation plan. In any event we see that different views about the possibility and efficacy of various types of potential government activities, and their costs, may logically lead to different views about appropriate allocation policies.

(b) *The time aspects of the decision environment.* Whether or not the indirect consequences of an allocation plan (or series of plans) are significant may depend on the time horizon and time commitment aspects of the decision environment. Once again compare models 2 and 3. If the time horizon is very short, say only five years rather than several generations, then the indirect consequences considered in model 3 may be trivial, and the appropriate investment policies may be the same for the two models. That is, it may take some time for the indirect consequences to take hold, so to speak.

Even more important is likely to be the question of the time commitment of the investment policy. For example, consider the possible difference between a one-shot-only investment policy versus one for a whole series of potential investment plans for, say, twenty years. The indirect consequences of a single plan may turn out to be trivial and may perhaps best be ignored. In this case the policies for models 2 and 3 can be the same. But the indirect consequences of a series of investment plans over

a twenty year period may be considerable. In this latter case the investment criteria and policies applicable for the two models may be very
different indeed. Also, the appropriate investment plan for a given year
that is looked upon as a one-shot-only affair, without reference to future
investment plans, may be very different from the appropriate investment
plan that is part of an integrated series.

The importance of the indirect consequences of an allocation plan is
determined, in part, by our views of the development process, which, in
turn, is distinguished by the nature and importance of the variables that
we assume to be endogenous to such a process. We now consider briefly
the treatment of some of these matters.

(c) *Population.* The question of how to treat the population aspect in
our decision environment enters in at least two different important respects. If the objective is to maximize some *per capita* variable then the
growth of population enters in a significant sense since it determines the
denominator of the ratio that determines the *per capita* value. The second
sense in which population may enter the problem is that the qualities of
the population (in the sense of acquired qualities such as learned skills,
education, health, and so on) may change over time and affect some of
the target variables. For example, the energy and skills of the population
may change over time as a consequence of the pattern of investment, and
as a result change the productive capacity of the population.

With respect to population size the usual argument revolves around the
fact that fertility patterns of various groups in a population may depend
on the roles, especially social, familial, and economic roles, that the individuals composing these groups generally play. For example, urban populations often have different fertility rates than rural populations, white
collar groups often have different fertility rates than either rural agricultural groups, or urban manual labourers, and so on. Since the pattern of
investment allocation is likely to involve both the demand and supply of
the labour, and in turn influence the economic and social role patterns, and
the distribution of role patterns, it may in this way also influence the consequent fertility rates of the population. It is through such indirect means
that the allocation plan may have an effect on population size and population growth.

More directly the allocation plan may determine both the aggregate output and the level of consumption which in turn may, to a certain extent,
influence mortality rates, and therefore the rates of population growth.
The main point to be considered here is that there is little question but
that we can visualize circumstances in which a connection exists between
the allocation plan (or series of plans) and the rate of population growth.

(d) *Investment and reinvestment rates.* In considering the effects of an
allocation plan (or plans) we must take into account not only the addition to the output stream that results from the allocation plan (or plans)
but also their possible influence on the rates of savings and investment in
the future periods. As before the importance of this element depends on
whether we look upon the rate of savings and investment as determined
exogenously or whether it is determined in part by the social and economic
environment created by the sequence of allocation plans. If it is the latter,
then we arrive at a different conclusion about investment policy, one that

is closer to that considered under model 3 than if it is the former. On *a priori* grounds it would appear that rates of savings and investment depend on income distribution and perhaps on the role composition of the population, and on the social and cultural environment in which the population finds itself. To think of it in terms of extremes the pattern of savings of peasants is likely to be very different from that of socially mobile white collar workers. Also, we might expect that the environment and the role composition of the population may be determined by the allocation plans that take place. As before a lot depends on whether or not we believe the savings and investment rates can be determined by direct governmental action, or the use of other social instruments, and also whether such determination is or is not costless.

(e) *The possible relation of social objectives to the development theory.* A point well worth commenting upon, but one which is quite different from our previous considerations, is the possibility that the objective of development may depend on both the development theory we have in mind and the possibilities of development given the investment fund available. For example, if we believe in the *critical minimum effort thesis* that the author has developed elsewhere[3] then we might take the view that if an investment fund is too small then there may not be any allocation that will lead to sustained development. In this case the objective may be made to depend on whether or not sustained development is possible. If the investment fund is such that a sustained development is a possibility then we might allocate the investment fund in accordance with policies that lead to high rate of reinvestment in the near future, and as a consequence not raise the consumption of the population in the early periods to the level that it might have achieved without the higher investment rate. On the other hand, if the investment fund is too small to generate sustained development, then we may decide that since development is not of the question in any event, that we should concentrate our efforts on maximizing the consumption level of the population even if in the long run this leads eventually to a return to the previous rate of consumption. We shall not elaborate on this aspect of the problem but merely point to the fact that appropriate investment policies may depend, under some circumstances, on criteria other than the maximization of the output stream.

(f) *Population and labour force qualities.* A second variable (or set of variables) of significance that is usually not considered in static or short run economic analysis is the changes in the quality of the population, in the resulting labour force, and in all of the characteristics and properties that we may associate with the notion of acquired population qualities. We cannot take up every aspect that might come under this global concept, but an enumeration of a few might indicate what we have in mind. Some of the qualities that may be of significance for productive purposes are the energy of the population, the acquired skills of the population, the flexibility of the labour force, the economic and social mobility of the population, and the general responsiveness of the population to economic incentives, and so on. The question that arises is whether changes in these

[3]H. Leibenstein. *Economic Backwardness and Economic Growth,* John Wiley and Sons, New York, Chapter 8.

properties are independent of the allocation plans that occur, and hence of the investment policies that determine them. It must be clear that we can think of some possibilities under which the allocation plans would affect the qualities of the population. For example, the nature and variety of consumption goods, which are, in part, determined by the allocation plans, will in turn have their influence on the energy level of the population. Also, expenditures on such things as education and educational facilities will in part determine the acquired skills of the population, and their productive capacities. Similarly, the environment created by a series of allocation plans, may, in part, determine the psychological attitudes of the population as well as their flexibility, mobility, and responsiveness to economic incentives.

A central aspect of the view just presented is that the qualities considered are entirely acquired rather than innate. They are characteristics that are determined by the social and economic environment under which the population lives, and in part, determined by the expenditure patterns of the population as such. But the expenditure patterns, both of an investment and consumption kind, may be determined in part by the nature of the allocation plans that take place. Thus we see that an obvious relationship between these elements and investment policy exists. Whether this relationship is really significant or not may be a debatable matter. But clearly our view of what investment policy is appropriate will depend on whether the elements that we have just considered are looked upon as endogenous or exogenous variables within our theory.

In this general connection we may look at model 3 as one that is consistent with the view that economic development involves not only growth in the capital stock, looked at in terms of the aggregate valuation of the physical non-human assets of the economy, but also that it depends on the transformation of the labour force and population as such. That is to say, the nature of industrial populations, the stimuli to which they respond, their energy, the motivations that lie behind their behaviour, as well as the things that they value and the skills that they possess, are very different from that of the typical peasant population that forms so large a part of the population in the typical underdeveloped area. If this type of transformation is looked upon as the paramount phenomenon of development then it would seem to follow that model 3 is more appropriate than the others considered.

On the other hand, if we view the process of development as something that does not affect in any marked degree the population as such, then of course model 1 and 2 may be adequate. It is to be noted, of course, that we may accept the view about the importance of the transformation of the population as part of the process of development and yet not accept the appropriateness of model 3. This would be correct if we believed that such a transformation occurs independently of the allocation plans in the initial and subsequent periods. In other words even if we accept the view that the transformation of the acquired qualities of the population is of paramount importance, we may believe that such a transformation is entirely socially (or governmentally) determinable. That is to say, it can be achieved directly without in any way involving the investment plans within any period, or it may be achieved through exogenous factors or influences that are primarily functions of time but which in no way are related to the investment plans period by period. Which view is correct is the subject for another occasion. Here we merely suggest that these are some of the issues that may be at the heart of the debate over appropriate investment allocation policies.

15. Notes on the Theory of the "Big Push"

P. N. Rosenstein-Rodan*

I. Methodology

"There is a minimum level of resources that must be devoted to . . . a development program if it is to have any chance of success. Launching a country into self-sustaining growth is a little like getting an airplane off the ground. There is a critical ground speed which must be passed before the craft can become airborne. . . ."[1] Proceeding "bit by bit" will not add up in its effects to the sum total of the single bits. A minimum quantum of investment is a necessary, though not sufficient, condition of success. This, in a nutshell, is the contention of the theory of the big push.

This theory seems to contradict the conclusions of the traditional static equilibrium theory and to reverse its famous motto, *natura non facit saltum*. It does so for three reasons. First, it is based on a set of more realistic assumptions of certain indivisibilities and "non-appropriabilities" in the production functions even on the level of static equilibrium theory. These indivisibilities give rise to increasing returns and to technological external economies. Second, in dealing with problems of growth this theory examines the path towards equilibrium, not the conditions at a point of equilibrium only. At a point of static equilibrium net investment is zero. The theory of growth is very largely a theory of investment. Moreover, the allocation of investment—unlike the allocation of given stocks of consumer goods (equilibrium of consumption), or of producers' goods (equilibrium of production)—necessarily occurs in an imperfect market, that is, a market on which prices do not signal all the information required for an optimum solution.[2] Given an imperfect investment market, pecuniary external economies have the same effect on the theory of growth as technological external economies. They are a cause of a possible divergence between the private and the social marginal net product.[3] Since pecuniary,

*From *Economic Development for Latin America,* edited by H. S. Ellis, IEA Proceedings (London: Macmillan & Company Ltd., 1951), pp. 57–66. Reprinted with the permission of Dr. P. N. Rosenstein-Rodan, The International Economic Association, St. Martin's Press Inc., The Macmillan Company of Canada, Ltd., and Macmillan & Company, Ltd. The author is Professor of Economics, Center for International Studies, Massachusetts Institute of Technology.

[1]Massachusetts Institute of Technology, Center for International Studies, *The Objectives of United States Economic Assistance Programs* (Washington, 1957, p. 70.
[2]See P. N. Rosenstein-Rodan, "Programming in Theory and in Italian Practice," in Massachusetts Institute of Technology, Center for International Studies, *Investment Criteria and Economic Growth* (Cambridge, Massachusetts, 1955).
[3]T. Scitovsky, "Two Concepts of External Economies," *Journal of Political Economy,* April 1954.

unlike technological, external economies are all-pervading and frequent, the price mechanism does not necessarily put the economy on an optimum path. Therefore, additional signalling devices apart from market prices are required.[4] Many economists, including the author, believe that these additional signals can be provided by programming. Third, in addition to the risk phenomena and imperfections characterizing the investment equilibrium, markets in under-developed countries are even more imperfect than in developed countries. The price mechanism in such imperfect markets does not provide the signals which guide a perfectly competitive economy towards an optimum position.

II. Terminology

Indivisibilities and external economies are portmanteau expressions which are loosely used. Fortunately, recent publications have clarified the concepts.[5] Not all indivisibilities give rise to external economies and not all external economies are due to indivisibilities. Some external economies are due to the impossibility of appropriating a factor—even if divisible. Pecuniary external economies are an almost superfluous concept in static equilibrium theory. They refer to those inter-industry relations which are due to the fact that production functions of different industries are not linear[6] and homogeneous. Their true function in the theory of static

[4]Futures markets and futures prices could perhaps provide such signalling devices. It is a moot point whether perfect futures markets for all goods can exist. The author's suspicion (without proof) is that they cannot exist for the same reasons for which perfect foresight is impossible. In reality they certainly do not exist.

"In an economy in which economic decisions are decentralized, a system of communications is needed to enable each person who makes economic decisions to learn about the economic decisions of others and co-ordinate his decisions with theirs. In the market economy, prices are the signalling device that informs each person of other people's economic decisions; and the merit of perfect competition is that it would cause prices to transmit information reliably and people to respond to this information properly. Market prices, however, reflect the economic situation as it is and not as it will be. For this reason, they are more useful for co-ordinating current production decisions, which are immediately effective and guided by short-run considerations, than they are for co-ordinating investment decisions which have a delayed effect and—looking ahead to a long future period —should be governed not by what the present economic situation is but by what the future economic situation is expected to be. The proper co-ordination of investment decisions, therefore, would require a signalling device to transmit information about present plans and future conditions as they are determined by present plans; and the pricing system fails to provide this." T. Scitovsky, *op. cit.* p. 150.

[5]See H. W. Arndt, "External Economics in Economic Growth," *Economic Record,* November 1955; T. Scitovsky, *op. cit.;* F. M. Bator, *Capital, Growth and Welfare: Essays on the Theory of Allocation,* a doctoral dissertation submitted at Massachusetts Institute of Technology, 1956, Part III; L. Lefeber, *External Economies and Transportation in the General Equilibrium System,* a doctoral dissertation submitted at Massachusetts Institute of Technology, 1957, Part I; M. Fleming, "External Economies and the Doctrine of Balanced Growth," *Economic Journal,* June 1955, confines his analysis largely to conditions of a static equilibrium.

[6]This is almost but not quite the same as saying that there are indivisibilities in the production functions. There can be continuous though non-linear production functions where, for instance, inputs and outputs are non-linearly linked. The decisive criterion is non-convexity of production possibility curves. In most cases that is due to indivisibilities.

equilibrium is to mark a place for a concept which will become important in the theory of growth. Technological external economies are rare in a static competitive economy with one important exception, the training of labour[7] and education. In the theory of growth, however, external economies abound. Given the inherent imperfection of the investment market, as well as imperfect knowledge and risks, pecuniary and technological external economies have a similarly disturbing effect on the path towards equilibrium. While the distinction between pecuniary and technological external economies becomes practically irrelevant in the theory of growth, three different kinds of indivisibilities and external economies may be distinguished.

First, there is indivisibility in the production function, especially indivisibility in the supply of social overhead capital (lumpiness of capital) which is discussed in Section III. Second, there is indivisibility of demand (complementarity of demand), discussed in Section IV. Third, there is indivisibility (kink) in the supply of saving, discussed in Section VI.

In one way the first indivisibility is fundamental. If it did not exist, the others would not arise. Linear homogeneous production functions are basic in this sense, but they are completely unrealistic. They imply no economies of scale or of agglomeration, no entrepreneurship, no phenomenon of minimum quantum or threshold, so that they threaten to obscure the nature of the economic process and the risks involved rather than throwing light on it. In reality there are indivisibilities in the production function. They create not only non-constant returns but also risks of investment and imperfect markets which give rise to the indivisibility (complementarity) of demand.

III. Indivisibility in the Production Function
(Lumpiness of Capital)

Indivisibilities of inputs, processes, or outputs give rise to increasing returns, that is, economies of scale, and may require a high optimum size of a firm. This is not a very important obstacle to development since with some exceptions (for instance in Central America) there is usually sufficient demand, even in small, poor countries, for at least one optimum scale firm in many industries. There may be room, however, only for one or a few firms with the obvious danger of monopolistic markets.

As Allyn Young pointed out, increasing returns accrue to a firm not only with the growth of its size but also with the growth of the industry and with the growth of the industrial system as a whole. Greater specialization and better use of resources become possible when growth helps to

[7]In a slave economy, investment in training slave workers may pay. In a non-slave economy in which mortgages on workers do not exist, a trained worker may contract at a higher wage rate with another firm which did not invest in his training. The supply of training facilities in a competitive economy will therefore be normally below optimum. The best way of training workers is probably on the job. Industrial workers in towns with many establishments and industries acquire skill by working, by talking to each other, exchanging experiences and changing jobs, much more quickly than isolated peasants. This fact alone, apart from better division of labour, is a source of increasing returns to the industrial system as a whole and a differential advantage of industrialization.

overcome indivisibilities generating pecuniary external economies. The range of increasing returns seems to be very wide indeed.[8]

Social overhead capital is the most important instance of indivisibility and hence of external economies on the supply side. Its services are indirectly productive and become available only after long gestation periods. Its most important products are investment opportunities created in other industries. Social overhead capital comprises all those basic industries like power, transport, or communications which must precede the more quickly yielding, directly productive investments and which constitute the framework or infrastructure and the overhead costs of the economy as a whole. Its installations are characterized by a sizeable initial lump and low variable costs. Since the minimum size in these basic industries is large, excess capacity will be unavoidable over the initial period in underdeveloped countries.[9] In addition, there is also an irreducible minimum industry mix of different public utilities, so that an under-developed country will have to invest between 30–40 per cent of its total investment in these channels. Since overall vision is required as well as a correct appraisal of future development, programming is undoubtedly required in this lumpy field. Normal market mechanisms will not provide an optimum supply.

Social overhead capital is characterized by four indivisibilities. First, it is indivisible (irreversible) in time. It must precede other directly productive investments. Second, its equipment has high minimum durability. Lesser durability is either technically impossible or much less efficient. For this and other reasons it is very lumpy. Third, it has long gestation periods. Fourth, an irreducible minimum social overhead capital industry mix is a condition for getting off the dead-end.

Because of these indivisibilities and because services of social overhead capital cannot be imported, a high initial investment in social overhead capital must either precede or be known to be certainly available in order to pave the way for additional more quickly yielding directly productive investments. This indivisibility of social overhead capital constitutes one of the main obstacles to development of under-developed countries.

IV. Indivisibility of Demand (Complementarity of Demand)

Relatively few investments are made in the small market of an underdeveloped country. If all investment projects were independent (which they are not) and if their number grew, the risk of each investment project

[8]The capital-output ratio in the United States has fallen over the last eighty years from around 4:1 to around 3:1, while income per head, wage-rates, and the relative importance of heavy industry were rising. This is due to technical progress (change in production functions), increasing returns on balance (increasing returns prevailing over decreasing returns), and to the rising demand for labour-intensive services characteristic of high-income economies. It is my conviction that increasing returns played a considerable part in it.

[9]We may distinguish in fact between the developmental social overhead capital which provides for a hoped for but uncertain future demand and the rehabilitation social overhead capital which caters to an unsatisfied demand of the past. The first with its excess capacity will necessarily have a big sectoral capital-output ratio (10–15:1); the second, through breaking bottlenecks, has a certain high indirect productivity and a much lower capital-output ratio.

would decline by simple actuarial rules. The lower marginal risk of each investment dose (or project) would thus constitute internal economies. In reality, however, various investment decisions are not independent. Investment projects have high risks because of uncertainty as to whether their products will find a market.

Let us restate our old example,[10] at first for a closed economy.[11] If a hundred workers who were previously in disguised unemployment[12] (so that the marginal productivity of their labour was equal to zero) in an underdeveloped country are put into a shoe factory, their wages will constitute additional income. If the newly employed workers spend all of their additional income on the shoes they produce, the shoe factory will find a market and will succeed. In fact, however, they will not spend all of their additional income on shoes. There is no easy solution of creating an additional market in this way.[13] The risk of not finding a market reduces the incentive to invest, and the shoe factory investment project will probably be abandoned. Let us vary the example. Instead of putting a hundred previously unemployed workers in one shoe factory, let us put ten thousand workers in one hundred factories and farms which between them will produce the bulk of the wage-goods on which the newly employed workers will spend their wages. What was not true in the case of one single shoe factory will become true for the complementary system of one hundred factories and farms. The new producers will be each other's customers and will verify Say's Law by creating an additional market. The complementarity of demand will reduce the risk of not finding a market. Reducing such interdependent risks naturally increases the incentive to invest.

If one unit of any wage-good could be produced as efficiently as many units, that is to say, if there were no indivisibilities in the production functions of wage-goods, a relatively small investment might suffice to produce a product mix which would satisfy, and create, the additional market. Indivisibilities make the minimum investment much larger.

The risk of any single investment in any one industry is increased by the fact that various goods are highly imperfect substitutes for each other in low income under-developed countries. The southwest corner of the indifference map shows very high degrees of convexity. Demand for most goods will therefore be highly inelastic. Low elasticities of demand make it much more difficult to fit supplies to demands. The difficulty of fitting demand to supply on a small scale constitutes a risk which is higher in a small than in a large and growing market. Complementarity of demand will reduce the marginal risk of growing and diversified investments but will be below a *minimum sensible* for small doses of investment. There is

[10]See P. N. Rosenstein-Rodan, "Problems of Industrialization of Eastern and South-Eastern Europe," *Economic Journal,* June-September 1943; R. Nurkse, *Problems of Capital Formation in Underdeveloped Countries* (Oxford, 1953).

[11]The assumption of a closed economy will be dropped in Section V.

[12]On the concept and measurement of disguised unemployment see P. N. Rosenstein-Rodan, *Notes on Disguised Unemployment,* Massachusetts Institute of Technology, Center for International Studies (Cambridge, Massachusetts, 1956), Part I.

[13]In an open economy the output of the shoe factory may replace former shoe imports, or may find export markets, although this too is uncertain. See Section V below.

therefore a minimum threshold at which the complementarity of demand manifests itself. The discontinuity in the complementarity of demand may therefore be called indivisibility of demand.

A minimum quantum of investment is required to produce the bulk of additional wage-goods on which additionally employed workers will spend their additional income. Unless it is probable that other investments will take place, many single investment projects may be too risky to be undertaken. The mobilization of sufficient investment to provide this minimum quantum is the first hurdle which under-developed countries must overcome, but it is not the only one. Even if saving and investment sufficient to provide a minimum quantum of wage-goods were forthcoming, the previous creation of a minimum quantum of social overhead capital constitutes a second hurdle which must be overcome. While the first minimum quantum of investment in wage-goods may amount to say $20 million, the minimum quantum of investment in social overhead capital may amount to $60 to $80 million. The effective minimum of total investment may thus amount to, and require a big push of, from $80 to $100 million.

V. International Trade Reduces the Size of the Minimum Push

Complementarity of demand was examined in Section IV above under the assumption of a closed economy. In an open economy a shoe factory may replace former imports or may be efficient enough to find export markets. The world market can be a substitute for the additional domestic market required in a closed economy. Can the world market provide enough continuity to obviate the need for a minimum quantum of investment? It is submitted that the mobility of products is in reality an imperfect substitute for the mobility of factors. International trade undoubtedly reduces the size of the minimum push required, so that not *all* the wage-goods need be produced in the developing country, but it does not eliminate it.

The great expansion of international trade in the nineteenth century led neither to an equalization nor even to a reduction in the inequality of factor rewards. Theoretically this fact may be due to three reasons:[1] first, transport costs as impediments to the mobility of factors; second, complete rather than partial specialization of production; and third, different production functions in different countries.

The fact that transport costs have been sharply reduced during the last 150 years should have led to a growing equalization of factor rewards. The increasing importance of partial, as opposed to complete, specialization of production should also have worked in this direction. The English Industrial Revolution may, indeed, have increased the share of complete specialization of production. In England during that period, export-gaining industries expanded more than import-saving industries. Nevertheless, subsequent industrial revolutions, for example, the industrial revolution in Germany, showed a greater expansion of import-saving than of export-

[1]See P. A. Samuelson, "International Trade and the Equalisation of Factor Prices," *Economic Journal,* June 1948, and "International Factor-Price Equalisation Once Again," *ibid.,* June 1949.

gaining production, although exact statistical information does not seem to exist.[15]

Therefore, the main explanation of why this tendency to a growing equalization of factor rewards did not materialize—why, in fact, labour rewards tended to become more unequal[16]—must rest on the assumption that production functions are different in various parts of the world. "The laws of nature may be the same everywhere, but the laws of nature and the economically relevant production function relating maximum output obtainable from specified concrete inputs are two quite different things. Effective knowledge ('know-how') is probably as important a variable in understanding economic history and geography as is specific factor endowment. . . . The 'effective' organization is different."[17] There is no doubt that differences in effectiveness of organization do exist in different countries and that effective knowledge cannot be acquired by reading a book or by editorial exhortation. It can be acquired, however, on the job! This possibility is a major source of increasing returns to the industrial system as a whole. Perhaps the most important yield of development is a cumulative increase in effective knowledge! The growth of international trade during the last 150 years has not reduced the inequality in this field.

We may conclude that international trade would not eliminate—although it would reduce—the indivisibility of demand, even if markets, other than the investment market, were more or less perfect. In reality, of course, markets are imperfect; and those in under-developed countries are probably more imperfect than those in the developed countries. International trade does much to reduce the danger of monopolies. It also effectively reduces the size of the minimum quantum of investment. But it does not dispense with the need for a big push.

VI. Indivisibility in the Supply of Savings

A high minimum quantum of investment requires a high volume of savings, which is difficult to achieve in low income, under-developed countries. There is a way out of this vicious circle. In the first stage when income is increased due to an increase in investment which mobilizes additional latent resources, mechanisms must be provided which assure that in the second stage the marginal rate of saving is very much higher than the average rate of saving. Adam Smith's dictum that frugality is a virtue and prodigality a vice has to be adapted to a situation of growing income. Economic history does not show that the English Industrial Revolution was preceded by a period of falling consumption. It only shows that the proportion saved from the increase in income was higher than the previous average rate of saving.

A zero (or very low) price elasticity of the supply of saving and a high income elasticity of saving thus constitute the third indivisibility.

[15]Much depends, of course, on the definition of the *same* or *similar* products in various countries.

[16]This was not due to a differentially higher increase in population in the under-developed countries. On the contrary, their increase in population was smaller than that of developed countries.

[17]P. A. Samuelson, *op. cit.*, (1948), p. 181.

These three indivisibilities and the external economies to which they give rise, plus the external economies of training labour, form the characteristic pattern of models of growth of under-developed countries.

VII. Psychological Indivisibility of the Development Drive

The economic factors discussed so far give only the necessary, but not the sufficient, conditions of growth. A big push seems to be required to jump over the economic obstacles[18] to development. There may be finally a phenomenon of indivisibility in the vigour and drive required for the successful development policy. Isolated and small efforts may not add up to a sufficient impact on growth. An atmosphere of development may only arise with a minimum speed or size of investment. Our knowledge of psychology is far too deficient to theorize about this phenomenon. This does not make it a less important factor. It may well constitute the difference between necessary and sufficient conditions for success. . . .

[18]The extent and relative importance of the three indivisibilities and external economies is greater in under-developed than in developed countries. The same applies to the degree of imperfect knowledge and of imperfect competition.

16a. Unbalanced Growth: An Espousal

Albert O. Hirschman[*]

Is Balance in Supply Required?

[Previously] . . . we criticized the idea that development must take place simultaneously in many activities to provide the element of "mutual support" that alone will make it possible to clear the market of the newly produced goods. Having discarded this "pure" theory of balanced growth we must still consider a far less rigorous version, one that insists that if growth is not to be stunted the various sectors of an economy will have to grow jointly in some (not necessarily identical) proportion; no sector should get too far out of line, not because of demand but because of supply of "structural" considerations. For instance, if secondary industry grows, the food and raw material input needed by the workers and the machines will go up; if some of these requirements are imported, then an increase in exports is necessary, etc., etc.

In this form, the balanced growth theory is essentially an exercise in retrospective comparative statics. If we look at an economy that has experienced growth at two different points in time, we will of course find that a great many parts of it have pushed ahead: industry and agriculture, capital goods and consumer goods industries, cars on the road and highway mileage—each at its own average annual rate of increase. But surely the individual components of the economy will not actually have grown at these rates throughout the period under review. Just as on the demand side the market can absorb "unbalanced" advances in output because of

*From *The Strategy of Economic Development* (New Haven: Yale University Press, 1958), pp. 62–65. The author is Professor of Economics, Columbia University.

cost-reducing innovations, new products, and import substitution, so we can have isolated forward thrusts on the supply side as inputs are redistributed among users through price changes, and at the cost of some temporary shortages and disequilibria in the balance of payments or elsewhere. In fact, development has of course proceeded in this way, with growth being communicated from the leading sectors of the economy to the followers, from one industry to another, from one firm to another. In other words, the balanced growth that is revealed by the two still photographs taken at two different points in time is the end result of a series of uneven advances of one sector followed by the catching-up of other sectors. If the catching-up overreaches its goal, as it often does, then the stage is set for further advances elsewhere. The advantage of this kind of seesaw advance over "balanced growth," where every activity expands perfectly in step with every other, is that it leaves considerable scope to *induced* investment decisions and therefore economizes our principal scarce resource, namely, genuine decision-making.

Classical economics, while not taking so positive a view of the imbalances of the growth process, at least was never particularly concerned about them because it relied on prices to signal, and on the profit motive to eliminate rapidly and reliably, any structural disequilibria that might arise in the course of growth. The critics of classical economics, on the other hand, have always pointed to cases in which these "market forces" would not act with adequate strength and speed. Having thus convinced themselves that the adjustment mechanism is beset with virtually insuperable obstacles, some of the critics naturally enough took the defeatist view that growth has to be balanced from the start or cannot take place at all.

This counsel of perfection is not only impractical but also uneconomical. We need not sacrifice the valuable development mechanisms brought into play by unbalanced growth, especially if we go beyond the overly narrow view of the adjustment process that has long dominated economic literature.

Tradition seems to require that economists argue forever about the question whether, in any disequilibrium situation, *market forces acting alone* are likely to restore equilibrium. Now this is certainly an interesting question. But as social scientists we surely must address ourselves also to the broader question: is the disequilibrium situation likely to be corrected at all, by market or nonmarket forces, or by both acting jointly? *It is our contention that nonmarket forces are not necessarily less "automatic" than market forces.* Certainly the almost monotonous regularity with which interventionist economists have come forward—and with which authorities have acted—when the market forces did not adequately perform their task testifies to the fact that we do not have to rely exclusively on price signals and profit-maximizers to save us from trouble.[1]

[1]Some traditional equilibrium mechanisms were unable to dispense entirely with help from agents outside the market. Thus, the restoration of balance-of-payments equilibrium and the damping of the business cycle was, for a long time, made to depend on correct manipulation by the central bank of the rate of interest, in reaction to developing disequilibria. But this role of the central banker has usually been rationalized as an exception to the rule; and in the minds of many economists, the central banker became a sort of honorary member of the market forces.

The case of unbalanced growth provides a good illustration. When supply difficulties arise in the course of uneven progress in sectors—such as education and public utilities—where private enterprise is not operating, strong pressures are felt by public authorities to "do something"; and since the desire for political survival is at least as strong a motive force as the desire to realize a profit, we may ordinarily expect some corrective action to be taken.[2]

There is no implication here that any disequilibrium whatsoever will be resolved by some combination of market and nonmarket forces. But if a community cannot generate the "induced" decisions and actions needed to deal with the supply disequilibria that arise in the course of uneven growth, then I can see little reason for believing that it will be able to take the set of "autonomous" decisions required by balanced growth. In other words, if the adjustment mechanism breaks down altogether, this is a sign that the community rejects economic growth as an overriding objective.

The inclusion of probable reactions of nonmarket forces not only serves to make economic analysis more realistic. It also protects us against a fallacious chain of reasoning that is fairly common in development economics and of which the doctrine of balanced growth is itself an excellent illustration. In this reasoning, one first selects some objective of economic policy that seems desirable enough; then one proves that the objective cannot be attained through the operation of market forces; and one concludes that state action surely will bring the objective about. But this conclusion is clearly a non sequitur. The fact that private entrepreneurs will be unable or unwilling to do certain jobs which we would like to see done does not in itself ensure that the government can handle them. We must examine whether these jobs are likely to be performed satisfactorily by public authorities, which function after all in the same society as the entrepreneurs. . . .

[2]Sectoral imbalances have of course been a conspicuous feature of Russian economic development. The resulting difficulties have been described in Soviet literature as "nonantagonistic contradictions" which are not only admitted to exist but apparently considered to perform a useful signaling and corrective function: "The characteristic trait of our difficulties and contradictions consists precisely in that they themselves indicate to us the basis and the means for their solution." V. Kozlovskii, *Antagonisticheskie i neantagonisticheskie protivorechiia* (Moscow, Moskovskii Rabochii, 1954), p. 70. These "nonantagonistic" contradictions which are successfully overcome by administrative action of the Communist party and the government are then opposed to the "antagonistic" contradictions which are said to afflict capitalism and which can be resolved only by revolution.

16b. Investment Choices and Strategies
Albert O. Hirschman*

Efficient Sequences versus Investment Criteria

We can now begin to consider one of the most crucial problems in development theory and policy: that of investment choices.

*From *The Strategy of Economic Development* (New Haven: Yale University Press, 1958), pp. 76–83.

Development requires the undertaking of a series of projects producing favorable effects on the flow of income, in a wide variety of fields: public administration, education, health, transportation, power, agriculture, industry, urban development, etc. The limitation of resources, be they savings available for investment or our "ability to invest," compels a choice among these projects. In traditional economics, the market performs this function by equating the productivities of the various projects at the margin. It is recognized, however, that in any economy a substantial proportion of funds must be devoted to projects (in education, health, some public utilities, etc.) whose output has no readily assigned or fully recoverable market value. Moreover, underdeveloped economies tend to exhibit certain systematic discrepancies between private costs and social costs, and in such cases reliance on the market would lead to misallocation of resources.[3]

These considerations and the practical needs of development planners have led to the elaboration of *investment criteria*. The problem that has been discussed in this connection can be formulated as follows: given a limited amount of investment resources and a series of proposed investment projects whose total cost exceeds the available resources, how do we pick out the projects that will make the greatest contribution relative to their cost? In answering this question, economists have ordinarily interpreted "contribution" as *direct contribution to output* once the project has been completed. This is only natural if growth is visualized as depending exclusively on aggregate output and income which, via the propensity to save, secrets the means for further growth. On these premises, the measurement of what has been called the "social marginal productivity" (SMP) of different projects—essentially a more or less sophisticated benefit-cost ratio—becomes the instrument that should in theory permit us to rank different projects in the order of their expected contribution to output and therefore to further growth.[4]

Recently, a far more elaborate concept has been proposed by Leibenstein: In addition to the output stream, investment criteria ought to take account also of the differential effects of the proposed ventures on the supply of entrepreneurship and of savings, on consumption habits, population increases, and a variety of other factors affecting further growth.[5] Leibenstein admits that a criterion embodying all these repercussions (in addition to SMP proper) would be of unusually difficult application.[6] In practice, his criticism seems likely to result in an agnostic "it all depends" attitude since it seriously impairs the usefulness of the SMP criterion without replacing it by a manageable new instrument.

[3]There are at least three important areas in which such systematic discrepancies are apt to occur: the wage rate (because of disguised unemployment), the exchange rate (because of overvaluation of the currency), and the interest rate (because of rationing of loan funds on the part of the banks). See J. Tinbergen, *The Design of Development* (Baltimore, 1958), pp. 39 ff.

[4]A. E. Kahn, "Investment Criteria in Development," *Quarterly Journal of Economics, 55* (Feb. 1951), 38–61; H. B. Chenery, "The Application of Investment Criteria," *Quarterly Journal of Economics, 57* (Feb. 1953), 76–96; J. Ahumada, "Preparación y evaluación de proyectos de desarrollo económico," *El trimestre económico, 22* (July–Sept. 1955), 265–96.

[5]Leibenstein, *Economic Backwardness and Economic Growth*, ch. 15.

[6]*Ibid.*, p. 268.

In attempting a different approach, we shall first draw a distinction between substitution choices and postponement choices. Consider any choice between project *A* and project *B*: If the decision favors *A*, this may mean either that *B* is *discarded permanently* or that it is *postponed*. In the former case, the choice is between technical substitutes such as alternative means of providing a city with power or water supply. Many important choices are of this kind. They relate to the best means of attaining a given end or to the best design of a project whose output itself is needed beyond question. In deciding such choices, the usual investment criteria retain considerable usefulness. Nevertheless, we feel that in underdeveloped countries additional considerations must be introduced and we will do so in Chapter 8.

Let us suppose for the time being that all substitution choices have been made and that we have before us a series of useful projects which are ideally designed to accomplish their respective purposes. In this situation, we are only faced with postponement choices.[7] We no longer choose *A* instead of *B*; rather, we choose the sequence *AB* instead of the sequence *BA*. What is the possible rationale for such a choice? If we suppose that our goal is to have both *A* and *B*, but that "now" we can undertake only either *A* or *B*, leaving *B* or *A*, respectively, for "later," then it is clear that the only conceivable reason for preferring *AB* to *BA* is that *B* will be possible sooner once *A* is in place than vice versa. In other words, our choice depends entirely on the pressure that the existence of *A* exerts toward the coming into existence of *B* as compared to the corresponding pressure that would emanate from *B* toward *A*. Once the problem is formulated in this way it becomes quite clear that the comparative productivity of *A* and *B* which will both have to be undertaken is likely to be a rather minor factor in the decision assigning the priority.

Although our reasoning has been drastically simplified, it takes hold of an important aspect of the development problem. Essential tasks always abound in underdeveloped countries since backwardness has so many different interrelated facets. From this interrelatedness we do not draw the balanced growth conclusion that a simultaneous attack is essential. But what might be called a sequential or chain solution is indeed required. In other words, isolated progress in one area is possible, but only for a limited period; if it is not to be choked off, it must be followed by progress elsewhere. Therefore to compare the productivity increases that result from two projects in, e.g., education and transportation, is an insoluble problem not only in practice but conceptually. Such comparisons must be made on the *ceteris paribus* assumption that progress is being achieved

---

[7]In an earlier paper, "Economics and Investment Planning: Reflections Based on Experience in Colombia" in *Investment Criteria and Economic Growth*, ed. M. F. Millikan (Cambridge, Mass., M.I.T., 1955, multilithed), I argued essentially that economists ought to confine themselves to the making of substitution choices. I still believe that the most urgent task of development planners usually consists in arriving at correct substitution choices; but I realize now that postponement choices cannot be evaded. They must be made at two different stages of the process of development planning: first before it is decided in which sector or sectors substitution choices are to be studied, for the decision seriously to study alternative means of fulfilling a given need usually already implies a decision to give priority to this need; and secondly, after substitution choices have been completed in several different sectors.

in only one of the areas; and on this assumption the longer-term productivity of both undertakings is simply *zero* since the improved transportation facilities will serve little purpose and will fast deteriorate if education is not also improved in due course and vice versa. Therefore, the question of priority must be resolved on the basis of a comparative appraisal of the strength with which progress in one of these areas will induce progress in the other.[8] In these basic types of development decisions, it is therefore not sufficient to supplement, qualify, and otherwise refine the usual investment criteria. We must evolve entirely new aids to thought and action in this largely uncharted territory of efficient sequences and optimal development strategies.

There is no doubt that the task that we have set ourselves is extremely complex. Let us suppose that we know which are the *n* steps that need to be taken to, say, double a country's per capita income. Then there exist in principle *n!* possible sequential arrangements of these *n* steps! Of course, there can be no question of neatly deducing, through a series of syllogisms, *the* most efficient sequence. Rather, we will strive to "suboptimize"[9] and to develop a few guideposts, principles, and illustrative models.

To begin with, there was a great deal of exaggeration in our statement that there exist *n!* sequences in which the *n* steps may be undertaken. Many sequences are unavoidably "one-way" for purely technical reasons (a road must be built before it can be paved); one also feels that other one-way sequences are imposed not because they are technically determined but because they are necessary if development is to be properly planned, i.e., is to proceed in an "orderly" fashion. But here there may be some doubt as to how far it is advisable to go. Observation tells us that rapid growth of countries, cities, industries, and individual firms hardly ever proceeds in a completely orderly fashion, but that an excess of disorderliness may exert in inhibiting and demoralizing influence on further growth. Can we then perhaps define an optimum degree of orderliness in development? To illustrate this problem, let *A, B, C,* and *D* in Figure 1 represent a group of development steps we wish to take and that ought to be taken in this order if ideal "orderliness" is to be achieved. Let us also suppose that step *A must* be realized before *B, C* or *D* can possibly be undertaken, but that with *A* accomplished the sequence is no longer imposed. In the absence of limiting factors, the sequence *ABCD* would be chosen because it provides the smoothest transition from state *A* to state *ABCD*. But we now introduce a limited resource, such as decision-making or organizational ability, or simply time, and assume that

[8]It may be objected that indivisibility could not be such as to prevent us from investing our resources partly in education and partly in transportation. However, the point we are making does not depend on indivisibility in the sense of "lumpiness." Let us assume that we have identified *n* essential and interrelated projects, costing 200 million dollars, but that we have only 100 million dollars at hand. Suppose that out of the *n* projects we can put together various collections of *m<n* projects costing 100 million dollars. Then again the criterion for picking any particular collection of *m* projects would be the strength with which their execution would induce the remaining projects. Thus indivisibility is assumed only in the trivial sense that some projects will necessarily be undertaken ahead of others.

[9]Charles Hitch, "Sub-optimization in Operations Problems," *Journal of the Operations Research Society of America, 1* (May 1953), 87–99.

different amounts of this resource are spent in going from one point to another. We want to minimize the use of this resource. If, say, ten units of this resource are spent in going from A to B, from B to C, and from C to D, then it is natural to think that to go from A directly to C will take a somewhat larger (say 12 units) and from A to D, perhaps a much larger amount (say 25 units), because of the absence of the intermediate preparatory stages. On the other hand, less than ten units (say 5) should be needed to "fill in" B or C after C or D, respectively, because once the later steps have been realized the lack of the intermediary ones makes itself felt in so pressing a manner that the decision to undertake them requires far smaller quantities of the scarce ability or time than when they represented genuine forward steps.

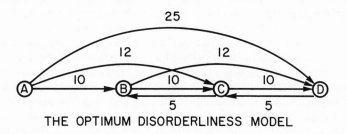

THE OPTIMUM DISORDERLINESS MODEL

Fig. 1

If we apply the foregoing illustrative figures, then the expenditure of our scarce resource that is involved in the various possible sequences is as follows:

A to B to C to D	30 $(10 + 10 + 10)$
A jump to C then fill in B, then D	27 $(12 + 5 + 10)$
A to B then jump to D, then fill in C	27 $(10 + 12 + 5)$
A jump to D, then fill in B and C	35 $(25 + 5 + 5)$

In this example the figures have been selected so as to show that a limited amount of "putting the cart before the horse" may be efficient as compared to both maximum orderliness and maximum disorderliness.

It may be helpful to attempt a translation of this model into more familiar terminology. Let us assume two ventures, m and n, which require equal amount of capital and have a yield of 10% and 8% respectively. At the beginning of period 1 the interest rate stands at 9%, hence only venture m is undertaken. At the beginning of period 2, with venture m in existence, the expected yield of venture n has risen to 10% and is now also launched. But we are free to suppose that, if n were undertaken first, m would be urgently required and that its expected yield would rise to 14% at the beginning of period 2. In this eventuality, investors would maximize income by selecting in period 1 the investment with the lower yield! Besides they would do everything to rush m to completion. Such strange results are avoided in traditional theory by the implicit assumption which we chose to discard here, that the profitability of different ventures is invariant with respect to the order in which they are undertaken.

The preceding examples are highly artificial as they imply that development proceeds along a single path. Nevertheless, they embody a number of concepts that are recurring throughout this essay: the difference between "permissive" and "compulsive" sequences, the possible rationality of violating "first things first" norms and the fact that the difficulty of taking a development decision is not necessarily proportional to the amount of capital it requires.

A more complex and perhaps more realistic model would be to consider development as the putting together of a jigsaw puzzle. The fitting in of individual pieces would represent the taking of discrete development steps. The problem would again be to minimize the time needed to put the puzzle together. The total time is of course equal to the sub of the time periods spent on fitting in the individual pieces, and the time needed for each piece could be made to depend inversely on the number of contacts with adjacent pieces already in place: with each piece surrounded by several neighbors, the larger the number of neighbors in place, the less time it will take to find and fit into its proper place the common neighbor of these neighbors. Each fitting is more or less "induced," depending on the ease or difficulty with which it may be made.[10] An efficient sequence for putting the puzzle together could be found by trial and error once we have information about the varying amounts of time needed for fitting in individual pieces. For instance, if the time needed fell rapidly toward zero the larger the number of neighbors already in place, then the efficient sequence would turn out to be completely different from the one that would be optimal if the increase in the facility with which pieces may be fitted in were subject to decreasing returns as the number of neighbors increased.

Up to this point, we have considered that the difficulty of taking any development steps (i.e., the fitting in of the individual jigsaw pieces) depends exclusively on the number of neighbors already in place. We can bring our model one step closer to reality by supposing that the taking of the different steps varies in intrinsic difficulty *besides* being affected by the number of neighbors. If this is the case, then the putting together of the puzzle becomes far more determinate than before: for now we would aim at surrounding by "neighbors" those pieces that are intrinsically most difficult to fit in, securing thereby far greater economies of effort than if we surrounded those pieces that are intrinsically of average or less-than-average difficulty.

These fanciful digressions may illustrate the kind of models in terms of which a general theory of "efficient sequences" might be built. I doubt,

[10]In the usual jigsaw puzzle the task of fitting in a piece also becomes progressively easier as the game progresses and the number of remaining loose pieces declines. Although this feature of a jigsaw puzzle could be related to the "take-off" concept and to Simon's learning model (cf. Ch. 2), it is rather a disturbing element from the point of view of the problem which we wish to illustrate at this juncture. To eliminate it, we may imagine that the jigsaw puzzle goes on forever: only a limited number of loose pieces can be chosen from at any point of time, but as soon as one piece is fitted, a new one is mixed in among the loose pieces on the table. Such a representation of our model is consistent with the view that the growth process is an infinite one, but that at any one point of time only a limited number of steps-to-be-taken is within the horizon of the decision-makers.

however, that it is useful to go very far in this direction. Our short discussion had primarily the purpose:

1. to make the concept of efficient sequence a little more palpable; and
2. to show that efficient sequences will necessarily vary widely from region to region and from country to country depending on the location and stubbornness of the principal development difficulties....

17. Comparative Advantage and Development Policy[1]

*Hollis B. Chenery**

In the great revival of interest in economic development that has marked the past decade, attention has centered on two main questions: first, what determines the over-all rate of economic advance? second, what is the optimal allocation of given resources to promote growth? Analysis of the growth rate has relied mainly on the Keynesian tools and has produced a multiplicity of aggregate growth models. The second question, however, reopens more ancient economic issues, and their analysis must start from the classical and neoclassical solutions. Only very recently have the two types of discussion tended to come together in the more comprehensive framework of general equilibrium analysis.

In the field of resource allocation, controversy centers around the implications of the classical principle of comparative advantage, according to which growth is promoted by specialization. The defenders of this principle draw their inspiration from David Ricardo, J. S. Mill and Alfred Marshall, while the lines of attack stem from Friedrich List, J. A. Schumpeter, A. A. Young and J. H. Williams. The chief criticism is that comparative advantage is essentially a static concept which ignores a variety of dynamic elements.

This issue is of great practical importance to the governments of under-developed countries, most of which take an active part in allocating investment funds and other scarce resources. The main purpose of the discussion has therefore been to discover workable principles for the formulation of development policy. The classical approach derives these principles from international trade theory, while its critics base their analysis on modern growth theory. Elements of a dynamic, general-equilibrium theory are needed to resolve the differences between the two approaches. The more general analysis is of very limited value, however, unless its empirical implications can be ascertained.

*From the *American Economic Review*, Papers and Proceedings, March 1961, pp. 18–51. The author is presently the Director of the Program Review and Coordination Staff, Agency for International Development.

[1] I am indebted to Moses Abramovitz, Bela Balassa, and Lawrence Krause for helpful comments. Research for this article was undertaken at the Cowles Foundation for Research in Economics under Task NR 047-006, Office of Naval Research. [This is the third in a series of survey articles for which the Rockefeller Foundation has provided support.—*Editor.*]

The present paper discusses the analysis of resource allocation in less developed economies from three points of view. Section I tries to ascertain the extent to which the allocation principles derived from trade theory and from growth can be reconciled with each other without losing their operational significance. Section II compares various approaches to the measurement of optimal resource allocation in terms of their logical consistency and their applicability to different conditions. Section III examines some of the practical procedures followed in setting investment policy in underdeveloped countries in the light of the earlier discussion. Finally, some of the theoretical issues are re-examined to indicate their practical importance.

I. Conflicts Between Trade Theory and Growth Theory

The main contradictions between comparative advantage and other principles of resource allocation derive from their different orientation and assumptions. The classical analysis focuses on long-run tendencies and equilibrium conditions, while modern theories of growth are concerned with the interaction among producing and consuming units in a dynamic system. Since both approaches are familiar, I shall only try to identify the differences in assumptions and emphasis that lead to different policy conclusions.

A. *The implications of comparative advantage for resource allocation.* The modern version of the comparative cost doctrine [20] is essentially a simplified form of static general equilibrium theory.[1] The optimum pattern of production and trade for a country is determined from a comparison of the opportunity cost of producing a given commodity with the price at which the commodity can be imported or exported. In equilibrium, no commodity is produced which could be imported at lower cost, and exports are expanded until marginal revenue equals marginal cost. Under the assumptions of full employment and perfect competition, the opportunity cost of a commodity, which is the value of the factors used to produce it in their best alternative employment, is equal to its market value. Market prices of factors and commodities can therefore be used to determine comparative advantage under competitive conditions. Long-term changes are not ignored, but they are assumed to be reflected in current market prices.

The Heckscher-Ohlin version of the comparative cost doctrine has been widely recommended as a basis for development policy because it provides a measure of comparative advantage that does not depend on the existence of perfect competition and initial equilibrium. This version states that a country will benefit from trade by producing commodities that use more of its relatively abundant factors of production. It will export these commodities and import commodities using more of its relatively scarce factors unless its pattern of domestic demand happens to be biased toward commodities using domestic factors. The critical

[1] An excellent discussion and synthesis of the several versions of trade theory is given by Caves [7]. The terms "comparative advantage" and "comparative cost" are used interchangeably in most discussions.

assumptions in this analysis are that factors of production are comparable among countries and that production functions are the same. These assumptions are not required by classical trade theory.

The applicability of the comparative cost doctrine to present-day conditions in underdeveloped countries has been re-examined by Viner and its validity has been reaffirmed with some modifications. Viner criticizes the Heckscher-Ohlin version because its assumption of comparable factors does not allow for observable differences in their quality [63, p. 16]. In his recent answer to critics of the comparative cost approach [64], however, Viner admits the necessity of interpreting comparative advantage in a dynamic setting in which the efficiency of production may change over time, external economies may exist, and the market prices of commodities and factors may differ from their opportunity cost. As Nurkse points out [64, p. 76], these modifications rob the original doctrine of much of its practical value. It is now necessary to have an explicit analysis of the growth process itself before it is possible to determine, even theoretically, where comparative advantage lies; market prices and current opportunity costs are no longer sufficient.

B. *Implications of growth theory for resource allocation.* Modern growth theory is concerned with the interactions over time among producers, consumers, and investors in interrelated sectors of the economy. In the writings of such economists as Rosenstein-Rodan [43], Lewis [29], Nurkse [36], Myrdal [34], Rostow [44], Dobb [12], and Hirschman [23], there is much more emphasis on the sequence of expansion of production and factor use by sector than on the conditions of general equilibrium. Growth theory either ignores comparative advantage and the possibilities of trade completely, or it considers mainly the dynamic aspects, such as the stimulus that an increase in exports provides to the development of related sectors or the function of imports as a carrier of new products and advanced technology. With this different point of view, growth theorists often suggest investment criteria that are quite contradictory to those derived from considerations of comparative advantage.

The conflicts between these two approaches to resource allocation may be traced either to differences in assumptions or to the inclusion of factors in one theory that are omitted from the other. Growth theory contains at least four basic assumptions about underdeveloped economies that differ strongly from those underlying the comparative cost doctrine: (1) factor prices do not necessarily reflect opportunity costs with any accuracy; (2) the quantity and quality of factors of production may change substantially over time, in part as a result of the production process itself; (3) economies of scale relative to the size of existing markets are important in a number of sectors of production; (4) complementarity among commodities is dominant in both producer and consumer demand.

Some of the implications of these factors are developed by Rosenstein-Rodan [43] and Nurkse [36] as arguments for "balanced growth," by which is meant simultaneous expansion of a number of sectors of production.[2] Assuming an elastic supply of either capital or labor, these

[2]The term "balanced growth" has been given a variety of meanings, but the idea of simultaneous expansion on several fronts is common to all of them.

authors show that investment will be more profitable in related sectors, because of horizontal and vertical interdependence, than in the same sectors considered separately. Market forces will not necessarily lead to optimal investment decisions because present prices do not reflect the cost and demand conditions that will exist in the future. This effect of investment in one sector on the profitability of investment in another sector, via increased demand or reduced costs, has been called by Scitovsky [47] a "dynamic external economy." The imputation of these economies to the originating sectors may seriously affect the estimate of comparative advantage.

If we assume fixed investment resources instead of an elastic supply, the same set of factors provide an argument for concentrated or unbalanced growth [48] [50]. In order to achieve economies of scale in one sector, it may be necessary to devote a large fraction of the available investment funds to that sector and to supply increased requirements in other sectors from imports (or to curtail them temporarily). The optimal pattern of investment will then be one which concentrates first on one sector and then on another, with balance being approached only in the long run. Streeten [53] has developed further dynamic arguments for unbalanced growth from the fact that technological progress may be more rapid if increases in production are concentrated in a few sectors, while Hirschman [23] argues for imbalance to economize on entreprenurial ability.

The historical significance of the balanced growth argument has been examined by Gerschenkron [18], Rostow [44], and Ohlin [38], in the context of nineteenth-century industrial development in Europe. They show that vertical interdependence has been important in stimulating the growth of related industrial sectors, although the nature and origin of these complexes differ from country to country. In one case they may be related to exports, in another to expansion for the domestic market. The importance of interdependence among producers emerges fairly clearly from these historical studies.

The net effect of the discussion of dynamic interdependence and balanced vs. unbalanced growth is to destroy the presumption that perfect competition, even if it could be achieved, would lead to the optimum allocation of resources over time. Since the doctrine of comparative advantage in its conventional form is a corollary of general equilibrium theory, the theoretical qualifications that apply to the latter also apply to the former. If, then, the doctrine of comparative advantage is to be useful for development policy, the essential elements of the growth analysis must be combined with it.

C. *Dynamic modifications of comparative advantage.* Classical trade theory does not exclude changes in the supply of factors and other data over time, but it does insist that under perfect competition the effects of such changes will be reflected in the market mechanism. If, on the other hand, we take comparative advantage as a principle of planning rather than as a result of market forces, we can include any foreseeable exogenous changes in technology, tastes, or other data without going beyond the framework of comparative statics.

Some of the modifications suggested by growth theory are dynamic in a more essential way, in that a particular change depends not only on the passage of time but on other variables in the system. For example, the rate of increase in the productivity of labor in an industry may depend on an increasing level of production in that industry. Some of these dynamic elements can also be analyzed by methods of comparative statics if our purpose is only to choose among alternative courses of action.

The four assumptions of growth theory discussed above (Section B) lead to the following requirements for the analytical framework to be used in determining comparative advantage in a growing economy.[3] (1) recognition of the possibility of structural disequilibrium in factor markets; (2) the inclusion of indirect (market and nonmarket) effects of expanding a given type of production; (3) simultaneous determination of levels of consumption, imports, and production in interrelated sectors over time when decreasing costs result from the expansion of output; and (4) allowance for variation in the demand for exports and other data over time.

These changes destroy the simplicity of the classical system, in which allocation decisions can be based on a partial analysis because adjustments in the rest of the economy are reflected in equilibrium market prices. In the dynamic analysis, it may not be possible to state that a country has a comparative advantage in producing steel without specifying also the levels of production of iron ore, coal and metal-working over time. In short, we are forced to compare alternative patterns of growth rather than separate sectors, and we cannot expect to find simple generalizations of the Heckscher-Ohlin type concerning the characteristics of individual lines of production.

Since there is no well-developed body of theory concerning the formal properties of the system just outlined,[4] I shall only try to indicate in a general way the modifications that some of these elements of growth theory will produce in the analysis of comparative advantage.

FACTOR COSTS. It is generally agreed that costs of labor and capital in underdeveloped countries do not reflect their opportunity costs with any accuracy because of market imperfections, but there is wide disagreement as to the extent of the typical discrepancies. Some types of labor may be overvalued while particular skills are undervalued. Factor costs may also change markedly over time as a result of economic development, so that an advantage based on cheap labor may prove quite limited in duration. As Lewis [29] and Hagen [21] show, the effects on comparative advantage of correcting for disequilibrium factor prices are often very substantial. (The effects of disequilibrium in factor markets are discussed further in Part II.)

EXPORT MARKETS. Two of the main arguments against the trade pattern produced by market forces concern (1) the fluctuating nature and (2) the

---

[3]Some of these criticisms of static analysis were made years ago by Williams [66], and a number of the elements were, of course, recognized by the classical economists themselves. I am not concerned with explicit criticism of the classical analysis, but with the possibility of reconciling it with growth theory.
[4]In his survey of modern trade theory, Caves [7] shows that attempts to introduce dynamic elements have been concerned mainly with particular aspects and have led not to new principles, but rather to extensions of static results.

low income and price elasticities of the demand for primary products. The existence of cyclical fluctuation is well established, but the income and price elasticities vary considerably among primary commodities. Their net effect on the terms of trade of primary producers over time is a matter of dispute [64]. These characteristics are often used as an argument for reducing specialization in underdeveloped countries and for expanding industry for local consumption rather than expanding primary exports [41] [51].

These factors can be admitted without seriously modifying the principle of comparative advantage. The market value of the stream of export earnings should be reduced to reflect the drawbacks to the economy resulting from its variable characteristics, and this social value should be used in comparing investment in primary exports to other alternatives. When export demand has a low elasticity, marginal revenue should be used in place of average revenue. Since it is quite likely that the market evaluation of the attractiveness of an investment in exports will differ from this social evaluation, some form of government intervention may be warranted. It is wrong, however, to conclude from this analysis that continued specialization in primary exports may not be the best policy, because even the corrected return on exports may be greater than that on alternative investments. The supply of foreign investment may also be greater for export production.

PRODUCTIVITY CHANGE. The possibility of rising efficiency as labor and management acquire increasing experience in actual production has long been recognized [66] and forms the basis for the infant industry argument. This argument has been generalized to include the effects of increasing production in any industry on the supply of skilled labor and management available to other industries. Since manufacturing is thought to have more important training effects than primary production [33] [41], the fact that improvements in factor supply are not reflected in the market mechanism may introduce a bias against manufacturing. The empirical basis for this argument has been questioned by several economists [46], [63], who assert that there is often as much scope for technological improvement in agriculture as in industry. Without trying to settle the empirical question that has been raised, it may be concluded that productivity change is an important factor and therefore that comparative advantage should be measured over time. It cannot be said, however, that allowance for this factor will always favor manufacturing.

DYNAMIC EXTERNAL ECONOMIES. As indicated above, dynamic external economies are received by an industry from cost reductions or demand increases in other sectors. Cost reductions may result from economies of scale, productivity increases, or new technology. The customary analysis of comparative advantage on a sector-by-sector basis would require that the cost reduction from simultaneously developing interrelated sectors be allocated separately to each. However, if a group of investments will only be profitable when they are undertaken together, comparative advantage can only be determined for alternative combinations of investments. As shown in [11], not only do market prices fail to produce the best investment allocation in this situation, but any structure of equilibrium prices may also be an inadequate guide in the presence of economies of scale.

There is considerable evidence that external economies are more important in the industrial sectors than in primary production because of internal economies of scale, training effects, and high demand elasticities. Their omission from the market mechanism is therefore likely to bias resource allocation against manufacturing. The quantitative significance of this factor is very hard to determine, however, since it involves simultaneous changes in a number of sectors.

UNCERTAINTY AND FLEXIBILITY. The limited ability of policy-makers to foresee changes in demand and supply conditions puts a premium on flexibility in the choice of a development strategy. This factor not only argues against specialization in one or two export commodities but it also favors the development of a diversified economic structure which will enable the economy to shift to new types of exports or import substitutes when changing trade conditions may require them. Kindleberger [26] sees this factor as the main explanation for his finding that the terms of trade have favored developed countries although they have not favored countries exporting manufactured goods in general.[5] The argument is similar to that of Stigler [52] concerning the optimum choice of techniques in a manufacturing plant. The optimum design for a changing market is likely to differ from the optimum under static conditions because in the former case the proper criterion is lowest-cost production for varying operating levels and with changes in product design. Similarly optimum development policy should result in a pattern of resource allocation that allows for unforeseen changes in supply and demand conditions even at the cost of some loss of short-term efficiency.

II. The Measurement of Optimum Resource Allocation

The development of an adequate theory is only the first step in formulating economic policy. In order to reach practical conclusions, it is also necessary to specify the environment in which the policy-maker functions. Relevant aspects of a particular society include its general objectives, the policy instruments to be considered, and the information available. The theory must then be combined with these elements in such a way as to yield guides to action or "decision rules" for particular situations.

Although the growing science of operations research is concerned with the development of decision rules for business and military operations, less progress has been made in developing an operational approach to long-run economic policy. Tinbergen [55] and Frisch [15] have outlined a general framework for policy analysis, but it has had relatively little impact on the discussion of the development of underdeveloped countries. In this field the failure to specify adequately the decision-making environment and to distinguish between decision rules and the corollaries of pure theory has led to great confusion.

Since the information needed for over-all economic analysis is available to a very limited extent in underdeveloped countries, there has been a considerable effort to derive decision rules or "investment criteria" that

[5]This argument is also discussed by Caves [7, pp. 264–66].

can be based on partial analysis. I shall group the various suggestions into three categories: (1) factor-intensity criteria; (2) productivity criteria; (3) programming criteria based on accounting prices. Although these various approaches often lead to contradictory results, each has some merit as a form of decision rule if properly qualified. In general, the theoretically more valid formulations require more information and must be replaced by cruder approximations when adequate data are not available. Since a major part of the literature in the development field has been devoted to the discussion of investment criteria, it is important to identify the sources of conflict among them and to specify the circumstances under which each may be approximately correct.

In economic theory, capital and labor are assumed to be separately allocated in single units to different uses. In national planning, however, it is more convenient to consider the decision to install a given productive process or plant, representing the allocation of a group of inputs in specified quantities, as the basic choice. Investment criteria are customarily formulated for "projects" of this sort, since they form the basis for the decisions of planning authorities. This procedure recognizes that very small productive units are uneconomical, and it permits a consideration of different scales of output. The choice of techniques can be considered as a choice among projects producing the same output from different input combinations. In this way the allocation procedure can be divided into two steps: the choice of the best technique for a given type of product, and the decision whether to produce the commodity at all. The principle of comparative advantage is more directly relevant to the second type of choice, but the two cannot be separated entirely.

A. *Factor-intensity criteria.* The simplest approach to any allocation problem is to concentrate on the scarcest resource. Since this is often capital in underdeveloped countries, it seems reasonable to choose the technique that uses the least capital to produce a given output. The same logic is applied to the choice of sectors of production: an underdeveloped country is advised to produce and export commodities that use relatively less capital per unit of output and to import items requiring more capital. Statements of this type occur in many economic writings of the past fifteen years. Buchanan [5] was among the first to state this criterion for investment in underdeveloped countries and to base policy recommendations upon it.

The "minimum capital-output ratio" criterion is only valid under the following restrictive conditions:[6] (1) Either capital is the only scarce factor in the system, or other inputs are so abundant relative to capital that the latter is the dominant element in determining cost differences. (2) Either the same output is produced by each investment alternative, or the market values used to compare the different products coincide with their social values. (3) Production takes place under constant costs.

The use of the capital-output ratio theoretically requires a measurement of the total capital used in producing a given commodity, including the capital used in producing all materials and services purchased. Alterna-

[6]A rigorous analysis of the validity of marginal and average factor-output ratios as indicators of optimum allocation in a two-factor system is given by Bator [4].

tively, the indirect use of capital can be allowed for by reducing the cost of purchased inputs from the value of output and expressing the criterion as the ratio of capital to value added. This procedure requires the further assumption that market prices correctly reflect the use of capital in the rest of the economy.

A closely related allocation criterion is the capital intensity: the ratio of capital to labor. This test is derived directly from the Heckscher-Ohlin version of the comparative cost doctrine. If the same production functions exist in all countries and if capital is scarce relative to labor in the underdeveloped countries, comparative advantage in the latter can be identified by low capital-labor ratios. This approach does not assume that labor has zero opportunity cost, as does use of the capital-output ratio, but only that the ratio of labor cost to capital cost is lower than in the country's trading partners. To allow for differences in the quality of labor among countries, it is sometimes suggested that the assessment of relative labor cost should be made for labor units of equal efficiency—e.g., the labor required in each country to perform a given type of operation with the same capital goods and organization.

A principal criticism of the use of both these ratios is that they ignore the existence of other factors of production, such as natural resources. If either labor or natural resources has a significant opportunity cost, the capital-output measure must be replaced by the more general marginal productivity of capital criterion, which is discussed in the next section.

To judge comparative advantage by the capital-labor ratio is to assume either that this ratio will be the same for the same industry in all countries, or that capital is equally substitutable for labor in producing all the commodities traded. Deviations from these assumptions, along with the omission of other inputs and variations in efficiency by sector, make the capital-labor criterion a very crude approximation indeed to a proper estimate of comparative advantage.

B. *Marginal productivity criteria.*[7] A more comprehensive allocation criterion is the social marginal product of a given unit of resources in a given use. Where the factor-intensity criteria are at best only correlated with the increase in national income produced by a project, the productivity criteria try to measure the increase. The marginal productivity test is in turn less general than the over-all programming approach, because it is based on a partial equilibrium analysis that is only valid for relatively small changes in the economic structure.

The several forms of marginal productivity criterion that have been proposed differ in the assumptions made about the social welfare function and in the extent to which allowance is made for the indirect effects of a given allocation. All versions are alike in assuming that the government controls, directly or indirectly, a certain fraction of the investible resources of the country and wishes to allocate them in such a way as to maximize future welfare.

Since the productivity criteria are usually applied to investment projects rather than to single units of capital, they are "marginal" only in the

[7]Surveys of these and other investment criteria are given by Castellino [6], Vaidyanathan [62], and the United Nations [61].

sense that a project normally constitutes a small fraction of the total capital invested in a given year. For very large projects a breakdown into smaller units would be more appropriate.

THE STATIC SMP CRITERION. As proposed by Kahn [25], the social marginal product (SMP) is a general equilibrium concept which is conventionally defined as the net contribution of a marginal unit (project) to the national product.[8] The related decision rule is to rank investment projects by their SMP and to go down the list until the funds to be allocated are exhausted. Alternatively, any project having an SMP above a given level can be approved.

Kahn uses the SMP criterion to show the fallacies in the factor-intensity measures that had been advocated by Buchanan [5], Polak [40], and other writers. He points out that: "The existence of a particular natural resource, specialized skills, particular climatic conditions, or the importance of a particular product or service may make the SMP of capital higher in a line which is more capital intensive than in another which is less so" [25, p. 40]. He also argues that even when there is substantial rural unemployment, a considerable amount of capital and other inputs are required to transport, train, and house the workers who are to be employed elsewhere. Kahn's arguments against the simple capital-intensity criteria appear to have been generally accepted, although he admits that a lower capital-output ratio may be a useful guide when other information is lacking.

Some modifications in the SMP criterion were suggested by the present author [8] to allow for artificial elements in the price system (tariffs, subsidies, etc.) and to provide for the evaluation of labor and foreign exchange at opportunity cost rather than at market value. Further allowances for the difference between market price and social value can be made by estimating the benefits to be provided to other sectors in the form of external economies, and by including overhead costs in the estimate of the cost of labor. All of these elements are included in Eckstein's synthesis and extension of the productivity approach [14].[9]

The SMP criterion is entirely consistent with the general programming approach discussed below, which derives opportunity costs from an explicit analysis of total factor use. In the absence of such an over-all analysis, the corrections suggested for the calculation of the productivity of investment are likely to be quite approximate. There is no logical conflict between the results of the SMP analysis and the dictates of comparative advantage because each is a corollary of a general equilibrium solution over a given time period.

THE MARGINAL REINVESTMENT CRITERION. A sharp criticism of the SMP criterion was made by Galenson and Leibenstein [17], who challenge some of its basic premises. They would substitute a different social welfare function in which the aim is to maximize per capita income at some time in

[8]To be more accurate, cost and output streams should be discounted to the present, but I shall not be concerned with differences in the time pattern of output of different projects.
[9]Eckstein points out that the assumption of capital rationing implies a social judgment as to both the amount of investment in the current period and the discount to be applied to future outputs, since the market rate of interest is rejected for both purposes.

the distant future rather than to maximize a discounted stream of income over time. They also assume severe restrictions on the policy instruments available to the government, and in particular deny its ability to affect the rate of saving by fiscal measures. Under these assumptions, it is necessary to take account of the division of income resulting from a project between profits and wages, since savings from the former are higher.

To maximize the total output at some distant future time, Galenson and Leibenstein easily show that the most "productive" project is not necessarily the one which maximizes national income in the near future but the one which leads to the highest savings. Since it is assumed that neither voluntary savings nor taxes can be extracted from wages, the most productive project will be the one with the highest profit rate per unit of capital invested.[10] The assumption that profits are saved and reinvested leads to the "marginal reinvestment quotient" as a decision-rule to be applied in place of the SMP.

Galenson and Leibenstein push their argument one step further and identify the most profitable project as the one with the highest capital-labor ratio. This result leads them to the paradoxical conclusion that the factor-intensity rule should be reversed: countries should prefer the most capital-intensive rather than the least capital-intensive techniques in order to promote savings and future growth. This conclusion involves an implicit assumption about the nature of production functions: that increasing the capital intensity will necessarily raise the average return to capital in each sector of production. This is obviously not true in general and is not necessarily true of existing productive techniques. The savings effect of a given project should therefore be measured directly and not assumed to vary in proportion to the capital-labor ratio.

Galenson and Leibenstein have been widely criticized for their extreme assumptions [4] [14] [24] [35], in particular for the use of a social welfare function in which the starvation of half the population in the near future would appear to be a matter of indifference and for the assumption that limitations on fiscal policy make a lower income preferable to a much higher one if the former has a higher savings component. Their analysis has nevertheless been useful in emphasizing that other effects of an investment besides its immediate contribution to the national product should be included in the productivity criterion.[11]

THE MARGINAL GROWTH CONTRIBUTION. Eckstein [14] has successfully reconciled the conflict between the Kahn-Chenery SMP approach and the Galenson-Leibenstein reinvestment approach, and in so doing he has provided a considerable generalization of each. First, he assumes that the social objective is to maximize the present value of the future consumption stream. With a zero discount rate, this objective approximates the long-term income objective of Galenson and Leibenstein, while with a high discount of future consumption it leads to the maximization of income in

[10]I omit the possibility of an effect on population growth, which leads Galenson and Leibenstein to state the criterion on a per capita basis.
[11]In [28], Leibenstein restates in more restrained form his arguments for including labor training, savings, population growth, and other indirect effects in a comprehensive productivity measure.

the short term. Second, Eckstein assumes that there is a different savings (reinvestment) coefficient associated with each project, but he allows for any savings rate out of wages and profits. From these assumptions, he derives a measure of the "marginal growth contribution" of a given project that consists of two parts: (1) an *efficiency term*, consisting of the present value of the consumption stream; and (2) a *growth term*, consisting of the additional consumption to be achieved by reinvesting savings.

The relative importance of the two terms depends largely on the rate of discount that is applied to future consumption. Even with a low rate of discount, the significance of the second term depends on how much variation there is in the fraction of income saved among different projects. If the savings ratio is not related to the form of income generated, then, as Bator [4] shows, there is no conflict between maximizing income in the short run and in the longer run. Eckstein's formula provides for all possible intermediate assumptions between the two extreme views of the determinants of savings.[12]

In principle, one might include other indirect dynamic effects, such as the value of the labor training provided, in the measurement of the total productivity of a given project. There is a danger of double counting if partial-equilibrium analysis is extended too far, however, and most indirect effects can be more readily evaluated in the more general programming framework considered below.

C. *Programming criteria and accounting prices.* The allocation rules discussed up to now are based on the existing economic structure and are strictly applicable only for relatively small changes in it. Although it may in many instances be necessary to rely primarily on these marginal criteria for lack of data on the rest of the economy, it is important to have some way of testing larger changes and of evaluating the errors that are introduced by the marginal procedure. Furthermore, without a more comprehensive analysis it is impossible to reconcile fully the conflicting policy implications of comparative advantage and growth theory.

The difficulties of partial analysis increase with the number of modifications that have to be applied to market prices in order to arrive at social value. Both the factor-intensity ratios and the partial productivity measures assume that there is one principal restriction on the system, the scarcity of capital. They do not allow for the fact that in allocating capital according to any one of these rules some other restriction on the system, such as the supply of foreign exchange, of skilled labor, or of a particular commodity, may be exceeded.

The programming approach to resource allocation begins with the problem of balancing supply and demand for different commodities and factors of production. Until quite recently, practical programming methods have been more concerned with ensuring the consistency of a given allocation of resources with certain targets than with testing the efficiency with which resources are used. Historically speaking, the programming approach is

---

[12]Sen [49] independently formulated a more general investment criterion that is very similar to Eckstein's, in which the SMP and reinvestment criteria are shown to be limiting cases.

thus the operational counterpart of the theory of balanced growth, from which much of its conceptual framework is derived.

One of the earliest attempts at formulating a comprehensive development program for an underdeveloped area was Mandelbaum's illustrative model for Southeastern Europe, undertaken during the war [31]. He starts, as many subsequent programs have done, from an estimate of the increase in national income required to absorb a prospective increment in the labor force. The allocation of capital and labor is made initially from demand estimates and by analogy to the structure of more advanced countries. The principle of comparative advantage is only introduced intuitively in modifying the initial projection. The main test of resource allocation is the balance of demand and supply for each sector and factor of production.

The development of mathematical programming methods makes it possible to carry out this type of analysis in a much more precise way. In several countries, consistent development programs have been formulated by using input-output analysis, as in the studies of the Economic Commission for Latin America [58] [59] [60]. It is only with the development of linear programming, however, that it is possible to reconcile the consistency criteria and the productivity criteria in a systematic way.

A link between the test of consistency (feasibility) in resource allocation and the test of productivity (efficiency) is provided by a consideration of the price implications of a given allocation. Assume that a set of production levels has been worked out so as to be consistent with the available supplies of labor, capital and natural resources, given the structure of consumer demand and the country's trading possibilities. These sector production and trade levels constitute a "feasible program." Any such program implies a unique set of commodity and factor prices if the economy is in equilibrium. If production activities are assumed to operate at constant costs, linear programming provides a method of calculating the "shadow prices" corresponding to the equilibrium conditions, in which the price of each commodity is equal to its cost of production.[13] Prices are determined by the solution to the following set of simultaneous equations, one for each production activity included in the program:

(1) $$a_{1j}P_1 + a_{2j}P_2 + \cdots + a_{nj}P_n = 0 \qquad (j = 1 \cdots n)$$

where a_{ij} is the input or output of commodity or factor i by activity j, and P_i is the shadow price of commodity or factor i. The input coefficients may be measured at existing prices or in other convenient units. In an open economy, activities of importing and exporting are also included in the system, and the price solution contains the equilibrium price of foreign exchange. An example of this calculation is given in Table 1, which will be explained shortly.

The use of shadow or "accounting" prices in evaluating investment projects has been suggested by Tinbergen [54] [56], Frisch [15] [16], and Chenery [9] [10]. Although Tinbergen does not use a linear programming

[13]The assumptions of linear programming and methods of finding solutions to programming models have been discussed in a number of recent publications, such as [13].

framework, his accounting prices for factors have the same meaning as shadow prices: the opportunity cost implied by a given resources allocation.[14] He suggests computing the costs associated with a project by using accounting prices; any project that shows a positive net return over cost (including capital cost) should be approved. This test is equivalent to the SMP criterion, as shown below.

The general linear programming problem is to maximize the value of a linear objective function subject to linear constraints. In development programs, the principal constraints are that the demands for commodities and factors should not exceed their supplies; the function to be maximized is usually taken as the national income. Alternatively, the objective may be the achievement of a given increase in output at minimum cost in investment (including foreign investment). Other social objectives, such as a minimum employment level or a specific degree of regional balance, can be included as additional restrictions on the program. The instrument variables can also be constrained to fall within specific limits, as in the models of Frisch.[15]

To illustrate the meaning and use of shadow prices in evaluating investment projects, I shall take up a very simplified programming model that is worked out in more detail elsewhere [11]. The truncated system given in Table 1 covers only a small part of the economy, but it will serve to illustrate the way in which interdependence influences investment decisions and the effect of having more than one scarce factor.

The model contains four production activities (X_1, X_2, X_3, X_4) and three import activities (M_1, M_2, M_3). Each activity is represented in Table 1 by a column of coefficients, a_{ij}, showing the amount of input $(-)$ or output $(+)$ of commodity i when the activity is operated at unit level. (These coefficients are the boldface figures in columns 1 to 7.) The net output is taken as unity in all cases. The production activity X_1, for example, represents the production of one unit of metal products from .22 units of iron and steel, .20 units of "other inputs," .70 units of labor, and .70 units of capital. The import activity M_1 provides an alternative way of supplying a unit of metal products by an expenditure (input) of .85 units of foreign exchange. A similar choice is provided between X_2 and M_2 (iron and steel) and between X_3 and M_3 (iron ore). The fourth production activity shows the resources used in the marginal export sector to provide a unit of foreign exchange.

[14]Tinbergen [56, p. 39] defines accounting prices as those "that would prevail if (i) the investment pattern under discussion were actually carried out, and (ii) equilibrium existed on the markets just mentioned" [i.e., labor, capital, foreign exchange markets]. The relation between accounting and shadow prices is discussed in Chenery [10] and Qayum [42].

[15]Frisch is one of the strongest advocates of the use of linear programming for development planning, as indicated in the preface to a recent methodological study: "In the beginning of 1959, during my work as a United Nations expert in Cairo, I was confronted with the problem of working out a methodology for *optimal investment programming* in a rapidly expanding underdeveloped country. I have always believed—and my Cairo experiences have confirmed it—that such a method must be formulated in terms which ultimately make the problem amenable to linear programming. Otherwise one is practically certain to be taken by surprise afterwards in unexpected balance of payments difficulties and other troubles" [16, p. 1].

Table 1. Evaluation of Production and Import Activities by Accounting Prices[1]

Commodities and Factors	Production Activities				Import Activities			Accounting Prices				Restrictions (12)
	X_1 (1)	X_2 (2)	X_3 (3)	X_4 (4)	M_1 (5)	M_2 (6)	M_3 (7)	Trial A (8)	Trial B (9)	Trial C (10)	Trial D (11)	
1. Metal Products	1.00 (3.41)				1.00 (3.41)			2.55	3.42	3.41	2.26	1000
2. Iron and Steel	−.22 (−.89)	1.00 (4.03)				1.00 (4.03)		3.60	4.82	4.03	3.50	1000
3. Iron Ore		−.08 (−.25)	1.00 (3.12)				1.00 (3.12)	3.30	4.42	3.12	2.19	0
4. Foreign Exchange				1.00 (4.01)	−.85 (−3.41)	−1.20 (−4.81)	−1.10 (−4.41)	3.00	4.02	4.01	2.92	0
5. Other Inputs	−.20 (−.62)	−.25 (−.78)	−.70 (−2.17)	−.10 (−.31)				3.00	3.20	3.10	2.20	—
6. Labor	−.70 (−1.05)	−.20 (−.30)	−.30 (−.45)	−1.00 (−1.50)				1.50	1.50	1.50	.50	—
7. Capital	−.70 (−.70)	−2.70 (−2.70)	−.50 (−.50)	−2.20 (−2.20)				1.00	1.00	1.00	1.00	—
Social Profitability[2]												
Trial a	−.59	−.41	+.25	−1.00	0	0	0					
Trial b	−.03	+.37	+1.23	0	0	0	0					
Trial c	+.15	0	0	0	0	−.78	−1.29					
Trial d	0	−.03	0	0	−.22	0	−1.02					
Production and Import Levels												
Trial a	0	0	0	2050	1000	1000	0					
Trial b	0	1000	80	850	1000	0	0					
Trial c	1000	1220	98	0	0	0	0					
Trial d	1000	0	0	1464	0	1220	0					

[1]Based on Chenery [11], Table 1. Prices satisfy equation (1) except for P_4 in trial 1. Figures in parentheses are $(a_{ij}P_i)$ for trial c.
[2]Calculated from equation (4).

In a complete programming model, the amounts of all commodities required for final use at a given level of income would be entered as restrictions on the solution. Similarly, the amounts of available capital and labor of different types would be specified. In this limited illustration, the problem is to supply requirements of 1000 each for metal products and iron and steel at minimum cost. Iron ore and foreign exchange are therefore taken to be intermediate goods having no net outside demand. "Other inputs," labor and capital are supplied from outside the model at prices reflecting their opportunity costs in the rest of the economy. The main difference in principle between this submodel and a complete programming system is that the prices of only the first four commodities are determined in the model in the present case, while in general all prices are so determined.

The four restrictions in the model consist of equations stating that the supply of each of the first four inputs must be equal to the specified demand:[16]

$$
\begin{aligned}
X_1 + M_1 &= 1000 \\
-.22X_1 + X_2 + M_2 &= 1000 \\
-.08X_2 + X_3 + M_3 &= 0 \\
X_4 - .85M_1 - 1.20M_2 - 1.10M_3 &= 0
\end{aligned}
$$

(2)

The objective is to minimize the amount of capital required to supply the given final demands, with the use of labor and "other inputs" valued at their opportunity costs in terms of capital. This is the same as supplying each commodity at minimum unit cost, since the amount of each to be supplied is fixed.

A feasible solution to the model contains either a production or an import activity for each of the three commodities plus the export activity for foreign exchange. The corresponding activity levels can be determined from equations (2) and are shown at the bottom of Table 1. The amounts of the outside factors (F_i)—labor, capital, and "other inputs"—required by each solution can then be determined from the following equations:

(3)

Other inputs: $F_5 = .20X_1 + .25X_2 + .70X_3 + .10X_4$

Labor: $F_6 = .70X_1 + .20X_2 + .30X_3 + 1.00X_4$

Capital: $F_7 = .70X_1 + 2.70X_2 + .50X_3 + 2.20X_4$

The programming model thus contains two types of equations: price equations of the type of (1), and equations for the supply and demand of commodities and outside factors, (2) and (3). As outlined in [10], the general procedure for solving a programming model of this type involves three steps: (a) finding a feasible program or set of activity levels that satisfies the supply-demand restrictions; (b) calculating the shadow prices associated with the given program; (c) using these prices to determine whether any improvement in the initial program is possible. This procedure is repeated as long as any further improvements can be made.

[16]I omit the possibility of overfulfilling demands, since there are no joint products in the present case.

The programming criterion used to compare projects or activities is the social profitability of each as measured from the shadow prices. Any profitable activity should be included in the program. It is the recalculation of prices that distinguishes this procedure from the partial programming approach suggested by Tinbergen. In either case, however, the test of social profitability of activity j can be expressed as:

$$(4) \qquad \Pi_j = \sum_i a_{ij} P_i$$

By definition, the activities that were used in determining the shadow prices will have a profitability of zero. The optimum solution is identified by the condition that all other activities have zero or negative profitability.

Some idea of the type of adjustment that results from moving from partial toward general equilibrium analysis may be given by determining solutions to the model in Table 1 under four different procedures: (a) the use of market prices; (b) correcting for the overvaluation of foreign exchange; (c) finding the optimum solution for the submodel alone; (d) finding the optimum solution for the submodel with changes in the opportunity costs of labor and other inputs determined from a general programming model. The accounting prices corresponding to each assumption are shown in columns 8 to 11 of Table 1. The calculation of social profitability of each activity, given the accounting prices, is illustrated in the table for trial c by giving cost and revenue figures in parentheses in columns 1 to 7.

TRIAL A. Assume that market prices are based on the cost of importing and are determined by setting profits on the import activities equal to zero, with a given foreign exchange cost of 3.00. The exchange rate is assumed to be overvalued, so that the price of foreign exchange is less than the cost of securing it through expanded exports. At these market prices, only activity X_3 (iron ore) is profitable, but there is no domestic demand for iron ore unless steel is also produced (the export price is lower than that of imports because of transport costs). The use of market prices therefore leads to imports of steel and metal products, since the opportunity cost of expanding exports is not taken into account. The corresponding activity levels are shown at the bottom of the table.

TRIAL B. Assume now that we correct for the existing structural disequilibrium by setting the price of foreign exchange equal to its opportunity cost of 4.02 as determined from the export activity X_4. Allowance is also made for a rise in the accounting price of "other inputs," some of which are imported. A new set of accounting prices for commodities 1–3 is determined from the cost of imports. Substituting these prices into equation (4) shows that X_2 and X_3 are both profitable ($\pi_2 = .37$, $\pi_3 = 1.23$). Investment should therefore take place in steel, iron ore, and exports on this test.

TRIAL C. To find the optimum solution to the submodel by linear programming, we can start from trial b and recalculate the shadow prices from the activities that are included: X_2, X_3, X_4, M_1. The four shadow prices P_1 to P_4 are determined by applying equation (1), taking the prices of the outside inputs (P_5, P_6, P_7) as given. The elimination of excess profits from the prices of iron ore and steel lowers the cost of producing metal products, providing an example of pecuniary external economies. Instead of a loss, activity X_1 now shows a profit of .15 and should be substituted for the import activity M_1. With the original prices for labor and capital, the optimum solution to the submodel is therefore to produce all three commodities and import nothing, since all import activities are unprofitable.

TRIAL D. If a similar analysis is carried out for the economy as a whole, it is likely that the initial estimate of the opportunity cost of labor (equal to its market price) will be revised. Assume that the shadow price of labor (equal to its marginal product in the rest of the economy) is only a third of its market price, or .5 units of capital. This lower labor cost will reduce the costs of production in different activities in proportion to their use of labor. Since exports are cheapened more than steel production by this calculation, it now becomes socially profitable to import steel and produce metal products. The optimality of this solution is shown by the prices in trial d, in which there is a loss of $-.03$ on X_3. The optimum quantity solution is shown at the bottom of the table. Valuing other inputs and labor at their accounting prices, it has a capital cost of 5760, compared to 8200, 7470, and 7290 in trials a, b, and c.

The programming approach of trials c and d adds two elements to the analysis of accounting prices. The first is the inclusion of repercussions on input prices from investment in supplying sectors. This is one of the main types of dynamic external economies which are omitted from partial analysis. It is much more significant when there are economies of scale. The second element is the revision of the initial estimate of the opportunity costs of labor, capital, and foreign exchange. This revision is determined by the relation between supply and demand for these factors and thus takes into account the requirements of feasibility.[17]

The profitability criterion (usually called the "simplex" criterion) that is used in linear programming is logically equilavent to the SMP test if the same prices are used in both. The two can be put in a comparable form as follows:

(4a)   Social profit on activity j: $$\Pi_j = \sum_i a_{ij}P_i - k_j$$

(5)   SMP of investment in activity j: $$(SMP)_j = \frac{\sum_i a_{ij}P_i}{k_j} = \frac{\Pi_j}{k_j} + 1$$

where $-k_j$ is used for the capital input coefficient instead of a_{rj}. An activity having a positive social profit in equation (4a) will have an SMP of greater than 1.0 in (5), and the same projects would be accepted by either test. If the prices used are not the equilibrium prices, however, the project rankings by the two formulae will not necessarily be the same.

[17]An example in which these successive adjustments are calculated in detail is given in [10]. Frisch has outlined a computational procedure for handling large numbers of investment projects without going beyond the capacity of simple calculating equipment [16].

Although the example given here contained only one technique of production for each commodity, linear programming methods readily encompass alternative techniques. In a trial application of linear programming to Indian planning, Sandee [45] includes three alternative ways of increasing agricultural output—increased use of fertilizer, irrigation, and extension services—which are substitutes over a limited range. The four alternative techniques for producing textiles cited by Galenson and Leibenstein [17] could also be more properly evaluated in a programming model in which the cost variation associated with their different requirements for materials, maintenance, and skilled labor could be included. However, it is only necessary to include alternative techniques in a programming model when the choice between them depends on the outcome of the solution. Probably in most cases the range of shadow prices can be foreseen accurately enough to determine in advance which technique is more efficient for a given country. The initial assumption can always be verified after the analysis has been completed by using the resulting prices.

Linear programming can be extended to include many of the indirect effects of investment that are suggested by growth theory. The production of trained labor, the effect on savings, or other indirect benefits can be considered as joint outputs whose value can be specified in the objective function. Similarly, indirect costs of production, such as the provision of housing to urban workers, can be included as additional inputs. The shadow prices computed from such an expanded system will therefore reflect nonmarket as well as market interdependence to the extent that it can be specified in quantitative form.

In formal terms, it is also quite easy to extend the programming model in time and to compute future prices for commodities and factors. The measurement of social profitability could then be made against a pattern of changing future prices. Given the degree of uncertainty attached to all future economic magnitudes, however, this is not likely to be a very useful procedure beyond the customary five-year planning period except in the most general terms. It would, however, be desirable to estimate the change in the equilibrium prices of foreign exchange and labor over a longer period of time, since these are the most important variables in choosing among investment projects.

D. *Investment criteria and comparative advantage.* The linear programming approach provides a convenient link to the principle of comparative advantage because the optimal pattern of trade is determined simultaneously with the optimum allocation of investment. The model is considerably more general than that of market equilibrium because it allows for different social objectives and takes account of costs and benefits other than those entering the market. The limitations to the programming model are of two sorts: the form of the restrictions that are specified, and the omission of relationships that cannot be expressed in quantitative form.

The introduction of inelastic demands or increasing costs does not create any more theoretical difficulty in a programming model than in the corresponding general equilibrium system, although the computational aspects of such models have not been widely explored. The accounting prices perform the same function as guides to proper allocation, but the test of social profitability must be applied in marginal rather than average terms. In development programs, this modification is particularly important in the case of exports, where the price elasticity of demand is often rather low.[18] As Nurkse [37] points out, marginal comparative advantage for the underdeveloped countries may for this reason be quite different from that inferred from the average costs and prices of primary exports.

The existence of increasing returns creates the same problem for the programming model as it does for equilibrium theory. Marginal-cost pricing is not sufficient to determine whether an investment should be undertaken, and the total cost of alternative solutions must also be considered. Although practical methods of solving programming models containing decreasing costs are now being developed, they do not give allocation criteria that rely only on accounting prices. It is approximately correct to say that beyond a certain output level country A has a comparative advantage in the production of steel, but the precise determination of the break-even point depends on the level of output in other sectors also.[19]

The most serious theoretical qualification to the principle of comparative advantage comes from the type of nonquantitative interdependence among sectors that is assumed by Hirschman [23]. If, as he supposes, one growth sequence is more effective than another because it economizes on decision-making ability or provides a greater incentive to political action, a set of criteria having little or nothing to do with comparative advantage is implied. The empirical significance of these psychological and sociological factors remains to be established, but they lead to a conflict that cannot be resolved in economic terms.

When the practical limitations on information and analysis are recognized, the possibilities of conflict between comparative advantage and growth theory are greatly increased, and Wiles [65] suggests that marginal efficiency calculations may be less important. An aversion to risk-taking may be a valid reason for limiting the extent of specialization in the export of primary products beyond the amount that would be optimum in the light of more accurate information. An inability to measure the extent of economies of scale, labor training, and other sources of external economies also makes possible a continuing disagreement as to their magnitude.

III. Comparative Advantage and Balance in Development Programs

The inconsistent procedures that governments employ in formulating development policies are probably the most important source of conflict between the dictates of comparative advantage and of growth theory.

[18]A programming model including this feature is given in Chenery [9].
[19]The nature of solutions to this type of problem is considered in [11], from which the data in Table 1 were taken. In this situation of decreasing average cost, the programming model may provide a greater improvement over the solution using partial criteria.

Official pronouncements on development policy usually allege that both types of criteria have been (or should be) utilized in drawing up the program that is put forward, but the procedure followed in reconciling conflicts between the two is rarely made explicit. Since the analytical basis of most development programs is quite limited, it is important to look into the procedure that is actually used in order to discover sources of bias.

Development programs must simultaneously confront two sets of problems. In the short run, progress is hampered by structural disequilibrium in factor markets and in the demand and supply of particular commodities. This disequilibrium is reflected in the balance-of-payments difficulties that beset most low-income countries as they try to accelerate the process of development. In the longer run, the choice among sectors becomes increasingly important because the pattern of growth in each period will depend on the choices made previously. Development programs that are influenced mainly by the existing structural disequilibrium therefore tend to stress the need for greater balance between domestic demand and supply, while those that take a longer view tend to pay more attention to comparative advantage.

Although the procedures actually followed cannot be ascertained with any accuracy by an outside observer, these two aspects can be identified from characteristic elements in the analysis. The balanced growth approach is generally associated with target-setting in key sectors, stress on the avoidance of bottlenecks, and attempts to equate the supply and demand of labor, capital, and the more important commodities. The extreme cases of this type of procedure are found in the communist countries. Less extreme examples, in which some attention is paid to comparative advantage, are the procedures of the Indian Planning Commission and the U.N. Economic Commission for Latin America.

Characteristic elements of the comparative advantage approach are attempts to measure the relative efficiency of different types of production, the weighing of balance-of-payments improvements against other benefits to the economy (by means of accounting prices or otherwise), and usually a greater emphasis on partial analysis than on over-all projections. Examples that will be cited are Puerto Rico, the Philippines, and Israel.

A. *Procedures emphasizing domestic balance.* The planning procedures developed in the USSR and applied with some modification in other communist countries represent in extreme form the use of balance as a criterion for resource allocation and the virtually complete omission of any test of comparative advantage. As revealed in recent studies by Montias [32] and Balassa [1], the main tool of Soviet-type planning is a very detailed system of material balances specified in quantitative terms. Policy objectives are translated into production targets in which priority is given to heavy industry and other sectors that are expected to contribute to further growth ("leading links"). Prices are used mainly as rationing devices and have no necessary connection with production costs. The cumbersome calculations involved in arriving at balance of supply and demand for a large number of commodities limit the alternatives that can be tried out, so the main effort is to find a feasible program [32].

The question of comparative advantage scarcely arises in the USSR because of its size and diversified resources, although similar problems arise in connection with the choice of production techniques. When the Soviet planning system was transplanted to the satellite countries, however, it ran into difficulties because of its inability to determine the advantages to be secured from trade. According to Balassa [1, p. 264], the idea of comparative advantage did not exist in Hungarian development policy (at least until very recently) although trade has a high ratio to GNP. Exports are determined by import "needs," and the institutional structure is such as to encourage exporters to meet targets for exports without regard to production costs. Since prices do not reflect resource use, it is impossible to determine where comparative advantage lies and to what extent the trade pattern deviates from the optimum.

Despite their violation of most short-term welfare considerations, the success of Soviet planning methods in producing a rapid rise in the national product makes them attractive to many underdeveloped countries. In India, for example, Mahalanobis' "plan-frame" for the second five-year plan [30] draws heavily on Soviet methodology. He starts from the assumption that the rate of investment is determined by the level of domestic production of capital goods: "As the capacity to manufacture both heavy and light machinery and other capital goods increases, the capacity to invest (by using home-produced capital goods) would also increase steadily, and India would become more and more independent of the import of foreign machinery and capital goods" [30, p. 18]. His analysis implies that export possibilities are so limited that they can be ignored, so that the composition of demand is limited by the composition of domestic output. In order to raise the level of investment, Mahalanobis concludes that investment in industries producing capital goods should be increased from less than 10 per cent to 30-35 per cent of total investment in the second five-year plan.

As Komiya [27] has shown, Mahalanobis' approach to development ignores price and demand considerations completely. The targets for the four sectors in his model appear to be based mainly on the goal of creating heavy industry, which is assumed to be the key to future growth. Criteria of efficiency and comparative advantage are entirely omitted from his analysis.

Although there are traces of the Mahalanobis approach in the second and third five-year plans formulated by the Indian Planning Commission, the final results are much less extreme. One basic problem is that exports are expected to rise only half as fast as national income between the first and third plan periods, while demand for the goods initially imported tends to rise much more rapidly. The inelastic demand for traditional Indian exports means that a considerable proportion of investment must be devoted to commodities that are presently imported. Within this category, the principles of comparative advantage should apply. In actuality, the emphasis has shifted somewhat from heavy industry in the second plan to agriculture in the third. In the latter document [19], increasing self-sufficiency in basic industrial commodities—steel, petroleum, machinery, etc.—is listed as a high-priority objective, but so is the maximum development of agriculture. Whether the resulting targets are consistent with comparative advantage is not considered in the published analysis.[20]

The balance-of-payment difficulties of many Latin American countries have also been a major factor in shaping the programming procedure developed by the Economic Commission for Latin America [57]. This approach has been applied in considerable detail in studies of Colombia [58], Argentina [59], and Peru [60]. One basic conclusion of these studies is that the growth of exports will be much slower than the growth of demand for goods that are currently imported. Investment therefore has to be heavily oriented toward import substitution, and the equality of supply and demand must be tested on a commodity basis to avoid balance-of-payments difficulties. In the three cases mentioned, this balancing process is carried out by means of an input-output analysis in which imported goods are distinguished from domestic products in each category.

In principle, comparative advantage can be used in the ECLA procedure as a basis for the choice of import substitutes, but this has apparently been done only to a limited degree. Since the main emphasis is on balance, there is a danger that the initial assumptions as to levels of exports will not be re-examined after the extent of import substitution required by a given program has been determined. The result may be a considerably lower productivity of investment in import substitutes than in exports if the two are not systematically compared. The drawbacks to this procedure are more serious in small countries like Colombia and Peru than in a large country like India, in which imports supply a smaller fraction of the total demand for commodities.

B. *Procedures Emphasizing Comparative Advantage.* Among countries having development programs, procedures that stress comparative advantage are less common than those emphasizing balance. Practically all policy statements list among their priority criteria factors presumably leading to comparative advantage, but there is little evidence as to how they are applied in drawing up programs.

The development procedures of the government of Puerto Rico come as close to being a pure application of comparative advantage as Soviet procedures are of principles of balanced growth. Unlike many low-income countries, Puerto Rico has an elastic demand for its exports to the U.S. market and can attract U.S. capital for profitable investments. The government's policy has been to give tax remission for ten years and to provide overhead facilities, labor training, and other inducements to industries that will benefit the island's economy. In deciding which industries to promote, the Economic Development Authority has studied the long-term comparative advantage of a large number of alternative projects, since comparative advantage will lead to both satisfactory profits and maximum income. Low-cost labor (even with allowance for differences in productivity) has been the main element in comparative advantage, since most industrial materials must be imported. Allowance is also made for

[20]On the basis of a simplified linear-programming model, Sandee [45, p. 25] finds that "up to 1970 more effective ways to employ capital for development exist than highly capital intensive steel-making," suggesting that an analysis of comparative advantage would indicate more reliance on imports. The nonmarket benefits of production are omitted from his analysis, however.

external economies in industries that will supply inputs to other sectors.[21]

Under this policy, the growth of per capita income has been as rapid (nearly 5 per cent annually) and the development of industry as marked (from 19 per cent to 25 per cent of GNP) over the years 1948-1958 as in any country following a deliberate policy of balanced growth. The planning procedure depends very largely on the particular relation of Puerto Rico to the United States and its small size. These factors make it unnecessary to worry about the elasticity of demand for exports or the dangers of dependence on foreign sources for essential imports, which so preoccupy the Indian and Latin American planners. With reliable export and import markets, domestic balance is not a problem.

Since the assumptions of the classical model are not approached so closely in most underdeveloped countries as in Puerto Rico, the calculation of comparative advantage usually departs farther from the market evaluation. In a more typical case the Philippine National Economic Council has outlined a procedure for applying the SMP formula under Philippine conditions [39]. This analysis starts from the market evaluation of the profitability of an investment and adds corrections for the project's effect on the balance of payments, its use of domestic materials, and its use of domestic labor, each with a suitable weight. This procedure may be justified by comparison to the linear programming criteria of social profit. In principle the proper correction to private profit is obtained by giving each a value equal to the difference between its shadow price and its market price.[22] In the Philippines, this would mean a bonus for labor and a penalty for foreign exchange use (or a bonus for foreign exchange saving). Higgins [22, pp. 654-62] shows that the weights assigned in the Philippines tend to exaggerate these effects. The use of the same weight for all domestic materials may lead to serious error, since not all are overvalued by market prices.

The government of Israel has developed one of the most systematic procedures for measuring comparative advantage as a basis for allocating investment funds and foreign exchange. In effect, the Ministry of Finance evaluates projects on the basis of accounting prices for foreign exchange and capital, taking into account the indirect use of foreign exchange in sectors supplying inputs such as power or industrial materials. The calculation is summed up as the cost in domestic resources of a dollar earned or saved, and it is applied equally to exports and to import substitutes. The calculation of domestic value added is also made by exporters as a basis for export subsidies [3, p. 23]. In allocating the government's development budget, priority is given to projects whose domestic cost of earn-

[21]The Puerto Rican experience is discussed by Baer [2]; the evaluation procedures are described in mimeographed reports of the Economic Development Authority.

[22]The social profit, $\bar{\pi}_j$, may be expressed as:

$$(4b) \qquad \Pi_j = \overline{\Pi}_j + \sum a_{ij} \Delta P_i,$$

where $\bar{\pi}_j$ is private profit per unit of output calculated at market prices and ΔP_i is the difference between the market price and shadow price of commodity i. The elements ΔP_i may be regarded as weights attached to each input or output coefficient.

ing or saving foreign exchange is less than the current estimate of its accounting price. This procedure can also be rationalized by means of the linear programming criterion of social profitability. Instead of measuring the value derived per unit of investment with accounting prices for foreign exchange and labor, as in the SMP formula, the cost per unit of foreign exchange acquired is computed using an accounting price for capital. When the same shadow prices are used, all three measures give the same result.

Although it is dangerous to generalize from the limited evidence on development policies that is available, there appears to be some relation between the type of procedure adopted and the characteristics of the economy in a number of the cases examined. Small countries are forced to pay more attention to comparative advantage because they cannot hope to produce the whole range of manufactures and primary products, while large countries may be tempted to follow more autarchic policies.[23] The importance given to balanced growth also depends to a large extent on the country's recent experience with its export markets and the state of its foreign exchange reserves and borrowing capacity. Puerto Rico and Israel can both count on substantial capital inflows which make it unnecessary for them to approach balanced trade in the near future, while India has much less leeway.

IV. Conclusions

This paper has considered development policy from the standpoint of economic theory, as a problem in operations research, and as it is actually carried on by governments. Much of the confusion in the field stems from a failure to distinguish these different levels of analysis. Theorists are prone to suggest decision rules that omit some of the relevant institutional limits, while economists who have been working in particular areas often arrive at conclusions that do not fit other cases. As in other fields of economics, most of the disagreement can be traced to implicit differences in assumptions.

There are a number of contradictions between the implications of trade theory and growth theory. To make the two theories consistent, it is necessary to discard the assumption of equilibrium in factor markets, to allow for changes in the quantity and quality of factors of production over time, and to take account of internal and external economies of scale. Although under these assumptions market forces do not necessarily lead to efficient resource allocation, a pattern of production and trade can be determined that maximizes income over time. The commodities to be produced and traded cannot be determined by a simple ranking procedure along the lines of classical comparative advantage because of the interdependence among sectors. At best, it may be possible to say, for example, that a country has a comparative advantage in steel production for a specified set of production levels in supplying and using sectors. In advanced countries, this qualification may be unimportant, but in the less developed ones it is crucial in a number of industries.

[23]Japan is one exception to this generalization, partly due to its dependence on imported raw materials.

Much of the attack on the use of comparative advantage is based on its omission of various nonmarket elements. It is assumed that the inclusion of the latter favors the development of industry, and special benefits are often attributed to capital goods and heavy industry. The intangible benefits stemming from trade in the form of new products, improved technology, and technical assistance tend to be overlooked in this discussion. Although I support the critics who wish to include more of growth theory in determining the desirability of specialization, I doubt that this extension will favor balanced growth to the extent that they suppose.

The other main theoretical attack on comparative advantage is aimed at its supposed support for continued specialization in primary exports. Granting the low elasticity of demand for many primary products, it is wrong to conclude that comparative advantage is thereby superseded by principles of balanced growth. The increasing shortage of foreign exchange makes it even more important to economize on its use and to seek efficient ways for increasing its supply. The comparison of domestic to foreign sources of supply that is implied by comparative advantage is no less relevant to this situation than to the case in which investment is more evenly divided between exports and import substitutes.

The aspects of growth theory which do not seem to be reconcilable with the notion of comparative advantage are the sociological and political effects of choosing one production pattern instead of another. While the concept of opportunity cost can be extended to include a number of non-market phenomena, such as labor training and overhead facilities, it can hardly be stretched to cover differences in fertility rates or political attitudes. So far as I can see, in the present state of knowledge of social phenomena, considerations such as these may be used to modify the results of economic analysis but cannot be directly incorporated into it.

At the level of operations research, the search for simple decision rules for investment in low-income countries seems to have been useful mainly in exposing the fallacies in some of the common rules of thumb. One can specify conditions under which ratios such as the capital intensity or the effect on the balance of payments would be a valid indicator of the desirability of an investment, but the apparent gain in simplicity is offset by the danger of applying the test in inappropriate circumstances. A more fruitful approach to partial equilibrium analysis is provided by the use of accounting prices to compute the social profitability of a given use of resources. This method allows simultaneously for several overvalued or undervalued inputs, and it can include whatever elements of general equilibrium analysis are available.

Since market forces cannot be relied on to balance supply and demand under conditions of initial disequilibrium and accelerated growth, a principal concern of development policy is to ensure the consistency of production levels with commodity demands and factor supplies. The technique of linear programming is designed to combine the test of consistency with the test of the social profitability of a given resource use. Although it cannot be applied very extensively in underdeveloped countries, as yet, the programming methodology serves as a guide to improved practical measures.

To most economists, a survey of the procedures actually followed in designing development policy would probably suggest that balance is over-emphasized and that the potential gains from trade are often neglected. This emphasis may be partly justified by the greater uncertainties attached to trade and by an aversion to risk that is greater than seems warranted to the outside observer. Better understanding of the working of the under-developed economies and better information for planning is needed to redress the balance and enable countries to secure the potential gains from trade without conflict with measures for domestic development.

References

1. B. A. Balassa, *The Hungarian Experience in Economic Planning*. New Haven 1959.
2. W. Baer, "Puerto Rico: an Evaluation of a Successful Development Program," *Quart. Jour. Econ.*, Nov. 1959, *73*, 645–71.
3. Bank of Israel, *Annual Report, 1959*. Jerusalem 1960.
4. F. M. Bator, "On Capital Productivity, Input Allocation, and Growth," *Quart. Jour. Econ.*, Feb. 1957, *71*, 86–106.
5. N. S. Buchanan, *International Investment and Domestic Welfare*. New York 1945.
6. O. Castellino, "La Scelta degli Investimenti nei Programmi di Sviluppo Economico," *L'Industria*, 1959, No. 1, 60–76.
7. R. E. Caves, *Trade and Economic Structure*. Cambridge 1960.
8. H. B. Chenery, "The Application of Investment Criteria," *Quart. Jour. Econ.*, Feb. 1953, *67*, 76–96.
9. _____, "The Role of Industrialization in Development Programs," *Am. Econ. Rev., Proc.*, May 1955, *45*, 40–57.
10. _____, "Development Policies and Programmes"; *Econ. Bull. for Latin America*, Mar. 1958, *3*, 51–77.
11. _____, "The Interdependence of Investment Decisions," in Abramovitz *et al.*, *The Allocation of Economic Resources*. Stanford 1959.
12. M. Dobb, *An Essay on Economic Growth and Planning*. London 1960.
13. R. Dorfman, P. A. Samuelson, and R. M. Solow, *Linear Programming and Economic Analysis*. New York 1958.
14. O. Eckstein, "Investment Criteria for Economic Development and the Theory of Intertemporal Welfare Economics," *Quart. Jour. Econ.*, Feb. 1957, *71*, 56–85.
15. R. Frisch, *A Method of Working out a Macroeconomic Plan Frame with Particular Reference to the Evaluation of Development Projects, Foreign Trade and Employment*. Oslo 1959 (mimeo.).
16. _____, *A Powerful Method of Approximation in Optimum Investment Computations of the Normal Type*. Oslo 1959 (mimeo.).
17. W. Galenson and H. Leibenstein, "Investment Criteria, Productivity, and Economic Development," *Quart. Jour. Econ.*, Aug. 1955, *69*, 343–70.
18. A. Gerschenkron, "Economic Backwardness in Historical Perspective," in B. Hoselitz, ed., *The Progress of Underdeveloped Areas*, Chicago 1952.
19. Government of India Planning Commission, *The Third Five Year Plan*. New Delhi 1960.
20. G. Haberler, "Some Problems in the Pure Theory of International Trade," *Econ. Jour.*, June 1950, *60*, 223–40.
21. E. Hagen, "An Economic Justification of Protectionism," *Quart. Jour. Econ.*, Nov. 1958, *72*, 496–514.
22. B. Higgins, *Economic Development*. New York 1958.

23. A. O. Hirschman, *The Strategy of Economic Development.* New Haven 1958.

24. _____, "Investment Criteria and Capital Intensity Once Again," *Quart. Jour. Econ.*, Aug. 1958, 72, 469–71.

25. A. E. Kahn, "Investment Criteria in Development Programs," *Quart. Jour. Econ.*, Feb. 1951, 65, 38–61.

26. C. P. Kindleberger, *The Terms of Trade: A European Case Study.* New York 1956.

27. R. Komiya, "A Note on Professor Mahalanobis' Model of Indian Economic Planning," *Rev. Econ. Stat.*, Feb. 1959, 41, 29–35.

28. H. Leibenstein, "Why Do We Disagree on Investment Policies for Development?" *Indian Econ. Jour.*, Apr. 1958, 5, 369–86.

29. W. A. Lewis, "Economic Development with Unlimited Supplies of Labor," *Manchester School*, May 1954.

30. P. C. Mahalanobis, "The Approach of Operational Research to Planning in India," *Sankhya*, Dec. 1955, 16, 3–131.

31. K. Mandelbaum, *The Industrialization of Backward Areas.* Oxford 1945.

32. J. M. Montias, "Planning with Material Balances in Soviet-type Economies," *Am. Econ. Rev.*, Dec. 1959, 49, 963–85.

33. H. Myint, "The Classical Theory of International Trade and the Underdeveloped Countries," *Econ. Jour.*, June 1958, 68, 317–37.

34. G. Myrdal, *Economic Theory and Underdeveloped Regions.* London 1957.

35. H. Neisser, "Investment Criteria, Productivity and Economic Development," *Quart. Jour. Econ.*, Nov. 1956, 70, 644–47.

36. R. Nurkse, *Problems of Capital Formation in Underdeveloped Countries.* Oxford 1953.

37. _____, *Patterns of Trade and Development.* Stockholm 1959.

38. P. G. Ohlin, "Balanced Economic Growth in History," *Am. Econ. Rev., Proc.*, May 1959, 49, 338–53.

39. The Philippines National Economic Council, *The Five-Year Economic and Social Development Program for Fiscal Years 1957–1961.* Manila 1957.

40. J. J. Polak, "Balance of Payments Problems of Countries Reconstructing with the Help of Foreign Loans," *Quart. Jour. Econ.*, Feb. 1943, 57, 208–40.

41. R. Prebisch, "Commercial Policy in the Underdeveloped Countries," *Am. Econ. Rev., Proc.*, May 1959, 49, 251–73.

42. A. Qayum, *Theory and Policy of Accounting Prices.* Amsterdam 1959.

43. P. Rosenstein-Rodan, "Problems of Industrialization of Eastern and South-Eastern Europe," *Econ. Jour.*, June-Sept. 1943, 53, 205–16.

44. W. W. Rostow, "The Take-Off into Self-Sustained Growth," *Econ. Jour.*, Mar. 1956, 66, 25–48.

45. J. Sandee, *A Long-Term Planning Model for India.* United Nations pub. New York 1959.

46. T. W. Schultz, "Latin American Economic Policy Lessons," *Am. Econ. Rev., Proc.*, May 1956, 46, 425–32.

47. T. Scitovsky, "Two Concepts of External Economies," *Jour. Pol. Econ.*, April 1954, 62, 143–51.

48. _____, "Growth—Balanced or Unbalanced," in M. Abramowitz *et al., The Allocation of Economic Resources*, Stanford 1959.

49. A. K. Sen, "Some Notes on the Choice of Capital Intensity in Development Planning," *Quart. Jour. Econ.*, Nov. 1957, 71, 561–84.

50. J. Sheahan, "International Specialization and the Concept of Balanced Growth," *Quart. Jour. Econ.*, May 1958, 72, 183–97.

51. H. W. Singer, "The Distribution of Gains Between Investing and Borrowing Countries," *Amer. Econ. Rev., Proc.*, May 1950, 40, 473–85.

52. G. Stigler, "Production and Distribution in the Short Run," reprinted in Am. Econ. Assoc., *Readings in the Theory of Income Distribution*. Philadelphia 1946.

53. P. Streeten, "Unbalanced Growth," *Oxford Econ. Papers*, June 1959, 11, 167–91.

54. J. Tinbergen, "The Relevance of Theoretical Criteria in the Selection of Investment Plans," in M. Millikan, ed., *Investment Criteria and Economic Growth*. Cambridge 1955.

55. _____, *Economic Policy: Principles and Design*. Amsterdam 1956.

56. _____, *The Design of Development*. Baltimore 1958.

57. United Nations, Department of Economic and Social Affairs, *Analyses and Projections of Economic Development*. New York 1955.

58. _____, *Analyses and Projections of Economic Development*. III. *The Economic Development of Colombia*. Geneva 1957.

59. _____, *Analyses and Projections of Economic Development*. V. *The Economic Development of Argentina*. Mexico City 1960.

60. _____, *Analyses and Projections of Economic Development*. VI. *The Industrial Development of Peru*. Mexico City 1959.

61. United Nations, *Manual of Economic Development Projects*. New York 1959.

62. A. Vaidyanathan, "A Survey of the Literature on Investment Criteria and Development of Underdeveloped Countries," *Ind. Econ. Jour.*, Oct. 1956, 4, 122–44.

63. J. Viner, *International Trade and Economic Development*. Oxford 1953.

64. _____, "Stability and Progress: The Poorer Countries' Problem," in D. Hague, ed., *Stability and Progress in the World Economy*. London 1958 (with comment by R. Nurkse).

65. P. Wiles, "Growth versus Choice," *Econ. Jour.*, June 1956, 66, 244–55.

66. J. H. Williams, "The Theory of International Trade Reconsidered," *Econ. Jour.*, June 1929, 39, 195–209. Reprinted in Am. Econ. Assoc., *Readings in the Theory of International Trade*. Philadelphia 1949.

18. Investment in Human Capital

Theodore W. Schultz[*]

Although it is obvious that people acquire useful skills and knowledge, it is not obvious that these skills and knowledge are a form of capital, that this capital is in substantial part a product of deliberate investment, that it has grown in western societies at a much faster rate than conventional (nonhuman) capital, and that its growth may well be the most distinctive feature of the economic system. It has been widely observed that increases in national output have been large compared with the increases of inputs

[*]Presidential Address at the American Economic Association, December 28, 1960; reproduced in the *American Economic Review*, March 1961. The author is Professor of Economics, University of Chicago. The author is indebted to his colleagues Milton Friedman for his very helpful suggestions to gain clarity and cogency and Harry G. Johnson for pointing out a number of ambiguities.

of land, manhours, and physical reproducible capital. Investment in human capital is probably the major explanation for the growth of national output.

Much of what we call consumption constitutes investment in human capital. Direct expenditures on education, health and internal migration to take advantage of better job opportunities are clear examples. Earnings foregone by mature students attending school and by workers acquiring on-the-job training are equally clear examples. Yet nowhere do these enter into our national accounts. The use of leisure time to improve skills and knowledge is widespread and it too is unrecorded. In these and similar ways the *quality* of human effort can be greatly improved and its productivity enhanced. I shall contend that such investment in human capital accounts for most of the impressive rise in the real earnings per worker that we have experienced.

I shall comment, first, on the reason why economists have shied away from the explicit analysis of investment in human capital, and then, on the capacity of such investment to explain many a puzzle about economic growth. Mainly, however, I shall concentrate on the scope and substance of human capital and its formation. In closing I shall consider some social and policy implications.

I. Shying Away from Investment in Man

Economists have long known that people are an important part of the wealth of nations. Measured by what labor contributes to output, the productive capacity of human beings is now vastly larger than all other forms of wealth taken together. What economists have not stressed is the simple truth that people invest in themselves and that these investments are very large. Although economists are seldom timid in entering on abstract analysis and are often proud of being impractical, they have not been bold in coming to grips with this form of investment. Whenever they have come even close, they have proceeded gingerly as if they were stepping into deep water. No doubt there are reasons for being wary. Deep-seated moral and philosophical issues are ever present. Free men are first and foremost the end to be served by economic endeavor; they are not property or marketable assets. Moreover, it has been all too convenient in marginal productivity analysis to treat labor as if it were a unique bundle of innate abilities that are wholly free of capital.

The mere thought of investment in human beings is offensive to some among us.[1] Our values and beliefs inhibit us from looking upon human beings as capital goods, except in slavery, and this we abhor. We are not unaffected by the long struggle to rid society of indentured service and to evolve political and legal institutions to keep men free from bondage. These are achievements that we prize highly. Hence, to treat human beings as wealth that can be augmented by investment runs counter to deeply held values. It seems to reduce man once again to a mere material component, to something akin to property. And for man to look upon himself as a capital good, even if it did not impair his freedom, may seem to debase him. No less a person than J. S. Mill at one time insisted that the people of a country should not be looked upon as wealth because

[1]This paragraph draws on the introduction to my Teller Lecture [16].

wealth existed only for the sake of people [15]. But surely Mill was wrong, because there is nothing in the concept of human wealth that implies otherwise. By investing in themselves, people can enlarge the range of choice available to them. It follows that this is one way free men can enhance their welfare.

Among the few who have treated human beings as capital, there are three distinguished names. The philosopher-economist Adam Smith boldly included all of the acquired and useful abilities of all of the inhabitants of a country as a part of capital. So did H. von Thünen who then went on to argue that the concept of capital applied to man did not degrade him or impair his freedom and dignity, but on the contrary that the failure to apply the concept was especially pernicious in wars, ". . . for here . . . one will sacrifice in a battle a hundred human beings in the prime of their lives without a thought in order to save one gun." The reason is that, ". . . the purchase of a cannon causes an outlay of public funds, whereas human beings are to be had for nothing by means of a mere conscription decree" [20]. Irving Fisher also clearly and cogently presented an all-inclusive concept of capital [6]. Yet the main stream of thought has held that it is neither appropriate nor practical to apply the concept of capital to human beings. Marshall [11] whose great prestige goes far to explain why this view was accepted, held that while human beings are incontestably capital from an abstract and mathematical point of view, it would be out of touch with the market place to treat them as capital in practical analyses. Investment in human beings has accordingly seldom been incorporated in the formal core of economics, even though many economists including Marshall have seen its relevance at one point or another in what they have written.

The failure to treat human resources explicitly as a form of capital, as a produced means of production, as the product of investment, has fostered the retention of the classical notion of labor as a capacity to do manual work requiring little knowledge and skill, a capacity with which according to this notion laborers are endowed about equally. This notion of labor was wrong then and it is patently wrong now with modern techniques of production. Counting individuals who can and want to work and treating such a count as a measure of the quantity of an economic factor is no more meaningful than it would be to count the number of all manner of machines to determine their economic importance either as a stock of capital or as a flow of productive services.

Laborers have become capitalists in the course of industrialization not from a diffusion of the ownership of corporation stocks, as folklore would have it, but from the acquisition of knowledge and skill that have economic value [9]. This knowledge and skill are in great part the product of investment and combined with other human investment predominantly account for the productive superiority of the technically advanced countries. To omit them in studying economic growth is like trying to explain Soviet ideology without Marx.

II. Economic Growth from Human Capital

Many paradoxes and puzzles about our dynamic, growing economy can be resolved once human investment is taken into account. A sketch of these issues will help us gain perspective. Let me begin with some that are minor though not trivial.

When farm people take nonfarm jobs they earn substantially less than industrial workers of the same race, age, and sex. Similarly nonwhite urban males earn much less than white males even after allowance is made for the effects of differences in unemployment, age, city size and region [21]. Because these differentials in earnings correspond closely to corresponding differentials in education, they strongly suggest that the one is a consequence of the other. Negroes who operate farms, whether as tenants or as owners, earn much less than whites on comparable farms.[2] Fortunately, crops and livestock are not vulnerable to the blight of discrimination. The large differences in earnings seem rather to reflect mainly the differences in health and education. Workers in the South on the average earn appreciably less than in the North or West and they also have on the average less education. Most migratory farm workers earn very little indeed by comparison with other workers. Many of them have virtually no schooling, are in poor health, are unskilled and have little ability to do useful work. To urge that the differences in the amount of human investment may explain these differences in earnings seems elementary. Of more recent vintage are observations showing younger workers at a competitive advantage; for example, young men entering the labor force are said to have an advantage over unemployed older workers in obtaining satisfactory jobs. Most of these young people possess twelve years of school, most of the older workers six years or less. The observed advantage of the former may therefore result not from inflexibilities in social security or in retirement programs, or from sociological preference of employers, but from real differences in productivity connected with one form of human investment, i.e., education. And yet another example, the curve relating income to age tends to be steeper for skilled than for unskilled persons. Investment in on-the-job training seems a likely explanation, as will be noted later.

Economic growth requires much internal migration of workers to adjust to changing job opportunities [10]. Young men and women move more readily than older workers. Surely this makes economic sense when one recognizes that the costs of such migration are a form of human investment. Young people have more years ahead of them than older workers during which they can realize on such an investment. Hence it takes less of a wage differential to make it economically advantageous for them to move, or, to put it differently, young people can expect higher return on investment in migration than older people. This differential may explain selective migration without requiring an appeal to sociological differences between young and old people.

The examples so far given are for investment in human beings that yield a return over a long period. This is true equally of investment in education, training, and migration of young people. Not all investments in human beings are of this kind; some are more nearly akin to current inputs, as for example expenditures on food and shelter in some countries

---

[2]Based on unpublished preliminary results obtained by Joseph Willett in his Ph. D. research at the University of Chicago.

where work is mainly the application of brute human force, calling for energy and stamina, and where the intake of food is far from enough to do a full day's work. On the "hungry" steppes and in the teeming valleys of Asia, millions of adult males have so meager a diet that they cannot do more than a few hours of hard work. To call them underemployed does not seem pertinent. Under such circumstances it is certainly meaningful to treat food partly as consumption and partly as a current "producer good," as some Indian economists have done [3]. Let us not forget that Western economists during the early decades of industrialization and even through Marshall and Pigou often connected additional food for workers with increases in labor productivity.

Let us pass on to three major perplexing questions closely connected with the riddle of economic growth. First, consider the long period behavior of the capital-income ratio. We were taught that a country which amassed more reproducible capital relative to its land and labor would employ such capital in greater "depth" because of its growing abundance and cheapness. But apparently this is not what happens. On the contrary, such empirical estimates as we have indicate that less of such capital tends to be employed relative to income as economic growth proceeds. Are we to infer that the ratio of capital to income has no relevance in explaining either poverty or opulence? Or that a rise of the ratio is not a prerequisite to economic growth? These questions raise fundamental issues bearing on motives and preferences for holding wealth as well as the motives for particular investments and the stock of capital thereby accumulated. For my purpose all that needs to be said is that these estimates of capital-income ratios refer to only a part of all capital. They exclude in particular and most unfortunately any human capital. Yet human capital has almost surely been increasing at a rate substantially greater than reproducible (nonhuman) capital. We cannot, therefore, infer from these estimates that the stock of *all* capital has been decreasing relative to income. On the contrary, if we accept the not implausible assumption that the motives and preferences of people, the technical opportunities open to them, and the uncertainty associated with economic growth during particular periods were leading people to maintain roughly a constant ratio between *all* capital and income, the decline in the estimated capital-income ratio[3] is simply a signal that human capital has been increasing relatively not only to conventional capital but also to income.

The bumper crop of estimates that show national income increasing faster than national resources raises a second and not unrelated puzzle. The income of the United States has been increasing at a much higher rate than the combined amount of land, man-hours worked and the stock of reproducible capital used to produce the income. Moreover, the discrepancy between the two rates has become larger from one business cycle to the next during recent decades [5]. To call this discrepancy a measure of "resource productivity" gives a name to our ignorance but does not dis-

---

[3]I leave aside here the difficulties inherent in identifying and measuring both the nonhuman capital and income entering into estimates of this ratio. There are index and aggregation problems aplenty and not all improvements in the quality of this capital have been accounted for, as I shall note later.

pel it. If we accept these estimates, the connections between national resources and national income have become loose and tenuous over time.
Unless this discrepancy can be resolved, received theory of production
applied to inputs and outputs as currently measured is a toy and not a
tool for studying economic growth. Two sets of forces probably account for
the discrepancy, if we neglect entirely the index number and aggregation
problems that be-devil all estimates of such global aggregates as total
output and total input. One is returns to scale; the second, the large improvements in the quality of inputs that have occurred but have been
omitted from the input estimates. Our economy has undoubtedly been
experiencing increasing returns to scale at some points offset by decreasing returns at others. If we can succeed in identifying and measuring the
net gains, they may turn out to have been substantial. The improvements
in the quality of inputs that have not been adequately allowed for are no
doubt partly in material (nonhuman) capital. My own conception, however, is that both this defect and the omission of economies of scale are
minor sources of discrepancy between the rates of growth of inputs and
output compared to the improvements in human capacity that have been
omitted.

A small step takes us from these two puzzles raised by existing estimates
to a third which brings us to the heart of the matter, namely the essentially unexplained large increase in real earnings of workers. Can this be a
windfall? Or a quasi-rent pending the adjustment in the supply of labor?
Or, a pure rent reflecting the fixed amount of labor? It seems far more
reasonable that it represents rather a return to the investment that has
been made in human beings. The observed growth in productivity per unit
of labor is simply a consequence of holding the unit of labor constant over
time although in fact this unit of labor has been increasing as a result of
a steady growing amount of human capital per worker. As I read our
record, the human capital component has become very large as a consequence of human investment.

Another aspect of the same basic question, which admits of the same
resolution, is the rapid postwar recovery of countries that had suffered
severe destruction of plant and equipment during the war. The toll from
bombing was all too visible in the factories laid flat, the railroad yards,
bridges, and harbors wrecked, and the cities in ruin. Structures, equipment,
inventories were all heaps of rubble. Not so visible, yet large, was the toll
from the wartime depletion of the physical plant that escaped destruction
by bombs. Economists were called upon to assess the implications of these
war-time losses for recovery. In retrospect, it is clear that they overestimated the prospective retarding effects of these losses. Having had a small
hand in this effort, I have had a special reason for looking back and won-
dering why the judgments that we formed soon after the war proved to be
so far from the mark. The explanation that now is clear is that we gave
altogether too much weight to nonhuman capital in making these assess-
ments. We fell into this error, I am convinced, because we did not have
a concept of *all* capital and, therefore, failed to take account of human
capital and the important part it plays in production in a modern economy.

Let me close this section with a comment on poor countries, for which there are virtually no solid estimates. I have been impressed by repeatedly expressed judgments, especially by those who have a responsibility in making capital available to poor countries, about the low rate at which these countries can absorb additional capital. New, outside capital can be put to good use, it is said, only when it is added "slowly and gradually." But this experience is at variance with the widely held impression that countries are poor fundamentally because they are starved for capital and that additional capital is truly the key to their more rapid economic growth .The reconciliation is again, I believe, to be found in emphasis on particular forms of capital. The new capital available to these countries from outside as a rule goes into the formation of structures, equipment and sometimes also into inventories. But it is generally not available for additional investment in man. Consequently, human capabilities do not stay abreast of physical capital and become limiting factors in economic growth. It should come as no surprise, therefore, that the absorption rate of capital to augment only particular nonhuman resources is necessarily low. The Horvat [8] formulation of the optimum rate of investment which treats knowledge and skill as a critical investment variable in determining the rate of economic growth is both relevant and important.

III. Scope and Substance of These Investments

What are human investments? Can they be distinguished from consumption? Is it at all feasible to identify and measure them, What do they contribute to income? Granted that they seem amorphous compared to brick and mortar, and hard to get at compared to the investment accounts of corporations, they assuredly are not a fragment; they are rather like the contents of Pandora's box, full of difficulties and hope.

Human resources obviously have both quantitative and qualitative dimensions. The number of people, the proportion who enter upon useful work, and hours worked are essentially quantitative characteristics. To make my task tolerably manageable, I shall neglect these and consider only such quality components as skill, knowledge, and similar attributes that affect particular human capabilities to do productive work. Insofar as expenditures to enhance such capabilities also increase the value productivity of human effort (labor), they will yield a positive rate of return.[1]

How can we estimate the magnitude of human investment? The practice followed in connection with physical capital goods is to estimate the magnitude of capital formation by expenditures made to produce the capital goods. This practice would suffice also for the formation of human capital. However, for human capital there is an additional problem that is less pressing for physical capital goods: how to distinguish between expenditures for consumption and for investment. This distinction bristles with both conceptual and practical difficulties. We can think of three classes of expenditures: expenditures that satisfy consumer preferences and in no way enhance the capabilities under discussion—these represent

---

[1]Even so our observed return can be either negative, zero or positive because our observations are drawn from a world where there is uncertainty and imperfect knowledge and where there are windfall gains and losses and mistakes aplenty.

pure consumption; expenditures that enhance capabilities and do not satisfy any preferences underlying consumption—these represent pure investment; and expenditures that have both effects. Most relevant activities clearly are in the third class, partly consumption and partly investment, which is why the task of identifying each component is so formidable and why the measurement of capital formation by expenditures is less useful for human investment than for investment in physical goods. In principle there is an alternative method for estimating human investment, namely by its yield rather than by its cost. While any capability produced by human investment becomes a part of the human agent and hence cannot be sold; it is nevertheless "in touch with the market place" by affecting the wages and salaries the human agent can earn. The resulting increase in earnings is the yield on the investment.[5]

Despite the difficulty of exact measurement at this stage of our understanding of human investment, many insights can be gained by examining some of the more important activities that improve human capabilities. I shall concentrate on five major categories:

1. Health facilities and services, broadly conceived to include all expenditures that affect the life expectancy, strength and stamina, and the vigor and vitality of a people.
2. On-the-job training, including old style apprenticeship organized by firms.
3. Formally organized education, consisting of elementary, secondary, and higher education.
4. Study programs for adults that are not organized by firms, including extension programs notably in agriculture.
5. Migration of individuals and families to adjust to changing job opportunities.

Except for education, not much is known about these activities that is germane here. I shall refrain from commenting on study programs for adults although in agriculture the Extension Services of the several states have played an important role in transmitting new knowledge and in developing skills of farmers [17]. Nor shall I elaborate further on internal migration related to economic growth.

Health activities have both quantity and quality implications. Such speculations as economists have engaged in about the effects of improvements in health,[6] has been predominantly in connection with population growth, which is to say with quantity. But surely health measures may also enhance the quality of human resources. So, also, may additional food and better shelter especially in underdeveloped countries.

The change in the role of food as people become richer sheds some light on one of the conceptual problems referred to above. I have already pointed

[5]In principle, the value of the investment can be determined by discounting the additional future earnings it yields just as the value of a physical capital good can be determined by discounting its income stream.
[6]Health economics is in its infancy; there are two medical journals with "economics" in their titles, two bureaus for economic research in private associations (one in the American Medical and the other in the American Dental Association), and not a few studies and papers by outside scholars. Dr. Mushkin's survey is very useful with its pertinent economic insights, though she may have underestimated somewhat the influence of the economic behavior of people in striving for health (Mushkin [14]).

out that extra food in some poor countries has the attribute of a "producer good." This attribute of food, however, diminishes as the consumption of food rises and there comes a point at which any further increase in food becomes pure consumption.[7] Clothing, housing and perhaps medical services may be similar.

My comment about on-the-job training will consist of a conjecture on the amount of such training, a note on the decline of the apprentice, and, then, a useful economic theorem on who bears the costs of such training. Surprisingly little is known about on-the-job training in modern industry. About all that can be said is that the expansion of education has not eliminated it. It seems likely, however, that some of the training formerly undertaken by firms has been discontinued and other training programs have been instituted to adjust both to the rise in the education of workers and to changes in the demands for new skills. The amount invested annually in such training can only be a guess. H. F. Clark[8] has been prepared to place it somewhere near to equal to the amount spent on formal education. Even if it were only one-half as large, it would represent currently an annual gross investment of about 15 billion dollars. Elsewhere, too, it is thought to be important. For example, some observers have been impressed by the amount of such training underway in plants in the Soviet Union.[9] Meanwhile, apprenticeship has all but disappeared, partly because it is now inefficient and partly because schools now perform many of its functions. Its disappearance has been hastened no doubt by the difficulty of enforcing apprenticeship agreements. Legally they have come to smack of indentured service. The underlying economic factors and behavior are clear enough. The apprentice is prepared to serve during the initial period when his productivity is less than the cost of his keep and of his training. Later, however, unless he is legally restrained, he will seek other employment when his productivity begins to exceed the cost of keep and training which is the period during which a master recoups on his earlier outlay.

Implicit in the above argument is the essence of the theorem, advanced by Gary Becker [1], which states that in competitive markets employees pay all the costs of their training and none of these costs are ultimately borne by the firm. Becker has pointed out several implications. The notion that expenditures on training by a firm generate external economies for other firms is not consistent with this theorem. The theorem indicates one force favoring the transfer from on-the-job training to attending school. Since on-the-job training reduces the net earnings of workers at the beginning and raises it later on, this theorem also provides an explanation for the "steeper slope of the curve relating income to age," for skilled than unskilled workers, a phenomenon referred to earlier.[10] What all this adds

[7]For instance, the income elasticity of the demand for food continues to be positive even after the point is reached where additional food no longer has the attribute of a "producer good."

[8]Based on comments made by Professor Harold F. Clark at the Merrill Center for Economics, Summer, 1959; also, see (Clark [4]).

[9]Based on observations made by a team of U. S. economists of which I was a member, to be published by the Committee for Economic Development.

[10]Professor Becker has also noted still another implication arising out of the fact that the income and capital accounts in on-the-job training are tied together which gives rise to "permanent" and "transitory" income effects that may have substantial explanatory value.

up to, is that the stage is set to undertake meaningful economic studies of on-the-job training.

Happily we reach firmer ground in education. Investment in education has risen at a rapid rate and may well account for a substantial part of the otherwise unexplained rise in earnings. I shall do no more than summarize some preliminary results about the total costs of education including income foregone by students, the apparent relation of these costs to consumer income and to alternative investments, the rise of the stock of education in the labor force, returns to education, and the contribution that the increase in the stock of education may have made to earnings and to national income.

It is not difficult to estimate the conventional costs of education in the United States consisting of the services of teachers, librarians, administrators, the costs of maintaining and operating the educational plant, and interest on the capital embodied in the educational plant. It is far more difficult to estimate another component of total cost, the income foregone by students. Yet this component should be included and it is far from negligible. For example, well over half of the costs of higher education consists of income foregone by students. As early as 1900, this income foregone accounted for about one-fourth of the total costs of elementary, secondary and higher education. By 1956, it represented over two-fifths of all costs. The rising significance of foregone income has been a major factor in the marked upward trend in the total real costs of education which rose, measured in current prices, from $400 million in 1900 to $28.7 billion in 1956 [18]. The percentage rise in educational costs was about three and a half times as large as in consumer income, which would imply a high income elasticity of the demand for education, if education were regarded as pure consumption.[11] Educational costs rose about three and a half times as rapidly as did the gross formation of physical capital in dollars. If we were to treat education as pure investment, this result would suggest that the returns to education were becoming relatively more attractive than those to nonhuman capital.[12]

Much schooling is acquired by persons who are not treated as income earners in most economic analysis, particularly, of course, women. To analyze the effect of growth in schooling on earnings, it is therefore necessary to distinguish between the stock of education in the population and the amount in the labor force. Years of school completed are far from satisfactory as a measure because of the marked increases that have taken place in the number of days of school attendance of enrolled students and because much more of the education of workers consists of high school and higher education than formerly. My preliminary estimates suggest that the stock of education in the labor force rose about eight and a half times between 1900 and 1956, whereas the stock of reproducible capital rose four and a half times, both in constant 1956 prices. These estimates

[11]Had other things stayed constant this suggests an income elasticity of 3.5. Among the things that did change the prices of educational services rose relative to other consumer prices offset perhaps in part by improvements in the quality of educational services.

[12]This, of course, assumes among other things that the relationship between gross and net have not changed or have changed in the same proportion. Estimates from my essay, "Education and Economic Growth," see [16].

are, of course, subject to many qualifications.[13] Nevertheless, both the magnitude and the rate of increase of this form of human capital have been such that they could be an important key to the riddle of economic growth.[14]

The exciting work under way is on the return to education. In spite of the flood of high school and college graduates, the return to this education has not become trivial. Even the low limits of the estimates at hand indicate that the return to such education has been in the neighborhood of the return to nonhuman capital. This is what most of these estimates show when they treat as costs all of the public and private expenditures on education and also the income foregone while attending school and when they treat all of these costs as investment, allocating none to consumption.[15] But surely a part of these costs is consumption in the sense that education creates a form of consumer capital which has the attribute of improving the taste and the quality of consumption of students throughout the rest of their lives. If one were to allocate a substantial fraction of the total costs of this education to consumption, say one-half, this would, of course,

[13]From [19], Sec. 4. These estimates of the stock of education are tentative and incomplete. They are incomplete in that they do not take into account fully the increases in the average life of this form of human capital arising out of the fact that relatively more of this education is held by younger people in the labor force than was true in earlier years; and, they are incomplete because no adjustment has been made for the improvements in education over time, increasing the quality of a year of school other than that related to changes in the proportions represented by elementary, high school and higher education. Even so the stock of this form of human capital rose 8.5 times between 1900 and 1956 where the stock of reproducible nonhuman capital increased only 4.5 times both in constant 1956 prices.

[14]In value terms this stock of education was only 22 percent as large as the stock of reproducible physical capital in 1900, whereas in 1956 it already had become 42 percent as large.

[15]Several comments are called for here: (1) the return to high school education appears to have declined substantially between the late thirties and early fifties and since then has leveled off, perhaps even risen somewhat, indicating a rate of return toward the end of the fifties about as large as that to higher education; (2) the return to college education seems to have risen somewhat since the late thirties in spite of the rapid influx of college trained individuals into the labor force; (3) Becker's estimates based on the difference in income between high school and college graduates based on urban males adjusted for ability, race, unemployment and mortality show a return of 9 percent to total college costs including both earnings foregone and conventional college costs, public and private and with none of these costs allocated to consumption (see his paper, "Under-investment in College Education?"; in the last issue of the *Proceedings* of this journal); (4) the returns to this education in the case of non-white urban males, of rural males, and of females in the labor force may have been somewhat lower (see Becker); and (5), my own estimates, admittedly less complete than those of Becker and thus subject to additional qualifiications, based mainly on lifetime income estimates of Herman P. Miller, "Annual and Lifetime Income in Relation to Education," used here with his permission, lead to a return of about 11 percent to both high school and college education as of 1958. See [12, Sec. 5].

Whether the consumption component in education will ultimately dominate in the sense that the investment component in education will diminish as these expenditures increase and a point will be reached where additional expenditures for education will be pure consumption (a zero return on however small a part one might treat as an investment), is an interesting speculation. It may come to pass as it has in food and shelter, but that point appears very remote presently in view of the prevailing investment value and the new demands for knowledge and skill inherent in the nature of our technical and economic progress.

double the observed rate of return to what would then become the investment component in education.

Fortunately, the problem of allocating the costs of education in the
labor force between consumption and investment does not rise to plague
us when we turn to the contribution that this education may have made
to earnings and to national income because a change in allocation only
alters the rate of return, not the total return. I noted at the outset that
the unexplained increases in U. S. national income have been especially
large in recent decades. On one set of assumptions, the unexplained part
amounted to nearly three-fifths of the total increase between 1929 and
1956.[16] How much of this unexplained increase in income may reflect a
return to education in the labor forces? A lower limit suggests that about
three-tenths of it came from this source, and an upper limit does not rule
out that more than one-half of it came from this source.[17] These estimates
also imply that between 36 and 70 percent of the hitherto unexplained
rise in the earnings of labor may be explained by returns to the additional
education of workers.

IV. A Closing Note on Policy

One proceeds at his own peril in discussing social implications and
policy. The conventional hedge is to camouflage one's values and to wear
the mantle of academic innocence. Let me proceed unprotected!

1. Our tax laws everywhere discriminate against human capital. Although the stock of such capital has become large and even though it is
obvious that human capital, like other forms of reproducible capital, depre-
ciates, becomes obsolete, and entails maintenance, our tax laws are all but
blind on these matters.

2. Human capital deteriorates when it is idle because unemployment
impairs the skills that workers have acquired. Losses in earnings can be
cushioned by appropriate payments but these do not keep idleness from
taking its toll from human capital.

3. There are more than a few hindrances to the free choice of professions. Professional associations and governmental bodies are in a position
to hinder entry. There is evidence that they do limit entry into medicine.
Such purposeful interference keeps the investment in this form of human
capital below its optimum. [7].

4. It is indeed elementary to stress the greater imperfections of the
capital market in providing funds for investment in human beings than
for investment in physical goods. Much could be done to reduce these imperfections by reforms in tax and banking laws and by changes in banking
practices. Long term private and public loans to students are warranted,
and they are feasible.

[16]Real income doubled rising from $150 to $302 billion in 1956 prices. Eighty-
nine billions of the increase in real income is taken to be unexplained, or about
56 percent of the total increase. The stock of education in the labor force rose
by $355 billion of which $69 billion is here allocated to the growth in the labor
force to keep the per worker stock of education constant, and $286 billion repre-
sents the increase in the level of this stock. See [19, Sec. 6], for an elaboration
of the method and the relevant estimates.

[17]In percent, the lower estimate came out to 29 percent and the upper estimate
to 56 percent.

5. Internal migration, notably the movement of farm people into industry, made necessary by the dynamics of our economic progress, requires substantial investments. In general families in which the husbands and wives are already in the late thirties cannot afford to make these investments because the remaining payoff period for them is too short. Yet society would gain if more of them would pull stakes and move because in addition to the increase in productivity currently, the children of these families would be better located for employment when they were ready to enter the labor market. The case for making some of these investments on public account is by no means weak. Our farm programs have failed miserably these many years in not coming to grips with the costs and returns from off farm migration.

6. The low earnings of particular groups in our population have long been a matter of public concern. Policy all too frequently concentrates only on the effects ignoring the causes. No small part of the low earnings of many Negroes, Puerto Ricans, Mexican nationals, indigenous migratory farm workers, poor farm people and some of our older workers, reflects the failure to have invested in their health and education. Past mistakes are, of course, by-gones, but for the sake of the next generation we can ill afford to continue making the same mistakes over again.

7. Is there a substantial under-investment in human beings other than in these depressed groups? This is an important question for economists. The evidence at hand is fragmentary. Nor will the answer be easily won. There undoubtedly have been over-investments in some skills, for example, too many locomotive firemen and engineers, too many people trained to be farmers, and too many agricultural economists! Our schools are not free of loafers and some students lack the necessary talents. Nevertheless, under-investment in knowledge and skill, relative to the amounts invested in nonhuman capital would appear to be the rule for a number of reasons. The strong and increasing demands for this knowledge and skill in laborers are of fairly recent origin and it takes time to respond to them. In responding to these demands, we are heavily dependent upon cultural and political processes and these are slow and the lags are long compared to the behavior of markets serving the formation of nonhuman capital. Where the capital market does serve human investments, it is subject to more imperfections than in financing physical capital. Our tax laws discriminate in favor of nonhuman capital. Then, too, many individuals face serious uncertainty in assessing their innate talents when it comes to investing in themselves, especially through higher education. Nor is it easy either for public decisions or private behavior to untangle and properly access the consumption and the investment components. The fact that the return to high school and to higher education has been about as large as the return to conventional forms of capital when all of the costs of such education including income foregone by students are allocated to the investment component, creates a strong presumption that there has been under-investment since, surely, much education is cultural and in that sense it is consumption. The evidence at hand is therefore not inconsistent with under-investment. In view of the reasons referred to, it is no wonder that there should be substantial under-investment in human beings, even though we take pride, and properly so, in the support that we have given

to education and to other activities that contribute to such investments.

8. Should the returns from public investment in human capital accrue to the individuals in whom it is made?[18] The policy issues in this question run deep and they are full of perplexities pertaining both to resource allocation and to welfare. Physical capital that is formed by public investment is not transferred as a rule to particular individuals as a gift. It would greatly simplify the allocative process if public investment in human capital were placed on the same footing. What then is the logical basis for treating public investment in human capital differently? Presumably it turns on ideas about welfare. A strong welfare goal of our community is to reduce the unequal distribution of personal income among individuals and families. Our community has relied heavily on progressive income and inheritance taxation. Given public revenue from these sources, it may well be true that public investment in human capital, notably that entering into general education, is an effective and efficient set of expenditures for attaining this goal. Let me stress, however, that the state of knowledge about these issues is woefully meager.

9. My last policy comment is on assistance to underdeveloped countries to help them achieve economic growth. Here, even more than in domestic affairs, investment in human beings is likely to be underrated and neglected. It is inherent in the intellectual climate in which leaders and spokesmen of these countries find themselves. Our exports of growth doctrines have contributed. These typically assign the stellar role to the formation of nonhuman capital, and take as an obvious fact the super abundance of human resources. Steel mills are the real symbol of industrialization. After all, the early industrialization of England did not depend on investments in the labor force. New funds and agencies are being authorized to transfer capital for physical goods to these countries. The World Bank and our Export-Import Bank already have much experience. Then, too, measures have been taken to pave the way for the investment of more private (nonhuman) capital abroad. This one-sided effort is underway in spite of the fact that the knowledge and skills required to take on and use efficiently the superior techniques of production, the most valuable resource that we could make available to them, is in very short supply in these underdeveloped countries. Some growth of course can be made from more conventional capital even though the labor that is available is lacking both in skill and knowledge. But the rate of growth will be seriously limited. It simply is not possible to have the fruits of a modern agriculture and the abundance of modern industry without making large investments in human beings.

Truly, the most distinctive feature of our economic system has been the growth in human capital. Without it there would have been only hard, manual work and poverty except for those who had income from property. There is an early morning scene in Faulkner's *Intruder in the Dust,* of a

<hr>

[18]I am indebted to Milton Friedman for bringing this issue to the fore in his comments on an early draft of this paper. See preface of [7] and also Jacob Mincer's pioneering paper, "Investment in Human Capital and Personal Distribution of Income," *Jour. Pol. Econ.,* Aug. 1958, *66.*

poor, solitary cultivator at work in a field. Let me paraphrase that line, "The man without skills and knowledge leaning terrifically against nothing."

References

1. G. S. Becker, preliminary draft of study undertaken for Nat. Bur. Econ. Research. New York 1960.
2. _____, "Underinvestment in College Education?" *Proc., Am. Econ. Rev.*, May 1960, *50*, 346–54.
3. P. R. Brahmanand and C. N. Vakil, *Planning for an Expanding Economy*. Bombay 1956.
4. H. F. Clark, "Potentialities of Educational Establishments Outside the Conventional Structure of Higher Education," *Financing Higher Education, 1960–70*, D. M. Keezer, ed. New York 1959.
5. Solomon Fabricant, *Basic Facts on Productivity Change*, Nat. Bur. Econ. Research, Occas. Paper 63. New York 1959. Table 5.
6. Irving Fisher, *The Nature of Capital and Income*. New York 1906.
7. Milton Friedman and Simon Kuznets, *Income from Independent Professional Practice*, Nat. Bur. Econ. Research. New York 1945.
8. B. Horvat, "The Optimum Rate of Investment," *Econ. Jour.*, Dec. 1958, *68*, 747–67.
9. H. G. Johnson, "The Political Economy of Opulence," *Can. Jour. Econ. and Pol. Sci.*, Nov. 1960, *26*, 552–64.
10. Simon Kuznets, *Income and Wealth in the United States*. Cambridge, England 1952. Sec. IV, Distribution by Industrial Origin.
11. Alfred Marshall, *Principles of Economics*, 8th ed. London 1930. App. E, pp. 787–88.
12. H. P. Miller, "Annual and Lifetime Income in Relation to Education: 1939–1959," *Am. Econ. Rev.*, Dec. 1960, *50*, 962–86.
13. Jacob Mincer, "Investment in Human Capital and Personal Income Distribution," *Jour. Pol. Econ.*, Aug. 1958, *66*, 281–302.
14. S. J. Mushkin, "Toward a Definition of Health Economics," *Public Health Reports*, U. S. Dept. of Health, Educ. and Welfare, Sept. 1958, *73*, 785–93.
15. J. S. Nicholson, "The Living Capital of the United Kingdom," *Econ. Jour.*, Mar. 1891, *1*, 95; see J. S. Mill, *Principles of Political Economy*, ed. W. J. Ashley. London 1909, p. 8.
16. T. W. Schultz, "Investment in Man: An Economist's View," *Soc. Serv. Rev.*, June 1959, *33*, 109–17.
17. _____, "Agriculture and the Application of Knowledge," *A Look to the Future*, W. K. Kellogg Foundation. Battle Creek, 1956, 54–78.
18. _____, "Capital Formation by Education," *Jour. Pol. Econ.*, Dec. 1960, *68*, Tables 3 through 7.
19. _____, "Education and Economic Growth," *Social Forces Influencing American Education*, H. G. Richey, ed. Chicago 1961.
20. H. von Thünen, *Der isolierte Staat*, 3rd ed., Vol. 2, Pt. 2, 1875, transl. by B. F. Hoselitz, reproduced by the Comp. Educ. Center, Univ. Chicago, pp. 140–52.
21. Morton Zeman, *A Quantitative Analysis of White-Nonwhite Income Differentials in the United States*. Unpublished doctoral dissertation, Univ. Chicago, 1955.

GROWTH MODELS

19. Notes on the Take-Off

Simon Kuznets*

Requirements for a Theory of Stages

The sequence of stages, of which the take-off is one, is offered by Professor Rostow as a scheme for viewing and interpreting modern economic development. It is, therefore, a gloss on the major distinction between modern and non-modern (traditional) types of growth; and I regret that in offering his scheme, Professor Rostow does not spell out the characteristics that are inherent in modern economic growth and distinguish it from the traditional and other types. Many come easily to mind: a high and sustained rate of increase in real product per capita, accompanied in most cases by a high and sustained rate of increase in population; major shifts in the industrial structure of product and labor force, and in the location of the population, commonly referred to as industrialization and urbanization; changes in the organizational units under whose auspices and guidance economic activity takes place; a rise in the proportion of capital formation to national product; shifts in the structure of consumer expenditure, accompanying urbanization and higher income per capita; changes in the character and magnitudes of international economic flows; and others that could be added. Behind all this is the increasing stock of useful knowledge derived from modern science, and the capacity of society, under the spur of modern ideology, to evolve institutions which permit a greater exploitation of the growth potential provided by that increasing stock of knowledge.

The distinction between modern economic growth and other types and our concentration on the former are justified by a basic working assumption—that we can study the characteristics of such growth most effectively if it is not merged with the evolution of economics before the 18th century or with the growth of such parts of the world as have not yet succeeded in tapping the sources of modern economic growth. If we assume that modern economic growth is different from other types and affected by new and different factors, we would only confuse matters and set ourselves an impossible task by treating the growth of Germany in the second half of the 19th century and that of France in the 13th century for example, as members of the same family of economic growth processes. In short, while allowing for historical continuity, we assume that modern economic

*Presented at the September 1960 meeting of the International Economic Association. The author is Professor of Economics, Harvard University. This article summarizes a paper later published in *Economic Development and Cultural Change,* July 1961.

growth is something quite new; and in order to observe it clearly, perceive its mechanism, and understand its driving forces, we must distinguish it from other types and study it by itself.

Distinguishing stages within modern economic growth is an operation similar to that which distinguishes modern from non-modern economic growth; and the basic working assumption that justifies the former parallels the one that justifies the latter. By claiming that stage A is distinct from stage B, we are saying that the characteristics commonly found in stage A are so distinct from those in stage B that it is methodologically improper to mix the two indiscriminately. Stages within an economic epoch or some such general construct, like the constructs themselves, are a classificatory device, governed by the working assumption that the generality of observation and invariance of analytical relations secured thereby are maximized.

An adequate test of such a working assumption comes at the end, not at the beginning, of a long period of study. But this does not mean that we need take seriously every suggestion of stages or other dividing lines within the sequence of modern economic growth—particularly if we recognize the major differences between it and non-modern growth. For if these differences are recognized, and the cumulative character of growth is taken as a matter of definition, it is all too easy to suggest "stages." Since modern economic growth presumably has roots in the past, a non-modern economy stage and a stage of preparation are clearly suggested: and we can easily divide the latter into several "phases"—initial preparatory phase; middle preparatory phase; final preparatory phase. Then, since, again by definition, modern economic growth is not attained in a few years, we can discuss the early or emergence period, the middle stage, maturity (biological analogy), post-maturity, and so on. The very ease with which separate segments can be distinguished in the historical movement from non-modern to modern economic growth and within the long span of the latter should warn us that any sequence of stages, even if offered as a suggestive rather than a substantive scheme, must meet some minimum requirements—if it is to be taken seriously. The following requirements are relevant:

(a) A given stage must display empirically testable characteristics, common to all or to an important group of units experiencing modern economic growth. This means the specification of modern economic growth; identification of the units that have manifested such growth; and establishment of empirically testable characteristics claimed to be common to these units at the given stage.

(b) The characteristics of a given stage must be distinctive in that, not necessarily singly but in combination, they are unique to that stage. Mere precedence (or succession) in time does not suffice: given the unidirectional character of growth (by definition), any period is necessarily characterized by larger economic magnitudes than earlier ones and by the structural shifts that accompany such larger magnitudes (particularly a rise in per capita income). Stages are presumably something more than successive ordinates in the steadily climbing curve of growth. They are segments of that curve, with properties so distinct that separate study of each segment seems warranted.

(c) The analytical relation to the preceding stage must be indicated. This naturally involves more than saying that the preceding stage is one of preparation for the given. More meaningfully, we need identification (again in empirically testable terms) of the major processes in the preceding stage that complete it and, with the usual qualifications for exogenous factors, make the next (our given) stage highly probable. Optimally, this would permit us to diagnose the preceding stage *before* the given stage is upon us, and thus would impart predictive value to the whole sequence. But even short of this difficult aim, it means specifying the minimum that must happen in the preceding stage to allow the given stage to emerge.

(d) The analytical relation to the succeeding stage must be indicated. Here too a clear notion (again in empirically testable terms) must be given of the occurrences in the given stage that bring it to a close—aside from mere passage of time. Optimally, such knowledge would permit us to predict, *before* the given stage is finished, how long it still has to run. But even short of such precision, we should know the essentials that occur during a given stage to bring about its end and clear the ground for the next stage.

(e) These four requirements relate to the common and distinctive characteristics of a given stage, viewed as one in an analytical (and chronological) sequence that links successive stages. However, these common and distinctive characteristics may differ among important groups of units undergoing modern economic growth. Consequently, the fifth requirement is for a clear indication of the universe for which the generality of common and distinctive characteristics is claimed; and for which the analytical relations of a given stage with the preceding and succeeding ones are being formulated.

Characteristics of the Take-Off

Against the background of the requirements just stated, we may consider Professor Rostow's discussion of the common and distinctive characteristics of the take-off stage, and the relations between it and the contiguous stages.

The three common characteristics explicitly listed by Professor Rostow are:

"(a) a rise in the rate of productive investment from (say) 5% or less to over 10% of national income (or net national product);

"(b) the development of one or more substantial manufacturing sectors with a high rate of growth;

"(c) the existence or quick emergence of a political, social and institutional framework which exploits the impulses to expansion in the modern sector and the potential external economy effects of the take-off and gives to growth an ongoing character."[1]

To these we may add three more characteristics, implicit or explicit in Professor Rostow's discussion.

(d) A marked rise in the rate of growth of national income (or net na-

[1]"The Take-Off into Self-sustained Growth," *The Economic Journal,* vol. LXVI, no. 261, March 1956, p. 32 (referred to henceforth as Rostow-I).

tional product) and of per capita income, in constant prices. This follows directly from the rise in the proportion of investment listed under (a) and Professor Rostow's discussion of the "Prima Facie Case" (*ibid.*, p. 34) which assumes no rise in the marginal capital-output ratio. The rate of growth of real income per capita rises from close to zero to about 2% per year.

(e) The leading sectors in the take-off [apparently a particularization of the manufacturing sector in (b)] have ranged historically "from cotton textiles, through heavy-industry complexes based on railroads and military end-products, to timber, pulp, dairy products and finally a wide variety of consumers' goods" (*ibid.*, p. 46). But in general these sectors were leading because of the enlarged demand for their products brought about by appropriate transfers of income, capital imports, etc.; because of their new production functions; because of their profitability and inducement to entrepreneurs to plough back profits; and because of the expansion and technical transformation in other parts of the economy affected by their expansion.

(f) The take-off is a relatively short period: in many of the countries identified by Professor Rostow appreciably less than thirty years, and in most of these close to two decades.

How distinctive are these characteristics? Do they occur in combination only in the take-off stage and not in any other stage—particularly the preceding transition or pre-conditions stage and the succeeding self-sustained growth or drive to maturity stage? Professor Rostow is not explicit on this point. Presumably the transition stage does not see a rise in the investment proportion from 5 to 10% or more. Yet much of what Professor Rostow would attribute to the take-off has already occurred in the pre-condition stage.[2] Thus, the agricultural revolution assigned to the pre-condition stage "must supply expanded food, expanded markets, and an expanded supply of loanable funds to the modern sector" (Rostow II, p. 24); much of social overhead capital is already invested in transport and other outlays—in the pre-conditions stage (*ibid.*, p. 24); and, in general, "the essence of the transition can be described legitimately as a rise in the rate of investment to a level which regularly, substantially and perceptibly outstrips population growth" (*ibid.*, p. 21). In short, one wonders whether the three specifically stated characteristics of take-off could not be found in the pre-conditions stage—unless explicit qualifications are attached, e.g., that the investment proportion in that earlier stage must stay below 5%; that the marked agricultural revolution does not immediately call for, and in fact is possible without, a contemporaneous rapid growth in some manufacturing sector; and that investment in overhead capital in transport, etc., is not necessarily accompanied by a rapid growth of one or more modern manufacturing sectors. Finally, one should note that characteristic (c) of the take-off mentions both the *existence* and the *quick emergence* of the political, social, and institutional framework favorable to exploiting "the impulses to expansion in the modern sector" as admissible alternatives.

[2]*The Stages of Economic Growth* (Cambridge, 1960), Chapter 3, pp. 17–35 (referred to henceforth as Rostow-II).

But if that framework already exists at the beginning of the take-off, its emergence must be assigned to the pre-conditions stage. How then does the latter differ from the take-off in which the framework emerges?

The line of division between the take-off and the following stage of self-sustained growth or drive to maturity is also blurred. Presumably the latter stage is marked by the existence of the proper social and institutional framework—which also exists during the take-off. Presumably this later stage also witnesses the rapid growth of one or more modern manufacturing sectors. Indeed, the only characteristics that are distinctly appropriate to the take-off and not to the next stage are the rise in the rate of productive investment to over 10% of national income or net national product; and the implicit rise in the rate of growth of total and per capita income. But are we to assume that both the rate of investment and the rate of growth of product (total and per capita) level off at the high values attained at the end of the take-off stage? And is it this leveling off, the cessation of the rise in the rate of investment and in the rate of growth, that terminates the take-off stage? No explicit statement is made by Professor Rostow; Rostow-II, Chapter 5, contains a list of dates when "maturity" was reached in a number of countries but little discussion of what took place between the end of the take-off stage, and the terminal point of the next stage.

Given this fuzziness in delimiting the take-off stage and in formulating its distinctive characteristics; given the distinctiveness only in the statistical level of the rate of productive investment (and the implicit rate of growth), there is no solid ground upon which to discuss Professor Rostow's view of the analytical relation between the take-off stage and the preceding and succeeding stages. At any rate, the brief comments that can be made within the scope of this paper will follow the review of the empirical evidence.

To what universe do the common characteristics claimed for the take-off period apply? In his most recent presentation, Professor Rostow distinguishes the "general" case of a traditional society from that of the small group of nations (the United States, Australia, New Zealand, Canada, and "perhaps a few others") "born free" (*op cit.*, pp. 6 and 17–18). The distinction is particularly important in the analysis of the pre-conditions stage, and Professor Rostow does not indicate whether the characteristics of the take-off stage in the originally traditional societies are different from those in the countries "born free." The distinction made in the discussion of pre-conditions is not repeated in the discussion of the take-off; unless the qualification about the rates of investment higher than 5% in some countries (Canada and Argentina) before the take-off stage (necessitated by heavy overhead social capital needs, see Rostow-II, p. 8) can be interpreted as such. But this qualification does not stress the distinction between traditional and free-born countries: social overhead capital needs were presumably heavy in Russia and for that matter, on a relative scale, in Switzerland. We may therefore infer that Professor Rostow, who includes the dates of the take-off period for both types of economy in the same list, assumes that the characteristics of the take-off are broadly the same for all countries undergoing modern economic growth.

Empirical Evidence on the Take-Off Stage

In dealing with the empirical evidence on the take-off, I am impeded by three difficulties. First, much of the specific evidence on the take-off period will presumably be presented in the individual country papers; and I am neither competent to assemble it nor eager to duplicate it. Second, quantitative evidence, and much of it must by the nature of the case be quantitative, is not available for some of the take-off periods suggested by Professor Rostow. Third, as already indicated, Professor Rostow's discussion does not yield a description of take-off characteristics sufficiently specific to define the relevant empirical evidence.

Thus I do not know what "a political, social and institutional framework which exploits the impulses to expansion in the modern sector, etc." is; or how to identify such a framework except by hindsight and conjecture; or how to specify the empirical evidence that would have to be brought to bear to ascertain whether such a framework is in "existence or in quick emergence." It seems to me that the passage just cited defines these social phenomena as a complex that produces the effect Professor Rostow wishes to explain; and then he treats this definition as if it were a meaningful identification.

It is easier to define the characteristic that specifies "the development of one or more substantial manufacturing sectors with a high rate of growth" once high is explained. But a review of empirical evidence on this point holds little interest if I am correct in assuming that the major distinctive characteristic of the take-off is a marked rise in the rate of growth of per capita and hence of total income. If the rate of growth does accelerate, some sectors are bound to grow more rapidly than others, as has been demonstrated in Arthur F. Burns' and my own work on production trends —partly in response to the differential impact of technological opportunities (including raw material supplies), and partly in response to the different income elasticities of the demand for various goods. Under these conditions, one or more manufacturing sectors, and one or more sectors of agriculture, transportation, services, etc. are bound to show high rates of growth. The pertinent question is why manufacturing—rather than agriculture, transport, or any other rapidly growing industry—should be specified as the leading sector.

In considering this question, the two constitutive characteristics of a leading sector must be kept in mind. First, sector A leads, rather than follows, if it moves not in response to sectors B, C, D, etc., within the country, but under the impact of factors which, relative to the given national economy, may be considered autonomous. These may be technological changes embodying some new inventions; changes in the resource base resulting from new discoveries; changes in foreign demand, which, being external to the given economy, may be considered autonomous; and breaks in social structure (political revolution, agrarian reform, and the like), which could be viewed as changes exogenous to economic processes proper. The point to be noted is that the autonomous nature of this characteristic, relative to the given national economy, rests upon the origin of the stimulus, not upon the scope of the response. The latter may depend largely upon many other factors besides the stimulus, factors that are part and parcel of a given economy and society.

This brings us to the second constitutive characteristic of a leading sector, the magnitude of its effects; or more specifically, the magnitude of its contribution to a country's economic growth. Sector A may be leading in the sense of responding to an autonomous stimulus, but unless its contribution to the country's economic growth is substantial, it does not "lead" the country's economic growth—no matter how high its own rate of growth. After all, a thousandfold rise in the production of plastic hula hoops over a decade does not make it a leading industry.

How to set the lower limit to a significant contribution is a question that can be answered only in terms of empirical, quantitative analysis. We must distinguish the direct contribution—what the autonomous growth of sector A, the result of its weight in the economy multiplied by its percentage rate of growth, adds to the growth of the economy, total and per capita; from what sector A contributes indirectly, through the effects of backward and forward linkages with sectors B, C, D, . . .; and, finally, from what it may contribute, again indirectly, through its effects on social structure and qualities of the population (e.g., urbanization, organizational form of the economic unit, education, and the like), which in turn affect a country's economic growth in a variety of ways. The magnitude and particularly the timing of these direct and indirect effects differ. A sector's direct and indirect contributions in a given period may be quite small— even though its own percentage rate of growth is high and the novelty of its technology makes it the cynosure of the eyes of its contemporaries and of latter-day historians; whereas in a later period its contributions may be far greater—even though its rate of growth has declined and the bloom of its novelty faded.

The establishment of these leadership characteristics of sectors—both in terms of the autonomous character of the impulse and the timing and magnitude of their direct and indirect contributions to a country's economic growth—is thus a task that involves intensive study, not merely of the leading sectors proper but also of those affected by them, extending into the quantitative framework of the whole economy. Leadership of sectors, or any other element in the acceleration of the rate of growth can be established only after careful analysis of the particular circumstances preceding and during the period of acceleration—country by country, and by the application of statistical, theoretical, and other tools to the historical evidence. This type of analysis, lacking in Professor Rostow's discussion, will, I hope, be provided in the country papers; it is beyond my powers here.

I can, therefore, turn to the purely statistical characteristics claimed for the take-off stage. But even here I find it difficult to specify Professor Rostow's meaning. I assume from the context that "rate of productive investment" refers to *net* rather than *gross* capital formation; and that the adjective "productive" means the inclusion of all components of the presently accepted definition of capital formation. But does he mean net *domestic* capital formation, i.e., all net additions to the stock of material reproducible capital within the country, whether financed by domestic savings or by capital imports (and excluding capital exports, when such occur); or net *national* capital formation (usually referred to as net capital formation without further qualification), i.e., only net additions to reproducible stock within the country financed by domestic savings plus capital exports, if any? Professor Rostow emphasizes changes within the country (under characteristic (c) above) that should help mobilize domestic savings, and much of his discussion is in terms of maximizing domestic savings, i.e., in terms of the net national capital formation proportion to national income. This emphasis is corroborated by the use of national income as denominator, since the proper denominator for the net domestic capital formation is net domestic product; although for most countries the two totals are statistically close. Yet in the analysis of capital—output relations, the appropriate ratio, particularly for a capital importing country, is that of net domestic capital formation to net domestic product. Professor Rostow cites long-term data for Sweden and Canada, and for one he uses the domestic capital formation proportion and for the other the national capital formation proportion. There is the further question whether the ratios of capital formation to national product should be based on totals in current or in constant prices: the former are more appropriate to the view of the proportion as a savings rate; the latter to the view of the proportion as affecting output.

Before presenting the statistical results, I shall attempt to resolve these doubts, and define the measures more precisely. For a capital exporting country we may use the ratio of net national capital formation to national income or net national product; and for a capital importing country we should use both net national and net domestic capital formation, as proportions of net national and net domestic product, respectively. Further, we shall use ratios based on current price totals only, partly because the available price indexes are crude and partly because in most cases the differences in long-term movement between the capital formation proportions based on current and on constant price totals are not appreciable. We can then ask whether in the periods of take-off dated by Professor Rostow the rises in these capital formation proportions are of the magnitude he suggests. I shall deal here with four countries, all included in Professor Rostow's "general" category: (a) Great Britain, (b) Germany, (c) Sweden, (d) Japan.

(a) For Great Britain Phyllis Deane has recently completed a major study. Her results indicate a net national capital formation proportion for England and Wales in 1770–1800, a period close to Professor Rostow's dates of 1783–1802, of about 6.5 percent—compared with about 5 percent indicated by Gregory King at the end of the 18th century. Miss Deane's estimates, which thenceforth apply to the United Kingdom, suggest a climb to about 9 percent for the period from the 1820's to the 1850's, and a further rise to a pre-World War I peak of 14 percent in the 1905–14 decade. The picture is thus one of a slow and relatively steady, rather than sudden and rapid, acceleration. The rate of growth of total national income (in constant prices) follows the same general pattern. For England and Wales, Miss Deane's estimates suggest an annual rate of growth for 1770–1800 of 1.5 percent, compared with 0.9 percent for 1740–70 and 0.3 percent for 1700–40. Then the rate of growth for the United Kingdom rises to well over 2.5 percent per year in the last quarter of the 19th century.

(b) For Germany (the territory of the German Reich in 1913) we have the studies by Professor Walther Hoffman of net capital formation and by Professors Hoffman and J. Heinz Müller of national income—both covering the period back to 1851. For 1850–73, the period dated by Professor Rostow as the take-off, we have the following proportions of net capital formation to national income (in current market prices): about 8.5 percent for the 1850's, 9.75 percent for the 1860's; 13.5 percent for the 1870's. The rise is appreciable, but is due in part to the favorable business cycle of the 1870's; and in the 1880's the net capital formation proportion is still below 14 percent. Then the proportion continues to rise to a peak of 16.5 percent in 1901–13. Here the net capital formation proportion increases only about 60 percent in the twenty-odd years dated as the take-off, and doubles only after a steady and sustained climb for about six decades. This steady rise in the net capital formation proportion is accompanied by a relatively stable rate of growth of net national product—about 2.5 percent per year for the entire period, somewhat more in the decades from 1851 to 1880, and somewhat less in the decades from 1880 to 1913.

(c) For Sweden the most recent estimates, by Dr. Östen Johansson, currently at the University of Stockholm, are a thorough revision of the older series which I used in my earlier paper and which Professor Rostow cites in his discussion. The major correction was for the understatement of construction in the early decades.

The directly available estimates yield a *gross* domestic capital formation proportion (to gross domestic product) of somewhat over 9 percent in 1861–70. On the assumption of a ratio of capital consumption to gross domestic capital formation of about 0.4, the net domestic capital formation proportion is almost 6 percent. The gross domestic capital formation proportion climbs, somewhat unsteadily, to 13.5 percent in 1901–10, and the implied net capital formation proportion to over 8 percent. The rise continues to a peak in 1941–50 of 21 percent gross, and roughly 13 percent net. In short, the net domestic capital formation proportion rises gradually, and doubles only after almost eight decades, not just two or three.

The *national* capital formation proportions present about the same picture, except that the steady climb begins after the 1880's. From an average of about 9.5 percent gross in 1861–80, the gross capital formation proportion rises to 11 percent in 1891–1910, to over 14 percent in 1911–20, and to 20.5 percent in 1941–50. The corresponding net national capital formation proportion would be somewhat less than 6 percent in 1861–90, almost 7 percent in 1891–1910, and slightly over 12 percent in 1941–50.

The rate of growth of total product is also gradual. Although it ranges from 1.8 to 5.4 percent per year for decadal periods (the high rate being for 1941–50), the average for 1871–80 (Professor Rostow's "take-off" dates are 1868–90) is about 2.3 percent per year, compared with 3.2 percent for the 1860's and 3.4 percent for 1891–1910. The averages for the longer periods suggest a perceptible although gradual acceleration in the rate of growth, from 2.6 percent for 1861–90 to 2.9 percent for 1891–1920, to 3.8 percent for 1921–50.

(d) For Japan the recent, and only acceptable, estimates of capital formation by Professor Henry Rosovsky of the University of California, cover a period beginning in 1888; and therefore include only part of 1878–1900, the take-off period dated by Professor Rostow. The *gross* domestic capital formation proportion excluding military investments (which were large in Japan) was between 10 and 11 percent in 1888–97; and the gross national proportion was slightly higher. On the assumption that capital consumption was about 0.4 of gross domestic capital formation, the corresponding net capital formation proportions were between 6 and 7 percent; and there is no ground for assuming that they were significantly lower in the preceding decade. Subsequently, the domestic capital formation proportion fluctuated around the same level until World War I; and it was only after that war that the domestic capital formation proportion rose significantly —to between 16 and 17 percent on a gross basis and to between 10 and 11 percent on a net basis. The *national* capital formation proportion moved somewhat more erratically, with substantial capital imports in 1900–10 and 1920–30; but the broad secular trend was the same. Not until four or five decades later were the capital formation proportions twice their initial size.

There is no evidence of a perceptible acceleration in the rate of growth of either total or per capita income. From 1878 to 1902 the average rate of growth of total income was about 4.9 percent per year; from 1893 to 1912 it was 3.2 percent; from 1908 to 1932, 4.9 percent; from 1918 to 1942, 4.9 percent.[3] The average rate of growth of income per member of the gainfully occupied population for the same four long periods was: 1878–1902 —3.7 percent per year; 1893–1917—2.6 percent; 1908–32—4.3 percent; 1918–42—4.0 percent.

Two or three more of the countries for which Professor Rostow suggests tentative dates of the take-off period could be added here. But the presentation of the full statistical evidence, even for a few countries, would far transcend the limits of this paper; and summaries like those above are barely adequate. We now have long-term records on capital formation and national product for twelve countries, excluding those in the Communist Bloc; and a detailed discussion of these is now in preparation.[4] All I can do here is summarize the evidence for the few countries in Professor Rostow's list and consider its bearing on his assumptions concerning the movement of the capital investment proportions, and the implicit movement of total product during what he defines as the take-off period. Unforunately, I do not now have adequate estimates for France, Belgium, and Russia, additional countries in Professor Rostow's list.

(i) In a number of countries, the net capital formation proportions, particularly domestic, at the beginning of the dated take-off periods are

These and the following rates are from Kazushi Ohkawa and others, *The Growth Rate of the Japanese Economy since 1878*. (Tokyo, 1957), Table 6, p. 21, and Table 7, p. 24.

[4]It will appear as Paper VI in the series being published in *Economic Development and Cultural Change*. Paper V, dealing with the international comparison of capital formation proportions for recent, post-World War II years, appeared in July 1960 (Volume VIII, no. 4, Part II). Since the detailed statistical data and sources are cited in these two papers, I decided not to repeat them here.

substantially higher than "5 percent or less." This is certainly true of Germany: of the United States, where the estimates by Professor Robert Gallman for the 1840's and the 1850's suggest a gross domestic capital formation proportion of between 15 and 20 percent; of Canada where Dr. O. J. Firestone's estimates indicate gross domestic capital formation proportions of 15 percent in 1870, 15.5 percent in 1890, and 13.5 percent in 1900. Also, in so far as net rates of 6 to 7 percent may be considered significantly higher than those of "5 percent or less," this is true of Great Britain, Sweden, and Japan.

(ii) In no case does the net domestic capital formation proportion even approach twice its initial size in the two or three decades dated as the take-off; and while the movements of the net *national* capital formation proportions are more erratic, they too fall far short of doubling during Professor Rostow's take-off periods.

(iii) There is no evidence to support the assumption of a marginal net domestic (or national) capital-output ratio of 3.5 to 1. The ratio is neither the same for different countries, nor stable over time. Thus for the United Kingdom, the marginal net national capital-output ratio at the beginning of the 19th century was about 3 (it was about 4 for England and Wales in 1770–1800, if the crude data can be trusted). In Germany in the 1850's the net national capital-output ratio was between 3 and 3.5; in Sweden in 1881–90, on a *gross* basis, the ratio was between 3 and 4, but on a net basis it would have been between 2 and 3.5; in Japan in 1888–97, the gross domestic capital-output ratio was about 3, and the net somewhat less than 2. Moreover, in many countries the net capital-output ratios show a marked trend over time. For example, in the United Kingdom, the marginal net national capital-output ratio, which was 3 in the first part of the 19th century, rose to almost 6 in the period from 1880–89 to 1910–13; and even the net *domestic* capital-output ratio rose from about 3 before the middle of the 19th century to 3.7 in the three decades before World War I. The net national capital-output ratio for Germany rose from between 3 and 3.5 in the 1850's to about 5.5 for the decades from 1891 to 1913.

(iv) In no case do we find during the take-off periods the acceleration in the rate of growth of total national product implied in Professor Rostow's assumptions of a doubling (or more) in the net capital formation proportion and of a constant marginal capital-output ratio. The capital formation proportions, if they rise, climb at a sustained rate and for a much longer period than the two or three decades of "take-off." Rates of growth of total product, if they show any long-term acceleration (and those for only a few countries do within the period beginning with the take-off stage) increase slowly—and certainly over a longer period than the short span of the take-off.

The summary above relates to a few countries, none of which is in the Communist Bloc, and is based upon crude estimates. But the data are firm enough to suggest rough orders of magnitude; and they bear directly upon what seem to be the essential statistical characteristics of the take-off period as Professor Rostow identifies them. Unless I have completely misunderstood Professor Rostow's definition of "take-off" and its statistical characteristics, I can only conclude that the available evidence lends no support to Professor Rostow's suggestions. . . .

Concluding Comments

The gist of the discussion in this paper can be summarized in a few brief propositions.

(a) Leadership of a sector depends upon the origin of its growth in an autonomous impulse, not in response to other sectors in the country; and upon the magnitude of its direct and indirect contributions to the country's economic growth. The autonomous impulse and the various types of contribution to growth differ in timing; and the identification and chronology of leading sectors requires specification and evidence lacking in Professor Rostow's discussion.

(b) The doubling of capital investment proportions and the implicit sharp acceleration in the rate of growth of national product, claimed by Professor Rostow as characterizing his "take-off" periods, are not confirmed by the statistical evidence for those countries on his list for which we have data.

(c) There is no clear distinction between the "pre-conditions" and the "take-off" stages. On the contrary, given the pre-conditions emphasized by Professor Rostow, viz., transformation of agriculture and overhead capital investments, there is a *prima facie* case for expecting the "pre-conditions" and the "take-off" stages to overlap.

(d) The analysis of the "take-off" and "pre-conditions" stages neglects the effect of historical heritage, time of entry into the process of modern economic growth, degree of backwardness, and other relevant factors on the characteristics of the early phases of modern economic growth in the different "traditional" countries.

(e) The concept (and stage) of "self-sustained" growth is a misleading oversimplification. No growth is purely self-sustaining or purely self-limiting. The characterization of one stage of growth as self-sustained, and of others, by implication, as lacking that property, requires substantive evidence and analysis not provided in Professor Rostow's discussion....

If we cannot accept Professor Rostow's sequence of stages, and particularly his notion of a distinct and commonly found "take-off" stage, what are we left with?

Let us begin by agreeing that modern economic growth displays certain observable and measurable characteristics, which in combination are distinctive to it, i.e., were not evident in earlier economic epochs; and that these characteristics can, in principle, be established with the help of quantitative and other data wherever such growth occurs. What these characteristics are is a matter for discussion; but I believe that agreement could easily be reached on some of them, e.g., those relating to rates of growth of national product, total and per capita, and to structural shifts that commonly accompany them. Let us assume for purposes of illustration that identification of such growth requires a minimum rise in per capita income sustained over a period of at least two or three decades, a minimum shift away from agriculture, and any other identifiable indispensable components of modern economic growth that we may specify.

With this specification of what modern economic growth is, it becomes possible, given the data, to place its beginning in the various countries in which modern economic growth occurred. The date of inception need not be a year, or even a quinquennium; it may be a band of some width, but still narrow enough to permit us to say that the two or three decades following it are the early phases of modern economic growth and the two or three decades prior to it are the ones directly preceding the beginning of modern economic growth in the country—without missing much in between. If, then, we consider it important to study just the early decades of modern economic growth, and/or those immediately preceding it, in the hope of finding characteristics and relations that would permit us to construct an adequate theoretical scheme, we may want to call the first two or three decades following the initiation of modern economic growth the "early growth phase" and the two or three decades preceding it the "late pre-modern phase."

Obviously, the two or three decades are just illustrative, and the period may vary in length from country to country: the phase segregated for concentrated study would have to be defined in terms of some reasonably realistic preliminary notions concerning the length of time during which the distinctive characteristics of early growth persist or during which the immediate antecedents must be studied. The firm point in this approach is the feasibility of dating the beginning of modern economic growth by some "hard" data, relating to one or several characteristics that are constituent elements in the very definition of modern economic growth. In doing this, all that we specify is the *early* phase of the segment of the long record of modern economic growth on which we wish to concentrate. The termination of the period is then to be decided on the basis of any substantive hypotheses concerning the distinctive characteristics of the early phase; although one would assume that since the span of modern economic growth in most countries is not much over a hundred years, there are narrow limits to the length of the early growth phase that an economist *of today* can set.

The term early phase of modern growth is far less appealing than "take-off": it does not carry the suggestive connotation of the latter. And the same is true of "late pre-modern period" compared with "pre-conditions," and of "middle growth period" compared with "self-sustained growth." But the appealing terms employing mechanical or biological metaphors carry the danger of misleading us into believing that the suggested connotations are relevant to observable reality. It is my conviction that at the present stage of our knowledge (and ignorance), it is the better part of valor to link the constraining influence of phase distinction to the bare lines of observable and measurable growth processes; and to concentrate discussion on the early decades of modern economic growth in these countries for which we can identify its beginning, with excursions into the pre-modern growth past and the post-early decades of modern growth when they seem warranted. The designation "early phase of modern economic growth" would, I suspect, fit the papers in this conference better than the specific reference to the "take-off."

20. Economic Development with Unlimited Supplies of Labour

W. A. Lewis

This essay is written in the classical tradition, making the classical assumption, and asking the classical question. The classics, from Smith to Marx, all assumed, or argued, that an unlimited supply of labour was available at subsistence wages. They then enquired how production grows through time. They found the answer in capital accumulation, which they explained in terms of their analysis of the distribution of income. Classical systems thus determined simultaneously income distribution and income growth, with the relative prices of commodities as a minor by-product.

Interest in prices and in income distribution survived into the neo-classical era, but labour ceased to be unlimited in supply, and the formal model of economic analysis was no longer expected to explain the expansion of the system through time. These changes of assumption and of interest served well enough in the European parts of the world, where labour was indeed limited in supply, and where for the next half century it looked as if economic expansion could indeed be assumed to be automatic. On the other hand over the greater part of Asia labour is unlimited in supply, and economic expansion certainly cannot be taken for granted. Asia's problems, however, attracted very few economists during the neo-classical era (even the Asian economists themselves absorbed the assumptions and preoccupations of European economics) and hardly any progress has been made for nearly a century with the kind of economics which would throw light upon the problems of countries with surplus populations.

When Keynes's *General Theory* appeared, it was thought at first that this was the book which would illuminate the problems of countries with surplus labour, since it assumed an unlimited supply of labour at the current price, and also, in its final pages, made a few remarks on secular economic expansion. Further reflection, however, revealed that Keynes's book assumed not only that labour is unlimited in supply, but also, and more fundamentally, that land and capital are unlimited in supply—more fundamentally both in the short run sense that once the monetary tap is turned the real limit to expansion is not physical resources but the limited supply of labour, and also in the long run sense that secular expansion is embarrassed not by a shortage but by a superfluity of saving. Given the Keynesian remedies the neo-classical system comes into its own again. Hence, from the point of view of countries with surplus labour, Keynesianism is only a footnote to neo-classicism—albeit a long, important and fascinating footnote. The student of such economies has therefore to work right back to the classical economists before he finds an analytical framework into which he can relevantly fit his problems.

*From *The Manchester School,* May 1954. The author is Principal, University College of the West Indies.

The purpose of this essay is thus to see what can be made of the classical framework in solving problems of distribution, accumulation, and growth, first in a closed and then in an open economy. It is not primarily an essay in the history of economic doctrine, and will not therefore spend time on individual writers, enquiring what they meant, or assessing its validity or truth. Our purpose is rather to bring their framework up-to-date, in the light of modern knowledge, and to see how far it then helps us to understand the contemporary problems of large areas of the earth.

I. The Closed Economy

We have to begin by elaborating the assumption of an unlimited supply of labour, and by establishing that it is a useful assumption. We are not arguing, let it be repeated, that this assumption should be made for all areas of the world. It is obviously not true of the United Kingdom, or of North West Europe. It is not true either of some of the countries usually now lumped together as under-developed; for example there is an acute shortage of male labour in some parts of Africa and of Latin America. On the other hand it is obviously the relevant assumption for the economies of Egypt, of India, or of Jamaica. Our present task is not to supersede neo-classical economics, but merely to elaborate a different framework for those countries which the neo-classical (and Keynesian) assumptions do not fit.

In the first place, an unlimited supply of labour may be said to exist in those countries where population is so large relatively to capital and natural resources, that there are large sectors of the economy where the marginal productivity of labour is negligible, zero, or even negative. Several writers have drawn attention to the existence of such "disguised" unemployment in the agricultural sector, demonstrating in each case that the family holding is so small that if some members of the family obtained other employment the remaining members could cultivate the holding just as well (of course they would have to work harder: the argument includes the proposition that they would be willing to work harder in these circumstances). The phenomenon is not, however, by any means confined to the countryside. Another large sector to which it applies is the whole range of casual jobs—the workers on the docks, the young men who rush forward asking to carry your bag as you appear, the jobbing gardener, and the like. These occupations usually have a multiple of the number they need, each of them earning very small sums from occasional employment; frequently their number could be halved without reducing output in this sector. Petty retail trading is also exactly of this type; it is enormously expanded in over-populated economies; each trader makes only a few sales; markets are crowded with stalls, and if the number of stalls were greatly reduced the consumers would be no whit worse off—they might even be better off, since retail margins might fall. Twenty years ago one could not write these sentences without having to stop and explain why in these circumstances, the casual labourers do not bid their earnings down to zero, or why the farmers' product is not similarly all eaten up in rent, but these propositions present no terrors to contemporary economists.

A little more explanation has to be given of those cases where the workers are not self-employed, but are working for wages, since it is harder to believe that employers will pay wages exceeding marginal productivity. The most important of these sectors is domestic service, which is usually even more inflated in over-populated countries than is petty trading (in Barbados 16 per cent of the population is in domestic service). The reason is that in over-populated countries the code of ethical behaviour so shapes itself that it becomes good form for each person to offer as much employment as he can. The line between employees and dependents is very thinly drawn. Social prestige requires people to have servants, and the grand seigneur may have to keep a whole army of retainers who are really little more than a burden upon his purse. This is found not only in domestic service, but in every sector of employment. Most businesses in under-developed countries employ a large number of "messengers," whose contribution is almost negligible; you see them sitting outside office doors, or hanging around in the courtyard. And even in the severest slump the agricultural or commercial employer is expected to keep his labour force somehow or other—it would be immoral to turn them out, for how would they eat, in countries where the only form of unemployment assistance is the charity of relatives? So it comes about that even in the sectors where people are working for wages, and above all the domestic sector, marginal productivity may be negligible or even zero.

Whether marginal productivity is zero or negligible is not, however, of fundamental importance to our analysis. The price of labour, in these economies, is a wage at the subsistence level (we define this later). The supply of labour is therefore "unlimited" so long as the supply of labour at this price exceeds the demand. In this situation, new industries can be created, or old industries expanded without limit at the existing wage; or, to put it more exactly, shortage of labour is no limit to the creation of new sources of employment. If we cease to ask whether the marginal productivity of labour is negligible and ask instead only the question from what sectors would additional labour be available if new industries were created offering employment at subsistence wages, the answer becomes even more comprehensive. For we have then not only the farmers, the casuals, the petty traders and the retainers (domestic and commercial), but we have also three other classes from which to choose.

First of all, there are the wives and daughters of the household. The employment of women outside the household depends upon a great number of factors, religious and conventional, and is certainly not exclusively a matter of employment opportunities. There are, however, a number of countries where the current limit is for practical purposes only employment opportunities. This is true, for example, even inside the United Kingdom. The proportion of women gainfully employed in the U.K. varies enormously from one region to another according to employment opportunities for women. For example, in 1939 whereas there were 52 women gainfully employed for every 100 men in Lancashire, there were only 15 women gainfully employed for every 100 men in South Wales. Similarly in the Gold Coast, although there is an acute shortage of male labour, any industry which offered good employment to women would be beseiged with applications. The transfer of women's work from the household to commercial employment is one of the most notable features of economic development. It is not by any means all gain, but the gain is substantial because most of the things which women otherwise do in the household can in fact be done much better or more cheaply outside, thanks to the large scale economies of specialisation, and also to the use of capital (grinding grain, fetching water from the river, making cloth, making clothes, cooking the midday meal, teaching children, nursing the sick, etc.). One of the surest ways of increasing the national income is therefore to create new sources of employment for women outside the home.

The second source of labour for expanding industries is the increase in the population resulting from the excess of births over deaths. This source is important in any dynamic analysis of how capital accumulation can occur, and employment can increase, without any increase in real wages. It was therefore a cornerstone of Ricardo's system. Strictly speaking, population increase is not relevant either to the classical analysis, or to the analysis which follows in this article, unless it can be shown that the increase of population is caused by economic development and would not otherwise be so large. The proof of this proposition was supplied to the classical economists by the Malthusian law of population. There is already an enormous literature of the genus: "What Malthus *Really* Meant," into which we need not enter. Modern population theory has advanced a little by analysing separately the effects of economic development upon the birth rate, and its effects on the death rate. Of the former, we know little. There is no evidence that the birth rate ever rises with economic development. In Western Europe it has fallen during the last eighty years. We are not quite sure why; we suspect that it was for reasons associated with development, and we hope that the same thing may happen in the rest of the world as development spreads. Of the death rate we are more certain. It comes down with development from around 40 to around 12 per thousand; in the first stage because better communications and trade eliminate death from local famines; in the second stage because better public health facilities banish the great epidemic diseases of plague, smallpox, cholera, malaria, yellow fever (and eventually tuberculosis); and in the third stage because widespread facilities for treating the sick snatch from the jaws of death many who would otherwise perish in infancy or in their prime. Because the effect of development on the death rate is so swift and certain, while its effect on the birth rate is unsure and retarded, we can say for certain that the immediate effect of economic development is to cause the population to grow; after some decades it begins to grow (we hope) less rapidly. Hence in any society where the death rate is around 40 per thousand, the effect of economic development will be to generate an increase in the supply of labour.

Marx offered a third source of labour to add to the reserve army, namely the unemployment generated by increasing efficiency. Ricardo had admitted that the creation of machinery could reduce employment. Marx seized upon the argument, and in effect generalized it, for into the pit of unemployment he threw not only those displaced by machinery, but also the self-employed and petty capitalists who could not compete with larger capitalists of increasing size, enjoying the benefits of the economies of scale. Nowadays we reject this argument on empirical grounds. It is clear that the effect of capital accumulation in the past has been to reduce the size of the reserve army, and not to increase it, so we have lost interest in arguments about what is "theoretically" possible.

When we take account of all the sources we have now listed—the farmers, the casuals, the petty traders, the retainers (domestic and commercial), women in the household, and population growth—it is clear enough that there can be in an over-populated economy an enormous expansion of new industries or new employment opportunities without any shortage of unskilled labour becoming apparent in the labour market. From the point of view of the effect of economic development on wages, the supply of labour is practically unlimited.

This applies only to unskilled labour. There may at any time be a shortage of skilled workers of any grade—ranging from masons, electricians or welders to engineers, biologists or administrators. Skilled labour may be the bottleneck in expansion, just like capital or land. Skilled labour, however, is only what Marshall might have called a "quasi-bottleneck," if he had not had so nice a sense of elegant language. For it is only a very temporary bottleneck, in the sense that if the capital is available for development, the capitalists or their government will soon provide the facilities for training more skilled people. The real bottlenecks to expansion are therefore capital and natural resources, and we can proceed on the assumption that so long as these are available the necessary skills will be provided as well, though perhaps with some time lag.

If unlimited labour is available, while capital is scarce, we know from the Law of Variable Proportions that the capital should not be spread thinly over all the labour. Only so much labour should be used with capital as will reduce the marginal productivity of labour to zero. In practice, however, labour is not available at a zero wage. Capital will therefore be applied only up to the point where the marginal productivity of labour equals the current wage. This is illustrated in Figure 1. The horizontal axis measures the quantity of labour, and the vertical axis its marginal product. There is a fixed amount of capital. *OW* is the current wage. If the marginal product of labour were zero outside the capitalist sector, *OR* ought to be employed. But it will pay to employ only *OM* in the capitalist sector. *WNP* is the capitalists' surplus. *OWPM* goes in wages to workers in the capitalist sector, while workers outside this sector (i.e. beyond *M*) earn what they can in the subsistence sector of the economy.

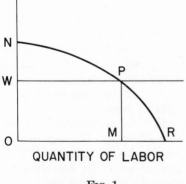

QUANTITY OF LABOR

Fig. 1

The analysis requires further elaboration. In the first place, after what we have said earlier on about some employers in these economies keeping retainers, it may seem strange to be arguing now that labour will be employed up to the point where the wage equals the marginal productivity. Nevertheless, this is probably the right assumption to make when we are set upon analysing the expansion of the capitalist sector of the economy. For the type of capitalist who brings about economic expansion is not the same as the type of employer who treats his employees like retainers. He is more commercially minded, and more conscious of efficiency, cost and profitability. Hence, if our interest is in an expanding capitalist sector, the assumption of profit maximisation is probably a fair approximation to the truth.

Next, we note the use of the terms "capitalist" sector and "subsistence" sector. The capitalist sector is that part of the economy which uses reproducible capital, and pays capitalists for the use thereof. (This coincides with Smith's definition of the productive workers, who are those who work with capital and whose product can therefore be sold at a price above their wages). We can think, if we like, of capitalists hiring out their capital to peasants; in which case, there being by definition an unlimited number of peasants, only some will get capital, and these will have to pay for its use a price which leaves them only subsistence earnings. More usually, however, the use of capital is controlled by capitalists, who hire the services of labour. The classical analysis was therefore conducted on the assumption that capital was used for hiring people. It does not make any difference to the argument, and for convenience we will follow this usage. The subsistence sector is by difference all that part of the economy which is not using reproducible capital. Output per head is lower in this sector than in the capitalist sector, because it is not fructified by capital (this is why it was called "unproductive"; the distinction between productive and unproductive had nothing to do with whether the work yielded utility, as some neo-classicists have scornfully but erroneously asserted). As more capital becomes available more workers can be drawn into the capitalist from the subsistence sector, and their output per head rises as they move from the one sector to the other.

Thirdly we take account of the fact that the capitalist sector, like the subsistence sector, can also be subdivided. What we have is not one island of expanding capitalist employment, surrounded by a vast sea of subsistence workers, but rather a number of such tiny islands. This is very typical of countries in their early stages of development. We find a few industries highly capitalised, such as mining or electric power, side by side with the most primitive techniques; a few high class shops, surrounded by masses of old style traders; a few highly capitalised plantations, surrounded by a sea of peasants. But we find the same contrasts also outside their economic life. There are one or two modern towns, with the finest architecture, water supplies, communications and the like, into which people drift from other towns and villages which might almost belong to another planet. There is the same contrast even between people; between the few highly westernised, trousered natives, educated in western universities, speaking western languages, and glorying in Beethoven, Mill, Marx or Einstein, and the great mass of their countrymen who live in quite other worlds. Capital and new ideas are not thinly diffused throughout the economy; they are highly concentrated at a number of points, from which they spread outwards.

Though the capitalised sector can be subdivided into islands, it remains a single sector because of the effect of competition in tending to equalise the earnings on capital. The competitive principle does not demand that the same amount of capital per person be employed on each "island," or that average profit per unit of capital be the same, but only that the marginal profit be the same. Thus, even if marginal profits were the same all round, islands which yield diminishing returns may be more profitable than others, the earliest capitalists having cornered the vantage points. But in any case marginal profits are not the same all round. In backward economies knowledge is one of the scarcest goods. Capitalists have experience of certain types of investment, say of trading or plantation agriculture, and not of other types, say of manufacturing, and they stick to what they know. So the economy is frequently lopsided in the sense that there is excessive investment in some parts and under-investment in others. Also, financial institutions are more highly developed for some purposes than for others—capital can be got cheaply for trade, but not for house building or for peasant agriculture, for instance. Even in a very highly developed economy the tendency for capital to flow evenly through the economy is very weak; in a backward economy it hardly exists. Inevitably what one gets are very heavily developed patches of the economy, surrounded by economic darkness.

Next we must say something about the wage level. The wage which the expanding capitalist sector has to pay is determined by what people can earn outside that sector. The classical economists used to think of the wage as being determined by what is required for subsistence consumption, and this may be the right solution in some cases. However, in economies where the majority of the people are peasant farmers, working on their own land, we have a more objective index, for the minimum at which labour can be had is now set by the average product of the farmer; men will not leave the family farm to seek employment if the wage is worth less than they would be able to consume if they remained at home. This objective standard, alas, disappears again if the farmers have to pay rent, for their net earnings will then depend upon the amount of rent they have to pay, and in overpopulated countries the rent will probably be adjusted so as to leave them just enough for a conventional level of subsistence. It is not, however, of great importance to the argument whether earnings in the subsistence sector are determined objectively by the level of peasant productivity, or subjectively in terms of a conventional standard of living. Whatever the mechanism, the result is an unlimited supply of labour for which this is the minimum level of earnings.

The fact that the wage level in the capitalist sector depends upon earnings in the subsistence sector is sometimes of immense political importance, since its effect is that capitalists have a direct interest in holding down the productivity of the subsistence workers. Thus, the owners of plantations have no interest in seeing knowledge of new techniques or new seeds conveyed to the peasants, and if they are influential in the government, they will not be found using their influence to expand the facilities for agricultural extension. They will not support proposals for land settlement, and are often instead to be found engaged in turning the peasants off their lands. (Cf. Marx on "Primary Accumulation.") This is one of the worst features of imperialism, for instance. The imperialists invest capital and hire workers; it is to their advantage to keep wages low, and even in those cases where they do not actually go out of their way to impoverish the subsistence economy, they will at least very seldom be found doing anything to make it more productive. In actual fact the record of every imperial power in Africa in modern times is one of impoverishing the subsistence economy, either by taking away the people's land, or by demanding forced labour in the capitalist sector, or by imposing taxes to drive people to work for capitalist employers. Compared with what they have spent on providing facilities for European agriculture or mining, their expenditure on the improvement of African agriculture has been negligible. The failure of imperialism to raise living standards is not wholly to be attributed to self interest, but there are many places where it can be traced directly to the effects of having imperial capital invested in agriculture or in mining.

Earnings in the subsistence sector set a floor to wages in the capitalist sector, but in practice wages have to be higher than this, and there is usually a gap of 30 per cent or more between capitalist wages and subsistence earnings. This gap may be explained in several ways. Part of the difference is illusory, because of the higher cost of living in the capitalist sector. This may be due to the capitalist sector being concentrated in congested towns, so that rents and transport costs are higher. All the same, there is also usually a substantial difference in real wages. This may be required because of the psychological cost of transferring from the easy going way of life of the subsistence sector to the more regimented and urbanised environment of the capitalist sector. Or it may be a recognition of the fact that even the unskilled worker is of more use to the capitalist sector after he has been there for some time than is the raw recruit from the country. Or it may itself represent a difference in conventional standards, workers in the capitalist sector acquiring tastes and a social prestige which have conventionally to be recognised by higher real wages. That this last may be the explanation is suggested by cases where the capitalist workers organise themselves into trade unions and strive to protect or increase their differential. But the differential exists even where there are no unions. . . .

So far we have merely been setting the stage. Now the play begins. For we can now begin to trace the process of economic expansion.

The key to the process is the use which is made of the capitalist surplus. In so far as this is reinvested in creating new capital, the capitalist sector expands, taking more people into capitalist employment out of the subsistence sector. The surplus is then larger still, capital formation is still greater, and so the process continues until the labour surplus disappears.

OS is as before average subsistence earnings, and OW the capitalist wage. WN_1Q_1 represents the surplus in the initial stage. Since some of this is reinvested, the amount of fixed capital increases. Hence the schedule of the marginal productivity of labour is now raised throughout, to the level of N_2Q_2. Both the surplus and capitalist employment are now larger.

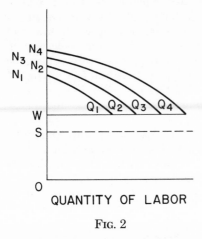

QUANTITY OF LABOR

Fig. 2

Further reinvestment raises the schedule of the marginal productivity of labour to N_3Q_3. And the process continues so long as there is surplus labour.

Various comments are needed in elaboration. First, as to the relationship between capital, technical progress, and productivity. In theory it should be possible to distinguish between the growth of capital and the growth of technical knowledge, but in practice it is neither possible nor necessary for this analysis. As a matter of statistical analysis, differentiating the effects of capital and of knowledge in any industry is straightforward if the product is homogeneous through time, if the physical inputs are also unchanged (in kind) and if the relative prices of the inputs have remained constant. But when we try to do it for any industry in practice we usually find that the product has changed, the inputs have changed and relative prices have changed, so that we get any number of indices of technical progress from the same data, according to the assumptions and the type of index number which we use. In any case, for the purpose of this analysis it is unnecessary to distinguish between capital formation and the growth of knowledge within the capitalist sector. Growth of technical knowledge outside the capitalist sector would be fundamentally important, since it would raise the level of wages, and so reduce the capitalist surplus. But inside the capitalist sector knowledge and capital work in the same direction, to raise the surplus and to increase employment. They also work together. The application of new technical knowledge usually requires new investment, and whether the new knowledge is capital-saving (and thus equivalent to an increase in capital) or labour-saving (and thus equivalent to an increase in the marginal productivity of labour) makes no difference to our diagram. Capital and technical knowledge also work together in the sense that in economies where techniques are stagnant savings are not so readily applied to increasing productive capital; in such economies it is more usual to use savings for building pyramids, churches, and other such durable consumer goods. Accordingly, in this analysis the growth of productive capital and the growth of technical knowledge are treated as a single phenomenon (just as we earlier decided that we could treat the growth of the supply of skilled labour and the growth of capital as a single phenomenon in long run analysis).

Next we must consider more closely the capitalist surplus. Malthus wanted to know what the capitalists would do with this ever-growing surplus; surely this would be an embarrassing glut of commodities? Ricardo replied that there would be no glut; what the capitalists did not consume themselves, they would use for paying the wages of workers to create more fixed capital (this is a free interpretation, since the classical economists associated the expansion of employment with an increase of circulating rather than of fixed capital). This new fixed capital would then in the next stage make possible the employment of more people in the capitalist sector. Malthus persisted; why should the capitalists produce more capital to produce a larger surplus which could only be used for producing still more capital and so *ad infinitum*? To this Marx supplied one answer: capitalists have a passion for accumulating capital. Ricardo supplied another: if they don't want to accumulate, they will consume instead of saving; provided there is no propensity to hoard, there will be no glut. Employment in the next stage will not be as big as it would have been if they had created more fixed capital and so brought more workers into the capitalist sector, but so long as there is no hoarding it makes no difference to the current level of employment whether capitalists decide to consume or to save. Malthus then raised another question; suppose that the capitalists do save and invest without hoarding, surely the fact that capital is growing more rapidly than consumption must so lower the rate of profit on capital that there comes a point when they decide that it is not worth while to invest? This, Ricardo replied, is impossible; since the supply of labour is unlimited, you can always find employment for any amount of capital. This is absolutely correct, for his model; in the neo-classical model capital grows faster than labour, and so one has to ask whether the rate of profit will not fall, but in the classical model the unlimited supply of labour means that the capital/labour ratio, and therefore the rate of surplus, can be held constant for any quantity of capital (i.e., unlimited "widening" is possible). The only fly in the ointment is that there may develop a shortage of natural resources, so that though the capitalists get any amount of labour at a constant wage, they have to pay ever rising rents to landlords. This was what worried Ricardo; it was important to him to distinguish that part of the surplus which goes to landlords from that part which goes to capitalists, since he believed that economic development inevitably increases the relative scarcity of land. We are not so certain of this as he was. Certainly development increases the rent of urban sites fantastically, but its effect on rural rents depends on the rate of technical progress in agriculture, which Malthus and Ricardo both gravely under-estimated. If we assume technical progress in agriculture, no hoarding, and unlimited labour at a constant wage, the rate of profit on capital cannot fall. On the contrary it must increase, since all the benefit of technical progress in the capitalist sector accrues to the capitalists.

Marx's interest in the surplus was ethical as well as scientific. He regarded it as robbery of the workers. His descendants are less certain of this. The surplus, after all, is only partly consumed; the other part is used for capital formation. As for the part which is consumed, some of it is a genuine payment for service rendered—for managerial or entrepreneurial services, as well as for the services of public administrators, whether these are paid salaries out of taxes, or whether they live off their rents or *rentes* while performing unpaid public duties as magistrates, lord-lieutenants, or the like. Even in the U.S.S.R. all these functionaries are paid out of the surplus, and handsomely paid too. It is arguable that these services are over-paid; this is why we have progressive taxation, and it is also one of the more dubious arguments for nationalisation (more dubious because the functionaries of public corporations have to be paid the market rate if the economy is only partially nationalised). But it is not arguable that all this part of the surplus (i.e. the part consumed) morally belongs to the workers, in any sense. As for the part which is used for capital formation, the experience of the U.S.S.R. is that this is increased, and not reduced, by transforming the ownership of capital. Expropriation deprives the capitalists of control over this part of the surplus, and of the right to consume this part at some later date, but it does nothing whatever to transfer this part of the surplus to the workers. Marx's emotional approach was a natural reaction to the classical writers, who sometimes in unguarded moments wrote as if the capitalist surplus and its increase were all that counted in the national income (cf. Ricardo, who called it "the net revenue" of production). All this, however, is by the way; for our present interest is not in ethical questions, but in how the model works.

The central problem in the theory of economic development is to understand the process by which a community which was previously saving and investing 4 or 5 per cent of its national income or less, converts itself into an economy where voluntary saving is running at about 12 to 15 per cent of national income or more. This is the central problem because the central fact of economic development is rapid capital accumulation (including knowledge and skills with capital). We cannot explain any "industrial" revolution (as the economic historians pretend to do) until we can explain why saving increased relatively to national income.

It is possible that the explanation is simply that some psychological change occurs which causes people to be more thrifty. This, however, is not a plausible explanation. We are interested not in the people in general, but only say in the 10 per cent of them with the largest incomes, who in countries with surplus labour receive up to 40 per cent of the national income (nearer 30 per cent in more developed countries). The remaining 90 per cent of the people never manage to save a significant fraction of their incomes. The important question is why does the top 10 per cent save more? The reason may be because they decide to consume less, but this reason does not square with the facts. There is no evidence of a fall in personal consumption by the top 10 per cent at a time when industrial revolutions are occurring. It is also possible that, though they do not save any more, the top 10 per cent spend less of their income on durable consumer goods (tombs, country houses, temples) and more on productive capital. Certainly, if one compares different civilisations this is a striking difference in the disposition of income. Civilisations in which there is a rapid growth of technical knowledge or expansion of other opportunities present more profitable outlets for investment than do technologically stagnant civilisations, and tempt capital into productive channels rather than into the building of monuments. But if one takes a country only over the course of the hundred years during which it undergoes a revolution in the rate of capital formation, there is no noticeable change in this regard. Certainly, judging by the novels, the top 10 per cent in England were not spending noticeably less on durable consumer goods in 1800 than they were in 1700.

Much the most plausible explanation is that people save more because they have more to save. This is not to say merely that the national income per head is larger, since there is no clear evidence that the proportion of the national income saved increases with national income per head—at any rate our fragmentary evidence for the United Kingdom and for the United States suggests that this is not so. The explanation is much more likely to be that saving increases relatively to the national income because the incomes of the savers increase relatively to the national income. The central fact of economic development is that the distribution of incomes is altered in favour of the saving class.

Practically all saving is done by people who receive profits or rents. Workers' savings are very small. The middle-classes save a little, but in practically every community the savings of the middle-classes out of their salaries are of little consequence for productive investment. Most members of the middle-class are engaged in the perpetual struggle to keep up with the Joneses; if they manage to save enough to buy the house in which they live, they are doing well. They may save to educate their children, or to subsist in their old age, but this saving is virtually offset by the savings being used up for the same purposes. Insurance is the middle-class's favourite form of saving in modern societies, yet in the U.K., where the habit is extremely well developed, the annual net increase in insurance funds from all classes, rich, middle, and poor is less than 1½ per cent of the national income. It is doubtful if the wage and salary classes ever anywhere save as much as 3 per cent of the national income, net (possible exception: Japan). If we are interested in savings, we must concentrate attention upon profits and rents.

For our purpose it does not matter whether profits are distributed or undistributed; the major source of savings is profits, and if we find that savings are increasing as a proportion of the national income, we may take it for granted that this is because the share of profits in the national income is increasing. (As a refinement, for highly taxed communities, we should say profits net of taxes upon profits, whether personal income or corporate taxes). Our problem then becomes what are the circumstances in which the share of profits in the national income increases?

The modified classical model which we are using here has the virtue of answering the question. In the beginning, the national income consists almost entirely of subsistence income. Abstracting from population growth and assuming that the marginal product of labour is zero, this subsistence income remains constant throughout the expansion, since by definition labour can be yielded up to the expanding capitalist sector without reducing subsistence output. The process therefore increases the capitalist surplus and the income of capitalist employees, taken together, as a proportion of the national income. It is possible to imagine conditions in which the surplus nevertheless does not increase relatively to national income. This requires that capitalist employment should expand relatively much faster than the surplus, so that within the capitalist sector gross margins or profit plus rent are falling sharply relatively to wages. We know that this does not happen. Even if gross margins were constant, profits in our model would be increasing relatively to national income. But gross margins are not likely to be constant in our model, which assumes that practically the whole benefit of capital accumulation and of technical progress goes into the surplus; because real wages are constant, all that the workers get out of the expansion is that more of them are employed at a wage above the subsistence earnings. The model says, in effect, that if unlimited supplies of labour are available at a constant real wage, and if any part of profits is reinvested in productive capacity, profits will grow continuously relatively to the national income, and capital formation will also grow relatively to the national income.

The model also covers the case of a technical revolution. Some historians have suggested that the capital for the British Industrial Revolution came out of profits made possible by a spate of inventions occurring together. This is extremely hard to fit into the neo-classical model, since it involves the assumption that these inventions raised the marginal productivity of capital more than they raised the marginal productivity of labour, a proposition which it is hard to establish in any economy where labour is scarce. (If we do not make this assumption, other incomes rise just as fast as profits, and investment does not increase relatively to national income). On the other hand the suggestion fits beautifully into the modified classical model, since in this model practically the whole benefit of inventions goes into the surplus, and becomes available for further capital accumulation.

This model also helps us to face squarely the nature of the economic problem of backward countries. If we ask "why do they save so little?" the truthful answer is not "because they are so poor," as we might be tempted to conclude from the path-breaking and praiseworthy correlations of Mr. Colin Clark. The truthful answer is "because their capitalist sector is so small" (remembering that "capitalist" here does not mean private capitalist, but would apply equally to state capitalist). If they had a larger capitalist sector, profits would be a greater part of their national income, and saving and investment would also be relatively larger. (The state capitalist can accumulate capital even faster than the private capitalist, since he can use for the purpose not only the profits of the capitalist sector, but also what he can force or tax out of the subsistence sector).

Another point which we must note is that though the increase of the capitalist sector involves an increase in the inequality of incomes, as between capitalists and the rest, mere inequality of income is not enough to ensure a high level of saving. In point of fact the inequality of income is *greater* in over-populated under-developed countries than it is in advanced industrial nations, for the simple reason that agricultural rents are so high in the former. Eighteenth century British economists took it for granted that the landlord class is given to prodigal consumption rather than to productive investment, and this is certainly true of landlords in under-developed countries. Hence, given two countries of equal incomes, in which distribution is more unequal in one than in the other, savings may be greater where distribution is more equal if profits are higher relatively to rents. It is the inequality which goes with profits that favours capital formation, and not the inequality which goes with rents. Correspondingly, it is very hard to argue that these countries cannot afford to save more, when 40 per cent or so of the national income is going to the top 10 per cent and so much of rent incomes is squandered.

Behind this analysis also lies the sociological problem of the emergence of a capitalist class, that is to say of a group of men who think in terms of investing capital productively. The dominant classes in backward economies—landlords, traders, moneylenders, priests, soldiers, princes—do not normally think in these terms. What causes a society to grow a capitalist class is a very difficult question, to which probably, there is no general answer. Most countries seem to begin by importing their capitalists from abroad; and in these days many (e.g. U.S.S.R., India) are growing a class of state capitalists who, for political reasons of one sort or another, are determined to create capital rapidly on public account. As for indigenous private capitalists, their emergence is probably bound up with the emergence of new opportunities, especially something that widens the market, associated with some new technique which greatly increases the productivity of labour if labour and capital are used together. Once a capitalist sector has emerged, it is only a matter of time before it becomes sizeable. If very little technical progress is occurring, the surplus will grow only slowly. But if for one reason or another the opportunities for using capital productivity increase rapidly, the surplus will also grow rapidly, and the capitalist class with it.

In our model so far capital is created only out of profits earned. In the real world, however, capitalists also create capital as a result of a net increase in the supply of money—especially bank credit. We have now also to take account of this.

In the neo-classical model capital can be created only by withdrawing resources from producing consumer goods. In our model, however, there is surplus labour, and if (as we shall assume) its marginal productivity is zero, and if, also, capital can be created by labour without withdrawing scarce land and capital from other uses, then capital can be created without reducing the output of consumer goods. This second proviso is important, since if we need capital or land to make capital the results in our model are the same as the results in the neo-classical model, despite the fact that there is surplus labour. However, in practice the proviso is often fulfilled. Food cannot be grown without land, but roads, viaducts, irrigation channels and buildings can be created by human labour with hardly any capital to speak of—witness the Pyramids, or the marvellous railway tunnels built in the mid-nineteenth century almost with bare hands. Even in modern industrial countries constructional activity, which lends itself to hand labour, is as much as 50 or 60 per cent of gross fixed investment, so it is not difficult to think of labour creating capital without using any but the simplest tools. The classical economists were not wrong in thinking of lack of circulating capital as being a more serious obstacle to expansion in their world than lack of fixed capital. In the analysis which follows in this section we assume that surplus labour cannot be used to make consumer goods without using up more land or capital, but can be used to make capital goods without using any scarce factors.

If a community is short of capital, and has idle resources which can be set to creating capital, it seems very desirable on the face of the matter that this should be done, even if it means creating extra money to finance the extra employment. There is no loss of other output while the new capital is being made, and when it comes into use it will raise output and employment in just the same way as would capital financed not by credit creation but out of profits. The difference between profit-financed and credit-financed capital is not in the ultimate effects on output, but in the immediate effects on prices and on the distribution of income.

Before we come to the effects on prices, however, we should pause a moment to notice what happens to the output of consumer goods in this model and the others while credit-financed capital is being created, but before it begins to be used. In the neo-classical model an increase in capital formation has to be accompanied by a corresponding fall in the output of consumer goods, since scarce resources can do one or the other. In the Keynesian model an increase in capital formation also increases the output of consumer goods, and if the multiplier exceeds 2, the output of consumer goods increases even more than capital formation. In our model capital formation goes up, but the output of consumer goods is not immediately affected. This is one of those crucial cases where it is important to be certain that one is using the right model when it comes to giving advice on economic policy.

In our model, if surplus labour is put to capital formation and paid out of new money, prices rise, because the stream of money purchases is swollen while the output of consumer goods is for the time being constant. What is happening is that the fixed amount of consumer goods is being redistributed, towards the workers newly employed, away from the rest of the community (this is where the lack of circulating capital comes into the picture). This process is not "forced saving" in the useful sense of that term. In the neo-classical model the output of consumer goods is reduced, forcing the community as a whole to save. In our model, however, consumer goods output is not at any time reduced; there is a forced redistribution of consumption, but not forced saving. And, of course, as soon as the capital goods begin to yield output, consumption begins to rise.

This inflationary process does not go on forever; it comes to an end when voluntary savings increase to a level where they are equal to the inflated level of investment. Since savings are a function of profits, this means that the inflation continues until profits increase so much relatively to the national income that capitalists can now finance the higher rate of investment out of their profits without any further recourse to monetary expansion. Essentially equilibrium is secured by raising the ratio of profits to the national income. The equilibrator need not however be profits; it might equally be government receipts, if there is a structure of taxes such that the ratio of government receipts to the national income rises automatically as the national income rises. This seems to be just about what happened in the U.S.S.R. In the crucial years when the economy was being transformed from a 5 per cent. to a (probably) 20 per cent net saver, there was a tremendous inflation of prices (apparently prices rose about 700 per cent in a decade), but the inflationary profits largely went to the government in the form of turnover tax, and by the end of the decade a new equilibrium was in sight.

It is not, however, always a simple matter to raise profits relatively to national income simply by turning on the monetary tap. The simplest and most extreme model of an inflation would be to assume that when the capitalists finance capital formation by creating credit, the money all comes back to them in the very next round in the form of an increase in their profits. In such a model profits, voluntary savings and capital formation can be raised to any desired level in a very short time, with only a small increase in prices. Something like this may well apply in the U.S.S.R. In real terms, however, this implies that there has been a fall in the share of the national income received by other people, including a fall in their real consumption, since they have had to release consumer goods for the previously unemployed who are now engaged in capital formation. It may be the farmers who are worse off, this showing itself in the prices of manufactures rising relatively to farm prices. Or it may be the workers in the capitalist sector who are worse off, because farm prices and the prices of manufactures rise faster than their wages. Or the blow may be falling upon salaried workers, pensioners, landlords or creditors. Now in the real world none of these classes will take this lying down. In the U.S.S.R., where the intention was that the capital formation should be at the expense of the farmers, it led in the end to organised violence on both sides. In our model it is hard to get away with it at the expense of the workers, since the wage in the capitalist sector must stand at a certain minimum level above subsistence earnings if labour is to be available. Generally, what happens as prices rise is that new contracts have to be made to take account of rising price levels. Some classes get caught, but only temporarily.

Now, if one pursued this argument logically, it would lead to the conclusion that equilibrium could never be reached—at any rate, so long as the banking system is content to supply all "legitimate" demands for money. If none of the other classes can be soaked, it seems impossible for profits to rise relatively to the national income for more than a temporary space, and it therefore seems impossible to reach an equilibrium level of savings equal to the new level of investment. The inflation, once begun goes on forever. This, however, is not possible for another reason, namely the fact that the real national income is not fixed, but rising, as a result of the capital formation. Therefore all that is required is that capitalists' real incomes rise faster than other people's. Beyond the first year or two, when the additional consumer goods begin to appear, it is not necessary for any class to reduce its consumption. By the time the process of recontracting has begun, output has also begun to rise, and it is therefore possible to end a *modus vivendi*.

We can give an exact description of this equilibrium in our modified classical model. In this model the average subsistence real income is given, and so also therefore is the real wage in the capitalist sector. It is not possible, by inflation or otherwise, to reach a new equilibrium in which the capitalist surplus has increased at the expense of either of these. If, therefore, the capitalists begin to finance capital formation out of credit, they lower the real incomes of the others only temporarily. Wages would then be chasing prices continuously but for the fact that, since output is growing all the time, profits are growing all the time. Hence the part of the investment which is financed out of credit is diminishing all the time, until equilibrium is reached. For example, suppose that an investment of £100 a year yields £20 a year profit, of which £10 a year is saved. Then, if capitalists invest an extra £100 a year, all of which in the first year is financed out of credit, by the eleventh year profits will be £200 a year greater, savings will be £100 a year greater and there will be no further monetary pressure on prices. All that will remain from the episode is that there will be £1,000 more useful productive capital at work than there would have if the credit creation had not taken place.

Thus we have two simple models marking the extreme cases. In the first, all the credit created comes back to the capitalists at once as profits (or to the state capitalists as taxes). Equilibrium is then reached easily, with the capitalists gaining at the expense of all others. In the other model the capitalists can only gain temporarily; equilibrium then takes much longer to reach, but it is reached eventually. In the first case we need only an expansion of money income; but in the second case it is the expansion of real income which eventually brings the capitalists the required proportion of the national income.

The fact that capital formation increases real output must also be borne in mind in the analysis of the effects of credit creation upon prices. The inflations which loom most in our minds are those which occur in war-time, when resources are being withdrawn from producing consumer goods. If the supply of money is increasing while the output of goods is falling, anything can happen to prices. Inflation for the purpose of capital formation, however, is a very different kettle of fish. For it results in increasing consumer goods output, and this results in falling prices if the quantity of money is held constant. . . .

We may now sum up this section. Capital formation is financed not only out of profits but also out of an expansion of credit. This speeds up the growth of capital, and the growth of real income. It also results in some redistribution of the national income, either temporarily or permanently, according to the assumptions one makes—in the model we are using, the redistribution is only temporary. It also prevents prices from falling, as they otherwise would (if money is constant and output rising), and it may drive prices up substantially if (as in our model) the distribution of income cannot be altered permanently by monetary measures, since prices will then continue to rise until real output has risen enough to effect the required redistribution. Thereafter prices fall further, since inflation raises prices while capital is being created, but the increased output which then results brings them down again.

One point remains. We have seen that if new money is used to finance capital formation the rise of prices eventually peters out, as savings grow into equilibrium with investment; and reverses itself, as the output of consumer goods begins to pour out. The new equilibrium, however, may take a long time to reach, and if also the flow of new money is substantial the resulting rise of prices may strike fear into the hearts of the public. People do not panic if prices rise for two or three years; but after that they may begin to lose confidence in money, and it may become necessary to call a drastic halt. This is the most important practical limitation on the extent to which capital formation can be financed in this way. This is why the banking authorities have always tended to alternate short periods of easy credit with sharp periods of restriction. Bank credit moves three steps up and one step down instead of moving up continuously. This also brings us to the threshold of the trade cycle. If capital were financed exclusively out of profits, and if there were also no hoarding, capital formation would proceed steadily. It is mainly the existence of an elastic credit system which makes the trade cycle an integral part of the mechanism of economic development in an unplanned economy. It is not necessary, however, for us to enter into analysis of the cycle since in this respect the model we are using does not yield results different from those of other models. . . .

21. Critical Observations on Some Current Notions in the Theory of Economic Development

Gottfried Haberler*

. . . The content of my paper will be somewhat negative and its tone grumbling, because I find myself out of sympathy with many recent contributions to the theory of economic development. I shall discuss critically four ideas that have played a great role in recent writings on economic development: 1) The notion of disguised unemployment in underdeveloped countries, 2) the notion of "balanced growth" or "big push," 3) the demonstration effect, 4) the theory of the secular deterioration of the terms of trade for underdeveloped countries.

I do not say that the whole literature on the subject is based on these notions. In fact it would be foolish to say that, if for no other reason than because I know only a small fraction of the immense literature on the subject. But it is safe to say, I believe, that these ideas have played a considerable role in a highly influential part of the literature and they permeate influential official thinking, e.g. many U.N. esp. E.C.E., ECLA and ECAFE publications.

I. Unemployment in Underdeveloped Countries.

. . . To my mind, the claims of the proponents of the theory of widespread disguised unemployment are tremendously exaggerated. I can perhaps better explain what I think is wrong with the theory of disguised unemployment by stating positively what in my opinion is actually true in varying degrees in various countries, not only in underdeveloped but in developed countries as well: If it were possible to improve methods of production in agriculture; *if* the skill of farm laborers is increased; *if* social habits could be changed, a new spirit implanted and the resistance to

*From *L'industria*, No. 2, 1957. The author is Galen L. Stone Professor of International Trade, Harvard University.

moving to and living in cities and to working in factories could be overcome; *if* technology in industry could be changed so as to employ unskilled rural workers; *if* capital and other cooperating factors (entrepreneurs, managers, skilled foremen, etc.) could be provided in larger quantities and better quality; *if* and to the extent that all these things happen or are done, agriculture can release a lot of labor without loss of output and industrial output be stepped up at the same time.

Now there is no doubt that all these things gradually do happen and did happen all the time in developed as well as underdeveloped countries. In fact, economic development largely consists of these changes. Furthermore, few would deny that many of these changes and improvements can be speeded up by appropriate policies (although, if the measures taken are inappropriate or the dosage incorrect the result will be a slow-down rather than a speed-up) and that for some of these changes to happen Government action is indispensable. But it is very misleading to speak of disguised unemployment. In that sense there always was disguised unemployment in developed as well as underdeveloped countries and practically everybody is a disguised unemployed person, even in the most highly developed countries, because each of us will produce more ten years hence when technology has made further progress, skill and training have been further improved, the capital stock increased, etc.

The cases where after removal of a part of the labor force, output remains unchanged (or even rises) without capital having been increased, technology improved, social habits changed, etc., or where such changes can be expected to be the automatic and immediate consequence of a prior reduction in labor input, must be comparatively rare and inconsequential compared with the increase in output due to the gradual introduction of all those changes and improvements.

The theory of disguised unemployment is often associated with the proposition that the capital-labor proportion is fixed—forgetting conveniently other productive agents. In other words production functions (isoquants) are said to have rectangular (or at least angular) shape. In some modern highly mechanized industries one may sometimes find situations faintly approaching this case. But the assumption that this should be the case in more primitive economies (agriculture) and should be a chronic situation seems to me preposterous.

It is true one can sometimes observe in underdeveloped countries a tendency to introduce a few modern highly mechanized plants with imported machinery, foreign supervisors and mechanics and using very little native labor. But these instances of "show case industrialization"[1] can in no way change the general picture. It should also be observed that they are not instances of the operation of the "demonstration effect," but almost always the consequence of faulty policies which artificially foster (e.g., by means of exchange allocation at often fantastically unrealistic rates) the establishment of uneconomic plants and industries.

[1] The phrase is W. H. Nichols' in *Investment in Agriculture in Underdeveloped Countries,* "American Economic Review," May 1955.

II. The Theory of "Balanced Growth" or "Big Push"

This theory asserts that if the typical underdeveloped country wishes to develop, it must push ahead fast and far, all along the line or it will not get anywhere at all. There is no room for slow piecemeal improvements. Owing to the low income and lack of purchasing power, the market is too small to permit any one industry to expand unless all others expand at the same time—thus providing a market for each others' wares.

This theory, again, is based on preoccupation with, and exaggeration of the importance of, a few highly mechanized giant plants or industries. These show cases catch the fancy of the onlooker and make him overlook the great mass of small and medium size run-of-the-mill plants and industries which are the backbone even of most highly developed countries.

The theory is contradicted by the patent fact that industrial advance is usually limited by lack of capital, including "social framework investment," insufficient supply of entrepreneurship, of skilled, trained and disciplined labor and not by the insufficient size of the market

The theory overlooks or discounts the possibility of increasing the size of the market by international trade.

On the basis of this theory, it is impossible to explain why any now developed country ever developed. How conservative and realistic, compared with modern theories, sounds the *Communist Manifesto* where the productive power of the unfettered capitalistic system and its capability of developing and industrializing backward countries are described in truly glowing terms.

III. The Demonstration Effect

Underdeveloped countries are supposed to be seriously handicapped by the operation of the "demonstration effect." The demonstration effect was introduced into economics by J. Duesenberry. He was, however, not speaking of underdeveloped countries and should not be held responsible for its use or abuse in that area.

The "demonstration effect" is supposed to work in the sphere of consumption as well as in that of production. . . .

The demonstration effect is best regarded as an explanation, motivation and excuse for inflationary policies. It is doubtful whether it would cause any troubles at all without lax monetary policies. It surely is not specifically related to underdeveloped countries. All of us, even in the most advanced countries, are under constant pressure by high power advertising to live beyond our means. Everywhere we see and read of things we should like to have and cannot afford. Instalment credit makes it easy to buy things that we should not buy. Some of us are tempted into making foolish purchases, which we later regret; but these slips are quickly corrected and no permanent harm results except if and to the extent that instalment credit intensifies inflationary expansion during the upgrade and deflationary contraction during the downgrade of the cycle; but this intensification of the cyclical swings is contingent upon the cyclical flexibility of credit in general and could be counteracted by monetary policy.

There is, however, an area in which the demonstration effect really operates and where it causes serious damage to the economies of underdeveloped countries. That is the area of public policy and collective spending.

Many backward countries have adopted and are still in the process of eagerly imitating the latest policies which it took the advanced industrial countries decades or centuries to develop. The latest most up-to-date legislation on social security, regulations of labor, minimum wages, working conditions, channeling of saving through governmental agencies and impounding them for public purpose—all these policies which the developed countries have adopted only in a late stage of their development are often introduced in underdeveloped countries as soon as they are freed from colonial status. Add equalization of income through progressive direct taxation, nationalization of existing enterprises and reservation for the Government of certain industries and you have an economic policy which greatly overtaxes the limited administrative capacities of underdeveloped countries.

IV. Terms of Trade

The theory has become popular that the terms of trade have shown a secular tendency to deteriorate for the underdeveloped countries, the so-called "peripheral" world; more precisely for the raw material producing or rather exporting countries.[2] This alleged historical trend is supposed to be the consequence of deepseated factors and hence capable of confident extrapolation into the future.[3]

To my mind the alleged historical facts lack proof, their explanation is faulty, the extrapolation reckless and the policy conclusions irresponsible —to put it mildly.

The historical generalization suffers, first of all, from an excessive degree of aggregation. It is improbable in the extreme that it should be possible to make a valid generalization for the very heterogeneous countries which constitute the underdeveloped part of the world. To pick a few examples from the Western Hemisphere: Can anyone seriously maintain that the long run[4] change in the terms of trade is the same for (a) agricultural exporters (Argentina, Uruguay), (b) mining countries (Bolivia), (c) coffee exporters (Brazil), (d) petroleum exporters (Venezuela). Many of these countries have undergone profound changes in their internal economy and trade structure which make long run comparisons extremely hazardous.

If we concentrate on a more homogenous group of countries whose export trade has not changed much, the fact still remains that the composition of their imports, that is of the exports of the industrial countries has changed

[2]It should not be forgotten that there are some highly developed and industrialized countries, whose exports consist largely of raw materials and foodstuff. To this group belong, for example, Australia and Denmark.

[3]See e.g. *The Economic Development of Latin America and its Principal Problems,* United Nations, 1950. For a more recent statement see Raul Prebisch in *National Policy for Economic Welfare,* Columbia University Bicentennial Conference. New York, 1955, pp. 277–280.

[4]During the short run cycle a greater uniformity may be present.

profoundly. Scores of new products are being produced and exported and the quality of those that existed 10 or 20 years ago has been improved to such an extent that they are virtually new commodities. No attempt has been made to allow for these quality changes. The above mentioned U.N. report confines itself to the remark: "It is regrettable that the price indexes do not reflect the difference in quality of finished products. For this reason, it was not possible to take them into account."[5] The report then proceeds as if this was a minor, quite unimportant qualification.

There has taken place another far-reaching structural change in world trade, the neglect of which completely vitiates long run comparisons in the terms of trade—namely, the revolution that has occurred in transport techniques and transport cost. When in the 1870's and 1880's the American Middle West was opened up and overseas wheat began to flow to Europe —the British terms of trade improved. But obviously that did not mean that the factoral terms of trade of the new exporting regions deteriorated. Agriculture in the old world was indeed hurt but surely not in the underdeveloped "regions of recent settlement" from where the new supplies originated.

In general, as has often been pointed out, if transport costs are reduced it is possible for the commodity terms of trade (exclusive of services) to improve for *both* importing and exporting countries or areas at the same time.

Waiving all these difficulties, or assuming that allowance has been made for them, there still remains the question of productivity changes. In other words, a given deterioration in the commodity terms of trade of a country need not reflect a deterioration of its single or double factoral terms of trade; it may reflect a differential increase in the productivity of the country's export industries.

No attempt has been made by the proponents of the criticized theory to grapple with any of the various defects which I have mentioned.

Suppose, however, we have satisfied ourselves that the terms of trade have in fact deteriorated in the last 100 years for a certain group of countries *posito non concesso*. No policy conclusions could be drawn unless it were possible to advance good reasons for assuming that this deterioration is likely to continue. In order to make such an extrapolation, it would be necessary to attempt an explanation of the alleged trend.

Two reasons are usually given why the terms of trade move against raw material exporters. The first is that prices of finished manufactured goods are bound to be kept high by monopolistic machinations of trade unions and cartels.

This argument, as it is usually presented, rests on a confusion of absolute and relative prices. It is true that industrial progress in the developed countries rarely takes the form of constant money wages and money incomes associated with falling prices, but rather the form of constant (or even rising) prices associated with rising money wages. This may be bad from the point of view of stability and is undoubtedly unjust for fixed income receivers. But there is no evidence that it has changed relative prices

[5]*Loc. cit.* p. 6.

as between industry and agriculture or between finished goods and raw materials.

The second reason advanced for the alleged trend is the operation of Engel's law. When incomes rise the world over, demand for foodstuffs and raw materials rises slower than demand for finished industrial products. Hence the terms of exchange move in favor of the latter against the former.

Engel's law is certainly one of the best established empirical generalizations in economics. But it cannot bear the heavy burden which is placed on it by the theory under review. It applies to food but not to every kind of food. In the case of industrial raw materials, the situation is much more complicated.

The main objection, however, is that the operation of Engel's law is only one factor among many others. The exhaustion of certain raw materials in some of the developed countries (e.g. coal in the U.K.; iron ore in the U.S.) which necessitates the massive importation of raw materials is an example of a counteracting tendency.[6]

This development can be regarded as a concrete manifestation of a broad and supposedly all-pervading tendency which has played an important role in classical and neo-classical economics—viz. of the law of diminishing returns.

There is a pessimistic streak—pessimistic from the point of view of the industrial countries, as well as from the point of view of the internal income distribution within each country—going through classical economics from Ricardo and Torrens via J. S. Mill to Keynes (in his debate on the terms of trade with Beveridge) and recently Austin Robinson.[7] It is based on the doctrine that agriculture and extractive industries are subject to diminishing returns while this is not true of manufacturing. Hence the terms of trade must inexorably turn against the manufacturing industries and industrial countries.

This is evidently the exact opposite of the thesis that Engel's law will turn the terms of trade against the primary producers. We have thus Engel's law pitted against the law of diminishing returns.

Around the turn of the century an influential and vocal group of nationalistic and protectionist German economists (among them A. Wagner and Pohle) warned about the dangers of further industrialization and advocated higher protection for agriculture to arrest or slow down the rapid urbanization and industrialization of Germany which was then at full swing. Their case was partly based on the prediction that the industrial countries would find it harder and harder to obtain food and raw materials from abroad, because the food and raw material producing countries, too, would industrialize and use their food and raw materials themselves.[8] Austin Robinson's recent article is reminiscent of those German voices. He reaches the same conclusion for present-day Britain as Wagner and Pohle did for Germany of their time.

[6]There are, of course, examples on the other side e.g. the substitution of "synthetic" for "natural" materials—which further illustrates the complexity and unpredictability of the broad development.

[7]*The Changing Structure of the British Economy,* "Economic Journal." Sept. 1954.

[8]See my *Theory of International Trade,* p. 285 *et seq.* for a brief summary and references to the literature.

Until now these dire predictions have proved entirely wrong. Industrialization and urbanization have proceeded relentlessly everywhere but the supply of raw materials and foodstuffs have kept pace.

It will perhaps be objected that both parties, the champions of Engel's law and those of the law of diminishing returns, cannot both be wrong simultaneously. For the terms of trade must shift either in favor of one or in favor of the other; it would be a strange coincidence if they did not change at all.

Now, the terms of trade may have shifted back and forth and this is probably what actually happened. But whatever the truth about the terms of trade, both parties can be wrong, and in fact are wrong, in my opinion, in the sense that a deterioration of its terms of trade does not prevent a country from being better off than before (although other things being equal a country would always be better off if foreign demand had been so elastic that a given improvement of technology in a country's export industry had left the commodity terms of trade unchanged instead of producing a deterioration).

Moreover, both parties cannot be right in their respective policy conclusions. For both groups recommend protection for contradictory reasons and purposes; the champions of Engel's law call for more severe import restrictions in underdeveloped countries in order to anticipate a deterioration of the terms of trade *against* the underdeveloped countries; the champions of the law of diminishing returns recommend more protection in the industrial countries in order to anticipate a deterioration of the terms of trade *against* the industrial countries.[9] The terms of trade cannot move in both directions at the same time. In fact, both parties are wrong in their policy recommendations, because it is irrational and irresponsible to base policy on highly uncertain guesses about future developments. Furthermore, even if we were sure that a certain change in the terms of trade was coming, there would be no sense in trying to anticipate it unless it was expected to come so suddenly that it would require a costly and rapid adjustment. In the German discussion 60 years ago much was made of the argument that industrialization and urbanization was an irreversible process. If by that is meant that once agriculture has been allowed to contract it is difficult to revive agricultural production, wartime experience seems to show that the argument is wrong. It is possible under modern conditions to expand agricultural production fairly quickly when the need arises.

Enough has been said, I believe, to demonstrate that the theory of the secular deterioration of the terms of trade for the underdeveloped countries is completely unfounded and the policy recommendations based on it are devoid of any solid basis.

V. Concluding Remarks

What does it all add up to? We can perhaps say that the four criticized notions and the policy recommendations derived from them are based on three basic convictions.

1. A profound distrust of the judgment of individual producers and con-

[9]It will be observed that the argument in question has nothing to do with the static, terms of trade or optimum tariff argument for protection.

sumers. The individuals are said to be often irrational and ignorant. The consumer does not know what is good for him. He is typically a spendthrift and is subject to the demonstration effect. Producers are equally irrational and incompetent. They employ workers whose marginal product is zero or negative, they copy methods of production which are unsuited for the resource pattern of underdeveloped countries, they are ignorant of potential external economies and fail to foresee and to anticipate changes in the terms of trade.

2. The economists, both native and foreign consultants on their fleeting visits to some backward area, are alert and informed about all these things which individual consumers and producers are ignorant of. They foresee changes in the terms of trade, recognize disguised unemployment and external economies and are not subject to the demonstration effect.

3. Economists are not only omniscient, but also know what to do to correct the various defects. And there is no doubt about their capability of persuading governments and politicians and of carrying out policies according to the diagnoses and prognoses provided by the economists.

All this sounds fantastic and it is undoubtedly exaggerated, but not to such an extent as to rob the picture that emerges of its relevance for the understanding of actual economic policy in many underdeveloped countries. In almost all backward countries economic policy is highly interventionist and protectionist, verging in some on integrated central planning.

The conclusion I wish to draw is not that an extreme *laissez-faire* policy is most conducive to stimulating economic development. The Government can certainly do much to speed up economic growth and there are many indispensable measures which only the Government can take. My conclusion is rather that by doing too much, by trying to do things that individuals and the market can do better, Governments overtax their limited capacities and are forced to neglect their basic and indispensable functions.

In his keynote talk opening the Columbia University Bicentennial Conference on "National Policy for Economic Welfare at Home and Abroad," an address full of beauty and wisdom, Sir Dennis Robertson asked the question: "What does the economist economize?" His answer was that the economist economizes, or should economize, "that scarce resource, Love"— meaning that they should not act and predicate their recommendations on the assumption that love, goodwill, cooperative spirit are available in unlimited quantities.

Similarly, on a lower and more pedestrian level, we may say that Governmental know-how, administrative efficiency, political honesty are a scarce and precious resource, especially scarce in underdeveloped countries. The supply and quality of this resource has improved over the last 150 years in most countries. It can be further increased but only slowly and at a heavy cost in terms of manpower and brain power—another precious and very scarce resource. It cannot be as easily taught or copied and imported from foreign countries as many productive technologies can be. On the other hand, it can be depleted and its quality impaired by excessive use and above all it can be misallocated and be spread too thin.

This is what happens in many underdeveloped countries. Prevailing policies misuse and misallocate, spread too thin and deplete and impair the limited supply of Governmental know-how. If Governmental energies and the best brains serving the administrative apparatus are spent on the thinking up and operating unworkable and infinitely complex systems of exchange control, rationing of imports, allocation of quotas, nationalizing, expropriating private enterprises, running grossly inefficient public enterprises—if Governments try to do things which private business, native or foreign, can do much more efficiently—it should be no wonder that those services, indispensable for economic growth, which only the Government can perform or which it can perform better, are sadly neglected. Such services and activities are elementary and higher education—if 40% and more of the population are illiterate as is the case, e.g. in most Latin American countries, economic growth must be retarded; public health; basic utilities such as water, communication, postal services, port installations as well as the elementary Governmental services of maintaining law and order. Many or all of these "social overhead investments" are sadly neglected in many or most underdeveloped countries; or they are not developed as fast as they should be in the interest of economic growth, because Governments pour a disproportionate part of their resources into activities, which are either outrightly wasteful or could be performed more efficiently and cheaply by private business, and cause inefficient use of private capital; e.g. by stimulating by all sorts of protectionist devices (including exchange control) of inefficient secondary industries.

Bad economic policies are, of course, not a monopoly of underdeveloped countries. But no doubt there they are especially bad and underdeveloped countries can least afford such waste. Economists in developed countries must take their full share of responsibility for this state of affairs.

INTERNATIONAL TRADE AND ECONOMIC GROWTH

22. International Trade and Economic Development

*Gottfried Haberler**

I

... I shall discuss the contribution, positive or negative, favorable or unfavorable, which foreign trade can make to the economic development of underdeveloped countries. I shall make a special effort to bring the tools of economic theory, i.e., the theory of international trade, to bear upon the problem on hand and shall also draw some policy conclusions from my analysis. ...

For present purposes I shall conform to the general usage and define development as the growth of per capita real income. A factor or institution or policy—international trade or a change of trade or trade policy, free trade or protection—are said to be conducive to economic development, if it can be shown that they speed up the rate of growth of per capita real income as compared with the rate that would obtain in the absence of the factor or policy or institution in question. ...

A well-trained, hard working and frugal people can make up to an astonishing degree for lack of natural resources, as the example of Switzerland shows. Nonetheless, it would be a mistake to expect a perfect correlation between the real level of development and output per head. It would be an even greater mistake to identify the level of development with the degree of industrialization, especially in the sense of having a large percentage of the working force employed in the manufacturing ("secondary") industries. Urbanization and having a large percentage of the working population employed in "tertiary" industries, i.e. in service industries such as education, entertainment, research, scientific and artistic pursuits, is probably a much better indicator of economic development than industrialization proper.[1]

It is true there may not yet exist an underdeveloped country that is highly industrialized, but some underdeveloped countries seem to be on the way to that status, and the results are not happy. Argentina, e.g., has managed to hurt its thriving agriculture badly and has steadily been going down, financially and economically. On the other hand, there may be no developed country in existence at the present time that is not industrialized in the sense that a large percentage of the labor force or population

*From National Bank of Egypt Fiftieth Anniversary Commemoration Lectures, Cairo, 1959.

[1]Needless to add that the growth of "tertiary" industries is a sign or symptom of development only when it comes "naturally." One cannot turn the argument around and assume that if the Government puts a large part of the people into tertiary occupations, say entertainment or even dentistry, by artificial means, it will automatically raise the level of economic development correspondingly.

(the two measures are not quite the same because of the larger families one finds often in the country) is in industry, mining and especially services. But some countries were highly developed before they ceased to be predominantly agricultural. New Zealand, Denmark and Australia are examples and there is nothing backward and underdeveloped about Nebraska and Iowa, American states that are predominantly agricultural. It is an extremely important fact that there exists no highly developed country that has not also a highly developed agriculture in the sense of a high degree of literacy, efficient application of modern methods of production, high input of machinery, fertilizer, etc. and high value of output per head.[2] Moreover, and this too is a very important fact, many highly industrialized countries (in the sense that a large percentage of the labor force is engaged in non-agricultural pursuits), have remained large net exporters of food and agricultural raw materials. The U.S., Canada, Australia, and Denmark are conspicuous examples.

These facts have important policy implications which are often ignored. The fact that in developed countries not only industry, but also agriculture, is more highly developed than in underdeveloped countries lends further weight to the warning that development policies should not concentrate exclusively on industry. And the fact that highly industrialized countries can remain efficient producers and cheap exporters of food and agricultural raw material should help to dispel the fear that it would be dangerous for industrial countries to fill a large share of their food and agricultural raw material requirements from foreign sources (possibly from underdeveloped countries) and to give up a correspondingly large part of their own high cost agriculture, on the ground that if they did that, later when industrialization has proceeded farther in many parts of the world, they may not be able to buy food and agricultural raw materials except at exorbitant prices.[3] Such fears were widespread among German economists around the turn of the century when Germany was making rapid strides towards industrialization. But one finds them also occasionally today. They are, e.g., implicit in certain versions of the Marxian theory (espoused also by non-Marxist writers such as G. Myrdal) that the underdeveloped countries of today are handicapped as compared with the now developed countries in the corresponding stage of their development because the underdeveloped countries today, when they push their development (identified by those writers with industrialization) are not surrounded by an underdeveloped world, as the now developed countries were in the early stages of their development—an underdeveloped world which provided industrializing countries with cheap supplies of raw material and food and a market for their industrial products. If my strictures draw the reply that it was the colonial status of the *then* underdeveloped countries which gave the now developed countries their comparative advantage over the underdeveloped countries *now*, my answer would be this:

[2] Physical output may be lower than in some less developed countries owing to comparatively poor soil and climate. Value output may still be high, if import restrictions keep the price of agricultural products high.
[3] Fear of blockade in case of war or fear of being at the mercy of unfriendly powers is, however, not so easy to dispel.

I am not going to discuss to what extent colonial rule has exploited the colonies and retarded their development. To some extent and in some cases it has undoubtedly done that. Not being an expert in that area, I shall not try to make any generalization. And fortunately I need not form a judgment on that matter because for the problem in hand another question is crucial, namely, the question to what extent the development of the colonial powers themselves was speeded by their possession of colonies. With respect to this question, I feel much more confident. My answer is that the possession of colonies was not a decisive or even very important factor in the development of the colonial powers. If it had been, it would be difficult to explain why colonial powers have done quite well after having lost their colonies (e.g. the Netherlands) and why other countries such as Germany,[4] Sweden, Switzerland, not to mention the USA, which never possessed colonies (or whose colonies were economically unimportant) developed just as well, or better, than others that had colonies.

But let me return to my main topic—the contribution of international trade to economic development. In this context growth of real income or output per head can be used with greater confidence as criterion, than in connection with the question as to which countries should be regarded as developed or underdeveloped, for in this case no inter-country comparisons are involved.[5]

II

I shall now positively and systematically state what I think the contribution of international trade to economic development was in the past and what it can be in the future. My overall conclusion is that international trade has made a tremendous contribution to the development of less developed countries in the 19th and 20th Centuries and can be expected to make an equally big contribution in the future, if it is allowed to proceed freely. It does not necessarily follow that a 100% free trade policy is always most conducive to more rapid development. Marginal interferences with the free flow of trade, if properly selected, may speed up development. But I do not want to leave any doubt that my conclusion is that substantially free trade with marginal, insubstantial corrections and deviations, is the best policy from the point of view of economic development. Drastic deviations from free trade can be justified, on development grounds—and this is very nearly the same thing as to say on economic grounds—only if and when they are needed to compensate for the adverse influence of other policies inimical to economic development, for example, the consequences of persistent inflation or of certain tax and domestic price support policies. Let me guard against a possible misunderstanding. If I say that drastic interferences with the market mechanism are not needed for rapid development, I refer to trade policy and I do not deny that drastic measures in other areas, let me say, land reform, education, forced investment (if the

[4]Germany did have some colonies before the first World War. But I don't think that any economist would argue that they were economically speaking of any consequence.
[5]Needless to add that statistical problems of measurement remain. What I am speaking of is theoretical criteria.

projects are well chosen) etc. may not speed up growth. But I shall in these lectures not further elaborate on those matters.[6]

I shall make use of the so-called classical theory of international trade in its neo-classical form associated with the name of Jacob Viner, James Meade, and Bertil Ohlin, to mention only a few. I shall not try to modernize the theory more than, say, Ohlin and Meade have done, although I shall make an attempt to spell out in some detail the implications of classical trade theory for economic development, an aspect which has perhaps been somewhat neglected. On the other hand, I shall, of course, avoid using the caricature of the theory which is often presented as a portrait by its critics.

Later I shall then take up in detail objections to the orthodox conclusions and shall consider alternative or rival theories put forward by the critics of the orthodox theory.

Let us then start with first things first. International division of labor and international trade, which enable every country to specialize and to export those things that it can produce cheaper in exchange for what others can provide at a lower cost, have been and still are one of the basic factors promoting economic well-being and increasing national income of every participating country. Moreover, what is good for the national income and the standard of living is, at least potentially, also good for economic development; for the greater the volume of output the greater can be the rate of growth—provided the people individually or collectively have the urge to save and to invest and economically to develop. The higher the level of output, the easier it is to escape the "vicious circle of poverty" and to "take off into selfsustained growth" to use the jargon of modern development theory. Hence, if trade raises the level of income, it also promotes economic development.

All this holds for highly developed countries as well as for less developed ones. Let us not forget that countries in the former category, too, develop and grow, some of them—not all—even faster than some—not all—in the second category.

In most underdeveloped countries international trade plays quantitatively an especially important role, that is, a larger percentage of their income is spent on imports, and a larger percentage of their output is being exported, than in the case of developed countries of comparable economic size. (Other things being equal, it is natural that the "larger," economically speaking, a country, the smaller its trade percentages.) Many underdeveloped countries are highly specialized also in the sense that a very large percentage of their exports consists of one or two staple commodities. . . .

This high concentration of exports is not without danger. One would normally not want to put so many of one's eggs into one basket. But the price of diversification is in most cases extremely high. I shall touch on that topic once more. At this point, let me simply say that a high level

[6]It also goes without saying that in countries where the Government runs the economy—in the communist countries—it has also to conduct foreign trade. But socialist state trading, if it is efficient and rational and motivated by economic objectives, would be along the line of comparative cost. I might add that socialist theoreticians fully agree to that, although many do deny that trade in capitalist countries is, in fact, conducted along these lines.

of concentrated trade will, in most cases, be much better than a low level of diversified trade. How much poorer would Brazil be without coffee, Venezuela, Iran and Iraq without oil, Bolivia without tin, Malaya without rubber and tin, Ghana without cocoa, and, I dare say, Egypt without cotton. The really great danger of concentration arises in case of deep and protracted slumps in the industrial countries—slumps of the order of magnitude of the Great Depression in the 1930's. In my opinion, and here I am sure the overwhelming majority of economists in the Western World agrees, the chance that this will happen again is practically nil.

The tremendous importance of trade for the underdeveloped countries (as well as for most developed ones, with the exception of the US and USSR, which could, if need be, give it up without suffering a catastrophic reduction in their living standard) follows from the classical theory of comparative cost in conjunction with the fact that the comparative differences in cost of production of industrial products and food and raw materials between developed countries and underdeveloped countries are obviously very great, in many cases, in fact, infinite in the sense that countries of either group just could not produce what they buy from the other.[7]

The classical theory has been often criticized on the ground that it is static, that it presents only a timeless "cross-section" view of comparative costs and fails to take into account dynamic elements that is, the facts of organic growth and development. Of modern writers, it was especially Professor J. H. Williams of Harvard and recently Gunnar Myrdal[8] who have voiced this criticism of the classical doctrine and have demanded its replacement by a dynamic theory. This type of criticism is, in fact, about as old as the classical theory itself. Williams mentions many earlier critics and especially the German writer Friedrich List who more than anyone else in the 19th Century has attacked the classical theory on exactly the same grounds, that is, for being "unhistorical and static,"[9] with the same vehemence and the same strange tone of bitterness and irritation as the modern writers.

Now it is true that the theory of comparative cost is static; it is also true that the economies of most countries are changing and developing and that the theory should take account of that fact. But it is not true that a static theory, because it is static, is debarred from saying anything useful about a changing and developing economic world. There is such a thing as "comparative statics," that is, a method for dealing with a changing situation by means of a static theory. How much can be done by means of comparative statics (as distinguished from a truly dynamic theory) de-

[7]In many cases very expensive and poor substitutes can be produced. There is not much sense in contemplating extreme situations. But if I were pressed to guess, I would say that the developed countries as a group, and a few of them individually, could get along without trade a little easier (although still at a terrific loss) than the underdeveloped countries.

[8]Williams: "The Theory of International Trade Reconsidered," *Economic Journal,* 1929. Myrdal: *Development and Underdevelopment,* National Bank of Egypt, 1956.

[9]It is strange that Myrdal, who quotes copiously from earlier and contemporary writers (see especially the full dress presentation of his views in *The International Economy,* New York, 1956) fails to mention List, to whose theory his own bears a most striking similarity, notwithstanding the fact that List's policy recommendations are more moderate than Myrdal's.

pends on the type of problem on hand. I contend that the problems of international division of labor and long-run development are such that the method of comparative statics can go a long way towards a satisfactory solution.[10] That does not mean, however, that a dynamic theory would not be very useful. Unfortunately, not much of a truly dynamic theory is available at present. What the critics of the static nature of traditional theory have given us over and above their criticism and methodological pronouncements is very little indeed and thoroughly unsatisfactory. But a well known Burmese economist, H. Myint, has recently reminded us that the classical economists, especially Adam Smith and J. S. Mill, were by no means oblivious of the indirect, dynamic benefits which less developed countries in particular can derive from international trade. Going beyond the purely static theory of comparative cost, they have analyzed the "indirect effects" of trade (as J. S. Mill calls them) and thereby presented us with at least the rudiments of a dynamic theory, which Myint aptly calls the "productivity" theory of international trade.[11] Let us then enquire how we can deal by means of the theoretical tools on hand with the problems of change and development. The tools on hand are the static theory of comparative cost and the semi-dynamic "productivity" theory.

For our purposes I will distinguish among the changes which constitute economic development of two types—those that take place independently of international trade and those that are induced by trade or trade policy.

As far as the first group—let me call them autonomous changes—is concerned, I can see no difficulty resulting from them for the applicability of the classical theory of comparative cost. Such changes are the gradual improvement in skill, education and training of workers, farmers, engineers, entrepreneurs; improvements resulting from inventions and discoveries and from the accumulation of capital—changes which in the Western World stem for the most part from the initiative of individuals and private associations, but possibly also from conscious Government policies.[12]

[10]The short run business cycle, on the other hand, is a type of problem of which a static explanation is rather useless. That is the reason why the *static* Keynesian system is so barren. In the short run, dynamic factors completely overshadow and distort the static Keynesian relationships—especially the liquidity preference and the investment function. Needless to add there are plenty of so-called "Keynesian type" dynamic models. But logically they have very little to do with the static Keynesian theory and nothing at all with the chapter on the "Trade Cycle" in *The General Theory*. This type of model building has been launched independently of Keynes by Frisch, Tinbergen and Lundberg. But nobody would deny that many others, who later became active in that field, thought they were merely dynamizing Keynes.

[11]H. Myint. "The 'Classical Theory' of International Trade and the Under-developed Countries," *Economic Journal*, June 1958, pp. 317–337. A. Smith, *Wealth of Nations*, Vol. 1, Cannan ed., p. 413. J. S. Mill, *Principles*, Ashley ed., p. 581. Myint distinguishes from the dynamic "productivity" theory, the "vent-of-surplus" theory and distinguishes the latter also from the static comparative cost theory. This distinction I find unconvincing. The "vent-of-surplus" (if it is not part and parcel of the productivity theory) seems to me simply an extreme case of differences in comparative cost—a country exporting things for which it has no use. This case does not call, it seems to me, for a special theory. But Myint is, of course, quite right that if this extreme situation exists (in modern parlance it might be described as disguised unemployment in export industries) it makes trade appear doubly productive and desirable.

[12]I am not speaking here of policies concerning international trade such as the imposition of import restrictions. Changes resulting from trade policy measures are trade induced and not autonomous changes.

These changes come gradually or in waves and result in gradually increasing output of commodities that had been produced before or in the setting up of the production of goods that had not been produced earlier. Analytically, such development has to be pictured as an outward movement of the production possibility curve (often called substitution or transformation curve). Depending on the concrete turn that autonomous development (including improvements in transportation technology) takes, the comparative cost situation and hence volume and composition of trade will be more or less profoundly affected. But since these changes only come slowly and gradually and usually cannot be foreseen (either by private business or Government planners) in sufficient detail to make anticipatory action possible, there is no presumption that the allocative mechanism as described in the theory of comparative cost will not automatically and efficiently bring about the changes and adjustment in the volume and structure of trade called for by autonomous development.

I turn now to the second type of changes in the productive capabilities of a country which are more important for the purposes of my lectures, namely, those induced by trade and changes in trade including changes in trade brought about by trade policy. Favorable as well as unfavorable trade-induced changes are possible and have to be considered. Alleged unfavorable trade-induced changes have received so much attention from protectionist writers from List to Myrdal (which has induced free trade economists, too, to discuss them at great length), that there is danger that the tremendously important favorable influences be unduly neglected. Let me, therefore, discuss the latter first.

If we were to estimate the contribution of international trade to economic development, especially of the underdeveloped countries, solely by the static gains from trade in any given year on the usual assumption of given[13] production capabilities (analytically under the assumption of given production functions or given or autonomously shifting production possibility curves) we would indeed grossly underrate the importance of trade. For over and above the direct static gains dwelt upon by the traditional theory of comparative cost, trade bestows very important indirect benefits, which also can be described as dynamic benefits, upon the participating countries. Let me emphasize once more that the older classical writers did stress these "indirect benefits" (Mill's own words).[14] Analytically we have to describe these "indirect," "dynamic" benefits from trade as an outward shift (in the northeast direction) of the production possibility curve brought about by a trade-induced movement along the curve.

First, trade provides material means (capital goods, machinery and raw and semifinished materials) indispensable for economic development. Secondly, even more important, trade is the means and vehicle for the dissemination of technological knowledge, the transmission of ideas, for the importation of know-how, skills, managerial talents and entrepreneurship. Thirdly, trade is also the vehicle for the international movement of capital especially from the developed to the underdeveloped countries.

[13]This includes autonomously shifting.
[14]In the neo-classical theory they have been somewhat neglected. The reason is perhaps that these factors do not lend themselves well to precise mathematical treatment.

Fourthly, free international trade is the best antimonopoly policy and the best guarantee for the maintenance of a healthy degree of free competition....

The first point is obvious. Recall the tremendous benefits which the underdeveloped countries draw from technological progress in the developed countries through the importation of machinery, transport equipment, vehicles, power generation equipment, road building machinery, medicines, chemicals, and so on. The advantage is, of course, not all on one side. I stress the advantage derived by underdeveloped countries (rather than the equally important benefits for the developed countries), because I am concerned here primarily with the development of the less developed countries.

The composition of the export trade of the developed industrial countries has been changing . . . in the direction of the types of capital goods which I have mentioned away from textiles and other light consumer goods. This shift has been going on for a long time; it is not a recent phenomenon. But it has proceeded rapidly in recent years, and there is no reason to doubt that it will continue.

Secondly, probably even more important that the importation of material goods is the importation of technical know-how skills, managerial talents, entrepreneurship. This is, of course, especially important for the underdeveloped countries. But the developed countries too benefit greatly from cross-fertilization aided by trade among themselves and the less advanced industrial countries can profit from the superior technical and managerial know-how, etc. of the more advanced ones.

The late-comers and successors in the process of development and industrialization have always had the great advantage that they could learn from the experiences, from the successes as well as from the failures and mistakes of the pioneers and forerunners. In the 19th Century the continental European countries and the U.S. profited greatly from the technological innovation and achievements of the industrial revolution in Great Britain. Later the Japanese proved to be very adept learners and Soviet Russia has shown herself capable of speeding up her own development by "borrowing" (interest free) immense amounts of technological know-how from the West, developing it further and adopting it for her own purposes. This "trade" has been entirely onesided. I know of not a single industrial idea or invention which the West has obtained from the East.[15] Today the underdeveloped countries have a tremendous, constantly growing, store

[15]This statement is made on the authority of Prof. John Jewkes of Oxford who has made a close study of sixty major industrial innovations (in the Schumpeterian sense) and comes to the following conclusion: "The cases taken as a whole reveal that no country has a monopoly of inventive power. The outstanding names and groups are widely spread over many industrial countries. One significant exception is that in none of sixty cases studied had contributions been made by Russian workers subsequent to the Revolution. Before that date numerous names of distinguished Russian contributors crop up." J. Jewkes, "The Sources of Invention," *Lloyd's Bank Review*, Jan. 1958, p. 23. The book that contains the material on which the quoted article is based was published under the same title by Macmillan, London, 1958. Note that what I say is that no industrial innovations have come from Russia to the West. That does not mean there are not any. Obviously, in the field of military technology they are doing quite well and it would be surprising if they had not made any innovations elsewhere. But they are probably minor compared with Western achievements and at any rate none has come out.

of technological know-how to draw from. True, simple adoption of methods developed for the conditions of the developed countries is often not possible. But adaptation is surely much easier than first creation.

Trade is the most important vehicle for the transmission of technological know-how. True, it is not the only one. In fact this function of trade is probably somewhat less important now than it was a hundred years ago, because ideas, skills, know-how, travel easier and quicker and cheaper today than in the 19th Century. The market where engineering and management experts can be hired is much better organized than formerly. There is much more competition in this field as well as in the area of material capital equipment. In the early 19th Century Great Britain was the only center from which industrial equipment and know-how could be obtained, and there were all sorts of restrictions on the exportation of both. Today there are a dozen industrial centers in Europe, the US, Canada, and Japan, and even Russia and Czechoslovakia all ready to sell machinery as well as engineering advice and know-how.

However, trade is still the most important transmission belt. What J. S. Mill said 100 years ago is still substantially true: "It is hardly possible to overrate the value in the present low state of human improvement, of placing human beings in contact with persons dissimilar to themselves, and with modes of thought and action unlike those with which they are familiar. . . . Such communication has always been, peculiarly in the present age one of the primary sources of progress."[16]

The third indirect benefit of trade which I mentioned was that it also serves as transmission belt for capital. It is true that the amount of capital that an underdeveloped country can obtain from abroad depends in the first place on the ability and willingness of developed countries to lend, which is of course decisively influenced by the internal policies in the borrowing countries. But it stands to reason—and this is the only point I wanted to make at this juncture—that, other things being equal, the larger the volume of trade, the greater will be the volume of foreign capital that can be expected to become available under realistic assumptions. The reason is that with a large volume of trade the transfer of interest and repayments on principle is more easily effected than with a small volume of trade; and it would be clearly unrealistic to expect large capital movements if the chance for transfer of interests and repayments is not good. There is, furthermore, the related fact that it is much easier to get foreign capital for export industries with their built-in solution of the retransfer problem than for other types of investments which do not directly and automatically improve the balance of payments. This preference of foreign capital for export industries is regrettable because other types of investment (such as investment in public utilities, railroads, manufacturing industries) may often (not always) be more productive and may make a greater indirect contribution, dollar per dollar, to economic development by providing training to native personnel and in various other ways than export industries which sometimes (by no means always) constitute foreign enclaves in native soil. If the direct and indirect contribution of non-export industries to national income and economic development are in fact greater

[16]Principles of Political Economy.

than those of the export industry, they should be preferred, because their indirect contribution to the balance of payments position will then also be such as to guarantee the possibility of smooth retransfer of principle and interest—*provided* inflationary monetary policies do not upset equilibrium entailing exchange control that then gets in the way of the transfer. But with inflationary monetary policies and exchange control practices as they are in most underdeveloped countries, the preference of foreign capital for export industries is readily understandable and must be reckoned with, and foreign capital in export is better than no foreign capital at all.

The fourth way in which trade benefits a country indirectly is by fostering healthy competition and keeping in check inefficient monopolies. The reason why the American economy is more competitive—and more efficient —than most others is probably to be sought more in the great internal free trade area which the US enjoys rather than in the antimonopoly policy which was always much more popular in the US than in Europe or anywhere else. The importance of this factor is confirmed by the fact that many experts believe that the main economic advantages of the European Common Market, towards the realization of which the first steps have just been taken, will flow from freer competition rather than merely from the larger size and larger scale production which it entails.

Increased competition is important also for underdeveloped countries, especially inasmuch as the size of their market is usually small (even if the geographic area is large). A reservation has nevertheless to be made. The first introduction of new industries on infant industry grounds may justify the creation of monopolistic positions, depending on the size of the country and the type of industry. But the problem will always remain how to prevent the permanent establishment of inefficient exploitative monopolies even after an industry has taken root and has become able to hold its ground without the crutches of imports restriction.

The general conclusion, then, is that international trade, in addition to the static gains resulting from the division of labor with given (or autonomously changing) production functions, powerfully contributes, in the four ways indicated, to the development of the productive capabilities of the less developed countries. Analytically we have to express that, in the framework of modern trade theory, by saying that trade gradually transforms existing production functions; in other words, that a movement along the production possibility curves in accordance with the pre-existing comparative cost situation, will tend to push up and out the production possibility curve.

I have stated my conclusions rather boldly and uncompromisingly. Some qualifications and reservations are obviously called for, because trade may have also unfavourable indirect (or direct) effects. . . .*

*Editor's note: An analysis follows of the conditions under which the infant industry argument is valid.

23. Instability in Export Markets of Underdeveloped Countries

*United Nations**

There have been marked fluctuations in proceeds from exports during the fifty years under review—whether measured on a cyclical basis or from year to year. While different commodities and countries have been variously affected, practically all showed a substantial degree of instability. Price fluctuations were not the major factor in the instability of export proceeds; on the whole, the volume of exports has fluctuated even more than the price. The contribution of fluctuating volume to the instability of export proceeds is especially evident in the sales of specific varieties and grades of primary commodities by under-developed countries.

Fluctuations in Unit Value or Market Price

The main findings of the study with respect to *price fluctuations,* for the four kinds of fluctuation distinguished—year-to-year, cyclical, long-term and within-year—are shown in Table 1. Year-to-year fluctuations in price averaged about 14 per cent; that is, in an average year of falling prices, export proceeds declined 14 per cent if the volume remained stable. A reduction of 14 per cent from a previous level of prices and proceeds might cancel the profits and destroy the economic justification of development projects which depend on the sale of primary commodities in foreign markets. Exporters of primary commodities might expect the following year's prices either to fall from 100 to 86, on an average, or to rise from 100 to 116,[1] with the possibility that the actual change might be outside these limits, that is, above 116 or below 86. Average year-to-year fluctuations in export prices of individual commodities ranged from 5 per cent to 21 per cent for different commodities. Copra, cotton, hemp, linseed, rubber and shellac were the commodities with the widest fluctuations in prices from year to year. No significant difference in stability was found in comparing United States import unit values with market prices.

The intensity of year-to-year price fluctuations increased successively in the three peace-time periods analysed—1901 to 1913, 1920 to 1939 and 1946 to 1950. The instability of prices during the Second World War was less than during the First World War, but in excess of the period before 1914.

In the larger sample of about 200 varieties and specified grades of commodities sold by underdeveloped countries in the United States market, the average year-to-year fluctuation in unit value was even greater than for broadly defined commodities, namely, 17 per cent instead of 14 per cent,

---

*From *Instability in Export Markets of Underdeveloped Countries,* New York, 1952.

[1] According to the method of measurement adopted in this study, a rise of 16 points represents 14 per cent of the higher point reached, that is, 116.

showing the greater degree of instability that specialized exporters encountered.

Analysis of exports to the United States from underdeveloped regions as a whole indicates that the vulnerability of underdeveloped countries to price fluctuations is much greater than that of other exporters to the United States, but it is less than the vulnerability of individual exporters selling particular commodities; some compensatory movements take place within underdeveloped regions.

Table 1. Summary of Year-to-Year, Cyclical, Long-Term and Within-Year Fluctuations in Prices of Major Primary Commodities,[1] 1901 to 1951*

(Average percentage fluctuation per year)

COMMODITY	YEAR-TO-YEAR	CYCLICAL UPSWING	CYCLICAL DOWNSWING	LONG-TERM RISING PHASE	LONG-TERM FALLING PHASE	WITHIN-YEAR
Bananas	5	3	3	1	2	–
Cocoa	17	16	18	5	4	32
Coffee	14	18	13	5	6	26
Copper	13	14	11	5	4	22
Copra	19	15	16	6	4	–
Cotton	18	16	19	5	5	30
Hemp	19	15	16	6	3	–
Hides and skins	13	12	13	6	4	–
Jute	16	15	20	4	7	32[2]
Linseed	18	19	15	6	4	–
Manganese	11	6	6	4	3	–
Nickel	5	4	3	3	1	–
Petroleum	10	9	9	6	4	–
Rice	12	13	16	3	4	–
Rubber	21	18	15	5	7	37
Shellac	19	22	15	9	6	–
Silk	14	12	21	6	6	–
Sisal	16	15	12	5	5	–
Sodium nitrate	5	6	9	4	3	–
Sugar	15	12	14	4	6	19
Tea	9	8	11	3	5	29[2]
Tin	14	11	14	3	4	26
Tobacco	10	10	10	6	4	–
Wheat	16	15	11	4	4	30[2]
Wool	15	14	13	4	5	27
Average, 25 commodities[3]	±13.7	+12.8	−13.0	+4.7	−4.3	26.7[4]

*Source: Unless otherwise noted, the sources of data for the tables in this study are those referred to in appendix A.
[1]Fluctuations represent changes in import unit values, except in the case of within-year fluctuations, which pertain to market prices.
[2]Excluding fluctuations during the Second World War.
[3]In all tables in which the symbols "±", "+" and "−" are given before the final averages, they apply to individual averages in the column.
[4]Average for 11 commodities.

Fluctuations in unit values or prices are not significantly lower when the purchasing power of such unit values or prices with respect to manufactured imports is taken into account. Fluctuations from year to year in the real purchasing power of export prices averaged between 13 and 14 per cent a year.

Cyclical declines in prices averaged about 27 per cent; on the average, the full cycle covered about 4½ years. Cyclical swings in the case of individual commodities ranged from 5 per cent to 40 per cent. Thus, on an average, underdeveloped countries exporting primary commodities experienced a decline from 100 to a little over 70, and a rise again to 100 in the prices obtained for their products within a period of four or five years, with the possibility that the actual fluctuation would be even greater. The vulnerability to price fluctuations was greatly increased by the fact that year-to-year movements tended to be in the same direction for two to three years at a time.

The annual rate of cyclical movements—both upswing and downswing—was about 13 per cent. Since this was almost equal to the average year-to-year movement of prices, the cyclical factor appeared to be the most important causative force in price instability.

Long-term price changes, as determined by a seven-year moving average, amounted to between 4 and 5 per cent a year in either direction; variations in individual commodities ranged from one per cent to 9 per cent. While the annual range of long-term changes was smaller than in either year-to-year or cyclical fluctuations, total long-term variations were marked—even exceeding cyclical changes.

Fluctuations within the period of a year averaged about 27 per cent (the percentage of change from the high point to the low point of each year). Thus, the proceeds from sales of exports by underdeveloped countries within a given calendar year might vary considerably, according to the season when sales took place or contracts were drawn up.

The data disclose evidence of correlation between degrees of price fluctuations among different commodities. Commodities which tended to be specially vulnerable—or stable—in respect of year-to-year price fluctuations also tended to be vulnerable—or stable—in respect of cyclical and long-term fluctuations.

Fluctuations in Volume of Exports

Average year-to-year fluctuations in the *volume* of exports of primary commodities, summarized in Table 2, were between 18 and 19 per cent a year, thus exceeding fluctuations in price by a considerable margin. Underdeveloped countries exporting primary commodities experienced an average drop in export volume from 100 to 81, or rise from 100 to 123,[2] from one year to another, with the possibility that the actual changes would be greater in magnitude. The range in average year-to-year fluctuation among different commodities was from 6 per cent in the case of wool to 33 per cent in the case of wheat. In respect of year-to-year fluctuations, changes in volume contributed more to instability of proceeds than change in price.

Fluctuations in the volume of exports in the period from 1920 to 1939 were smaller than those before 1914, but they increased sharply after 1945. Fluctuations were equally wide during both world wars. In each of the sub-periods studied, volume was less stable than price.

[2]A rise from 100 to 123 represents an increase of about 19 per cent of the higher point reached, that is, 123.

Table 2. Summary of Year-to-Year, Cyclical and Long-Term Fluctuations in Export Volume of Major Primary Commodities, 1901 to 1950

(Average percentage fluctuation per year)

| | | CYCLICAL | | LONG-TERM | |
| | | | | RISING | FALLING |
COMMODITY	YEAR-TO-YEAR	UPSWING	DOWNSWING	PHASE	PHASE
Cocoa	17	19	19	3	2
Coffee	12	15	12	2	2
Copper	16	18	12	5	3
Cotton	21	19	20	4	4
Hemp	17	12	11	2	2
Jute	17	15	16	4	5
Linseed	31	27	18	6	7
Petroleum	18	11	12	4	5
Rice	21	23	16	4	5
Rubber	29	25	21	5	7
Silk	13	9	6	3	–
Sodium nitrate	22	24	25	5	6
Sugar	18	15	17	4	5
Tea	10	12	10	3	4
Tin	18	16	17	4	5
Tobacco	16	19	17	5	4
Wheat	33	32	39	6	6
Wool	6	5	5	2	3
Average, 18 commodities	±18.7	+17.6	−16.8	+4.0	−4.1

While year-to-year fluctuations in volume were greater than in price, total cyclical movements were similar. However, owing to the fact that cyclical movements in volume tended to be shorter and more concentrated than in price, the annual rate of cyclical fluctuation in volume was higher than the corresponding rate for price cycles. Total amplitude of cyclical fluctuations in volume ranged from under 10 per cent to over 50 per cent for different commodities. On an average, cyclical variations caused export volume to decline from 100 to 73 and to return to 100 within four years.

Changes in export volume due to long-term factors were similar in magnitude to long-term price trends—about 4 per cent a year.

Year-to-year fluctuations in the volume of exports to the United States were greater for underdeveloped regions as a whole than for the average of all exports to the United States; the oversea sterling area had the greatest fluctuation.

There was a close relation in the rank of individual commodities in respect of the various types of fluctuation in volume. Commodities which were particularly stable—or unstable—in respect of year-to-year changes in volume were also particularly stable—or unstable—in respect of cyclical and long-term changes.

Fluctuations in Total Export Proceeds

Year-to-year fluctuations in *export proceeds* from eighteen major primary commodities, summarized in Table 3, averaged 23 per cent between 1901 and 1950. Thus, on the average, underdeveloped countries exporting primary commodities experienced a drop in export proceeds from 100 to 77, or a rise from 77 to 100, from one year to another; in about half the cases, the instability was even greater. There was little change in the degree of year-to-year instability in export proceeds between 1901 and 1945, but since the war there has been a more marked increase in fluctuations.

Varieties and grades of particular commodities showed much greater instability of proceeds—amounting to 37 per cent, on the average, for over 200 varieties analysed with respect to sales in the United States.

Cyclical fluctuations in proceeds amounted to about 37 per cent in total amplitude, and the average cycle covered a period of a little over four years. On the whole, export proceeds fell from 100 to 63 and subsequently rose again to 100, all within the space of a little over four years. The annual rate of cyclical rise or fall was close to the average year-to-year rise or fall, indicating that most of the instability of proceeds is related to cyclical factors.

Changes in export proceeds due to long-term factors were at the rate of about 6 per cent a year, but the cumulative effect was often considerable.

There appeared to be a definite correlation in the rank of different commodities in respect of their year-to-year, cyclical and long-term fluctuations in total export proceeds. Commodities tended to be stable—or unstable—in all three respects.

Table 3. Summary of Year-to-Year, Cyclical and Long-Term Fluctuations in Export Proceeds from Major Primary Commodities, 1901 to 1950

(Average percentage fluctuation per year)

| | YEAR-TO-YEAR | | CYCLICAL | | LONG-TERM | |
COMMODITY	MONEY VALUE	REAL TERMS	UPSWING	DOWNSWING	RISING PHASE	FALLING PHASE
Cocoa	20	24	24	23	6	4
Coffee	21	19	18	20	5	5
Copper	21	21	26	20	5	6
Cotton	26	23	25	24	6	4
Hemp	22	22	12	27	5	8
Jute	22	20	20	24	7	6
Linseed	28	27	24	27	6	7
Petroleum	19	19	16	11	7	6
Rice	21	23	18	17	5	3
Rubber	36	35	26	28	9	8
Silk	19	12	24	19	6	6
Sodium nitrate	22	21	26	32	5	7
Sugar	23	27	21	23	6	7
Tea	15	15	14	13	5	6
Tin	25	23	20	24	5	7
Tobacco	18	18	18	18	5	6
Wheat	33	32	42	33	8	7
Wool	15	16	16	15	4	6
Average, 18 commodities	±22.6	±22.0	+21.7	−22.1	+5.8	−6.1

Interrelation of Fluctuations in Price, Volume and Proceeds

All types of fluctuations in proceeds measured in the study—year-to-year, cyclical and long-term—and fluctuations measured for different periods, were in each case higher than those in volume or in price alone. This indicates that changes in price and in quantity had a destabilizing effect on each other. This was also found to be true in each of the sub-periods studied and with respect to the combined export proceeds of all underdeveloped regions and areas. In each case, fluctuations in proceeds were greater than fluctuations in price or quantity alone.

Analysis of years of falling proceeds, during which declines averaged 25 per cent, show that two-fifths of this decrease was accounted for by a drop in price, the rest by a decline in volume. For over 200 grades and varieties of commodities sold in the United States market, the decrease in price contributed less than the decline in quantity to the average drop in proceeds. The contribution of price decreases to declines in proceeds was less than one-fifth of the total—indicating that fluctuations in proceeds for specified varieties and grades were mainly determined by changes in volume.

Substantial differences were found in the relative importance of fluctuations in price and in volume, so far as particular commodities or particular countries were concerned. In general, however, neither price stabilization alone, at the existing level of instability in export volume, nor volume stabilization alone, at the existing level of instability in price, was sufficiently great to result in substantial stability of proceeds.

There was some correlation in the rank of different commodities with respect to instability of prices, instability of volume and instability of proceeds. Commodities which were particularly liable to wide year-to-year price fluctuations also tended to be liable to wide year-to-year fluctuations in volume and in proceeds, and vice versa.

An explanation of the cumulative effect of instability in prices and in proceeds, in the absence of a clear-cut correlation between the direction of changes in price and in volume, was found in the relatively greater instability of volume. Year-to-year fluctuations in volume were frequently twice as high as fluctuations in price, and thus resulted in greater instability in proceeds even when the fluctuations were in the opposite direction. Lack of clear correlation between the direction of price changes and of volume changes was in large part the result of grouping food and industrial raw materials together. In the case of food, price and volume tended to move in opposite directions; while in the case of industrial raw materials, the change was in the same direction. . . .

24. The "Classical Theory" of International Trade and the Underdeveloped Countries[1]

*H. Myint**

There has recently been a considerable amount of controversy concerning the applicability of the "classical theory" of international trade to the underdeveloped countries.[2] The twists in this controversy may be set out as follows. The critics start with the intention of showing that the "nineteenth-century pattern" of international trade, whereby the underdeveloped countries export raw materials and import manufactured goods, has been unfavourable to the economic development of these countries. But instead of trying to show this directly, they concentrate their attacks on the "classical theory," which they believe to be responsible for the unfavourable pattern of trade. The orthodox economists then come to the defense of the classical theory by reiterating the principle of comparative costs which they claim to be applicable both to the developed and the underdeveloped countries. After this, the controversy shifts from the primary question whether or not the nineteenth-century pattern of international trade, as a historical reality, has been unfavourable to the underdeveloped countries to the different question whether or not the theoretical model assumed in the comparative-costs analysis is applicable to these countries. Both sides then tend to conduct their argument as though the two questions were the same and to identify the "classical theory" with the comparative-costs theory.

It will be argued in this paper that this has led to the neglect of those other elements in the classical theory of international trade which are much nearer to the realities and ideologies of the nineteenth-century expansion of international trade to the underdeveloped countries. In Sections I and II we shall outline these elements and show that they are traceable to Adam Smith and to some extent to J. S. Mill. In Section III we shall show how one of Adam Smith's lines of approach can be fruitfully developed to throw a more illuminating light on the past and present patterns of the international trade of the underdeveloped countries than the convential theory. In Section IV we shall touch upon some policy implications of our analysis and show certain weaknesses in the position both of the orthodox economists and of their critics.

I

The neglected elements in the classical theory of international trade may be traced to Adam Smith, particularly to the following key passage in the *Wealth of Nations:*

*From *The Economic Journal*, June 1958. The author is Senior Lecturer in Economic Development of Underdeveloped Countries, Oxford University.

[1]This paper has benefited from comments by Sir Donald MacDougall, Professor H. G. Johnson, R. M. Sundrum and G. M. Meier.

[2]Of the very extensive literature on the subject, we may refer to two notable recent works, the first stating the orthodox position and the second the position of the critics: J. Viner, *International Trade and Economic Development,* and G. Myrdal, *An International Economy.*

Between whatever places foreign trade is carried on, they all of them derive two distinct benefits from it. It carries out that surplus part of the produce of their land and labour for which there is no demand among them, and brings back in return for it something else for which there is a demand. It gives a value to their superfluities, by exchanging them for something else, which may satisfy a part of their wants, and increase their enjoyments. By means of it, the narrowness of the home market does not hinder the division of labour in any particular branch of art or manufacture from being carried to the highest perfection. By opening a more extensive market for whatever part of the produce of their labour may exceed the home consumption, it encourages them to improve its productive powers, and to augment its annual produce to the utmost, and thereby to increase the real revenue and wealth of society (Vol. I, Cannan ed., p. 413).

There are two leading ideas here. (i) International trade overcomes the narrowness of the home market and provides an outlet for the surplus product above domestic requirements. This develops into what may be called the "vent for surplus"[3] theory of international trade. Later we hope to remove some of the prejudice aroused by this "mercantilist" sounding phrase. (ii) By widening the extent of the market, international trade also improves the division of labour and raises the general level of productivity within the country. This develops into what may be called the "productivity" theory. We shall be mainly concerned with the "vent for surplus" theory and the light it throws upon the growth of international trade in the underdeveloped countries in the nineteenth century. But first it is necessary to consider the "productivity" theory briefly.

The "productivity" doctrine differs from the comparative-costs doctrine in the interpretation of "specialisation" for international trade. (a) In the comparative costs theory "specialisation" merely means a movement along a static "production possibility curve" constructed on the given resources and the *given techniques* of the trading country. In contrast, the "productivity" doctrine looks upon international trade as a dynamic force which, by widening the extent of the market and the scope of the division of labour, raises the skill and dexterity of the workmen, encourages technical innovations, overcomes technical indivisibilities and generally enables the trading country to enjoy increasing returns and economic development. This distinction was clearly realised by J. S. Mill, who regarded the gains in terms of comparative-costs theory as direct gains and the gains in terms of Adam Smithian increases in productivity as "indirect effects, which must be counted as benefits of a high order." Mill even went on to extend this doctrine to countries at "an early stage of industrial advancement," where international trade by introducing new wants "sometimes works a

[3] This term is borrowed from Professor J. H. Williams, who in turn quoted it from a passage in J. S. Mill's *Principles,* in which Mill was criticising this particular aspect of Smith's theory of international trade. Professor Williams is the only modern economist to sponsor this "crude" doctrine. While he is mainly concerned with the loss to a country on being deprived of the export market for its surplus product, we shall pay special attention to the gain to a hitherto isolated underdeveloped country on obtaining a "vent" for its surplus productive capacity. Cf. J. H. Williams, "The Theory of International Trade Reconsidered," *Economic Journal,* June 1929, pp. 195–209.

[4] Cf. *op. cit.,* Chapters II and III, Book I. This aspect of Smith's theory has been made familiar by Professor Allyn Young's article on "Increasing Returns and Economic Progress," *Economic Journal,* December 1928, pp. 527–42.

sort of industrial revolution" (*Principles,* Ashley ed., p. 581). (*b*) In the comparative costs theory "specialisation," conceived as a reallocation of resources, is a completely reversible process. The Adam Smithian process of specialisation, however, involves adapting and reshaping the productive structure of a country to meet the export demand, and is therefore not easily reversible. This means that a country specialising for the export market is more vulnerable to changes in the terms of trade than is allowed for in the comparative-costs theory. We shall come back to this point later.

In the expansive mental climate of the late nineteenth century the "productivity" aspect of international specialisation completely dominated the "vulnerability" aspect. At a semi-popular level, and particularly in its application to the underdeveloped countries, Smith's "productivity" doctrine developed beyond a free-trade argument into an export-drive argument. It was contended that since international trade was so beneficial in raising productivity and stimulating economic development, the State should go beyond a neutral and negative policy of removing barriers to trade and embark on a positive policy of encouraging international trade and economic development. Under its influence, many colonial governments went far beyond the strict *laissez-faire* policy in their attempts to promote the export trade of the colonies.[5] Further, although these governments were frequently obliged to use "unclassical" methods, such as the granting of monopolistic privileges to the chartered companies or the taxing of the indigenous people to force them to take up wage labour or grow cash crops, they nevertheless sought to justify their policy by invoking the Adam Smithian doctrine of the benefits of international division of labour. This partly explains why some critics have associated the "classical theory" with "colonialism" and why they have frequently singled out Adam Smith for attack instead of Ricardo, the founder of the official classical free-trade theory.

It is fair to say that Smith's "productivity" doctrine is instructive more in relation to the ideological than to the actual economic forces which characterised the nineteenth-century expansion of international trade to the underdeveloped countries. It is true, as we shall see later,[6] that both the total value and the physical output of the exports of these countries expanded rapidly. In many cases the rate of increase in export production was well above any possible rate of increase in population, resulting in a considerable rise in output per head. But it is still true to say that this was achieved not quite in the way envisaged by Smith, viz., a better division of labour and specialisation leading on to innovations and cumulative

[5] See for instance, L. C. A. Knowles, *The Economic Development of the British Overseas Empire,* Vol. I, pp. 119–20, 248–9 and 486–7. However, in Section IV below we shall argue that, in spite of the attention they have received, these export-drive policies were not successful enough to cause a significant "export-bias."

[6] See footnotes on pp. 324 and 327 below. See also Sir Donald MacDougall's *The World Dollar Problem,* pp. 134–43. Sir Donald's argument that the productivity of labour in the underdeveloped countries has been rising faster than is generally assumed is mainly based on figures for productivity *per capita.* These figures are not inconsistent with our argument that on the whole the expansion of the export production has been achieved on more or less constant techniques and skills of indigenous labour, by increasing working hours and the proportion of gainfully employed labour rather than by a continuous rise in productivity per man-hour.

improvements in skills and productivity per man-hour. Rather, the increase in output per head seems to have been due: (i) to once-for-all increases in productivity accompanying the transfer of labour from the subsistence economy to the mines and plantations, and (ii) what is more important, as we shall see later, to an increase in working hours and in the proportion of gainfully employed labour relatively to the semi-idle labour of the subsistence economy.

The transfer of labour from the subsistence economy to the mines and plantations with their much higher capital-output ratio and skilled management undoubtedly resulted in a considerable increase in productivity. But this was mostly of a once-for-all character for a number of reasons. To begin with, the indigenous labour emerging from the subsistence economy was raw and technically backward. Moreover, it was subject to high rates of turnover, and therefore not amenable to attempts to raise productivity. Unfortunately, this initial experience gave rise to or hardened the convention of "cheap labour," which regarded indigenous labour merely as an undifferentiated mass of low-grade man-power to be used with a minimum of capital outlay.[7] Thus when the local labour supply was exhausted the typical reaction was not to try to economise labour by installing more machinery and by reorganizing methods of production but to seek farther afield for additional supplies of cheap labour. This is why the nineteenth-century process of international trade in the underdeveloped countries was characterised by large-scale movements of cheap labour from India and China.[8] This tendency was reinforced by the way in which the world-market demand for raw materials expanded in a series of waves. During the booms output had to be expanded as quickly as possible along existing lines, and there was no time to introduce new techniques or reorganize production; during the slumps it was difficult to raise capital for such purposes.

This failure to achieve Adam Smith's ideal of specialisation leading on to continuous improvements in skills can also be observed in the peasant export sectors. Where the export crop happened to be a traditional crop (e.g., rice in South-East Asia), the expansion in export production was achieved simply by bringing more land under cultivation with the same methods of cultivation used in the subsistence economy. Even where new export crops were introduced, the essence of their success as peasant export crops was that they could be produced by fairly simple methods involving no radical departure from the traditional techniques of production employed in subsistence agriculture.[9]

Thus instead of a process of economic growth based on continuous

[7] Cf. S. H. Frankel, *Capital Investment in Africa,* pp. 142–6, and W. M. Macmillan, *Europe and West Africa,* pp. 48–50.
[8] Cf. Knowles, *op. cit.,* pp. viii and 182–201.
[9] Thus A. McPhee wrote about the palm-oil and ground-nut exports of West Africa: "They made little demand on the energy and thought of the natives and they effected no revolution in the society of West Africa. That was why they were so readily grafted on the old economy and grew as they did" (*The Economic Revolution in West Africa,* pp. 39–40). Some writers argue that there was a studied neglect of technical improvements in the peasant sector to facilitate the supply of cheap labour to other sectors. Cf., for example, W. A. Lewis, "Economic Development with Unlimited Supplies of Labour," *Manchester School,* May 1954, pp. 149–50. For a description of imperfect specialisation in economic activity in West Africa see P. T. Bauer and B. S. Yamey, "Economic Progress and Occupational Distribution," *Economic Journal,* December 1951, p. 743.

improvements in skills, more productive recombinations of factors and increasing returns, the nineteenth-century expansion of international trade in the underdeveloped countries seems to approximate to a simpler process based on constant returns and fairly rigid combinations of factors. Such a process of expansion could continue smoothly only if it could feed on *additional* supplies of factors in the required proportions.

II

Let us now turn to Smith's "vent for surplus" theory of international trade. It may be contrasted with the comparative-costs theory in two ways.

1. The comparative-costs theory assumes that the resources of a country are given and fully employed before it enters into international trade. The function of trade is then to reallocate its given resources more efficiently between domestic and export production in the light of the new set of relative prices now open to the country. With given techniques and full employment, export production can be increased only at the cost of reducing the domestic production. In contrast, the "vent for surplus" theory assumes that a previously isolated country about to enter into international trade possesses a surplus productive capacity[10] of some sort or another. The function of trade here is not so much to reallocate the given resources as to provide the new effective demand for the output of the surplus resources which would have remained unused in the absence of trade. It follows that export production can be increased without necessarily reducing domestic production.

2. The concept of a surplus productive capacity above the requirements of domestic consumption implies an inelastic domestic demand for the exportable commodity and/or a considerable degree of internal immobility and specificness of resources. In contrast, the comparative-costs theory assumes either a perfect or, at least, a much greater degree of internal mobility of factors and/or a greater degree of flexibility or elasticity both on the side of production and of consumption. Thus the resources not required for export production will not remain as a surplus productive capacity, but will be reabsorbed into domestic production, although this might take some time and entail a loss to the country.

These two points bring out clearly a peculiarity of the "vent-for-surplus" theory which may be used either as a free-trade argument or as an anti-trade argument, depending on the point of view adopted. (*a*) From the point of view of a previously isolated country, about to enter into trade, a surplus productive capacity suitable for the export market appears as a virtually "costless" means of acquiring imports and expanding domestic economic activity. This was how Adam Smith used it as a free-trade argument. (*b*) From the point of view of an established trading country faced with a fluctuating world market, a sizeable surplus productive capacity which cannot be easily switched from export to domestic production makes it "vulnerable" to external economic disturbances. This is in fact how the present-day writers on the underdeveloped countries use the same situation depicted by Smith's theory as a criticism of the nineteenth-century pattern of international trade. This concept of vulnerability may be dis-

[10]A surplus over domestic requirements and *not* a surplus of exports over imports.

tinguished from that which we have come across in discussing the "productivity" theory of trade. There, a country is considered "vulnerable" because it has adapted and reshaped its productive structure to meet the requirements of the export market through a genuine process of "specialisation." Here, the country is considered "vulnerable" simply because it happens to possess a sizeable surplus productive capacity which (even without any improvements and extensions) it cannot use for domestic production. This distinction may be blurred in border-line cases, particularly in underdeveloped countries with a large mining sector. But we hope to show that, on the whole, while the "vulnerability" of the advanced countries, such as those in Western Europe which have succeeded in building up large export trades to maintain their large populations, is of the first kind, the "vulnerability" of most of the underdeveloped countries is of the second kind.

Let us now consider the "vent-for-surplus" approach purely as a theoretical tool. There is a considerable amount of prejudice among economists against the "vent-for-surplus" theory, partly because of its technical crudeness and partly because of its mercantilist associations. This may be traced to J. S. Mill, who regarded Smith's "vent-for-surplus" doctrine as "a surviving relic of the Mercantile Theory" (*Principles*, p. 579).

The crux of the matter here is the question: why should a country isolated from international trade have a surplus productive capacity? The answer which suggests itself is that, given its random combination of natural resources, techniques of production, tastes and population, such an isolated country is bound to suffer from a certain imbalance or disproportion between its productive and consumption capacities. Thus, take the case of a country which starts with a sparse population in relation to its natural resources. This was broadly true not only of Western countries during their mercantilist period but also of the underdeveloped countries of South-East Asia, Latin America and Africa when they were opened up to international trade in the nineteenth century. Given this situation, the conventional international-trade theory (in its Ohlin version) would say that this initial disproportion between land and labour would have been equilibrated away by appropriate price adjustments: i.e., rents would be low and relatively land-using commodities would have low prices, whereas wages would be high and relatively labour-using commodities would have high prices. In equilibrium there would be no surplus productive capacity (although there might be surplus land by itself) because the scarce factor, labour, would have been fully employed. Thus when this country enters into international trade it can produce the exports only by drawing labour away from domestic production. Now this result is obtained only by introducing a highly developed price mechanism and economic organisation into a country which is supposed to have had no previous economic contacts with the outside world. This procedure may be instructive while dealing with the isolated economy as a theoretical model. But it is misleading when we are dealing with genuinely isolated economies in their proper historical setting; it is misleading, in particular, when we are dealing with the underdeveloped countries, many of which were subsistence economies when they were opened to international trade. In fact, it was the growth of international trade itself which introduced or extended the money economy in these countries. Given the genuine historical setting of an isolated economy, might not its initial disproportion between its resources, techniques, tastes and population show itself in the form of surplus productive capacity?

Adam Smith himself thought that the pre-existence of a surplus productive capacity in an isolated economy was such a matter of common observation that he assumed it implicitly without elaborating upon it. But he did give some hints suggesting how the "narrowness of the home market," which causes the surplus capacity, is bound up with the underdeveloped economic organisation of an isolated country, particularly the lack of a good internal transport system and of suitable investment opportunities.[11] Further his concept of surplus productive capacity is not merely a matter of surplus land by itself but surplus land combined with surplus labour; and the surplus labour is then linked up with his concept of "unproductive" labour. To avoid confusion, this latter should not be identified with the modern concept of "disguised unemployment" caused by an acute shortage of land in overpopulated countries. Although Smith described some cases of genuine "disguised unemployment" in the modern sense, particularly with reference to China, "unproductive" labour in his sense can arise even in thinly populated countries, provided their internal economic organisation is sufficiently underdeveloped. In fact, it is especially in relation to those underdeveloped countries which started off with sparse populations in relation to their natural resources that we shall find Smith's "vent-for-surplus" approach very illuminating.

III

Let us now try to relate the "vent-for-surplus" theory to the nineteenth-century process of expansion of international trade to the underdeveloped countries. Even from the somewhat meagre historical information about these countries, two broad features stand out very clearly. First the underdeveloped countries of South-East Asia, Latin America and Africa, which were to develop into important export economies, started off with sparse populations relatively to their natural resources. If North America and Australia could then be described as "empty," these countries were at least "semi-empty." Secondly, once the opening-up process had got into its stride, the export production of these countries expanded very rapidly, along a typical growth curve,[12] rising very sharply to begin with and tapering off afterwards. By the Great Depression of the 1930s, the expansion

---

[11]*Op cit.*, Vol. I, pp. 21 and 383. This is similar to what Mrs. J. Robinson has described as "primitive stagnation." Cf. *The Accumulation of Capital*, pp. 256–8.

[12]For instance, the annual value of Burma's exports, taking years of high and low prices, increased at a constant proportional rate of 5% per annum on the average between 1870 and 1900. Similar rates of expansion can be observed for Siam and Indonesia (Cf. J. S. Furnivall, *Colonial Policy and Practice*, Appendix I; J. H. Boeke, *The Structure of Netherlands Indian Economy*, p. 184; and J. C. Ingram, *Economic Change in Thailand since 1850*, Appendix C). African export economies started their expansion phase after 1900, and the official trade returns for the Gold Coast, Nigeria, and Uganda show similar rates of increase after that date, although the expansion process was arrested by the depression of the 1930s.

process seems to have come to a stop in many countries; in others, which had a later start, the expansion process may still be continuing after the Second World War.

There are three reasons why the "vent-for-surplus" theory offers a more effective approach than the conventional theory to this type of expansion of international trade in the underdeveloped countries.

1. The characteristically high rates of expansion which can be observed in the export production of many underdeveloped countries cannot really be explained in terms of the comparative-costs theory based on the assumption of given resources and given techniques. Nor can we attribute any significant part of the expansion to revolutionary changes in techniques and increases in productivity. As we have seen in Section I, peasant export production expanded by extension of cultivation using traditional methods of production, while mining and plantation sectors expanded on the basis of increasing supplies of cheap labour with a minimum of capital outlay. Thus the contributions of Western enterprise to the expansion process are mainly to be found in two spheres: the improvements of transport and communications[13] and the discoveries of new mineral resources. Both are methods of increasing the total volume of resources rather than methods of making the given volume of resources more productive. All these factors suggest an expansion process which kept itself going by drawing an increasing volume of hitherto unused or surplus resources into export production.

2. International trade between the tropical underdeveloped countries and the advanced countries of the temperate zone has grown out of sharp differences in geography and climate resulting in absolute differences of costs. In this context, the older comparative-costs theory, which is usually formulated in terms of qualitative differences[14] in the resources of the trading countries, tends to stress the obvious geographical differences to the neglect of the more interesting quantitative differences in the factor endowments of countries possessing approximately the same type of climate and geography. Thus while it is true enough to say that Burma is an exporter of rice because of her cliamte and geography, the more interesting question is why Burma should develop into a major rice exporter while the neighbouring South India, with approximately the same type of climate and geography, should develop into a net importer of rice. Here the "vent-for-surplus" approach which directs our attention to population density as a major determinant of export capacity has an advantage over the conventional theory.[15]

---

[13]This is what Professor L. C. A. Knowles described as the "Unlocking of the Tropics" (*op. cit.*, pp. 138–52).

[14]Cf. J. Viner, *International Trade and Economic Development*, pp. 14–16.

[15]Those who are used to handling the problem in terms of qualitative differences in factors and differential rent may ask: why not treat the surplus productive capacity as an extreme instance of "differential rent" where the transfer cost of the factors from the domestic to export production is zero? But this does not accurately portray the situation here. The transfer cost of the factors is zero, not because land which is used for the export crop is not at all usable for domestic subsistence production but because with the sparse population in the early phase there is no demand for the surplus food which could have been produced on the land used for the export crop. As we shall see, at a later stage when population pressure begins to grow, as in Java, land which has been used for export is encroached upon by subsistence production.

3. Granted the importance of quantitative differences in factor endowments, there still remains the question why Smith's cruder "vent-for-surplus" approach should be preferable to the modern Ohlin variant of the comparative-costs theory. The main reason is that, according to the Ohlin theory, a country about to enter into international trade is supposed already to possess a highly developed and flexible economic system which can adjust its methods of production and factor combinations to cope with a wide range of possible variations in relative factor supplies (see Section II above). But in fact the economic framework of the underdeveloped countries is a much cruder apparatus which can make only rough-and-ready adjustments. In particular, with their meagre technical and capital resources, the underdeveloped countries operate under conditions nearer to those of fixed technical coefficients than of variable technical coefficients. Nor can they make important adjustments through changes in the outputs of different commodities requiring different proportions of factors because of the inelastic demand both for their domestic production, mainly consisting of basic foodstuff, and for their exportable commodities, mainly consisting of industrial raw materials. Here again the cruder "vent-for-surplus" approach turns out to be more suitable.

Our argument that, in general, the "vent-for-surplus" theory provides a more effective approach than the comparative-costs theory to the international trade of the underdeveloped countries does not mean that the "vent-for-surplus" theory will provide an exact fit to all the particular patterns of development in different types of export economies. No simple theoretical approach can be expected to do this. Thus if we interpret the concept of the surplus productive capacity strictly as pre-existing surplus productive capacity arising out of the original endowments of the factors, it needs to be qualified, especially in relation to the mining and plantation sectors of the underdeveloped countries. Here the surplus productive capacity which may have existed to some extent before the country was opened to international trade is usually greatly increased by the discovery of new mineral resources and by a considerable inflow of foreign capital and immigrant labour. While immigrant labour is the surplus population of other underdeveloped countries, notably India and China, the term "surplus" in the strict sense cannot be applied to foreign capital. But, of course, the existence of suitable surplus natural resources in an underdeveloped country is a pre-condition of attracting foreign investment into it. Two points may be noted here. First, the complication of foreign investment is not as damaging to the surplus-productive-capacity approach as it appears at first sight, because the inflow of foreign investment into the tropical and semi-tropical underdeveloped countries has been relatively small both in the nineteenth century and the inter-war period.[16] Second, the nineteenth-century phenomenon of international mobility of capital and labour has been largely neglected by the comparative-costs theory, which is based on the assumption of perfect mobility of factors within a country and their imperfect mobility between different countries. The sur-

[16]Cf. R. Nurkse, "International Investment To-day in the Light of Nineteenth Century Experience," *Economic Journal*, December 1954, pp. 744–58, and the United Nations Report on *International Capital Movements during the Inter-war Period*.

plus-productive-capacity approach at least serves to remind us that the output of mining and plantation sectors can expand without necessarily contracting domestic subsistence output.

The use of the surplus-productive-capacity approach may prove in particular to be extremely treacherous in relation to certain parts of Africa, where mines, plantations and other European enterprises have taken away from the tribal economies the so-called "surplus" land and labour, which, on a closer analysis, prove to be no surplus at all. Here the extraction of these so-called "surplus" resources, by various forcible methods in which normal economic incentives play only a part, entails not merely a reduction in the subsistence output but also much heavier social costs in the form of the disruption of the tribal societies.[17]

When we turn to the peasant export sectors, however, the application of the "vent-for-surplus" theory is fairly straightforward. Here, unlike the mining and plantation sectors, there has not been a significant inflow of foreign investment and immigrant labour. The main function of the foreign export-import firms has been to act as middlemen between the world market and the peasants, and perhaps also to stimulate the peasants' wants for the new imported consumers' goods. As we have seen, peasant export production expanded by using methods of production more or less on the same technical level as those employed in the traditional subsistence culture. Thus the main effect of the innovations, such as improvements in transport and communications[18] and the introduction of the new crops, was to bring a greater area of surplus land under cultivation rather than to raise the physical productivity per unit of land and labour. Yet peasants export production usually managed to expand as rapidly as that of the other sectors while remaining self-sufficient with respect to basic food crops. Here, then, we have a fairly close approximation to the concept of a pre-existing surplus productive capacity which can be tapped by the world-market demand with a minimum addition of external resources.

Even here, of course, there is room for differences in interpretation. For instance, there is evidence to suggest that, in the early decades of expansion, the rates of increase in peasant export production in South-East Asian and West African countries were well above the possible rates of growth in their working population.[19] Given the conditions of constant

[17]Cf. The United Nations Report on the *Enlargement of Exchange Economy in Tropical Africa,* pp. 37 and 49–51.

[18]It may be noted that the expansion of some peasant export crops, notably rice in South-East Asia, depended to a much greater extent on pre-existing indigenous transport facilities, such as river boats and bullock carts, than is generally realised.

[19]For instance, cocoa output of the Gold Coast expanded over forty times during the twenty-five year period 1905–30. Even higher rates of expansion in cocoa production can be observed in Nigeria combined with a considerable expansion in the output of other export crops. Both have managed to remain self-sufficient with regard to basic food crops. (cf. West African Institute of Economic Research, *Annual Conference,* Economic Section, Achimota, 1953, especially the chart between pp. 96 and 98; *The Native Economies of Nigeria,* ed. M. Perham, Vol. 1, Part II). In Lower Burma, for the thirty-year period 1870–1900, the area under rice cultivation increased by more than three times, while the population, including immigrants from Upper Burma, doubled. (Cf. also, Furnivall, *op. cit.,* pp. 84–5.)

techniques, no significant inflow of immigrant foreign labour and continuing self-sufficiency with respect to the basic food crops, we are left with the question how these peasant economies managed to obtain the extra labour required to expand their export production so rapidly. A part of this labour may have been released by the decline in cottage industries and by the introduction of modern labour-saving forms of transport in place of porterage, but the gap in the explanation cannot be satisfactorily filled until we postulate that even those peasant economies which started off with abundant land relatively to their population must have had initially a considerable amount of under-employed or surplus labour. This surplus labour existed, not because of a shortage of co-operating factors, but because in the subsistence economies, with poor transport and little specialisation in production, each self-sufficient economic unit could not find any market outlet to dispose of its potential surplus output, and had therefore no incentive to produce more than its own requirements. Here, then, we have the archetypal form of Smith's "unproductive" labour locked up in a semi-idle state in the underdeveloped economy of a country isolated from outside economic contacts. In most peasant economies this surplus labour was mobilised, however, not by the spread of the money-wage system of employment, but by peasant economic units with their complement of "family" labour moving *en bloc* into the money economy and export production.

The need to postulate a surplus productive capacity to explain the rapid expansion in peasant export production is further strengthened when we reflect on the implications of the fact that this expansion process is inextricably bound up with the introduction of the money economy into the subsistence sectors. To the peasant on the threshold of international trade, the question whether or not to take up export production was not merely a question of growing a different type of crop but a far-reaching decision to step into the new and unfamiliar ways of the money economy.

Thus let us consider a community of self-sufficient peasants who, with their existing techniques, have just sufficient land and labour to produce their minimum subsistence requirements, so that any export production can be achieved only by reducing the subsistence output below the minimum level. Now, according to the conventional economic theory, there is no reason why these peasants should not turn to export production if they have a differential advantage there, so that they could more than make up for their food deficit by purchases out of their cash income from the export crop. But, in practice, the peasants in this situation are unlikely to turn to export production so readily. Nor is this "conservatism" entirely irrational, for by taking up export production on such a slender margin of reserves, the peasants would be facing the risk of a possible food shortage for the sake of some gain in the form of imported consumers' goods which are "luxuries" to them. Moreover, this gain might be wiped off by unfavourable changes in the prices of both the export crop they would sell and the foodstuffs they would have to buy and by the market imperfections, which would be considerable at this early stage. Thus, where the margin of resources is very small above that required for the minimum subsistence output, we should expect the spread of export production to be inhibited or very slow, even if there were some genuine possibilities of gains on the comparative costs principle.[20]

In contrast, the transition from subsistence agriculture to export production is made much easier when we assume that our peasants start with some surplus resources which enable them to produce the export crop *in addition* to their subsistence production. Here the surplus resources perform two functions: first they enable the peasants to hedge their position completely and secure their subsistence minimum before entering into the risks of trading; and secondly, they enable them to look upon the imported goods they obtain from trade in the nature of a clear net gain obtainable merely for the effort of the extra labour in growing the export crop. Both of these considerations are important in giving the peasants just that extra push to facilitate their first plunge into the money economy.

Starting from this first group of peasants, we may picture the growth of export production and the money economy taking place in two ways. Firstly, the money economy may grow extensively, with improvements in transport and communications and law and order, bringing in more and more groups of peasants with their complements of family labour into export production on the same "part-time" basis as the first group of peasants. Secondly, the money economy may grow intensively by turning the first group of peasants from "part-time" into "whole-time" producers of the export crop.[21] In the first case, surplus resources are necessary as a lubricant to push more peasants into export production at each round of the widening circle of the money economy. Even in the second case, surplus resources are necessary if the whole-time export producers buy their food requirements locally from other peasants, who must then have surplus resources to produce the food crops above their own requirements. Logically, there is no reason why the first group of peasants who are now whole-time producers of the export crop should buy their food requirements locally instead of importing them. But, as it happens, few peasant export economies have specialised in export production to such an extent as to import their basic food requirements.

[20]Of course, this argument can be countered by assuming the differences in comparative costs to be very wide. But, so long as export production requires withdrawing some resources from subsistence production, some risks are unavoidable. Further, remembering that the middlemen also require high profit margins at this stage, the gains large enough to overcome the obstacles are likely to arise out of surplus resources rather than from the differential advantages of the given fully employed resources. The risk of crop-failure is, of course, present both in subsistence and export production.

[21]In either case the expansion process may be looked upon as proceeding under conditions approximating to constant techniques and fixed combinations between land and labour once equilibrium is reached. The distinctive feature of peasant export economies is their failure to develop new and larger-scale or extensive methods of farming. It is true that in subsistence agriculture "fixed factors," such as a plough and a pair of bullocks, were frequently used below capacity, and one important effect of cash production was to increase the size of the holding to the full capacity of these "fixed factors." But this may be properly looked upon as equilibrium adjustments to make full use of surplus capacity rather than as the adoption of new and more land-using methods of production. Increasing the size of holding to make a more effective use of a pair of bullocks is different from the introduction of a tractor! Our assumption of constant techniques does not preclude the development of large-scale ownership of land as distinct from large-scale farming.

The average economist's reaction to our picture of discrete blocks of surplus productive capacity being drawn into a widening circle of money economy and international trade is to say that while this "crude" analysis may be good enough for the transition phase, the conventional analysis in terms of differential advantages and continuous marginal productivity curves must come into its own once the transition phase is over. Here it is necessary to distinguish between the expansion phase and the transition phase. It is true that in most peasant export economies the expansion process is tapering off or has come to a stop, as most of the surplus land suitable for the export crop has been brought under cultivation. This, of course, brings back the problem of allocating a fixed amount of resources, as we shall see in the next section when we consider issues of economic policy. But even so, the surplus-productive-capacity approach is not entirely superseded so long as the transition from a subsistence to a fully developed money economy remains incomplete. In most underdeveloped countries of Asia and Africa[22] this transition seems not likely to be over until they cease to be underdeveloped.

The continuing relevance of the surplus-productive-capacity approach may be most clearly seen in the typical case of a peasant export economy which with its natural resources and methods of production has reached the limit of expansion in production while its population continues to grow rapidly. According to the surplus-productive-capacity approach, we should expect the export capacity of such a country to fall roughly in proportion as the domestic requirement of resources to feed a larger population increases. This common-sense result may, however, be contrasted with that obtainable from the conventional theory as formulated by Ohlin. First, it appears that the Ohlin theory puts to the forefront of the picture the *type* of export, i.e., whether it is more labour-using or land-using as distinct from the total export capacity of the trading country. Secondly, in the Ohlin theory there is no reason why a thickly populated country should not also possess a high ratio of (labour-intensive) exports to its total output.

The ideal pattern of trade suggested by the Ohlin theory has a real counterpart in the thickly populated advanced countries of Europe, which for that very reason are obliged to build up a large export trade in manufactures or even in agriculture as in the case of Holland. But when we turn to the thickly populated underdeveloped countries, however, the ideal and the actual patterns of international trade diverge widely from each other. Indeed, we may say that these countries remain underdeveloped precisely because they have not succeeded in building up a labour-intensive export trade to cope with their growing population. The ratio of their export to total production could, of course, be maintained at the same level and the pressure of population met in some other way. But given the existing conditions, even this neutral pattern may not be possible in many underdeveloped countries. Thus, in Indonesia there is some evidence to

<hr>

[22]Cf. the United Nations Report cited above on the *Enlargement of the Exchange Economy*. Even in the most developed peasant export economies the money economy has not spread to the same extent in the market for factors of production as in the market for products.

suggest that the volume of agricultural exports from the thickly populated Java and Madura is declining absolutely and also relatively to those of the Outer Islands, which are still sparsely populated.[23] Of course, there are other causes of this decline, but population pressure reducing the surplus productive capacity of Java seems to be a fundamental economic factor; and the decline spreads from peasant to plantation exports as more of the plantation lands, which were under sugar and rubber, are encroached upon by the peasants for subsistence production.[24] In general, given the social and economic conditions prevailing in many underdeveloped countries, it seems fair to conclude that the trend in their export trade is likely to be nearer to that suggested by the surplus-productive-capacity approach than to that suggested by the theory of comparative costs.[25]

IV

This paper is mainly concerned with interpretation and analysis, but we may round off our argument by touching briefly upon some of its policy implications.

1. We have seen that the effect of population pressure on many underdeveloped countries, given their existing social and economic organisation, is likely to reduce their export capacity by diverting natural resources from export to subsistence production. If we assume that these natural resources have a genuine differential advantage in export production, then population pressure inflicts a double loss: first, through simple diminishing returns, and secondly, by diverting resources from more to less productive use. Thus, if Java has a genuine differential advantage in growing rubber and sugar, she would obtain a greater amount of rice by maintaining her plantation estates instead of allowing them to be encroached upon by peasants for subsistence rice cultivation. The orthodox liberal economists, confronted with this situation, would, of course, strongly urge the removal of artificial obstacles to a more systematic development of the money economy and the price system. Now there are still many underdeveloped countries which are suffering acutely from the economic rigidities arising out of their traditional social structure and/or from discriminatory policies based on differences in race, religion and class. Here the removal of barriers, for instance, to the horizontal and vertical mobility of labour, freedom to own land and to enter any occupation, etc., may well prove to be

[23] Cf. J. H. Boeke, *Ontwikkelingsgang en toekomst van bevolkings-en ondernemingslandbouw in Nederlandsch-Indie* (Leiden, 1948), p. 91. I owe this reference to an unpublished thesis by Mr. M. Kidron.
[24] The same tendency to transfer land from plantation to subsistence agriculture may be observed in Fiji with the growing population pressure created by the Indian immigrant labour originally introduced to work in the sugar plantations. The outline is blurred here by the decline in the sugar industry. The reason why this tendency does not seem to operate in the West Indies is complex. But it may be partly attributable to the tourist industry, which helps to pay for the food imports of some of the islands.
[25] The surplus-productive-capacity approach also partly helps to explain why underdeveloped countries, such as India, which started off with a thick population tend to retain large and persistent pockets of subsistence sectors in spite of their longer contacts with the world economy, while the subsistence sectors in thinly populated countries, such as those in West Africa, tend to disappear at a faster rate in spite of their much later start in international trade.

a great liberating force.[26] But our analysis has suggested that it is much easier to promote the growth of the money economy in the early stage when a country is newly opened up to international trade and still has plenty of surplus land and labour rather than at a later stage, when there are no more surplus resources, particularly land, to feed the growth of the money economy. Thus in a country like Java there is a considerable amount of artificial restriction, customary or newly introduced, which the liberal economists can criticise, e.g., restriction on land ownership. But given the combination of population pressure, large pockets of subsistence economy and traditional methods of production which can no longer be made more labour-intensive, it seems very doubtful whether the mere removal of artificial restrictions can do much by itself without a more vigorous policy of state interference. The truth of the matter is that in the underdeveloped countries where, for various reasons described above, the exchange economy is still an extremely crude and imperfect apparatus which can make only rough-and-ready responses to economic differentials, it may require a considerable amount of state interference to move toward the comparative-costs equilibrium. Thus given that Java has genuine differential advantages in the production of rubber and sugar, a more optimal reallocation of her resources may require, for instance, the removal of her surplus population either to the thinly populated Outer Islands or to industries within Java and a vigorous export-drive policy supplemented by bulk purchase and subsidies on the imported rice. Here we come to a fundamental dilemma which is particularly acute for the orthodox liberal economists. On a closer examination it turns out that their free-trade argument, although ostensibly based on the comparative-costs principle, is buttressed by certain broad classical presumptions against protection and state interference:[27] e.g., the difficulty of selecting the right industry to protect, the virtual impossibility of withdrawing protection once given, the tendency of controls to spread promiscuously throughout the economic system strangling growth, and so on. These presumptions gain an added strength from the well-known administrative inefficiency and sometimes corruption of the governments of some underdeveloped countries. Thus even if we believe in the "nineteenth-century pattern" of international trade based on natural advantages, how can we be sure that the state is competent enough to select the right commodities for its export-drive policy when it is considered incompetent to select the right industry for protection?

2. We have seen that the rapid expansion in the export production of the underdeveloped countries in the nineteenth century cannot be satisfactorily explained without postulating that these countries started off with a considerable amount of surplus productive capacity consisting both of unused natural resources and under-employed labour. This gives us a common-sense argument for free trade which is especially relevant for the underdeveloped countries in the nineteenth century: the surplus produc-

---

[26]This is why the case for the "liberal" solution is strong in places such as East and Central Africa, where due both to the general backwardness of the indigenous population and the presence of a white settler population, both types of rigidity prevail (cf. *The Royal Commission Report on East Africa*).

[27]Cf. J. Viner, *International Trade and Economic Development*, pp. 41–2. See also Sidgwick, *Principles of Political Economy*, Book III, Chapter V.

tive capacity provided these countries with a virtually "costless" means of acquiring imports which did not require a withdrawal of resources from domestic production but merely a fuller employment for their semi-idle labour. Of course, one may point to the real cost incurred by the indigenous peoples in the form of extra effort and sacrifice of the traditional leisurely life[28] and also to the various social costs not normally considered in the comparative-costs theory, such as being sometimes subject to the pressure of taxation and even compulsory labour and frequently of having to accommodate a considerable inflow of immigrant labour creating difficult social and political problems later on. One may also point to a different type of cost which arises with the wasteful exploitation of natural resources.[29] But for the most part it is still true to say that the indigenous peoples of the underdeveloped countries took to export production on a voluntary basis and enjoyed a clear gain by being able to satisfy their developing wants for the new imported commodities. Thus our special argument for free trade in this particular context still remains largely intact. The orthodox economists, by rigidly insisting on applying the comparative-costs theory to the underdeveloped countries in the nineteenth century, have missed this simpler and more powerful argument.

3. We have seen in Section I that the deep-rooted hostility of the critics towards the "classical theory" and the nineteenth-century pattern of international trade may be partly traced back to the time when Western colonial powers attempted to introduce export-drive policies in the tropical underdeveloped countries; and tried to justify these policies by invoking the "classical theory" of free trade and the Adam Smithian doctrine of international trade as a dynamic force generating a great upward surge in the general level of productivity of the trading countries. To the critics, this appears as a thinly disguised rationalisation of the advanced countries' desire for the markets for their manufactured products and for raw materials. Thus it has become a standard argument with the critics to say that the nineteenth-century process of international trade has introduced a large "export bias" into the economic structure of the underdeveloped countries which has increased their "vulnerability" to international economic fluctuations.

In Section II we have seen that once we leave the ideal world of the comparative costs theory in which the resources not required for the export market can be re-absorbed into domestic production, every country with a substantial export trade may be considered "vulnerable." Thus a coun-

---

[28]It may be formally possible to subsume the surplus-productive-capacity approach under the opportunity-cost theory, by treating leisure instead of foregone output as the main element of cost. But this would obscure the important fact that the underdeveloped countries have been able to expand their production very rapidly, not merely because the indigenous peoples were willing to sacrifice leisure but also because there were also surplus natural resources to work upon.

[29]The social cost of soil erosion can be very great, but this may be caused not merely by an expansion of export production but also by bad methods of cultivation and population pressure. The problem of adequately compensating the underdeveloped countries for the exploitation of their non-replaceable mineral resources belongs to the problem of the distribution of gains from trade. Here we are merely concerned with establishing that the indigenous peoples do obtain some gains from trade.

try may be said to be vulnerable because it has built up a large ratio of export to its total production simply by making use of its pre-existing surplus productive capacity. *A fortiori,* it is vulnerable when it has genuinely improved upon its original surplus productive capacity. How does the idea of "export bias" fit into our picture?

The term "export bias" presumably means that the resources of the underdeveloped countries which could have been used for domestic production have been effectively diverted into export production by deliberate policy. The implication of our surplus-productive-capacity approach is to discount this notion of "export bias." In the peasant export sectors, at the early stage with sparse populations and plenty of surplus land, the real choice was not so much between using the resources of export production or for domestic production as between giving employment to the surplus resources in export production or leaving them idle. In the later stage, when the population pressure begins to increase as in the case of Java, we have seen that the bias is likely to develop against, rather than in favour of, the export sector. Even when we turn to the mining and plantation sectors, it is difficult to establish a significant "export bias" in the strict sense. Here the crucial question is: how far would it have been possible to divert the foreign capital and technical resources which have gone into these sectors into the domestic sector? The answer is clear. For a variety of reasons, notably the smallness of domestic markets, few governments of the underdeveloped countries, whether colonial or independent, have so far succeeded in attracting a significant amount of foreign investment away from the extractive export industries to the domestic industries. In criticising the colonial governments it should be remembered that the only choice open to them was whether to attract a greater or a smaller amount of foreign investment within the export sector and not whether to attract investment for the domestic or the export sector.

This is not to deny that the colonial governments had a strong motive for promoting export production. Apart from the interests of the mother country, the individual colonial governments themselves had a vested interest in the expansion of foreign trade because they derived the bulk of their revenues from it.[30] In their search for revenue they have pursued various policies designed to attract foreign investment to the mining and plantation sectors, such as granting favourable concessions and leases, favourable tariff rates for rail transport, taxation policy designed to facilitate the supply of labour, provision of various technical services, etc.[31] But on the whole it is still true to say that the most important contribution of the colonial governments towards the expansion of the colonial exports is to be found, not in these export-drive policies, but in their basic services, such as the establishment of law and order and the introduction of modern transport, which enabled the pre-existing surplus productive capacity of the colonies to be tapped by the world market demand. If we wish to criticise the export-drive policies of the colonial governments it would be

[30]This is true for the governments of most underdeveloped countries, whether colonial or independent, past or present.
[31]For a discussion of the question of the possible export bias through the operation of the 100% sterling exchange system of the colonies, see A. D. Hazlewood, "Economics of Colonial Monetary Arrangements," *Social and Economic Studies,* Jamaica, December 1954.

more appropriate to do so, not on the ground of "export bias" but on the ground that they may have diverted too great a share of the gains from international trade and of the public services of the colonies to the foreign-owned mines and plantations at the expense of indigenous labour and peasant export producers.

It may be argued that we have given too strict an interpretation of the "export-bias" doctrine which is merely meant to convey the general proposition that, whatever the exact cause, the nineteenth-century process of international trade has landed many underdeveloped countries with a large ratio of raw materials exports to their total national products, making it desirable to reduce their "vulnerability" to international economic fluctuations. But the trouble is that the "export bias" doctrine tends to suggest that the raw-materials export production of the underdeveloped countries has been artificially over-expanded, not merely in relation to their domestic sector, but absolutely. Given the strong feelings of economic nationalism and anti-colonialism in the underdeveloped countries, this can be a very mischievous doctrine strengthening the widespread belief that to go on producing raw materials for the export market is tantamount to preserving the "colonial" pattern of trade. Thus already many underdeveloped countries are giving too little encouragement to their peasant export sectors by diverting too much of their capital and technical resources to industrial-development projects, and are also crippling their mining and plantation export sectors by actual or threatened nationalisation and various restrictions and regulations. The effect is to reduce their foreign-exchange earnings so urgently needed for their economic development. Of course, no competent critic of the nineteenth-century pattern of international trade would ever suggest the drastic step of reducing exports absolutely; some would even concede the need for vigorous export drive policies.[32] But having built up a pervasive feeling of hostility and suspicion against the "nineteenth-century" or the "colonial" pattern of international trade, they are not in a position to ram home the obvious truths: (a) that, even on an optimistic estimate of the possibility of international aid, the underdeveloped countries will have to pay for the larger part of the cost of their economic plans aiming either at a greater national self-sufficiency or at the export of manufactured goods; (b) that the necessary foreign exchange for these development plans can be earned by the underdeveloped countries at the present moment only by the export of raw materials (though not necessarily the same commodities for which they were supposed to have a differential advantage in the nineteenth century); and (c) that therefore to pursue their development plans successfully it is vitally important for them to carry out the "export-drive" policies, which in their technical properties may not be very different from those of the colonial governments in the past.[33] In trying to carry out their development plans on the foreign-exchange earnings from raw-materials export they would, of course, still

[32]Cf., for example, Gunnar Myrdal, *An International Economy*, p. 274.
[33]Colonial governments have frequently defended their export-drive policies as the means of taxing foreign trade to finance services needed for internal development. But because they were colonial governments, their motives were suspect. At first sight we might imagine that the new independent governments of the underdeveloped countries would be free from this disability. But unfortunately, given the atmosphere of intense nationalism and anti-colonialism, this

be "vulnerable"; but this should be considered separately as a problem in short-term economic stability[34] and not as a criticism of the nineteenth-century pattern of international trade in relation to the long-term development of the underdeveloped countries. From a long-term point of view, even countries which have successfully industrialised themselves and are therefore able to maintain their population at a higher standard of living by building up a large export trade in manufactures, such as Japan or the thickly populated countries of Western Europe, will continue to be "vulnerable."[35]

---

is not true. In some cases the hands of the newly independent governments seem to be tied even more tightly, and economic policies admitted to be desirable are turned down as "politically impossible." Here those economists who regard themselves as the critics of the classical theory and the nineteenth-century pattern of international trade have a special responsibility. Instead of dealing tenderly with the "understandable" emotional reactions which they have partly helped to create, they ought to be emphatic in pointing out the conflicts between rational considerations and "understandable" mental attitudes. The underdeveloped countries are too poor to enjoy the luxury of harbouring their emotional resentments.

[34]Cf. the United Nations Report on *Measures for International Economic Stability* and Myrdal's comments on it, *op. cit.,* pp. 238–53.

[35]It is particularly in relation to the thickly populated advanced countries of Western Europe which have specialised and adapted their economic structure to the requirements of the export market that Professor J. H. Williams found Adam Smith's "vent-for-surplus" approach illuminating. We have, in this paper, interpreted the "surplus" more strictly in its pre-existing form without the improvements and augmentation in productive capacity due to genuine "specialisation." (Cf. J. H. Williams, "International Trade Theory and Policy—Some Current Issues," *American Economic Review, Papers and Proceedings,* 1951, pp. 426–7.)

25. The Long-Run Terms of Trade Between Agriculture and Manufacturing

Theodore Morgan *

There is a widely held opinion that the terms of trade between agriculture and manufacturing industry have been shifting historically to the advantage of manufacturing; and that this shift is what should be expected, both in the past and in the future. The alleged trend is used as an argument for industrialization in underdeveloped countries, or for "balanced development," at the expense of agricultural development.

The first section below discusses the United Kingdom data on which this opinion has mainly been based, criticizes it from the point of view of its use, and adds data for an additional time period and for six other countries. Part II comments on several doctrines that imply adverse, and perhaps worsening, terms of trade for producers of primary products must be expected.

*From *Economic Development and Cultural Change,* October 1959. © 1959 by The University of Chicago. Reprinted by permission of The University of Chicago Press. The author is Professor of Economics, University of Wisconsin. Discussions with Professor P. T. Ellsworth were helpful in the development of this paper. Miss Jacqueline L. Hodgson was most effective in the work of collecting and charting the data.

Since non-agricultural products are of minor significance in the primary product series below, the terms "primary products" and "agricultural products" are used here interchangeably. The charts shown below on the terms of trade between agricultural and manufactured products are always in the form of prices of agricultural products divided by prices of manufactured products, so that a rise in any series means that agriculture is gaining a price advantage.

The British Data

The most widely known data on the terms of trade between primary and manufactured products are in the League of Nations' *Industrialization and Foreign Trade*,[1] reproduced and added to in the United Nations' *Relative Price of Exports and Imports of Under-Developed Countries*.[2] Both studies use British data[3] as a sample of prices in world trade. British data have considerable attractions for this purpose: they are available over a long period; Britain has had a large share of world trade; and British imports have had the convenience of being mainly primary products, its exports mainly manufactured goods. Chart I shows the three series of the United Nations' study.

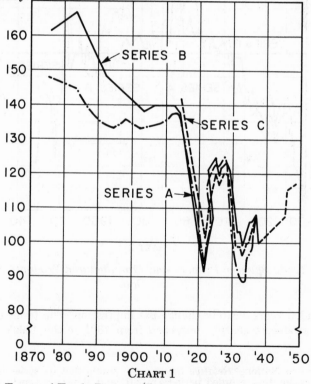

CHART 1

Terms of Trade Between Primary and Manufactured Products, 1876–1948. British Data.

[1]Geneva, 1945, pp. 154–157. The main author is Folke Hilgerdt.
[2]Lake Success, New York, 1949, pp. 21–24.
[3]There is a minor exception. Sources of data are omitted below, but can be found in the original article.

Chart 1 seems to show clearly that there was from 1876 on a trend of prices unfavorable to primary producers. The trend is plain despite wide price fluctuations. On the strength of this trend, predictions have been made that primary producers will in future years continue to suffer price-wise, and several theories have been elaborated as to why the trend should be accepted as a continuing fact.[4]

But the Chart 1 series are inadequate as the basis for such an interpretation on two counts. (*a*) First of all, data are available for a longer stretch of time, within which Chart 1's 1876 to 1948 period are only an atypical segment.[5] Consider Chart 2, which also presents British data. Series A, for 1801 to 1953, uses the same data as the Series A of Chart 1, 1876 to 1938, and the same sources for earlier and later years. Series B is shown as a check on Series A.[6]

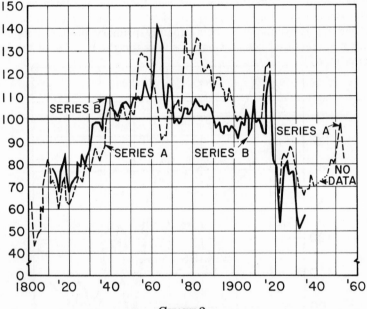

CHART 2

Terms of Trade Between Primary and Manufactured Products, 1801–1953. British Data.

The added years entirely change the impression. The terms of trade of primary producers sharply *improved* from 1801 to the 1860's or 1870's,

[4]See below.
[5]The United Nations' *Relative Prices,* etc., grants that its series begins close to the peak for the recorded period (p. 23), and states its conclusions as applying only to the movement from the 1870's on.
[6]Series B is Schlote's index for the prices of primary products divided by his index for the prices of finished manufactures. Werner Schlote, *Entwicklung und Strukturwandlungen des englischen Aussenhandels von 1700 bis zur Gegenwart,* Jena, 1938; translated as *British Overseas Trade, from 1700 to the 1930's,* Oxford, 1952.

when the decline that has been so much emphasized began.[7] One might plausibly fancy a long wave portrayed in these 153 years, but no single trend. There is marked short-term and long-term instability.[8]

(b) In addition, the British data do not measure fairly the prices received by primary producers of the world *within any given span of years*. Systematic bias is built into the British data in two ways, both of which increasingly understate the position of the world's primary producers as the decades go by. These two sources of bias have been pointed out elsewhere, and we can summarize the arguments briefly.

First, qualitative improvements in products are inadequately taken account of. As economic growth proceeds, these improvements take in all lines of production. Among primary products, one can readily think of the pebbles in the rice, dirt in the salt, and the uncertain condition of meat and fish in underdeveloped countries; and of the perishable foods that are not available at all. Among manufactured products the contrasts range still wider: for example, the carpenters' tools and building equipment of underdeveloped countries as contrasted with those of developed areas, or the bullock cart as contrasted with the truck, or the brick cooker as contrasted with the electric range. On the whole, I would judge that without doubt the improvements have been less in primary than in manufactured products. In the actual statistics that we have, corrections for improvements in quality are rare and incomplete;[9] and small changes, which cumulatively are very important, are not taken account of at all. The result is that all the data available—both the British series, and all others—understate the trend in the relative price position of primary producers.

In the second place, the British data cannot validly be used to measure the terms of trade against manufactures that primary producers experi-

[7]Suggestions on the causes of these changes, and of the changes shown in terms of trade data for six other countries, are brought together below.

[8]Imlah's investigation supports the approximate accuracy of the Sauerbeck index of British wholesale primary prices used in Series A of Charts 1 and 2. (Albert H. Imlah, "Real Values in British Foreign Trade, 1798–1853," *Journal of Economic History*, November 1948, pp. 133–152.)

[9]The only consistent attempt to meet the problem of continued quality improvements that I have found in the data underlying the eight charts of this paper is in the construction of part of the Indian price series (Chart 4 below).

A. N. McLeod points out that better quality secondary tertiary products can lower costs of primary producers, and so increase their real incomes, even while their terms of trade are turning against them. ("Trade and Investment in Under-developed Areas: A Comment," *American Economic Review*, June 1951, p. 414.)

R. E. Baldwin argues that omission of new commodities, or their inclusion at relatively small beginning year weights, tends to bias a price index upward, since new commodities usually fall considerably in price soon after they are introduced. ("Secular Movements in the Terms of Trade," *American Economic Review*, Papers and Proceedings, May 1955, pp. 267–268.)

Buchanan and Ellis feel that "the real weakness of the terms-of-trade basis of a supposed inferiority of primary production lies . . . in its failure to allow for the vast increase in the quality of manufactured goods." (*Approaches to Economic Development*, Twentieth Century Fund, New York, 1955, p. 262.)

Haberler has recently pointed out an extreme, but important, case of this distortion: "Unit value indexes of machinery represent for the most part declared values divided by weight!" (*Review of Economics and Statistics*, Supplement, February, 1958, p. 5.) Suppose that machinery price per pound remains the same while—as in fact has been happening—it is, over the decades, getting more effective per pound. Then the index is constant, but the real price is falling.

enced *within* their own countries. The reason is that transportation costs have been falling. During the past century and more, primary producers of the world outside of Britain have been receiving a price for their products that fell short of the price in Britain and other importing countries by a smaller and smaller amount. During the same period, primary producers of the world have been paying prices for their imports of manufactures that exceeded the prices of manufactures in Britain and other industrial countries by a smaller and smaller amount. Both distortions work in the same direction: producers of primary goods have been doing much better in the past century and more than the British data indicate.

Transportation costs have been falling because of the appearance and increasing use of more and better roads, canals (including Suez and Panama), railroads, steam-propelled ships, and trucks. Previously isolated economies and isolated kinds of production have been brought more and more into world commercial relationships. Wright generalizes that freight transportation on U. S. turnpikes and dirt road cost, in the mid-nineteenth century, "10 to 20 cents a ton mile, a rate prohibitive for long distance shipments." But railroads carried freight for long distances at 2 and 3 cents a ton mile, and canals seldom exceeded 1 cent.[10] There are abundant examples of commodity prices falling in New York or in the United Kingdom, while as a result of falling shipping rates, the prices of the same commodities were rising in the regions where they were being produced.[11]

Just before the second World War, an average of 10 percent of the value of total world trade probably went into transportation costs.[12] The share must have been far higher a century or more earlier—the above data suggest the neighborhood of 3 to 7 times higher, or 30 to 70 percent.

The widely used British data therefore are unreliable as a measure of the long-run relative price position of primary producers of the world for the two reasons we have surveyed—the relatively short time period the British data cover, and bias due both to quality improvements (especially) in manufacturing, and to falling transportation costs.[13]

[10]Chester W. Wright, *Economic History of the United States,* New York, 1949, p. 287.
[11]Such examples are given in J. M. Powers, *The Purchasing Power of Gold,* Report to the Bureau of Labor, Minnesota, 1947. The years covered are 1875–1895. Ellsworth gives some striking examples for the period 1884–1903: P. T. Ellsworth, "The Terms of Trade between Primary Producing and Industrial Countries," *Inter-American Economic Affairs,* Summer 1956, pp. 55–56. C. M. Wright also lists such data: "Convertibility and Triangular Trade as Safeguards against Economic Depression," *Economic Journal,* September 1955, pp. 425 ff.
Estimates of the average fall of shipping rates after 1870 are given in A. K. Cairncross, *Home and Foreign Investment, 1870–1913,* Cambridge, 1953, pp. 170 ff.; and in C. P. Kindleberger, *The Terms of Trade: A European Case Study,* New York, 1956, pp. 20–21, 336–339.
[12]*Relative Prices,* etc., p. 132.
[13]These two weaknesses exist also in other series derived from European or U. S. data. The U. S. data presented below are subject to the "bias" criticism; and both criticisms are relevant to Kindleberger's series, (*op. cit.,* Ch. 11); to that of Lewis ("World Production, Prices and Trade, 1870–1960," *Manchester School,* May 1952); and to GATT's series (Contracting Parties to the General Agreement on Tariffs and Trade, *International Trade,* 1952, Geneva, June 1953). Even so, Kindleberger concludes from his analysis of these data that, on

Data from Other Countries

As a check on the above reasoning, we show below in Charts 3 to 8 the prices of primary products divided by the prices of manufactures for six countries other than the United Kingdom.

Chart 3 gives two series for the United States. Series 1D" runs from 1787 to 1953, and is for domestic wholesale prices. In this series, the data for 1787 to 1889 are mainly quotations from New York, and (because of the trend in transportation costs) understate considerably the position of the average U.S. primary producer of the included goods. Series 2C, for 1913 to 1948, is calculated from United States statistics for prices of imported primary goods and imported manufactured goods—both f.o.b. This second series seems comparatively reliable for measuring the trend of relative prices in the countries with which the United States was trading, in that the transportation bias tends to cancel out.

There is no question about the general trend of the long U.S. series (1D).

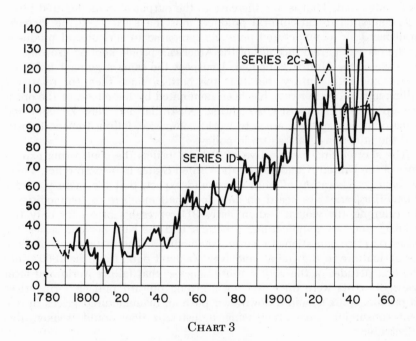

CHART 3

Terms of Trade Between Primary and Manufactured Products, 1787–1953. United States Data.

---

face value, "there is no long-run tendency for the terms of trade to move against primary products in favor of manufacturing"; and that if allowance is made for the improvement in quality of manufactures, "the terms of trade may have turned against manufactures and in favor of raw materials per unit of equal quality" (p. 263). Cf. below.

"In this chart, and in the following charts, a *D* following the number of a series means that the data are calculated from domestic wholesale prices, and a *C* means that the data are export and/or import prices.

Primary production has gained greatly—by 300 to 400 percent—*vis-a-vis* manufactures by a drastic shift of relative prices in its favor.

[Data for 5 other countries follow here. Editors' note.]

Tables 1, 2 and 3 summarize the experiences of the seven countries within each of the three different time perspectives indicated.

The over-all impression from these three tables is, I submit, that of the wide variety of experience of different nations. The variety suggests highly diverse demand and supply experience for particular commodities of the different countries covered. Table 1 underlines the importance of *not* generalizing on the experience of other countries or regions, from the experience of one. The remarkable data for the United States, showing continued and drastic improvement in the price position of agriculture over a century and a half, probably bears testimony mainly to the relatively rapid realization of the special advantages of the United States in many a line of manufacturing—as natural resources were discovered and utilized, capital accumulated and technology improved, and labor and management skills advanced. That is, the increase in the output of manufactured products compared to agricultural products must have exceeded the increase in demand for manufactured products compared to agricultural products, as the per capita real incomes of the American people kept on growing. In the case of the United Kingdom, I suspect the same argument holds up to the mid-19th century, but that the pattern since then (of relatively falling agricultural prices) has been dominated by the effects of the opening up of North America, Argentina, Australia, and New Zealand and some other agricultural areas to world commerce, falling transport costs, and the adoption of a free trade policy.

The shorter time perspective of Table 2 brings the contrasting experience of the United Kingdom and the United States into sharp relief. There is some corroboration of what one would expect, that the more violently fluctuating series are based on data for small numbers of commodities— for example, the violent Indian series 3D represents prices for only two primary and two manufactured products, and the New Zealand series 2 is based on price quotations for seven commodities. The rising terms of trade for agriculture in the Indian and New Zealand data, from the 1860's into the first decades of the 20th century, suggest that falling world and local transport costs were then exerting a strong upward pull on farm prices in producing areas, and a downward push on manufactured prices in distant consuming areas. Increasing industrialization would weaken this effect later.

Finally, there are the 50-odd years of Table 3. Beginning with about 1910, the U.S. series no longer shows a sharp upward trend, but at most, only a moderate upward movement. The changed trend may reflect relatively more rapid technological progress in American agriculture compared to manufacturing. In recent years, the simple explanation of a number of good seasons is relevant.

From the decade 1910–1920 on, all these series show conspicuous instability. Two wars and the great depression, with their correlated changed basic demands for and supplies of particular goods, and correlated shifts

Table 1. Data Covering Approximately 150 Years—1800 to 1950

COUNTRIES	ESTIMATE OF RELIABILITY OF DATA	EXACT YEARS COVERED	GENERAL MOVEMENT OF PRICES OF PRIMARY PRODUCTS DIVIDED BY PRICES OF MANUFACTURES
United Kingdom	Good (earlier years) to excellent (later years)	1801–1953	Major rise (to the mid-19th century), then major fall
United States	Good (earlier years) to excellent (later years)	1787–1953	Major rise through whole period

Table 2. Data Covering Approximately 90 Years—1860's to 1952

COUNTRIES	ESTIMATE OF RELIABILITY OF DATA	EXACT YEARS COVERED	GENERAL MOVEMENT OF PRICES OF PRIMARY PRODUCTS DIVIDED BY PRICES OF MANUFACTURES
United Kingdom	(see above)	1860–1953	Major fall (but a rise in the last 20 years of series)
United States	(see above)	1860–1953	Major rise (wider fluctuations in last 40 years of series)
India	Excellent in total	1861–1953	Rise—fall—rise
Japan	Good	1873–1952	Customs data: mild rise, then major fall to 1930's. Domestic data: rise to 1930's, then decline (violent fluctuations)
New Zealand	Excellent	1861–1952	Major rise (violent fluctuations)

Table 3. Data Covering Approximately 50 Years—1900's to 1952

COUNTRIES	ESTIMATE OF RELIABILITY OF DATA	EXACT YEARS COVERED	GENERAL MOVEMENT OF PRICES OF PRIMARY PRODUCTS DIVIDED BY PRICES OF MANUFACTURES
United Kingdom	(see above)	1900–1953	Major fall to the 1930's; moderate rise in recent years
United States	(see above)	1900–1953	General rise
India	(see above)	1900–1953	Fall to 30's, then a rise
Japan	(see above)	1900–1952	Customs data: fall to the 30's; Domestic data: no clear trend (violent fluctuations)
New Zealand	(see above)	1900–1952	Upward trend in earlier years; no clear trend since the 20's (violent fluctuations)
Union of South Africa	Good	1910–1952	Fall—rise—fall
Brazil	Good	1901–1950	Rise—fall—rise—fall—rise (violent fluctuations)

in commercial policy, have caused increasingly violent price changes. For most series, the depression years bring a sharp worsening in the price position of agriculture; but after those years there has been sharp improvement.[15]

II. Two Theories of the Terms of Trade

The data do not show any general worsening of the price position of primary producers. Hence theories that purport to explain why a worsening must take place invite special scrutiny.

Raul Prebisch has developed an attractively plain thesis to explain the British data, 1876–1948.[16] He generalizes that "the advantages of technical progress have been mainly concentrated in the industrial centers and have not directly extended to the countries making up the periphery of the world's economic system."[17] The cause is said to be that "the characteristic lack of organization among the workers employed in primary production prevents them from obtaining wage increases (in the boom) comparable to those of the industrial countries and from maintaining the increases to the same extent (in depression)."[18]

---

[15]Primary producers may, of course, be burdened by falling relative prices for their products, at the same time that their real incomes are rising. Suppose that the real price of A's product is falling, but that his productivity is rising faster than that price falls. Then his real income rises—and it might rise faster than that of producer B, the real price of whose product is rising.

A's situation resembles that of primary producers in the United States, Argentina, and some other "underdeveloped" areas of the nineteenth century. Rich agricultural areas of the world were being settled and were being made accessible to work markets. Even if and where the terms of trade of primary producers in such areas were deteriorating, their real income advance *could* have been much faster than that of typical manufacturing producers of the world.

A more extreme case is possible. Assume that factors are employed somewhere in the domestic economy with lower productivity than exists for them in the export sector, and that they have not hitherto moved into export sector employment. That is, there is malallocation of these factors due to their immobility. Now production for export expands, and these factors are drawn into the export sector. The factors will gain to the extent their (rising) marginal productivity in the employment they are leaving still remains below their (falling) marginal productivity in the export sector. The real prices of the products of the export sector may be falling.

In summary: the real income of these factors can be rising, *without* their achieving rising productivity, and *with* worsening terms of trade. (Cf. R. E. Baldwin, "Secular Movements in the Terms of Trade," *American Economic Review,* Papers and Proceedings, May 1955, pp. 259–269).

[16]Above, Chart 1. Prebisch is the author of the United Nations, *The Economic Development of Latin America,* Lake Success, New York, 1950. The data that he used are from a preliminary version of the study later published by the United Nations as *Relative Prices,* etc., *op. cit.*

[17]*Op cit.,* p. 8. Prebisch, in fact, goes further and argues that falling terms of trade of the primary producers has transferred part of the fruits of their own technical progress to the great industrial centers (pp. 10, 14).

[18]*Ibid.,* p. 13. H. W. Singer's similar view is not explicitly based on the unionization argument. *American Economic Review,* Supplement, May 1950, p. 478; *Review of Economics and Statistics,* Supplement, February, 1958, p. 87.

Gunnar Myrdal accepts deterioration of terms of trade for underdeveloped countries as a general fact, and concludes simply that they have had "rather bad luck" (*An International Economy,* New York, 1956, pp. 230–238); and that the play of market forces works normally toward greater economic inequality between localities and regions, rather than toward less (*Rich Lands and Poor,* New York, 1957, pp. 23–66).

This reasoning appears inconclusive on two counts. (1) Are money wages and prices that rise freely and fall sluggishly either necessary, or sufficient, to cause relatively high prices in the world market? No, for world supply and demand are the determinants of world price levels. Any country whose unions had been especially successful in hiking money wage rates would find itself in a competitive squeeze. Its sales of exports would slip, its balance of payments turn adverse; and if domestic prices did not in the longer run fall, the exchange value of its currency would fall instead. (2) Higher money wages do not necessarily cause higher domestic prices. They do so only if they rise faster than productivity. But even if they do the question still remains as to whether unions secure higher money wage rates, for labor of given quality, than the wage rates of non-union labor. Net conclusions from inquiries in this field are notably cautious.[19]

The first argument (1) of the above paragraph is relevant also to W. Arthur Lewis' view that "over-concentration on exports" brings with it the penalty of adverse terms of trade to underdeveloped areas that do nothing to raise the productivity of peasants producing food for domestic consumption. The latter "constitute a reservoir of cheap labour available for work in mines or plantations or other export enterprises."[20] But any one underdeveloped country runs the risk, as it raises its costs of producing exports, of pricing itself out of the world market. And if all underdeveloped countries together raise their costs and price quotations, they can find themselves in a worse net position, if demand for the export product falls off sharply. For example, how much would underdeveloped countries exporting rubber (or cotton, or rice) be advantaged by a sharp rise in price quotations for those commodities?

In his recent exhaustive study,[21] Kindleberger finds that "in the European context, the terms of trade favor the developed and run against the underdeveloped countries" (p. 239). He was able to compute only the merchandise terms of trade for this purpose (p. 232). The data are for 1872, on, and do not take into account the effects of specially rapid quality improvements in manufactures, and the relevance (from the point of view of primary producers on their home grounds) of falling transportation costs.[22]

After considering and rejecting several other explanations, Kindleberger

[19]Cf. the symposium in the Proceedings, *American Economic Review,* May 1954, pp. 279–331. The principal contributors were C. Kerr, M. Bronfenbrenner, and H. M. Levinson. Kerr does conclude firmly that labor's share of income has been no larger in unionized than in non-union industries (p. 288).

[20]*The Theory of Economic Growth,* London, 1955, p. 281.

[21]*Op. cit.*

[22]The qualification in the above quotation is well taken. One could hold that "in the European context, the terms of trade . . . run against the underdeveloped countries" and also believe that in the underdeveloped countries themselves, the terms of trade have not generally run against them. The Kindleberger data support the former; the data of this paper support the latter statement.

Hence it does not follow, as Kindleberger concludes, that "the views of Singer and Prebisch [that the terms of trade of underdeveloped countries have deteriorated] . . . derive support" from his data. "The Terms of Trade and Economic Development," *Review of Economics and Statistics,* Supplement, February 1958, p. 85. It is the experience of underdeveloped countries on their home grounds that is relevant to their policies.

suggests that the terms of trade he feels to exist—that is, that price trends have been unfavorable to underdeveloped countries—are due to "systematic differences in the capacity of the two types of countries to shift resources" (p. 253).[23] Underdeveloped countries are said to be less able to shift their resources off downward price escalators and on to upward price escalators, than are developed countries.

But he also finds that the terms of trade between manufactures and primary products do *not* run against primary products. Thoroughly heterogeneous price experience among the commodities measured, especially when they are divided up among different regions of export and import, is given as the explanation.[24]

The data of this paper suggest that emphasis ought to be centered on the heterogeneity of price experience. Particular supply influence, and particular demand changes, for different commodities, countries and times, have dominated the historical picture.

What are the implications for policy in underdeveloped countries of these data? First, and so obvious that it need not be stated save that it is often overlooked: the barter terms of trade we have been looking at have only limited relevance to policy in underdeveloped countries with respect to specialization in primary products versus manufacturing. Both a single factor terms of trade concept (the volume of imports obtainable through devoting a unit of factors to export production), and the income terms of trade (the volume of imports obtaintable from total export earnings) are likely to be more significant for policy.[25] And both of these latter terms of trade concepts are apt to show a more favorable trend than does the barter terms of trade.

Second, insofar as the barter terms of trade data are to be used as a guide to policy: (*a*) European data or world data should not be relied on, but instead the price changes experienced in the country in question. (*b*) No easy assumption should be made that primary products as a whole are likely to rise or fall in real price. Instead, the prospects of each potential export and import and import-substitute commodity ought to be scrutinized separately. Underdeveloped countries should be vividly aware that price raising policies by one or a few of the world producers of a commodity invite disaster as other producers gratefully expand into the widened

[23]In the *Dollar Shortage* (New York, 1950), Kindleberger presented a different thesis:
> The certainty of loss arises from agricultural and primary product countries from the assumption of continuously increasing efficiency of production in these and in manufactured products, and . . . the application in these circumstances of Engel's law on a national basis (p. 122).

This reasoning raises two main questions: (1) whether a modification of Engel's law to make it apply to real expenditures over successive time periods, is valid; and (2) whether the world's per capita income has been rising, or rising enough, so that such a modified Engel's law has had a chance to work. Kindleberger has not followed this reasoning in his later book on European terms of trade.

[24]*The Terms of Trade*, etc., *op. cit.*, pp. 263–264.

[25]Cf. Viner's analysis of terms of trade concepts in his *Studies in the Theory of International Trade*, New York, 1937, pp. 558–565; and the relevant comments of G. M. Meier, *Review of Economics and Statistics*, Supplement, February 1958, pp. 88–90.

markets; and they should be equally aware that a general, cartel-type, attempt by all producers of a commodity to raise its price (e.g., rubber, sugar, wheat, tin, steel) is a cordial invitation to new producers to start up production, to customers to shift over to existing substitutes, and to industrial chemists and engineers to invent new substitutes. (c) Even the most careful predictions of future prices are nearly certain to be partially or wholly wrong. Hence, as many writers in this field have emphasized, underdeveloped countries should center strong emphasis on improving the flexibility and adaptability of their economies, so as to be able to shrink the output of things in which their advantage is shrinking, and expand rapidly the output of things in which they have expanding advantage.

OCCUPATIONAL DISTRIBUTION IN THE COURSE OF GROWTH

26. Economic Progress and Occupational Distribution

P. T. Bauer and B. S. Yamey*

1. The principal purpose of this article is to examine the validity and significance of the widely held view that economic progress is generally associated with certain distinct, necessary and predictable changes in occupational distribution, in particular with a relative increase in the numbers engaged in tertiary activities. Our method is largely analytical; but since a strong empirical basis is claimed for the generalisation we are examining, we have found it necessary to make frequent descriptive reference to the composition of economic activity in economies at different stages of development. Most of the description is concentrated in the first section of the article, which describes and analyses the volume and significance of trading activity in British West Africa. The remaining sections of the article examine the analytical and statistical foundations of the generalisation and suggest that these are defective.

I

2. The few available occupational statistics of backward economies, especially in the colonies, purport to show that the great bulk of the population is occupied in agriculture. This impression is also often conveyed in official statements on economic activity in these territories. An example may be taken from *An African Survey*:

> In the Northern Province of Nigeria, at the census of 1931, about 84% of occupied males whose returns permitted them to be classified were shown as engaged in agriculture and fishing, about 9% in manufacture, and under 3% in commerce and finance.... For Southern Nigeria less detailed information is available. The returns, which are less reliable than those for Northern Nigeria, would suggest that the proportion of males engaging in agriculture is about 82% and that concerned with handicrafts about 4.7%.

Trade and transport are not mentioned. No attempt is made to reconcile this with another statement (on the same page) that almost 30% of the population of Nigeria lived in towns of over 5,000 inhabitants. In the same vein the official *Annual Report on Nigeria* states year after year that the great majority of the population is occupied in agriculture: trade is not among the other occupations listed.

*From *The Economic Journal,* December 1951. P. T. Bauer is Professor of Economics of Underdeveloped Countries and Economic Development, London School of Economics. B. S. Yamey is Professor of Economics, London School of Economics.

In contrast to these statements and statistics a remarkable multitude of traders, especially of small-scale sellers of both local produce and of imported merchandise, is a most conspicuous feature of West Africa. This is so apparent that it has not escaped attention. It is freely said by responsible administrators that in the southern parts of Nigeria and the Gold Coast everybody is engaged in trade, and this is hardly an exaggeration.

3. For reasons to be explained it is not possible to give specific quantitative information about the volume of trade or of the numbers engaged in it. Certain sporadic but conservative data, relating, for example, to numbers of market stallholders and hawkers' licences, indicate that the number of selling points, including children hawking very small quantities of goods, is very large in the principal markets. But the figures give an imperfect idea of the multitude of people engaged either part-time or whole-time in selling small quantities of goods or conveying them to dispersed points of sale. In the aggregate there is an enormous amount of activity the quantitative significance of which is obvious to the observer.

4. The seriously misleading impression created by official statistics and statements derives from the inappropriateness of classification by distinct occupational categories in an economy in which occupational specialisation is imperfect. The economic activity of a large proportion of the population of West Africa is better described as the performance of a number of different things rather than as the pursuit of a definite occupation. In many of the so-called agricultural households the head of the household trades part-time even during the normally short farming season, and more actively outside the season, whilst members of the family trade intermittently throughout the year. Even if only main activities are considered, it is doubtful whether five-sixths of the population is engaged in agriculture; when it is realised that even the head of the family is likely to have part-time economic activities and that many of his dependents (including children) are engaged at least periodically in trade, it becomes clear that the official statistics in their present form are apt to mislead.

The imperfect specialisation of economic activity is not confined to the agricultural community. Many African doctors and lawyers and almost all the leading chiefs have extensive trading interests. Government employees and servants of the European population trade part-time, either importing merchandise or dealing in merchandise and foodstuffs bought locally. The fluidity of activity extends to personal relations where they bear closely on economic life. A prominent African trader in Lagos whose children are being educated at expensive universities and schools in England includes his wife among his principal retailer customers. Similar commercial relations exist between other prominent Africans and their wives and children.

Even where the conceptual and statistical difficulties arising from imperfect occupational specialisation are fully appreciated it is difficult to collect the required information on subsidiary activities of individuals, particularly on part-time trade. Africans frequently do not regard trade as an occupation, especially when carried on by dependents, and would not refer to it as such when questioned, because they regard it as part of existence and not as a distinct occupation. In many cases it may not be possible to draw the line between the social and commercial activities of, say, a group of women traders in the market. There is, however, no doubt that the commercial element is generally substantial.

5. Once the level of economic activity has risen from that of a subsistence economy to that of an emerging exchange economy—a process which is encouraged and promoted by the activities of traders—the task of distribution may require a substantial volume of resources. Much depends upon physical and climatic conditions. But the circumstances of West Africa are certainly not exceptional in requiring a large volume of distributive activity. The large number of dispersed farmers and holdings, poor natural communications and long distances and the difficulties of prolonged storage in the open, together postulate a substantial volume of resources in distribution and transport for raising and maintaining the economy above the subsistence level even at an early stage in economic development. In this type of economy the indispensable tasks of assembly, bulking, transport, breaking of bulk and dispersal may require a large proportion of available resources. Moreover, in an economy which has recently emerged from the subsistence level, some transactions are still likely to be on a barter basis. Barter tends to use more resources, especially labour, than a fully developed money economy to transact a given volume of trade.

6. There is in West Africa widespread involuntary idleness of unskilled labour, resulting from lack of other co-operant resources, especially capital, to set it to work. This lack of employment is a major feature of comparatively undeveloped economies which in the aggregate comprise probably over half of the population of the world, including India, China, Java, large parts of Eastern and Southern Europe and much of Africa. The dependence of the volume of employment on the amount of the stock of capital used to be a major topic of political economy. The subject gradually receded from economic discussion as economists became preoccupied mainly with unemployment in advanced industrial economies, resulting not so much from lack of co-operant resources as from fluctuations in aggregate demand or various other influences discouraging investment and enterprise. Interest in the subject has revived with the growing realisation of its importance. Very recently unemployment in the "empty economy" has brought the problem nearer home.

The missing co-operant factor (or factors) of production can be capital, land or technical and administrative skill. The type of scarcity or its incidence varies greatly in different regions and even districts in West Africa as elsewhere. But in many regions the low level of capital and of suitable administrative and technical skills constitutes the principal shortage.

7. Entry into small-scale trade is easy, as at this level no technical or administrative skill is required and only very little capital. Trade is attractive even for very low rewards in view of the absence of more profitable alternatives.[1] Women and children are also available for trade, partly for social reasons; for example, in some areas the wife is expected to make a

[1]The relative increase in the numbers engaged in retail distribution in Great Britain and elsewhere during the depression of the early 1930s is a more familiar example which can be largely explained in terms of reduced supply price arising from the absence of suitable alternatives.

contribution to the family's income; also there is little for women to do in the house and there are few schools for children.[2]

8. The type of resources to be found in trade and transport depends, given the state of technique, upon the relative terms at which different productive resources are available. In an economy, such as West Africa, where capital is scarce and expensive and unskilled labour abundant and cheap, the large volume of resources in distribution and transport consists very largely of labour. As compared with more advanced economies there is a mass emphasis on labour rather than on capital. This tendency, which may proceed very far and reveal unsuspected possibilities, permeates West African trading arrangements; a few examples will illustrate it.

9. In West Africa there is an extensive trade in empty containers such as kerosene, cigarette and soup tins, flour, salt, sugar and cement bags and beer bottles. Some types of container are turned into household articles or other commodities. Small oil-lamps are made from cigarette and soup tins, whilst salt bags are made into shirts or tunics. But more usually the containers are used again in the storage and movement of goods. Those who seek out, purchase, carry and distribute second-hand containers maintain the stock of capital. They prevent the destruction of the containers, usually improve their conditions, distribute them to where they can best be used, and so extend their usefulness, the intensity of their use and their effective life. The activities of the traders represent a substitution of labour for capital. Most of the entrepreneurs in the container trade are women and children. The substitution is economic as long as six or eight hours of their time are less valuable (in view of the lack of alternatives) than the small profit to be made from the sale of a few empty containers. So far from the system being wasteful it is highly economic in substituting superabundant for scarce resources; within the limits of available technical skill nothing is wasted in West Africa.

For various reasons, of which the low level of capital is one, the individual agriculturalist produces on a very small scale. Moreover, the same lack of capital is reflected in the absence of suitable storage facilities and of cash reserves. As a result each producer has to dispose of small quantities of produce at frequent intervals as they become available during and immediately after the harvesting season. This postulates a large number of intermediaries, who, because of the high cost of capital, employ methods of transportation using relatively little capital and much labour. Donkey and bicycle transport are examples, while in some cases there is still head loading and human porterage, especially in the short-distance movement of local crops. The available transport equipment is used continuously with the assistance of large quantities of labour (subject to frequent breakdowns owing to poor roads and low technical skill).

The same phenomenon of the more intensive use of capital, that is its more rapid turnover, can be observed in the breaking of bulk into the

[2]It is possible that the numbers attracted into trade in West Africa are increased because of a largely institutional rigidity in money wages. But even if money wages were to fall to the equilibrium level the number who would find trade attractive would still be very large as long as the underlying economic factors remained broadly unchanged.

minute quantities in which imported merchandise is bought by the ultimate consumer. The purchase of a box of matches is often still a wholesale
transaction as the buyer frequently breaks bulk and re-sells the contents
to the final consumer in small bundles of ten to fifteen matches. Similarly,
at the petty retail stage sugar is sold in lots of three cubes, trade perfume
by the drop, salt by the cigarette tin and cheap biscuits by the small heap
of three or six. The small purchases are the result of low incomes and
low capital, and the activities of the numerous petty retailers represent
a substitution of labour for capital.

In Nigeria the small number of telephones and the low rate of literacy
render it necessary for the importing firms and the large distributors to
use the services of numerous intermediaries to keep contact with smaller
traders and to distribute their goods to them at an economic rate of turnover. The intermediaries reduce the size of stocks which need to be held.
This is of particular importance, since the low level of fixed capital tends
to enhance the economy's requirements of working capital. The large accumulation of unrailed groundnuts in the producing region of Nigeria is a
familiar instance of a general problem.

The narrowness of markets and the backwardness of communications are
reflected in inter-regional price differences which provide profitable opportunities for successful arbitrage (particularly in locally produced goods),
from region to region. This attracts traders and intermediaries, and also
makes it profitable for non-trading travellers to take part in trade, which
they frequently do on a casual basis.

10. The foregoing may be summarised as follows: in West Africa, as in
other emerging economies, the indispensable task of commodity distribution is expensive relatively to available resources; of the available resources,
capital is scarce and unskilled labour is abundant; the multiplicity of
traders is the result of the mass use of unskilled labour instead of capital
in the performance of the task of distribution. There is an extensive demand for the services of intermediaries, and there is a large section of the
population available to perform these services at a low supply price in
terms of daily earnings.

II

11. The description and analysis of Section I show that there are severe
limitations and qualifications to the view that a high proportion of labour
in tertiary production is both a consequence of and a pointer to a high
standard of living. As is well known, this generally held view derives from
the statistical investigations and analysis of Mr. Colin Clark and Professor A. G. B. Fisher. Thus according to Mr. Colin Clark:

Studying economic progress in relation to the economic structure of different countries, we find a very firmly established generalisation that a
high average level of real income per head is always associated with a high
proportion of the working population engaged in tertiary industries. . . .
Low real income per head is always associated with a low proportion of the
working population engaged in tertiary production and a high percentage
in primary production, culminating in China, where 75–80 per cent of
the population are primary producers. High average real income per head
compels a large proportion of producers to engage in tertiary production.

Professor Fisher writes:

We may say that in every progressive economy there has been a steady shift of employment and investment from the essential "primary" activities, without whose products life in even its most primitive forms would be impossible, to secondary activities of all kinds, and to a still greater extent into tertiary production. . . .

The shifts of employment towards secondary and tertiary production revealed by the census are the inescapable reflection of economic progress.

12. It would appear that the general proposition of Mr. Clark and Professor Fisher is based partly on analytical reasoning and partly on statistical evidence. Both types of verification appear to be defective.

The analytical reasoning purporting to sustain the generalisation seems to be based on the view that tertiary production is less essential than primary or secondary production; and that its products are in the nature of luxuries which cannot be afforded in economies with low real incomes. In essence the argument is that the income elasticity of demand for tertiary products is higher than that for the products of primary and secondary activities; and that therefore the demand for tertiary products increases relatively more rapidly with economic progress. Moreover, it is argued that technical progress is relatively slower in tertiary production. For both reasons taken together the proportion of occupied labour in tertiary production is supposed to rise with economic progress. The next section calls into question the validity of this reasoning; in Section IV it is suggested that the statistical verification claimed for the generalisation is inconclusive.

III

13. The analytical basis of the generalisation of Mr. Clark and Professor Fisher is open to criticism on several independent grounds of which the following are the most important. First, a substantial proportion of tertiary products are not luxuries with a relatively high income elasticity of demand; conversely, some products of primary and secondary production, possibly on a large scale in their aggregate, are such luxuries. Secondly, there may be large-scale substitution of capital for labour in tertiary production in the course of economic progress. Thirdly, the concept of the income elasticity of demand applied to a whole economy raises problems of aggregation which render doubtful any universal proposition about changes in its average value in conditions of change and economic growth; and this is particularly doubtful when relative factor prices and the distribution of incomes change.

14. For reasons already mentioned in Section I the distributive task in the early stages of economic development is likely to be expensive in terms of *all* resources. A considerable volume of trading and transport is necessary to develop and sustain an exchange economy at an early stage of its development; it is an essential prerequisite for the development of specialisation and thus to the raising of productivity in primary production. Thus the proportion of resources engaged in tertiary production, notably in trade and transport, is likely to be high. It is possible that this proportion may fall at certain stages because the distributive task becomes relatively

easier and less expensive in resources as the economy develops. The task may become lighter with the growth of internal security, the development and improvement of communications and the growth and stabilisation of markets, all of which contribute towards more regular and continuous commercial contacts, more intensive use of available resources in distribution and an increase in the size of trading units. These improvements are likely to have differential effects on productivity in various types of economic activity. It is not unlikely that trade and transport may be particularly favourably affected, and thus that the proportion of resources engaged in them may decline. This decline may continue until the fall is arrested by the possibly increasing volume of other kinds of tertiary products (including more elaborate distributive services) which may be called for at higher levels of real income.

Tertiary production, as it is usually understood, comprises a heterogeneous collection of different services. Some of these are qualitatively indispensable through economic development and quantitatively important at an early stage; others are not indispensable at all stages and are quantitatively important only in more advanced economies. The term "tertiary" carries the misleading suggestion that all these services belong to the latter category of luxuries.

15. There is no *a priori* reason to believe that as wealth increases a greater proportion of the luxuries consumed must be products of tertiary activities. The durable consumer goods of the North American economies provide numerous examples on a large scale of heavy expenditures on the products of secondary activities with growing wealth. Expensive motor cars, jewelry, works of art, mass produced but high-grade textiles and hand-made bespoke clothes and shoes are products of secondary activities.[3]

16. The proportion of all resources in tertiary production will not provide an index of economic progress. Moreover, even if it did it would not follow that the proportion of occupied labour engaged in tertiary production must rise with economic progress. This proposition would be valid only if additionally it were legitimate to assume that labour and other productive reasources were employed in tertiary production in fixed proportions. This would be true only if substitution were not possible in the whole range of tertiary production, or if the relative terms upon which labour and other factors of production could be obtained remained unchanged throughout the whole course of economic progress. These assumptions are inadmissible. Technical possibilities of substitution between productive resources are obviously possible in tertiary production; and clearly the terms on which labour and capital are available are certain to change in a growing economy.

In Section I examples have been given to show the emphasis in the use of labour rather than capital in tertiary production in an under-developed economy. An example has also been given (the trade in used containers) to show how a tertiary activity expands with a lavish use of labour to make

---

[3]Perhaps more fancifully purchases of fur coats, oysters, caviare, lobsters, pheasants and orchids sustain hunting, fishing and farming which are primary activities.

good a shortage in the products of secondary production. Conversely, examples abound in more advanced industrialised economies where capital replaces labour in tertiary activities and where secondary production expands to economise on labour-intensive tertiary activities. There are familiar examples on a large scale in domestic services, laundry and repair services, and restaurant and retailing services, where capital equipment is now used instead of labour. The purchase of pre-cooked or prepared canned or processed food, or of paper cups and plates intended for one use only, represents an extension of secondary production to replace the tertiary activities in the kitchen. The mass substitution of capital for labour in tertiary activity in North America is as striking as the reverse substitution in West Africa.[4]

17. The neglect of the "substitution effect" destroys the general validity of the quantitative law connecting society's real income and the proportion of occupied population in tertiary production. Technical progress may greatly affect the demand for labour in primary, secondary and tertiary production, the possibilities of substitution between labour and other resources and the relative supply prices of productive resources.

Changes in relative factor prices and differential rates of technical progress in different branches of production will also affect the relative prices at which different luxuries (that is, goods or services with relatively high income elasticities of demand whether the products of primary, secondary or tertiary production) there would be a tendency for consumers to substitute luxuries which are produced by secondary production to those produced by tertiary production.[5]

18. In any society it is unlikely that all members spend the same proportion of their incomes on tertiary products. Differences may arise either because of differences in incomes or because of differences in tastes and individual circumstances. The share of the total national expenditure on tertiary products is obviously an average for the population as a whole. There is no ground for assuming a unique relationship between changes in this average and the changes in national income. Indeed, this average may well fall if the bulk of any increase in the national income accrues to members whose relative expenditure on tertiary products is below the average. In these circumstances the average can be pulled down, even though the income elasticity of demand of each member for tertiary products exceeds unity (which, of course, is by no means necessary). This is a very likely contingency in societies such as India and China, where a large proportion of the population live near starvation levels and where there are great differences in the proportion of individual incomes spent on tertiary products. If in such communities there is a general increase in productivity the proportion of the total national expenditure devoted to the products of primary and secondary activity is almost certain to increase. The same

[4]Of course even in West Africa the time may come when eight hours of a woman's time may be more valuable than the profit margin on the sale of three beer bottles.
[5]There is no a priori reason why technical progress should always be relatively more rapid in primary and secondary production than in tertiary production. But even if it were, it would support Mr. Clark's generalisation only if the possibility of substitution mentioned in the text is disregarded.

increase in productivity is likely to reduce the superfluity of very cheap labour formerly available for employment in certain types of tertiary activity, notably domestic service, petty trade and menial tasks generally, and may thus accentuate the relative decline in tertiary activity.

A reduction in the national average expenditure on tertiary products may also be brought about as a result of other causes not necessarily connected with increasing productivity. Thus graduated taxation and social-security payments may reduce the share of national expenditure on tertiary products through their effects on the pattern of demand and on the supply price of labour.

19. An important practical conclusion follows from the possibility that there may be a fall in the average proportion of expenditure on products of a relatively high income elasticity of demand with an increase in income if this proposition is extended internationally. If a large proportion of an increase in world income accrues to countries or to individuals who spend a smaller proportion than the world average on products of a luxury type it follows that the demand for luxuries would suffer a relative decline. This would tend to turn the terms of trade in favour of the producers of relative necessities and against the producers of relative luxuries. On an international scale the luxuries would be mainly the products of industrialised countries. There is implicit in this possibility a threat to the standard of living of some of these countries. It reinforces the more familiar argument based on population increase, especially in the primary producing countries. The relative demand for the essentials of life can clearly increase either because there are more mouths to feed or because an increase in incomes accrues largely to the relatively poor.[6]

20. The foregoing analysis may now be summarised. Even if acceptable statistics were found which should show that the proportion of tertiary activities has increased in particular countries with economic progress the findings would not be evidence of any necessary or predictable tendency. Tertiary production is an aggregation of many dissimilar activities, including domestic service, government service, transport, retail and wholesale distribution, entertainment, education and others. There is no reason why the demand for every one of these should follow a common trend. The only feature common to all tertiary production is that the output is non-material. This does not appear to provide a logical category of significance in the analysis of demand or of economic progress. Moreover, on the supply side the proportion of the labour force in tertiary production depends upon a number of different forces, the individual and total effect of which is in no way unambiguously determined by secular changes in the national income. Thus any observed correlation between economic progress and occupational distribution should be regarded as more in the nature of a statistical accident than as an indication or proof of a significant economic law.

[6]The two cases differ in their effects. Thus where there is a mere increase in numbers average income per head must fall, and those whose terms of trade are adversely affected are necessarily worse off absolutely. In the other case average income per head must rise, and those whose terms of trade are adversely affected need not necessarily be worse off absolutely.

IV

21. The empirical verification seems to be based upon occupational statistics which generally show both a high proportion of the occupied population in tertiary industries in advanced countries compared with underdeveloped countries and also an increasing proportion in time series for individual developing countries. These types of comparison seem to be vitiated principally on two counts. First, occupational statistics cannot take into account important difficulties arising out of imperfect economic specialisation. Secondly, the comparability of these statistics is affected by shifts of labour between unpaid and paid activities.

22. Clear-cut occupational classifications are inappropriate in under-developed countries where specialisation is imperfect. We are not concerned with possible inadequacies in the coverage and the arithmetical accuracy of the statistics but with their significance as a picture of economic activities. As has already been stated in Section I above, in these economies statistics convey a false impression of activities by concentrating on one activity of the head of the household to the exclusion of his other activities and of those of the other members of his household.[1] Over a considerable period of development many activities, especially trading, porterage and domestic service, would not be regarded as separate occupations either by official enumerators or by the subjects themselves. This applies particularly where occupations are carried on by part-time workers or dependents. As specialisation becomes more definite and pronounced and as these activities are carried out by specialists, the performers and their performance are more easily identified and recognised and their quantitative extent looms larger, possibly much larger, in occupational statistics, even though in total the volume of these activities may be unchanged or even reduced.

23. It would seem that the classification of economic activities into three types, while superficially convenient and clear, conceals large arbitrary elements which greatly reduce its value. The activities of the agricultural producer selling his crops can be regarded partly as primary and partly as tertiary; this is particularly evident where he sells to the final consumer. Yet until they are taken over by an intermediary his activities will be regarded as primary. Where the intermediary is a member of the family the activity may continue to be classed as primary. Its tertiary character is likely to be recognised only when the intermediary is an independent middleman. Since the emergence of an intermediary is likely to reduce the total effort in marketing a given volume of produce, tertiary activity may appear to be increasing at a time when it is actually decreasing.

It should not be thought that these difficulties of classification disappear entirely in more advanced economies. On a smaller scale similar difficulties appear in the classification of the activities of different departments of a manufacturing firm or of most forms of large-scale enterprise. Again, the activities of the cobbler and the milliner are likely to be classified as tertiary when these are carried out in establishments (shops) dealing with

[1] It is not even certain on what criteria the principal activity of the head of the household is chosen for statistical purposes.

the public. Yet under factory conditions the activities would be treated as secondary production. A classification of economic activity which is tacitly based on a particular assumed but undefined degree of specialisation and disintegration of functions appears to have little value for economic analysis or statistics. When census material is used it is more than likely that the assumed degree of specialisation differs between countries and periods.

24. The difficulty of classifying and comparing economic activity where there are differences in the degree of occupational specialisation largely undermines the statistical approach to the study of the relationship between occupational distribution and economic progress. There is much scattered evidence of the importance of some of the main tertiary activities in underdeveloped societies to-day,[ ] as well as in earlier periods in the history of Great Britain and Western Europe, especially when the services of part-time workers and dependants are also considered.[ ] However, because of the inherent statistical difficulty meaningful quantification seems to be impossible either in support or in refutation of Mr. Clark's generalisation, both with reference to a time series for one country and with reference to international comparisons.

25. The substitution of unpaid labour, with or without capital, for paid labour (or vice versa) is a form of substitution which affects the proportion of occupied labour in tertiary production and which illustrates and emphasises a conceptual difficulty present in a wide range of problems of economic statistics, particularly of indices of economic welfare. Such substitution takes place at all levels of economic progress, and not necessarily in the same direction at any given level. An obvious example in an advanced economy is the substitution of the activities of the household for those of the paid domestic servant; conversely, the household may frequently purchase the services of restaurants, laundries and repair agencies. Economic progress provides no general indication of the direction in which the shift between paid and unpaid labour will take place. Retail trade provides examples. In a poor economy the poverty of consumers does not allow them to buy in advance of requirements and to store their purchases. The tasks of holding stocks and of breaking bulk into the small quantities required for almost daily consumption devolve upon the paid intermediary. In these instances the activities of middlemen arise in response to the needs of poor consumers, to whom they secure access to commodities which would otherwise be outside their reach. By contrast, in advanced economies to-day housewives may store substantial quantities of consumer goods, especially of food, and may actually break bulk themselves. This development has gone far in North America. The tertiary activity remains, but unpaid labour of consumers and their own capital are being substituted for the services of the intermediary.

[ ]In this respect conditions in West Africa are not exceptional. The large number of full-time or part-time domestic and menial servants in India and the Middle East is another obvious example.
[ ]Thus there may have been a declining proportion of labour in tertiary activity in the early part of the industrial revolution with a rapid growth in factory production, particularly when allowance is made for paid domestic service performed by dependent members of agricultural households.

The examples in the preceding paragraph underline the arbitrariness of certain distinctions which are fundamental to national income and employment statistics. The shifting lines of demarcation suggest the advisability of caution in the use of such statistics as indices of economic welfare or as the basis of extrapolation.

LAND AND THE PEASANTS

27. Land Reform: Defects in Agrarian Structure and Obstacles to Economic Development

United Nations*

AGRARIAN STRUCTURE IN UNDER-DEVELOPED COUNTRIES

To a very large extent, the problem of the under-developed countries of the world is the problem of the poverty of their farm populations. Unduly low standards of living in rural areas are not confined to the under-developed countries; they can be found also in countries which have reached a high level of economic development. But in the under-developed countries the problem is of a different dimension, because the economy of these countries is mainly agricultural. Table 1 shows the proportion of agricultural population to total population in Asia, Africa, Central and South America as compared with the proportion in North America and Europe.

Table 1. Proportion of World Population in Agriculture, 1949*

AREA	TOTAL POPULATION (MILLIONS)	AGRICULTURAL POPULATION (MILLIONS)	AGRICULTRAL POPULATION AS PERCENTAGE OF TOTAL
North America[1]	163	33	20
Europe	391	129	33
Oceania	12	4	33
South America	107	64	60
Central America[2]	50	33	67
Asia	1,255	878	70
Africa	198	146	74
World total	2,177	1,285	59

*Source: Food and Agriculture Organization of the United Nations, *Yearbook of Food and Agriculture*, 1950, page 15.
[1]Canada and the United States.
[2]Including Mexico.

Of the total population of the world, some 60 per cent, or almost 1,300 million people, are dependent upon agriculture. Of these, over 1,000 million live in Asia, Africa, Central and South America, and only 162 million in Europe and North America. Whereas in Europe only one person out of three, and in North America only one person in five, is dependent on agriculture, in Asia and Africa three out of every four obtain their living from the land.

*From *Land Reform: Defects in Agrarian Structure and Obstacles to Economic Development*, 1951.

In the predominantly agricultural countries, the level of output per acre is generally lower than it is in the predominantly industrial countries; the level of output per person in agriculture is very much lower, because, generally speaking, the density of the farm population per acre is much greater, while the average yield per acre is less. As a long-term trend, these differences in productivity tend to become greater. The following table shows comparative levels of productivity in the agricultural and industrialized areas, by continents, before and after the Second World War.

Table 2. Productivity of the Agricultural Population by Continents and for the World, Pre-war and 1947–48*

Continent	Yield Per Hectare			Yield Per Person in Agriculture		
	Pre-war (Metric Tons)	1947–48	1947–48 as Per Cent of Pre-war	Pre-war (Metric Tons)	1947–48	1947–48 as Per Cent of Pre-war
World average	1.24	1.30	105	0.42	0.42	100
North and Central America	1.07	1.50	140	1.80	2.57	143
South America	1.28	1.39	109	0.58	0.48	83
Europe	1.51	1.34	89	1.04	0.88	85
Oceania	1.06	1.20	113	1.94	2.38	123
Asia	1.26	1.20	95	0.24	0.22	92
Africa	0.77	0.73	95	0.12	0.12	100

*Source: Food and Agriculture Organization of the United Nations, *Monthly Bulletin of Food and Agricultural Statistics*, vol. 2, No. 9, September 1949; arranged in order of yield per hectare in 1947–48.
¹Excluding the Union of Soviet Socialist Republics.

The differences in productivity per person in agriculture give some indication of the range of difference in rural living standards. Where the output per person in agriculture averages approximately 2½ tons, as it does in North America, the standard of living of the farm population will clearly be higher than where it is less than one-quarter of a ton, as in Asia, or one-eighth of a ton, as in Africa.

The causes of low productivity in agriculture and of low standards of living of the farm population are many: poor soils and unfavourable climates; backward techniques and inadequate equipment; excessively high densities of rural population; low prices received by the farmer. All these are important in varying degrees.

Among the most important factors which affect rural living standards is the agrarian structure. This term is here used to mean the institutional framework of agricultural production. It includes, in the first place, land tenure, the legal or customary system under which land is owned; the distribution of ownership of farm property between large estates and peasant farms or among peasant farms of various size; land tenancy, the system under which land is operated and its product divided between operator and owner; the organization of credit, production and marketing; the mechanism through which agriculture is financed; the burden imposed on rural populations by governments in the form of taxation; and the services supplied by governments to rural populations, such as technical advice and educational facilities, health services, water supply and communications.

The different forms of agrarian structure and different systems of land tenure which exist in the under-developed countries of the world are the result in part of different forms of society and in part of the influence of foreign institutions. In many of the under-developed regions of the world, tribal or feudal institutions still form the social framework, even though under European influence the economic and political basis of tribal and feudal society has changed.

Since this report is concerned primarily with the effects of different forms of agrarian structure on the economic development of the societies in which they occur, neither the historical origins nor the legal forms are touched on, except where these relate to one of the many ways in which agrarian structure may be an obstacle to economic development and economic welfare. The agrarian structure may reduce the standard of living of the peasant by imposing on him exorbitant rents or high interest rates; it may deny him the incentive or opportunity to advance and it may check investment because it offers him no security; it may lead to the prevalence of farms which are too small to be efficient units of production or too large to cultivate intensively. The influence of the land tenure system varies greatly from region to region and there are no defects which are present to the same degree in all the under-developed countries, though certain ones are very widespread.

In the following sections of this chapter some of the outstanding features of the land systems in the under-developed countries are considered; no attempt has been made to deal with every aspect of the subject as defined above. Only the more important features have been selected, for the purpose of indicating their effects in broad outline; those selected are common to more than one country and more than one continent. Examples have been chosen from different countries where the problems of development arise in an acute form, and where unsatisfactory agrarian structures have particularly noticeable effects. The instances which are given are examples only; they could be greatly multiplied. Nor are the countries selected to illustrate different aspects of agrarian problems necessarily the ones in which these problems are most acute, since lack of data strictly limits the number of examples in any particular case. In many countries the necessary data for analysis of the agrarian structure—statistics of farm population, agricultural income, land ownership or size of farms, for example— are lacking. Wherever possible, official sources have been used, but since for some countries such material is not available, estimates made by independent observers have necessarily been used in some cases.

Farm Size and Layout

The outstanding feature of the agrarian structure in many under-developed countries is the extremely small size of the average farm holding. The definition of what acreage constitutes a small farm varies greatly from country to country. In most parts of the United States and in England a farm of 30 hectares (75 acres) would be considered a small farm, while in eastern Europe, where the average size of farm holdings is 5 hectares

(12½ acres), or in some Asian countries, where it is one hectare (2½ acres), such a farm would be considered very large indeed. Nor is it possible to establish a general criterion of what size of farm constitutes a minimum size for economic operation, since this standard must necessarily vary with the type of cultivation and land utilization in different countries. Clearly the minimum size for economic operation will be smaller if the plough is drawn by bullocks than if it is drawn by a tractor.

Uneconomic holdings. In many under-developed countries, however, the question of what acreage constitutes a minimum economic holding, in the sense of what acreage will permit full utilization of the farmer's equipment, is less important than the question of what acreage provides a subsistence minimum, either directly by growing food or indirectly by providing an income from commercial crops. The standard is measured not in terms of a necessary scale of operation, but of a minimum standard of food consumption. Even on this basis, acreage alone is not a sufficient criterion, since there are great differences in the intensity of cultivation, and differences in cropping rates: an acre of land in an irrigated double-cropped river valley in India may produce six times as much as an acre of non-irrigated single-cropped land.

None the less, even when allowance is made for differences in intensity of cultivation, it is possible to state that there are many countries in which large numbers of farms are too small to provide a subsistence minimum for the cultivator and his family, or to provide them with full employment; and too small also to permit of any improvement in methods of cultivation. This feature of the agrarian structure may be the result of the extreme subdivision of farms resulting from the pressure of population on the land, or of inequality in the distribution of land ownership; or it may result from the operation of both these factors together. Extreme subdivision of farm units tends to promote concentration of ownership and increase inequality in the distribution of property, because the small owners are generally unable to gain a subsistence from their farms, and in consequence become indebted to landowners and money-lenders who thereby acquire possession of the land.[1]

Where the density of the agricultural population is extremely high, the average farm holding is as a rule extremely small. The relation of farm population to the cultivated area varies greatly between different countries, and between different continents. Appendix tables I to III show the relation of total population to arable land in under-developed countries (figures for the farm population cannot be given, since for many countries occupational statistics are not available). From these tables it appears that the countries where density of total population in relation to the area of arable land is highest are, in order of highest density, Japan, Egypt, Haiti, Korea, Indonesia, Lebanon, Indochina, Ceylon, China and India.[2] In all these countries there is less than one-third of a hectare (less than

[1] See section on credit and agricultural indebtedness.
[2] Three Latin American countries, Bolivia, Colombia and Peru, show a similar relationship. But here the area of arable land per person is not a sufficient indication of excessive density of farm population as it is in Asia, because pasture farming plays a much larger part in the economy, and also because much cultivable land is not classified as arable.

one acre) per head of total population. The significance of these figures is clear if the relationship between rural population and land resources is considered on the basis of estimates of the rural population. Japan has a farm population of 34.5 million on 5.9 million hectares of arable land.[3] Egypt has a rural population of between 14 and 15 million on 2.5 million hectares; in Indonesia, Java and Madura have a rural population of between 45 and 50 million on 10 million hactares of cultivated land; the average size of holdings in 1938 was 0.86 hectare. India has a rural population of 285 million living on 98 million hectares of arable land. Though the density of the rural population per hectare in India is lower than in the three countries mentioned above, the effects of a high density on the living standard are more acute, in that the level of productivity per hectare is far lower; crop yields are much smaller, and double cropping is only practised on a small proportion of the land, whereas in Egypt, Japan and Java, yields are very high and double cropping is general. In China, the density of the rural population is extremely high in many regions: surveys of 17,000 farms in twelve provinces reveal a farm population of some 1,500 persons per square mile, or half an acre of land for each person on farms.[5] Thus the average density in these regions is twice as high as in India, but average crop yields are also twice as high.

In these overcrowded conditions, the average farm holding would be small, even if all the land were equally distributed. Where the average holding is small, the greater the degree of inequality in the size of farm holdings, the larger will be the number of farm units below average size, and the larger therefore the number of holdings below the subsistence minimum. In Japan, for example, the average size of farm is one hectare, or 2½ acres; the recent reform has made farm sizes much more equal, yet 41 per cent of farm holdings are still under 1.2 acres.[6]

In India, where the problem of uneconomic holdings assumes vast proportions, the average size of farms in most states is between 4 and 5 acres. It is estimated that an economic holding in India must have a minimum of five acres, of which 2.3 acres must be wellwatered land.[7] Since only about one-third of India's total sown acreage can count on adequate rainfall or irrigation, there are hardly two acres of wellwatered land available per average holding, so that an additional four acres of dry land would be required to make up an economic holding. Thus even the average acreage of a farm holding falls below the subsistence minimum; and a large proportion of holdings falls below the average.

Table 3 shows the percentage of farm holdings which fall below the average in different Indian states. It should be noted that these figures

[3] This figure is somewhat larger than that given for the cultivated area on pages 54 and 55 because it includes the whole of Japan. Supreme Command, Allied Power, *Japanese Agricultural Land Statistics,* Natural Resources Report 101 (Tokyo, 1948), page 11.
[4] Estimated as 80 per cent of total population, as reported in the census of 1951.
[5] J. Lossing Buck, "Fact and Theory about China's Land," *Foreign Affairs,* (New York, October 1949).
[6] Supreme Command, Allied Powers, *Japanese Land Reform Program,* Natural Resources Report 127 (Tokyo, 1950) page 86. Prior to the reform, 34 per cent of Japanese farms were under 1.2 acres.
[7] M. B. Nanavati and J. J. Anjaria, *India's Rural Problem* (Bombay, 1945).

refer to holdings and not to properties, and include tenants as well as owners. The figures indicate the scale of operations, not of ownership, and show the effect of population pressure and inequality in the size of holdings, not the much greater inequality in ownership of land.

*Table 3. India: Percentage of Families with Different Sizes of Land Holdings**

PROVINCES	NUMBER OF ACRES PER HOLDING			
	UNDER 2	2 TO 5	5 TO 10	10 AND OVER
Assam[1]	38.9	27.4	21.1	12.6
Bombay:[2]				
Gujarat	27.5	25.7	22.3	24.5
Deccan	19.8	16.7	18.8	44.7
Carnatic	12.2	19.2	21.7	46.9
West Bengal	34.7	28.7	20.0	16.6
Madhya Pradesh (Central Provinces)[3]	49.0		21.0	30.0
Orissa	50.0	27.0	13.0	10.0
Madras	51.0	31.0	7.0	11.0
Uttar Pradesh (United Provinces)[4]	55.8	25.4	12.8	6.0
Punjab[5]	37.9[6]	17.9[7]	20.5	23.7

*Source: *Report of the Congress Agrarian Reform Committee.*
[1]Based on a sample survey of 2,613 families in Darrang District, Assam. The size of the holdings in the original data were in *bighas*; the converted figures are only approximate.
[2]Based on a sample survey by Shri Sankpal, Director, Bureau of Economics and Statistics, Bombay; indicates percentage of cultivators instead of families.
[3]Figures based on information collected in 1938; indicates percentage of tenants.
[4]Percentage of cultivators.
[5]Figures refer to undivided Punjab; source, P. A. Wadia and K. T. Merchant, *Our Economic Problem* (Bombay, 1946).
[6]Under two and one-half acres.
[7]Two and one-half to five acres.

These figures may be supplemented by the estimates in the report of the Indian Famine Commission, which calculated the gross output of grain crops on peasant holdings in different states. According to these figures, the average production per holding is about two tons in Madras, Bengal and Uttar Pradesh, and about three tons in the Punjab. The proportion of the total number of holdings producing less than one ton was 74 per cent in Madras, 50 per cent in Bengal and Bombay; in Uttar Pradesh, 50 per cent produced under 1½ tons.[8] When it is recalled that a large section of the rural population of India are neither owners nor tenants and do not have any proprietary interest in the land they cultivate, the magnitude of the problem of the uneconomic holding is evident.

Where estates are large units of operation, and not merely large landholdings leased to tenants in small lots, the average size of peasant farms is usually very small. The effect of this type of agrarian structure on farm sizes is shown most clearly by the statistics in Table 4, showing the distribution of land in Egypt. These figures show the distribution of property, as

[8]*Report of the Indian Famine Commission,* vol. II, part IV: *Land Tenures in India,* reprinted as an extract from the *Report of the Indian Society of Agricultural Economics* (Vora & Company, Bombay, 1946).

Table 4. *Distribution of Land Ownership in Egypt, 1947*

SIZE OF HOLDING	NUMBER OF OWNERS	PER CENT OF TOTAL	AREA OWNED (FEDDANS)	PER CENT OF TOTAL
1 feddan and under[1]	1,921,000	72.1	785,000	13.1
1 to 5 feddans	587,000	22.1	1,219,000	20.4
5 to 50 feddans	143,000	5.4	1,774,000	29.7
Over 50 feddans	11,000	0.4	2,200,000	36.8
Total	2,662,000	100.0	5,978,000	100.0

[1]One feddan equals 1.038 acres or 0.42 hectare.

distinct from the scale of operation, which would be somewhat affected by the practice of leasing part of the large holdings to tenants. In addition to approximately two million cultivators owning less than one feddan, there is a large class of landless labourers who work on large estates and own no land.

In greater or less degree, the problem of large numbers of extremely small farms affects India, parts of China, and all South East Asia except Burma. It is present also in the Caribbean countries, and in Egypt and Japan in an extreme degree. In so far as results from an excessively high density of rural population, it is not a problem which can be dealt with by change in the agrarian structure alone.

Though it is in the rurally over-populated countries that this problem assumes its most serious dimensions, farms of non-economic size can also be found in countries which do not suffer from great congestion on the land. In the Philippines, for example, the average size of farm holdings is four hectares (10 acres) but more than half the farms are under two hectares, because of extremely unequal distribution of ownership and because of the concentration of population in Luzon and the Visayan islands.

Even in countries of very extensive cultivation with large reserves of land, over-cultivated small holdings exist. Their part in the economy is a different one, in that the small holding may not be the sole source of the cultivator's income as it is in some parts of Asia, but a subsistence holding to supplement wages. Where such holdings are the sole source of the cultivator's income, they are usually over-cultivated. A recent report of the International Bank for Reconstruction and Development has drawn attention to the ill effects of *minifundia*.[9]

In the sparsely populated countries of South America, there would appear good reason to believe that many holdings are uneconomically large. In Argentina, 85 per cent of the privately held agricultural land is in estates larger than 500 hectares (1,250 acres), while 80 per cent of the farm population own no land.[10] Table 5 shows the distribution of land ownership in Brazil, a country where tenancy is not prevalent and where the distribution of property broadly indicates the scale of farming operations.

[9]See pages 20 and 21 [page 312 this edition].
[10]Wendell C. Gordon, *The Economy of Latin America* (New York, 1950), page 35.

Table 5. Classification of Farm Establishments in Brazil According to Size, 1940

SIZE OF HOLDING (HECTARES)	NUMBER OF ESTABLISHMENTS (THOUSANDS)	PER CENT OF TOTAL	Area Utilized for Agriculture TOTAL (THOUSANDS OF HECTARES)	PER CENT OF TOTAL	Cultivated Area (THOUSANDS OF HECTARES)	PER CENT OF TOTAL	NUMBER PERMANENTLY EMPLOYED (THOUSANDS)	PER CENT OF TOTAL
Under 5	414.4	21.8	1,092.7	0.6	762.6	4.1	1,153	11.4
5 to 20	555.8	29.2	6,358.3	3.2	2,586.0	13.7	2,047	20.1
20 to 100	659.7	34.6	28,554.6	14.4	6,370.8	33.8	3,447	33.9
100 to 500	212.3	11.1	44,609.2	22.6	4,891.0	26.0	2,248	22.1
500 to 1,000	31.5	1.7	21,575.8	10.9	1,572.9	8.3	589	5.8
1,000 and over	30.7	1.6	95,529.6	48.3	2,651.9	14.1	676	6.7
Total	1,904.4	100.0	197,720.2	100.0	18,835.2	100.0	10,160	100.0

Source: Agricultural census of Brazil.

Almost half the land is held in estates of over 1,000 hectares, and the half of the farms which are under 20 hectares in size account for less than 20 per cent of the cultivated area. A characteristic feature of the agrarian structure in Latin America is the large area of grazing land on the large estates, shown in the table by the large share of the total agricultural area (as distinct from the cultivated area) held by establishments of more than 1,000 hectares. The ownership of land on this scale tends to prevent more intensive cultivation and better forms of land utilization.[11]

Fragmentation of holdings. The splitting up of a farm holding into numerous different plots scattered over a wide area is a feature of the field layout in countries at all levels of economic development. It is not associated with any particular form of land tenure. It may be seen in countries as highly developed as Switzerland, France and southern Germany.[12] In eastern Europe, notably in Poland and in the Balkan countries, the process has gone to extreme length; a farm of twelve acres, in Yugoslavia, for instance, may be divided into thirty separate plots. It is a widespread condition in Asia, particularly in India and China, and in the Middle Eastern countries.

Fragmentation has several causes. It originated in remote times from the traditional field layout in which holdings were divided into several strips located in different parts of a village. In the course of time these original strips have been divided and subdivided, as a result of the increase of the farm population, and of inheritance laws which encourage the subdivision of land among many heirs. In western Europe, where pressure of rural population is not acute, the principle of succession established in the Code Napoleon exercises a major influence, while in eastern Europe and in Asia, the pressure of population would appear to be the predominant cause, though laws of succession reinforce an inevitable trend.

[11]See page 19 [page 311 this edition].
[12]Food and Agriculture Organization of the United Nations, *Consolidation of Fragmented Agricultural Holdings.* Agricultural Studies No. 11, prepared by B. O. Binns, (Washington, D.C., September 1950).

The evils of fragmentation need no emphasis: waste of time and effort, the impossibility of rational cultivation are obvious effects. None the less, the consolidation of holdings is not an easy reform to carry through. The conservatism of the peasant is one obstacle, the high cost per acre of surveying and exchanging many small plots is another. Even in a country so advanced as Switzerland the process of consolidation has been slow.

In the under-developed countries consolidation of holdings has been attempted with some success in Jordan, where it accompanied the surveying and registration of land, that is, settlement of title,[13] and also in Lebanon. In India, a degree of success in the consolidation of holdings has been achieved by the co-operative method, begun on a voluntary basis in the Punjab in 1921, and continued there and in Madhya Pradesh (formerly the Central Provinces) and Uttar Pradesh (formerly the United Provinces) under legislation which enforces consolidation on a partly compulsory basis, when a majority of the farmers (usually two-thirds) agrees to a scheme.

The method of consolidation through co-operative societies is as follows: The right-holders in a village form a "consolidation of holdings society" and get themselves registered as such. The members undertake to agree to a scheme of re-allocation of land approved by a percentage of members. This percentage is generally two-thirds of the members holding not less than two-thirds of the entire cultivated land in the village. In actual practice, however, no scheme is ordinarily enforced unless it is acceptable to every member. All holdings of members are thereafter pooled. The managing committee then places, subject to the approval of the general meeting, each field in its appropriate class and draws up a scheme of re-allocation in consultation with the members concerned. In the re-allocation, an effort is made to ensure that each member gets the same area and classes of land in compact blocks as he had originally in scattered holdings. After the scheme has been approved new blocks are marked out and necessary steps are taken to have possession redistributed. Separate staff trained in revenue work is provided by the Government to assist these societies, a part of the cost, usually based on the area consolidated, being borne by the members of the societies.[14]

By 1949 about 1,600,000 acres had been consolidated in the Punjab, Madhya Pradesh and Uttar Pradesh, and the number of plots within this area had been reduced from 4,250,000 to 646,000.[15] Very obvious advantages have been gained. An orderly arrangement of fields has taken the place of the former patchwork of divided holdings. The chief benefit of consolidation in the Punjab is that it has enabled owners to irrigate their holdings by sinking new wells. Improvements such as raising of embankments, levelling of land, saving of water and digging of manure pits have also been made. In some consolidated villages "better living co-operatives" have been successfully started.

[13]See pages 25 and 26 [pages 316 and 317 this edition].
[14]Extract from Note on Consolidation of Holdings in India, prepared by the Government of India for the Food and Agriculture Organization of the United Nations.
[15]These figures and the information which follows are from Note on Consolidation of Holdings in India, and from Note on Consolidation of Holdings in Pakistan, prepared by the Government of Pakistan for the Food and Agriculture Organization of the United Nations.

In spite of these advantages, the process of consolidation by this method has proved extremely slow. Much demonstration and persuasion were needed to convince the villagers of the benefits to be obtained. Apart from this psychological difficulty, the complications of the land tenure system, which imposes various liens and mortgages on different plots, were a major hindrance. It should be noted that consolidation by the co-operative method has been successful in the Punjab, partly because the configuration of the land is more favourable and also because peasant proprietorship prevails; in East Bengal, where the landlord-tenant system is predominant, no substantial contribution could be made by this method owing to the obstacles provided by the land system.

A new approach to the problem was made by the Bombay Prevention of Fragmentation and Consolidation of Holdings Act of 1947 and by the East Punjab Holdings (Consolidation and Prevention of Fragmentation) Act of 1948. These acts empower the Government to define the standard of area for a minimum size of plot, prohibit the transfer or partition of land which will create new "fragments" of land less than the standard size, and empower the Government also to introduce and enforce schemes for consolidation, without any reference to the willingness of landlords.

Tenancy

Tenancy is a feature of the land tenure system in many under-developed countries. The proportion of tenants to the number of farmers varies widely from one country to another. In Asia, the proportion as a rule is very high. As a broad generalization, it would appear that in Burma, China, India and Japan, prior to the recent changes, about half of the land was worked by tenants cultivating small holdings leased to them by landowners and that the majority of the cultivators were either tenants or part owners and part tenants.[16] In South East Asia, tenancy is an important feature of the land system in Burma, Cochin-China, the Philippines and central Thailand.

For the countries of the Middle East no estimate of the proportion of tenants to owners can be made owing to the lack of statistical data. There are some regions where peasant proprietorship is established. In Cyprus, Egypt, Lebanon and Turkey most of the farmers own land. Apart from these countries, tenancy is widely prevalent. In Syria, it is estimated that about half of the land is owned by large landowners, and cultivated by small share tenants; in southern Iraq, large landowners own most of the land, letting it to share tenants through a series of intermediary lessees. In Iran, also, tenancy is the prevalent form. It is estimated that only 15 per cent of the claimed land[17] belongs to small holders, as against about half to some 100,000 large landowners, the balance consisting of state domain or religious endowments. A sample survey conducted in 1949 showed that 60 per cent of rural families owned no land at all, 25 per cent owned less than one hectare and 10 per cent between one and three hectares.[18] . . .

[16] See chapter 2.
[17] Large areas are not claimed, and the ownership of many plots is in dispute.
[18] Gideon Hadary, "The Agrarian Reform Problem in Iran," *Middle East Journal* (spring issue, 1951).

Although there is much variation in practice, some examples of the level of rents may be given. The most commonly practised division of the crop in India (before the recent changes) was half to the landlord and half to the peasant cultivator, who provided his own labour and that of his bullocks, while the landlord provided the land, and in some cases, half the seed.[19] In Indonesia, the Philippines and Thailand, equal sharing of the crop between tenant and landlord seems to be a common practice. Rents in Ceylon vary from one-sixth to one-half of the crop, depending on the region and the type of crop.

In countries of the Middle East, 50 per cent is the usual division in Syria for dry crops; in southern Iraq, where landowner and sub-landlord provide water, their share in the crop may be higher. In Iran, there is great variation from district to district in the share taken by the landowner. For dry crops, which are grown only in certain parts of the country, the landowner's share, when land only is provided, varies widely. For irrigated crops, when the landowner provides water and the peasant labour, seed and oxen, there is also great variation: one-third, one-half, and two-thirds are customary divisions.

A description of the actual method by which rent is collected may serve to show the essential features of the share rent system as it is practised in these countries.[20]

In those countries of Latin America where land is plentiful and labour scarce, share rents are considerably lower than they are in Asia and in the Middle East. Little statistical information on the subject is available, but from the 1948 legislation in Argentina for the compulsory reduction of rents to 20 per cent of the gross crop, it appears that before the introduction of the law the customary share of the gross crop payable as rent was 38 per cent for corn and 36 per cent for wheat. In the countries of Latin America where land is less plentiful, rents are higher, and in some countries reach levels comparable with those prevailing in Asia.

The payment of rent in the form of fixed amounts of produce, or payment in fixed sums of money, are less common forms of tenancy in underdeveloped countries. From the standpoint of the tenant, these forms are clearly preferable, since with a fixed rental he has an incentive to increase production and he gains the full benefit of any improvement on the land in so far as his tenancy is secure. Fixed produce rents were until recently the customary form of payment in Burma[21] and in Japan; they are still prevalent in many parts of India. In Japan, rents were assessed each year in advance of the harvest, and varied from 50 per cent to 70 per cent of the gross product.[22]

Where payment of rent is made on a fixed cash basis, the entire burden of risk is passed on to the cultivator. Cash rents are not, however, a general feature of tenancy systems in under-developed countries, and, as a rule,

[19]*Report of the Indian Famine Commission*, vol. II, part IV, pages 25–26.
[20]*Cf.* A. K. Lambton, *Landlord and Peasant in Persia*, a study to be published by the Royal Institute of International Affairs, London.
[21]B. O. Binns, *Agricultural Economy in Burma* (Rangoon, 1948) page 17.
[22]Supreme Command, Allied Powers, *The Japanese Village in Transition*, Natural Resources Report 136, prepared by A. F. Raper (Tokyo, 1950), page 249.

are found only in certain regions and for special crops. Such rents are extremely high. An investigation in Madras, for example, showed that in the districts of Guntur and West Godavari rents of 300 to 350 rupees per acre were charged on lands growing tobacco, and rents of 400 to 500 rupees per acre on lands growing sugar cane.[23] In Egypt, a country of highly intensive farming and cash crop production, cash rent is the general form. Such rents are extremely high; in pre-war times they ranged from £E 4 per acre on newly reclaimed land to £E 10 per acre in the congested districts. During the war they rose in proportion to the price increase and in congested districts reached £E 25 per acre. These figures represent almost half the market value of the crops grown on an acre; most of the expenses of cultivation are borne by the tenant.

Labour rents are not a usual form of tenancy except in some countries of Latin America, in parts of India and in Iran. In Latin America, this form is common in Bolivia, Chile, Colombia, Ecuador, Peru and Venezuela, among estate labourers who receive a small piece of land from the estate owner in return for which they must work unpaid for a certain number of days per week. In remote regions of Iran, the feudal obligation of labour service on land cultivated by the landlord can still be exacted from villagers. In India, this form of payment is rare; it may be noted that the recent Bombay tenancy act prohibits it.[24]

Security of tenure. Cultivators who hold land under these forms of tenancy as a rule hold it on a customary basis, with no legal agreement to define their obligations. In India, the rights and obligations of tenants with occupancy rights are defined by legislation, but the actual cultivators, in many cases share-croppers, enjoy no such legal protection. Where customary rights are not recognized, there is great insecurity and great poverty among the share-croppers. In Burma, where holdings are generally larger than in India, and tenants are better off, there is also great insecurity; investigations in different parts of the country in the nineteen thirties showed that the number of tenants who had cultivated the same plot of land for more than three years represented, in most cases, only a quarter to a third of the total, while the number of those whose tenancy did not go back more than one year ranged between a sixth and a half.[25] In some countries of the Middle East, the peasant does not even cultivate the same plot of land from year to year; the landlord or his agent frequently gives the most fertile plots to favoured tenants who please him in one way or another. The peasant therefore has usually one aim, to get the best out of his land during his short tenancy, regardless of the effect on the fertility of the soil.

Great insecurity also characterizes the conditions of tenancy in Latin America. The term "tenant" in these regions covers many heterogeneous forms: the fixed money-rent tenant with some form of agreement; the tenant with a share-cropping arrangement of some type; paid migrant

---

[23]A. V. Sayana, *Agrarian Problems of Madras Province* (Madras, 1949).
[24]See page 53.
[25]J. Russell Andrus, *Burmese Economic Life* (Stanford University Press, California, 1947), page 72.

labourers who squat on small areas rent-free; permanent *colonos* or *inquilinos* settled on estates, paying for subsistence holdings by unpaid labour. Conditions of tenancy in all these forms are usually described as fluid or informal; there is possibly even less security than in Asia, because customary obligations are less powerful.

It is evident that the tenancy system in the conditions described above is a powerful obstacle to economic development, in three ways. In the first place, the tenant has little incentive to increase his output, since a large share in any such increase will accrue to the landowner, who has incurred no part of its cost. In the second place, the high share of the produce taken by the landowner may leave the peasant with a bare subsistence minimum, with no margin for investment; in a bad year, he gets more heavily in debt; in a good year, he can reduce his indebtedness. Thirdly, it means that wealth is held in the form of land, and that the accumulation of capital does not lead to productive investment. In Asia, the landowner is also a money-lender, and in this capacity depends more on interest on loans to small cultivators than on increased income from the improvement of land.

In such conditions it is important to emphasize that the existence of large-scale property ownership does not secure any of the advantages of large-scale operation or investment. The tenants secure no benefit of working with better equipment, or with better seed; their methods of work are the same as those of the small owner. Landowners are less interested in maintaining the fertility of the soil, or in increasing agricultural production, than in holding wealth in a secure form. Even in irrigated regions where the landowner in theory provides water, the actual maintenance of ditches or channels must be undertaken by the tenants themselves, under the supervision of sub-landlords or landowners' officials. In some countries, the landowners' share in the gross crop may not represent the sum total of the peasant's obligations; he may also have to surrender a further share to sub-landlords, or to undertake the transportation of the landowner's share in the crop.

Estates and Plantations

In the Caribbean, throughout South America, in South East Asia, in Ceylon and in parts of East Africa, the agrarian structure is dominated by large estates. Unlike the large landholdings of Asia and the Middle East, referred to in the preceding section, these estates are large centrally managed and operated units of production, employing paid labour. This type of farm organization exists in widely differing conditions: in regions with much unused land and sparse population, and in regions where there is a great shortage of land and an excess of labour. In the former setting, the large estate may be a cattle ranch, covering great areas of grazing land. In the second setting, it is a plantation, with highly intensive cultivation, a large investment of capital and large labour requirements per acre. In their social effects both types of estate have a common feature: they offer the farm population unsatisfactory conditions of employment, and no degree of responsibility or initiative in management. In their economic effects they differ widely and must be considered separately.

Large estates with extensive agriculture. This type of farm organization, the *latifundia,* is a special feature of the agrarian structure of Latin America. With the exception of parts of Costa Rica, El Salvador, Haiti and Mexico, large estates take up the greater part of the cultivable land area throughout the continent. In Latin America as a whole, about one and one-half per cent of the individual landholdings exceed 15,000 acres. The total of these holdings constitutes about 50 per cent of all agricultural land. While much of the land is not suitable for crop production, a substantial proportion consists of idle lands that have been held for generations. Large plantations are also included in these great land-holdings, but do not account for the greater part of the land so held. At the other extreme are the small landowners who practise subsistence farming on a few over-cultivated or unproductive acres. While there are also farmers with medium-sized holdings, the bulk of the remaining rural population consists of small tenants and landless labourers.

A peculiarity of the agrarian structure in Latin America is the absence of a clear line of division between the last two categories. In the more advanced countries, a proportion of the land is leased to tenant farmers on fixed rentals. But elsewhere tenancy arrangements are less systematized. When labour is scarce, squatters settle temporarily on the borders of an estate, cultivating a small area for their own requirements, and working on the estate without paying rent. A characteristic feature in many countries, notably in Bolivia, Chile, Guatemala and Peru, is the patron-tenant relationship, under which the tenants (*colonos*) receive a piece of land for cultivation in return for a specified number of days' work per week on the estate. This relationship is associated with a low social status and an extremely low living standard for the farm workers.

Clearly, high levels of productive efficiency and rising standards of living are not likely to be achieved in an agrarian structure of this kind. Some of the effects of the tenancy system on farm productivity have already been considered in the preceding section. Here attention may be drawn to the broad effects of this form of agrarian structure on the utilization of land.

One obvious effect of this type of structure is that agricultural production is not adjusted to the demand for food, particularly foods of high nutritional value. The prevalence of large estates devoted to extensive grazing prevents an expansion of food production to meet the needs of the urban population, as well as the needs of the rural population itself. Throughout Latin America there is a shortage of dairy produce, which could be overcome by the introduction of better breeding stock, more attention to soil conditions and better pasture management. Several South American countries, with a predominantly agricultural population and large land resources, import food for their urban population, part of which could be supplied by more intensive cultivation of the land, or by bringing idle land into cultivation. In Venezuela, for example, within easy reach of the capital now there are fertile regions utilized for extensive grazing which, with a different system of land tenure, could become a market garden area for Caracas. In other regions, all the produce from the areas of intensive cultivation on less fertile and steeply sloping hillsides has to be transported by human beings or pack animals across less intensively cultivated fertile areas to the town.[26]

The pattern of land utilization is thus the reverse of that which market conditions and natural resources require. The hillside land, which is best suited for pasture and woodland, is intensively cultivated for subsistence crops by hoe culture which destroys the top soil, while the valley floors, more suited for arable cultivation, are used for grazing. The report of the mission to Colombia of the International Bank for Reconstruction and Development has laid special emphasis on this problem:

> Some large-scale farms, particularly producers of sugar-cane and rice, appear to be quite efficient and to have gained high labour productivity through the use of considerable mechanized equipment. It must be recognized, however, that these farms also have the effect of denying landless families, or families with too little land to make a satisfactory living, access to land. Many large-scale farms that may be considered efficient in economic terms are not providing living standards for the families who live or work on them. For example, it would be quite unusual if the returns from a large farm, occupied by the owner and 24 workers (25 farm families altogether), were providing more than two or three of the families with enough income to be significant purchasing units or to maintain satisfactory levels of living. On the other hand, in many areas (for example, Nariño, Santander and Boyacá) the problem of *minifundia,* or excessive parcelization of the land into uneconomic patches, prevents efficient land use. Large numbers of farm families are trying to eke out an existence on too little land, often on slopes of 50 or even 100 per cent (45 degrees) or more. As a result, they exploit the land very severely, adding to erosion and other problems, and even so are not able to make a decent living. This pattern of land use is one of the most important causes of low labour productivity in agriculture and of resulting widespread poverty in rural areas.[27]

If the medium-sized farms played a larger part in the economy, there is reason to believe that the volume of agricultural production would rise, and that standards of living, both urban and rural, could be raised also. Provided that such farms could be established in the grazing lands, methods of land utilization could also be improved. In Brazil, the pattern of agricultural production would appear to be changing in favour of the small and medium-sized farms, of which the numbers are increasing, chiefly as a result of the tendency to sell off land from the older coffee plantations. Market conditions also favour this change. The only limiting factor to a further expansion of small and medium-sized holdings is everywhere the shortage of capital, which prevents the small tenants or subsistence cultivator from increasing the size of his holding. At present, however, the provision of capital to the small farmer is not adequately organized. Co-operative credit societies play very little part in the credit system.[28] If this obstacle were removed, the conditions for the development of family farms in many regions would be highly favourable. Shortage of land is not a limiting factor in most Latin American countries, and,

[26]Raymond E. Crist, "Land Tenure Problems in Venezuela," *American Journal of Economics and Sociology* (New York, January 1942).
[27]International Bank for Reconstruction and Development, *The Basis of a Development Program for Colombia* (Washington, D. C., 1950), page 63.
[28]See page 40, and pages 74 to 77.

given adequate credit facilities, farms in the more advanced countries should be able to attain an economic size. In the less advanced countries, and in non-cultivated areas, the provision of educational and technical assistance by the government and the extension of health services would be a necessary accompaniment of any change in the agrarian structure.

Plantations. Large estates which practise intensive farming cannot generally be said to impede economic development; on the contrary, large increases in land productivity and high yields per acre are usually a feature of the plantation system. The demand for a reform of the estate system in plantation economies is motivated by social considerations: the need for more equal distribution of income and greater possibilities of social advance.[29] In many regions today this type of agrarian structure

The sugar plantation economy of the West Indies is one example among many which might be given to the conflicts which now centre on this type of agrarian structure. In this region the disproportion between population and natural resources is very great. The density of the farm population in the islands is among the highest in the world, ranging from thirty to fifty persons in agriculture for every hundred acres of cultivated land. The cultivated land is owned predominantly by large estates, either centrally operated or leased to tenants on small holdings. Such holdings are fragmented and occupy only a minor part of the total area. The sugar industry has been subject to long periods of depression, in which estates have gone out of cultivation and unemployment has increased.

In this situation the demand for land reform has taken the form of a demand for land settlement, as a means of relieving unemployment, and as a means of improving the conditions of employment. That there is possible scope for increasing employment by the division of the sugar-cane plantations seems unlikely since the cultivation of sugar-cane requires an intensive use of labour to the acre. With the existing density of farm population it would appear that no reorganization of the agrarian structure is likely to increase the employment possibilities. None the less, from the social point of view, the plantation system is everywhere unpopular.

The sugar industry in the West Indies has reached a political impasse. It cannot continue on its present basis because that basis gives too much political offence. This offence shows itself not only in a general atmosphere of hostility, but also in strikes, riots, the burning of canes, and in some colonies even in uncertainty from year to year whether the state of labour relations will permit the whole crop to be taken off. This state of tension is a luxury which the West Indies cannot afford. New forms of organization must be tried, and must be tried urgently.[30]

Since the need for maintaining employment must be a paramount consideration in these overcrowded islands, whatever new forms of organization are created must aim at promoting intensive use of the land. It is

[29]International Labour Organization, Committee on Work on Plantations, *Basic Problems of Plantation Labour* (Geneva, 1950).
gives rise to acute social tension.
[30]W. Arthur Lewis, *Issues in Land Settlement Policy,* a report to the Caribbean Commission West Indian Conference, 1950.

generally believed that the division of the plantations into small farms would be likely to reduce the area planted to sugar-cane, which would reduce the demand for labour and also the volume of agricultural production. So far as plantation crops other than sugar are concerned, the difference in yields between large and small farms is not great enough to outweigh the social advantages which would be gained by resettlement on smaller farms. So far as sugar-cane is concerned, the division of plantations under present conditions would probably result in a decline in yields. The yield of sugar per acre is from 50 to 100 per cent greater on the plantations than it is on small farms.[31] Whether it is possible to conclude from these figures that small-scale production is not an economic alternative as a long-run development is uncertain. The small farm at present produces on inferior land and with insufficient capital. The experience of the United States Farmers Home Administration has shown that it is possible for small farmers, given adequate technical assistance and credit, to produce crops, as for instance cotton, in which the large estate was considered to have an uncontested superiority. None the less, unless such assistance were forthcoming, it seems certain that a division of the estates would be followed by a decline in yields.

Up to the present, little attempt has been made to solve this problem except by settlement in small holdings and by special measures in Puerto Rico. Some settlement in small holdings has taken place in Jamaica (about 100,000 acres up to 1950), chiefly on land not utilized by the plantations; in Puerto Rico (some 44,000 acres up to 1941); and to a smaller extent in other islands. In Puerto Rico, an attempt to limit the size of corporate holdings to a maximum area of 500 acres was made by a provision in the Organic Act of 1900 which was again embodied in the Organic Act of 1917. In practice these provisions were disregarded, and large corporations increased their holdings. Until 1936 no direct attempt was made to enforce the law. In 1940 a decision of the United States Supreme Court upheld the provision, and in 1941 a new approach was made through the Land Law of Puerto Rico, which established a Land Authority with power to purchase land from the large corporate estates in excess of the legal maximum. The scheme covers three types of holdings: the proportional-profit farm, established on land best suited to commercial production; individual holdings from 5 to 25 acres; and building lots for rural settlements. By June 1950 the Land Authority had acquired 102,816 acres of land under the 500-acre law, equivalent to some 50 per cent of the area held by corporations; it had also established 420 family farms on 5,910 acres. From 1944 to 1949 it was operating 48 proportional-profit farms. Under this scheme land is leased in tracts of 500 acres or more to farmers, farm managers or agronomists, who employ labourers on a profit-sharing basis. The managerial share of net profits varies between 5 per cent and 15 per cent. Labourers are paid the regular agricultural wage, and in addition receive part of the net profit of the farm, in proportion to the days each has worked and the wage rates for each type of work. Cane workers on these farms have received an in-

[31] *Ibid.*

crease in income, through the distribution of profit, ranging from $6 to $40 per labourer per year.

Technically, the operation of the farms has been successful. Relations between labour and management have not been smooth in the past, but have improved in recent years. Whether in fact the system will prove to be an effective method of combining large-scale operation with social advance remains to be seen; so far it would appear to be the only practical approach to the problem that has been made in the region, with the exception of Jamaica, where one such experiment has been carried out.[32]

In the Caribbean region, the main objections to the plantation system are social. In other regions of the world, however, the plantation system, in addition to similar social consequences, has had serious economic disadvantages. The sugar plantations of Java, for example, though successful in that they produced a high return on private capital, dominated the whole economy of the districts in which they were situated, and had adverse effects on crop rotation by facilitating the cultivation of sugar at the expense of rice. They also had unfavourable effects on food production for local needs and on the volume and conditions of employment. As a result, the area of sugar production in Java has long been a "classical stage for social unrest"[33] as it has been in the Caribbean.

In certain areas of Africa—particularly in eastern, central and southern Africa—there has been a development of plantation agriculture mainly under the auspices of non-indigenous enterprise. These plantations are devoted almost exclusively to the production of cash crops, most of which are for export. In the main, the labour force on which these plantations depend is drawn from indigenous tribal and village groups. Formerly, these workers depended entirely on subsistence agricultural and pastoral activities for their livelihood; most of them are still rooted in their subsistence tribal and village groups, from which they come as migrant workers, often on temporary contracts.[34] In some parts of eastern and southern Africa, plantation crops have been developed on the basis of immigrant labour from Asia, particularly the Indian sub-continent, as, for example, in the case of the Natal sugar industry in the Union of South Africa. In Kenya and Tanganyika, where the labour corps is largely African, plantations are mainly owned by European and Asian immigrant settlers.

The most important plantation crops in Africa are sisal, sugar, tea, coffee, tobacco, wattle, rubber, pyrethrum and essential oils. Sisal, sugar, tea and pyrethrum are at present almost exclusively produced on non-indigenous plantations as export crops. Coffee, wattle and tobacco are grown for sale both on plantations and by peasant cultivators. Certain other crops, such as sisal, are likely to continue as plantation crops on account of the relatively large capital outlays required in their production and the economic advantages which they offer through mechanized

[32]Luis Rivera Santos, *Land Tenure in Puerto Rico and the Virgin Islands*, a report to the Caribbean Commission West Indian Conference, 1950; and Walter E. Packard, "The Land Authority and Democratic Processes in Puerto Rico," in *Inter-American Economic Affairs* (Washington, D. C., 1948).
[33]For a full treatment of these effects, see E. H. Jacoby, *Agrarian Unrest in Southeast Asia* (Columbia University Press, New York, 1949), page 56.
[34]For a discussion of the effects on subsistence agriculture, see page 31.

methods of cultivation. Apart from these special considerations, however, the general trend of African commercial agriculture appears to be toward peasant rather than plantation forms of cultivation.

There is no clear indication from the available evidence on Africa whether plantation production is likely to prove more advantageous to the territories concerned than peasant production. The kind of crop cultivated undoubtedly has a bearing on the question. Equally, if not more, important is government policy in respect of assistance to indigenous agriculture through such agencies as, for example, credit institutions, co-operatives and marketing facilities. Other relevant considerations are wage rates and conditions of labour on plantations as compared with the lot of individual, and in some cases co-operatively organized, peasant producers. The effect of either type of agrarian structure on production of food for local consumption is also a crucial question.[35]

Settlement of Land Title: Water Rights

In certain countries the occupying owners of land have no legal title to the land they occupy, because no system of registration of title exists. This is a serious defect, in that lack of title means lack of secure tenure and leads to continual disputes as to ownership. This condition occurs in several Latin American countries, for example, Bolivia, Colombia and Venezuela, and most notably in Haiti.[36]

A complex situation arises in the Middle Eastern countries, where the work of land settlement (that is, registration of title) has not as yet been completed, and where the legal position as to water rights remains highly confused. The situation is in many respects peculiar to the region: it is a result both of a high degree of administrative inefficiency in the past, and a conflict between law and custom in the present. In the days of the Ottoman Empire, grants of individual freehold ownership were made, but no system of land registration was effectively enforced, and in fact no title could be legally established. Two forms of communal ownership were widely recognized by custom: a semi-communal village system (mushaa) under which periodic re-allotment of shares in the land among different families was practised; and tribal rights of occupancy over large areas of land. Where these forms of customary ownership existed, the individual titles to land issued by the Ottoman Government were disregarded. In consequence, at the time that the Mandatory Powers took over the government of Iraq, Lebanon, Palestine, Syria and Transjordan, the land system was in a state of complete chaos.

Although much progress was made under the mandates, it cannot be said that this chaotic condition was entirely removed. Generally speaking, it proved possible to introduce satisfactory settlement of title on an individual freehold basis wherever the semi-communal village system had lapsed, and individual cultivation was established by custom. This was the case in

[35]See page 31 *et seq.*
[36]For an account of the situation in Haiti, see *Mission to Haiti*, the report of the United Nations Mission of Technical Assistance to the Republic of Haiti (New York, July 1949), pages 87–88; and for the Mission's recommendations see pages 108 and 112 of the report.

Lebanon, Palestine, Jordan (then Transjordan) and parts of Syria. In Jordan the legal settlement of title has brought about a noticeable improvement in methods of cultivation; for example, terracing of slopes has been carried out in many villages, and other methods of preventing erosion have been introduced; forest areas have been demarcated and registered as government property, so that over-grazing can be prevented. Social conditions have improved, in that crimes of violence arising from disputes over land have shown a noticeable decline. This achievement may be attributed partly to greater administrative efficiency; the work of land survey and that of title registration were carried out simultaneously by the same department, while in other Middle Eastern countries the division of these functions between different authorities has delayed the work. Another reason for the successful settlement of title was that the semi-communal system had to a great extent lapsed, and the grant of individual freehold title corresponded to the desires of the cultivators.

While the grant of individual freehold title to land has had on the whole beneficial results in Middle Eastern conditions, it carries with it certain dangers. One result has been to facilitate the alienation of peasant-occupied land to large landowners or speculators. To prevent this danger, the French survey authorities in Syria occasionally followed the practice of settling title on a semi-communal basis, by registering individual title to a share in the total area of the village, without tying the title to a specific piece of land. This, of course, was highly disadvantageous from the standpoint of encouraging better cultivation.

On the other hand, the division of communal land into individual freehold properties has often resulted in the creation of strip holdings, each farmer owning one or more strips of land up to two or three kilometres long and only a few metres wide. Such a pattern has serious technical disadvantages and may, in addition, facilitate soil erosion. Hence, in Jordan, Lebanon, Palestine and Syria, it has been found necessary for the government to go one step further and consolidate the strips into more compact holdings.[37]

In Iraq, the policy of granting individual freehold title has had very questionable results. Large blocks of tribal land were registered as the property of the heads of the tribe, with the result that sheikhs became large landowners, appropriating the tribal land as their estate, while the tribesmen became tenants. The land remains extensively cultivated, with shifting cultivation practised in a partially irrigated zone, and high share rents are exacted from the tenants. In some districts the settlement of title has not been accepted by the occupiers, and attempts to enforce such claims have resulted in outbreaks of violence. Both in Syria and Iraq, large areas of land remain as government domain, in which title has not been settled.[38] The absence of settlement of title, or the mistaken principle on which title has been settled, are undoubtedly major obstacles to the expan-

[37]See pages 11 to 14 [pages 305–307 this edition].
[38]In Syria, the distribution of government lands has recently begun in El Jezira and in the Homs-Hama district. Cultivators can now acquire legal title to ownership of the land they occupy by the payment of a nominal rent over a period of three years.

sion of cultivation in dry zones and to the intensification of agriculture in the irrigated or irrigable zones. Unless the costs of survey and court fees are kept low, however, settlement of title may work against the small occupier and in favour of the large landowner.

The lack of adequate legislation on water rights is another defect, the importance of which it is difficult to exaggerate in countries where shortage of water is the main factor limiting agricultural progress. Under the Ottoman Land Code, water rights were regarded as the personal property of individuals and not as annexed to the land to which they should appertain. Such rights may be sold apart from the land, and wealthy landowners or speculators are therefore enabled to acquire water rights and thus compel small farmers to sell their land. This defect of the legal system is also an obstacle to the regulation of irrigation schemes, since it impedes the acquisition of water rights by the State.

It is evident that, in such conditions, the settlement of title is not merely a question of new legislation or more efficient administration. To evolve a satisfactory principle for the grant of title necessarily involves consideration of other factors; the desire on the part of small cultivators for security of tenure must be connected with the need for control of water resources over wide areas of land, as well as the need for preventing soil erosion. From the experience in Middle Eastern countries it can be seen that the grant of individual freehold title does not necessarily always produce a satisfactory settlement. Where communal tenures still exist, and are disintegrating, the question of what form of title is to be granted becomes an extremely complex one. The question of settlement of title must therefore be further considerd in relation to communal tenure. The following section includes some further examples of experience in this field: those in Buganda, in the Belgian Congo and in French West Africa are of particular interest as illustrating the results of different methods and policies.

Communal Tenure

A type of agrarian structure entirely different from those which have hitherto been described is the system of communal tenure in which control over land is exercised through a social group. Systems of this kind are to be found surviving in parts of South East Asia, India and the Middle East, in some of the Caribbean countries and in the northern and western republics of South America. The question of settlement of title which arises when such a system has already disintegrated has been mentioned in the previous section, with reference to the Middle East. In the following paragraphs the relation of economic development to this form of tenure is considered as it is seen in Africa south of the Sahara, where communal tenure is the most widespread form of agrarian structure.

In this region communal tenure exists in a variety of forms, with certain fundamental features in common. Land is held on a tribal, village, kindred or family basis, and individuals have definite rights in this land by virtue of their membership in the relevant social unit. Hence, title to land has a communal character and it is usufructuary, rather than absolute. A chief, for example, may be the custodian of the land but he is not its owner. The normal unit of land ownership is generally the extended family or kindred group, and once the land is granted to such a group it remains its property. In theory land may be pledged and redeemed, but only in such manner that it shall not be permanently lost.

Though different physical conditions result in a variety of forms of cultivation in various parts of Africa, communal tenures have been most frequently associated with shifting subsistence agriculture. Shifting cultivation in any of its forms implies a relatively plentiful supply of land in relation to population. As the area of land in relation to the population declines, more intensive methods of cultivation become necessary. This has already happened in many parts of Africa as a result of a number of closely related factors, including population increase, the introduction of commercial crops and the alienation of land either on a concession basis or to immigrant settlers. Soil deterioration and soil erosion, already serious problems in these areas, further reduce the available land. New techniques of agriculture are thus imperative, not only for the purposes of commercial cropping and subsistence production, but also for maintaining the fertility of the soil and for reconditioning land already eroded.

Under the pressure of these influences, traditional systems of land tenure are necessarily being adjusted. Frequently, however, conflicts of interest arise between the development of commercial cropping, and the requirements of farming methods designed to prevent loss of soil fertility, since overcropping for commercial reasons is a common danger and may contribute seriously to soil deterioration. Moreover, commercial crops may be developed at the expense of local food crops. New methods also frequently involve some capital expenditure—for example, for the fencing of pasture lands, for fertilizer and for new agricultural implements. In many instances, the lack of proved experience tending to show that the additional returns justify new forms of effort and expenditure may be more important obstacles to change than the existing form of land tenure.

Indeed, available data suggest that the communal systems of land tenure in Africa have not proved in themselves so inflexible as to prevent adaptation to new conditions. In certain parts of Africa, for example in the Gold Coast and Uganda, the traditional communal land system has been changing rapidly to one of individual private holdings in land, mainly in response to the desire to exploit land for commercial purposes. In other areas of Africa, the communal system has been less completely modified. In the Belgian Congo commercial and subsistence crops have been developed under government direction, without fundamentally affecting the customary system of land tenure in force. In the Gezira Scheme in the Sudan, where private rights to land in this area had long been recognized, the right-holders largely retained ownership of their land, although they leased it to the Government for a forty-year period, and acquired rights of tenancy when the Government obtained control over the land for purposes of development. The question of the influence of land tenure in Africa is therefore not whether traditional systems present *per se* a powerful obstacle to economic development, but rather whether the new forms arising from the increasing invasion of subsistence economy by an economy based on exchange will lead to economic development, without in the long run destroying much of the land for agricultural production, or resulting in abuses detrimental to the social and economic welfare of the community.

It is necessary therefore to consider the effects of the different forces which are now breaking up the communal system, and then to consider the role of government policy in relation to agriculture. Among the factors which are changing the communal system into more individual forms of land tenure the most general is the introduction of cash cropping; no large indigenous group in Africa remains entirely uninfluenced by it. In some regions shortage of land has been a determining factor, while in others the introduction of new crops and new methods of cultivation has played a part. The expansion of industrial employment has been a very disruptive influence. Land alienation is also important, especially in eastern and southern Africa, where there is permanent European settlement on a considerable scale, and also in French Equatorial Africa and the Belgian Congo, where large-scale land concessions to Europeans have been granted....

SUMMARY AND CONCLUSIONS

1. For many centuries the Agrarian structure, and in particular systems of land tenure, prevent a rise in the standard of living of small farmers and agricultural labourers and impede economic development, both by preventing the expansion of the food supply and by causing agriculture—usually the major economic activity of the country—to stagnate. Among the features of the agrarian structure which have most serious effects are the uneconomic size of farms; the mal-distribution of land ownership with concentration of large estates insufficiently utilized and the landlessness of a large part of the rural population; the fragmentation of holdings; the high rents and insecurity of tenure characteristic of many tenancy systems; indebtedness and lack of adequate credit facilities for the small farmer; absence of settled title to land and water; plantation economies which offier low wages and no share in management to the cultivators; taxation policies which impose undue burdens on the small farmers and farm labourers; and in general an unsatisfactory set of incentives for a rising and sustained agricultural production.

2. Examples of these features have been given to illustrate their effects in several countries. No attempt could be made fully to assess the influence of these features in all under-developed countries in view of the lack of sufficiently precise statistical and other information. Nor has any attempt been made to analyse in full the agrarian structure in any one country. Although the treatment has thus been selective and summary, the evidence suggests the widespread occurrence of these several features throughout the under-developed areas of the world, their significance varying from area to area.

3. Examples have also been given of several different types of reforms designed to remedy these defects, such as the great change from tenancy to ownership which is now in process in many countries of Asia; registration of title; the creation of credit and marketing co-operatives; types of large-scale organization designed to give security of tenure to small owners on

a communal basis; the redistribution of estate land to farm labourers in Mexico; the creation of producers' co-operatives in eastern Europe. Taxation policies designed to lighten the tax burden on the small farmers have been introduced in some countries. In many cases, and particularly where change is recent, lack of official information has prevented any detailed analysis of experiences gained by governments as the result of such reforms.

4. So far as generalization on the basis of these experiences is possible, it would appear that changes in the land tenure system are more likely to lead to a rise in the standard of living of the farmers and farm workers when they form a part of a general programme for the improvement of agricultural organization than when they are undertaken in isolation. Many of the benefits which might be expected to result from reform of the tenure system will be nullified if steps are not taken to provide appropriate services and facilities to the newly established small farmer, either individually or as a member of an association. It has been indicated that the provision of credit facilities, co-operative marketing, advisory technical and health services are among the major services and facilities needed. Where it is desired to enable small farmers to make use of better equipment, or to introduce new methods of farming, the organization of production in some form of producers' co-operatives has definite advantages. Tax policies designed to lighten the burden on the small farmer and on farm labourers should play an essential part in such general programmes.

5. The conclusion may be drawn that in many countries conditions exist which could be improved by the adoption, with appropriate adjustments and safeguards, of general programmes combining measures such as those described here. The extent to which measures for the reform of the agrarian structure, and in particular measures for the redistribution of land ownership, can be effective in promoting a general rise in the standard of living, depends in great part on the relation between population, land and other resources. Where there is no shortage of land, and where there are favourable market conditions, there is good reason to expect a change in the size of farms to be beneficial where it takes the form of redistributing land from large extensively cultivated estates to farm workers or tenants for more intensive operation in smaller (not necessarily very small) units. Where additional land can be brought under cultivation, surplus rural population can be absorbed and productive work can be provided for unemployed or under-employed members. The benefit derived from such a change would be influenced by the availability of such ancillary services and facilities as are noted above. Such change would be beneficial to the farm population in that the income of the farm workers would be raised and employment increased; it would be beneficial also to the economy as a whole in that better land utilization would increase the food supply and so raise the national income, thus enlarging the domestic market for industry. Where large owner-operated estates practise intensive farming, subdivision of large units might lead to a decline in production unless accompanied by further measures such as the establishment of co-operatives and the provision of credit, fertilizers and machinery. In such a case new forms of organization would need to be considered.

6. In countries where the relationship between population and land is unfavourable and where the density of the farm population is increasing, large estates generally take the form, not of owner-operated farms, but of large concentrations of small units of land leased to tenants. In these conditions the redistribution of land ownership involves a change in status which may lead to an improvement in the cultivator's income, and so raise his standard of living: it may also increase farm production by increasing both the cultivator's ability and his willingness to invest. But under such circumstances the redistribution of ownership will not be likely to enlarge the smaller holdings: the average farm size will still be very small, and large numbers of uneconomic holdings will still remain. Thus, land reform in these conditions will not in itself remove one of the most serious defects of the agrarian structure, the large number of excessively small farms, nor is it likely to offer land or fuller employment to most of the landless labourers. Such agrarian reform, though it may improve the condition of the farm population and may be a necessary stage in the improvement of the state of agriculture, cannot itself overcome the disparity between land and population.

7. To secure economic development in such circumstances will require a broader range of measures with specific emphasis on greater intensification and greater diversification of production to absorb the excess population. Intensification of agricultural production will require the provision of more capital to agriculture, since the labour-intensity of cultivation is already very high. In addition, some countries confronted with this situation have developed small-scale rural industries for the purpose of providing more employment in the rural community. Properly equipped and guided, such industries can fulfill a useful function, chiefly because they provide the basis for the development of industry on a wide scale. It is particularly at this point, however, that proposals for land reform may need to be integrated with economic development plans as a whole, for the correction of the disparity between land and population in such conditions requires action of a much broader character. It is beyond the scope of this report to explore the appropriate relationship between changes in agrarian structure on the one hand and plans for the general economic development of under-developed countries on the other. Clearly there will be, and indeed should be, inter-action between the policies adopted in these two fields of action.[39]

8. The report has also considered only in outline the types of change which appear likely to have beneficial results on production, on living standards and on investment. It has not attempted to consider the practical methods by which changes in the agrarian structure can be most successfully carried out. Many important practical aspects have not been examined, chief among them the financial and administrative arrangements involved.

9. General Assembly resolution 401 (V) *inter alia* requests the Economic and Social Council:

[39]United Nations, *Measures for the Economic Development of Under-Developed Countries,* May 1951; see especially chapter VIII, section on industry and agriculture, page 58.

... to prepare recommendations to the General Assembly with a view to the improvement of the conditions of agricultural populations, paying special attention to such measures as the following:

(a) Institution of appropriate land reform;

(b) Appropriate action on the part of the governments concerned to render financial aid to agricultural workers and tenants and to small and medium-sized farmers through cheap agricultural credit facilities, comprehensive technical assistance and the promotion of rural co-operatives;

(c) Construction or development, either by direct government action or suitably financed co-operative group, of

(i) Small factories and workshops for the manufacture, maintenance, repair and servicing of the most essential agricultural machinery and for the storage of spare parts;

(ii) Locally-based enterprises for the processing of agricultural products;

(d) Taxation policies designed to lighten, to the greatest possible extent, the tax burden on tenants and small and medium-sized farmers;

(e) Promotion of family owned and operated farms and of co-operative farms, as well as of other measures to promote the security of tenure and the welfare of agricultural workers and tenants and of small and medium-sized farmers.

10. The analysis presented here suggests that in the widely varying circumstances occurring in under-developed countries the measures noted for special attention by the General Assembly, while each of great value, are not all of equal importance for all countries and hence the recommendation of any special measure or group of measures cannot be expected to meet all situations. At the same time the analysis suggests that the effect of a single measure will be less if it is applied in isolation than if it is applied in conjunction with other measures which will reinforce and sustain it. A comprehensive attack by a combination of measures appears to be the most likely to achieve the desired result and each government will desire to devise its own policies combining in varying degrees the several types of measures mentioned, bearing in mind also the relationship between such a programme and general plans for promoting economic development. Governments of countries in which agrarian conditions "constitute a barrier to their economic development" should be strongly urged to examine the results which have been achieved by such measures in other under-developed countries with a view to devising or developing a programme of action suited to the circumstances of their countries.

11. Resolution 401 (V) recommends to the governments of the under-developed countries concerned "that they avail themselves of the facilities available to them through the United Nations expanded programme of technical assistance, in order that they may obtain expert advice in the planning of such measures as those listed in the preceding paragraph, for the purpose of improving agrarian conditions." This recommendation gains force in the light of the foregoing suggestion that governments devise programmes according to their particular requirements, as in assessing the relative merits of the measures available and the relationship between such measures and broader plans for economic development there would arise many opportunities for utilizing technical assistance from the United Nations and specialized agencies. Additional research on the effectiveness

of past measures in these fields will also be needed as a basis for training experts.

12. Given the serious importance for the under-developed countries of agrarian conditions which obstruct their economic development and in view of the Economic and Social Council's continuing responsibility to promote the economic development of under-developed countries and of the responsibility of governments to take joint and separate action for the purposes of Article 55 of the United Nations Charter, including the promotion of "conditions of economic and social progress and development," the Council may wish to consider making arrangements which will keep it informed of, and assist it in making recommendations with regard to:

(a) Major problems confronting the governments of under-developed countries in their efforts to overcome obstacles to the improvement of the conditions of their agricultural populations; and

(b) Technical assistance services requested and rendered to governments by the United Nations and specialized agencies in respect of this problem with particular regard to types of assistance requested which could not be provided.

13. Such arrangements might be based on the submission by the Secretary-General, in consultation with the Food and Agriculture Organization, of a report to the Economic and Social Council every two or three years covering recent developments in the field, particularly the aspects noted above. To prepare such a report the Secretary-General would need the assistance of governments in furnishing the necessary information, and both the United Nations and the Food and Agriculture Organization would need to devote increased resources to the study and analysis of problems and progress in this field of action.

28. Communism and the Peasants

*David Mitrany**

The most effective side of the Communist advance, and the least understood, has been the association between Communists and peasants in eastern Europe and in Asia.

Marxism was a doctrine for the industrial proletariat, and a movement by the proletariat for taking over the most advanced strongholds of industrial capitalism. In fact, Communism has so far nowhere come within reach of power in Western industrial countries; it has secured power only in undeveloped peasant countries. In every instance, from 1917 in Russia to 1949 in China, Communism has risen to victory on the back of disaffected peasantries. So far, it has always been a proletarian revolution without a proletariat, a matter of Communist management of peasant discontent. But while this shows that in the countries where this happened

*From *The Annals of the American Academy of Political and Social Science,* July 1951. The author is Professor, School of Economics and Politics, Institute for Advanced Studies, Princeton.

the peasants were ripe for revolt, it does not show that they inclined to Communism. As regards eastern Europe, at any rate, the evidence is all the other way.

Marxist View of Peasants

That actual association between Communists and peasants rests on a double paradox. Neither side expected or wanted the alliance. All Marxists, whether Socialists or Communists, have for the past century refused to have anything to do with the peasants politically, or to help the peasants in any way socially. As early as 1848, in the *Communist Manifesto*, Marx declared the peasants to be an anachronism and moribund as a class. To Marx and Engels, concentration in ownership and especially in production was the mark of economic advance. In *Das Kapital* Marx simply assumed that agriculture, like industry, must develop into ever larger units of production. He therefore laid it down as the goal of socialist policy to have a relatively small number of very large farm units which would be farmed with "armies of laborers."

That doctrine remained a sacred prescription with Marxists everywhere. Even the British Labor party, which has always been more Fabian than Marxist, insisted on the need to nationalize the land and agriculture right up to 1945; that is, until it came to power. As regards political action, Marx also looked upon the peasants as merely the least stupid among the beasts of the farmyard, and therefore as quite incapable of any revolutionary action. He even found it in him to praise capitalism for having rescued, as he said, large numbers of people from the idiocy of rural life. At no time did Socialists or Communists try to work out a political program of common action with the peasants, nor did they ever mitigate the demand for the dictatorship of the proletariat, even in the eastern countries where the peasants formed the bulk of the population.

Peasants' View of Marxism

As for the peasants, they never had any use for the ideas and policy of Marxism. To them, the traditional peasant homestead was not merely a means of living but a way of life. They were inclined to be devout, and found the harsh materialism of Marxist doctrine repugnant. Everywhere they had a tradition of mutual self-help, but not of class. All of them, rich and poor, disliked the economic and cultural domination of the towns, and had little understanding for the abstract revolutionary creed of Marxism or liking for its idea of a centralized planned economy. All they wanted was more land and a decent administration, and everywhere they seemed to prefer to get that by normal political action and to pay for it.

There is no instance of any substantial peasant group joining politically with Socialists or Communists. In western Europe the peasants formerly struggled together with the radical townspeople and the workers against autocracy and aristocratic privileges, but the rise of Marxist Socialism drove them rather into the arms of Conservative parties and groups. In central and eastern Europe, where peasants were numerous and workers few, peasants formed strong and progressive democratic parties of their own.

Leninist Adaptation

No one, therefore, could have foreseen that the peasants of eastern Europe and of Asia would become the instrument for the victory of Communist regimes. That was made possible by two things, one positive and one negative. On the one side there was the remarkably astute insight of Lenin; on the other, the curious indifference of the West. After the collapse of the rising of 1905, Lenin realized that revolution could not succeed in Russia unless it had the support of the peasant masses. From that moment he worked assiduously in his writings and in his actions to bring about at the crucial moment the possibility of joint action between Communists and peasants; and to that end he modified, against severe criticism from purer Marxists, the ideas and prescription of Marx on the agrarian problem.

Lenin did not give up the central idea of an economic system based on industrial development and on centralized control, or the idea of the necessary dictatorship of the proletariat so as to lead the revolution to an effective conclusion. But he insisted that when the revolution occurred, land would have to be given to the mass of the peasants, in small equal holdings of the kind which the peasants thought to be fair. Secondly, he believed and taught that the ultimate aim of a collectivized agriculture could be achieved only by converting the peasants to voluntary acceptance of the idea, and that it would therefore be a long, gradual process. It was, indeed, the handing over of the land to the peasants at once, without restriction and without compensation, that made possible the Bolshevik victory in October 1917.

Western Indifference

Western liberals never adapted their ideas and actions in a similar way to the realities of the democratic problem in eastern Europe and elsewhere. They took a deep interest in the struggle of the eastern people for national liberation, and in general infused a more liberal content into international relations. Yet it was the same liberal trend, concerned as it was above all with democratic political forms, that showed little sense that independence would not mean much to those people unless it brought them social improvement, and that the core of the social problem in the East was the fate of the peasants. Western Socialists added to an equal indifference a positive dislike of the peasants, in the true Marxist tradition.

When, at the end of the first World War, the empires of central and eastern Europe collapsed, the liberal peacemakers at Versailles showed concern only for national self-determination; in spite of the Russian Revolution, they ignored the social implications of that collapse, while the Socialists blundered into trying to set up in Munich and Vienna and Budapest Socialist regimes in the midst of a peasant countryside. One English Socialist, at least, later realized the mistake. He wrote:

To the Balkan peoples the indissoluble connection between national unity, individual liberty and peasant proprietorship seemed as self-evident as it did to Tom Paine; to Western industrial workers it had no sort of significance; to the Communists it was an outworn ideology which must be ruthlessly crushed. Once again as in 1848 the democratic revolution failed to reach completion, but this time the Western democrats failed to show any concern over its failure.

It is still more strange that, in spite of the swelling totalitarian current, Western liberals and Socialists in general did not change their attitude during the interwar period and during the second World War. In central and eastern Europe, outside Russia, an impressive peasant movement sprang up after 1919. Without exception, those Peasant parties were progressive and democratic, they stood firmly for international peace, and while they all supported a policy of friendly relations with the Soviet Union, they would have nothing to do with Communism as such. They were out to secure better government and a better life for the masses in their respective countries, and for that very reason they became the butt of persecution and violence on the part of the old landed and privileged groups in those countries. The cry was always against the Communist wolf, but it was the peasant shepherds that were imprisoned or murdered or ostracized.

In no instance, however, did a Western government protest against that violence, in the way that those governments have repeatedly protested against the denial of free elections in those parts since 1945. Though the Peasant parties and movement were clearly the only safe bulwark against totalitarianism from either Left or Right, the Western governments showed no hesitation in working with the oppressive and brittle dictatorial regimes of Marshal Pilsudski and Admiral Horthy, of Prince Paul and King Boris and King Carol.

The Cost

Western liberalism and Socialists in general were to pay heavily for such neglect of the peasants. During the Second World War, when the support of the peasants was vital, their political leaders were given prominent positions in all the Eastern governments in exile. But when the war ended with the victorious Soviet advance, the Western governments were unable to secure for the peasants equal standing in the so-called governments of popular union which, under strong Communist pressure, were set up in the countries of eastern Europe. With great difficulty they secured a place for Mikolajczyk in the Polish government, but he soon found himself checked in his work and had to flee the country to save himself. In Rumania, in Hungary, in Bulgaria, in Yugoslavia, the old Peasant leaders were imprisoned or hanged unless they were able to escape, so the chief of them are in exile again, this time in Washington, where they have set up an International Peasant Union. Dictatorship from the Left has thus continued and completed the work of destroying the democratic Peasant movement which dictatorship from the Right had started in central and eastern Europe.

As for the Socialists, they not only found themselves as Marxists impotent to resist Communist pressure and tactics; they actually shared in the undermining of the Peasant groups, only to be themselves destroyed as separate political groups. Indeed, throughout the eastern half of Europe the democratic Socialists have been wiped out even more thoroughly than have the Peasant groups.

Communist Use of Peasants

The curious side, and the significant lesson, of those events is that while the Socialists tried to remain good Marxists, the Communists only cared to remain good Leninists. To them the only goal that mattered was power, and to that end their tactics were as adaptable as their policy was un-Marxist.

The position was very different from that in 1917. Then the Bolsheviks had been faced with a widespread peasant revolution, and the only thing they could do was to go along with it. In 1945, the Soviet armies and Communist groups were in control throughout the eastern half of Europe, and they would have found it easy to impose the nationalization of the land and the collectivization of agriculture, which in the meantime had been completed in Russia. Instead, they did the very opposite. While they destroyed the political peasant movement, socially they applied the full peasant program. Large estates and farms, and even the holdings of the richer peasants, were broken up and distributed in very small lots to the mass of poor peasants. This was done even in the Soviet zone of Germany, and everywhere quickly, without any preparation or plan, mostly through local peasant committees, and inevitably with serious if temporary detriment to agricultural production.

The picture is completed by the skillful and effective way in which the Chinese Communists used the long sufferings and the land hunger of the peasants to open up for themselves the road to power. The land problem is, if anything, more acute in the countries of Asia than it ever was in eastern Europe. Not long ago an American writer, Mr. Erich Jacoby, showed in a careful study how in the past decades peasant subsistence farming had been pressed back by commercial farming for export; production had risen, but not the "level of living." When opening the Indian National Commission for Cooperation with UNESCO, in the spring of 1949, Mr. Nehru told the assembly that "the agrarian problem is naturally the most important problem in Asia, and a body connected with UNESCO must have full appreciation of this."

Hence, in China as in eastern Europe, land reform was the first and most important reform carried out when Communists took charge anywhere. The attitude of the Communists did not mean, however, that they had abandoned Communism and that they had come to love the peasants. It only meant, as Stalin has more than once explained, that they had learned to turn the peasants, during the revolutionary struggle, from a possible reserve of the bourgeoisie into an active reserve of the proletariat. That was indeed the lesson which the Soviet leaders passed on to their lieutenants in every place where peasants still formed a powerful section of the working population. Not only in eastern Europe and in Asia, but in Italy and France and elsewhere, the Communists work hard to gain access to the countryside, and to that end do not hesitate to leave their Marxism at home.

Un-Marxist Action

There is, indeed, a very interesting theoretical side to this story. From the point of view of Marxist theory and practice, the whole Communist action is as un-Marxist as it could well be. It is true that in the meantime in Russia, and to some extent in the eastern countries of Europe, the policy has been reversed and agriculture has been or is being collectivized. But this does not happen in the Marxian way. To Marx, growing concentration in production was simply a law of economic nature. Hence he assumed and prescribed it as the only possible trend for Socialist society. Yet, unlike the growth in industry, in agriculture such concentration has nowhere come to pass as part of the natural evolution of economic life under capitalism. As for the Communist system, concentration in agriculture has had to be imposed by force and maintained by force.

In a genial moment, during one of their wartime meetings, Marshal Stalin confided to Mr. Winston Churchill that collectivization had been a "second revolution," and one tougher and more dangerous than the first. The Marshal did not complete the picture by explaining that that second revolution was directed not against feudal landlords and bourgeois capitalists, but against the hardest-working section of the working class. But that no doubt explains why, fully a generation after the Communist triumph in Russia and with Russian collectivization completed, at the moment of their great military and political victory the Soviets in 1945 nowhere tried to apply their Marxist program, but instead applied an extreme peasant program.

The political consequence of this is also bound to be highly un-Marxist. No doubt, wherever they have the chance, the Communists will try to revert, as they have done in Russia, to the agrarian formula of Marxism. But given the nature of the countries in which they have come to power, they can do so only insofar as they can build up a large industry and in the process also a large proletarian class. To that end they must impose prolonged and heavy sacrifices upon the mass of the peasant population. The probability therefore is that, as in Russia, the policy of forced economic development will go hand in hand with a long period of uncompromising political dictatorship.

Marxist Theory Disproved

In the light of the erstwhile socialist ideal, the upshot is certainly strange. Through a combination of undialectical circumstances, the Communists have come to power, from 1917 in Russia to 1949 in China, only as leaders of peasant-agrarian revolutions. Because of that, the agrarian side of Marxist theory, with its "scientific" claims, is the only side which so far has been tested in practice. In the process, that theory has been proved wrong in every respect. Marx's analysis of the evolution of agriculture has nowhere been proved right; his prescription for the organization of agricultural production has never come to be practiced as part of a normal economic evolution.

The Marxist view of the backwardness and political incapacity of the peasants has been made ridiculous by the dependence of the Communist advance on the peasants' political temper and stamina; but the expectation of a natural revolutionary alliance between proletariat and poor peasants through class division in the village, in spite of much Communist effort and propaganda, has never materialized. In no instance has communism as such been supported consciously and deliberately by the peasants, and in no instance has the victory of the Communists been simply the success of their own efforts and program. In every instance the Marxist agrarian idea, when tried, has had to be applied by force and to rely on force for its survival; while the Socialist groups which wanted to remain democratic have in every instance had to abandon it altogether.

The historical reality of the whole revolutionary episode since 1917 is therefore a vast peasant uprising over half of Europe and most of Asia, the final demolition of feudal conditions on the land. Marxism has had nothing to contribute to that, whether as a theory or as a movement. The Communist part in that great historical upheaval was accidental and has remained artificial. Insofar as it has been successful politically, it has been the very negation of Marxist doctrine. The Communist advance has been a series of tactical victories. It would have had little chance had not the Western liberal movement of the new middle class, and the social movement of the new working class, been afflicted with an introverted urbanism which caused them to remain as indifferent to as they were ignorant of the tremendous social and political implications of the peasant problem in eastern Europe and in Asia.

29. Public Interest in Private Property (Land)

*Raymond J. Penn**

The most profound development in the last few centuries of world history unquestionably has been what Karl Polanyi calls the Great Transformation—the transition of society from a feudal to a market economy.

Under feudalism, the common denominator of all social relations was the tenure under which men held land. The whole fabric of feudal society was tacked down at all strategic points to the land. Political power, social prestige, material wealth, and justice—all of these for any man were related to and dependent upon his land tenure status. . . .

Sometimes we in the United States are apt to forget that feudalistic customs constitute a heavy barrier in many lands against the introduction of democratic principles of social organization. We forget that, in many parts of the world, agrarian feudalism lasted until late in the nineteenth century; that, in some countries, the break from feudalism has begun only since World War I; and that, in parts of many countries even to-day, a paramount social question is, "How can we break the fetters of a feudalistic land system?"

*From *Land Economics*, May 1961. The author is Professor of Agricultural Economics, University of Wisconsin. The author is indebted to Professor Bryant Kearl, University of Wisconsin, for many of the ideas and for invaluable aid in putting this manuscript into final form.

The ideas presented in this article constitute the theoretical portion of a paper presented by the author at the Conference on Land Problems and Policies, held in Santiago, Chile, under the sponsorship of the International Cooperation Administration in February 1961. ICA representatives from twenty Latin American countries were in attendance.

The problem of eliminating the vestiges of agrarian feudalism is of course bound up with the equally difficult problem of determining upon some other land system that will allow men the freedom and equality which feudalism does not allow, but that will still give men that degree of security which will assure the needed production of food and raw materials, the conservation of natural resources, and human satisfactions in living. In all parts of the world there are literally millions upon millions of people to whom this question is the great unsolved riddle of social organization.[1]

This quotation from a paper by the late Leonard A. Salter, Jr., published after his death, states quite clearly the central issues of land development and agricultural reform.

It is hard for us in the United States to realize how many people, in how many parts of the world are trying to untie themselves from feudalism. In varying degrees, both the poor farmer of the Andean Mountains and the agricultural worker on the large irrigated farm have seen that land ownership carries with it more than the right to manage the land and the income from it. In a sense, ownership of land carries with it ownership of government—the right to tax, the right to enact and enforce police regulations, and the right to judge. In addition, decisions on investments in social capital—education, transportation, hospitals, power projects—appear to be the prerogative of land ownership.

So, to the "campesino" ownership of land is both the symbolic and the real source of a new kind of life. It gives him food to stay alive, but it also gives him the right to build his own house in which to raise his family. It gives him, too, the right to tax himself to build a school. Is it any wonder then that land reform assumes major importance to those people who are still living under vestiges of feudalism, or at least outside of the market ecenomy? To a simple view, what Latin America wants is to industrialize, to expand production and increase the domestic market; in short, to raise the standard of living of the people.

From any point of view, these Latin American countries can do this only if all of their people are part of the economic system. They must produce to sell: and they must have the power to purchase. This requires a shift from feudalism to some form of market economy—an economy where division of labor is possible and where there is some reasonable security of expectations.

All countries are, of course, at different stages in this development from feudalism to a market economy. The process of the shift is different from one country to another, too. However, nearly everything I have read and the very little I have seen of Latin America leads me to believe that the basic issue is how to absorb the nearly 50 percent of the population into productive jobs in the economy.

Let me point out that the problem would be relatively easy if it were only what it appears to be—making more land resources available to the landless. It is that, yes, but it is much more. The pressure for land reform is, in actuality, pressure for a major change in the structure of the econ-

[1]Leonard A. Salter, Jr., "Do We Need a Land Policy?" *The Journal of Land & Public Utility Economics,* November 1946, pp. 310–311.

omy. I submit that what the landless of Latin America want, and what the economy of Latin America demands, is more than the breaking up of large landholdings. It is the breaking up of the bundle of rights which have so long been a prerogative of the large landholder and denied to the landless.

It is perhaps natural that we in the United States take a much more limited view of land reform. Our own nation was founded at a time when Europe was breaking away from feudalism; and our Constitution was established on the liberal ideas of those who knew what feudalism was and why it must be abandoned. The Constitution sets up courts, a police force and legislative authority apart from the ownership of land. Thus feudalism never really got established in the United States and some rather violent "rent wars" in New York in the 1840's dealt the final blow to the patron system.

Property in the United States still carries with it rights to land and the products from that land. It also imposes responsibilities on others to respect those rights. But the landless and those who own only a little have ways open to protect themselves and to advance. They can go to court and can count on fair treatment if the landowner abuses them. They can put pressure on the legislature for social security, minimum wages, safety requirements, and unemployment protection. Credit sources make land purchase more feasible. They can acquire property rights in industry; or, through their union, even feel that they have some security in the form of the laborer's right to a job.

So let me repeat, it is natural for us in the United States to look at land development and land reform issues in Latin America and also in other parts of the world in such a restricted way that we may miss the issue completely.

There is another reason why one needs to differentiate between the meaning of property in the United States and in countries that still have some feudalism. We think of United States firms as going into foreign countries and operating pretty much as they do in the United States, with labor and capital sharing the same rights and responsibilities as they do in the United States. Generally, however, this is not the case. When a company acquires property in another country it will generally follow the rules of that country. Willingly or not, it will find itself exercising the landowner's prerogatives of that country. It may furnish better than average facilities and conditions of employment for its laborers. Yet a United States company in a feudal country becomes a symbol of the general ownership structure of the past and, as such, the target of land reform programs. To put it bluntly, United States industry cannot operate in a feudal country without accepting the rules of feudalism and thus sharing the villain's role for those who want to strengthen the economic and legal position of the landless and jobbers.

Up to now we have been talking about the nature of private property in land and how the concept may be different in different countries or even in different parts of the same country. Now we come to the question of using resources in the public interest. Most of us would agree that the national interest (and simple justice) require that the use of resources be designed to bring the greatest good to the greatest number. This is what we mean by the *public interest*.

In the United States we feel we have a sort of built-in automatic regulator of public interest. In theory at least, each person does what he considers best for himself. He buys or sells land or any other product. He makes the most profit he can. Prices will fluctuate, production and demand will adjust, and competition will force each of us into his most productive employment. Hence, the sum of the maximum incomes of individuals will result in maximum public welfare.

On the strength of this idea the United States proceeded late in the nineteenth century to give almost complete and inviolate private property rights in land. It is my feeling that this was possible only because of the large amounts of unoccupied land in the United States. At any rate, the United States encountered a number of problems in land use and in each instance the issue developed because individual responses to the automatic pricing mechanism were different from what the public wanted. For instance, the best interest of the heavily mortgaged farmer was to cultivate as intensely as possible even though the farm would wash away and a resource be destroyed as a result. The timber owner could make the most profit for himself by clear-cutting his land. The stockbroker would profit most by selling stock to an uninformed customer for more than it was worth. Our response to these abuses was not to abandon the price mechanism as a way of allocating resources, but to modify it by specific restrictions on what individuals could do.

In the twentieth century, with rapid increases in population, expansion of cities, greater demand for land and water, etc., the public interest in land use has come into focus more clearly than before. In the United States today I think we may fairly say that community land use planning (zoning, local government and services, etc.) is a public policy matter second only to international relations. Land use planning is our response to the challenge of protecting the public interest against unrestricted use of land by its owner contrary to the public interest.

The idea that private property in the United States was absolute and inviolate led Karl Marx into an erroneous forecast. He thought the power accompanying ownership of productive resources would become so concentrated in the hands of a few, and these few would abuse the rights of the many so outrageously, that revolt would be inevitable. Marx missed the forecast because he saw only one part of the picture. He failed to see that an individual without private property rights may still, under a far-sighted governmental structure, have procedures available and freedom to develop new ones that will act in the larger public interest—restraining private interest if and when that becomes necessary.

I would like to draw a sharp distinction between public interest and public authority or government. Governmental authorities often come to believe that their actions are the only ones invested with public interest. This is true everywhere; it is true in the United States all too often. A conservation department considers its decrees synonymous with public interest and accuses its opponents of selfishness or dishonesty or both. A highway department puts its road-building program above any other land use or use of tax money in the public interest. Fortunately there are always groups or agencies to challenge such arrogance, often even within the government itself. In those countries with one-hand control of government or with a dictatorship of a few, and with restrictions on freedom of speech and press, it is much more serious to consider government authority and public interest one and the same.

Public interest it seems to me should be the view of the public—of the people. Actions of individuals are often in the public interest; sometimes even when they conflict with government policies. Resolving conflicts between individuals, even on what might be thought of as private matters, may also be in the public interest. And of course projects which cannot be done by individuals or whose benefits are widely dispersed are the most commonly considered to be in the public interest.

What does it take to define and determine what is in the public interest? Three things, I think. People must have an opportunity to express their desires, the right to get together in groups and arrive at decisions, and some bargaining power to put the group decisions into effect.

Procedures are important. We need procedures to help in arriving at group decisions (planning or policy formation). We need procedures which give the people power in putting their plans (their wills) into operation. And of course we need procedures to protect minorities. The force of public interest thus defined can be brought to bear not alone on the recalcitrant individual but also on the government agency that is failing to do a job that is needed—and may even be brought to bear on the government itself.

I submit that the most important ingredient in economic development is for people (the public) to have authority to express their interest. Land ownership was, at one time, the only channel through which this could be done. Today other procedures of a society give the public their force. The procedures must be flexible so that the structure can be continually changing to meet the needs of the times. When an institution or a rule is inadequate for current needs, it must be changed—either with orderly procedures or in a more violent manner. Witness the sit-down strikes in the 1930s or the Iowa judge unable to foreclose on a farm; these were violent reactions to rules too rigid for the public interest. The violence of the change is, I think, in direct proportion to the inappropriateness of the rule or institution and the rigidity with which it is held.

Public interest and procedures to give it expression in a continuing and orderly manner have not been conspicuous in Latin America. But such procedures must and will be developed. Latin America will not follow our procedures but they may find our experience useful in their own planning. Let me very briefly review the procedures we use in the United States to exert public interest on the use of land.

1. *Police power.* People, through their government, can pass such laws as are necessary for health, safety, security, and national welfare in regulating an individual's land use. We are required to stop at a stop sign, we cannot open a store in a residential area, we cannot plow up sod in some soil conservation districts in the Great Plains. This is strong authority;

so it is limited. It is not to be used unless it is necessary to protect the *public health, safety, morals* and general welfare. It cannot be arbitrary and it must have some relations to the desired goal. It cannot confiscate the property. In addition, it must involve *due process of law* for the individual. He must be notified, have an opportunity to be heard, and have access to the court if he feels damaged.

2. *Taxation.* People can levy taxes on land and income to support their government. These taxes must be uniform—similar pieces of land must pay the same tax. Taxes must be used for public purposes to finance the government. We in the United States have a rule that taxes are not to be used for regulation; though one from Wisconsin must say that with tongue in cheek. History has ample evidence that the power to tax is the power to destroy. All the more reason why it must be exercised locally, democratically, and with a broad sensitivity to the public interest.

3. *Eminent domain.* If the public must have a person's land it can be taken. This, too, is a power so strong that rigid limits have been placed on it. Any land taken by the government must be used for a public purpose. Highways, railroads and public utilities, schools, etc. are considered public but, in general, we could not use this authority to take land from one private person and give it to another for private use, as would be done in a land distribution program. Urban redevelopment (slum clearance), however, has used this authority to take private land, change its use, and return it to private use. The owner is compensated for the land taken but his only basis for contesting the action is the adequacy of the compensation and the validity of the public interest.

4. *Spending power.* Governments can have major effect on land use by the decisions made about spending. Roads, schools, power projects, airports, defense and other government purchases all can have a major effect on land. Subsidies, as well as taxes, can guide the nature of private land use. Considerable public expenditures will be needed in most of the settlement projects I have seen in Latin America. Spending power is important in economic development anywhere.

These, then, are some of the basic tools by which the people express their public interest in private land in the United States. Often, without changing ownership these tools give the government power over private property when it can demonstrate that its actions are in the public interest. Tools such as these are, of course, the particular peculiar combination that has grown out of the United States history and culture. Other cultures will find other ways in which people can give their interest form and force. Successful development of ways to express the public interest may let us substitute moderate changes in the structure of the economy for violent changes in the economic system. One way or other, however, peoples will break with feudalism (as we ourselves did) and establish the authority of the public interest against the authority of centralized government or economic class.

I have directed my attention in this paper primarily to land problems and policies as they relate to economic development. But *land* policies and *trade* policies and *national fiscal* policies and *total economic development* are all part of the same structure. Perhaps I can be excused, as a land economist, for feeling that land policies are strategic to these other areas of vital national concern. But as a social scientist of wider interest and as a person of deep democratic convictions, I must also make it clear that land ownership is a burning issue in Latin America only because of the other powers that, in a feudalistic society, accompany the ownership of land. The peoples of Latin America feel a passionate concern about owning land because owning land is their route to personal security, to autonomy, to freedom from arbitrary subjection to the will of others. It is, however, only one of several routes. It may, in fact, be a disappointment and a delusion if the other requisites of political and economic security are not present.

DEVELOPMENT
POLICY

PROGRAMMING

30. The Essence of Programming

*Jan Tinbergen**

I. Nature of General Programming

...It is clear that a policy of deliberate development, to be successful, must satisfy a number of important conditions. Any action on a large scale requires careful preparation, and this is unquestionably true in the formulation of development policy. Preparation is of course a prerequisite to the numerous practical decisions to be taken by the technicians and organizers of the separate projects, but it is likewise needed at an earlier stage. To assure consistency and to avoid large-scale waste and disorganization, care should be taken that the component parts of the program form a coherent and co-ordinated whole. It is the purpose of general programming to see to this coherence and co-ordination. General programming has to supply a bird's-eye view of the pattern of future development of the country, and to show the possible and the most desirable development of the national product and its components, i.e., imports and production of the broad industrial groups, as well as its destination: exports, consumption, investment and government use. . . .

One of the most typical elements which programming is able to add to factual information may be called "consistency." The figures for the development of the individual industries have to obey a number of conditions of consistency. The total resources—land, capital, skilled labor—to be employed by them together cannot exceed the available quantities of these resources. Quantities produced have to be sold; in order that they may be sold their prices have to satisfy certain conditions; and these prices are dependent on the prices of land, capital and labor. Imports are needed; but they must be paid for by exports or by the importation of capital, and so on. The activities of certain industries have to be interrelated, since one uses the products of the other, or both supply products to a third. Taxes collected by the government, together with loans and deficit financing, will have to cover the total expenditure planned. Programming tries to establish a set of figures satisfying all these conditions. If the provisional program taken as a point of departure cannot possibly be brought into line with such requirements, it will have to be revised. Large practical errors may be avoided if such revisions are made in advance and are not forced upon the policy-maker by unexpected events. This is what programming tries to avoid.

*From *The Design of Development* (Baltimore: The Johns Hopkins Press, 1958). The author is Professor, Netherlands School of Economics.

Apart from the element of consistency, programming also tries to give some guidance as to the *completeness* of the picture. It helps to reveal which elements of information are lacking and gives hints as to where to look for these elements. More specifically, it leads to inquiries as to where the particular skills needed and where the willingness to take initiative are to be found.

II. Rough Outline of General Programming

The aim of general programming is to arrive at a framework of figures for the possible development of an economy.

The possibilities for development are dependent on certain factors such as the willingness of the government and the people to make special efforts, on foreign assistance in the field of investment or education, and on a number of short-term factors, such as crop yields, world market fluctuations, etc. In order to show that influence can be exerted by changes in such factors it is often useful to draw up a number of *alternative programs* each of them based on specified assumptions. The existence of an alternative program will be very useful if some of the factors turn out to be less favorable, or more favorable than was originally anticipated. This procedure of using alternatives may, in addition, be applied in order to illustrate the influence of uncertainties in some of the data. Each of the alternative programs will have to be calculated with the aid of the same techniques now to be described. These techniques are based on certain relationships between economic and other phenomena which have been tested, to a greater or lesser extent, by statistical research, and on a number of basic economic "laws," with which an equilibrated economic development must comply. Usually a first outline is derived from "macro-economic" figures; this is then refined in a second, "micro-economic" program. A macro-economic program merely projects the development of such general totals as national income and outlay (private consumption and investment and public outlay), imports, exports and imports of capital, and total national capital. A micro-economic program fills in this framework with figures in individual industries, and, as the case may require, on regions of even specific important plants.

The *macro-economic* program is usually based on a forecast of population over the period to be studied, say ten years. Both total population and active population are estimated. An assumption is then made as to the growth of productivity, i.e., product per active person. This assumption may play one of two roles. On the one hand it may be—since productivity is decisive for income per head—an indication of the development in material well-being it is desired to attain; on the other hand, it may be an indicator of what is assumed to be possible. Here the alternatives already discussed may have to be distinguished. Statistical experience has shown that over longer periods of time this growth has been rather stable, the most common figure, taking the average for all industries of a country, being 1.5 per cent per annum. There may be special reasons, e.g., in the case of the recovery of a war-damaged economy, to assume higher figures. Higher figures may also be used where the government proposes to make a special effort. In such a case it should be made clear, however, what the usual figure has been and to what extent a special effort is being demanded. Multiplying the "active population" figure by "productivity" will give the volume of gross product or "total resources available." It is these resources that will be available under the hypotheses made—indicating either the most probable rate of development or the most desirable one, or the rate to be expected if specified events occur.

A rough estimate of the volume of *imports* may then be made, based on the average import content of the country's product—an estimate which will have to be revised as soon as some insight has been gained as to the composition of future national product. With certain further assumptions as to possible capital imports, an estimate of the necessary exports follows. The question whether these exports can be sold and at what prices is an important element of programming. The value of national resources minus imports equals national income and with the aid of tax rates and a savings rate it may very roughly be estimated how tax revenue and savings are likely to develop.

One vital problem may now be considered: will savings plus estimated capital imports be sufficient to raise the national capital to the extent required to attain the assumed national income?

The relationships which are relevant to this question have been dealt with in a concise and simple way by the introduction of the so-called *"capital coefficient."* Experience shows that, at least for countries, the ratio between investments and the resulting increase in net national income varies less than was long believed. Something can be said about its order of magnitude, although the margin of uncertainty is still fairly high. Or, to put it in a different way: there appears to be a fairly constant ratio between a country's wealth and its income per annum. For economies like the United States and the United Kingdom, ratios of about three to one have been found to obtain over a remarkably long period. It is often maintained that for new investments in underdeveloped countries a higher ratio should be expected, since there must be established a number of basic facilities which are relatively "capital-intensive" in most countries. On the other hand, there are examples (e.g., Mexico) of recent developments showing an even lower capital coefficient. It would seem often safe to assume that for development programs a capital coefficient of 4 is needed, but we will also consider the consequences of lower values, even down to 2. The historical record of any given country will be the best guide, provided that it covers a sufficiently long period.

The significance and limitations of the application of capital coefficients are familiar. For the moment the existence of a roughly constant ratio of this kind will be taken for granted. Its meaning is that the annual percentage increase in national income to be obtained from a program of investment of, say, 8 per cent of national income amounts to 2 to 4 per cent. From a program of 12 per cent—an ambitious one for many countries—a 3 to 6 per cent annual increase in national income will be obtained. Now, the aim of development is not simply to increase national income but also to increase national income per capita and at a fairly fast rate. If there is an annual increase of 1 per cent in population, however, an increase of 1 per cent in national income does not increase income per capita. Several countries show population increases of 2 to 3 per cent annually. It follows that a rate of investment of 2 to 12 per cent is needed merely to maintain the level of income per head: 2 per cent in the favorable case of a 1 per cent population increase with a capital coefficient of 2; 12 per cent, however, in the unfavorable case of a population increase of 3 per cent with a capital coefficient of 4. With the assumed population growth of 1 per cent per annum, and an objective of an increase of income per capita at the rate of 3 per cent, which is modest if a real change is wanted, an investment program of 8 to 16 per cent would be needed. Even with a rate of growth of 3 per cent per annum it would take two decades before the average income of South Asia is brought to the modest level of Mexico's.

More generally, to raise income per head by 3 per cent a year requires an investment program of at least 2 and perhaps 4 times $(x+3)$ per cent of national income, where x is the rate of increase in population.

A study of actual figures for most countries discloses that the above analysis sets a lower limit to development programs which may well be, at the same time, about the maximum attainable in the short-run. For the numerous countries with a 2.5 per cent rate of population growth programs of 11 to 22 per cent would follow; for the principal countries in South Asia with population increases of 1 to 1.5 per cent, programs of 8 to 18 per cent of national income would follow, well above what has so far been possible. This underlines the urgency of the tasks ahead, not only for the governments concerned, but also for the international community as a whole. At the same time the figures presented illustrate, more eloquently than words, the importance of checks on the increase in population. Any reduction in percentage population increase means a two- to four-fold reduction in the rate of savings needed to achieve a given rise in the standard of living.

From the examples cited, another feature of the process of development becomes apparent, namely, that small changes in the savings ratio, if it is modest, may either bring the country from a state of stagnation into one of development or the other way around. If a country's population is growing at the rate of 1.5 per cent a year, and if again the capital coefficient is taken to be 4, then a savings rate of 6 per cent means stagnation, whereas a rate of 8 per cent means an increase in income per capita of 0.5 per cent annually.

It may be necessary, even at this stage, to take account of the *time-lags* involved in the execution of larger investment projects. The relation between total product and total capital refers to capital in the form of productive equipment and stocks ready for use. Production of investment goods will have to start early enough to allow for the length of the production process. Accordingly, investment activity in a given year may be partly dictated by the capital needs in some future year. This is of particular importance when a long period of construction is involved as, e.g., in the case of large dams or mine pits. In the stage of macro-planning, it may be sufficient to adopt an average time-lag for all investment activity. Later on, in the stage of micro-planning, a more precise calculation, depending on the type of investment activity, will be needed.

The long time needed for the execution of certain investment projects is also reflected in the existence of a large volume of works in progress and commitments to finish them which considerably narrow down, in each year, the possibility of starting new projects. Only a relatively modest part of the necessary equipment and labor is released for such new projects.

A word may be added about the *statistical sources* to be used in deriving the coefficients needed in programming. Preferably as much information as possible should be taken from the historical record of the country itself, provided that a sufficiently long period is covered. Coefficients on import content or capital coefficients should not be derived on the basis of a few years only, since there are considerable random fluctuations in annual figures. Averages over some ten years are often safer, since they also rule out possible cyclical influences. If no such figures are available, figures for comparable countries may be used; even comparability is not essential if general research has shown that there are no marked differences between countries. Certain statistical regularities are quite general indeed, such as, e.g., the distribution of expenditures over various categories or the capital coefficient. General though they may be, the coefficients are not too precisely known and their margin of uncertainty often is more important than their systematic variation from one country to another. This again stresses the desirability of working with alternative programs.

III. Projection of a Country's Markets

The next stage of programming, the "micro" stage, will then be reached, in trying to answer the question: what types of goods will have to be produced? This different question must, in principle, be considered from two angles, well known to the economist: "demand" and "supply." To begin with, we assume—for the time being that prices will not change. What then are the sales of the various classes of goods to be expected? There are two markets to be considered, home and abroad. Home demand derives from the increasing national income. We know something about how an increased income is spent: relatively fewer "necessities," more "luxuries." This tendency is international and indications can be derived, in this case, from foreign statistics. Numerous studies with respect to foreign demand are available, showing how increased foreign incomes are being spent. Of course, the "art" of such an analysis is to find figures that cover the most comparable groups of people in other countries. And common sense, as has already been stressed, is always needed to correct any estimate.

General speaking, there are three sources of data on demand for final consumer goods. The first source is *family budget* statistics. These data are obtained from a relatively small number of families, which may mean a large margin of error; in addition, there will be a bias, to the extent that families willing to provide this information may have a spending pattern different from other families. Usually family budget statistics give a detailed list of the goods bought, and in this respect they are, in principle, complete. In addition, they give quantities bought or amounts spent for different income classes, showing the influence of income on demand. It must also be kept in mind that total demand for a certain commodity is exerted not only by "families in existence" but also by "families in preparation," i.e., engaged couples buying furniture, etc. Finally, there may be industrial demand and institutional demand (schools, hotels, shipping companies, etc.).

The second source for final demand data may be direct observation of *retail trade*. From this source, total demand for a country may be derived, without data on its distribution over different income groups.

The same is true for the third source of demand data, that calculated from *production, imports* and *exports* and, where appropriate, changes in *stocks*. In this case, the influence exerted by changes in income can be ascertained only by comparisons for different years (if national income is known year by year) or as between countries (if national income is known country by country).[1] The advantage of the figures of the second and third sources is their completeness: neither, and particularly not the third source, is based on samples, but each covers the whole of consumption.

The relation between income and expenditure over a period does not necessarily correspond to that revealed by family budget statistics. It may vary with time. Demand changes from year to year may be called short-term changes. If incomes fall there will, e.g., be a tendency to maintain demand for necessities and to reduce demand for luxuries and durables, which might be called postponable demand. Long-term adaptations of demand to a changed income will, however, also have to reserve some income for durables. It may be assumed that comparisons between demand of different income classes as found in family budget statistics, will reveal something about such long-term adaptations.

Market projections have some particular importance for arriving at a reasonable estimate of what is possible in the field of *import substitution*. In a growing economy, an increasing number of products, formerly imported, may be produced at home as soon as a sufficient volume of sales are reached by a plant of optimum size. This process of import substitution should, however, not diverge too much from what a reasonable international division of labor suggests, a point to be discussed subsequently. Substitution may take place gradually, as resources become available. For example, if wire is being imported, efforts may first be made to produce wire locally from imported rods; only at a later stage, when sufficient new capital is available, will it be possible for the rods themselves to be produced at home.

The most difficult part of the analysis comes with consideration of international competition. Thus far it has been assumed that prices do not change. This implies that the quantities demanded can be supplied at unchanged prices. Probably this is not true. Every country has particular industries in which production is relatively cheap, others in which it is expensive. This brings us to the cost side of the problem. At what prices can increased quantities be supplied? In principle, the individual industrial projects known to the administration have to supply the answer. To the extent that such projects are known, some provisional answer will be possible.

---

[1] A continuous flow of new investigations is gradually narrowing down the uncertainties in our knowledge on the spending of income and also attempting to discover the similarities and dissimilarities between countries. An example is Colin Clark, *Conditions of Economic Progress*, 2nd Edition, London 1951.

If the price at which a product can be supplied in future is higher than the existing level, demand will be less; if the price is lower, demand will be greater than was initially estimated. We have to know demand elasticities in order to tell by how much the initial estimates will have to be corrected. Sometimes we know these elasticities. Here again, international comparisons will be a useful source of knowledge.

Our knowledge both of possible future production costs and demand elasticity is very incomplete, however. The set of individual industrial projects available will, as a rule, not cover all industries and products. Some sectors may be fairly completely covered by the projects available, others only partly so or not at all. It may be wise to consider each type of sector separately. We shall have to supplement the limited knowledge derived from the projects by reasonable guesses, which will no doubt turn out to be to some extent erroneous. This state of affairs is not new at all, but merely confronts the programmer with the fact of "incomplete information" so familiar to employers. The production pattern must then be estimated; it should include all practicable possibilities for producing relatively cheaply and, in fields for which no cost figures are available, should assume expanded production in proportion to demand increases, as far as production factors are available.

The principle upon which the selection of the goods to be supplied rests is the well-known principle of comparative cost. Each country should produce the goods in which it has the greatest comparative advantages in costs. This will maximize national as well as international production, under certain conditions, to be sure. . . .

The elements so far presented lead to a fairly complicated mechanism of interdependencies, but do not give a complete picture of the complications. Two other important phenomena should be mentioned. As already observed, export commodities must satisfy two conditions: they should be sufficient to meet import needs (apart from imports of capital, etc.), and they should actually be saleable. Each new addition to production facilities itself requires production of the investment goods involved. If additional shoe production is needed, it must be preceded by construction of the shoe factory. This itself requires activity by the building trade and by say, toolmakers, and these activities must be inserted in the program. In addition, some time will elapse between the start of construction and completion of the factory. Such "time-lags" must also be taken into account, as emphasized in Section 2.

The methods that may be employed to make up a program satisfying all the conditions of an economic and a technical character summarized thus far range from primitive trial-and-error to highly sophisticated mathematical techniques. Choice of methods depends upon experts and the nature of the data available. The annual programming of the British economy has been done with the aid of trail-and-error methods rather than mathematical procedures, whereas the latter have been more to the foreground in the Netherlands. Recently, Professor Frisch made use of some of the most modern techniques in advising on Indian development programs. Among the scientific tools he uses is the so-called "linear programming," a technique increasingly applied in private business. It is designed to establish production programs consistent with the requirements of inter-industry supplies. . . .

IV. The Role to be Played by Individual Projects

As is self-evident, any pattern of future production must ultimately materialize as a set of individual projects, largely in the private sphere. Here we arrive at the very essence of the development phenomenon. One of the reasons why development has not been achieved in a number of countries is the absence of sufficient spontaneous projects of the requisite kind. Development policy should aim at inducing private producers and investors to undertake them. . . .

The role to be played by individual projects in making up the general pattern of development is to provide information, even if only scattered, on the costs of production of specified commodities. Two main difficulties are encountered by the programming agency. First, for the projects to be helpful at all, they must be sound. Their soundness will have to be tested. Secondly, they are too few and the question therefore arises whether they can be "constructed" with the help of general information of the type available to the programming agencies. The two questions are related. Part of the testing will consist of finding out whether a program "fits" in the general picture of the country's development. This requires consideration of the development of markets and the testing of cost estimates with the help of general information.

What has been said on *market projections* therefore also applies here. The possibilities and usefulness of this device may now be examined more closely.

The knowledge of demand and its probable development is of relatively little importance for the single small producer. To him market prices will be the most important indicator; if they imply a profit he will produce; if they do not, he will have to stop production sooner or later. The quantity of his own production hardly influences the market.

It is otherwise for a larger producer. His supply may very well influence the market and for his investment plans to be well-devised he will want some knowledge about future demand. Accordingly the number of large firms undertaking demand studies of their market is already considerable and is increasing.

The same is true of production programs of countries as a whole. Even if production is in the hands of relatively small individual producers the total of their product will often be important in relation to the market as a whole, and expansion beyond what the market can take would mean waste. On the other hand, the extent of the market will depend on the rise in income generally and hence it will be related to the program. As far as internal demand is concerned, it may even be argued that investments should be distributed among the various industries exactly as the increased income is distributed among the various goods demanded. Such an investment program for the home market might be called a *harmonious program*. Demand analysis can make a considerable contribution toward making a program harmonious. It may also help to strengthen confidence in a sustained growth of markets.

Although the international market is less influenced by production increases in any one country, there have nevertheless been numerous instances in which this influence has been marked. This is true particularly of raw materials which are produced in a small number of countries, such as jute, cotton, rubber, coffee, etc. Here, too demand analysis is very useful to the programming country.

Recently considerable progress has been made in the field of econometric demand analysis. Programming agencies may advantageously make use of the results. This type of analysis requires the recruitment of experts or subcontracting with institutes specializing in this field. These are to be found in a number of developed, as well as in underdeveloped, countries. Significant results can, however, now be obtained with the aid of more pedestrian methods. And common sense should, of course, always have the final word.

The *testing of cost estimates* is the most important aspect of the testing of individual projects. Costs vary a good deal more among countries and individual plants than do market developments. A distinction should be made between processes that are more or less the same everywhere and processes very much dependent on the particular factor endowments of the country. For the first category, a number of standard figures are available, such as the investment costs per ton of steel, or per ton of cement, the quantities of coke per ton of pig iron, or of power per ton of aluminum. Still it should not be overlooked that alternative methods are often available, and that the choice to be made in an underdeveloped country does not necessarily coincide with the choice to be made elsewhere.

It is the second category of processes, those depending on factor endowment, that is much more variable. The essential problem for each country is to find out in which fields its comparative advantages lie. As a rule they will be related to geographical factors such as mineral deposits, quality of the soil, climate and transportation facilities. Particular comparative advantages will then show themselves in low costs of certain raw materials and of transportation. In certain cases a particular skill of the population may add to the advantages.

The only really satisfactory method of exploring a country's potentialities would be a systematic collection of the cost figures; this will as a rule not be possible in the short run, but might be kept in mind as a useful piece of research. Any such systematic ascertainment of cost figures implies a thorough technical exploration of production facilities and the collaboration of numerous technical experts. This aspect of the problem falls outside the scope of this report. In this field the role of the politician, the administrator and the general economist is a limited one. The importance of having accurate and many-sided information of this kind should, however, be recognized; to acquire it requires scientific and technical surveying and research in which the government would have to participate financially to a considerable extent.

The data needed on the cost side of an economic analysis relate, first of all, to the cost of producing a unit of the product or groups of products in question. To the extent that there may be differences between the costs of existing plants and of new plants, these differences or, more generally, the distribution of costs among the various enterprises involved should be ascertained. It should also be determined how costs vary with prices of the raw materials, labor and other means of production. This assumes knowledge of the quantities of these means of production used, per unit of product. The degree of detail needed would depend on the degree of detail of the program: if say, only ten industrial groups were singled out, a subdivision of costs for each of these groups would of course be sufficient. A very important further datum would be the capital investment per person employed. . . .

V. Avoidance of International Duplication

The essence of programming is the avoidance of inconsistencies. One evidence of this, already noted, is the devising of a harmonious program as far as home markets are concerned. Expansion of exports should likewise be based on demand analysis, in this case for foreign markets. There might be still a danger of inconsistencies if two or more countries independently planned to expand the same line of production. Such unco-ordinated programs might result in over-production. Therefore it is desirable that duplication be avoided.

Sometimes bilateral contacts will be sufficient to avoid duplication in its most pronounced form. Although in principle it is a time-consuming procedure and rather haphazard, often it will be the most practical course to take. The arguments given in favor of programming do not end at national borders. Programming ought to be coordinated internationally. Without such coordination other types of duplication also occur, as for example, duplication in analysis. It is not very efficient for sixty countries all to be studying world market development to some extent. They had much better use as their basic data the results of a few centralized studies. These studies should bear on the probable development of world markets and some of their determinants. The estimates should be based on a number of explicit assumptions as to population, productivity, weather conditions, general policy, etc., and possibly certain alternatives should also be presented. The studies might be undertaken by existing international agencies; in fact, they are already being made in some fields.

There should not be a monopoly in this field; much benefit may be derived from sound criticism and discussion.

VI. Types of Programming to be Applied Under Varying Circumstances

The question may now be put to what extent the programming techniques to be applied must depend on the particular circumstances of each case. Although there is probably less need for differences in approach than is sometimes believed, it cannot be denied that the emphasis must sometimes be shifted from one element of programming to another, and that the outcome of the planning process is necessarily dependent on the characteristics of the given situation.

In what follows, some of these characteristics together with consequences for the program are illustrated.

1. Probably the most important factor is the *stage of development* a country has reached. In the earlier stages of development, the historical record will not provide much of a glimpse of future possibilities; the most important lines of production may still have to be determined and established and probably there is need, first of all, for some general facilities for which public investment is required. Detailed programming at this stage would hardly be appropriate, but a rough idea of the rate of development and the most characteristic comparative cost advantages of the country will be necessary. In the later stages, on the other hand, the probable course of development will be more clearly discernible and more diversified action will be called for, distributed over more sectors and based on a more detailed type of programming. Accordingly, the content of the program will be different. In the early stages data on the costs and external markets of potential products will be important and those on the development of the internal market and its compartments of less significance. In the later stages a more precise study of internal demand becomes useful. The appraisal of some public investment projects will be very important in the early stages, while an effort to stimulate private projects in manufacturing industry should be postponed to a later period. It may even be simpler, in making the programming estimates, to start with the cost side, rather than with the demand side.

2. Another important feature of the economy is the degree of activity and initiative in the private sector. Where the private sector is rather passive, either more initiative must originate in the public sector, or other types of stimulation must be provided.

3. The type of programming needed will also depend to some extent on the particular *bottlenecks* with which the country is faced. They may either be general or specific in nature. The most important examples of the former are capital scarcity and scarcity of foreign currency. If *capital* is the bottleneck, every care must be taken to assure its most effective use. The supply of capital will be decisive for the rate of development found to be possible; preference will have to be given to labor-intensive activities and measures will have to be taken to induce investors to follow this preference. Such a situation contrasts with that prevailing in a country like Iraq where there is now a surplus of capital and where other factors will therefore be decisive.

Another general bottleneck may be *foreign exchange,* and here exports take the key position. A distinction may again be made between situations in which exports are limited in variety and those in which they are diversified. If only one or a few products are decisive, the furtherance of these products ranks high in policy determination, and accordingly a correct analysis of the prospects for these products is of primary importance in programming.

Bottlenecks of a more specific character are exemplified by a *transportation bottleneck.* In such cases, a road building program or the construction of harbor facilities would seem to be among the more urgent projects. Other examples are a scarcity of certain types of *skilled labor,* calling for training measures, or local scarcities of *dwellings,* requiring a building program.

4. A fourth important influence on the character of programming is to be found in the *general attitude of the people* with regard to government measures: the degree of public spiritedness and the willingness to cooperate, and in the quality of administration. Under favorable conditions more elaborate measures may be taken to further development in the private sector. Accordingly, more detailed research may perhaps then be appropriate. Thus it is conceivable that subsidies might be paid for employing workers in order to stimulate labor-intensive activities. This is possible only if the purpose of such a measure is understood and if the management of the enterprises and the administration of taxes is sufficiently reliable to permit this rather subtle type of regulation.

5. Finally, another factor which will necessarily influence the programming technique is the *quality and nature of the data available*. This will not usually be completely independent of the stage of development or the general level of education, but nevertheless it may vary as between countries otherwise comparable. Clearly there is less scope for the making of refined calculations if the data available are poor than if they are reliable and abundant. Nevertheless, there is a tendency to over-emphasize the influence of the quality of data on the type of programming required. More guess-work is needed if the data are poor, but the logic of programming is not necessarily different.

The same statement applies to the influence of circumstances as a whole on programming. While it is true, that as just indicated, there is some such influence, it should not be forgotten that the basic logic of the development process is not different. It is the relative size of the sectors and their increase in time, and the relative importance of the instruments of policy, which vary and thereby change the practical appearance of the problems, but the core of programming, the attempt to arrive at a consistent picture of potentialities and desirabilities, does not change; neither do the fundamental relations between the main economic phenomena.

POPULATION POLICY

31. Economic Problems of Population Change

*Frank W. Notestein**

For practical purposes, too much of the work done on the economic problems of population is dominated by points of view that lie at opposite poles. At one extreme the optimum population theorists treat the subject as if the major problem were that of deciding on the number of people needed to maximize *per capita* income, or some other goal of their choice. This work is done, or proposed, almost as if the essential questions would be solved once such a number were ascertained. Problems of transition are neglected as if they did not exist—as if numbers could be changed at will and without repercussions on the economy and society. The abstraction is a dangerous one. It neglects the fact that the nature of the social-economic changes selected to achieve the desired population size partly determines the population size that is desirable. Processes of population change are neither completely flexible nor frictionless.

The opposite extreme is equally unfortunate. It tends to treat population growth as following an established and predictable course. In this view, which is usually implicit rather than explicit, all that is necessary is to extract a prediction from some authority, and then set about the problems of meeting the economic needs of the predicted population—set about it, that is, on paper, not in fact. This procedure also suffers from a fatal defect. There is no immutable course of population growth that can be forecast. Future trends will depend on many things, important among which will be the nature of the steps taken to meet the economic problems of population growth. The nature of the economic changes ahead will be quite as important in determining the size of the population as will the nature of the population growth in determining the magnitude of the economic problems.

One extreme overlooks the processes of population change, and the other treats them as independent of the situation in which they arise. Both fail, therefore, to focus attention on the major questions which are those of the interrelated processes of social, economic, and demographic evolution. The result has been a good deal of rather idle speculation. There is not very much point, for example, in finding the extent to which India or China is "overpopulated" when the avoidance of continuing population increase would apparently involve a catastrophic loss of life.

Those who treat population change as independent of its social-economic setting have contributed even more to the confusion in matters of food and

*From *Proceedings of the Eighth International Conference of Agricultural Economists*, 1953. The author is president of The Population Council.

population. Will mankind's numbers eventually outrun the possibility of obtaining a minimum adequate supply of food, minerals, and energy? This question of ultimate carrying capacity is meaningful only in a very restricted way. Any reasonable consideration of the subject will show that the highest conceivable limit would be reached if growth, even at current rates, were to continue for any span of time that could be considered significantly long in the history of the human race. The plan is important because it establishes a principle. Growth must stop sometime, and it must do so either by a reduction of the birth-rate or by an increase of the death-rate. If man covers low death-rates in the future, as he always has in the past, he must eventually reduce birth-rates. The principle established, however, the question becomes one of means and timing, and the real problems are those of process.

Difficulties also arise when the analysis relates to the needs of a predicted population in the near future. By disregarding the social and economic processes involved we can think almost exclusively in engineering and scientific terms. We can talk about the marvels of science and technology as if there were no intervening terms. In a word, we can forget that we are social scientists who should know that both the application of new knowledge and the processes of new discovery depend on social settings that have been infrequently present in the world. We forget that we already know much more than we apply, and that we shall not see science and technology smoothly applied in some never-never land of economic, social, and political vacuum. There is great danger that social, economic, and political difficulties will intervene to bring drastic checks to population increase long before the theoretical possibilities of advanced technology are exhausted. It is in this sense that the problems of social-economic organization and change, rather than those of technology, seem the important ones.

This is the thesis, and a warning of the bias with which my paper proceeds. To make the case it will be necessary to see what we know of the processes of change, to find the major gaps in our knowledge and to ask the meaning of our knowledge and ignorance for research and action.

The European Setting

Europe and the industrial countries of the New World furnish us with the most important information. They provide the longest statistical record, and they have gone furthest in the transition toward a balance of low birth- and death-rates. An understanding of their experience gives us considerable information about the kinds of processes likely to be found in other parts of the world as technological development gets under way.

First of all it must be recognized that Europe's population growth during the past three centuries was unique in the world's history. Her population multiplied fivefold, and the population of European extraction increased probably more than sevenfold throughout the world.[1] The major source of this increase was a reduction of mortality. The decline of the

[1]Dudley Kirk, *Europe's Population in the Interwar Years,* Geneva, League of Nations, 1946, p. 17.

death-rate was gradual for a long time, as public order and the agricultural, commercial, and industrial revolutions lifted incomes, and as sanitary and medical knowledge advanced. In the late nineteenth century a precipitous decline in mortality got under way and has continued to the present with the virtual elimination of deaths from contagious and infectious diseases. The expectation of life at birth probably was below 35 years in the mid-sixteenth century. Today in advanced countries it is seldom below 65 years and it exceeds 70 years in the best modern experience.[2]

Meanwhile birth-rates remained generally unchanged until the last quarter of the nineteenth century.[3] Although they were lower than in Colonial America, or in the Orient today, they were high by present standards. Indeed, they had to be high. We may take it for granted that all populations surviving to the modern period in the face of inevitably high mortality had both the physiological capacity and the social organizations necessary to produce high birth-rates.

Peasant societies in Europe, and almost universally throughout the world, are organized in ways that bring strong pressures on their members to reproduce. The economic organization of relatively self-sufficient agrarian communities turns almost wholly about the family, and the perpetuation of the family is the main guarantee of support and elemental security. When death-rates are high the individual's life is relatively insecure and unimportant. The individual's status in life tends to be that to which he is born. There is, therefore, rather little striving for advancement. Education is brief, and children begin their economic contributions early in life. In such societies, moreover, there is scant opportunity for women to achieve either economic support or personal prestige outside the roles of wife and mother, and women's economic functions are organized in ways that are compatible with continuous childbearing.

These arrangements, which stood the test of experience throughout the centuries of high mortality, are strongly supported by popular beliefs, formalized in religious doctrine, and enforced by community sanctions. They are deeply woven into the social fabric and are slow to change. Mortality dropped rather promptly in response to external changes because mankind has always coveted health. The decline of fertility, however, awaited the gradual obsolescence of age-old social and economic institutions and the emergence of a new ideal in matters of family size.

The new ideal of the small family arose typically in the urban industrial society. It is impossible to be precise about the various casual factors, but apparently many were important. Urban life stripped the family of many functions in production, consumption, recreation, and education. In factory employment the individual stood on his own accomplishments. The new mobility of young people and the anonymity of city life reduced the pressures toward traditional behaviour exerted by the family and community. In a period of rapidly developing technology new skills were needed, and new opportunities for individual advancement arose. Educa-

[2]Louis I. Dublin, Alfred J. Lotka, and Mortimer Spiegelman, *Length of Life,* New York, The Ronald Press, 1949.
[3]A. M. Carr-Saunders, *World Population,* Oxford, The Claredon Press, 1936, pp. 84–105.

tion and a rational point of view became increasingly important. As a consequence the cost of child-rearing grew and the possibilities for economic contributions by children declined. Falling death-rates at once increased the size of the family to be supported and lowered the inducements to have many births. Women, moreover, found new independence from household obligations and new economic roles less compatible with child-rearing.

Under these multiple pressures old ideals and beliefs began to weaken, and the new ideal of a small number of children gained strength. A trend toward birth restriction started in the urban upper classes and gradually moved down the social scale and out to the countryside. For the most part this restriction of childbearing was accomplished by the use of folk methods of contraception that have been widely known for centuries throughout the world. However, they were not widely used until the incentive for birth restriction became strong. Later, presumably in response to the new demands, the modern and more efficient methods of contraception were developed and gained widespread acceptance.[4] By the middle nineteen-thirties birth-rates throughout the modern West had reached very low levels. The transition to an efficient recruitment of life on the basis of low birth-rates and low death-rates was virtually completed. Because the decline of the birth-rate lagged behind that of the death-rate, pending the reorientation of attitudes and beliefs about child-bearing, the transition produced an unparalleled period of population growth.

In brief, this is the standard interpretation of the demographic transition. There are other views but they will not stand close scrutiny. One of them is that modern technology has reduced reproductive capacity by producing better diets. This theory fails, among other things, to account for the finding that when the urban women of today do not practice contraception they conceive about as readily as their predecessors did two centuries ago.[5] Neither can the invention of modern contraceptive methods be thought of as the fundamental cause. The trend toward decline was well under way before modern methods had any appreciable importance.

The cases that do not fit easily into the standard interpretation are also important to an understanding of the decline in fertility. Birth-rates have declined outside the urban-industrial setting and, on occasion, have failed to decline in it. American birth-rates were dropping early in the nineteenth century, but the drop was from extremely high levels to those more nearly characterizing Europe. In France, however, rural birth-rates apparently were dropping in the eighteenth century. An early rise of rationalism and a secular point of view may have been involved, but this explanation raises more questions than it answers. Similarly, birth-rates were falling rapidly between the world wars in the Balkans, and notably in Bulgaria which is almost wholly agricultural. Here we may note the presence of popular education, an awareness of the outside world, rapidly improving health

[4]Regine K. Stix and Frank W. Notestein, *Controlled Fertility,* Baltimore, The Williams & Wilkins Company, 1940, pp. 144–58.
[5]Biological and Medical Committee of the Royal Commission on Population of Great Britain. "Reproductive Capacity and the Birth Rate" (*Papers of the Royal Commission on Population,* vol. iv), London, His Majesty's Stationery Office, 1950.

and an extreme shortage of land newly intensified by international restrictions on migration.

Ireland is the most outstanding and difficult case. It is the only country that reduced its population during the last century. The main factor was wholesale emigration beginning after the potato famine. Its birth-rate, however, also fell sharply. The decline came in an essentially rural culture and almost exclusively by means of rising age at marriage and increasing spinsterhood. There has been very little control of fertility within marriage. Here, then, is a rural society in which the motives for reducing fertility became so strong that reproduction was controlled by a measure of self-restraint that other populations have been unwilling to accept. The situation seems so unusual as to make its repetition in other parts of the world unlikely.

On the other side of the matter, birth-rates have failed to decline in a number of urban settings, notably in Egypt and the Far East.⁶ In these instances, however, the city dwellers do not represent major proportions of the total population. We may note, moreover, that health conditions are poor, there is little popular education, the middle classes are weak, and often much of the labour force is transient, retaining its familiar roots in the countryside. It is also true that the higher economic groups are controlling their reproduction to some extent.

It is evident that urbanization provides no mystical means for the reduction of fertility. The small family ideal and strong motivation for the reduction of births have arisen in a variety of conditions. At present we cannot either list all of the factors involved or attach precise weights to the factors we can list. There is, however, good reason to believe that among the important factors are: the growing importance of the individual rather than the family, and particularly the extended family group; the development of a rational and secular point of view; the growing awareness of the world and modern techniques through popular education; improved health; and the appearance of alternatives to early marriage and childbearing as a means of livelihood and prestige for women.

Some of these factors have been present in most of the situations in which fertility has declined in rural areas. Many have been absent where urban fertility has failed to decline. But it is in the urban-industrial society that all have been present in greatest force. Looking at the scene as a whole, it is difficult to escape the conclusion that the development of modern technology lies at the root of the matter. The societies that developed the technology which produced the declines in mortality were ultimately transformed by the very requirements of that technology in ways that brought forward the small family ideal and the practice of birth restriction.

The population of the modern West may or may not increase considerably in the future. When death-rates are low, rather small changes in the proportions married and in the number of children born to married

⁶Clyde V. Kiser, "The Demographic Position of Egypt," *Demographic Studies of Selected Areas of Rapid Growth*, New York, Milbank Memorial Fund, 1944, pp. 97–121; Kingsley Davis, *The Population of India and Pakistan*, Princeton, Princeton University Press, 1951, pp. 67–82.

women can make the difference between growth and decline. But the almost automatic increase of the transitional period seems to be over. From the point of view problems of food, one important fact should be noted: these populations can check their growth by a further restriction of births any time the wisdom of such a course becomes generally obvious.

Evidence from Non-European Experience

One of the crucial questions in demographic analysis is whether that part of the world's population whose fertility remains very high would react as Europeans did if submitted to similar circumstances. There can be no certain answer. On the evidence thus far considered we may note only that the principles drawn upon in our account are very general ones —hence probably widely transferable under appropriate circumstances.

This view is strengthened by Japan's experience, which does not differ in essentials from that of Europe. Here, too, the death-rate led the birth-rate in the decline. Moreover, the urban-rural and regional differences in fertility are reminiscent of those in the West. Perhaps the greatest difference lies in the fact that a relatively large part of the decline in fertility was due to rising age at marriage. However, contraception is practised extensively in the urban centres, and currently abortion is rife throughout the nation.[7] During its period of modernization the population has grown from about 30 to more than 84 millions. Moreover, although birth-rates have declined sharply since 1920, the transition is by no means complete. By the time it is complete the period of modernization may have lasted from a century to a century and a half and have resulted in a three-to-fourfold multiplication of numbers.[8]

The hypothesis that the principles of the European analysis are transferable to other peoples receives indirect support of another sort. Where, as in Formosa and Ceylon, economic development has taken a different course, the population trends have also been different. In both cases colonial Governments have facilitated a rapid expansion of production in agriculture and rather little has been done about non-agricultural production. In both cases efficient government, rising production, and effective public health programmes have reduced death-rates sharply.

Between 1905 and the early years of the last war, the Japanese transformed Formosa from one of the most unhealthy regions in the Far East to one of the healthiest. Without benefit of sulfa drugs, antibiotics, or modern insecticides, the death-rate was reduced to 20 per 1,000 by 1940.[9] Since the war, and with the assistance of funds, medical supplies, and technicians from the United States, the death-rate has been further reduced. In Ceylon the essentials of the story are not too much different for

[7]Irene B. Taeuber and Marshall C. Balfour, "The Control of Fertility in Japan," *Approaches to Problems of High Fertility in Japan,* New York, Milbank Memorial Fund, 1952, pp. 102–28.
[8]Marshall C. Balfour, *et al., Public Health and Demography in the Far East,* New York, The Rockefeller Foundation, 1950, pp. 13–50.
[9]George W. Barclay, "Colonial Development and Population in Taiwan." Unpublished thesis, Princeton University, 1952.

our purposes.[10] The early reductions in death-rates were somewhat less impressive, but the recent ones even more spectacular. Under the impact of a vigorous antimalarial programme, the death-rate dropped from 20 per 1,000 in 1946 to 13 in 1950.[11]

Meanwhile nothing much has happened to the birth-rate of either area. That of Formosa has, if anything, risen, and that of Ceylon probably has remained rather steady. The 1940 figure was 44 per 1,000 in Formosa, and the 1950 figure was 40 per 1,000 in Ceylon. Moreover, this effective stability of birth-rates is exactly what one would expect on the basis of our European analysis. In both regions agricultural development has been accomplished with a minimum of disturbance to the existing social order. Foreign technicians have provided the necessary initiative and supervision. There has been little general education and little occasion to learn new skills in an unfamiliar setting. Even in the field of public health the control of disease has meant an emphasis on doing things for people, rather than on teaching people to do things for themselves. In short, the programmes of agricultural development administered by outsiders have enhanced production and improved health, but they have also left relatively untouched the details of social organization, and the customs, attitudes, and beliefs of the population which throughout the centuries served to maintain high birth-rates.

The results in the cases under consideration are rates of natural increase that have exceeded 2 per cent per year for a considerable time and that are currently running to nearly 3 per cent. Such rates, if maintained, double the stock every 23 years. The case of Puerto Rico is in principle the same. The natural increase is about 3 per cent per year and there are already more than 650 persons per square mile.[12] Thus far rapid agricultural development under colonial and semi-colonial management appears to have delayed the demographic transition. It has speeded the decline of the death-rate, and done so with almost startling efficiency in the past decade. But it appears to have delayed the sorts of social change from which the restriction of childbearing might be expected to emerge.

Both the Japanese experience and the different course of events produced by a different sort of economic development in such areas as Ceylon, Formosa, and Puerto Rico tend to confirm the hypothesis that the principles drawn from the European demographic transition are widely applicable throughout the world.

The Problems of Densely Settled Areas of High Fertility

To say that the principles drawn from the European analysis apply to the world's present areas of high fertility is, of course, a far cry from saying that we may expect events to take a similar course. Possibly they will in the parts of the world that, like Europe at the beginning of its transi-

[10]Irene B. Taeuber, "Ceylon as a Demographic Laboratory: Preface to Analysis," *Population Index*, vol. xv, No. 4 (Oct. 1949), pp. 293–304.

[11]United Nations, *Demographic Yearbook,* 1951, New York, 1952 (Sales No. 1952, XIII.I).

[12]*Ibid.*

tion, are relatively lightly populated in relation to the resources potentially available. But in the densely settled regions of Asia the initial conditions are strikingly different from those of Europe a century ago. It is to these regions, containing more than half of the world population, that we shall devote our attention because they present the major problems both of food supply and of population change.

It would, of course, be advantageous if the transition to low birth- and death-rates could come as an automatic by-product of economic development. Difficult social, political, and moral questions could then be avoided. Economic development is generally wanted, at least in principle, and is urgently needed to meet the immediate problems of poverty and disease. With an automatic demographic transition, changes that are immediately wanted could become the unrecognized carriers for the changes that are ultimately necessary. However, many factors suggest that the regions under discussion face no such easy prospect.

Much remains unknown about the actual demographic situation, and still less is known about the details of the economy and of the resources available. Moreover, the situation is by no means uniform from region to region. For our purposes, however, the general picture is clear. The populations are heavily agrarian; probably more than three-quarters of the people are dependent on agriculture. The amount of cultivated land per person is extremely small, and significant extensions would be expensive. The vital rates are not known precisely, but there is good reason to believe that birth-rates are generally above 40 per 1,000.[13] This figure is higher than any ever recorded in western Europe. In spite of universally high birth-rates, population growth is by no means universally rapid. Indeed, by Western standards it has been rather slow, because death-rates are in general extremely high. Again, exact figures are not available for the major populations. However, the expectation of life at birth is probably not as much as thirty-five years in India, and may be even lower in China.

Starting from this position, what is the magnitude of the economic task if the transition to low birth- and death-rates is to come as the by-product of a successful programme of economic development? Since no special effort would be made to induce declining birth-rates, our previous analysis would lead us to expect no immediate or substantial change. Birth-rates would remain for several decades at about their present level—say 40 per 1,000 population. Moreover, efforts to reduce death-rates would be fostered. Few people would hold that a demographic situation was at once sufficiently relaxed to make unnecessary any effort to reduce the birth-rate, and so desperate that reasonably available techniques for preventing death should be withheld. What, then, would happen to population increase?

A death-rate of more than 20 per 1,000 would be most unlikely under the assumed conditions of economic development which would provide progressively rising *per capita* incomes and reasonable health protection. A birth-rate of 40 and a death-rate of 20 yield an increase of 20 per 1,000, or 2 per cent per year. This rate doubles a population in 35 years and

[13]United Nations, *Demographic Yearbook,* 1949–50, New York, 1950 (Sales No. 1951. XIII.i), p. 14.

trebles it in 52 years. Formosa experienced such a rate of increase during the period of Japanese control and, as we have seen, in several regions the current increase is even more rapid. Under our assumption of a programme of economic development, which is to be continuously successful in improving living conditions, birth-rates would eventually begin to fall. In the early stages, however, the reduction would be offset by the continued decline of the death-rate. It seems likely that, under these imaginary conditions, the rate of population growth would be between 2 and 3 per cent per year for several decades—perhaps for two generations.

A programme of economic development sufficiently successful to yield progressively increasing *per capita* income would therefore need to be a programme that improved living conditions for populations growing at between 2 and 3 per cent per year. At least this would be the case under our assumption that no special efforts were required to reduce birth-rates or to check the decline of the death-rate. Such an expansion of the economy is no mean undertaking even when land and other resources are relatively abundant, populations are literate, and the incomes are high enough to facilitate capital accumulation. But it is a staggering task in the absence of such conditions.

Let us consider some of the problems that would be faced in the Orient. It may be taken for granted that the labour force in agriculture ought not to expand. If *per capita* incomes are to increase, the need is for more, not less, land per worker. The increase should be drained off to the non-agricultural sector of the economy. Such a transition would involve an enormous effort. It would mean that a sector of the economy on which less than one-quarter of the population is dependent would have to absorb the total increase. On this reckoning a 2 per cent rate of increase in the total population would require the non-agricultural sector of the economy to expand at an average annual rate of 5 per cent per year for the first thirty years. Among other things, such an increase would require a rapid expansion in non-agricultural investment and in non-agricultural skills. Meanwhile, a relatively constant agricultural labour force would have to increase its production at rates well above 2 per cent per year in order to provide an improving food supply for populations growing at 2 per cent. Heavy investment in agriculture would also be required. Under these imaginary conditions a 4 per cent annual rate of expansion in total production would scarcely seem adequate.[1]

Moreover, there would be long-run problems of sheer size involved. It seems most unlikely that the regions concerned could expand their agricultural production rapidly enough to provide adequate diets for two billion people in thirty-five years. To do so might well require trebling agricultural production. England and Japan solved their analogous problems by selling their industrial and commercial services to the world in exchange for food, but their populations constituted no substantial part of the world's total. Here, however, we are dealing with more than half of

[1]United Nations, *Measures for the Economic Development of Under-Developed Countries.* Report by a group of experts appointed by the Secretary-General of the United Nations, New York, 1951 (Sales No. 1951.II.B.2), p. 46.

the world's population. The problems of securing the necessary resources, production, and markets for trade on this scale would seem insuperable.

Unfortunately this is not the end of the difficulty. Much might be accomplished if there were ideal conditions of social-economic organization, appropriate skills, and populations well oriented to the factory and market economy. The actual situation is the vastly different one in which new Governments are endeavouring to rule huge numbers of uneducated peasants who are increasingly aware of their difficult position. Great unrest, great uncertainty, and great yearning for a better life are present, and complicate the attainment of the discipline needed to build a strong economic machine.

It may be argued that the picture is overdrawn. We have dealt with an annual increase of 2 per cent, whereas in most of the regions under consideration the rate of population growth has been less than 1 per cent. But recall the problem. We are discussing what will occur. Instead we are considering what would be required if reliance were to be placed on the automatic processes of social-economic change to bring the transition to low birth- and death-rates.

With existing high birth-rates and modern methods of controlling disease, a smaller rate of increase—say 1 per cent—would mean either: (a) that gains in production were too small to permit the attainment of reasonable health in spite of efforts in that direction or (b) that mortality was intentionally held high to relieve the pressure of population increase. The latter could scarcely be envisioned except as a temporary means of avoiding the perpetuation of the former. In reality, therefore, both alternatives come to the same thing. They amount to holding death-rates up, as a substitute for reducing birth-rates. That amounts, in turn, to admitting that rates of economic development that permit increases of only 1 per cent are inadequate to yield sustained improvements in living conditions if birth-rates stay high.

The conclusion is one that an examination of the past records of India, Java, and Egypt amply justifies. Indeed, as their records show, the dangers are greater than we have indicated. Programmes of economic development that just manage to meet the needs of gradually expanding numbers run the risk of being worse than useless. Being insufficient to change the conditions of life, they run the risk of expanding the base populations without reducing their capacity for still further growth.

To me it seems evident that almost insuperable difficulties are involved in achieving the sort of economic development required to permit reliance upon the automatic processes of social-economic change for the transition to low birth- and death-rates. The difficult initial conditions, and the new efficiency with which disease can be controlled, require measures that will speed the reduction of birth-rates, if programmes of economic development are to achieve their objectives. But this conclusion has an embarrassing consequence. If it is valid, the already difficult task of economic development becomes more complicated than ever. The objective is no longer restricted to the increase of production. It now also becomes that of speeding the processes of social change in directions that yield falling birth-rates, which in turn will permit more rapid increases in *per capita* income. In effect, we must move from economics to sociology and back again, travelling always in a political world.

Moreover, the problem is that of stimulating social change without inducing a measure of social disorganization that leads to catastrophe. By definition, the stimulation of social change involves weakening loyalties to the institutions and beliefs that have served to give stability and continuity. When these bonds are weakened, internal pressures may well become explosive. The very efficiency of modern medical techniques enhances this risk. It is now quite possible to keep people alive in spite of appalling living conditions. There is much less danger than there used to be that the failure to enhance production will lead to the curtailment of population growth by epidemic and starvation. Now the danger is that even the best efforts will fail to improve living conditions among populations newly aware of their disadvantaged positions.

Rising internal pressure and the weakening of traditional social bonds can easily result in political explosions; indeed, they are doing so. It is not at all unlikely that political explosion, and the economic disorganization which accompanies it, will provide the major check to population increase in the future. Populations living close to the level of subsistence, yet dependent on increasingly complex economic organizations, are vulnerable to the failures that complexity entails in times of disorganization. Today, the risks appear to be those of political upheaval, its attendant economic disorganization, and the resulting catastrophic loss of life. To be sure, times of upheaval can also be times of rapid social change that could assist in the resolution of long-run problems. Before the fact, however, the direction of the change is difficult to predict. Moreover, the loss of life could be great. In view of this risk, the advocate of social upheaval must be completely convinced of the futility of a humanitarian policy of social evolution.

It is in this tense situation that the resolution of long-run problems requires the stimulation of social change. The difficulties are insidious. No Government and no international organization can afford to take the long view when pressed by immediate emergencies. The situation two decades from now attracts little attention when a major catastrophe looms this year. Hand-to-mouth action is literally essential; yet it may intensify future problems.

The problems are by no means limited to demographic matters. It seems likely, for example, that immediate increases in the production of food can best be obtained by steps that involve minimum disturbance of the existing social-economic organizations, interference with vested interests, and difficulty in obtaining community co-operation. In short, immediate gains in production can probably be maximized by minimizing the changes in the institutional organization of the economy. Yet, in the long run, fundamental changes in the institutions, attitudes, and beliefs are probably as essential to the attainment of high economic productivity as they are to stimulating the decline of the birth-rate. The social organization of a peasant society is ill-adapted to the achievement of high technological proficiency.[15] There is much easy talk about the necessity for each society to follow a line of development consonant with its own values, but those who seek to reap either the productive possibilities of modern technology or the lasting benefits of good health will, in all probability, have to undergo a reorientation of their value structures. At least such a reorientation has occurred in all populations that have made substantial progress toward these goals.

The difficulty is that the need for immediate efficiency requires a minimum of disturbance, whereas, long-run success requires rapid social-economic evolution. In the West and in Japan the possibility of a severalfold multiplication of population permitted the necessary compromises between immediate and eventual needs. The apparent impossibility of such multiplication in the regions under discussion is the major source of the difficulty. Hence the need for attaining new efficiency in the processes of social change.

It is this line of reasoning that led to our initial proposition that the important economic problem of population is not either that of locating some ideal goal in terms of size, or that of finding the means of attaining adequate living conditions for some inevitable rate of increase. The real problem is that of population change. Within the limits of the possible, what course of events will minimize human suffering?

Implications for Research

To answer such a question our knowledge is at present wholly inadequate in the fields of economics, sociology, and demography. In demography our theory of the broad processes of population change seems to have been sufficiently tested to prove its general validity. It is adequate to delineate the nature of the problem at hand. But it does not answer the concrete questions on which information is needed either for purposes of prediction or for the formulation of policy. It does not do so because it tells us almost nothing precise about costs, magnitudes, and rates of change; and it gives us a minimum of information about the effects of particular courses of action. Yet the formulation of wise policy will require as detailed knowledge as it is possible to secure. Whatever the situation may be in economics, in demography it seems to me that there is less need for work on the over-arching theory of change than for knowledge at lower levels of generality.

We may illustrate the needs in the case of fertility. We have argued that reduction of the risk that economic development may fail to achieve its goal requires an early decline in fertility. In effect this means endeavouring to reduce the birth-rates within the peasant society. Both theory and experience indicate that such a reduction is difficult to bring about, but also that it is not necessarily impossible. What do we need to know to

[15]Wilbert E. Moore, *Industrialization and Labor: Social Aspects of Economic Development*. Published for the Institute of World Affairs, New School for Social Research, Ithaca, Cornell University Press, 1951.

permit an intelligent effort to be made? There are two broad lines of approach. In the first place, direct measures may be taken. In the second place, background factors of the economy and society can be manipulated to some extent.

One direct measure is to lift the age at marriage. What would be the best measures of community education, legislation, and incentive taxation to take in this direction? The problems are suitable ones for experiment, but we know almost nothing about them.

Direct efforts can also be made to reduce childbearing by spreading the practice of birth control in its various forms. We know that resistance is great but that, under suitable conditions, something might be accomplished. Although people in most peasant societies want large families, the truly huge family is not always considered desirable, particularly by the mothers. Some interest in the possibility of limiting childbearing is always present. The extent of such interest does not make itself evident currently, because the majority of the population takes it for granted that the restriction of childbearing is not really a practical matter. An intensive programme of public education, coupled with competent technical advice, might accomplish a good deal. But here again the questions are what precise programmes, with what results, and at what costs. The questions are readily amenable to investigation and experiment. It is within the bounds of possibility that the wise use of modern methods of communication and training to promote higher marriage age and the practice of birth control would bring a considerable reduction of the birth-rate even in peasant societies.

The problems will not be easily solved because local willingness to attack them energetically presupposes an understanding of their importance. Dominant beliefs and attitudes often are not congenial to the spread of such an understanding. Little enthusiasm can be expected for activities designed to reduce the birth-rate if, as is often the case, the community thinks it needs more children instead of fewer, and views action taken to limit childbearing as immoral. In this siuation the second type of approach, which endeavours to stimulate interest in family limitation by manipulating the background factors, may prove to be even more important. We may give only a few examples of the sorts of questions needing examination.

If, as our analysis suggests, the dominance of the extended family is an important element in supporting high birth-rates, what can be done to weaken that institution? An obvious approach is to provide more effective means of fulfilling the functions now served by the extended family. Many of these fall in the field of elementary economic security. What are the alternative possibilities and what are their costs? At present it is often economically advantageous to have many children. How could the lines of interest be changed in the most acceptable form by means, for example, of taxation and of changes in property institutions? These questions have not been seriously examined.

For the purpose of inculcating an innovative point of view and a rationalistic approach to life, could not something be done about the ways in which agricultural innovations are introduced to the community? Could not the community organizations for the improvement of agriculture be utilized in ways that would give added prestige to families with educated children? In short could not existing interest in better crops be used to extend interest in other forms of economic and social change?

There would seem to be even more direct possibilities connected with public health activity. Could health programmes be used to transform the existing ideal of many children into the ideal of a few healthy children? In general, would it not be possible to construct programmes of agricultural development and public health in ways that would stimulate many of the social changes that came as a by-product of urban-industrial development in Europe? Very little work has been done on this problem.

There are any number of such questions. How can programmes of land development be managed to increase the mobility of young people, thereby weakening the pressures toward traditional behaviour exerted by the elders of the family and community? It is the women who best understand the difficulties of bearing and rearing large numbers of children. What measures can be taken to enhance their status? What economic and social alternatives to early marriage and abundant childbearing could be provided for them? Are cottage industries so important to the economy as to be worth the dangers of adding new economic functions that are fully compatible with high reproductive performance?

Although we have argued that urban-industrial development will not be sufficient to bring the demographic transition, it is also clear that it will be necessary in economic terms and useful in relation to population trends. How can such development be guided in ways that speed the rise of marriage age and the restriction of childbearing?

What are the possibilities in the field of popular education? How can its scope and content be arranged to stimulate an innovative and rational view of life, to enhance the importance of the individual as opposed to the extended family group, to improve the status of women, and to substitute the ideal of a healthy prosperous family for that of a large family? What are the possibilities, and what are the costs?

Perhaps the most fundamental of all questions are those of the allocation of scarce resources to meet unlimited needs. How much of the product of economic development can be allowed to go into immediate consumption, and how much must be deflected to capital equipment, education, health, and the provision of elemental security? The answers may well be essentially political, and the decisions are inevitably hard. They are being taken every day, implicitly. Nevertheless, there are differences of opinion as to what existing programmes may be expected to accomplish in the near future, and whether, if they succeed in their immediate aims, they may not do more harm than good in the long run. Such differences of opinion are eloquent testimony to the complexity of the problems and to the paucity of our knowledge.

We have confined our suggestions about the scope of needed research to questions of human fertility because that is the fundamental variable. In many situations, however, migration also offers a possibility of relief during the period of transitional growth. Here, too, our information on the economic, social, and demographic aspects of specific plans is grossly and needlessly defective.

Little in the way of concrete action may be expected until the political leadership of the regions concerned becomes aware of the need for curtailing population growth. In a number of regions such an awareness shows signs of developing at the highest levels, but it is not as yet broadly based.[16] Widespread studies by local scholars of the processes of population change under a variety of conditions of economic development could do much to stimulate interest. The subject is charged with emotion, and citizens of prosperous nations are inevitably open to suspicion as to their disinterestedness. It seems likely that local political leaders can be brought to an understanding of the relation of population growth to health and prosperity most effectively through the work of their own scholars studying the practical problems of population, social, and economic development.

Given an understanding of the problems by local leaders, and a large store of detailed information about the costs and potential results of a wide range of possibilities, the problems may yet find their resolution. It is quite possible that we can learn to speed the reduction of fertility with something of the efficiency with which we already reduce mortality. If so, we shall greatly enhance the chance that economic development can mean sustained improvements in health and living conditions for the world's poorest peoples.

If there is a moral to this analysis for the economist, it lies in the fact that he should stray from the well-worn and familiar paths if he is to be truly useful. His problems are not simply those of production, distribution, and consumption within the framework of well-established institutions. In view of the demographic situation, his hopes for long-run success in ameliorating living conditions must lie in speeding the change of institutions. In short, to be useful the economist must also be a general social scientist, for, in view of the demographic situation, the key problems are the interrelated ones of social, economic, and political change.

[16]Frank W. Notestein, "Policy of the Indian Government on Family Limitation," *Population Index,* vol. xvii, No. 4 (Oct. 1951), pp. 254–63 (see also vol. xviii, No. 1 (Jan. 1952), p. 20).

FINANCIAL POLICY

32. Monetary Policy in Underdeveloped Countries
Arthur I. Bloomfield*

The Institutional Setting of Monetary Policy in
Underdeveloped Countries

Among the many institutional characteristics common to underdeveloped countries in general are some of special relevance in influencing the potential role, scope, and effectiveness of monetary policy.

Money does not play the same pervasive role that it does in economically advanced countries. A substantial portion of the agricultural production, which bulks so large in the aggregate output of most underdeveloped countries, is usually of a subsistence rather than market character. In many rural areas in these countries, moreover, barter transactions rather than purchase and sale predominate, money being used mainly for the payment of taxes or for the purchase of a narrow range of essential goods from the market sector of the economy. A considerable part of the aggregate economic activity of underdeveloped countries is thus often outside the scope of monetary policy.

As is well known, externally-generated fluctuations play an especially important role in the economic life of the majority of underdeveloped countries in view of their heavy dependence upon exports. Since their exports consist mainly of primary products subject to wide swings in world demand and prices, underdeveloped countries tend to undergo wide externally-generated swings in their external reserves, money supply and money incomes. The primary changes in the money supply associated with such swings are not easily subject to the direct control of the central bank nor, as will be noted, can they easily be offset by central bank action on that part of the money supply which is so subject.

Changes in the volume of central bank credit to the government and its agencies are often another important cause of changes in the money supply in underdeveloped countries because of strong development drives, inadequate tax systems and narrow markets in government securities. The central bank may have great difficulty in controlling such credit if the government is insistent upon undue recourse to the central bank to finance its expenditures.

It is mainly, therefore, on that segment of the money supply which is generated by the commercial banks' credit operations with the private

*From C. J. Friedrich and S. E. Harris, eds., *Public Policy* (Harvard University, 1956). Arthur I. Bloomfield is Professor of Economics and Finance, Wharton School of Finance and Commerce, University of Pennsylvania.

sector of the economy[1]—which is usually a relatively small segment of the money supply in most underdeveloped countries—that the central bank is able to exert its most direct influence. Thus, if the money supply tends to rise unduly because of large externally-induced acquisitions of exchange reserves or large central bank-financed budget deficits, it would probably be too much to expect the central bank to be able to *contract* commercial bank credit to the private sector, which will in fact be increasing its demand for accommodations[2] at a time when the commercial banks have a large amount of reserves with which to lend. At best, the central bank may be able to do no more than prevent the commercial banks from adding further to the money supply on the basis of these added reserves, i.e., prevent a secondary expansion of the money supply. However, when an inflationary expansion of the money supply originates from an undue increase in commercial bank credit to the private sector, the central bank should be able to keep such expansion in check.

Difficulties would similarly tend to occur when there is an externally-induced decline in exchange reserves, the money supply and money incomes because of a drop in world demand for the country's exports. The central bank may be able at best to prevent the commercial banks from bringing about a secondary contraction in the money supply and additional deflationary pressures. If it *were* successful at such a time in inducing some credit expansion to the private sector, the drain on exchange reserves would tend to be increased, especially in the light of the high marginal propensity to import characteristic of most underdeveloped countries. How far such counter-cyclical action could be pursued by the central bank, and in fact by the government, would thus depend upon the amount of exchange reserves that had previously been accumulated and upon whether or not and how far imports and other payments abroad were officially restricted.

In most underdeveloped countries, the banking habit is not as yet widespread. Banking touches only a relatively small part of the population. The use of checking accounts and other bank services is confined primarily to traders, businessmen and government entities. Savings accounts, however, are somewhat more widely used by the general public. Some 50 per cent or more of the money supply (as conventionally defined) usually takes the form of currency in circulation. One consequence of this high degree of preference for currency is to keep down the deposit-creating capacity of the commercial banks on the basis of any given accretion of reserves, since any given increase in bank loans and invest-

---

[1] And by the central bank's credit operations with the private sector in those cases where the central bank engages in a commercial banking business. A distinction should be drawn between the foreign-trade and the domestic components of the private sector. Commercial bank credit usually goes mainly to the former.

[2] To take but one obvious example: a rising export surplus resulting from increased foreign demand and prices leads to larger demands upon the banks for credits to finance the larger aggregate value of foreign trade. In addition, the expansion in domestic activity, money incomes and money supply associated with a rising export surplus or a central bank-financed budget deficit stimulates increased demands from the private sector for bank credit in general.

ments leads to a significant drain of currency into circulation, thereby depleting bank reserves and tending to reduce the ability of the banks further to expand their credit operations.[3] This may be a factor of some help to the monetary authorities on occasions when bank reserves are changing rapidly and cannot easily be controlled.

Underdeveloped countries are also characterized by the limited scope or virtual absence of money markets and especially of capital markets. There are few organized markets in bills or commercial paper. There is often a lack of discountable paper, commercial bank loans being commonly made on an over-draft basis. The markets in short- and long-term government securities are usually very narrow, as are the markets in corporate stocks. These factors limit the scope and effectiveness of central bank open-market operations and to some extent discount operations as well. . . .

It follows from the underdeveloped nature of the money and capital markets that the interest rate structure in underdeveloped countries is largely unintegrated and that over a large part of the economy interest rates are relatively insensitive to the actions of the monetary authorities. Even within given sectors or localities of the market there is often a wide diversity of interest rates because of wide differences in the type and quality of risk or because of the forces of custom and tradition. There is an especially wide gap between interest rates in the so-called organized and unorganized sectors of the money market. Interest rates undeniably play a lesser role than they do in more developed countries in influencing the volume and direction of investment. In the *modus operandi* of monetary policy, the availability of credit factor is likely to be more important, relative to the cost factor, than it is in more developed countries. (In some cases, in fact, the authorities fix maximum loan rates for banks or official lending institutions.)

In most underdeveloped countries there is a marked lack of balance in the allocation of commercial bank credit. Commercial banks, in large part because of their traditional concern for a very high degree of liquidity, tend to concentrate heavily on short-term loans to finance foreign trade, domestic commerce, inventory holdings and related short-term transactions. Such loans are also likely to be more profitable than other types of lending. Loans for productive purposes to industry and agriculture, and especially medium- and long-term loans, usually constitute only a relatively negligible part of bank portfolios. Commercial banking facilities are concentrated mainly in urban centers. Established concerns tend to be favored over new ones, and large concerns over small ones. Branches of foreign banks, which play so important a role in the banking structure of underdeveloped countries, focus predominantly on servicing the foreign-trade sector of the economy.

Because of these banking habits and of a lack of "credit-worthiness," large sections of the population, especially farmers and small businessmen, cannot satisfy their credit needs through normal banking channels and must rely in large part upon moneylenders, merchants, and land-

---

[3] The degree of multiple deposit creation is likely to be further held down by the relatively high marginal propensity to import, which tends to result in substantial external drains on bank reserves when bank credit is expanded.

owners at exorbitant interest rates. While such lenders cannot, to be sure, "create" money, they can affect the income-velocity of money by influencing its rate of turnover and by providing money-substitutes, e.g., open-book credits; to some degree they can thus influence the aggregate volume of spending and the level of economic activity. Yet for the most part they are outside the reach of the monetary authorities.

Commercial banks in most underdeveloped countries tend to maintain the ratios of their reserves to deposit liabilities well in excess of the legal minima, where such are imposed. A substantial fraction of any increment of reserves, over and above that needed for legal requirements, tends to be held idle. This is another factor, along with the large internal and external drains noted earlier, tending to keep down the coefficient of multiple credit expansion. This tendency to maintain relatively large excess reserves reflects such factors as the lack of an adequate supply of short-term liquid assets that would provide suitable secondary reserves, the volatility of externally dependent underdeveloped countries, the susceptibility of the banks to large and sudden withdrawals of currency and the absence in many cases of a long-standing tradition of discounting at or borrowing from the central bank.

Since commercial banks in the majority of underdeveloped countries do not discount at or borrow from the central bank to any great extent or on a frequent or regular basis,[4] the potential effectiveness of the discount mechanism as a credit-control instrument in such countries is weakened. Since, moreover, the commercial banks tend to permit their holdings of excess reserves to undergo substantial fluctuations, the exact degree of their response to any given change in their reserves tends to be less predictable than in the more developed countries where banks usually keep relatively small excess reserves. Further limitations are thus imposed on the effective use of the traditional instruments of credit control.

Although all too little is known about the behavior of money in underdeveloped countries, there is reason to believe that the income-velocity of money in such countries tends, in the short run at least, to be much more stable than in developed ones. This stems from the fact that holdings of inactive money balances tend to be relatively small (although in some Far Eastern countries a substantial amount of currency may be hoarded), or at least are not subject to large or sudden short-run shifts.[5] If the income-velocity of money does change significantly in the short run, it is generally because of changes in the rate of turnover of transactions balances, e.g., due to expectations of sharply rising or falling prices. Increases in the money supply (after allowance for the resulting drains through imports) thus tend ordinarily to be more closely correlated with increases in national money income in underdeveloped than in developed countries;

[4]There are, however, some notable exceptions to this rule, such as Japan, South Korea, Chile, Colombia, Paraguay, Guatemala, Costa Rica and Nicaragua.
[5]It would be interesting to see how those who emphasize the "speculative motive" or "liquidity-preference proper" as "the" determinant of interest rates, with other demands for money being regarded as inelastic, would apply their doctrine to underdeveloped countries. We suspect that some substantial modifications would be necessary.

additions to the money supply tend quickly to be spent on consumption or to provide the finance for investment, thereby raising incomes, and usually prices, until the added money is absorbed in larger transactions and finance balances. To the extent that the authorities have a firm control over the supply of money, this relative short-run stability of velocity would clearly be a factor working in favor of the effectiveness of monetary policy. But, for reasons already suggested, such control is often especially difficult to attain in underdeveloped countries.

The role and scope of monetary policy in underdeveloped countries are greatly influenced by the strong development drives to which most of them are subject. These drives, superimposed upon economies of low savings propensities, low taxable capacities and relatively inelastic out-puts, make these countries highly sensitive to inflationary pressures and call for constant vigilance by the monetary authorities. They contribute to strong political pressures upon the central bank to extend credit unduly. They often make it necessary for the central bank to be more concerned with the development process, and to engage in a wider range of activities and operations, than is traditional with central banks in the more devel-oped countries.

It is evident from the foregoing discussion that monetary policy faces special problems and limitations in underdeveloped countries which lie deep in the institutional structures of such countries. It follows also that monetary policy in underdeveloped countries should not necessarily be evaluated in terms of the same standards and criteria applied in the more developed ones. The methods of implementing monetary policy, and the range and scope of central bank action, may well have to differ.

Objectives and Principles of Monetary Policy in Underdeveloped Countries

Fundamentally, the basic objectives of monetary policy, and indeed of fiscal policy, do not differ greatly in underdeveloped countries from those in more developed ones, despite the widely differing economic and social frameworks. Internal financial stability, high and rising levels of per capita income, and external payments balance: these are the major goals sought in each case. But there is likely to be a very substantial difference in emphasis on these goals in the two sets of countries. In developed coun-tries, the avoidance of inflation and deflation is usually the primary objective. In underdeveloped countries, on the other hand, the promotion of economic growth tends to overshadow all other goals of national eco-nomic policy; all too frequently, in fact, internal and external stability have been sacrificed in an attempt to achieve this basic objective. . . .

The problem of increasing and mobilizing real resources and of channel-ing them into expenditures serving the needs of balanced development— as well as the implementation of other measures designed to promote development—are primarily a responsibility of the government through its tax, expenditure, debt and other financial and economic policies. The formulation of the over-all development program itself is also primarily a government responsibility. The major objective and responsibility of the central bank should be to strive to achieve and maintain reasonable internal financial stability through control of the availability and cost of money. To the extent that the central bank is able, with the cooperation of the government, to achieve this objective, it will not only prevent the inequities and misuse of resources associated with inflation (or deflation), but also provide a necessary, though not sufficient, condition for increased saving, for attracting foreign investment and for promoting more balanced economic growth. As we shall see, the central bank can also contribute in other ways, within the framework of a policy aimed at stability, to encourage development. The maintenance of internal financial stability, it need hardly be added, would also help to foster, though not necessarily to assure, the maintenance of external payments stability as well.[6] External payments stability would in turn tend to facilitate the process of economic development. . . .

A major objective of policy must be to attempt to see to it that development takes place within a framework of reasonable financial stability, i.e., that aggregate spending is kept within the limits of available real resources at current prices.

Obviously, the central bank alone cannot assure such stability. At best its role can be only a contributory one, however strategic that role might be. The financial policies of the government must carry a large part of the load. There must in any case be the closest possible coordination between the policies of the central bank and the government if there is to be hope of a job well done. For example, an irresponsible fiscal policy could easily upset the efforts of the central bank to maintain internal and external stability, just as an ill-advised monetary policy could counteract the effects of a prudent fiscal policy. Besides, trade, payments and exchange policies must be closely integrated with both, especially in the face of large and persisting imbalances in international payments.

While the achievement and maintenance of monetary stability is the dominant contribution that the central bank can make to balanced economic development in underdeveloped countries, it can also promote this objective in other ways. Within the framework of a policy aimed at stability, it can seek to influence the flow of bank credit, and indeed of savings, in directions more in keeping with development ends. Thus, through selective credit controls applied to the banking system, through help in establishing and supporting special credit institutions and through influence over the lending policies of such institutions and of other institutional investors, it can help to some degree to rechannel real resources in desired directions, both between the public and the private sector, on the one hand, and within the private sector itself, on the other. The central bank can also play a useful role in increasing and mobilizing savings by helping to develop a market in government securities, by helping to establish special savings institutions, by encouraging a spread of banking

---

[6]By external payments stability we refer to a situation where the average payments and receipts of a country on current and ordinary long-term capital account are in reasonable balance over the course of the cycle without resort to import quotas, exchange restrictions on current account or excessive tariffs.

facilities and of the banking habit, by promoting the liquidity and solvency of the banking system and by other related measures.

In its attempt to maintain monetary stability, the central bank must constantly strive, despite the limitations to which it is subject, to adjust the aggregate money supply to the demands of the public for money balances at constant prices. These demands grow as the economy grows, thereby making possible a certain, though in most cases limited, rate of growth in the money supply without inflationary consequences. If the money supply is allowed to grow at a rate in excess of the public's demand for money at constant prices, there will be an upward pressure on prices; if it grows at a slower rate, there will be deflationary pressures and some retardation of production. In its attempt to keep the money supply growing at the "right" rate, however, the authorities will have to take account of undesirable developments that might occur in the balance of payments. If the pursuit of this goal involves large and persisting drains on exchange reserves, the authorities might have to slow up the rate of credit expansion; if it involves a large and persisting payments surplus, they might perhaps want to increase it.

Although the growth of real income is the major factor determining the public's demand for money, the rate of expansion in the money supply consistent with internal financial stability will not, of course, be exactly equal to the rate of growth of income. For one thing, the shrinkage of the non-monetary sector as the economy grows will in itself involve an increasing demand for money at constant prices. Moreover, the demand for money is likely to be stimulated by such factors as the growing differentiation of production, the spread of banking habits and the relative expansion of purely financial transactions. All these factors, which make for a decline in the income-velocity of money over time, would enable an expansion in the money supply at a rate somewhat greater than that of real income without inflationary consequences. On the other hand, when the public has little confidence that monetary stability can be maintained, there will be a move to economize on money holdings and the income-velocity of money will rise.

In its attempt to keep the money supply adjusted to the needs of the economy at constant prices, the central bank faces the special problem, noted in an earlier section, arising from wide externally induced swings in exchange reserves and in the money supply that occur from time to time in many underdeveloped countries.¹ These swings tend to disrupt the efforts of the central bank to maintain internal stability and militate against the steady course of economic development programs. Large externally induced surpluses in the balance of payments usually provide the economy with a greater amount of money than needed and tend to generate undesirable inflationary pressures. Conversely, large externally-induced deficits may involve undesirable deflationary pressures and a dangerous rate of drain on exchange reserves which would threaten to impair the country's ability to finance the imports of equipment and raw

¹In the longer run, with the development and diversification of the economy, the absolute and relative importance of such swings is likely to be reduced and their internal effects to be more easily offset or absorbed.

materials necessary for the continued implementation of the country's development program.

As noted earlier, there is little that the central bank can do by measures of credit policy to offset the primary expansions and contractions in the money supply resulting from such externally generated swings. To be sure, open-market sales or purchases of securities by the central bank to or from the *non-bank* public could, if substantial enough, help to offset these primary changes (and also the associated effect on commercial bank reserves), but the securities market is invariably too narrow to enable such offsetting to be carried very far. In general, the central bank's main responsibility at such times should be to try to prevent the secondary changes in the money supply that would tend to occur. To the extent that an underdeveloped country *is* able to control the magnitude of externally induced swings in the balance of payments and their primary impact on the money supply and money incomes, the problem is predominantly one, not for credit policy, but for fiscal payments and trade or exchange policy....

As one general rule, however, it may be stated that where export booms are believed to be temporary, the authorities should attempt to minimize their inflationary impact on the economy, and the distortions which such impact would tend to create, and thereby to conserve as large a part as possible of the accruing foreign exchange receipts, which would otherwise tend to be partly drained away through enlarged imports, often of a relatively unessential character. When exports fall off and the balance of payments becomes adverse because of slackening world demand, the authorities should similarly try to maintain the level of internal incomes and to use the previously accumulated reserves to finance those deficits and to maintain the level of essential imports. On the other hand, when the externally induced shifts in the balance of payments are believed to reflect more permanent or structural forces, it might be desirable to allow them to exert their impact on internal prices, incomes and expenditures. Alternatively, the exchange rate might have to be adjusted, or the country's investment program reoriented, in the light of the altered international economic position—both of which would likewise have internal repercussions. Admittedly, however, it is not always easy for the authorities to determine whether the change in exports is likely to be temporary or not. It goes without saying, moreover, that, regardless of official attempts at insulation, some degree of inflation and deflation is inevitable in export economies in the face of major export booms and recessions emanating from abroad. National measures alone are insufficient....

One of the problems to which the government and the central bank must constantly be alert is the need for instituting appropriate corrective measures in the face of large and persisting drains on exchange reserves, however generated. At just what point such measures should be instituted, however, and just what measures should be taken (e.g., credit restriction, fiscal retrenchment, exchange depreciation, or imposition or tightening of trade and payments controls) are obviously highly difficult questions to answer in any given case. In an effort to provide a criterion or warning signal for policy in this respect, a number of the newer central bank statutes in underdeveloped countries impose central bank reserve requirements of a novel type;[5] and, when the ratios in question fall to a certain "critical" level, specific actions must be taken. In other cases, where no such requirements, novel or otherwise, are imposed, "guiding principles" are inserted in the statutes to assist the authorities in the timing and choice of corrective measures to meet reserve drains. Analogously, some of the statutes also contain "guiding principles" or criteria for credit policy in the face of inflationary or deflationary movements at home.

While "criteria," "guiding principles" and "rules" are unquestionably of value in assisting the monetary authorities in the formulation and implementation of appropriate policies, especially in those underdeveloped countries where central banks were only recently established and where the requisite administrative skills and experience may be lacking, they cannot be expected to provide hard and fast rules to guide the authorities correctly under all possible circumstances. No formulas have as yet been discovered to assure appropriate monetary policy in all cases. There is no substitute in any given situation for sound and informed judgment, reached on the basis of a detailed examination and understanding of all available facts and criteria of relevance, and growing out of the lessons of experience.

Instruments of Credit Control in Underdeveloped Countries

We turn now to a discussion of the various instruments of general and selective credit control that have been employed by central banks in underdeveloped countries in recent years.

The scope for open-market operations in most underdeveloped countries, especially as an instrument of credit restraint, is narrowly limited for reasons mentioned earlier. Although the majority of central banks in underdeveloped countries are formally equipped with the power to engage in such operations, in most cases this power has been relatively inoperative. . . .

It is widely recognized that a market must first be developed before open-market operations can become an effective means of implementing monetary policy. . . .

Discount operations have likewise not been of much significance in the majority of underdeveloped countries as an instrument through which the central bank has been able to influence the availability and cost of credit. In many of these countries, especially in Asia and the Middle East, the reserves of the commercial banks are usually so ample as to preclude the need for any regular recourse to central bank credit via rediscounts and borrowing.[9] In periods of inflationary pressure when measures of credit

[5]e.g., Central bank reserves are related to average sales of foreign exchange in a preceding period or to the volume of money held by the public. Such devices are confined entirely to certain Latin American central banks, such as those of Guatemala, the Dominican Republic and Ecuador. Experience with them, however, has not in general been satisfactory.
[9]As noted earlier, this degree of liquidity is often a reflection in part of the absence of a tradition of borrowing at the central bank. It might also be noted that specialized government financing institutions in some cases rely on central bank credit to a greater extent than do the commercial banks.

restraint are called for, moreover, the banks are often being fed liberally with additional reserves through the balance of payments or government borrowings at the central bank. Foreign-owned commercial banks usually prefer to replenish their reserves when necessary by borrowing from their head offices abroad or by rediscounting their holdings of trade bills in foreign money markets where this is possible. In some cases where banks would like short-term accommodation from the central bank, they might be hampered by insufficient holdings of paper eligible for rediscounting or borrowing, despite the relatively generous provisions governing such accommodation in many of the central bank statutes. Finally, the under-developed state of the money and capital markets, and the absence in most cases of any long-standing tradition of central bank leadership or of conventional arrangements, tend to make rates of interest in the organized sector of the market relatively insensitive in most cases to changes in central bank discount rates. With the growth of the economy, however, the force of these various obstacles should progressively abate. . . .

In those developed countries where such power exists, changes in reserve requirements are usually regarded as a somewhat blunt instrument of general credit control, to be used relatively infrequently when needed to wipe out or to release at a stroke a large block of excess reserves and, incidentally, to reduce or increase the deposit-creating capacity of the commercial banks on the basis of any given amount of reserves. In under-developed countries, on the other hand, given the relative ineffectiveness of open-market and discount operations and the wide swings in bank reserves, resort to this device may have to be had more frequently, notably on occasions when reserves are rising unduly because of inflows of foreign exchange or central bank-financed budget deficits. In many cases, however, the increases in reserve requirements may have to be very substantial if they are to impinge significantly upon the liquidity positions of the banks.

Changes in reserve requirements may often involve serious inequities, since they strike alike at banks with large and with small excess reserves and at banks which are expanding credit rapidly and at those which are not. An alternative method, which many of the newer central banks are also empowered to undertake, would be the imposition in periods of rapidly rising bank reserves of very high supplementary reserve requirements against *increases* in deposits, while leaving the regular requirements unchanged. This would avoid the above-mentioned inequities and also strike more directly at the root of the problem. If, in the extreme case, the supplementary ratio were fixed at 100 per cent, the commercial banks could theoretically expand their loans and investments only to the extent that they already had excess reserves, which they were willing to use, or could get reserves by borrowing at, or selling holdings of securities to, the central bank or by repatriating their pre-existing foreign exchange assets. Even in these cases there could be only a one-to-one expansion in bank loans and investments relative to reserves. . . .

Among other instruments of credit control at the disposal of various central banks in underdeveloped countries is the power to impose ceilings on the loans and investments of the commercial banks or on the rate of increase of such assets within specified periods of time. This instrument can also be used as a selective credit control device to check the growth of specific categories of loans and investments as compared with others. As a weapon of quantitative control, the portfolio ceiling device would seem to be recommended mainly for situations of extreme emergency when all other, less direct, methods of stopping or slowing up a dangerous expansion have failed or are likely to fail. For it involves an objectionable degree of direct interference in bank loan and investment policies and may also involve serious inequities as among individual banks. . . .

It will be observed that many of the credit control measures discussed in the foregoing paragraphs are of a selective character designed to encourage or discourage specific types of bank loans and investments and thus to influence the allocation of bank credit and of real resources in desired directions. Many underdeveloped countries, in fact, have been much more concerned with such measures than they have been with general credit controls. The specific objectives sought by the use of selective credit controls have been many: to discourage credit for speculative or relatively unessential purposes and to encourage it for more socially productive ones; to meet more adequately the credit needs of specific sectors of the economy which cannot obtain sufficient bank credit at reasonable cost; to meet more adequately the needs for specific types of credit (e.g., medium- and long-term credit), even in relatively well-organized sectors of the economy; to assist in discouraging excessive or unessential imports; to counteract, without the need for stronger general credit measures, an inflationary movement which is being significantly promoted by excessive credit to one or a few specialized sectors of the economy (or to shelter certain sectors from the effects of restrictive general credit policies); to assist in developing a government securities market; or to promote economic diversification as such. Nearly all of these objectives, it might be noted, are directly or indirectly related to the broader objective of promoting balanced economic growth.

With such a variety of objectives, and with such a diversity of measures used, it is exceedingly difficult to draw any general conclusions as to the degree of effectiveness that selective credit controls may have had in underdeveloped countries in achieving the objectives sought. These controls have probably been more effective in influencing the distribution of bank credit between the private and public sectors than they have been in influencing the distribution of credit within the private sector itself. In the latter case, the effectiveness of these controls has tended to be limited by a number of well-known factors that require no detailed elaboration. . . .

33. Taxation and Economic Development

*Richard Goode**

The relation between taxation and economic development may be illuminated either by an intensive study of one country or by an examination of

*From *Proceedings of the 46th Annual Conference of the National Tax Association*. The author is with the Brookings Institution.

problems that appear to be characteristic of many countries. For the present paper I have chosen the more general survey. In following this approach, however, we should not lose sight of the fact that there is great diversity among countries that are usually considered economically underdeveloped. Fiscal institutions and problems grow out of local conditions. An acceptable program for reform must take full account of this fact. Nevertheless, I believe that the problems of poverty and its alleviation are similar enough in different parts of the world to allow some useful generalizations to be made about tax policy in the underdeveloped countries. . . .

Objectives of Policy

In relation to economic development, taxation must be considered from two points of view. First, an adequate amount of taxation is needed to provide a noninflationary means of financing government expenditures that will promote development. Second, the kinds of taxes that are levied need to be selected in the light of their probable effects on the capacity and willingness of the population to work, save, and invest, and on the attractiveness of local opportunities to foreign investors. These two objectives are conflicting in the sense that too much emphasis on one is likely to interfere with progress by complicating the attainment of the other. But they are complementary in that too little attention to either consideration may give rise to conditions that are an obstacle to economic development.

This formulation of the objectives of tax policy is intended to draw attention to the fact that the way to economic development is not along the easy path of low taxation and minimum government activity. The state has a large role to play in creating the conditions in which progress can be made. In every country the quality of public health and educational services is an important determinant of labor efficiency. Governments of most underdeveloped countries are finding it necessary to take an active part in providing public utility services such as transportation, communications, electric energy, water, storage, and marketing facilities and in establishment of credit institutions. Availability of these basic services opens up a wide range of opportunities for private investment and innovation in agriculture, manufacturing, and commerce. In addition many governments are investing directly in large-scale undertakings of strategic importance such as steel, cement, and fertilizer plants.

The fact that government development expenditures may be highly productive does not obviate the need for financing them through taxation. Government spending for these purposes, like private investment, constitutes an immediate claim on available output. Unless other claims are voluntarily postponed as a result of private saving or are restrained by taxation, money demand will expand. In most underdeveloped countries real output cannot be immediately increased in response to greater demand. Although these countries often have large reserves of unemployed or underemployed labor and land, they lack the capital and organization needed to put these resources to work. If large development outlays are financed by credit expansion or money creation, the inevitable result is inflation. Inflation will discourage private saving and upset the balance of payments. It will also result in grave inequities.

Since a broad market for government bonds exists in few underdeveloped countries and savings institutions are usually weak, the only important source of noninflationary finance that is ordinarily open to the government is taxation. If a project yields a salable product or service, receipts from this source may supplement taxes at a later time. But, even for self-liquidating projects, these receipts do not provide the funds required in the original construction period.

Most governments that are determined to hasten economic development will find it necessary to raise much more revenue than their tax systems have yielded in the past. Without this additional revenue they cannot provide the expansion of services and the new social capital that are urgently needed for development purposes or can do so only by adopting highly inflationary methods of financing. Failure of the government to assume its proper responsibilities on either the spending or the taxing side may seriously handicap economic development.

Governments in underdeveloped countries face the difficult task of trying to find measures that will provide a significant increase in revenue but that will not unduly interfere with labor efficiency or private capital formation. Two of the many other influences that bear on tax policy deserve special mention. Weakness of the revenue administration and lack of voluntary and informed taxpayer compliance favor traditional measures such as import and export duties and simple taxes on domestic consumption and production. On the other hand, the social and political forces that establish development as a prime objective of government policy bring with them from other parts of the world new ideas on taxation—for example, ideas about ability to pay and progressivity—that may clash with administrative expediency.

Taxation of Consumption

Taxes on consumption items have long been the major source of revenue in most underdeveloped countries. Such taxes are established and relatively easy to administer, particularly in the form of import duties. These considerations alone suggest that consumption taxes should be expected to contribute a large part of the additional revenue that most underdeveloped countries require.

A strong economic argument can also be advanced in favor of taxation of consumption in the underdeveloped countries. One of their greatest needs is a rapid increase in capital formation. In order merely to maintain a constant level of real income per head, it seems to be necessary to undertake net new investment equal to roughly 3 to 4 percent of the national income for every 1 percentage point annual increase in population. Economic progress can occur only if output grows faster than population. If the population is growing at an annual rate of 1 percent, which is the approximate average for the underdeveloped countries of Asia, net capital formation amounting to 6 to 8 percent of national income will be required to provide a modest improvement of 1 percent a year in income per head. Better sanitation and public health measures, moreover, are likely to bring about a sharp reduction in the death rate before a corresponding decline in the birth rate occurs. The rate of population growth may rise to 2 or 2.5 percent a year, which is the range that includes Ceylon and many Latin American countries. Then a 1 percent annual increase in income per head will require net new investment amounting to 10 to 15 percent of national income. Countries with a high rate of population growth may find it necessary to invest more than one-fifth of national income in order appreciably to narrow the gap between their standard of living and that of the richer nations. To appreciate the significance of this figure one should note that net capital formation in the United States averaged only 14 percent of national income (in constant prices) over the period 1869–1928.[1]

A part of the required capital formation may be financed by foreign loans, equity investments, and grants. But most of it will have to come from local savings. A prescription for a country wishing to establish a progressive "mixed economy," which seems to be the goal that appeals to most underdeveloped countries, might therefore be compounded of three elements: first, tax consumption to finance basic government expenditures; second, favor savings in order to encourage private capital formation; and, third, impose further taxes on consumption to provide government savings if private savings are insufficient to finance the minimum required increase in capital formation.

In the underdeveloped countries, concentration of taxes on consumption is not subject to the economic objection that has often been raised against this policy in the industrialized countries. There is little risk that consumption taxes will bring depression or stagnation because of lack of markets. Nearly all underdeveloped countries that are making a deliberate effort to increase public and private investment face a problem of inflation rather than of insufficient demand. To be sure, heavy taxes on particular items of consumption may inhibit the growth of industries producing these goods. But this is usually necessary to prevent absorption of resources needed for other purposes.

The policy of taxing consumption is, however, subject to an economic objection or limitation that scarcely exists in the more advanced countries. In many parts of the world the masses of the population are so poor that a further reduction in their consumption would not only cause great hardship but might actually impair health and working efficiency. Even when the people are not this close to the subsistence level, it is hard to persuade them to sacrifice present consumption for a future gain which may or may not accrue directly to themselves.

These considerations have led most students to the conclusion that an underdeveloped country cannot be expected to force a significant reduction in per capita consumption as a means of providing resources for develop-

[1] The average rate of growth of national income in constant prices was about 3.6 percent per year. Simon Kuznets, "Proportion of Capital Formation to National Product," *American Economic Review*, Vol. XLII, No. 2 (Papers and Proceedings, May 1952), pp. 507–08.

ment. Almost all official and quasi-official development plans that have been drawn up in recent years accept this proposition.

If present consumption cannot be reduced, it may still be possible to find development resources at home by capturing a large fraction of any increase in per capita income. The Indian Five Year Plan for Economic Development, for example, contemplates that one-half of the increase in per capita income will be invested. This high marginal rate of savings may be contrasted with an average rate of government and private savings in the recent past equal to only about 5 percent of national income. In a poor country it cannot be expected that the population will voluntarily save a large fraction of an increase in available income. It may be necessary, therefore, to rely on taxation to prevent an increase in consumption in proportion to any rise in per capita income.

Although the rule that taxation must restrain the rise in consumption is, I think, a valid and indeed a fundamental principle of economic development, its statement in aggregate terms may obscure some of its specific implications. Taxes cannot be directed with a high degree of selectivity at the particular individuals who are disposed to increase their consumption outlays. In the first place, such a procedure would be administratively infeasible. Second, and more important, the policy of imposing a differentially heavy tax on all increases in consumption, or income, would be economically unwise. Development requires workers to shift to new occupations, farmers to improve their cultivation techniques, businessmen to expand their operations and to adopt new methods. It will be difficult to bring about these changes in view of the strong hold of tradition and other obstacles to mobility. A tax system that appropriates most of the individual rewards in the form of increased consumption that may be associated with income-expanding activities is likely to make the reallocation of resources quite impossible.

In actual application, therefore, the rule means that the consumption of many persons must be reduced while that of others is allowed to increase. From the economic point of view, the ideal would be to impose the heaviest taxes on those who are above the subsistence standard and who make the smallest contribution to the expansion of output. In a low-income country, where there is likely to be a sharp distinction between the consumption patterns of the rich and the poor, it may be technically feasible to exempt most absolute necessities from taxation and to concentrate excises and import duties on items that are purchased almost exclusively by the middle- and upper-income groups. There is less scope for selective taxation of nonproductive elements in the community, but to some extent this objective will be furthered by taxing items for conspicuous consumption and, in some societies, by taxation of land and residential buildings.

Excises and import duties will usually be the main constituents of a program designed to limit the expansion of consumption, but income taxes can be a useful supplement to these measures. For a variety of reasons most underdeveloped countries cannot expect to place major reliance on income taxes at the present time.[2] Nevertheless, their limited use can give

[2]Richard Goode, "Reconstruction of Foreign Tax Systems," *Proceedings of the 44th National Tax Conference,* 1951, pp. 213–15.

recognition to the principles of ability to pay and progressivity that are now gaining acceptance in the underdeveloped countries.

In view of the importance that attaches to additional saving, the question arises whether the underdeveloped countries should exempt savings from the income tax. Although this practice would be much more acceptable in a capital-poor country than in the developed countries, I doubt that it is desirable. The first reason for this judgment is that assessment of the tax on this basis would require information regarding the change in the taxpayer's assets during the year as well as all the information that is needed to assess an ordinary income tax.[3] Balance sheet data would be helpful even in connection with the regular income tax, but the countries with the most advanced administrative organizations have not considered it feasible to require this information generally for purposes of the individual income tax.

The economic objection to a general exemption of savings is that it cannot be assumed that all savings will automatically be invested for productive purposes. In the underdeveloped countries there is a strong disposition to hold liquid assets. Sometimes these take the form of hoards of national currency, but more often gold, foreign exchange, and excessive inventories are preferred. Hoarding of national currency is comparatively innocuous, although it complicates the problem of monetary management, but the other types of hoarding deprive the community of the use of real assets. There is also general agreement that in many underdeveloped countries an excessive portion of savings has been invested in luxury housing and other types of construction in the cities.

Betterment Taxes and Price Policy of Public Enterprises

Although general taxation of increases in individual incomes is neither feasible nor desirable, the state can safely appropriate a large share of the increase in income directly attributable to its own capital projects. The most effective way of doing this is through betterment taxes and prices charged for services of government enterprises. This area deserves more attention than it has received in most underdeveloped countries.

Irrigation systems, drainage and flood control projects, roads, and similar public works typically increase the economic yield of the land that they serve. The discounted value of the expected increase in yield tends to be capitalized in the value of the land. If the state finances the project out of general revenues without exacting a special contribution from owners of the land, they will receive a large windfall gain.

On grounds of equity the state is justified in levying a betterment tax, or a special assessment in usual American terminology, equal to the whole or a large part of the estimated increase in value of land attributable to the project. If properly determined, such a levy will not interfere with full use of the facility or impose a hardship on the land owner. The increased

---

[3]As is clearly recognized by advocates of the principle. See Irving Fisher and Herbert W. Fisher, *Constructive Income Taxation* (New York: Harper Bros., 1942); William Vickrey, *Agenda for Progressive Taxation* (New York: Ronald Press, 1947), pp. 5–6.

yield will cover the betterment tax. If the owner retains his land, he has only to take advantage of the service to meet the tax; if he sells the land, the price will reflect the capitalized value of the benefit. Betterment taxes do not solve the immediate problem of financing the project because land owners must ordinarily be allowed to discharge their liabilities in a series of instalments. But revenue from this source will help finance future improvements in other areas.

Remunerative prices for the services of public enterprises such as irrigation, electrical energy, and transportation facilities can be justified by much the same reasoning as betterment taxes for special-benefit public works. When prices are below full cost, users of the service are subsidized at the expense of other taxpayers. It may sometimes be advisable to set prices below cost in order to introduce the service to skeptical or uninformed customers or to assure full-scale operation of a completed facility. But when taxable capacity is limited and budget demands are pressing, as they are in most underdeveloped countries, full-cost pricing should be the general rule. Costs should include current operating expenses, plus estimated depreciation and obsolescence computed on the basis of replacement cost rather than original cost. Adjustment of charges to reflect replacement cost is important in view of the world-wide increase in prices that has occurred over the past ten or fifteen years.

Tax Exemption for Investment or New Enterprises

For countries seeking development, particularly industrialization, tax exemption often has great appeal as a possible stimulus to the desired type of activities. Tax-exemption programs differ widely in scope. Some are confined to national income taxes; others extend to virtually all national taxes and also to state and local levies. Two of the most comprehensive and best-known programs are those of Puerto Rico and Mexico.

The efficacy of tax exemption has been widely debated, but much less effort has gone into detailed appraisal of actual experience. The difficulties encountered in such a study are formidable but perhaps no greater than in empirical investigations of other important tax questions. The present discussion is not a contribution to needed research in this area; it consists merely of an abbreviated statement of some of the issues. At the outset I freely confess what will soon be apparent—that I share with most other students of public finance a bias against special tax exemptions as a means of stimulating economic activity.

A few generalizations can be made about the scope and form of tax exemptions. First, there seems to be a tendency to concentrate unduly on exemptions from income and profits taxes. These taxes are seldom the heaviest borne by a new or expanding enterprise in an underdeveloped country. Furthermore, because they adjust automatically to current conditions and to business success or failure, income and profits taxes are less burdensome than cost-increasing or receipts-reducing taxes such as excises, payroll taxes, export duties, customs duties on imported equipment and supplies, property taxes, and license fees. Generally, it seems probable that the stimulus to business and hence the nonfiscal return to the government will be larger when a given amount of exemption is related to these comparatively inflexible taxes than when it takes the form of freedom from income and profits taxes.

Second, if exemptions are to be offered, there is, I believe, a presumption in favor of stating them in the most general way that will accomplish the purpose. This may force a dilution of the benefit, but it avoids many problems associated with any attempt to be highly selective. For example, it seems better to offer exemption to new investment than to new businesses, because, other things equal, expansion of an existing business is at least as productive as formation of a new firm and is likely to be more feasible in view of the limited supply of entrepreneurial ability. . . . To be sure, not all types of productive activities are equally desirable from the point of view of economic development, but it is hard for the best-informed planning commission to determine in advance just what activities can and should be expanded. It is usually much more satisfactory to specify the activities that will not receive exemption than to try to list in detail those that should receive the benefit.

Tax exemption is often adopted on the mistaken notion that it is simple and inexpensive. If a considerable degree of selectivity is attempted, the program proves to be highly complex to devise and administer. The cost is nearly always indeterminate. The most favorable experience would be enjoyed when exemptions went only to productive activities that would not otherwise have been undertaken. Even if this were the case, however, some cost to the economy and to the treasury would be involved if, as is highly probable, the new activities were possible only by diversion of some labor and capital from taxed fields. Moreover, it is almost certain that some part of the exemption will be entirely wasted because it is granted for activities that would have been undertaken without the exemption. The existence of special exemptions is a standing invitation to others to attempt to obtain similar benefits, and these pressures cannot always be resisted. To the extent that the exemptions do result in a revenue loss, government expenditures must be curtailed or higher taxes must be imposed on other industries or consumers. Exemption from local taxes that normally finance the provision of services for the industry itself, such as policing, fire protection, and sanitation, clearly places an additional burden on other members of the community.

The broad political objection to special exemptions from general taxes has been often stated, but it will bear repetition. These exemptions are equivalent to the payment of a subsidy from the government budget. Subsidies are not necessarily undesirable, but a clear understanding of public affairs will be promoted by a requirement that they be explicitly supported in competition with other demands.

I believe that both economic and political considerations suggest that it is ordinarily better to try to stimulate development by a general tax reform for the purpose of lessening tax obstacles, supplemented if necessary by direct government expenditures and subsidies, than to attempt to accomplish the same objective through special tax exemption. Taxes that are clearly inconsistent with development objectives should be abolished outright. For example, there seems to be no good reason why an under-developed country should impose import duties on capital equipment or special taxes on the use of machinery or modern processes. In the taxation of business profits, adequate allowances for all legitimate operating costs and for amortization of capital outlays are desirable. Liberal amortization seems to be especially important. It substantially reduces investment risks and lowers or eliminates income taxes on a firm during an expansion period. Although space does not permit full consideration of the subject here, my opinion is that rapid amortization would have many of the advantages of temporary exemption from income tax without some of the disadvantages of the latter. On the expenditure side, there may be a case for government assistance to business through loans or equity investment or for construction of buildings for lease and the provision of special services.

Foreign Private Investment

So far this paper has dealt mainly with the mobilization of local resources for the purposes of development with only incidental reference to foreign loans and investment. I believe that this emphasis reflects a realistic appraisal of the probable roles of domestic and foreign capital in development of most countries. But most underdeveloped countries would welcome an inflow of foreign private capital if it could be obtained on acceptable terms. Governments of the industrialized countries may wish to encourage foreign private investment as a partial substitute for official loans and grants.

Taxation, of course, is only one of the many factors affecting the attractiveness of investment opportunities in the eyes of foreign businessmen. Other phases of government policy that are often of equal or greater importance include inconvertible currencies and exchange controls, labor legislation, and outright limitations on entry, as well as less tangible items such as attitudes toward private enterprise and property and toward foreign business in general.[4] The fact that other policies may often be more significant is no reason for neglecting taxation, but it does suggest that tax revision alone is not likely to remove the impediments to foreign private investment.

From the point of view of the capital-importing country, the appropriate objective in regard to foreign investment is to obtain the maximum contribution to local income. This contribution is a function of the value of total output attributable to foreign investment and of the proportionate share of local participation in the value of that output. Taxation is one way of enlarging the local share at the expense of remittances of profits, interest, and amortization to nonresidents. The offsetting consideration is that high taxes may discourage maintenance and expansion of foreign in-

[4] U. S. Department of Commerce, Office of International Trade, *Factors Limiting U. S. Investment Abroad*, Part 1, *Survey of Factors in Foreign Countries* (1953); idem, *Study of Factors Limiting American Private Foreign Investment: Summary of Preliminary Findings and Recommendations* (July 1953); United Nations, *The Effects of Taxation on Foreign Trade and Investment* (1950.XVI.1).

vestment. The arrangement that will be most advantageous to the capital-importing country will not necessarily be that which produces the maximum of capital inflow or that which yields the greatest amount of tax revenue. The optimum will be the system that strikes the best balance between these two and thereby brings the largest attainable contribution to local income.

The extractive industries, which account for a large part of foreign direct investment in the underdeveloped areas, often present in sharp focus the issue of local versus foreign participation. Typically these industries produce mainly for the export market and obtain their capital equipment and much of their supplies from abroad. In many instances, wages and other local costs are a relatively small percentage of the value of output, and taxes are a major determinant of the local share. For example, in Venezuela taxes constituted three-fifths of total local-currency expenditures of the foreign-owned oil companies in 1949–50.[5] In Chile taxes accounted for more than one-third of total local participation in the value of copper exported by the large U.S. companies during the period 1946–51, and differential foreign exchange rates impose, in effect, a substantial additional tax which is not included in these figures.[6] In taxing the export industries, some of the underdevelped countries may be motivated by a desire not only to obtain a larger share in the value of their natural resources but also to secure funds to lay the basis for diversification of their economies. In this way they hope to reduce their vulnerability to fluctuations in the demand for primary products due to changes in business conditions originating in the industrialized countries.

Foreign investors, of course, would like to obtain as large a return as possible. The return that they do obtain will depend in part on the tax system of the underdeveloped country. It does not follow that the interests of investors and of the capital-importing country are in irreconcilable conflict any more than it is true that one party to every exchange transaction must be cheated.

I venture these rather trite remarks only because I fear that there is a tendency to discuss the influence of taxation on foreign private investment too much in absolute terms. The underdeveloped countries need to recognize that withdrawal of large amounts of profit and amortization is not necessarily exploitation. Foreign investors must accommodate themselves in many instances to special taxation, which is often discriminatory in effect if not in form.

At recent sessions of the United Nations Fiscal Commission and the Economic and Social Council there has been much discussion of the interrelations between the income and profits taxes of the capital-exporting and capital-importing countries. The major capital-exporting countries appear to recognize the prior right of capital-importing countries to tax income from foreign-owned enterprises. When the capital-exporting country allows a credit for foreign taxes, as the United States does, double taxation is avoided, but the tax of the capital-exporting country applies if

[5]Banco Central de Venezuela, *Memoria,* 1950, p. 36.
[6]Banco Central de Chile, *Balanza de Pagos de Chile,* 1951, p. 21.

the capital-importing country does not take advantage of its right to tax the profits of foreign enterprises. Some of the underdeveloped countries complain that this arrangement deprives them of the opportunity of holding out low income tax rates as an attraction to foreign investment. These countries and business groups in the capital-exporting countries have urged that the capital-exporting countries exempt from taxation income received from foreign investments.

This proposal contemplates that the capital-exporting countries shall grant a special tax concession to foreign private investment and that the capital-importing countries shall make this concession effective by maintaining low income tax rates. The consequences of such an arrangement are uncertain. On the one hand it is clear that taxation is only one of many influences on the international flow of investment and that income taxes are often not the most obstructive form of taxation. In this connection it is interesting to note that in the years 1946–51, 64 percent of estimated net direct-investment capital movements from the United States to Latin America, Asia, and Africa were in petroleum,[1] an industry on which U.S. income taxes are relatively low and foreign taxes are probably on the average relatively high. Furthermore, there seems to be no observable tendency for capital outflow to be directed toward low-tax countries. One-fifth of the total in 1946–51 went to Canada. On the other hand, it is undoubtedly true that, all other things remaining the same, a reduction of income taxes would have some favorable effect on the volume of foreign investment.

On the whole, I am inclined to be rather skeptical that modification of the income tax laws of the capital-exporting countries would make an important contribution to satisfaction of the needs of the underdeveloped countries. Furthermore, most of the underdeveloped countries that wish to offer more favorable treatment to foreign investment still have scope for adjustment of taxes other than those on income and profits and for revision of foreign exchange regulations and other government policies. Under the circumstances, it is perhaps not unreasonable for the capital-exporting countries to hesitate to impair the progressivity of their tax systems by granting an exemption of uncertain effectiveness as a stimulus to foreign investment.

Conclusion

Tax policy can fill an important, although a secondary, role in economic development. An adequate amount of tax revenue and remunerative prices for services of public enterprises are required for noninflationary financing of development expenditures by governments. Careful selection of tax measures can help minimize obstacles to progress. Research on the relation between taxation and economic development and application of the findings are tasks that should challenge the energy and ingenuity of experts throughout the world.

[1]Exclusive of overseas dependencies of ERP countries. *Survey of Current Business,* November 1949, December 1951, September 1952.

34. The High Cost of Economic Development

*Martin Bronfenbrenner**

The Role of Inflation

... Inflation need not encourage economic development and, if carried too far and too rapidly, will usually operate to discourage it. Under conditions of hyper-inflation, capital shifts from its ordinary activities (including the developmental) to the speculative purchase of gold, land, precious stones, foreign securities, and foreign exchange as inflation hedges. Specific capital goods, too, find their way to hoards in inventories to wait for higher prices and so are used for further production more slowly than normally is the case. The velocity of circulation of inventory, so to speak, will fall and the real national output and income suffer in consequence.

On the other hand, the monetary resources created through inflation may be made available in the first instance for development purposes. If so, inflation, within certain limits, encourages development in a number of ways, none of them costless in real terms. A few of the more important patterns are listed below.

1. Inflation permits the employment, or the fuller employment, of labor and capital resources which would otherwise be wholly or partially unemployed. The fullness of employment elsewhere in the economy makes general expansion, developmental or otherwise, impossible without price increases or rigid controls, while substantial under-employment remains in important sections and industries. This is the familiar "bottleneck" situation. In the underdeveloped countries the primary "pocket of under-employment" is in family agricultural industry and in rural areas—that is to say, in upwards of 80 percent of both the population and the area of the countries concerned. Inflation appears to be required before the surplus family labor of the Oriental farm can be hired away, or the essential labor of the farmer himself secured during the agricultural off-season.

2. Particularly if "development authorities" exist, such as governmental bodies or public corporations, inflation may proceed through money or credit created directly for these authorities. The development authorities are thereby given first priority in acquiring the scarce resources they need before their prices have risen to their full extent. This is an aspect of the phenomenon of forced saving or forced frugality which has been discussed periodically in economic literature since the days of Bentham. Monetary or credit expansion gives the development authority the resources needed at the expense of the rest of the population. It should be noted that inflation encourages development through forced saving in an open economy to a greater extent than in a closed one because foreign exchange is often the most strategic resource which expansion makes

*From *Land Economics,* August 1953. The author is Professor of Economics, Carnegie Institute of Technology.

available preferentially to the development authority.[1] On the other hand, inflation through forced saving does not encourage development to the same extent if the resources created are made available initially for consumption, wage increases, residential housing, general education, social services, or other purposes worthy in themselves but somewhat competitive with rapid material development. Successive doses of forced saving may also be decreasingly effective if the holders of development goods and foreign exchange learn to discount future inflation in advance and raise their prices immediately upon the first rumor of currency or credit expansion.

3. Development is encouraged when the authorities are permitted by credit expansion to raise the relative prices of the types of labor and capital goods required for development projects without imposing on other sectors of the economy the reductions in money wages and prices which would otherwise be required. The case of labor is particularly important in this connection in countries where the wages of skilled labor, foremen, and the like have traditionally been low relative to clerical and office workers, and where it is difficult to recruit labor for development projects at the going wage rates.

4. A slow inflation, or even a rapid one, in its early stages induces laborers to work more intensively for real incomes which are no higher and which may be lower than their previous level. To a lesser extent owners of land and capital may be induced to put their property to work more intensively in the same way when money incomes rise. We are dealing here, of course, with the effects of the well-known "money illusion." The product of the extra labor and other output which the money illusion generates will seldom be limited to anything which can be termed development, but it can be concentrated in those fields by development authorities adept and cynical enough to combine the pressures of forced saving with those of money illusion.

In speaking of credit creation and monetary expansion we have ignored tacitly the possibility of simultaneous offsets in the form of increased taxes or monetary contraction elsewhere in the economy. But in fact such offsets are difficult if not impossible in most underdeveloped countries by reason of their embryonic systems of banking and taxation. We may state as a general principle that inflation is often inevitable when economic development is financed by credit creation, even when the necessary heavy capital goods are imported free of charge or on a barter basis.

Taking the first point first, regarding offsets to credit creation: In countries without developed income taxes or other progressive tax systems, the distributive effects of inflation, bad as they are, may still be superior to those of the higher indirect taxes on land and on essential commodities which are the only feasible alternatives. Similarly, in countries without developed systems of commercial and central banking, especially where

[1]This observation I owe to Professor Takata who uses it to explain in part why the process of inflation, which appears to have been effective in furthering Japanese economic development during the Meiji Era (1867–1912) when Japan was opened to foreign trade, failed to promote reconstruction during 1945–1948 when international intercourse was regulated strictly by the Allied Occupation.

large sectors of the economy operate on a barter basis, it is difficult to employ monetary policy as an alternative to inflation in view of the slow and tortuous process of its operation. Direct controls, too, are practically unenforceable outside the major urban centers of most underdeveloped countries.

It is less easy to realize that inflation remains a problem even when heavy capital goods for development projects are imported free of charge, as in the American aid programs in South Korea, Thailand, and elsewhere in Asia.[2] Granted that the fixed capital be supplied gratis, there will be inflation unless the labor and other domestic-currency costs of putting it to work are paid for by means other than inflation. To minimize inflation through this process the Mutual Security Agency of the United States has required of Thailand and the Republic of Korea (to continue the same examples) the setting up of counterpart funds in local currency equal in value to the capital goods being supplied gratis for the purpose of meeting those local currency costs. Since the counterpart funds may be set up from the proceeds of loans as well as from those of taxes, however, the effectiveness of this procedure is somewhat questionable.[3]

Graphic Analysis

Certain of these arguments regarding the role of inflation in economic development can be illustrated, and their implications clarified, by a graphical analysis derived in its mean essentials from the work of Professor Don Patinkin.[4] Figure 1, however, is an ordinary "Keynesian cross," with no distinctive Patinkin embellishments.

The horizontal axis of this figure represents national disposable income (after income taxes) in money terms. The vertical axis represents its components, also in money terms. These components are usually classified as: consumption expenditures, private net domestic investment, government expenditure for goods and services, and the export surplus. (The second and fourth of these may be negative.) Total expenditure or aggregate demand DD cuts at A the 45-degree line of equality between income and the sum of its components, which may be looked upon as a supply curve. The income level E corresponding to point A is therefore an apparent equilibrium point.

DD, it should be noted, is a total expenditure function and not merely a consumption function. By considering it stable in *money* income and its components, we must abstract from price changes so drastic as to render this assumption ridiculous. (We do not identify the maximum price level change consistent with a stable expenditure function in money terms.)

[2]For a more detailed treatment of the Korean case in particular, see ECAFE, *Economic Survey of Asia and the Far East,* 1951, pp. 295–300.

[3]The counterpart funds mentioned here differ from the fund set up in Occupied Japan where the actual proceeds of the sale of aid goods to the population were impounded. The Japanese type is more effective as an anti-inflationary device since the purchase of the aid goods supplied gratis to the Japanese Government was not financed directly or indirectly through consumer credit expansion. (The Counterpart Fund set up in connection with the American wheat loan to India in 1951 was of the Japanese type.)

[4]Don Patinkin, "Involuntary Unemployment and the Keynesian Supply Function," *Economic Journal,* September 1949, pp. 365–68.

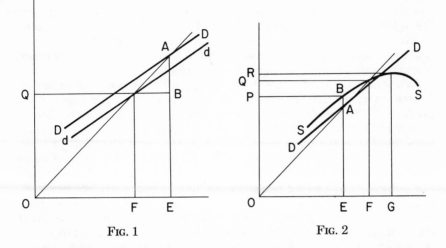

FIG. 1   FIG. 2

At full employment, however, the total real income produced is only F (which equals Q), real income being measured in the prices of the beginning of the period under consideration. F is less than E, and is drawn to the left of E on the horizontal axis. There is an inflationary gap AB, filled in practice by price increases, which makes of E something other than a full equilibrium income level. Measures to reduce DD to dd, so as to eliminate "over-employment" and the inflationary gap and provide full equilibrium at income level F, are usually suggested in such a situation. This is because F itself, the real income supplied at full employment, is conventionally considered independent of any income level either money or real. Usually the easiest way to reduce aggregate demand from DD to dd has been the cutting of economic development projects, armament expenditures, or social welfare programs. Nothing in the formal analysis, however, suggests where the reductions should be made. (Nothing in the formal analysis of the opposite case, where E lies to the left of F, suggests where demand should be supplemented to eliminate the gap, this time deflationary, and maintain full employment.)

Following Patinkin, I propose to complicate this presentation in the interests of realism by allowing for the effect of aggregate money income on aggregate real supply at full employment. This involves making the level of full employment output a variable, and substituting for the horizontal line FB of Figure 1 a curve SS expressing the variation.

Let us use the vertical axis of Figure 2 to represent simultaneously the monetary components of income (on the demand side) and real income (on the supply side). By real income is meant, as usual, money income at prices prevailing at the outset of the period under consideration. Money income is related to real income at full employment by an aggregate full employment real supply function SS, which replaces the line QB of Figure 1. The aggregate *full-employment real* supply function SS should be distinguished clearly from the aggregate *money* supply function at *varying* employment levels represented by the 45-degree line. The crossing of SS and the 45-degree line gives the full-employment income level F and the real full employment output Q, at the given price level. When E lies to the left of F, as it does in Figure 2, a deflationary gap BA results, which is filled by price-cutting and/or by employment at a level less than full. Real income and output, moreover, fall from Q to P even at full employment and below P if unemployment persists.

As a stability condition, SS should lie above DD at low levels of money income, meaning that aggregate demand falls short of full-employment production. On the other hand, SS should lie below DD at higher levels, meaning that aggregate demand exceeds production even at full employment, producing the phenomena of "inflationary gap" and "over-employment." A horizontal SS satisfies these conditions and is in fact assumed as a first approximation by most economists. Patinkin pictures SS as a straight line with a small upward slope. In our own presentation, SS increases, although at a decreasing rate, to a point corresponding to an income level G, normally to the right of F. Here SS reaches a maximum real output R and then turns downward. The maximum real output R and the corresponding money income level G are points of especial importance in considering economies with problems of reconstruction, development, or mobilization. We shall hear more of them later on.

Why does SS slope upward, usually to a point considerably beyond full-employment equilibrium? The upward slope represents partially the effects of general money illusion; labor and other productive services offer longer hours or more intensive activity in return for higher money incomes, even under conditions of mild inflation. At the same time, a program of forced saving, as in the interest of a development program, can partially divert a given quantity of real aggregate demand from consumer's goods to capital goods and to foreign exchanges. If this is done, the effects on real production will be favorable. These are not complete explanations of the upward slope, however, particularly toward the left side or low-income portion of the diagram. Here it may be caused largely by more favorable expectations and by diminishing uncertainties as demand increases; price changes need not be involved at all. Furthermore, we may look at the upward slope in reverse; that is to say, as a cut in real production at full employment when money incomes fall. This cut represents the effects of resistance by workers and other factory owners to cuts in their money returns. The effects of strikes and slowdowns, labor force reductions, inadequate capital replacements, etc., are thus included.

Why may SS turn downward above G? Probably the most important single reason in most countries is a shift of economic activity from current production to the hoarding of inventories and foreign exchange as inflation deprives the money illusion of its force. The involuntary unemployment which sometimes features hyper-inflations results from the same shift in activity. A secondary force, in countries dependent on imported raw materials, is their increased prices and reduced volumes as inflation raises the value of foreign exchange. Finally there is a tendency, familiar to economists since the Mercantilist era, for factor supply curves to turn backwards after real income rises to a series of critical points, none of which necessarily corresponds with the maximum point on SS in Figure 2. In the language of utility analysis, the marginal utility of real income falls as its amount increases, and the marginal utility of leisure rises, together with that of direct consumption of productive resources until, at a series of critical points, the supply functions of the various productive services reverse themselves. When enough of these reversals have occurred, total production can also be expected to fall as the economy turns from hard labor to lotus-eating. The point of falling total production from this cause may conceivably come before full-employment demand is satisfied (i.e., to the left of F in Figure 2). This situation would result in maximum output being reached under *deflationary* pressure at somewhat *less* than full employment. It can be imagined most readily in countries with extremely unequal distributions of income where work is done by a labor force with simple tastes and limited demands and output is consumed by a leisure class which does no work. While an interesting theoretical curiosity, this case does not seem realistic for any economy of which the writer has knowledge.

The aggregate demand and supply functions DD and SS have been drawn not only as stable but also as independent of such variables as the distribution of income. The independence of total expenditure (including induced investment) and the income distribution is probably legitimate as a first approximation although Socialist and laboristic writers may wish explicit recognition of the possibility of an upward drift resulting from increasing the degree of equality and the relative share of labor. The independence of total supply and the income distribution is more questionable, in view of evidence (incompletely verified, it is true) from centrally-planned economies ascribing rapid rises throughout the length of SS to shifts in income distribution in favor of the laboring class as a whole and particularly the more highly-skilled elements therein.

For countries in the throes of economic development, the inflationary gap of Figure 1 is usually more meaningful than the deflationary setting of Figure 2. Figure 3, which combines the essential elements of the other two, is submitted as presenting most realistically the persistent policy dilemma which confronts developing countries. Here, as in Figure 1, we have over-full employment with an inflationary gap. Given the aggregate demand or expenditure curve DD, E is the equilibrium level of money income. But equilibrium monetary demand A exceeds full-employment real supply B; AB is the inflationary gap. If demand were cut back to the level indicated by dd, full equilibrium could be established at the income level F, and the inflationary gap eliminated. So far so good, but there would occur at the same time a consequence less welcome, namely, a cut PQ in real production. At the same time, real production could be increased beyond P (called forth at income level E), as far as R (elicited by income level G). This could de done by further increases in the aggregate demand schedule, from DD to D'D'. But, if demand rises to D'D', the inflationary gap increases with it. On the diagram, when production increases by PR the inflationary gap increases from AB at income level E to A'B' at income level G. In practice, a larger proportionate inflationary gap leads

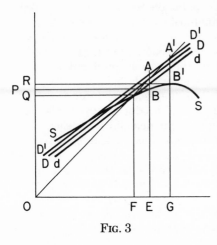

FIG. 3

to a more rapid rate of price increase in an open inflation, and increases the difficulty of maintaining controls in a suppressed one.

Faced with aggregate money demand functions and full-employment real supply functions like DD and SS respectively, a developing country and its development program find themselves under simultaneous pressure from opposite directions. Should real output be increased at the cost of inflation for however long a period may be necessary to complete a given development plan for a given stage in such a plan? Or, on the other hand, should price stability be purchased at the cost of development retarded in the short run? There is conservative, orthodox pressure for withdrawal to dd, which would give full equilibrium, full employment, and stable prices at F.[5] There is radical and nationalistic pressure for precisely the opposite maneuver, or a rise in demand from DD to D'D', for maximum production and development at G, and usually simultaneously for direct controls to moderate the social and economic inequities of the inflationary process. (Where controls raise SS, moving point B' to the northeast on Figure 3 and increasing both G and R, so much the better. As a general rule, however, controls appear to lower B' and therefore R, to encourage evasion at the expense of production and to lessen the production advantage of the inflationary policy alternative.)

In the terminology of Professor A. P. Lerner's *Economics of Employment*,[6] point F (or Q) corresponds to "low full employment" and point

[5]The International Monetary Fund is currently (1942–53) taking the lead in exercising pressure in this conservative direction. See an address by Ivar Rooth, Managing Director of the Fund, reprinted in *International Financial News Survey*, November 28, 1952, p. 175, in which the Fund's position is stated: "National policy in all countries must start with eliminating inflation, through strong budgets and tight credits. Obviously this is not consistent with the view that there must not be unemployment at any time in any sector of the economy. . . . In the under-developed countries there must be some moderation in their policy of rapid development at any cost." A fuller and more scholarly presentation of the same position is found in E. M. Bernstein and I. G. Patel, "Inflation in Relation to Economic Development," International Monetary Fund *Staff Papers*, III, November 1952, pp. 367–84, after analysis of the disappointing experience of several countries, notably the Latin American Republics and the Philippine Islands, with inflation as a major tool of economic development.

[6]*Op. cit.*, (New York: McGraw-Hill, 1951), Ch. 13. Lerner favors direct controls, particularly over wage rates, to avoid inflationary pressure in the neighborhood of "high full employment." Professor Slichter, on the other hand, presenting what appears to be a similar analysis, accepts secular inflation as not only inevitable but the desirable consequence of striving for "high full employment," and doubts the feasibility of direct controls over wage rates. See "How Bad Is Inflation?" *Harper's Magazine*, August 1952, pp. 53–57. Professor J. M. Clark appears to concur: "Aims of Economic Life as Seen by Economists," in A. Dudley Ward, *op. cit.*, p. 45.

G (or R) to "high full employment." Professor Lerner estimates the range between F and G (or between Q and R) as sufficient under American conditions to provide employment for the marginal 8 to 10 percent of the American labor force. The estimate is of the roughest and cannot be applied to other countries. Suppose, however, that this range amounted to only half Lerner's estimate, or only five percent of real national output. In terms of national output as a whole this increment would not be impressively large. But in terms of developmental investment, which is apt to be the most flexible item when we consider varying aggregate demand by conscious policy between such limits as dd and D'D', it is much more significant. The development program itself can rarely absorb more than 25 percent of the national output and usually absorbs less than 10 percent. The choice between dd and D'D', then, may mean the difference between no development program at all and a really substantial effort in this direction.

Faced with the political and social actualities of the mid-twentieth century, developing countries generally have chosen the route via high full employment but have borne with no particular equanimity the costs associated with their choice, meaning the burdens and injustices of inflation. (Such exceptional cases as the Burman deflation of 1949–52 deserve special note, commendatory or otherwise.)[1] There is danger in many countries that the location of G be estimated too far to the right and R too far upward. As a result, inflation may be overdone through the effort to do too much too fast; real output may be reduced by the effort to make it exceed its peak. Japan in 1946–47 illustrates such an outcome. Successive Finance Ministers, in a deliberate attempt to squeeze the ultimate in production for the reconstruction of a war-ravaged country with substantial "disguised unemployment" in its agricultural regions, over-shot their mark and pushed money income far beyond G. Reconstruction might have been considerably more rapid had there been fewer incentives to wait and hoard materials rather than to produce.

The dilemma of price stability versus maximum output, of low versus high full employment, should not be conceived as limited to under-developed countries or to countries recovering from war or other catastrophe. After the outbreak of the Korean War in 1950, the United States and much of Western Europe balanced more or less precariously at income levels such as E in Figure 3. These money incomes are too high to eliminate inflationary pressure and at the same time too low to elicit maximum productive effort. Both direct controls and indirect offsets to military expansion are more available to these countries than to, say, Chile or Thailand; but political pressures and the legitimate fear of cutting output even temporarily have delayed and prevented their use.

Under these circumstances, such economic conservatives in the United States as Senators Taft and Byrd, and ex-President Hoover, advocated drastic retrenchment in government expenditures. The net effect of their recommendations would be a reduction of aggregate demand from DD at

[1] For an analysis of Burman Experience, see ECAFE, *Economic Survey of Asia and the Far East,* 1951, *op. cit.,* pp. 292–95.

least to dd, and quite possibly lower. Proposals for sharply increased taxes and for general credit restriction would operate in the same direction. On the other hand, the Truman Administration and the Council of Economic Advisers supported policies of maximum production, holding aggregate demand at DD or raising it toward D'D' despite the resulting increases of inflationary pressures.[5] The position of a developed country relative to rearmament or mobilization has, it would seem, basic similarity to that of an undeveloped country relative to its development program.

Successive Periods

If an expansionary (inflationary) alternative is in fact taken in the situation of Figure 3 and if equilibrium monetary demand generates an inflationary gap, will the resulting inflation be temporary and self-liquidating, or will it be long-term and perhaps explosive? The question is fundamental for policy decisions but cannot be solved by the apparatus we have developed here. This apparatus deals with a single period but we can nevertheless extend it to an elementary sort of "period analysis."

Let us consider only D'D' and SS on Figure 3, supposing the decision has been made to maximize real output and the speed of economic development. What will be the position of these functions, D'D' and SS, in the next period after prices have risen or controls have been imposed? D'D' will move upward unless controls are extraordinarily effective. Higher prices require more expenditure out of given money incomes if living standards and real investment are not to suffer. The effects on SS are more complex. Any rise in the price level will raise SS vertically, by definition. If real output means output measured in prices at the beginning of the period, its schedule must rise from period to period as prices rise even if physical output be unchanged. (Ambiguity in this definition of "real output" is unfortunate and regrettable.) There will in addition be a vertical rise in SS as the development program takes hold, increasing the amount of capital available and the productivity of productive agents generally. At the same time, however, SS will probably shift to the right unless controls are completely effective or money illusions exceptionally powerful. Otherwise, greater money returns to both labor and capital will be required to induce any given amount of effort or employment as prices rise. The net effect on SS, then, is movement in a roughly northeasterly direction on the diagram, whereas the effect on D'D' is a movement to the north.

We can concentrate our attention on SS, and more particularly on its maximum point B' (corresponding to real output R), assuming aggregate demand more amenable to centralized control. If B' moves at a 90-degree

[5]The clash of views was brought out with especial clarity in hearings before the Sub-Committee on General Credit Control, Joint Committee on the Economic Report, United States Congress, on the occasion of the freeing of government security markets by the Federal Reserve System in 1951. The hearings were reviewed by Herbert Stein, "Monetary Policy and the Management of the Public Debt," *American Economic Review,* December 1952, esp. p. 872 f., on the testimony and examination of Chairman Leon Keyserling of the Council of Economic Advisers.

angle with the horizontal, i.e., directly northward on the diagram, it will eventually rise to coincide with A¹. There will be full equilibrium, and the inflation will have been of the once-and-for-all variety. If B¹ moves at an angle between 45 and 90 degrees in the northeasterly quadrant, successive inflationary gaps will become smaller and smaller from period to period and a new full equilibrium will eventually be established at a new and higher price level. The closer the critical angle to 90 degrees, the smaller will be the requisite inflation and the sooner its completion. If, on the other hand, B¹ should move at an angle of 45 degrees or less, the inflationary gaps would rise, or at least not decline, in successive periods. Inflation would be progressive or explosive. It could be checked only by drastic measures which involve real risks of substantial and continued reductions in output and employment.

Needless to say, the choice of policy between maximum-output and maximum-stability in the dilemma of Figure 3 should depend largely upon the economist's or statesman's best judgment of the movements of points like B¹, once inflation begins. The right answer for one underdeveloped country may be completely wrong for its immediate neighbor, let alone for another country across the oceans on another continent. We can merely list a number of qualitative factors which, when present, will guide B¹ to a near-vertical path and render development by mild or marginal inflation relatively safe in a free economy.

1. Strong money illusions held by owners of productive services.
2. Strong monetary authorities, capable of restricting the monetary circulation when the pace of inflation rises, despite the objections of organized agriculture, business, and labor, and at the cost of temporary unemployment.
3. General agreement on desirable distribution of income between the major segments of the economy.
4. Direct control apparatus selected and enforced for minimum interference with production and minimum price increases.
5. Rapid reflection of economic development in increased per capita output of consumption goods.

Five contrary factors, which when present will guide B¹ to a near-horizontal path, make any inflation dangerous, and increase the attractions of the "sound finance" counselled by the International Monetary Fund are:

1. Recent experience with inflation; money illusion largely dispelled.
2. Agriculture, business, and labor strongly organized, with political or economic power to enforce their monetary demands.⁹ Monetary authority weak, decentralized, or absent.
3. Sharp class conflicts regarding the distribution of income and wealth.
4. Direct controls badly chosen or ineffectively enforced. Generally under-developed public administration.
5. Long lag between inception of development programs and increased output of consumption goods.

⁹Space limitations prevent full development of this phase of the argument but, if for each dollar increase of money national income the total money claims of organized productive agents increase by more than a dollar, as they will if each organized group actively takes advantage of inflation to raise its distributive share, the result is instability. See M. W. Reder, "Problems of a National Wage-Price Policy," *Canadian Journal of Economics,* February 1948, pp. 46–61.

Cursory examination of the economies of most under-developed countries in the period since 1945 or 1950 seems to show the second group of factors more potent than the first, and therefore to explain the conservative shift of sentiment within the international financial organizations. On the other hand, no such shift of opinion is apparent in the under-developed countries themselves or in the United Nations organization proper.

35. The Impact of Foreign Exchange

*Walter Krause**

... The primary rationale for placing foreign-exchange impact in a pivotal position is that the immediate bottleneck handicapping industrial development in the typical underdeveloped country is found in foreign-exchange stringency, and that, therefore, the effect of any new industrial enterprise upon total foreign-exchange supplies logically represents a core consideration.[1] The contention is that an enterprise has special merit if it helps ease the foreign-exchange situation, since added development then becomes easier, not harder; on the other hand, an enterprise loses in merit if its presence serves to impair the foreign-exchange situation further and thus automatically precludes additional development.[2]

Beyond this primary rationale, a major secondary rationale also exists: tests based on foreign-exchange impact are held to be practical, especially in the sense of being easy to apply. Some persons are convinced that tests rooted in comparative advantage are likely to prove impractical; attempts to judge new enterprises on this basis serve to raise a great many questions, both of theory and fact, so that over time the performance record is in danger of becoming one of "much talk and little new industry." These persons are inclined to regard action as much more probable when tests are based instead on foreign-exchange impact. They contend that greater action is fostered because only problems of immediate consequence are pivoted into a central position, with other issues left for later argument—presumably when industrial development is well underway and a country can afford the luxury of the debates likely to be associated with efforts toward the refinement of testing techniques. In essence, as these persons see the matter, what underdeveloped countries need is some new industry

*From Walter Krause, *Economic Development: The Underdeveloped World and the American Interest* (Belmont, California: Wadsworth Publishing Company, Inc., 1961), pp. 134–138. © 1961 by Wadsworth Publishing Company, Inc. The author is Professor of Economics, University of Iowa.
[1]Other deterrents to industrial development are not thereby ignored; the point is simply that *the* shortcoming that forges to the forefront to inhibit the "very next step" in the course of industrial development tends, with almost uncanny regularity, to be foreign-exchange stringency. Relative to this point, the reader is urged to refer again to Ch. 4.
[2]Typically, a major rationale for establishment of a screening committee proceeds in terms of the need for control over the evolving investment pattern so as to assure beneficial foreign-exchange impact from new investments (or to preclude adverse foreign-exchange effects).

now—whenever such can be had on a workable basis; absolute perfection is not necessary all along the line.

The key consideration, then, is foreign-exchange impact. Stated briefly, any enterprise that is *foreign-exchange-earning* or *foreign-exchange-saving* is regarded to have merit in terms of this approach (and the more foreign exchange earned or saved, per given amount of investment, the more meritorious an enterprise is presumed to be). But what, precisely, is a foreign-exchange-"earning" or "-saving" enterprise? A foreign-exchange-earning enterprise is one whose output enters export markets, and whose presence has the net effect of adding to a country's foreign-exchange-earning capacity, so that the country's foreign-exchange reserves are increased by virtue of the new enterprise. Outstanding examples of foreign-exchange-earning enterprises include those devoted to the processing of raw materials prior to export. On the other hand, a foreign-exchange-saving enterprise is one whose output substitutes for previous imports. In order to "save" foreign exchange, new domestic production must cost less in associated foreign-exchange outlays than did imports displaced by it. Foreign exchange is not saved if the volume of domestic production is expanded to such an extent that associated foreign-exchange outlays exceed those previously made on imports of the product in question (or if any expansion in volume is not offset by substitutions in import composition such that total foreign-exchange outlays on the product and its substitutes are held below those previously made on the product and its substitutes). During early stages of industrial development, foreign-exchange-saving enterprises tend especially to be those concerned with articles of widespread domestic consumption, e.g., textiles, soap, and cigarettes.

Numerous advocates of industrial development are inclined to favor foreign-exchange-saving enterprises over those in the foreign-exchange-earning category—meaning that they prefer production for the domestic market to production for export. The explanation for this preference appears rooted, for the greater part, in a fear that reliance upon foreign-exchange-earning enterprises will give a country nothing better than some elementary processing of raw materials prior to exportation, which frequently is regarded as a "low" form of industrial development at best, and, at worst, just more colonialism in operation. Significantly, however, foreign-exchange-saving enterprises can save foreign exchange only insofar as imports occurred previously. Therefore, developmental potential in the foreign-exchange-saving category is limited by the size of the existent balance-of-payments configuration. On the other hand, foreign-exchange-earning enterprises are not limited in this manner; their earnings are not circumscribed within some previous or current balance-of-payments framework, but occur *outside* and beyond any such balance-of-payments framework. Therefore, developmental potential in the foreign-exchange-earning category is limited only by a country's capacity to produce and to secure foreign markets.

Always, however, an eased foreign-exchange situation—whether a result of foreign-exchange supplies being freed-up through the saving of foreign exchange or increased outright through the earning of foreign exchange—helps a country to sustain additional foreign-exchange commitments associated with further development, so that the process of growth is fostered. Foreign-exchange-earning and foreign-exchange-saving enterprises represent new development, in and of themselves, and, in addition, they "open the door" for further development in that they help ease the foreign-exchange situation. This is the essential appeal. As proponents, drawing upon the old adage that "the proof of the pudding is in the eating," like to put the matter (in support of basic tests related to foreign-exchange impact): industry ordinarily results thereby, and industry now is preferable to industry later (or maybe never).

Point of Controversy

As evidenced by the foregoing, a basis exists for controversy as between two distinct goals: maximization of *efficiency* versus *extrication* from a balance-of-payments straitjacket. Under terms of the first, the problem is seen as one of how to allocate resources and effort so as to maximize productive efficiency, i.e., of how to secure maximum output per given input. According to its proponents, pursuit of this goal requires each country to concentrate on activities in compliance with the law of comparative advantage, or some interpretation of it. Under terms of the second, the problem is seen as one of "how to get things moving"—or, "moving faster." According to its proponents, pursuit of this goal requires that special attention be given foreign-exchange impact. Given the differing points of emphasis, criticism and counter-criticism readily emerge. On the one hand, advocates of efficiency as the basic consideration fear that demotion of it as a test, in favor of tests related to foreign-exchange impact, is likely to result in the foisting upon an economy of enterprises that are destined to prove inefficient over the long-run, and hence prone to prove a drag upon the economy. On the other hand, advocates of foreign-exchange impact as a test question preoccupation with efficiency, particularly when underemployment is widespread (representing, perhaps, the greatest source of inefficiency of all); as they view the matter, even "inefficient" activity is defensible, if the only alternative is activity of even lesser caliber, or no activity at all.

The issue, as outlined, is a much-discussed one in certain quarters (e.g., within those US Government agencies concerned with the flow of official capital to underdeveloped countries), but discussion seems more often to lead merely to greater precision in the statement of divergent views than to a reconciliation of those views. In practice, no great conflict springs from the status of export-type enterprises. Foreign-exchange-earning enterprises must be able to compete in an international market in order to survive; hence, tests of efficiency, stemming from some interpretation of the law of comparative advantage, are not entirely precluded. Clashes of viewpoint, insofar as they arise, tend to show up more particularly in reference to enterprises oriented to the domestic market. There individual positions tend typically to divide on whether, or how, to take the following three factors into account. First, does one allow for, or disregard, the presence of underemployment or of unemployment? Second, does one allow for, or disregard, implications attributable to the presence of exchange control and to the "artificial" exchange rates that typically exist and serve to distort international price relationships? Third, does one permit, or disallow, new enterprises catering to new domestic demands, i.e., demands of a type that place the new enterprises in the position of being neither foreign-exchange-earning nor foreign-exchange-saving? To say the least, the situation is made to order for disagreement. And disagreement there is!

A Statement of View

Achievement of a world situation in which reasonably high real percapita income and near-full employment are realized represents an "ideal" that many persons—including this author—are prepared to view as a worthy goal. But if the global environment thus envisaged as a goal is to be achieved, a transition period of some duration needs to be undergone. Seemingly, one should inquire what policies are appropriate when the ideal situation prevails, and what policies are appropriate during the transition period preceding its attainment; perhaps the two differ.

Significantly, the traditional law of comparative advantage assumes an environment that conforms more to the one pictured here as a goal than it does to the one actually prevailing or reasonably to be expected during the transition period preceding attainment of the goal. Accordingly, in the opinion of this author, the traditional law of comparative advantage is subject to important shortcomings as a guide in determining the types of industries a present-day underdeveloped country might reasonably contemplate in the course of its efforts to achieve development. Some deviation from, or modification of, the law of comparative advantage (in this form) seems warranted to help ease and speed the transition—as many persons have maintained in times past and as is much in evidence, for example, in infant-industry-type arguments. Yet, it seems inadequate simply to recognize a shortcoming in the law of comparative advantage and to condone deviation from it; some standards in terms of which basic decisions can be made still seem needed. Thus, the important question is what tests might prove workable during the transition. It is in this connection that "foreign-exchange impact" as a test acquires special relevance.

The central argument for foreign-exchange impact as a test—with which this author is in basic agreement—is that it "makes sense" in the here and now; it offers meaningful guidance for underdeveloped countries in the selection of the specific industries that can hope to survive and prosper, and that hence can help in the transition to that now-distant global environment in which conditions are reasonably akin to those assumed for the traditional law of comparative advantage—at which time the law of comparative advantage can well be looked to for the guidance its framers intended. In short, foreign-exchange impact is viewed as a meaningful test for the *short-run,* pending that time when evolution of an environment akin to that assumed by the law of comparative advantage serves to give meaning to its application as the *ultimate* test.

PLANNING AND PLANS

36. Proud Borrower and Shy Investor

The Economist*

Once upon a recent time, a private investor set out from his home in the west to seek good risks in underdeveloped countries. On his first night on a strange shore, he sought his fortune in the bar of the Palm Palace Hotel. Here he fell in, first, with a fine landlord-politician of the place, and later with a fellow countryman in business there.

"Investment here?" said the first. "Our land is crying out for it. You are welcome. We need a dam for our great river and a hydro-electric station beside it, so that we can settle peasants and run factories; we need our marshes drained, some silos and a new port; we need cement, paper, and fertiliser plants; there is no road to the interior, but would you be interested in our minerals?"

"Investment here?" said the second. "Don't touch it. I cannot move for the red tape of ill-run departments; my profits are frozen at will; my right to hire and fire is tampered with, not only by law but also by politicians who press me to sack their opponents. I am up against disregard of undertakings; a long-term operational agreement that I made only last year is already being questioned because someone thinks I ought to be able to afford better terms. Take my advice and the next plane for countries that offer better security."

This conversation might have taken place anywhere in three or four continents. Both in sovereign states and in dependencies all over the world, would-be borrowers for purposes of "development" see no incompatibility between setting their cap at the new investor and, simultaneously, behaving without consideration to the old. In fact, the talk took place in the Middle East, and, since this is the destination of a large trade mission which is leaving London next week, the examples given in this article are all taken from there. They are given subject to the comment that all can be matched elsewhere.

Concrete examples are available in almost every Middle Eastern state. Lebanon, for instance, proclaims its anxiety to attract investment from overseas, but is at the same time engaged in expropriating an urban electricity company without proper compensation. Syria, though less keen on new foreign investment, is joining with Lebanon in squeezing the two foreign oil pipeline companies that enjoy transit rights through their lands for better terms. Saudi Arabia, which sees the Arabian American Oil Com-

*From *The Economist* (November 7, 1953). Although dated in its references, this article has not lost its relevance to contemporary situations.

pany as an inexhaustible source of benefits, seldom tires of renegotiating recent agreements in quest of better terms. Iraq may yet carry out threats to nationalise a foreign electricity company without compensation for loss of profits. Almost everywhere in the Middle East, Dr. Mossadegh's battle with the Anglo-Iranian Oil Company is vested with such an aura of nationalist triumph for Persia that its reverse aspect—the deterrent that it constitutes to further foreign investment—is ignored.

General Neguib's Egypt, however, offers an interesting potential exception to the rule. The Egypt of his predecessors was even more apt than its neighbours to throttle foreign enterprise in the name of nationalism, regardless of its need for foreign capital. In 1947 and 1948 it passed anti-foreign company and mining laws that caused many foreign concerns to put a brake on development and some to withdraw from the country altogether. Today, the Neguib government has instituted a new production council and a committee for the investment of foreign capital, and the chairman of the two bodies has publicly remarked that "if we want to understand how to attract capital, we must study what we did that caused it to flee." The new government has revised the mining law, is talking of amendments to the companies law, and has produced a new law on the investment of foreign capital in economic development projects that is meant to protect the investor against the freezing of his assets.

These moves present so sharp a contrast to the blind nationalism of past policy that most Egyptians have not been able to go into reverse overnight, and foreign investors still hang back because they see the survivors among their predecessors handicapped by the acts of officials who have not caught up with the new thinking. But a start has been made.

The underdeveloped countries have their retort to many of the complaints. It was voiced at a panel discussion held at the International Bank in September on the problem of creating in underdeveloped countries a climate conducive to foreign investment. Its spokesman was the Egyptian Minister of Finance, who asked:

You demand transferability for both profits and capital. But are you doing the necessary to enable importing countries to earn your currency or are you, by trade barriers, barring them from earning it in an honest way? You complain of labour legislation. But is it too much for the people in less developed countries to claim the right to a bite of the cake that is produced there?

Naturally, there is a happy mean in such matters. But the chief reason why it is not yet attained in underdeveloped areas, and why the investor with money to place remains shy of commitments there, lies more in the waywardness and xenophobia of the countries that wish to borrow than in the present practices of the west.

Local myopia is often founded on beliefs and prejudices that have nothing to do with economics. The Arab, Persian or Egyptian, however keen to attract capital, judges that he can behave as loftily as he likes to the West because he has suffered at its hands and is owed compensation. A second premise is that he is indispensable. These two ideas have been encouraged by western behaviour—by greedy concessionaires of Ottoman days, by leading figures in two world wars who represented the Middle East as "vital to western interests" but failed to establish any impression that Middle Eastern interests also were at stake, by oil companies that paid a royalty of three cents a barrel until they sensed that the Middle East was discovering the better terms secured by Venezuela, by politicians who partitioned Palestine and then—in Arab eyes—acknowledge guilt by paying conscience money towards the upkeep of its refugees.

In recent years the twin premises have been further encouraged. One end-product of such enterprises as Mr. Bevin's Middle East Office, President Truman's Point Four, the United Nations' agency for the relief of the Arab refugees, and President Eisenhower's recent grant of $43 million to Persia, is an enhancement of the conceit that western bounty is due as of right, and that, no matter how often western streetnames are torn down and American or British offices sacked, the West will turn the other cheek. Normally, the technique for a concern needing capital is to display the security and yield obtained by earlier investors. Underdeveloped countries, in their arrogance, offer no such attractions, and the would-be lender is understandably shy.

He is also held back by another big consideration. All categories of private investor—whether individuals, fiduciaries responsible for insurance and trust funds, or corporations whose managements are responsible to stockholders—look, when investing abroad, for one or more of the classic inducements to invest. Of these, one is a large and sure market; the biggest markets being in the west, the investor abroad has tended to put his capital into raw materials that he can market at home, that are really an extension of his home economy and that bring local benefits only as a by-product of his operation. These conditions are not on offer in the Middle East today; it wants the other side of the medal.

An alternative inducement is the financing of part of the enterprise by local participants. In the Middle East, however, the absence of the habit of investment in any project offering a small but regular yield has long been proverbial. Your Egyptian, Persian or Kuweiti wants at least a 30 per cent dividend; mistrusting his neighbor, he also wants it quickly, and completely within his personal control; he therefore puts his savings into land, houses or merchandise. He does not see that his participation would carry weight with foreign lenders, and is querulous about the dimensions of American aid to Western Europe as opposed to American aid to himself. A wider move than has yet been made to establish joint-stock companies in collaboration with western lenders would vastly increase his country's prospects of capital development.

The American government's idea in launching aid programmes for underdeveloped countries was that public aid would fade away and private investment step in. But what happens in Western Europe is not happening in the Middle East. Nor will it happen quickly. Especially in xenophobic countries, the private investor is not the man to whom to turn for basic requirements such as vast irrigation schemes or networks of communications. As Sir George Schuster pointed out in the discussion at the International Bank already quoted, "the scope for private investment capital, and the things that need to be done to open the way to a fuller flow of private investment capital, are quite different." It is unrealistic to hope for the latter without first providing the basic capital works that will make investment pay, and to finance these recourse must undoubtedly be had to continued foreign public aid. Yet here, at least in the Middle East, is the threat of a vicious circle. The greater the public aid that is proffered from the West, the more lasting the Middle East's belief that the West is under an unredeemed obligation to it.

But compromises are not beyond the bounds of imagination. At a meeting last spring of the Finance Ministers of the Arab League there was some talk of an Arab Development Bank, and some at least of the propounders of the idea envisaged International Bank participation not only in its capital formation but in its management. Here is a germ that, if developed, might produce a new type of mixed International Finance Corporation undertaking major works. Such public bodies offer a double advantage; they are, owing to their strength and spread, more proof than private companied against the risk of expropriation that is at present the main deterrent to individual investors, and they are the essential forerunners of the mixed private companies that are—until underdeveloped territories give birth to a large body of indigenous savers and investors—the best answer to their need for capital.

Until he gets that answer the new private investor will be a scarce commodity there. He may poke his head round the door, but, after colloquy, he will tend to leave in search of the better risks that are to be had in the western lands themselves. The remedy lies in the hands of the "underdeveloped" peoples, but it shows too little sign of being used. Indeed, their rich men, far from setting the example for a local change of investing habits, are prone also to place their private investments in those countries of greater security.

37. Indian Planning Experience

*Anne O. Krueger**

I. Introduction

India's attempt to foster economic growth is of particular interest for several reasons. First, of course, the success or failure of Indian efforts will be of critical significance, not only for the welfare of her 400 million people, but also for the political stability of the country and the whole of

*The author is particularly indebted to her colleagues at the University of Minnesota, Professors Martin Bronfenbrenner and Marcel Richter, for helpful comments and suggestions.
This paper was initially written in the fall of 1959. Although certain sections were added in June 1962, the main body of the paper has been left unaltered.
The author is Professor of Economics, University of Minnesota.

Southeast Asia, since other countries have both the Indian and the Chinese experiences to observe. Secondly, the Indian effort is unique in that it was the first popularly elected government of an underdeveloped country to attempt to organize its economy under "planning" with, at the same time, the vast majority of its economic activities organized either traditionally or under free enterprise. India, in contrast to the West where development took place largely under private enterprise and to the Soviet bloc where there is no representative government, has attempted to maintain individual freedoms and yet let the government guide the economy.

Indian planning cannot be well defined; it is what it is. The Planning Commission draws up a document, or series of documents, in which it sets forth an investment allocation plan, estimates of national income in future years, and the like. Yet the Planning Commission has no authority to carry out the Plan, even of government investments, which are carried out both by various agencies in the central government, the various states, and private firms. Despite this, the Plans are important. The prevailing political attitudes of the Indian people and government attach primary importance to economic growth, and the Plan carries considerable weight. Moreover, the very act of drawing up such a document focuses attention on the important aspects of Indian economic problems, and serves as an impetus to the various government agencies who are consulted to consider alternatives from an economic standpoint.

Because of the unique nature of Indian planning, the best approach to understanding it will be consideration of the plans, followed by consideration of some of the important issues raised by the Indian experience.

II. The First Five Year Plan

When independence came to India, bloodshed and crisis accompanied it. The first years of independent India were devoted largely to the development of political institutions and to meeting the major crises that arose. The partition led to economic as well as political crises: shortages of many consumer goods; the refugee problem; and disruption of the transport and communication systems. The efforts of the government were devoted largely to alleviating those difficulties.

That the First Five Year Plan was formulated under these conditions attests to the importance the government of India places on economic development. The first committees on planning were established as early as 1948, the First Plan was in operation by 1951. It was, in large measure, a collection of projects that had already been inaugurated by the Center and States. Under the pressure of events, little or no consideration had been given as to the form by which government development efforts should take place; the question of how "planning" should operate in a society where virtually all economic activity was in the hands of small-scale operators was unconsidered.

Despite the rather makeshift nature of the over-all Plan, the planners attempted long-range projections of the possible course of national income, investment and consumption. These projections are of importance primarily because they are still in vogue, and important in Indian thinking. The Plan did not make clear whether the projections were estimates of what was feasible, or whether they related to what the planners regarded as desirable. In either case, per capita income, it was declared, could be doubled by 1977, if investment rose each year by 50% of additional income in that year.[1]

It is clear that the First Plan was regarded as a preliminary to development, rather than as a part of the development effort itself.[2] It was recognized that the agricultural base of the country was extremely weak, and that primary effort should be devoted to strengthening agriculture sufficiently so that other projects could follow. Additionally, restoration of the railroads and other overhead services was given great emphasis. Together, agriculture, irrigation and power projects were to receive 38% of total public development expenditures[3] (total public outlay was set at 2,069 million Rupees), while transport and communications were allocated 24%, social services 16%, and large and small industry together only 8%. Private sector investment, of course, was expected to supplement public investment, so that over-all industrial investment was to have a slightly greater share of total investment than the Plan figures would indicate.[4] Even with this qualification, it is clear that government efforts during the First Plan period were devoted primarily to improving social overhead services and agricultural productivity.

For present purposes, it is unnecessary to trace the vicissitudes of the First Plan in any detail. During the first two years of the Plan, inflationary pressures were strong, and little evidence was forthcoming that the Plan expenditures had any effectiveness. However, due to a number of factors, the last three years of the First Plan were successful beyond all hopes of the original plan, so that the results of the First Five Year Plan, on paper, were impressive. Whereas it had been estimated that per capita income might rise 10–11% during the five years, it actually rose 18%. Food output, for which the target had been a 14% increase, actually rose by 20% —this was 142% of the planned increase in the case of foodgrains.[5]

Although many government enterprises, especially in the industrial sector, did not meet their Plan targets, this was more than offset by the private sector's overfulfillment of the rate of output assigned to it in the Plan.

Even more astonishing than the overfulfillment of optimistic expectations was the fact that it was accomplished with spending at less than the anticipated level,[6] with a foreign trade surplus and a falling price level. There was no evidence of strain, but rather the Plan left considerable slack in the economy.

---

[1]*First Plan,* p. 21.

[2]"The Five Year Plan is essentially a plan of preparation for laying the foundation for more rapid development in the future. . . ." *Ibid.,* p. 7

[3]Strictly speaking, not all of public sector expenditures were to be for development; however, the proportion of non-development to developmental expenditures in each sector was approximately the same.

[4]This is because private investment in industry constitutes a higher proportion of total private investment than did government investment in industry to total investment of the First Plan.

[5]Government of India Planning Commission, *Review of the First Five Year Plan,* p. 14–5. May 1957, New Delhi.

[6]Actual outlay in the public sector was approximately Rs. 1,960 crores.

The reasons for this apparently astonishing success were many, and not all obvious. The Plan was, of course, partly responsible. Additionally, two other factors were important: extremely favorable weather (as well as improved irrigation facilities) and (an illusory element) improved statistical coverage. While it is impossible, even in light of later information, to estimate with any degree of precision the extent to which these factors either singly or in combination contributed to increased food crops, the most frequent guess is that nearly half of the total increase in food output was due to these two factors. The importance of the availability of food for any investment program in a country as poor as India cannot be overestimated. This increase in food output, regardless of whether it was due to weather or the Plan, clearly was a necessary precondition for the fiscal ease which accompanied the Plan expenditures.

Even the large increase in industrial production was not entirely due to Plan expenditure. There had been considerable excess capacity at the start of the First Plan, so that output increases were the combined result of increased utilization of existing plant and the introduction of new plant and equipment: use of available data would have indicated a marginal capital-output ratio (net investment to net increase in output) of 1.8: 1, clearly much too low had all output increases been attributable to increased capital. (Available investment figures significantly understate achieved investments since no figures are available for non-monetized farm improvements.)

On some other fronts, even the modest goals set forth in the Plan were not met: the number of pupils in primary schools by 1955–56 was 60% of the target; electrical capacity was only 84% of target. More important, perhaps, than the failures to meet output targets, was the appearance of a considerable body of open unemployment in the cities, and distress in cottage industry as factory industry prospered. By the end of the First Plan, the Government was extremely conscious of the need for creation of employment opportunities, as well as a rapid increase in the standard of living.

III. The Second and Third Five Year Plans

Amid all the evidence of success during 1954–55, the question of priorities for the Second Plan began to receive serious consideration.

Before much discussion had occurred, however, P. C. Mahalanobis, a physicist and statistician by training, wrote and published a *Plan Frame* wherein he expounded the view that the key to rapid development lay in the concentration on heavy industry: "machines to make machines" should receive primary emphasis in the Second Plan. He proposed a big push in the government owned heavy industry sector, particularly iron and steel, and machine tool production, a major step-up in the rate of plan expenditures (from Rs. 2 billion to Rs. 6 billion), and 39% of expenditure devoted to heavy industry.[1] He then argued that in order to provide the

[1] Mahalanobis has developed a formal model in support of his view. It is concerned with the problem of allocation, but space will not allow a detailed explanation and critique here. The reader is referred to P. C. Mahalanobis, "The Approach of Operational Research to Planning in India," *Sankhya*, December 1955.

necessary employment, labor-intensive cottage industry should be subsidized from a tax on the factory consumer-goods industries.

The argument that iron and steel are the index of development had, of course, much psychological appeal. Additionally, Mahalanobis contended that concentration on heavy industry, while requiring heavy foreign exchange expenditures in the short run, would in the long run cut down India's imports considerably, also a persuasive point to the Indian people.

Although Mahalanobis' proposals as put forward in the Plan Frame were watered down considerably in the final Second Plan, Mahalanobis' basic ideas and emphasis were accepted by the Planning Commission,[*] and still form the basic philosophy for Indian planning. The basic idea behind Plan allocation was that the rate of development of heavy industry would determine the rate of growth of the entire economy, and that attention should be devoted to the supply of consumer goods only in so far as provision of these goods would enable the hiring of more workers for the production of investment goods. The goals of increasing output and providing sufficient employment were regarded as being almost entirely separate and, if anything, competing rather than complementary.

Within this theoretical approach, then, the Second Plan was formulated. Public expenditure was to rise from the First Plan level of Rs. 2,000 crores to Rs. 4,800 crores—a drastic increase in the scale of effort, and in the government share in total investment. Table 1 indicates scheduled outlays in the Second Plan as compared with the First. Emphasis shifted considerably to industry, and away from social services and agriculture, even though the absolute sum devoted to the latter sectors was also increased.

Table 1: *Allocation of Expenditures of Government in the First and Second Plans**

	FIRST PLAN		SECOND PLAN	
	RS. CRORES[1]	% OF TOTAL	RS. CRORES	% OF TOTAL
I. Agriculture and comm. dev.	357	15.1	568	11.8
II. Irrigation and power	661	28.1	913	19.0
III. Industry and mining	179	7.6	890	18.5
IV. Transport and communication	557	23.6	1,385	28.9
V. Social services	523	22.6	945	19.7
Total	2,356	100	4,800	100

*Source: *Second Five Year Plan*, pp. 51–52. It should be remembered that the price level in 1955–56 was slightly lower than it was in 1951–52.
[1]One crore=10,000,000

This level of expenditure, along with the efforts of the private sector, was expected to increase national income by 25% over the Second Plan period (an assumed marginal capital: output ratio of 2.3: 1—extremely low, especially in view of the emphasis on heavy industry and transport).

[*]Professor Shenoy was the only dissenter on the Planning Commission. See his "Dissent," in Government of India, *Planning Commission, Papers Relating to the Formulation of the Second Five Year Plan*, p. 19. New Delhi, 1956.

It has already been mentioned that emphasis on capital-intensive heavy industry dictated a separate approach to the employment problem through the subsidization of cottage industry and restriction of factory consumer goods output. Even on the optimistic assumptions of the planners, India would be unable to do more than create employment for additional workers entering the labor force; the large backlog of unemployment would not be touched during the Plan period.[9]

Despite the wave of optimism surrounding the successful completion of the First Plan, it was apparent to the Planning Commission that the strain on the economy in carrying out the Second Plan would be considerable. Of total public plan expenditures, 25% were to be financed by deficit financing and 25% from a foreign trade deficit, not withstanding the optimistic taxation and small savings yields estimated in the Plan. With all this, there was a Rs. 600 crores gap between anticipated level of expenditures and level of financing.

The contrast between the First and Second Plans was extremely sharp. Whereas the First Plan concentrated on activities surrounding the agricultural sector, the Second Plan paid relatively much less attention to that sector. The First Plan's allocation did not require the development of much additional government enterprise, and the level of expenditures and direction of activities was such that the public and private sectors were not competing for the same resources. In the Second Plan, the level of expenditure was so much higher that there could not help but be competition between the two sectors for scarce resources, while the direction expenditures required considerable extension of the sphere of government enterprise. Whereas in the First Plan little conflict between goals existed, and the aim of the Plan was to increase output, the Second Plan aimed in two directions (at least) at the same time: with one program it aimed at raising output, with another, at increasing employment.

Almost from the very start of the Second Plan, difficulties and crises arose.[10] By the end of 1956–57, a huge foreign trade deficit had been incurred: within one year the drain on foreign exchange reserves was greater than that planned for the entire Second Plan, despite a favorable turn in the terms of trade and increased demand for India's exports. This surge in imports took place even before the "big push" envisaged in the Second Plan got under way, and at first was not attributable to the plan at all, but rather to buoyancy in the private sector. As the drain on foreign exchange reserves intensified, the government tightened import licensing drastically, cutting down even on raw materials essential to some lines of industrial production. However, government import requirements under the Plan had by that time risen. Additionally, the Indian government felt that it must increase its defense effort, which required additional expenditures both locally and in foreign exchange. The price level began to rise under the pressure of government spending for development and defense.

[9]*Second Plan,* p. 112.
[10]It should be noted, however, that the flow of statistics is sufficiently slow in India so that the foreign exchange problem was not clearly recognized until 1957; even then, no one knew how many additional import licenses were outstanding. This is a serious problem in Indian planning; the 1954–55 and 1955–56 data indicate that the import boom had already started—had these been available, at an earlier date, decisions might have been different.

The wholesale price level (1952–53 = 100), which had stood at 90.8 in March of 1955, and 98.1 in March of 1956, rose to 105.6 by March of 1957, despite the huge import surplus.

To make matters worse at that juncture, weather conditions, which had so favored Indian crops during the First Plan, changed, and food output declined drastically in 1957–58. In all, the first half of the Second Plan was disastrous: output targets were not met while expenditures on various projects ran well above the planned level, the foreign exchange crisis continued unabated, and demoralization set in.

By March 1958, at the end of a very bad crop year, the planners were forced to curtail their goals for 1960–61, and the level of Plan expenditures in real terms along with it. In paring the Plan, they attempted to retain the "hard core" of Plan projects (i.e., heavy industry), but cut down on the desired goals. In actuality, this was done by retaining the Rs. 4,800 crores expenditure figure (reallocating it between categories) even though the price level had risen by ten per cent.[11]

In reality, total government expenditures during the Second Plan were Rs. 4,600 crores, which when adjusted for price increases in the interim represented a reduction of approximately 13% below the initially scheduled outlay. Table 2 below gives some of the major economic indicators for the Second Plan period.

Table 2: Indian Economic Performance During the First and Second Plans*

	1950–51	1955–56	1956–57	1957–58	1958–59	1959–60	1960–61	Average Annual Increase During Second Plan
Net national output constant prices[1]	88.5	104.8	110.0	108.9	116.5	118.5	126.9	3.8
Per capita output constant prices[2]	250.3	267.8	275.6	267.4	280.2	279.0	292.5	1.8
Agricultural production[3]		116.8	124.3	115.9	132.0	128.7	139.1	3.6
Industrial production[4]	100.0	122.4	132.6	137.3	139.7	151.9	170.3	6.9
Price level[5]		92.5	105.3	108.4	112.9	117.1	124.8	6.5
Trade balance[6]		−464	−639	−454	−300	−450		−
Reserves[7]		1,866	1,435	942	722	814	670	−

*Sources: For first five indicators, Government of India, *Economic Survey 1961–62*, March 1962. Trade balance from Government of India, Planning Ecommission, *Third Five Year Plan*, p. 108. Reserve data taken from *International Financial Statistics*, May 1962.
[1]Rs. crores at 1948–49 prices.
[2]Rupees, in 1948–49 prices.
[3]Index, crop year ending June 1950=100.
[4]Index, on calendar year basis, 1951=100.
[5]Index, 1952–53=100.
[6]Rs. crores; 1961 estimates are preliminary; exports fob, imports cif.
[7]In millions of U.S. dollars, on last day of each calendar year.

[11]Planning Commission, "Appraisal and Prospects of the Second Five Year Plan," May 1958. New Delhi.

While it is clear that the actual results of the Second Plan were well below the intended 5% annual rate of growth of national income, the rate of growth of income did increase slightly as compared with the First Plan; however, this was not reflected in the growth of per capita income, which grew more slowly in the Second Plan, as a result of the spurt in the rate of population growth.

Moreover, the Second Plan's accomplishments were accompanied by significant strain on the economy, as can be seen by the decline in reserves (despite huge foreign emergency loans and considerably more foreign aid than was anticipated), and the relatively rapid rate of increase in the price level. Much of this pressure is not reflected in the figures, since foreign capital was used to offset many of the imports; some of these, as for instance foodgrains (where 20 million tons were imported during the Second Plan as compared with planned imports of 6 million tons) served to damp increases in the price level, as the Indian government tried actively to maintain price stability in the markets of staple foods.

Although there are no adequate capital formulation data available for India, the Planning Commission estimates that the rate of domestic saving reached 8.5% by the end of the Second Plan period. Since foreign capital inflow equalled about 3% of Indian output, total capital formulation was about 11.5%; it should be noted that more than ¼ of Indian investment, therefore, hinged on the willingness of foreign countries to lend on a long term basis for Indian development.

The Third Five Year Plan: The formulation of the Third Five Year Plan began at the time when Indian economic fortunes seemed at their lowest. Two conflicting and offsetting pressures were foremost in the Planners' thinking: on the one hand, the results of the Second Plan had shown clearly that investments planned beyond the resources of the country could lead to foreign exchange crisis and curtailment; on the other hand, the pressing political and economic pressures for a higher standard of living dictated even greater efforts for a more rapid rate of economic growth. Strangely enough, in all the discussion, there was little questioning of the basic philosophy that had underlined the Second Plan. Although, as will be seen below, greater awareness of the importance of agricultural production, foreign exchange, and the role of the private sector resulted from the experience of the Second Plan, no change in the emphasis on the desirability of self-sufficiency in capital goods occurred.

Hence, the goals of the Third Plan are very similar to those of the Second, and the few shifts in allocation that occurred were, other than heavier emphasis on agriculture and a slightly increased role of the private sector, *de minimus*. The Third Plan aims at raising national income 5% annually, and the statement of other goals is little changed, save for the significant addition of goal number two: "to achieve self-sufficiency in foodgrains and increase agricultural production to meet the requirements of industry and exports."[12]

Total investment is expected to rise from Rs. 1,600 crores in the last year of the Second Plan to Rs. 2,600 crores in 1965–66; this is a 54% in-

[12]*Third Five Year Plan,* p. 48.

crease in total investment, with a 70% increase in public investment and a 32% increase in private investment. Domestic savings are expected to rise to 11.5% at the end of the Third Plan period, which with foreign aid, will result in investment of 14% of national income.[13]

Although it is anticipated that employment will increase by 14 million during the Third Plan period, the labor force will increase by some 17 millions—indicating the difficulty encountered as the rate of population growth increases.

The allocation pattern differs only in detail from the Second Plan: of the larger total investment public investment will be allocated 14% for agriculture (compared with 11% in the Second Plan), investment in power facilities will increase from 10 to 13%, and 3% will be invested in increasing inventories to prevent bottlenecks of the kind that occurred during the Second Plan period. The share of large-scale industry will remain unchanged, and the major per cent reduction in share will be the transport and communications sector, whose allocation of public investment funds will fall from 28% in the second plan period to 20% in the Third. When the anticipated pattern of private investment is taken into account, these changes are even smaller; the share of transport, communications and social services in investment will decline, and that of agriculture and organized industry will increase.

More significant, perhaps, than these shifts in allocation is the increased awareness of the planners of the importance of foreign exchange and resource pressures. Foreign exchange requirements of investment are more carefully set forth,[14] and there is considerable emphasis on the necessity for price stability. During the Second Plan, it was recognized that the degree of strain placed upon the economy was too great, and additional taxation was seriously attempted, with considerable success. Table 3 presents in outline the intended and actual financing of the Second Plan as compared with the planned financing of the Third.

Table 3. *Financing of the Second and Third Plans**

| | Rs. Crores | | |
| SOURCES OF REVENUE | SECOND PLAN | | THIRD PLAN |
	ORIGINAL	1960 EST.	
Central government sources	1950	1510	3040
Additional taxation	450	1052	1710
External assistance	800	1090	2200
Deficit financing	1200	948	550
Total	4400	4600	7500

*Source: *Third Plan,* p. 95.

As was earlier pointed out, the anticipated financing of the Second Plan left a large margin for doubt as to whether the resources would be forthcoming. The same statement may equally well be made with regard to the Third Plan. The central government sources' increase is predicated upon

[13]*Third Five Year Plan,* pp. 49ff.
[14]*Ibid.,* p. 110.

a significant increase in receipts from current taxes and a surplus in government owned enterprises—neither of these items have shown any surplus at all in the past—indeed, in the Second Plan, the central government ran a small deficit in its current budget as a result of defense expenditures. Likewise, the external assistance is predicated on total foreign capital inflow of Rs. 3,200 crores, some 550 being necessary for amortization and interest on current loans, and some 450 anticipated to go to private industry. Thus, although the anticipated financing of the Third Plan is considerably more realistic than that of the Second, it is evident that, once again, extreme pressure is liable to be placed on Indian foreign and domestic resources and it is doubtful whether all these sources of funds will be forthcoming.

In summary, the Third Plan moves in generally the same direction as the Second. While it is overly optimistic in many regards, it is not so grossly unrealistic as the Second Plan. While undoubtedly some curtailment will be necessary and many of the goals not attained, a repetition of the drastic reductions of 1957–58 is unlikely, and there is ground for hope that the over-all results of the Third Plan will be generally better than those of the Second. Much, of course, depends on the degree to which other countries are willing to continue and expand their foreign assistance to India, and, as in the past, much will depend upon vagaries of the weather and consequently agricultural production. In the first year of the Third Plan, agricultural production rose about 8% and industrial production about the same amount; this was accompanied by significant pressure on India's foreign exchange, but no visible pressure on prices. As such, the Third Plan started more favorably than did the Second.

Summary of the Indian experience. It should be clear from the above that the Indian experience with planning has been too short and too particular to offer very many generalizations. However, many significant issues have been raised by the Indian experience, which may have some relevance for development policy in other countries. In many respects, it is still too early to interpret the meaning of the Indian experience, even for the first eleven years of planning. Nonetheless, any attempt to assess Indian prospects for development must depend largely on evaluation of these issues to which we now turn attention.

IV. Questions and Lessons Arising from the Indian Experience

The questions and problems which have emerged from the Indian experience are many and varied. The writer has chosen four of the problems of more general interest for consideration. The issues to be considered here are: the role of government in development programs, conflicts between goals, investment criteria, and the degree of strain on the economy most conducive to rapid development.

A. *Public-private sector relationships in Indian planning.* The most critical issue, in the opinion of the writer, raised by Indian experience is that of the relationship between government and private economic activities in a development program under a representative government.

Several pertinent facts will serve to illustrate the sort of problems that arise. Public enterprises produced in 1960–61 4.0% of Indian output, yet had received more than 60% of all Indian investment in the Second Plan. Yet the private sector has overfulfilled its output and investment targets in both Plans while the public sector has not attained either.[15] The large increases in output occurring during the First Plan outside agriculture originated almost entirely in the private sector. Yet private investment is largely choked off by government regulation, the channelling of investment funds into the government sector, and the like. During the foreign exchange crisis, it was private capital goods imports that were choked off in order to maintain the planned government investment program.

Indians tend to assume that any difficulties arising in connection with the Plan are caused, not by the Plan itself, but rather by underlying development problems. Virtually no account has been taken of the "opportunity cost" of additional government investment in terms of the resources diverted from the private sector of the economy. Yet the successes and failures of the two Plans can be largely explained by the way in which government activities affected the private sector.[16] There can be little question but that private enterprise was stagnant at the time of the formulation of the First Five Year Plan. Even during the first two years of the First Plan, when government expenditures were still low, private industry remained stagnant. However, as expenditures in the First Plan picked up, private industry also came to life. The important point in this regard is that almost all investment during the First Plan that was undertaken by the government was complementary to the private sector. Irrigation, power facilities, transport and communications—these were the big items in the First Plan, and virtually all of them contributed to the vitality of the private sector.

Investment activities in the private sector started increasing rapidly, and the favorable trade balance usually maintained by the private sector was reversed as private capital goods imports started mounting rapidly by 1954 under the stimulus of the Plan and increased demand resulting from it.[17] This boom in the private sector was cut off only in 1956–57 when the government, faced with needed imports for the plan, and a heavy drain on foreign exchange, imposed rigid controls on imports. The rate of increase in industrial production at that time slowed down drastically.

In the Second Plan, a large part of government investment was channelled into activities that compete with the private sector, and, for that matter, divert funds from the private sector. Steel plants, heavy machinery building, fertilizer plants, and the like, do little in the short run to stimulate production in other industry; indeed, the prices of many of these goods have risen as their availability from abroad has been reduced and

[15] *Third Plan,* p. 105. Private investment during the Second Plan was Rs. 3,300 crores whereas Rs. 2,400 crores were planned.
[16] This is consistent with the view that agricultural output was crucial to the First Plan, since government activities were complementary to the private sector.
[17] For a further discussion of the capital goods imports originating in the private sector, see A. Krueger and N. K. Choudhry "The Balance of Payments Crisis," *Eastern Economist,* August 1959.

critical bottlenecks have emerged, especially in coal, raw jute, and other raw materials.

This problem is really a manifestation of a structural difficulty underlying the entire planning process in India: an understanding tendency, on the part of the planners, to pay a great deal of attention to the government sector of the economy, where they can make their decisions directly operative, and to devote relatively little thought to the needs of the private sector.

This myopia, as it were, in favor of government enterprise, is quite strong and has two bases: the political leaning of the country (particularly the disrepute into which the Indian capitalist class has justly fallen) and the greater ease of planning in the government sphere where activities are directly under control. These factors lead to a general bias in favor of the public sector.

To some extent, the Indian planners have been more alert to the needs of the private sector since the 1957–58 Plan cutbacks. Although the official statement of the Indian government on the relationship of the private and public sectors has not been altered, and the public sector is still to receive more than 60% of investment funds in the Third Plan, the confidence of private businessmen in India with regard to their future has somewhat increased. While licenses and dealing with government officials are necessary for imports, expansion, borrowing of funds, and the like, they are somewhat more readily attained than was the case at the beginning of the Second Plan, and the private sector's output, which fell off during 1957–58, has resumed its rate of expansion.

In addition to this basic difficulty, there are very real problems involved in extending the scope of the public sector. Not only does additional government activity have direct costs in terms of the private enterprise resources it bids away, there are administrative and other problems within the government sector itself.

Despite the relatively high quality of administration, the Plans have suffered in several respects due to bureaucratic inertia. One illustration will suffice: as of mid-1958, 40% of the irrigation facilities installed during the First Plan period were still unusable due to failure to install the supplementary field canals. Similar administrative failures are reported frequently; in the large, they probably constitute a considerable deterrent to the pace of development.[18]

In addition to the presence or absence of the necessary administrative talent, the very organization of the Indian government has led to certain difficulties. The federal form of government, while necessary for many reasons, has not been conducive to effective planning: there are essentially fourteen state plans in operation, as well as the program of the center. This means that the Planning Commission sets up tax and expenditure targets for the states; once its task is done, it has no power of enforcement.[19]

[18]W. Malenbaum, *East and West in India's Development*, pp. 33–34. Washington, 1959.

[19]To give some idea of the importance of this factor, Rs. 2,102 crores (out of Rs. 4,800 crores) of the public expenditures in the Second Plan were to be expended by the states; the states were to raise Rs. 822. crores toward total plan

A second organizational difficulty exists entirely at the federal level, and could be remedied within the present Indian constitutional framework. It is this: the Planning Commission is, at present, a purely advisory body. Thus, although it draws up (with the assistance of those governmental agencies concerned) the Plan, it has no responsibility for carrying it out. There is no government agency with responsibility for over-all supervision of the development program. During the foreign exchange crisis, for example, the Ministry of Commerce was unable even to indicate how many import licenses were outstanding; it, in turn, had no information on the probable extent of government import requirements. The cost of such lack of coordination is undoubtedly very high.

B. *Conflicting goals.* The problem of the aims of government economic policy is thorny in all underdeveloped countries.

In general, several types of conflict are possible: maximum present consumer welfare conflicts with maximum future consumer welfare; socially-conscious governments usually find their social welfare programs in conflict with their development goals; the desire for a relatively equal income distribution conflicts with the use of incentives as a tool for attainment of economic growth.

All these conflicts have been recognized in the literature, and have been regarded as the "price" of economic development, one some underdeveloped countries may be unwilling to pay. Recently, however, it has been recognized that another type of conflict may occur: maximum growth may also entail a considerable volume of unemployment.[20]

This problem has been a major worry to the Indian government: the Second Five Year Plan stated its principal objectives as follows:

a. Sizeable increase in national income so as to raise the level of living in the country.
b. rapid industrialization with particular emphasis on the development of basic and heavy industries;
c. a large expansion of employment opportunities
d. reduction in inequalities in income and wealth and a more even distribution of economic power.[21]

It was recognized that there could be considerable conflict between these goals.[22] As already indicated the final choice was concentration on investment in heavy industry coupled with taxation of factory consumer goods to subsidize cottage industry to provide employment. In allocating investment funds in this manner, the planners seem to have maximized the degree of conflict between goals in this choice. In the Third Plan the stated objections remain unchanged, save for the addition of a new aim, that of agricultural self-sufficiency, mentioned above.[23]

---

financing. In the first Plan, the proportion of State to total expenditure was even higher. The difficulties that arise from this form of organization should be obvious, and little more need be said here. *Second Plan,* p. 87. See also Planning Commission, *Review of First Five Year Plan,* p. 27.

[20]R. S. Eckaus, "Factor Proportions in Underdeveloped Countries," *American Economic Review,* September 1955, pp. 539–568, presented a formal proof of this proposition.
[21]*Second Plan,* p. 24.
[22]*Ibid.,* p. 25.
[23]*Third Five Year Plan,* p. 48.

The ends of industrialization, employment, and growth, however, have conflicted strongly. Heavy and basic industries have a low labor-capital ratio; hence, few additional jobs are provided by this type of investment.[24] With limited capital, this use of investment funds means fewer jobs than could otherwise be created. Moreover, it is frequently contended that investment of the type undertaken in the Second and Third Plans has a very low employment multiplier: that is, for every job created directly by planned investment, there is a very small additional increment of employment along with it. Few other investments are induced as a result of the initial outlay, either through increased consumption or through ancillary investment projects undertaken.[25]

The decision to concentrate on heavy industry conflicts with the aim of increasing employment as much as possible, and also conflicts with the goal of maximum growth of output.[26] The high capital-output ratio in this sector implies that there will be less additional output per unit of capital when it is invested in this sector than in others with a lower capi-

---

[24]The Indian government, with its social consciousness, has been very responsive to trade union pressures. As a result, the urban wage level is quite high, and one cannot but suspect that this increased the flow of migrants from country to city, while simultaneously reducing the volume of employment—and possibly output in the cities. The degree to which high wages are responsible for open unemployment is difficult to estimate. One factor, of course, is that the number of "retainer" positions with private industry has been reduced. Consequently, employment provided during the first two plans has been somewhat greater than the statistics would indicate, if one assumes that these low product workers would have been dismissed anyway.

[25]W. Malenbaum, *East and West in India's Development*, p. 35. Washington, D. C., 1957.

[26]This is especially true, given India's foreign exchange constraint. The foreign exchange required for various types of investments in the Third Plan are as follows:

Sector	Total Investment	Rs. Crores Foreign Exchange Component	% Foreign Exchange Required
A. *Public*			
Agriculture	610	30	5.0
Major and medium irrigation	650	50	7.7
Power	1012	320	31.6
Village and small industries	100	20	20.0
Large and medium industries	1470	690	47.1
Transport and communications	1486	320	21.6
Social services and miscellaneous	572	90	15.7
Inventories	200	–	–
Total	6100	1520	24.9
B. *Private*			
Large and medium industries, minerals, and transportation	1350	495	36.6
Village and small industries	325	15	4.1
Other	2625	Neg.	–
Total public and private	12400	2030	16.4

tal output ratio.[27] In a country where capital is extremely scarce, this implies a lower rate of growth of total output.[28]

Although a different investment allocation pattern would have reduced the magnitude of the employment problem and increased the growth rate, it is not at all clear that any alternative policy could have solved the problem, given the Indian resource endowment. The First Plan, in which the conflict between employment and growth was far less important, saw a huge increase in open urban unemployment.[29] Yet even at that stage, one cannot help but question whether a different approach to the unemployment issue might have yielded better results. In the First Plan, it was estimated that it would require Rs. 3,000 capital investment in order to provide one additional job. Clearly, the figure can vary with the type of employment envisaged: a more satisfactory approach would have been the choice of projects that appeared promising *and* whose labor input was high relative to the capital input,[30] and the calculation of the required amount of capital from these estimates.

Whatever contributing factors—price distortion, poor planning emphasis, etc.—may aggravate unemployment, the basic fact of Indian poverty is a scarcity of capital (including services) per worker. Any solution that utilizes available capital inefficiently will, in the long run, aggravate and perpetuate the unemployment problem. Much of Indian cottage industry is clearly inefficient. There is even indication that capital, as well as labor, per unit of output is higher in cottage industry than in factory industry.[31] Any subsidization of this inefficiency, as has been undertaken as a result of the emphasis on heavy industry, is unwise, and harmful to development *and* employment in the long run. Only an increase in capital (including human skills) can provide any solution to the unemployment problem.

To the extent that short-run measures are necessary for humanitarian reasons, they should not affect efficient production, and should minimize the resource diversion from investment that occurs. Well-digging, construction of roads, schools, and many other employment opportunities can be provided that do not interfere and stultify the economic performance of other sectors of the economy to anything like the same degree as subsidization of cottage industry at the expense of factory industry has done.

C. *Investment criteria in development programs.* The question of proper allocation of investment funds on both theoretical and empirical grounds

[27]It is quite possible that investment in industries with high capital-output ratios may still make sense since the required labor input is often considerably lower than in industries with lower capital to output ratios. However, the burden of proof must lie with those who want to push highly capital-intensive industries in a labor surplus country.

[28]This assumes that labor has a marginal product of zero or very close to it or that the marginal value product of labor does not vary significantly as between different industries.

[29]Planning Commission, *Review of the First Five Year Plan*, p. 10.

[30]W. Malenbaum, "India and China: Contrasts in Development," p. 298, *American Economic Review,* June 1959.

[31]V. V. Bhatt, "Capital Output Ratios in Certain Industries: A Comparative Study of Certain Countries," *Review of Economics and Statistics,* Vol. XXXVI No. 3 (August 1954).

is an extremely difficult one, and cannot be considered here in any of its broad ramifications.

In the Indian experience, the only contribution to investment allocation theory, in any important sense, is the Mahalanobis model,[32] upon which the Second Five Year Plan was based.

Within India, there is some evidence that the Planners have learned by experience, and that the Third Five Year Plan may be more realistic in its investment allocation. Particularly, there seems to be some increased awareness of the importance both of agricultural productivity increases, and also of the potentialities of expanding consumer goods exports.[33]

D. *The degree of strain most conducive to development.* In Indian thought with regard to planning, there have been two implicit assumptions that the present writer regards as being detrimental. The first of these is the tendency to confuse the desirability of a given program with its feasibility, and the second is the assumption that the larger the size of plan expenditures, the greater will be the growth of income.

Each of these unspoken assumptions has in turn fed on the other. This can be most clearly seen in the case of the Second Plan. Clearly it is and was desirable that a huge increase in income occur. The Second Plan was formulated, partly with a view to what "must" be done, and partly with a view to that which was feasible. But the assumption that the bigger the Plan, the better, led to a Plan in which only 25% of total expenditures could be covered by taxation and other visible revenues. As further illustration of this same phenomenon, after all expenditures and targets for the Second Plan had been finalized, the Government lifted the output target in the agricultural sector by 10 million tons of foodgrains, leaving outlays unchanged.[34]

The fact that a "big" plan is not necessarily a good plan is manifest in the cutbacks that had to be made during the execution of the Second Plan. The waste of resources that occurs when projects must be abandoned half-finished and imports must be cut across the board is tremendous. Additionally, of course, the political and psychological costs of failure are enormous.

Despite the experience of the Second Plan, the Third Plan will be considerably "bigger" once again. Although its financing is not as grossly unrealistic as that anticipated for the Second Plan, it has already been shown that the size of Third Plan expenditures will depend critically

[32]As noted earlier, space does not permit more than a passing reference to Mahalanobis' model. See earlier reference, which includes the *Plan Frame.* See also P. C. Mahalanobis, "Some Observations on the Process of Growth of National Income," *Sankhya,* December 1953. We are not concerned here with the four-sector model, which has been much less important, and which is criticized in Ryutaro Komiya, "A Note on Professor Mahalanobis' Model of Indian Economic Planning," *Review of Economics and Statistics,* February 1959. Since this article was written, Professor Martin Bronfenbrenner has written an excellent, simple exposition of the Mahalanobis model, as well as a thorough examination of its fundamental assumptions. See his "A Simplified Mahalanobis Model," *Economic Development and Cultural Change,* 1961.

[33]See, for example, Madan, "The Third Five Year Plan," Reserve Bank *Bulletin,* July 1959.

[34]*Economic Weekly,* July 1956.

upon a huge inflow of foreign resources and in addition will place considerable strain on the Indian Economy.

Since no one can say what would have happened with a different plan, or with no plan at all, it is unlikely that the emphasis on "big" plans will change. However, as experience with planning continues, awareness of the consequences of "too big" plans will undoubtedly bring greater realism to Indian planning.

V. Prospects For Future Indian Development

Any attempt at balanced assessment of India's achievements and future potential must perforce be extremely tentative. It is clear that the first years since independence have seen the start of tremendous social and economic change. The problems in India are so vast, however, that despite tremendous change, hardly a dent has been made in the long road to development and a minimally acceptable standard of life.

The progress of the past eleven years on the socio-economic front has been encouraging. Output increased from 1950–51 to 1960–61 by 40%, while per capita income in constant prices rose 17%. Even more significant, however, from the viewpoint of long-term growth, is that the seeds of change have been planted in every village in India.

Quite aside from the necessity of reweaving the social fabric, if development is to succeed, the population problem in India is immediate and pressing. Despite all the attention devoted to employment in the Second Plan period, the additional employment created was not expected to absorb even new entrants into the labor force. Already India's population is growing by more than 5 million people per year, and her labor force by over 2.0 million. Given as many people as already exist on the land, it is wishful thinking to expect any net addition to output through the use of more labor in that sector. While there are some new lands that may be opened up, these are far fewer than was generally thought ten years ago. Thus, the problem of increasing efficiency sufficiently to prevent per capita output from falling is an already serious one.

The Indian government has recently started to step up its efforts to cut down the rate of increase of population. Free sterilization is available in hospitals, and parents are encouraged to avail themselves of the facilities after having several children. While no data are yet available (even the number of Indians is still a question) there is some reason to hope that the current effort may have some success in reducing the birth rate.

As the population problem has increased in intensity, the Indian government has shown increasing awareness of it, and willingness to do something about it. Despite the fact that more action will be taken, it is doubtful that the population increase, at least in absolute numbers, will be noticeably reduced in the foreseeable future, as health measures are brought to the villages and the absolute base of the population grows.

From a welfare viewpoint, the population problems themselves indicate that even rapid success in raising output will lead to only moderate success in terms of individual welfare. Moreover, the fact that some attention must be diverted from raising output to increasing employment is virtuallly certain to retard growth in the short run. The degree to which this happens will, of course, depend on the Indian government's policy in future plans.

In addition to population problems, the very low standard of living and per capita output that prevails—despite ten years' success—itself constitutes a further difficulty. The temptation to utilize additional output to increase the level of consumption, rather than investment, will remain strong for the foreseeable future.

No matter what course development follows, the efficiency of the agricultural sector of the economy is crucial to the success of the development effort. For, with 75% of her people dependent on agriculture for a livelihood, output per person must be substantially raised in that sector if the standard of living is to be increased. While it is conceivable under certain circumstances that the transfer of people off the farms while output remains constant might occur (i.e., a zero marginal product of workers in agriculture), with a greater proportion of total food output being marketed as this migration occurs, it is rather unlikely to occur in actual practice. For, with the low nutritional standards that exist in India, there is every indication that consumption per person on the farms rises as the size of the family farm rises. Additionally, as workers find productive occupations in urban areas, their consumption of foodgrains also tends to rise, so that city workers consume more food per capita than farm residents.[35]

This implies that, first, output on the farms must be increased simply in order that people on the farms may be better off, and secondly, so that workers may be transferred to productive occupations, thereby raising per capital farm output.[36]

Additionally, the experience of the good crop years in both the First and Second Plan periods seems to indicate that the level of Plan outlays that can be withstood without inflation is heavily dependent on the output of food and other consumer goods. Since food occupies an important part of the consumer budget, and the income elasticity of demand for food seems to be relatively high starting from the present low levels of income, investment programs that raise incomes can be supported to the extent that consumer goods are available.

[35]Reserve Bank of India *Bulletin,* May 1959.
[36]Cf., *infra.,* p. 8.

38. Malayan Economic Planning

*The Federation of Malaya**

First Five-Year Plan: 1956–1960

The major economic problems facing the Federation are those associated with population growth (the rate of natural increase exceeds 3 per

*From *The Federation of Malaya's First and Second Five-Year Plans.*

cent per annum), a dependence on the variable fortunes of two export commodities, rubber and tin, and low productivity (and low incomes) in the rural areas in which approximately two-thirds of the population reside.

To meet the challenge posed by these problems, the Federation Government embarked on a general plan of development for the five-year period 1956–60. This plan envisaged total investment by the Federation and State Governments and public authorities of $1,150 million, about double the amount during 1951–55. Actual investment fell short of the target by about 15 per cent. This was, however, not entirely unexpected. When the plan was adopted in 1956, it was realised that possible financial stringency and lack of skilled technical, managerial and administrative personnel might result in the plan having to be extended to 1961 or 1962. As it turned out, transition to independence, though orderly and gradual, resulted in some readjustment in the Government's administrative machinery; the world-wide recession in 1957–58 reduced the amount of Government finance available for development expenditure; and the Emergency continued until 1960 to absorb considerable time and resources. Amounts allocated to projects which had top priority, however, such as the public utilities, rubber replanting, land development, telecommunications, housing, roads and bridges, were fully spent or exceeded.

In the private sector, investment amounted to about $2,000 million, a level much higher than in the previous five years. The main increase was in the manufacturing field where there was gratifying response to the Government's offer of specially-prepared industrial sites complete with services, liberal company taxation concessions under the Pioneer Industries (Tax Exemption) Ordinances, 1958, and the possibility of tariff protection in deserving cases. The outstanding example of the success of the Government's industrial programme is the Petaling Jaya industrial estate where more than 80 of the 150 factories which have been allotted sites are already in production. Total paid-up capital of companies which were granted pioneer status from 1958 until 31st December, 1960, amounted to $28.6 million, of which almost half was subscribed from local sources.

In the agricultural sector, which provides employment for about 58 per cent of the labour force and accounts for about 47 per cent of total national output, a large part of the increase in investment took place under the stimulus of various Government programmes designed to promote rubber replanting and new planting with high-yielding material. As a result, the total area under high-yielding trees represented about half of the total rubber acreage planted at the end of the Plan period. In addition, there were large increases in the production of rice, palm oil, smallholding fruits and vegetables resulting from the Government's land and irrigation schemes. The Federal Land Development Authority, in conjunction with the State Governments, started 22 land development schemes in nine different States which are now in various stages of completion. However, the full extent of the benefits of public investment in agriculture cannot be expected to be seen for several years.

The increase in output of the economy resulting from investment during the Plan period of nearly $3,000 million was about 20 per cent and this more than kept pace with the rising rate of population growth.

Second Five-Year Plan: 1961–1965

With the ending of the First Five-Year Plan, 1956–60, the major economic problems facing the country were looked at afresh in the light of the progress made under the Plan. These problems remain: population is expected to continue to increase by more than one million in the next five years; there will be an estimated 340,000 new entrants to the labour force, and there will be an estimated 200,000 more children of primary school age. In order to maintain and improve living standards in face of these problems, the task of accelerating the rate of economic growth consistent with financial stability will require a much greater effort on the part of both the Government and the people than that expended during the last five years.

The Second Five-Year Development Plan published on 6th February, 1961, provides for public investment of $2,150 million which is more than double that of 1956–60 and the private sector is expected to invest about $2,900 million, 40 per cent higher than in the first Plan period, making a total gross investment outlay of $5,050 million. Through the Plan the Government aims to provide adequate employment opportunities, raise per capita output and living standards, and improve levels of economic and social well-being among the rural population.

With an investment of this magnitude during the next five years, expansion of output in the economy is expected to exceed 4 per cent a year, more than the expected annual rate of population growth of 3.3 per cent. The table below shows the output and employment targets envisaged as a result of investment expenditure under the Plan.

The pattern of allocation in the public sector is shown in the table below:—

Public Investment—1956–60, 1961–65

| | | FIRST FIVE-YEAR PLAN 1956–60 | |
SECTOR	PLAN TARGET 1961–65 $ MILLION	TARGET $ MILLION	APPROX. PERCENTAGE ACHIEVED %
Agriculture	545.3	265.6	86
Transport	362.0	222.5	93
Public Works Department Plant and Equipment	68.7	13.0	181
Communications	72.9	63.3	82
Utilities	402.0	214.5	111
Industry	27.0	15.8	77
General	121.1	141.3	52
Social Services	491.0	212.7	65
	2,090.0	1,148.7	85
Defence	60.0	35.0*	–
Total	2,150.0	1,183.7	–

*Actual Expenditure.

The attempt to diversify the Federation economy and reduce its relative dependence on rubber underlies the whole system of priorities in the Plan.

The $545 million allotted to agriculture forms the basis of the Government's many-sided rural development programme. Within the agricultural sector itself, the level of investment on irrigation for rice and other crops, palm oil development, rehabilitation of coconut areas, forestry, fisheries and animal husbandry will be greatly increased, and, in addition, emphasis will be laid on opening up new land for the rural community and expanding the cultivable area.

Another significant feature of the Plan is the importance given to developing the social services, particularly education ($260 million) and health ($145 million). A major portion of the funds will be expended in the rural areas.

Of the $402 million to be spent on public utilities, $245 million will be devoted to increasing the supply of electricity and $145 million to water. Electricity services will be extended to many rural areas and the existing supply of water to the rural population will be greatly increased. Of the $362 million allotted for transport, $190 million is for construction and improvement of roads and bridges especially in rural areas where roads must be built in anticipation of traffic and spearhead the opening up of new land and other development activities. The remaining $172 million has been allotted to railway modernisation ($65 million), improvement to port facilities, chiefly at Port Swettenham and Butterworth ($55 million), and a new international airport ($52 million) for Kuala Lumpur.

The proposed programmes will, in course of time, transform the Federation into a more progressive economy providing the people with higher living standards and also lay the foundation for further and stable economic growth.

39. Economic Development and Social Welfare

The Republic of Colombia*

One of the first acts of the present administration was to propose to Congress Law 19 of 1958, which created two organizations: the Council for Economic Policy and Planning and the Administrative Department for Planning and Technical Services. In close collaboration with other departments of the Government, these organizations have been carefully studying the development potential of Columbia in order to ascertain the best policy for the Government to follow with regard to the private as well as to the public sectors.

The Government intends to state overall national economic development policy periodically, and to revise its statements from time to time in the light of new facts. The task of formulating a realistic plan for national development is difficult. Still, it is advisable for the Government at this time to submit to public consideration a general statement regarding its economic policy.

*From *Economic Development and Social Welfare: A Platform of the Government and the Council for Economic Policy and Planning of the Republic of Colombia,* 1960.

The Nature of Economic Development

The limited scope of the economic studies undertaken so far have created the erroneous impression that an economic development policy is not necessarily a policy for the improvement of the living conditions of the people as a whole. Hence, it is necessary to assert that, in the view of the Colombian Government, economic development has no other objective than that of producing within the shortest period of time, with the full application of all public and private resources, a gradual rise in the standard of living of the entire population and a better distribution of income.

There are not many roads open to an underdeveloped country to attain higher standards of living. It should not, in making a choice, take a road that might lead to the quickest results, but rather one which would follow its own political philosophy and principles.

The common notion of an underdeveloped country is that of a country that has not yet reached the same degree of industrial evolution as the more powerful nations in the world. Hence, the weaker economic classes erroneously identify economic development with the prosperity of industry and industrialists. But, an underdeveloped country is essentially one where the most serious problems of social injustice and misery are to be found. The solution of these problems has not been found, has even been made more difficult, where demagogic methods pretend to eliminate the steps necessary for the creation of collective welfare. Underdevelopment, in fact, means the lack of Government resources to provide public education, to care for public health or to extend communications to all the regions of the country. It means unsatisfactory land distribution and low productivity, progressively impoverished small holdings and large tracks of unused lands. It means inefficiency and the inability to solve technical problems because of the lack of professional and technical personnel. An underdeveloped country finds it difficult to acquire equipment not produced in the country against the export of a single product whose price fluctuates in foreign markets. Underdevelopment is bad housing, malnutrition, low wages, and the unemployment of millions of people who leave the countryside in search of uncertain employment in urban centers.

No partial solutions to these problems can be adequate. Nor can solutions be enacted. Colombia cannot have sufficient food, housing, communications, schools, good wages or greater production simply because these things are decreed. Only an orderly economic development of the country will achieve these objectives.

Alternative Ways for Economic Development

... The Government, from the very beginning and with the preparation of its economic and social platform in 1958, has conformed its policies to the program of economic development. Above all, this program has to fit into the frame-work of Colombia's constitutional and political system. The principles of state intervention and the subordination of private to public interests are established in the constitution and these principles have been further defined and developed by legislation.

Although the State is responsible for directing and coordinating the country's economic activity, this responsibility should be consistent with the conception of freedom that allows private enterprise and individuals to carry on their activities, business, and professions. The Government has no authority to propose solutions for economic development in the manner adopted by Communist regimes. Therefore, the economy has to be guided through indirect measures such as monetary, fiscal and commercial policies. In underdeveloped countries someone must have authority to give certain incentives and a certain direction to the national economy. That someone must perforce be the State. Without guidance or planning, it is not possible to achieve economic development. The State, on the other hand, cannot do everything, and, in democratic countries, the role of the State is to formulate policies which, by means of incentives and disincentives, influence private enterprise, and exert direct action within the public sphere. . . .

Economic Development Objectives

It is clear that if the country chooses to adopt and execute a plan of economic development, it will be taking the most arduous road. It is easier to become resigned to a relatively stagnant situation and to enjoy the benefits of stability without attempting to intensify the progress of the country. This attitude prevailed for centuries in the colonial economy and in the early stages of the Republic, to the profit of a small minority who found in this situation the most effective way of retaining their privileges. But the country's external relations, which greatly improved during the first quarter of this century, encouraged by favorable circumstances in international trade, and by the investment of capital from the United States, brought about a constant increase in income which has only recently diminished.

The Council for Economic Policy and Planning has been examining the preliminary results of studies on economic development undertaken by the Department of Planning and Technical Services, with the assistance and advice of experts from the Economic Commission of Latin America (ECLA) and from the Technical Assistance Operations of the United Nations. They have reached the conclusion that the present rate of growth of 3.5% per annum, which could be maintained with some effort, is totally insufficient, if the present rate of population growth continues. The situation would be even more serious if, as can be foreseen, population grows at an even faster rate.

The present 3.5% annual increase in the gross national product, although equal to that of the more developed countries, will not solve the need for employment which will be generated in the years to come. Moreover, any further deterioration of world coffee prices would be disastrous, even if the efforts undertaken by the country were limited to maintaining public expenditures and investments at the reduced level that prevails today. Neither should we be able to contemplate the necessary expansion of our education, health and housing programs.

Let us examine some provisional but not exaggerated figures for investment requirements in some of the basic sectors of the economy:

A. According to the latest available figures published by the Bureau of Statistics, the school-age population today is 2.6 million while the number of pupils actually attending school is 1.5 million. This means that there are at present 1.1 million children without educational facilities.

To meet this shortage, assuming an average of 40 pupils per classroom, a fairly high figure, it would be necessary to build approximately 28,500 additional classrooms. If we go further and provide for the increase in the school population until 1975, 57,000 additional classrooms would have to be constructed by that time. The cost per classroom is estimated at 15.000 pesos, including equipment, or a total investment of 855 million pesos, 57 million pesos per year.

B. In health, the problem is no less serious. At present there are three hospital beds per 1,000 inhabitants. The Government intends to reduce this shortage by 33%. This implies, in the period mentioned above, the building of hospitals with a total of 15,000 beds, at a cost of 450 million pesos, of which the Government would have to provide 75% or 300 million, or 75 million per year.

C. In the municipal field, in order to eliminate the present shortage of water works and sewerage, and to meet the demands of the increase in population up to 1970, the Institute of Municipal Development should undertake the following investments:

Water works	Colombian $	760.000.000
Sewerage	Colombian $	540.000.000
Total	Colombian $	1.300.000.000

This represents, from 1960 to 1970, an annual investment of approximately 130 million pesos.

D. For the completion of the road building now being carried out by the nation, 680 million pesos are required as from 1961. If the level of investment budgeted for 1960 is attained, the Government would have to commit its resources for the next four years in order to conclude the work, without having the possibility to construct any new roads. These figures exclude conservation and maintainance expenses for the new roads.

E. The shortage of housing in 1959, as estimated by the Land Credit Institute, comes to about 250,000 houses. This is only in towns having a population of over 10,000 and does not take into account the large requirements of rural areas. The Institute estimated that more than 40,000 new families will be formed in 1960. On the other hand, approximately 15,000 houses were built in 1959.

F. The capacity of the electric power installed in the country totals 860,000 kilowatts, 0.061 kilowatts per inhabitant. If Colombia wishes to increase its capacity to 0.100 kilowatts per inhabitant, a figure comparable to the present installed capacity per inhabitant in Mexico, the shortage amounts to 540,000 kilowatts. Since there are new plants under construction, with a capacity of 340,000 kilowatts, which will be completed in the course of the next three years, the deficit would still be approximately 200,000 kilowatts. Again, if the present rate of increase in the population is taken into account, the shortage can be estimated at 300,000 kilowatts.

The country's population will continue to grow at an annual rate of not less than 2.5%, an increase of close to 2 million inhabitants by 1965. Besides implying urgent requirements for consumer goods and public services, this would represent a considerable increase in the nation's labor-force. The increase of the Gross National Product and the expansion of investment in the last six years would not provide enough employment for all this available man-power during the next five years. According to estimates made by the United Nations, the Colombian labor-force would increase by more than 600,000 persons from 1960 to 1965, or an average of 120,000 persons per year. The volume of new employment consistent with a growth rate of 3.5% would only come to 459,000 workers, while 150,000 persons would have to remain unemployed or employ themselves in less productive tasks, thus increasing concealed unemployment.

A Growth Rate of Five Per Cent Per Annum

The Government wants to set a higher goal for Colombia's economic development in the next five years. The goal is to increase the Gross National Product at a rate of 5% per annum. Such a growth rate would require a great effort and the cooperation of all Colombians. The Government sets this rate as an objective of its economic policy and hopes that it will be accepted by all the sectors of the country, including industry, labor, business, agriculture and transport. . . .

The Department of Planning and the technical assistance experts of the United Nations and the ECLA have, during the past eight months, concentrated on working out the production possibilities of the various sectors of the national economy. It has been necessary to make a diagnosis of the economy as a whole to appreciate its capacity for growth, verify the main difficulties to be met with in carrying out the program, analyze the perspective of the balance of payments, define the characteristics of future development of agriculture and industry, foresee the fiscal, monetary and exchange policy which would be most adequate to improve the conditions of investment and consumption, and estimate the population and available labor force within the period. This study will be completed in June and the Council of Economic Policy and Planning will then be able to present a detailed development program.

Nevertheless, the Government and the Council consider that even now, on the basis of preliminary studies, it is possible to select an objective of growth which, within the country's financial possibilities, will require special effort and sacrifice. The reward for this effort would be attractive. If the country maintains a rate of growth of 5% per year, the real income per person would be doubled within 25 years. In this way we should have broken the vicious circle to which the less developed countries are subject. Moreover, should Colombia succeed in maintaining a 5% growth rate over the next five years, it may be possible to accelerate economic expansion after 1965, say to 6% per annum. A growth rate of 5% maintained over 25 years would raise per-capita income to 1.960 pesos, which is equivalent to that of such developed countries as Holland, Denmark or Austria and represents a level considerably higher than the present one of 1.060 pesos.

It is important to understand that the rate of growth must be the highest that is compatible with stability; that is to say, it cannot be the result of inflation. Further, the growth of Colombia should become a permanent feature of its economic system, so that over a number of years progress will depend on the Government's active intervention to a lesser extent than is necessary in the initial years of the program.

Meaning of the Objective of a 5% Growth Rate

A 5% per annum growth rate would increase the Gross National Product from 16,878 million pesos in 1959 to 21,984 million pesos in 1965 and to 35,810 million pesos in 1975.

A 5% rate is less than the one maintained during 1925–30 which was 5.7% per year. After 1930, the rate decreased considerably until it reached 3.5%. To obtain an increase of 5% now is a very hard task, because in the past higher rates of growth were accompanied by balance-of-payment situations considerably more favorable than the present one.

The 5% growth rate is higher than that of the majority of the less developed economies of the Free Western Democracies. Obviously, it is higher than the expansion rate of the fully developed countries in the Western World, but it is inferior to the rate of growth achieved by certain socialist countries of Eastern Europe and Asia, where the political system allows the drastic suppression of consumer-goods production in favor of capital goods. The United States, over the past ten years, has maintained an average 3% per annum increase in its real income. Argentina's rate of growth has averaged only 1% per annum.

This is an ambitious development goal, because it must be reached at the time when Colombia's import capacity is much lower than it was during the period 1925–1930 and than in the immediate post-war years. Moreover, we cannot count today upon an industrial development as powerful as that which took place between 1933 and 1939 when the bases of our industrial growth were laid.

To achieve the proposed goal, the following basic conditions must be maintained:

a. Sufficient formation of capital goods to make possible an immediate increase in the productive capacity of the country.

b. Investment of funds where productivity will be highest.

c. Increased productivity of already existing capital resources, either by a more rational organization of work or by a more intensive use thereof.

d. Availability of sufficient foreign exchange to purchase the essential imports which are needed to maintain employment and increase production.

e. An intensive program of import substitution as part of the solution to the balance-of-payments problem.

f. Sufficient aid from external credit and the intensification of direct foreign investment.

g. Sufficient fiscal resources of the public sector, i.e., of the Central Government, the Departments, and Municipalities, and autonomous public agencies, needed to carry out essential public investments and to increase expenditures for education, health, housing, etc., which are conditions fundamental to the achievement of higher income levels.

h. An expansion of manufacture consistent with the rate of development proposed and an intensification of industry in those lines where demand will be greatest.

i. Sufficient development of agriculture both to provide raw materials for industry and to supply food for an increasing population, whose requirements will increase with income, thus avoiding shortages and a rise in prices.

j. Enough employment to absorb the larger labor-force resulting from the increase in population. . . .

40. The Requirements for Development

*Maurice Zinkin**

The qualities required for economic development are not the highest of which man is capable; for both the individual and the nation there are more important ends in life than becoming rich. It is still pleasanter and more proper to die for one's country than to save for it; and loving our neighbour, not making money, is the way to salvation.

Economic progress is, in short, only doubtfully also moral progress. Riches subject man to nearly as many temptations as poverty. Economic development is only good in so far as it is achieved without an increase in envy, uncharitableness and exploitation. The sweating of labour in the first half of the nineteenth century in England permitted some very necessary accumulation, the enclosures of the second half of the eighteenth century saved England from starvation in the Napoleonic Wars; but they were not good for the souls of the sweaters and enclosers.

Economic development, therefore, would appear at first sight something over which no one could get excited; and so it was, on the whole, in ancient India or mediaeval Europe. But today it has become mixed up with a whole series of moral considerations to which it is somewhat doubtfully relevant. Those who love their country now believe that to be great she must be powerful; and to be powerful she must first be rich. Those who love their neighbour now regard the salvation of his body as more important than the salvation of his soul; there is much rejoicing over a 5 per cent increase in the national income, little over new endowment for temples. Those who love God often feel that He is better worshipped by high taxes than by prayer.

Economic progress is, therefore, sought today, in Asia as elsewhere, for reasons which are not economic. That provides a drive profounder than any known before, for the sacrifices men will make for religion are far greater than those they will make for riches. But it also has its dangers.

*From Maurice Zinkin, *Development for Free Asia* (London: Chatto & Windus Ltd., 1956).

Because the qualities and the policies required for development are so often religiously uninspiring, the resources needed for economic progress are perpetually being diverted to satisfy some non-economic principle, often with only the dimmest idea of the economic sacrifice involved. High cost industries are built up, because they are thought to contribute to national power. Amenities for labour more expensive than productivity justifies are enforced, so that labourers shall have a better life. High incomes are taxed almost out of existence to increase equality. Location of industry is interfered with so that every part of the country shall have its 'fair' share of development. Such large farmers as know about agriculture have their holdings cut down so that more of the landless can enjoy the pleasures of ownership. And so on. The criteria applied in judging economic problems mostly have nothing to do with economics; and the result is naturally that, though there may be more equality, or greater regional fairness, or possibly, fewer revolutions, there is also less development.

That does not necessarily mean that these non-economic criteria are wrong. Economic and non-economic standards of value are not better or worse than each other, they are different. Which should be applied in any particular case is for a man's conscience rather than his reason to decide. It is an irrelevance to tell those who believe cows to be sacred that they would be better off if useless cattle were killed. All that can properly be said is that sometimes those who apply non-economic criteria are not altogether aware of their economic cost. Those who shout for equality now might do so less loudly if they knew it would make their children poorer. Those who build high cost factories to make their country more powerful today might be less enthusiastic if they realised how much weaker the waste of resources will make their country in the long run. Any major decision, national or personal, should in the end be guided by men's beliefs, and not their interests; but before the decision is made the facts should be understood.

The requirements which have to be fulfilled for Asia to get rich are clear. Getting rich must be a major objective, for which people are prepared to sacrifice old habits as well as present consumption. They must save instead of hoarding, or spending on festivals or ceremonies. They must invest productively instead of buying jewellery and brocades. They must admire innovations, and inventions, and successful entrepreneurs rather than writers of commentaries and men who conform to perfection to the methods of their ancestors. Business must become as respectable as administration. The State must take the initiative in change, it must develop public utilities, put through social reform, make available extension services and widen the scope of co-operation; but, because it has so much it ought to do, it must refrain from doing what can be done by others. It must restrain itself from unnecessary nationalisations and meddling controls. There must be politicians who can lead their people to change, and bureaucrats who can make actual the politicians' dreams. There must be equality for women and the traditionally oppressed, so that society may draw upon the initiative of all, but economic equality must not be excessive, so that some will have the leisure and the money to study or take risks. Education must be reformed to bring forward an adequate supply of the technically trained and economically adaptable. Above all, in deciding between alternative possibilities of action, the most profitable should be chosen, not that which will be most advantageous to a special interest, or will benefit the most backward, or the best behaved, or the largest number. If wealth is the aim, wealth must be the criterion, not power, or autarchy or even fairness.

The needs of development cannot be absolute. There must be occasions when defence or justice will override them with propriety. But for that there is a price. The poor will remain poorer for longer.